E.D.R.*

Ratings for

*Every Darn Radiator

(and convector) you'll probably ever see

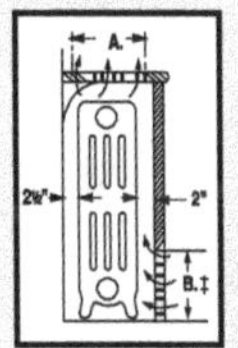

DAN HOLOHAN

For Elise Della Rocca, our favorite "E.D.R."
Thanks for all that you do for us.

You get the HIGHEST rating!

If it's old, you'll probably find it here!

When you replace an old steam boiler you have to know the ratings of the radiators because the boiler's ability to produce steam must match the piping and radiation's ability to condense steam. You can't just go by the rating on the old boiler because buildings change over time. Radiators that were once there may be gone or someone may have removed sections. The only way to pick the right boiler is to survey the system and add up the radiation load. And that's where this book can help. Here you will find all the radiator and convector ratings I've managed to gather over the years. Most of what you see here comes from antique books that I found in used bookstores across America. If it's an old radiator or convector, you'll probably find it here.

If you're replacing a hot water boiler, this book will also come in handy because you'll be able to figure the radiator's ability to heat the room, based on its E.D.R. rating. Make sure you adjust the BTUH per square foot E.D.R. rating for the average water temperature you'll be using. Here's a chart that will help:

Average Water Temperature °F	Output in BTUH per sq. ft. E.D.R.
150	110
155	120
160	130
165	140
170	150
175	160
180	170
185	180
190	190
195	200
200	210
205	220
210	230
215	240

This thing we call E.D.R.

This book is filled with radiator ratings. The term we use to explain a radiator's ability to emit BTUs, Equivalent Direct Radiation, came about as radiators started to get fancy. The original term, Square Feet of Radiation, came from this radiator.

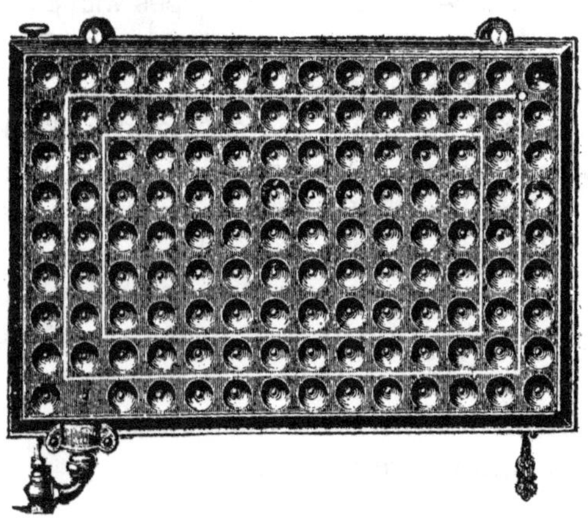

Stephen J. Gold invented this one and he called it a "mattress radiator." One square foot of radiation equaled one square foot of surface area. This was the first commercially successful radiator in America.

Each square foot of radiation puts out 240 BTUH when there's 215 degrees inside the radiator (that's about 1 psi steam) and 70°F air surrounding the radiator. Make the air cooler, and the radiator puts out more heat. The opposite is also true.

Toward the end of the 19th Century, foundries began to elevate radiator making to an art form (you'll see what I mean in the following pages). To increase the available surface area, while decreasing the overall size of a radiator, manufacturers began to give their units more nooks and crannies than a beehive. The challenge for them became one of measuring the actual surface area of these old beauties. They solved the problem in a most ingenious way. They took a vat and filled it with paint. They put the vat on a scale and weighed it. Then they plugged all the holes in the radiator, hung it from a chain, and lowered it into the vat of paint.

They left it in there for a while as the paint worked its way into every angle, twist and turn. Then they raised the radiator from the vat and let the excess paint drip back into the vat. Next, they weighed the vat one more time, knowing that the paint that was no longer in the vat would now be clinging to the outside surface of the radiator. Finally, they'd put that much paint in a can, and then they painted the floor with it. The amount of floor surface they could cover with the paint became the square foot E.D.R. rating of the radiator. Pretty cool, eh?

As time went by, they figured out how to measure a radiator's output by weighing the condensate that came out of it. After they had this more-modern method worked out they went back and checked it out against the Paint Method. The measurements were remarkably similar!

AN OLD RADIATOR Q&A

Q: Can I successfully cut down the size of an antique cast-iron radiator?

A: Maybe. It all depends on how the long-gone manufacturer assembled the radiator. A cast-iron radiator goes together in sections, like a loaf of sliced bread. Each section attaches to the next with round metal fittings called nipples. Nipples looks like very short pieces of pipe, which may or may not have threads on them.

Threaded nipples are unusual in that one side has a left-hand thread, while the other side has a right-hand thread. As the manufacturer turned the nipple one way between the two sections, it pulled both sections tightly together. After a few years of normal use and corrosion, the threaded nipples and radiator sections became one, never to separate again. Because of this, threaded nipples aren't available anymore. If you're looking to reduce the size of one of these old beauties, you're out of luck.

And then there are push nipples, which are still available. A push nipple is a smooth piece of pipe that's beveled. The bevel makes the push nipple wider in the middle than it is at either end. Rather than screw the radiator sections together, the manufacturers who used push nipples pushed one section into the other, taking advantage of the nipple's bevel to create a tight seal.

If your radiator has a threaded rod running between its sections, rest assured it has push nipples. Now all you have to do is get the beast apart. Loosen and withdraw the threaded rod. Next, apply equal parts of patience, pry bar, and elbow grease. If you're careful and persistent you should be successful. Remove the offending section and reassemble the radiator.

If the old push nipples don't look so good, get new ones. And don't waste your time shopping around for these because there's only one place you can go: Oneida County Boiler Works (Phone: 315-732-7914). Give them a call. They'll want you to send a sample of the old nipple (no matter what condition it's in) and they'll take good care of you. They regularly help people from all over the country, and they assure me that Oneida is the only company around that still supplies these fittings. "If people could get 'em any closer to home, they wouldn't be calling us!" they say. I believe them.

Once you get the new push nipple in place, tighten the push rods, and pull the radiator sections back together. (Gosh, I make that sound so easy.)

Q: What's the best way to disconnect, move, and reconnect radiators for, say, floor repairs?

A: First, take care with those old pipes. Make sure you're using two wrenches when you're loosening the union connections. Assume the position, and then turn one wrench while holding back with the other. Don't take any shortcuts here because if you attack old pipes with a single wrench the torque you create can, and probably will, break the pipe.

A hand truck with a few strategically placed blocks of wood will help you move the old beast out of the way. And if you're planning to take that old radiator down a flight of stairs proceed cautiously, and with plenty of help because an antique radiator can weigh hundreds of pounds.

Q: If I decide to move a cast-iron radiator, where should I reinstall it?

A: Ideally, a cast-iron radiator should be under the window (that's where the greatest heat loss is), and it should be as wide as the window. Its top should never peek above the windowsill because this lessens the convective movement of air around the radiator. Speaking of which, for maximum convective efficiency, the radiator should be 2-1/2 inches away from the wall. It took the old-timers years to figure that out.

Q: What's the difference between a steam and a hot water radiator?

A: It's the way the radiator sections go together. They may be nippled together at both the top and bottom, or just at the bottom.

Older steam radiators have nipples across just the bottom portion of the sections. This is because steam is lighter than air. When the steam enters the bottom of a radiator (as it always will in a one-pipe steam radiator), it flows upward into the sections, displacing the air as it goes.

Hot water radiators, on the other hand, have nipples across both the upper and lower portion of the radiator sections. Even though hot water rises, it doesn't move as quickly as steam. The double set of nipples encourages better circulation of the hot water across the entire radiator and leads to greater efficiency.

Around 1905, when two-pipe steam became popular, contractors began to use hot-water radiators on steam systems. The old steam radiators with their single set of bottom nipples quickly faded and became obsolete.

Q: What's the difference between a one-pipe and a two-pipe steam radiator?

A: As the name implies, a one-pipe steam radiator has just one pipe connected to it, and that pipe is always at the bottom. Both steam and condensate (the water that forms when steam condenses) share this pipe. One-pipe steam systems can use either steam or hot water radiators, however.

Two-pipe steam systems usually have the steam entering through a pipe at the top of the radiator. The condensate leaves the radiator through a pipe at the bottom. Since the steam moves across the top of the radiator, and the condensate drips down along the radiator's inside passages, two-pipe radiators generally provide a more-even sense of warmth.

There will usually be a steam trap (which is an automatic, temperature-sensitive valve) at the point where the radiator and the condensate pipe come together. You should check these with a thermometer once a year. You're looking for at least a 10-degree drop in temperature across the trap. If the trap's not working, you can replace the internal parts. Most plumbing and heating supply houses will be able to get the parts for you.

A two-pipe steam system will almost always use hot water radiators. There is one notable exception, though, and it's called the two-pipe, air vent system. You'll know you have this one if you see two pipes, one on each side of the radiator (at the bottom), and both pipes have hand valves. These radiators also have air vents. From a historical perspective, the two-pipe, air vent system is the missing link between one-pipe steam and two-pipe steam.

Q: Does a two-pipe steam radiator have to have a steam trap?

A: No, but it has to have <u>something</u> to keep the steam from entering the condensate return lines. That "something" may be an internal orifice, a tiny check valve you can't see, a hidden metal ball or a water seal. There were about three dozen companies doing business between 1905 and 1930 that made these steam-stopping gizmos. They're all out of business now. So do not remove any weird-looking device until you've answered three essential questions:

1. What is it?
2. What does it do?
3. What the heck happens if I take it out?

If you can't answer those questions, put your hands in your pockets, and back slowly away from that radiator.

Q: Can I take out a steam radiator and put in a hot water radiator?

A: Yes.

Q: Can I take out a hot water radiator and put in a steam radiator?

A: Yes, if it's a one-pipe steam system.

Q: Where does the air vent belong on a cast-iron steam radiator? How about on a hot water radiator?

A: If it's a one-pipe steam radiator, the vent belongs on the side of the radiator that's opposite the pipe. Because the lighter-than-air steam will head first for the top of the radiator, you should install the air vent about halfway down the radiator, and not at the top.

Two-pipe steam systems (with the exception of that "missing link" one-pipe, air-vent system) should not have air vents on the radiators. If the two-pipe radiator won't heat without an air vent, check the steam trap. Misapplied radiator air vents can lead to nightmarish system problems.

Each hot water radiator should have an air vent at the top, on the side opposite the inlet pipe. You'll use this vent to "bleed" air from the radiator when you're first starting the system.

Q: Where can I buy antique radiators?

A: You can take pot luck at your local junk yard, or you can call Fran Fahey at A-1 New and Used Plumbing & Heating Supplies, 30 Prospect St., Somerville, MA (Phone: 617-625-6140). Fran operates a veritable supermarket of antique radiators in all shapes, styles and sizes, and all A-1 radiators, he assures me, are in A-1 shape. Fran told me he has repaired and pressure-tested every one of them. He'll ship anywhere in the country, and he'll also fix your old radiator or remove a section (providing it has push - not threaded - nipples).

Q: Can I repair a leaking cast-iron radiator?

A: It depends on where the leak is and how bad it's leaking. Steam radiators, because they're under much less pressure than hot water radiators, are usually the easier of the two varieties to fix.

To begin, first determine where the leak is. This, of course, is easier said than done. Use an inspection mirror. That will allow you to see around corners and up into spaces not viewed within the past 100 years.

If you find a pinhole leak at a push nipple, you can replace the push nipple. If the radiator is cracked, say, after a hard-freeze, you may not be able to repair it at all, however. It all depends on the severity of the crack, and where it is.

Q: Are there stop-leak products for cast-iron radiators (as there are for automotive radiators?)

A: None that you can pour into the radiator, but J-B Weld Company of Sulphur Springs, TX (903-885-7696) may have the answer. The company's literature states that the City of Dallas, Texas used J-B Weld to repair a cracked Caterpillar engine block. That sure got my attention!

A representative of the company told me that old-house owners have reported great success with his company's product, J-B Weld on old cast-iron radiators.

But to fix a leak, you first have to be able to get at it, so consider this. Before using J-B Weld, you have to drain the radiator and remove any paint, primer, or rust. Next, you have to thoroughly clean the surface with a non-petroleum-based cleaner such as acetone or lacquer thinner, removing all dirt, grease and oil. Then you have to rough up the surface with a file, mix the two elements of the product in 50/50 proportions, and apply it to a thickness of no less than 1/32-inch. Don't get any on your skin or in your eyes. Finally, you let it dry for at least 15 hours, and see what you've got. (Can you do all that?) I asked if the product will take the temperature along with the expansion and contraction common in cast-iron radiators. The manufacturer told me the product actually "softens" when heated and will move with the metal. It's not the sort of 'softening' you'll notice, though. You'd have to get the temperature up to 400°F, to see that (the product is good up to 600°F.) Typically, a radiator in a steam-heating system will get up to about 229°F, tops. So if you can get at the leak, it sounds like this stuff will work.

The challenge, of course, is that an antique radiator can have more nooks and crannies than a Thomas' English muffin, and a good leak knows where to hide. But if you're in love with that old radiator, it's certainly worth a try. The company sells only to wholesalers, and only in quantity, but you can buy J-B Weld for about five bucks at most automotive and hardware retail stores.

Q: Do I need to flush an old radiator from time to time?

A: No. Hot water radiators operate within a "closed" system where there's little or no corrosion taking place. Flushing these radiators will only cause you to add more water to the system, which will create more corrosion, and so on, and on. Why cause problems?

Steam systems are open to the atmosphere so the radiators do see more corrosion than their hot water brethren. However, cast iron radiators come with their own mud legs, and these can hold many years' worth of scale and rust.

Take a look at the way your radiators connect to your pipes. Notice how the inlet valve or outlet steam-stopping device is always a bit higher than the bottom of the radiator? This is true even when the valve is installed near the bottom of the radiator. The scale and rust settle into that low-slung "pocket" and stays there.

Keep this in mind if you decide to pitch your one-pipe steam radiators back toward their inlet valves to give you better condensate drainage. Take care not to pitch those old beauties too much. If you do, you just might slosh one-hundred-year's worth of sludge into that inlet valve. You'll know you made this mistake by the water hammer that pounds on the pipes and the condensate that squirts from the air vents. That's when it's time to flush the radiator.

Does the color of a radiator matter?

I came across this circular sent out by the US Department of Commerce's National Bureau of Standards on July 19, 1935. I hope you find it as fascinating as I did.

Painting of Steam and Hot Water Radiators

For a number of years this subject has received considerable attention from the public, and it is apparent that the essential facts have not always been understood. The object of this note is to supply the more important facts in the case.

It will appear that as far as their effect on the performance of radiators is concerned, paints fall into two classes. First, those in which the pigment consists of small flakes of metal, such as the aluminum and bronze paints, most commonly used for painting radiators, which produce a metallic appearance and will be called metallic paints. Second, the white and colored paints, in which the pigment consists not of the metals but of oxides or other compounds of the metals. Thus white lead paints, or those containing compounds of zinc or other metals, will be called non-metallic paints. These non-metallic paints are obtainable in practically all colors, including white and black, while the metallic paints have the color of the metal or alloy of which the flakes are composed.

We will state at the outset the principal conclusion, which will be explained in more detail later, that the last coat of paint on a radiator is the only one that has an appreciable effect. And that a radiator coated with metallic paint will emit less heat, under otherwise identical conditions, than a similar radiator coated with non-metallic paint. In order to obtain the same amount of heat from the two radiators just considered the temperature of the one painted with metallic paint must be somewhat higher. Under these conditions, exactly the same amount of heat is being supplied to the two radiators. And since neither the boiler efficiency nor the heat wasted in the pipelines is appreciably affected by small changes in radiator temperatures, practically the same amount of fuel is required to supply the heat in each case. In other words, while it may be desirable for various reasons to avoid the use of metallic paints on radiators, no appreciable saving in fuel will result from the use of non-metallic rather than metallic paints.

The purpose of a heating system is to maintain the rooms in a house at some temperature higher than that prevailing out of doors. The heat that is developed by burning fuel is transferred to the rooms by means of the radiators. A radiator neither creates nor destroys heat and a large radiator, while it can put more heat into a room than a small one, must be supplied with all of the heat it puts in. In the sense that they ultimately transfer all the heat supplied into the room, all radiators are 100% efficient. The word "efficiency" is, however, used in other ways, and it is now customary to use it on all possible occasions, but it is hardly correct to say that putting metallic paint on a radiator reduces its efficiency when the effect is merely to reduce its capacity. The size of the radiators in a house can only affect the fuel required for heating by increasing or decreasing the heat wasted in transmission from boiler to radiator and that lost up the chimney. Only when the radiators are so small as to render the whole heating plant ineffective is an appreciable saving of fuel to be expected by installing larger radiators. After these preliminary explanations, we may proceed to consider the kind of effects that may be obtained by the use of various kinds of paint. The heat emitted from a radiator is removed in two ways. First, the air streaming past the radiator and rising from it is heated and carries the heat to other parts of the room. Second, the hot surface of the radiator emits heat by radiation just as the glowing electric and gas heaters do. Most types of steam and hot water radiators emit less than half their heat by radiation and evidently the name "radiator" although universally used is not a particularly appropriate one.

To take concrete case, a particular sectional cast iron radiator, if painted with any non-metallic paint, might transfer into the room 180 Btu per hour for each square foot of its surface, if supplied with the necessary amount of heat from a boiler. The burning of one pound of good coal produces about 12,000 Btu, and if the coal is used in a domestic heating plant, perhaps half of this, or 6,000 Btu, might finally be transferred from the radiators into, the rooms. Most of the other half of the heat produced is inevitably lost via the chimney.

The area of one section of a cast iron radiator is about two square feet for the smaller sections, and up to seven or eight square feet for the larger sections, so that a 10-section radiator would have a surface area between 20 and 80 square feet. Of the 180 Btu per hour transferred, about 2/3 or 120 Btu would go to heating the air that passes over the radiator. The 120 Btu transferred directly to the air would not be increased or decreased by repainting the radiator. The remaining 60 Btu not carried off by the air is emitted as radiant energy. The amount of radiant energy which can be emitted per hour by the hot surface is dependent upon the kind of paint used for the last coat. It was assumed that the radiator was painted with non-metallic paint. If it be repainted with a metallic paint, such as aluminum or bronze, it will no longer be able to radiate 60 Btu per hour, but may be able to radiate only 30 Btu, so that instead of transferring 180 Btu to the room per hour, it can now transfer only 150 Btu. The coat of aluminum or bronze paint is not an insulating covering like a covering of magnesia or asbestos, but it has a similar effect, although for an entirely different reason. The resulting reduction in heat emission is entirely due to the reduction in the radiating power of the exposed surface, rather than to the insignificant insulating value of the thin layer of paint. It is therefore evident that undercoats of paint, regardless of kind, have no significant effect on the performance of the radiator, except in the practically impossible case where the paint was thick enough to act as an insulating covering. In repainting a radiator, it is therefore unnecessary to remove the old paint. The effect of adding the metallic paint is equivalent to removing 1/6 of the radiator, or nearly 17%, or as if one section out of six had been removed. Thus, a radiator of five sections painted with white or colored paint should be about as effective as another of six sections of the same kind painted with metallic paint since each would transfer the same amount of heat to the room, provided the necessary amount of heat were supplied to each.

In the following applications, the numerical values given above will be used as if they were exact, but it must be understood that they are merely representative and would not apply exactly to any particular case except by chance. The effect of painting on the capacity of a radiator depends upon the size and design of the radiator. The reduction in capacity produced by the application of aluminum paint is less for large radiators than for small ones, especially so in the case of large radiators having many columns or tubes per section. In a large tubular type radiator having seven tubes per section, more than three-quarters of the heat is carried away by the air directly and painting with aluminum consequently reduces the capacity of the radiator only about 10%. If only the visible portions of a radiator are painted with aluminum paint, the reduction in capacity is also obviously less than if the entire surface is covered.

Application 1: Suppose a house in which all the radiators are painted with aluminum paint, and that the radiator in one room is found to be too small, so that when the other rooms are warm enough, this one is too cold. If the radiator in this room is painted with non-metallic paint, either white or colored, the heat emitted by it can be increased from 10 to 20% without affecting conditions in the other rooms, although it will be necessary to burn more fuel to supply the additional heat in the one room. If the increase is sufficient, the expense of installing a radiator may thus be avoided.

Similarly, it is possible, by using bronze or aluminum paint on radiators in rooms which are overheated, and colored or white paints in rooms not sufficiently heated, to improve conditions without going to the expense of installing new radiators of larger or smaller sizes.

Application 2: In installing radiators in a new house, somewhat smaller radiators may be installed if they are to be painted with colored paints, rather than bronze or aluminum paints.

Application 3: If the radiators on a hot water system are painted with metallic paint and are all too small, so that the water must be kept hotter than it is desired in order to heat the house, they may be repainted with non-metallic paint, and it should, then be possible to heat the house with the water in the system not quite so hot. There will be no noticeable saving of fuel.

Application 4: Since basements usually overheated so that much of the heat supplied there is wasted, some economy can be effected by painting the heater and pipes, with metallic paint. This cannot, however, serve as anything more than a poor substitute for a covering of good insulating material about inch thick; which is capable of making an appreciable saving in the coal bill. The insulating material will remain effective for years, while the paint becomes ineffective if covered with dust.

Application 5: If a radiator is situated next to an outside wall, as most of them are, it is evident that the heat supplied directly to this wall is more or less wasted. Some slight economy may be obtained, therefore, by using metallic paint on the side facing the wall and non-metallic paint on the visible portions. The gain is not large enough to be important, but on the other hand, in putting non-metallic paint over metallic, it is not worth while to go to the trouble of repainting' the side next the wall.

Radiator Enclosures

If you're thinking about boxing in an old radiator there are a few things you need to consider. The size and shape of the enclosure can affect the radiator's output, decreasing it or increasing it a bit or a lot. These drawings will help you decide what's best for you.

And by the way, if you're looking for radiator enclosures, go to the Internet and use any search engine and the keywords, "Radiator Enclosures." You'll turn up quite a few companies.

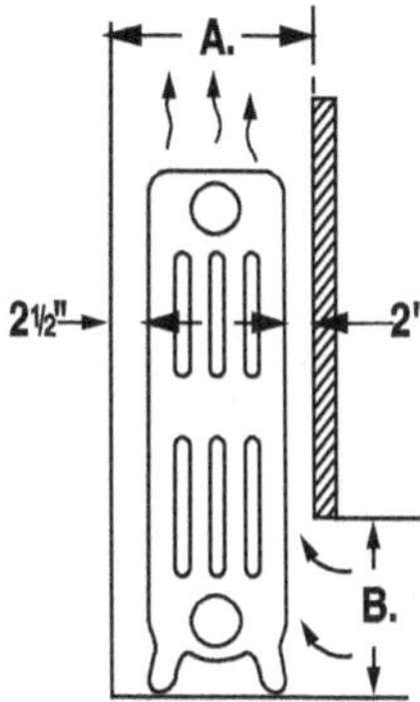

When you put a barrier in front of a radiator it creates a chimney effect and increases the radiators output because more air moves across the radiator's surface. In this case, you can deduct 10% from the size of the radiator you'd need without the barrier. In other words, if the room called for a radiator of 100 square feet E.D.R., you'll get the same effect with a radiator of 90 square feet E.D.R. if you use the barrier and take advantage of the chimney effect.

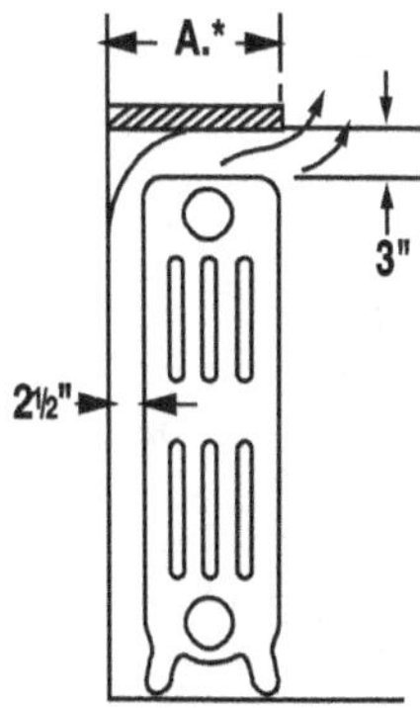

Here, we're putting a barrier on top of the radiator. That slows the flow of heated air that's moving across the radiator and decreases the radiator's output by 20%. If the barrier ("A" in the drawing) is just 50% the depth of the radiator, the loss will be 10%. If it's 150% the depth of the radiator, the loss will be 35%.

And that can get confusing so let's do a few examples. Say the barrier is as deep as the radiator. Assuming the room needs a radiator with 100 square feet E.D.R. you'd have to install a radiator with a rating of 120 square feet E.D.R. to get the same effect. Make sense? If the barrier is half as deep as the radiator you'll need 110 square feet E.D.R.. And if the barrier hangs over the edge of the radiator by half as much again, you'll need 135 square feet E.D.R. to get the same heat as you'd get from an uncovered radiator with a rating of just 100 square feet E.D.R. So shelves make a big difference. If the room feels cool, look to the shelf.

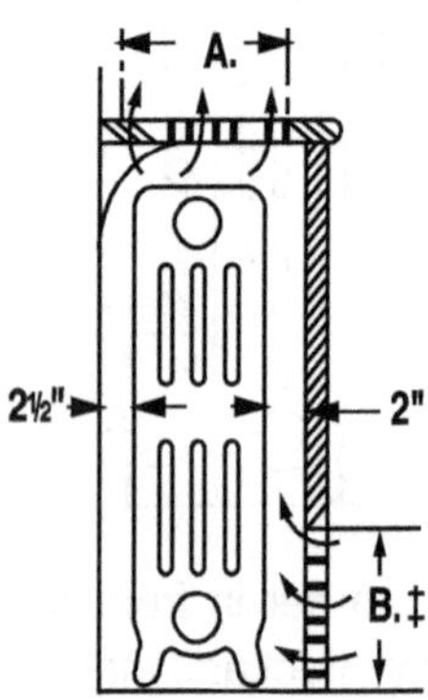

Okay, now we have a barrier in front of the radiator and it's creating a chimney effect. But we also have a barrier on top. This top barrier, however, has holes in it. The overall effect is to increase the radiator's output by 5%. So if the room needs 100 square feet, you can get by with 95 square feet. And check the footnotes to see how the openings relate to each other.

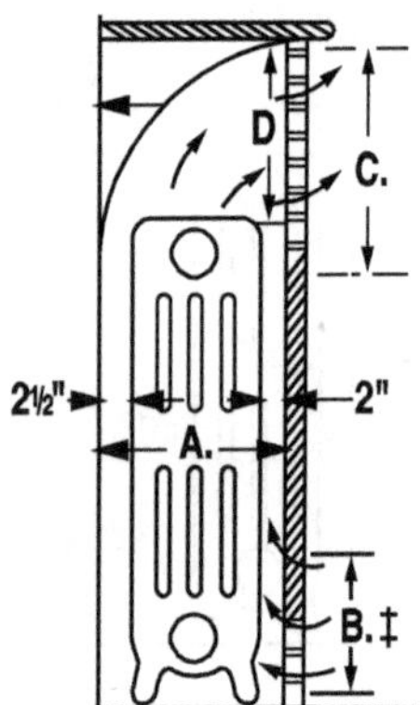

This enclosure is so well done that the radiator doesn't even know it's there! There's no difference in output between this radiator and an uncovered radiator.

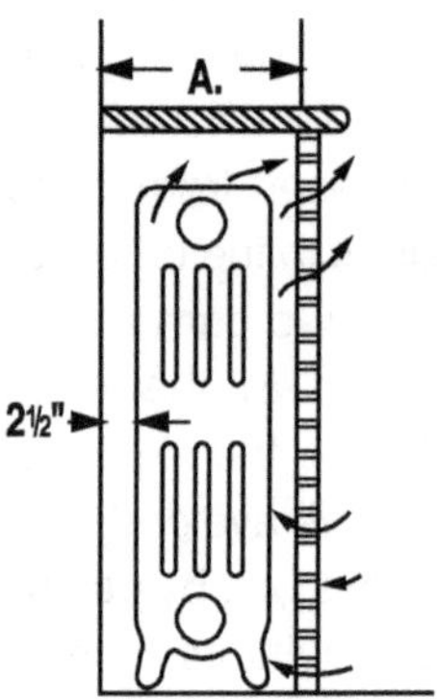

Covering the top of the radiator and having a decorative screen across the front of the radiator reduces the radiator's output by 30%. So if you need 100 square feet E.D.R. you'll have to install 130 square feet E.D.R. to get the same effect. Surprised? Don't be. Just think like air. There's little or no chimney effect here and if you were air, you couldn't get out the top, right?

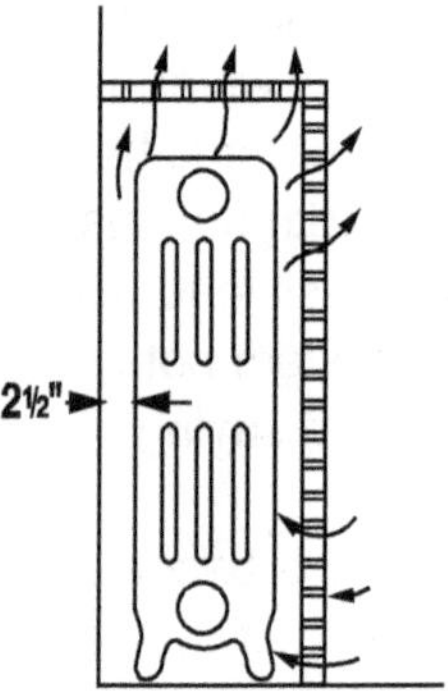

Now we have a grill in the front and a grill up top and the overall effect is to reduce the radiator's output by 5%. So if you need 100 square feet E.D.R., you'd have to install a radiator capable of 105 square feet E.D.R.

* If A is 50% of width of radiator, add 10%; if 150%, add 35%.

‡B = 80% of A. C = 150% of A. D = A.

The Ratings

(You'll find that some radiators seem identical to others, but there are subtle differences that the manufacturers made over the years.)

(These pages, from Rolla C. Carpenter's 1895 book, *Heating and Ventilating Buildings*, detail some of the earliest experiments ever done to establish radiator ratings. Although the charts lack pictures of these early radiators, the descriptions are good and you should be able to find what you need if and when you encounter one of the more ancient radiators. - D. H.)

HEAT GIVEN OFF FROM RADIATING SURFACES.

51. Results of Tests of Radiating Surface.—The results of the experiments of Péclet have been given quite fully, and they will be found to agree well with best modern tests when the conditions are similar. The radiating surface ordinarily employed for steam or hot-water heating consists of a number of pipes closely grouped together so as to occupy as little space as possible. In some instances long coils or series of parallel rows of pipe are employed arranged horizontally, but ordinarily the pipes are vertical, and grouped together in two to four rows. The usual height of radiator is 36 to 40 inches with the bottom placed about 3 inches from the floor, making the actual height of radiating surface about 3 feet. In some instances radiators are lower. in which case the results per unit of surface are considerably increased.

The value of a radiator in which the surface is grouped so as to prevent the free escape of radiant heat will depend largely upon the effectiveness with which the air-currents strike the heating surfaces. There is a tendency for heated air to move in a vertical current in contact with the radiator surface, and thus to keep the upper portion in a very hot atmosphere, which has the effect of materially lessening its efficiency. The practical effect of these restrictions is to reduce the heating power of radiators which are composed of a large amount of surface closely grouped. The following summary of a series of radiator tests made by J. H. Mills shows that with very small radiators the results are in practical accordance with those of Péclet's experiments, but as the radiators increase in size they fall off about in proportion to the loss of effective radiating surface.

Sq. Ft. of Radiating Surface.	Difference of Temperature.	B. T. U. per Sq. Ft. per Hour per Degree Difference of Temperature.	
		Peclet's Formula.	Actual.
10	155	1.86	2.10
20	150	1.84	2.08
30	158	1.87	2.06
40	175	1.92	1.75
50	155	1.86	1.73
60	165	1.89	1.67

The following experiments were made by Tredgold * for the time of cooling of water in vessels of various kinds. The writer has reduced the results to heat-units given off per square foot of surface per hour.

SUMMARY OF TREDGOLD'S EXPERIMENTS.

Material Cooling.	Material of Radiator.	Temperature of Hot Body.	Temperature of Room.	Difference of Temperature.	Heat-units Emitted per Sq. Ft. per Hour.		
					Total Heat-units.	Per Deg. Diff. Temp.	By Péclet's Formula.
Hot water...	Tinned iron cylinder....	180	55.5	124.5	255	1.43	1.17
Hot water....	Glass	180	56.5	123.5	426	2.37	2.36
" "	Wrought-iron block....	180	57	123	434	2.41	2.36
" "	Rusty wrought iron....	180	57	123	486	2.70	2.5

* Tredgold's Warming and Ventilating of Buildings, second edition, pages 56 to 60.

The following table is abstracted from one published in "Warming and Ventilation of Buildings," by J. H. Mills:

EXPERIMENTS ON DIFFERENT STEAM-HEATED SURFACES AND DIFFERENT MATERIALS.

WROUGHT-IRON, CAST-IRON, STEEL, AND BRASS PIPES. CORRUGATED, RINGED, AND PLAIN SURFACES.

		Square Feet of Surface.	Temperature. Steam.	Temperature. Air of Room.	Temperature. Difference. B – C.	Lbs. of Water Condensed per Sq. Ft. per Hr.	Heat-units per Degree Diff. Steam and Air.
J. H. Nason, 1862.	Description of heating surface	A	B	C	D	F	I
	Plain wrought-iron pipe, 1", 100' in a single horizontal line	33.30	212	70	142	.41	2.89
	Plain cast-iron pipe 3" diameter outside, 5' long	4.02	212	70	142	.344	2.42
	" " " 3" " " 5' " but thinner than above	4.02	212	70	142	.344	2.42
	Ribbed cast-iron pipe, S. Williams; core 3" in diam., 5' long; ribs ⅜' deep, ½" between cylinders, 1" cylinders	8.87	212	70	142	.24	1.69
	Ribbed cast-iron pipe, No. 1, J. Nason & Co., 3" outside	10.70	212	70	142	.275	1.95
	" " " " 2, " " " 3" " heavier ribs than No. 1	9.20	212	70	142	.280	1.98
	Plain cast-iron pipe, J. Nason & Co. } Placed side by side and tested together.	4.02	212	70	142	.36	2.54
	Ribbed " " " " " }	10.70	212	70	142	.245	1.72
	Curved rib cast-iron radiator, Morris, Tasker & Co	14.14	212	70	142	.269	1.89
	Box-radiator, cast iron, with straight vertical ribs	44.30	212	70	142	.21	1.60
	Vertical cast-iron ringed-pipe radiator, 7 Sec. "Clogston"	21.00	212	70	142	.237	1.67
J. H. Mills, 1888.	Cast-iron pipe 3" diam., in single line	25.00	222	70	152	.312	2.06
	Wrought-iron pipe 3" diam., in single line	26.00	228	70	158	.312	1.98
	Steel pipe 4" diam., in single line	25.00	230	68	162	.39	1.86
	Brass 1" horizontal pipe; 4-branch circulation	10.00	230	62	168	.351	2.09
	Wrought-iron. 1" horizontal pipe, 4-branch circulation	10.00	228	65	163	.412	2.53
	Plain brass vertical tube-radiator ⅛" diam., 2 × 4	12.00	230	62	163	.269	1.60
	Corrugated brass vertical tube-radiator ⅛" diam., 2 × 16	48.00	228	60	168	.214	1.26
	Vertical wrought-iron tube-radiator, Walworth, 1 row of 20 pipes	20.00	228	77	151	.369	2.43
	" " " " " " 2 " " 16 "	32.00	228	70	158	.343	2.04
	" " " " " " 3 " " 16 "	48.00	228	72	156	.219	1.80
	"Union" radiator, cast iron, 6 sec., 29" high	25.00	228	70	158	.32	2.03
	"Triumph" radiator, A. A. Griffing Iron Co., cast-iron, 8 loops	40.00	230	65	165	.275	1.67
	Peirce "Excelsior" cast-iron radiator, 10 sections	40.00	228	63	165	.219	1.70
	"Art" radiator, cast iron, 6 panels	18 00	228	74	154	.264	1.71
	" " " " 12 " double	36.00	228	70	158	.199	1.25
	Detroit Radiator Exeter Machine Co., cast-iron, 8 loops	40.00	228	73	155	.256	1.65
	Single bar of Gold's Pin Indirect Radiator, 3" × 6" × 3½'	10.00	228	70	158	.375	2.37
	Howard Oxbow Radiator, 2 loops, cast iron. Date 1866	25.00	228	70	158	.347	2.20

The following table gives the abstract of a large number of radiator tests made under the supervision of the author: *

Name or Kind of Radiator.	Dimensions.				Tests of Kelsey & Jackson.		Tests of Camp & Woodward.		Tests of Dunn & Mack.		Péclet's Coefficient.
	No. Sections.	Rows of Tubes.	Surface, Sq. Ft.	Height, Inches.	Difference of Temperature, Deg. Fahr.	Coefficient.	Difference of Temperature, Deg. Fahr.	Coefficient.	Diff. of Temp., Deg. Fahr.	Coefficient.	
W. I. vertical pipes	12	4	53.6	36	94	1.62					
W. I. vertical pipes, Nason	16	3	47.94	36	90	1.669	145	1.70	......	...	1.81
					146.6	1.83	144	1.69	......	....	1.81
							133	1.62	......	....	1.78
W. I. hot water, Western No. 2	12	4	41.19	32½	.....	.....	......	.....	133.2	1.62	1.78
									130.1	1.56	1.77
									137.6	1.60	1.79
W. I. steam, Western No. 2	12	4	43.33	32½	......	......	......	.....	144.8	1.81	1.81
									148.2	1.68	1.82
									158.5	1.79	1.87
Steel, hot water, Western No. 1	12	4	45.13	35	.....	.....	......	......	146.2	1.60	1.82
									147.6	1.79	1.82
									159.5	1.95	1.87
Steel, steam, Western No. 1	12	4	47.24	35	......	......	......	......	144.6	1.59	1.81
									143.0	1.50	1.81
									155.0	1.55	1.86
Cast iron, Bundy	16	1	45.11	37	......	......	......	......	153.2	1.76	1.85
									154.4	2.14	1.85
" " "	10	3	79	37	149	1.64	......	......	159.4	2.02	1.87
" " Bundy Élite	9	3	41.8	36	......	......	......	......	153.1	1.88	1.85
									157.1	1.71	1.86
									171.1	1.96	1.91
" " "	...	..	......	...	......	......	......	......	......	...	...
" " Reed	13	1	48.7	...	......	......	151	1.688	......	...	1.83
							147	1.627	......	...	1.82
							136	1.523	......	...	1.78
" " Royal Union	11	3	49.12	37	151	2.08	151	1.688	150	1.73	1.83
							139	1.565	137.5	1.88	1.79
							130	1.582	157	1.88	1.87
" " " "	26	3	52.81	17	......	......	......	......	153	2.46	
									152	2.37	
									159	2.75	
" " Perfection Steam	13	1	49.9	....	91	1.63	147.8	1.456			
							147	1.374			
							144	1.433			
" " " "	12	1	48.17	37¼	......	......	.....	....	147.0	1.77	1.82
									156.3	1.59	1.86
									166.5	1.89	1.89
" " " "	10	2	40.2	37¾	......	......	......	......	151.5	1.59	1.83
									145.4	1.51	1.81
									165.6	1.71	1.89
" " Perfection Hot Water.	12	1	48	37	89	1.664					
					150	1.55					
" " Ideal Steam	10	1	40	38	......	......	......	......	155.3	1.73	1.86
									158.7	1.70	1.87
									155.1	1.74	1.86
" " " Hot Water	10	1	40	38	140	1.61	......	......	154.5	1.91	1.85
									167.6	2.01	1.90
									158.4	1.99	1.87
" " National Steam.	10	1	40	38	......	......	......	.....	154	1.67	1.86
									153	1.69	1.85
									160	1.76	1.88
" " Whittier Ex. Surface	3	1	38.65	30	142	1.13	......	......	152.6	1.51	1.83
									164.3	1.56	1.89
" " Michigan Indirect	...	1	58.2	....	91	1.434	......	......	151.0	1.45	1.83
	...	..	......	....	140	1.27					
2-inch pipe, single, horizontal	...	..	......	....	......	......	......	......	155.6	3.3	
									167.1	3.7	
									194.5	4.3	
									213.2	4.3	
1-inch pipe, single, horizontal.,	....	..	.....	...	......	......	......	......	151.9	5.5	
									165	5.7	
									182.4	5.8	

* Vol. 1., Transactions American Society Heating and Ventilating Engineers.

TESTS OF RADIATORS WITH EXTENDED SURFACE SO AS TO FORM AIR-FLUES, COMPARED WITH PLAIN CAST-IRON RADIATORS.*

	Description of Radiator.	Number of Loops.	Height above Floor, Inches.	Width of Loop, Inches.	Area Surface, Sq. Ft.	Steam-pressure.	Temperature. Steam.	Temperature. Room.	Temperature. Difference.	Wt. Steam Condensed per Hour per Sq. Ft., Lbs.	Ditto, per Deg. Diff. Temp.	B.T.U. per Sq Ft. and per Deg. per Hr.	B.T.U. per Sq. Ft. per Hr.	B.T.U. by Peclet's Rules
		1	2	3	4	5	6	7	8	9	10	11	12	13
A	Extended surface, Joy flue	9	37	8⅝	57.8	3.96	225	52.1	173	3.12	0.00170	1.65	302	312
a	Do. do. do.	1	37	8⅝	6.40	4.0	226	67.6	158	0.332	0.00212	2.05	323	312
A'	Same as *A* with flues planed off.	9	37	8⅝	40.4	3.9	224	57.8	172	0.329	0.00197	1.97	318	388
a'	Do. do. do.	1	37	8⅝	4.24	3.9	224	70.5	154	0.379	0.00247	2.39	369	288
B	Crescent Flue Radiator	9	36½	8⅝	60.8	3.81	223	73.6	149	0.245	0.00136	1.30	248	280
b	Do. do. do.	1	36½	8⅝	6.23	4.0	225	68.8	156	0.360	0.00231	2.24	350	296
C	Plain Bundy, single row	14	39½	2½	40.25	3.94	224	65.7	158	0.345	0.00243	2.33	335	312
c'	Do. do. do.	1	39½	2½	2.83	4.1	226	66.2	159	0.375	0.00237	2.26	365	312
D	Princess flue radiator	9	38	8⅝	63.1	3.96	225	71.5	153	2.21	0.00145	1.39	214	285
d	Do. do. do.	1	38	8⅝	7.18	4.1	226	70.5	155	0.301	0.00194	1.9	292	294
D'	Same as *D* with extended surface removed.	9	38	8⅝	41.2	3.97	225	71.7	153	0.292	0.00191	1.85	284	285
d'		1	38	8⅝	4.50	4.0	222	66.2	159	0.365	0.00231	2.24	355	312

52. Tests of Indirect Heating Surfaces.—The tests which have been made on indirect heating surfaces show very great difference in results, varying from those given by Peclet for the loss due to convection alone, to results which are 8 or 10 times as great. This difference in result is no doubt due in each case to the velocity of air which comes in contact with the surface. When the indirect radiators are not freely supplied with air, or the velocity is low, the amount of heat which is discharged is small; when the velocity of the air is high, the amount of heat taken up is proportionally greater. According to experiments made by the writer, the coefficient of heat transmission increases as the square root of the velocity of the air.

The amount of air passing over a given surface of the radiator can be estimated quite accurately by the amount of heat given off, which we can reasonably suppose in this case to be

* Test by Denton & Jacobus, July, 1894.

all utilized in warming the air. At a temperature of about 60 degrees, 1 heat-unit will warm 55 cubic feet of air 1 degree (see Table VIII), so that the number of cubic feet of air warmed is equal to 55 times the total number of heat-units given off from 1 square foot of heating surface per hour, divided by the difference of temperature of entering and discharge air.

NOTE.—Let T = temperature discharge air, t' that of entering air, H = total number of heat-units given off per square foot of surface, a the number of square feet of surface. Then,

$$\text{Cubic feet of air per square foot heating surface} = \frac{55H}{(T - t')a}.$$

The following tests, made under the direction of the writer, give actual results obtained in testing steam-pipes in a current of air moving at different velocities:

SUMMARY OF RESULTS.—TEST OF 2″ STEAM-PIPE WITH BLOWER.

Steam-pressure by Gauge.	Average Difference of Temperature of Steam and Air of Room.	Velocity of Air Passing over Pipe, Feet per Second.	Heat Transmission in B. T. U. per Square Foot per Hour for each Degree of Temperature.	Increase in Temperature of Air, Deg. Fahr.	Cubic Feet of Air per Square Foot per Hour.
4.45	123.72	9.8	6.32	26.7	148
5.09	120.30	9.4	6.37	28.4	142
5.38	113.68	4.1	4.29	42.0	63
5.86	113.44	4.5	4.72	42.4	69
5.27	119.32	6.7	5.46	34.9	102
5.15	116.20	5.5	5.46	37.4	83
5.20	117.77				
12.48	134.29	7.1	5.53	35.9	112
13.70	132.73	6.7	5.19	37.3	101
12.10	127.84	6.0	5.24	40.9	91
12.25	125.75	5.5	5.19	43.1	83
13.73	125.93	4.3	4.53	48.3	65
13.55	122.87	4.4	4.99	51.4	66
12.97	128.24				
25.35	157.05	8.6	5.67	37.1	130
27.10	158.27	9.1	5.91	37.7	136
27.54	153.70	6.7	5.36	44.8	101
28.21	153.28	6.3	5.41	45.4	100
27.10	146.68	4.3	4.20	52.6	65
26.70	147.19	4.6	4.61	53.7	70
26.97	152.69				

EXPERIMENTS ON INDIRECT RADIATORS.*

Number.	Names of Radiators, Engineers' and Dates of Experiments.	Square Feet Surface.	Gauge-pressure, Steam.	Temperatures: Steam.	Temperatures: Entering Air.	Temperatures: Exit Air.	Diff. Temp.: Enter and Exit Air.	Diff. Temp.: Steam and Enter Air.	Oz. Water condensed per Foot per Hour.	Air, Cubic Ft. per ft. per Hour.	Units of Heat: Per Ft. per Hour.	Units of Heat: Per Deg. Diff. Temp. Stm. & Air.
1	C. B. Richards, 1873-4. Gold's pin		1	215	0	160	160	215	5.44	111	340	1.58
2	Novelty		1	215	0	156	156	215	5.09	102	318	1.48
3	G. Whittier		1	215	0	135	135	215	4.40	106	275	1.28
4	Pipe coil		1	215	0	147	147	215	4.88	108	305	1.42
5	W. J. Baldwin, 1885. Gold's pin	60	10	239	71	168	97	168	3.83	128	239	1.42
6	Compound coil	60	10	239	71	170	98	167	3.84	126	240	1.43
7	W. Warner, 1880, Gold's pin	70	3	222	42	145	103	180	4.60	145	288	1.60
8	J. H. Mills, 1879. Walworth	40	5	227	33	142	109	194	5.00	149	313	1.61
9	Mills	60	5	227	78	162	84	139	4.98	158	255	1.71
	100 Cubic Feet of Air per Foot per Hour, Average.									126	286	1.50
10	Dr. Gray, 1875, Gold's pin	90	20	259	33	125	92	226	6.54	231	409	1.81
11	J. R. Reed, 1875, Whittier	68	3	222	45	129	84	177	5.09	197	318	1.80
12	C. B. Richards, 1873-4. Gold's pin		1	215	0	139	139	215	9.15	214	572	2.66
13	Novelty		1	215	0	132	132	215	8.70	214	544	2.53
14	G. Whittier		1	215	0	102	102	215	6.66	212	416	1.94
15	Pipe coil		1	215	0	106	106	215	6.98	214	436	2.03
	200 Cubic Feet of Air per Foot per Hour, Average.									214	449	2.13
16	J. R. Reed, 1875. Whittier	68	3	222	52	110	58	170	5.50	308	344	2.02
17	G. Whittier	68	3	222	52	114	62	170	5.86	307	366	2.15
18	Gold's pin	58	3	222	52	127	75	170	7.92	343	495	2.91
19	C. B. Richards, 1873-4. Gold's pin		1	215	0	129	129	215	12.65	319	791	3.68
20	Novelty		1	215	0	121	121	215	11.90	320	744	3.46
21	G. Whittier		1	215	0	87	87	215	8.53	319	533	2.48
22	Pipe coil		1	215	0	89	80	215	8.64	323	540	2.51
23	J. H. Mills, 1876, Gold's pin	76½	10	239	81	159	78	158	8.49	354	531	3.36
24	W. J. Baldwin, Nov., 1885. Gold's pin	60	5	227	82	150	68	145	8.16	390	510	3.52
25	Compound coil	60	5	227	82	152	70	145	8.16	379	510	3.52
	300 Cubic Feet of Air per Foot per Hour, Average.									336	536	2.96
26	J. H. Mills, 1876, Gold's pin	76½	10	239	90	158	67	148	8.91	433	557	3.76
27	W. J. Baldwin, 1885. Gold's pin	60	5	227	70	137	67	158	8.93	433	558	3.55
28	Compound coil	60	5	227	70	135	65	158	8.40	420	525	3.34
29	C. B. Richards, 1873-4. Gold's pin		1	215	0	121	121	215	15.92	428	995	4.63
30	Novelty		1	215	0	113	113	215	14.86	428	929	4.32
31	G. Whittier		1	215	0	77	77	215	10.14	428	634	2.95
32	Pipe coil		1	215	0	76	76	215	10.02	428	626	2.91
	400 Cubic Feet of Air per Foot per Hour, Average.									428	689	3.64
33	J. H. Mills, 1876. Gold's pin	77	6	230	88	158	70	142	10.04	467	628	4.42
34	Walworth	67½	6	230	88	142	54	142	8.88	534	555	3.91
	500 Cubic Feet of Air per Foot per Hour, Average.									501	592	4.17
35	J. H. Mills, 1876. Walworth	85	20	259	90	160	70	169	13.69	636	856	5.06
36	Gold's pin	76½	20	259	90	166	76	169	15.16	649	948	5.61
	600 Cubic Feet of Air per Foot per Hour, Average.									643	902	5.34
37	J. H. Mills, 1876. Walworth	85	3	222	90	142	52	132	11.61	726	726	5.50
38	Gold's pin	76½	3	222	90	145	55	132	12.54	741	784	5.94
	700 Cubic Feet of Air per Foot per Hour, Average.									734	755	5.72
39	J. H. Mills, 1876. Gold's pin	77	5	227	94	145	51	133	13.43	855	839	6.31
40	Nason	85	7½	233	79	135	56	154	15.30	888	956	6.21
	800 Cubic Feet of Air per Foot per Hour, Average.									872	898	6.26

* From John H. Mills' work on Heat, by permission.

COMPARISONS OF WATER AND STEAM CIRCULATION, WITH INDIRECT RADIATORS, *NATURAL* AND *FORCED* AIR-SUPPLY. BY J. H. MILLS.

No. for Reference.	Radiators boxed in Stacks, open below, and with Outlet above for heated Air, the duty of Radiator being determined by the Volume and Temperatures of the heated Air.	Square Feet of Surface.	Square Inch of Outlet.	Temperatures.				Difference of Temperature.		Cubic Feet of Air.		Units of Heat per Sq. Ft. per Hour.	
				Water or Steam.		Air to be Warmed.							
	Engineers, Radiators, and Dates.			Flow	Return.	Cold.	Warm.	Steam or Water and Cold Air.	Warm and Cold Air. *F – E.*	Velocity of Hot Air, Ft per Sec.	Per sq. ft per Hour at Uniform Den.	Total.	Per Deg. Dif. Steam or Water & Air.
	Radiators with Water Circulation.												
1	W. J. Baldwin, 1886. Box coil, nat. draught, water	74	192	192	176	85	134	99	49	1.97	106	99	1.00
2	W. J. Baldwin, 1886. Compound coil, nat. draught, water	48	192	195	185	85	143	105	58	1.5	117	131	1.25
3	J. H. Mills, 1885. Albany cast, nat. draught, water	60	78	202	172	38	128	149	90	4.5	123	213	1.43
4	J. H. Mills, 1885. Box coil, nat. draught, water	55	82	205	162	45	135	138	90	4.7	145	251	1.82
5	W. J. Baldwin, 1886 Box coil	74	144	206	186	78	150	118	72	3.8	149	206	1.75
6	W. J. Baldwin, 1886 Compound coil	48	144	206	194	78	166	122	88	2.5	148	250	2.05
7	J. H. Mills, 1885. Gold's pin	100	144	214	178	28	143	168	115	5.	146	323	1.92
8	J. H. Mills, 1885. Mills' indirect	100	144	214	181	28	138	169	110	5.3	157	332	1.96
9	Staggered Tube Coil Radiator, Shakelton's, water	55	50	198	159	34	116	144	82	7.8	158	249	1.73
10	J. H. Mills, 1885. Mills' indirect, Shakelton's, water	100	144	196	155	40	111	135	71	6.6	204	279	2.07
11	J. H. Mills, 1885. Gold's pin, Shakelton's, water	100	144	196	155	40	114	135	74	7.	211	300	2.22
	Averages			202	173	53	134	135	82	4.6	151	239	1.75
	Comparison of Steam and Water under similar Conditions and Temperatures.												
12	J. H. Mills, 1884, Box coil, nat. draught, water.	55	50	210	163	50	146	137	96	5.8	107	198	1.45
13	C. B. Richards, 1874, Box coil, nat. draught, steam.			215		0	147	215	147		106	305	1.42
14	J. H. Mills, 1884, Mills' indirect, water.	100	144	220	180	28	136	172	108	4.9	146	303	1.76
15	J. H. Mills, 1879, Mills' indirect, steam.	60		227		78	162	149	84		151	255	1.71
16	W. J. Baldwin, Compound coil, water.	48	144	206	194	78	166	122	88	2.5	148	250	2.05
17	W. J. Baldwin, Compound coil, steam.	60	144	220		62	170	158	108		146	303	1.92
18	J. H. Mills, 1884, Gold's pin, water.	100	144	240	200	26	157	194	128	5.7	163	401	2.07
19	W. J. Baldwin, 1885, Gold's pin, steam.	60	144	220		62	157	158	95		161	295	1.87
	Averages, water.			219	184	46	157	156	105		141	288	1.83
	Averages, steam.			221		51	159	170	109		141	289	1.73
20	J. H. Mills, Walworth 10-foot flue, Indirect Radiator, steam	66	217	231	192	84	138	147	54	6.7	461	479	3.26
21	J. H. Mills, Walworth forced draught, Indirect Radiator, steam	66	217	228	180	94	135	134	41	22.1	1360	1077	8.04
22	June 16, 1876, Gold's pin, 10-foot flue, Indirect Radiator, steam	76	217	231	184	84	155	147	71	6.3	360	492	3.35
23	June 16, 1876, Gold's pin, forced dr't, Indirect Radiator, steam	76	217	228	150	94	145	134	51	19.7	1143	1121	8.36
24	Nason, 10-foot flue, Indirect Radiator, steam	85	217	228	178	83	133	145	50	10.1	534	513	3.54

NOTE.—For Nos. 5, 15, 17, and 19 the heat recorded is that due to the amount of steam condensed (see Table XII).

From the general results shown in the table page 80 it is seen that the heat-units given off per square foot per degree difference of temperature equals very nearly the square root of four times the velocity in feet per second. That is,

$$h = \sqrt{4v}.$$

The tables pages 81 and 82 contain an extensive summary of tests of indirect radiators, abstracted from Mills' work on Heating and Ventilation, and are of especial interest as showing the close agreement in results, whether water or steam is used. The higher results in this table agree fairly well with the rule stated; those for natural draught are much smaller, and approximately equal to the square root of the velocity in feet per second.

53. Conclusions from Radiator Tests.—The general results of radiator tests can be summed up as follows: First, that the values for heat transmission in recent tests of direct radiators vary greatly and differ more from an average result than from those given by Péclet, and consequently his results can be used with confidence as applying to modern radiators. Second, the results of the test show greater differences in favor of low radiators as compared with high ones than was shown in the experiments of Péclet. Third, the experiments do not show any sensible difference for different materials used in radiators or for hot water or steam, provided the difference in temperature between the air in the room and that of the fluid in the radiator is the same. Fourth, the internal volume of radiators is of value only in lessening the friction of the fluid. It has no special influence on the results. Fifth, the extended surface radiators, or radiators in which the cast iron projects from the surface into the air, show large results when estimated on the basis of projected or plain surface, but show very small results when estimated on the basis of measured surface. Sixth, thin radiators, or those with one row of tubes, always show higher efficiency than thick ones or those with numerous rows of tubes. Seventh, comparative tests of radiators should only be made between radiators of similar forms, or at least those which have about the same amount of surface.

THE CRANE "STANDARD"

RETURN BEND

WROUGHT IRON TUBE RADIATORS.

THE CRANE "STANDARD"

RETURN BEND

WROUGHT IRON TUBE RADIATORS.

LIST OF SIZES.

Number of Rows.	Tubes in each Row.	Heating Surface. Square Ft.	Height. Inches.	Length, Inlet to Outlet. Inches.	Width. Inches.	Size of Inlet. Inches.	Size of Outlet. Inches.	Height from floor to center of Openings. Inches.
1	4	4	33½	9½	4⅜	¾	¾	3¾
1	6	6	33½	13½	4⅜	¾	¾	3¾
1	8	8	33½	17½	4⅜	¾	¾	3¾
1	10	10	33½	21½	4⅜	¾	¾	3¾
1	12	12	33½	25½	4⅜	¾	¾	3¾
1	16	16	33½	33½	4⅜	1	¾	3¾
2	4	8	33½	9½	6	1	¾	4¼
2	6	12	33½	13½	6	1	¾	4¼
2	7	14	33½	15½	6	1	¾	4¼
2	8	16	33½	17½	6	1	¾	4¼
2	9	18	33½	19½	6	1	¾	4¼
2	10	20	33½	21½	6	1	¾	4¼
2	12	24	33½	25½	6	1	¾	4¼
2	15	30	33½	31½	6	1¼	1	4¼
2	18	36	33½	37½	6	1¼	1	4¼
2	21	42	33½	43½	6	1¼	1	4¼
2	24	48	33½	49½	6	1¼	1	4¼
2	28	56	33½	57½	6	1¼	1	4¼
2	32	64	33½	65½	6	1¼	1	4¼
2	38	76	33½	77½	6	1¼	1	4¼

Single pipe system and staggered tube radiators same dimensions as above.

All our radiators are tested to 75 pounds pressure before leaving the shop.

THE CRANE "STANDARD"

RETURN BEND

WROUGHT IRON TUBE RADIATORS.

LIST OF SIZES.

Number of Rows.	Tubes in each Row.	Heating Surface. Square Ft.	Height. Inches.	Length. Inlet to Outlet. Inches.	Width. Inches.	Size of Inlet. Inches.	Size of Outlet. Inches.	Height from floor to center of Openings. Inches.
3	4	12	34	9½	7½	1	¾	4¼
3	8	24	34	17½	7½	1	¾	4¼
3	10	30	34	21¾	7½	1	¾	4¼
3	12	36	34	25½	7½	1¼	1	4¼
3	16	48	34	33½	7½	1¼	1	4¼
3	20	60	34	41½	7½	1¼	1	4¼
3	24	72	34	49½	7½	1¼	1	4¼
3	28	84	34	57½	7½	1½	1¼	4¼
3	32	96	34	65½	7½	1½	1¼	4¼
3	38	114	34	77½	7½	1½	1¼	4¼
4	4	16	34	9½	10¼	1	¾	4¼
4	8	32	34	17½	10¼	1¼	1	4¼
4	10	40	34	21½	10¼	1¼	1	4¼
4	12	48	34	25½	10¼	1¼	1	4¼
4	14	56	34	29½	10¼	1¼	1	4¼
4	16	64	34	33½	10¼	1¼	1	4¼
4	18	72	34	37½	10¼	1¼	1	4¼
4	20	80	34	41½	10¼	1½	1¼	4¼
4	22	88	34	45½	10¼	1½	1¼	4¼
4	24	96	34	49½	10¼	1½	1¼	4¼
4	26	104	34	53½	10¼	1½	1¼	4¼
4	28	112	34	57½	10¼	1½	1¼	4¼
4	30	120	34	61½	10¼	1½	1¼	4¼
4	32	128	34	65½	10¼	1½	1¼	4¼

Single pipe system and staggered tube radiators, same dimensions as above.

All our radiators are tested to 75 pounds pressure before leaving the shop.

ROMAN RADIATORS.

The Roman Radiator is practical in construction, yet it is built upon proper lines. No expense has been spared to keep it up to the highest standard of excellence. Modern dwellings demand a radiator that will conform harmoniously with its surroundings—one that will properly distribute the heat, and at the same time be pleasing to the eye. A radiator cannot be made a thing of beauty, but it can be made to harmonize with the decoration of the rooms, and so be less conspicuous than at first it appears.

Radiators can be placed under seats, under windows, and in places where they will do the best work without detracting from the accepted scheme of decoration.

ROMAN RADIATORS.

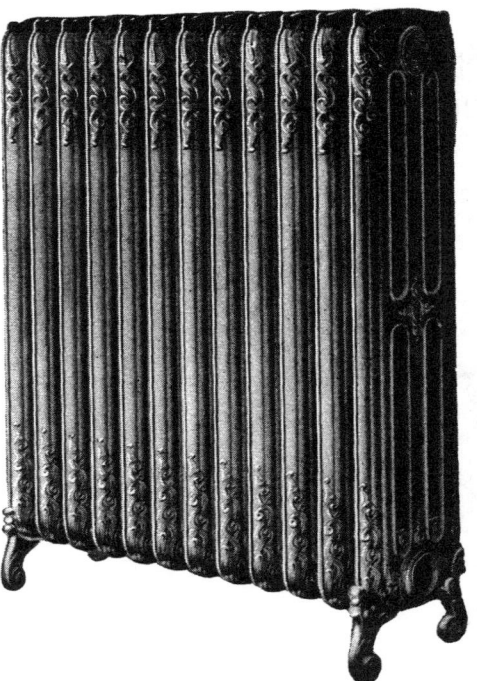

THREE COLUMN.

FOR STEAM OR WATER.

ROMAN THREE COLUMN RADIATORS.

No. of Sections	Length in inches	Heating Surface—Square Feet				
		45 in. high, 6½ sq. ft. per sec.	38 in. high, 5½ sq. ft. per sec.	32 in. high. 4¾ sq. ft. per sec.	26 in. high. 4 sq. ft per sec.	20 in. high, 3¼ sq. ft. per sec.
3	7½	19½	16½	14¼	12	9¾
4	10	26	22	19	16	13
5	12½	32½	27½	23¾	20	16¼
6	15	39	33	28½	24	19½
7	17½	45½	38½	33¼	28	22¾
8	20	52	44	38	32	26
9	22½	58½	49½	42¾	36	29¼
10	25	65	55	47½	40	32½
11	27½	71½	60½	52¼	44	35¾
12	30	78	66	57	48	39
13	32½	84½	71½	61¾	52	42¼
14	35	91	77	66½	56	45½
15	37½	97½	82½	71¼	60	48¾
16	40	104	88	76	64	52
17	42½	110½	93½	80¾	68	55¼
18	45	117	99	85½	72	58½
19	47½	123½	104½	90¼	76	61¾
20	50	130	110	95	80	65
21	52½	136½	115½	99¾	84	68¼
22	55	143	121	104½	88	71½
23	57½	149½	126½	109¼	92	74¾
24	60	156	132	114	96	78
25	62½	162½	137½	118¾	100	81¼
26	65	169	143	123½	104	84½
27	67½	175½	148½	128¼	108	87¾
28	70	182	154	133	112	91
29	72½	188½	159½	137¾	116	94¼
30	75	195	165	142½	120	97½
31	77½	201½	170½	147¼	124	100¾
32	80	208	176	152	128	104
Price per sq. foot.		41c.	42c.	46c.	50c.	57c.

TAPPINGS:—All Radiators are tapped 2", and bushed as follows:

Containing 26 feet or under, 1 inch.
Containing above 26 ft. but not exceeding 60 ft., 1¼ in.
Containing above 60 ft. but not exceeding 112 ft., 1½ in.
Containing above 112 feet, 2 inch.

Width of section, 9½ inches; width across feet, 10¼ inches.

Distance from floor to center of 2 inch Tapping, 4½ inches.
Distance from floor to center of 1½ inch Tapping, 4½ inches.
Distance from floor to center of 1¼ inch Tapping, 4⅜ inches.
Distance from floor to center of 1 inch Tapping, 4¼ inches.

Radiators are made at and shipped from the plant near Pittsburg, Pa.

Ventilating Base can be attached to the above pattern.

NOTE.—In ordering, always mention whether for steam or water, and if for steam, whether for one or two pipe, or for atmospheric or vapor system. For steam, one pipe tapping will be regularly supplied, unless otherwise ordered. Single pipe tappings may be made solid without bushings.

ROMAN RADIATORS.

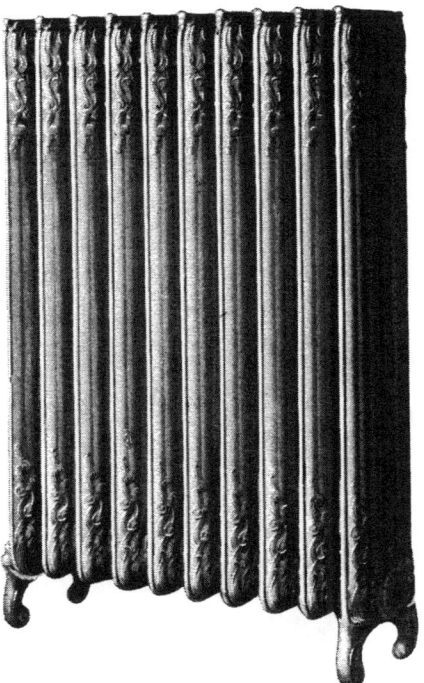

TWO COLUMN.

FOR STEAM OR WATER.

ROMAN TWO COLUMN RADIATORS.

No. of Sections	Length, 2½ in. per Section	Heating Surface—Square Feet				
		45 in. high, 5 sq. ft. per sec	38 in. high, 4 sq. ft. per sec	32 in. high, 3⅓ sq. ft. per sec.	26 in. high, 2⅔ sq. ft per sec.	20 in. high, 2 sq. ft. per sec.
2	5	10	8	6⅔	5⅓	4
3	7½	15	12	10	8	6
4	10	20	16	13⅓	10⅔	8
5	12½	25	20	16⅔	13⅓	10
6	15	30	24	20	16	12
7	17½	35	28	23⅓	18⅔	14
8	20	40	32	26⅔	21⅓	16
9	22½	45	36	30	24	18
10	25	50	40	33⅓	26⅔	20
11	27½	55	44	36⅔	29⅓	22
12	30	60	48	40	32	24
13	32½	65	52	43⅓	34⅔	26
14	35	70	56	46⅔	37⅓	28
15	37½	75	60	50	40	30
16	40	80	64	53⅓	42⅔	32
17	42½	85	68	56⅔	45⅓	34
18	45	90	72	60	48	36
19	47½	95	76	63⅓	50⅔	38
20	50	100	80	66⅔	53⅓	40
21	52½	105	84	70	56	42
22	55	110	88	73⅓	58⅔	44
23	57½	115	92	76⅔	61⅓	46
24	60	120	96	80	64	48
25	62½	125	100	83⅓	66⅔	50
26	65	130	104	86⅔	69⅓	52
27	67½	135	108	90	72	54
28	70	140	112	93⅓	74⅔	56
29	72½	145	116	96⅔	77⅓	58
30	75	150	120	100	80	60
31	77½	155	124	103⅓	82⅔	62
32	80	160	128	106⅔	85⅓	64
Price per sq. foot,		**41c.**	**42c.**	**46c.**	**50c.**	**57c.**

TAPPINGS:—All Radiators are tapped 2", and bushed as follows:

Containing 26 feet or under, 1 inch.
Containing above 26 ft. but not exceeding 60 ft., 1¼ in.
Containing above 60 ft. but not exceeding 112 ft., 1½ in.
Containing above 112 feet 2 inch.

Width of section, 7¾ inches; width across feet, 8¼ inches.

Distance from floor to center of 2 inch Tapping, 4½ inches.
Distance from floor to center of 1½ inch Tapping, 4½ inches.
Distance from floor to center of 1¼ inch Tapping, 4⅜ inches.
Distance from floor to center of 1 inch Tapping, 4¼ inches.

Radiators are made at and shipped from the plant near Pittsburg, Pa.

Ventilating Base can be attached to the above pattern.

NOTE.—In ordering, always mention whether for steam or water, and if for steam, whether for one or two pipe, or for atmospheric or vapor system. For steam, one pipe tapping will be regularly supplied, unless otherwise specified. Single pipe tappings may be made solid without bushings.

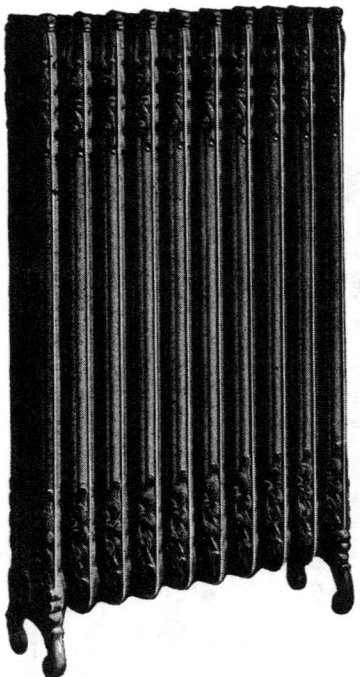

SINGLE COLUMN.

FOR STEAM OR WATER.

ROMAN SINGLE COLUMN RADIATORS.

No. of Sections	Length, 2½ in. per Section	Heating Surface—Square Feet			
		38 in. high, 3 sq. ft. per sec.	32 in. high, 2½ sq. ft. per sec.	26 in. high, 2 sq. ft. per sec.	18 in. high, 1½ sq. ft. per sec.
2	5	6	5	4	3
3	7½	9	7½	6	4½
4	10	12	10	8	6
5	12½	15	12½	10	7½
6	15	18	15	12	9
7	17½	21	17½	14	10½
8	20	24	20	16	12
9	22½	27	22½	18	13½
10	25	30	25	20	15
11	27½	33	27½	22	16½
12	30	36	30	24	18
13	32½	39	32½	26	19½
14	35	42	35	28	21
15	37½	45	37½	30	22½
16	40	48	40	32	24
17	42½	51	42½	34	25½
18	45	54	45	36	27
19	47½	57	47½	38	28½
20	50	60	50	40	30
21	52½	63	52½	42	31½
22	55	66	55	44	33
23	57½	69	57½	46	34½
24	60	72	60	48	36
25	62½	75	62½	50	37½
26	65	78	65	52	39
27	67½	81	67½	54	40½
28	70	84	70	56	42
29	72½	87	72½	58	43½
30	75	90	75	60	45
Price per sq. foot,		42c.	46c.	50c.	58c.

TAPPINGS:—All Radiators are tapped 2", and bushed as follows:

Containing 26 feet or under, 1 inch.
Containing above 26 ft. but not exceeding 60 ft., 1¼ in.
Containing above 60 ft. but not exceeding 112 ft., 1½ in.
Containing above 112 feet, 2 inch.

Width of section, 5¼ inches; width across feet, 5¾ inches.

Distance from floor to center of 1½ inch Tapping, 4⅜ inches.
Distance from floor to center of 1¼ inch Tapping, 4¼ inches.
Distance from floor to center of 1 inch Tapping, 4¼ inches.

Radiators are made at and shipped from the plant near Pittsburg, Pa.

NOTE.—In ordering, always mention whether for steam or water, and if for steam, whether for one or two pipe, or for atmospheric or vapor system. For steam, one pipe tapping will be regularly supplied, unless otherwise specified. Single pipe tappings may be made solid without bushings.

MERCURY RADIATORS.

THREE COLUMN.

FOR STEAM OR WATER.

MERCURY THREE COLUMN RADIATORS.

No. of Sections	Length in inches	HEATING SURFACE—SQUARE FEET					
		45 in. high, 6 sq ft. per sec.	38 in. high, 5 sq. ft. per sec.	32 in. high, 4½ sq.ft per sec	26 in. high, 3¾ sq.ft per sec	23 in. high, 3¼ sq. ft. per sec.	20 in. high, 2¾ sq. ft. per sec.
2	5	12	10	9	7½	6½	5½
3	7½	18	15	13½	11¼	9¾	8¼
4	10	24	20	18	15	13	11
5	12½	30	25	22½	18¾	16¼	13¾
6	15	36	30	27	22½	19½	16½
7	17½	42	35	31½	26¼	22¾	19¼
8	20	48	40	36	30	26	22
9	22½	54	45	40½	33¾	29¼	24¾
10	25	60	50	45	37½	32½	27½
11	27½	66	55	49½	41¼	35¾	30¼
12	30	72	60	54	45	39	33
13	32½	78	65	58½	48¾	42¼	35¾
14	35	84	70	63	52½	45½	38½
15	37½	90	75	67½	56¼	48¾	41¼
16	40	96	80	72	60	52	44
17	42½	102	85	76½	63¾	55¼	46¾
18	45	108	90	81	67½	58½	49½
19	47½	114	95	85½	71¼	61¾	52¼
20	50	120	100	90	75	65	55
21	52½	126	105	94½	78¾	68¼	57¾
22	55	132	110	99	82½	71½	60½
23	57½	138	115	103½	86¼	74¾	63¼
24	60	144	120	108	90	78	66
25	62½	150	125	112½	93¾	81¼	68¾
26	65	156	130	117	97½	84½	71½
27	67½	162	135	121½	101¼	87¾	74¼
28	70	168	140	126	105	91	77
29	72½	174	145	130½	108¾	94¼	79¾
30	75	180	150	135	112½	97½	82½
31	77½	186	155	139½	116¼	100¾	85¼
32	80	192	160	144	120	104	88
Price per sq. foot,		41c.	42c.	46c.	50c.	53c.	57c.

TAPPINGS:—All Radiators are tapped 2", and bushed as follows:

Containing 26 feet or under, 1 inch.
Containing above 26 ft. but not exceeding 60 ft, 1¼ in.
Containing above 60 ft. but not exceeding 112 ft., 1½ in.
Containing above 112 feet, 2 inch.

Width of section, 9 inches; width across feet, 9¾ inches.

Distance from floor to center of 2 inch Tapping, 4½ inches.
Distance from floor to center of 1½ inch Tapping, 4½ inches.
Distance from floor to center of 1¼ inch Tapping, 4⅜ inches.
Distance from floor to center of 1 inch Tapping, 4¼ inches.

Radiators are made at and shipped from the plant near Pittsburg, Pa.

NOTE.—In ordering, always mention whether for steam or water, and if for steam, whether for one or two pipe, or for atmospheric or vapor system. For steam, one pipe tapping will be regularly supplied, unless otherwise specified. Single pipe tappings may be made solid without bushings.

MERCURY RADIATORS.

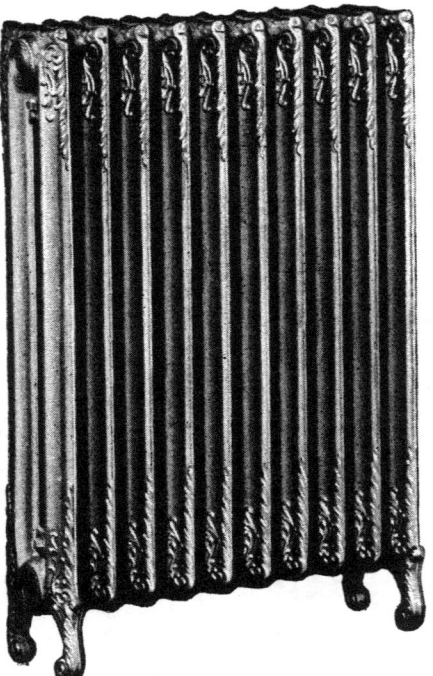

TWO COLUMN.

FOR STEAM OR WATER.

MERCURY TWO COLUMN RADIATORS.

No. of Sections	Length 2½ in. per Section	Heating Surface--Square Feet					
		45 in high, 5 sq. ft. per sec.	38 in. high, 4 sq. ft. per sec.	32 in. high, 3⅓sq.ft. per sec.	26 in. high. 2⅔sq.ft. per sec.	23 in. high, 2⅓sq ft per sec	20 in. high. 2 sq. ft. per sec.
2	5	10	8	6⅔	5⅓	4⅔	4
3	7½	15	12	10	8	7	6
4	10	20	16	13⅓	10⅔	9⅓	8
5	12½	25	20	16⅔	13⅓	11⅔	10
6	15	30	24	20	16	14	12
7	17½	35	28	23⅓	18⅔	16⅓	14
8	20	40	32	26⅔	21⅓	18⅔	16
9	22½	45	36	30	24	21	18
10	25	50	40	33⅓	26⅔	23⅓	20
11	27½	55	44	36⅔	29⅓	25⅔	22
12	30	60	48	40	32	28	24
13	32½	65	52	43⅓	34⅔	30⅓	26
14	35	70	56	46⅔	37⅓	32⅔	28
15	37½	75	60	50	40	35	30
16	40	80	64	53⅓	42⅔	37⅓	32
17	42½	85	68	56⅔	45⅓	39⅔	34
18	45	90	72	60	48	42	36
19	47½	95	76	63⅓	50⅔	44⅓	38
20	50	100	80	66⅔	53⅓	46⅔	40
21	52½	105	84	70	56	49	42
22	55	110	88	73⅓	58⅔	51⅓	44
23	57½	115	92	76⅔	61⅓	53⅔	46
24	60	120	96	80	64	56	48
25	62½	125	100	83⅓	66⅔	58⅓	50
26	65	130	104	86⅔	69⅓	60⅔	52
27	67½	135	108	90	72	63	54
28	70	140	112	93⅓	74⅔	65⅓	56
29	72½	145	116	96⅔	77⅓	67⅔	58
30	75	150	120	100	80	70	60
31	77½	155	124	103⅓	82⅔	72⅓	62
32	80	160	128	106⅔	85⅓	74⅔	64
Price per sq. foot,		41c.	42c.	46c.	50c.	53c.	57c.

TAPPINGS:—All Radiators are tapped 2", and bushed as follows:

Containing 26 feet or under, 1 inch.
Containing above 26 ft. but not exceeding 60 ft., 1¼ in.
Containing above 60 ft. but not exceeding 112 ft., 1½ in.
Containing above 112 feet, 2 inch.

Width of section, 7¾ inches; width across feet, 8¼ inches.

Distance from floor to center of 2 inch Tapping, 4⅛ inches.
Distance from floor to center of 1½ inch Tapping, 4⅛ inches.
Distance from floor to center of 1¼ inch Tapping, 4⅜ inches.
Distance from floor to center of 1 inch Tapping, 4¼ inches.

Radiators are made at and shipped from the plant near Pittsburg, Pa.

Ventilating Base can be attached to the above pattern.

NOTE.—In ordering, always mention whether for steam or water, and if for steam, whether for one or two pipe, or for atmospheric or vapor system. For steam, one pipe tapping will be regularly supplied, unless otherwise ordered. Single pipe tappings may be made solid without bushings.

FLUTED RADIATORS.

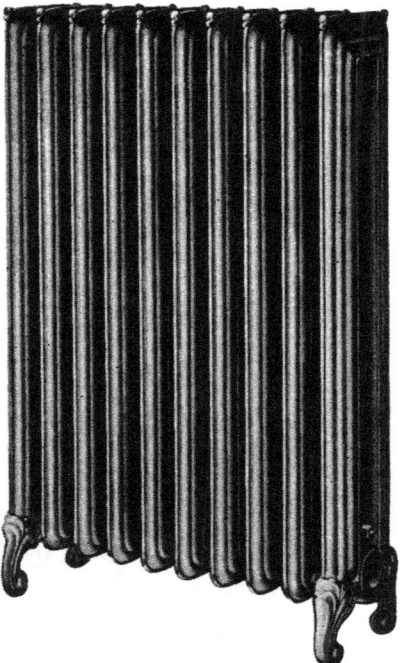

FOR STEAM ONLY.

FLUTED TWO COLUMN RADIATORS.

No. of Sections	Length in inches	Heating Surface—Square Feet				
		45 in. high, 5 sq. ft per sec.	38 in high, 4 sq. ft per sec.	32 in. high, 3⅓ sq. ft. per sec	26 in high, 2⅔ sq. ft. per sec.	20 in. high, 2 sq. ft. per sec.
2	5	10	8	6⅔	5⅓	4
3	7½	15	12	10	8	6
4	10	20	16	13⅓	10⅔	8
5	12½	25	20	16⅔	13⅓	10
6	15	30	24	20	16	12
7	17½	35	28	23⅓	18⅔	14
8	20	40	32	26⅔	21⅓	16
9	22½	45	36	30	24	18
10	25	50	40	33⅓	26⅔	20
11	27½	55	44	36⅔	29⅓	22
12	30	60	48	40	32	24
13	32½	65	52	43⅓	34⅔	26
14	35	70	56	46⅔	37⅓	28
15	37½	75	60	50	40	30
16	40	80	64	53⅓	42⅔	32
17	42½	85	68	56⅔	45⅓	34
18	45	90	72	60	48	36
19	47½	95	76	63⅓	50⅔	38
20	50	100	80	66⅔	53⅓	40
21	52½	105	84	70	56	42
22	55	110	88	73⅓	58⅔	44
23	57½	115	92	76⅔	61⅓	46
24	60	120	96	80	64	48
25	62½	125	100	83⅓	66⅔	50
26	65	130	104	86⅔	69⅓	52
27	67½	135	108	90	72	54
28	70	140	112	93⅓	74⅔	56
29	72½	145	116	96⅔	77⅓	58
30	75	150	120	100	80	60
31	77½	155	124	103⅓	82⅔	62
32	80	160	128	106⅔	85⅓	64
Price per sq. foot,		41c.	42c.	46c.	50c	57c.

TAPPINGS:—All Radiators are tapped 2", and bushed as follows:

Containing 26 feet or under, 1 inch.
Containing above 26 ft but not exceeding 60 ft., 1¼ in.
Containing above 60 ft but not exceeding 112 ft., 1½ in.
Containing above 112 feet, 2 inch.

Width of section, 7¾ inches; width across feet, 8¼ inches.

Distance from floor to center of 2 inch Tapping, 4½ inches.
Distance from floor to center of 1½ inch Tapping, 4½ inches
Distance from floor to center of 1¼ inch Tapping, 4⅜ inches.
Distance from floor to center of 1 inch Tapping, 4¼ inches.

Radiators are made at and shipped from the plant near Pittsburg, Pa.

Ventilating Base can be attached to the above pattern.

NOTE.—In ordering, always mention whether for one or two pipe system. One pipe tapping will be regularly supplied, unless otherwise ordered. Single pipe tappings may be made solid without bushings.

PLAIN RADIATORS.

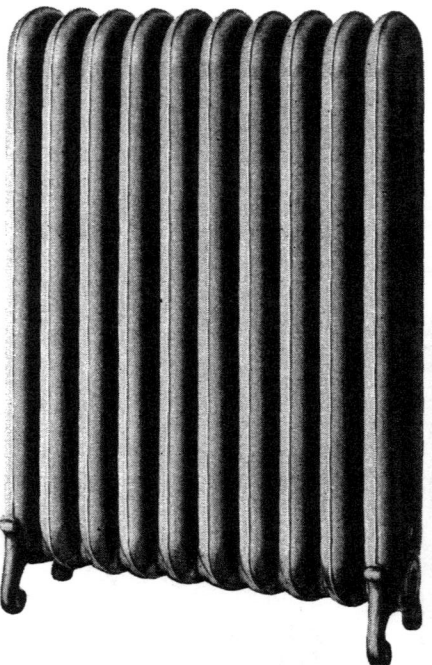

TWO COLUMN.

FOR STEAM OR WATER.

PLAIN TWO COLUMN RADIATORS.

No. of Sections	Length in inches	Heating Surface—Square Feet				
		45 in. high, 5 sq. ft. per sec.	38 in. high, 4 sq. ft. per sec.	32 in. high, 3⅓ sq. ft. per sec.	26 in. high, 2⅔ sq. ft per sec.	20 in. high, 2 sq. ft. per sec.
2	5	10	8	6⅔	5⅓	4
3	7½	15	12	10	8	6
4	10	20	16	13⅓	10⅔	8
5	12½	25	20	16⅔	13⅓	10
6	15	30	24	20	16	12
7	17½	35	28	23⅓	18⅔	14
8	20	40	32	26⅔	21⅓	16
9	22½	45	36	30	24	18
10	25	50	40	33⅓	26⅔	20
11	27½	55	44	36⅔	29⅓	22
12	30	60	48	40	32	24
13	32½	65	52	43⅓	34⅔	26
14	35	70	56	46⅔	37⅓	28
15	37½	75	60	50	40	30
16	40	80	64	53⅓	42⅔	32
17	42½	85	68	56⅔	45⅓	34
18	45	90	72	60	48	36
19	47½	95	76	63⅓	50⅔	38
20	50	100	80	66⅔	53⅓	40
21	52½	105	84	70	56	42
22	55	110	88	73⅓	58⅔	44
23	57½	115	92	76⅔	61⅓	46
24	60	120	96	80	64	48
25	62½	125	100	83⅓	66⅔	50
26	65	130	104	86⅔	69⅓	52
27	67½	135	108	90	72	54
28	70	140	112	93⅓	74⅔	56
29	72½	145	116	96⅔	77⅓	58
30	75	150	120	100	80	60
31	77½	155	124	103⅓	82⅔	62
32	80	160	128	106⅔	85⅓	64
Price per sq. foot,		41c.	42c.	46c.	50c.	57c.

TAPPINGS:—All Radiators are tapped 2", and bushed as follows:

Containing 26 feet or under, 1 inch.
Containing above 26 ft. but not exceeding 60 ft., 1¼ in.
Containing above 60 ft. but not exceeding 112 ft., 1½ in.
Containing above 112 feet, 2 inch.

Width of section, 7⅝ inches; width across feet, 8½ inches.

Distance from floor to center of 2 inch Tapping, 4⅛ inches.
Distance from floor to center of 1½ inch Tapping, 3⅞ inches.
Distance from floor to center of 1¼ inch Tapping, 3⅞ inches.
Distance from floor to center of 1 inch Tapping, 3⅞ inches.

Radiators are made at and shipped from the plant near Pittsburg, Pa.

NOTE.—In ordering, always mention whether for one or two pipe system. One pipe tapping will be regularly supplied, unless otherwise specified. Single pipe tappings may be made solid without bushings.

STAR RADIATORS.

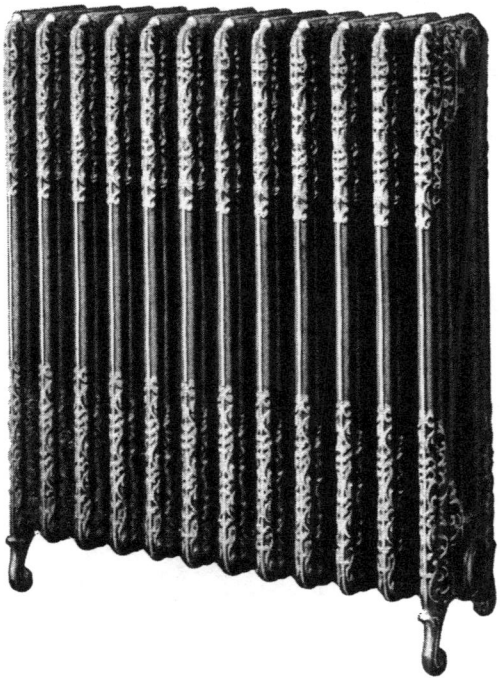

A wide Radiator used in place of a Four Column.

STAR RADIATORS.

No. of Sections.	Length in inches.	Heating Surface—Square Feet			
		38 in. high, 7 sq. ft per sec.	26 in. high, 5 sq. ft. per sec	20 in. high, 4 sq. ft. per sec.	15 in. high, 3 sq. ft. per sec.
2	5	14	10	8	6
3	7½	21	15	12	9
4	10	28	20	16	12
5	12½	35	25	20	15
6	15	42	30	24	18
7	17½	49	35	28	21
8	20	56	40	32	24
9	22½	63	45	36	27
10	25	70	50	40	30
11	27½	77	55	44	33
12	30	84	60	48	36
13	32½	91	65	52	39
14	35	98	70	56	42
15	37½	105	75	60	45
16	40	112	80	64	48
17	42½	119	85	68	51
18	45	126	90	72	54
19	47½	133	95	76	57
20	50	140	100	80	60
21	52½	147	105	84	63
22	55	154	110	88	66
23	57½	161	115	92	69
24	60	168	120	96	72
25	62½	175	125	100	75
26	65	182	130	104	78
27	67½	189	135	108	81
28	70	196	140	112	84
29	72½	203	145	116	87
30	75	210	150	120	90
Price per sq. foot,		**42**c.	**50**c.	**57**c.	**62**c.

TAPPINGS:—All Radiators are tapped 2″, and bushed as follows:

Containg 26 feet or under, 1 inch.
Containing above 26 feet but not exceeding 60 ft., 1¼ in.
Containing above 60 feet but not exceeding 112 ft., 1½ in.
Containing above 112 feet, 2 inch.

Width of section, 11¼ inches; width across feet, 11¼ inches.

Distance from floor to center of Tapping (38 in. height) 4¾ in.
Distance from floor to center of Tapping (26 in. height) 4¾ in.
Distance from floor to center of Tapping (20 in. height) 3 in.
Distance from floor to center of Tapping (15 in. height) 3 in.

Radiators are made at and shipped from the plant near Pittsburg, Pa.

Ventilating Base can be attached to the 26-in. and 38-in. heights of the above pattern.

NOTE.—In ordering always mention whether for steam or water, and if for steam, whether for one or two pipe, or for atmospheric or vapor system. For steam, one pipe tapping will be regularly supplied, unless otherwise specified. Single pipe tappings may be made solid without bushings

UTILITY RADIATORS.

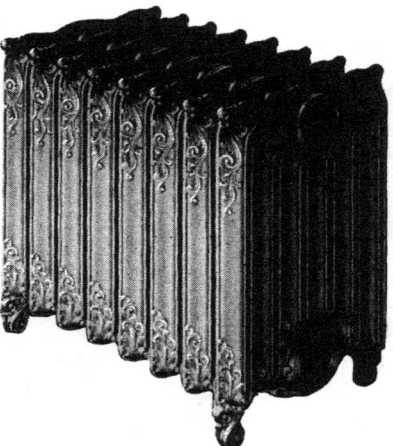

A Six Column Radiator for windows and seats.

Can be made curved or angle to suit the various forms of rooms or spaces.

UTILITY RADIATORS.

No. of Sections	Length in inches	Heating Surface—Square Feet				
		26 in. high, 7 sq. ft. per sec.	22 in. high, 6 sq. ft. per sec.	18 in. high, 5 sq. ft. per sec.	14 in. high, 4 sq. ft. per sec.	13 in. high 4 sq. ft. per sec.
2	5½	14	12	10	8	8
3	8¼	21	18	15	12	12
4	11	28	24	20	16	16
5	13¾	35	30	25	20	20
6	16½	42	36	30	24	24
7	19¼	49	42	35	28	28
8	22	56	48	40	32	32
9	24¾	63	54	45	36	36
10	27½	70	60	50	40	40
11	30¼	77	66	55	44	44
12	33	84	72	60	48	48
13	35¾	91	78	65	52	52
14	38½	98	84	70	56	56
15	41¼	105	90	75	60	60
16	44	112	96	80	64	64
17	46¾	119	102	85	68	68
18	49½	126	108	90	72	72
19	52¼	133	114	95	76	76
20	55	140	120	100	80	80
21	57¾	147	126	105	84	84
22	60½	154	132	110	88	88
23	63¼	161	138	115	92	92
24	66	168	144	120	96	96
25	68¾	175	150	125	100	100
26	71½	182	156	130	104	104
27	74¼	189	162	135	108	108
28	77	196	168	140	112	112
29	79¾	203	174	145	116	116
30	82½	210	180	150	120	120
Price per sq. foot,		50c.	53c.	58c.	64c.	66c.

TAPPINGS:—All Radiators are tapped 2", and bushed as follows:

Containing 26 feet or under, 1 inch.
Containing above 26 ft. but not exceeding 60 ft., 1¼ in.
Containing above 60 ft. but not exceeding 112 ft., 1½ in.
Containing above 112 feet, 2 inch.

Width of section, 11¼ inches; width across feet, 11¼ inches.

Distance from floor to center of 2 inch Tapping, 3 inches.
Distance from floor to center of 1½ inch Tapping, 2¾ inches.
Distance from floor to center of 1¼ inch Tapping, 2¾ inches.
Distance from floor to center of 1 inch Tapping, 2¾ inches.
In 13-inch size, distances are 1 inch less.

Radiators are made at and shipped from the plant near Pittsburg, Pa

NOTE.—In ordering, always mention whether for steam or water, and if for steam, whether for one or two pipe, or for atmospheric or vapor system. For steam, one pipe tapping will be regularly supplied, unless otherwise specified. Single pipe tappings may be made solid without bushings.

ROMAN DINING ROOM RADIATORS.

FOR STEAM OR WATER.

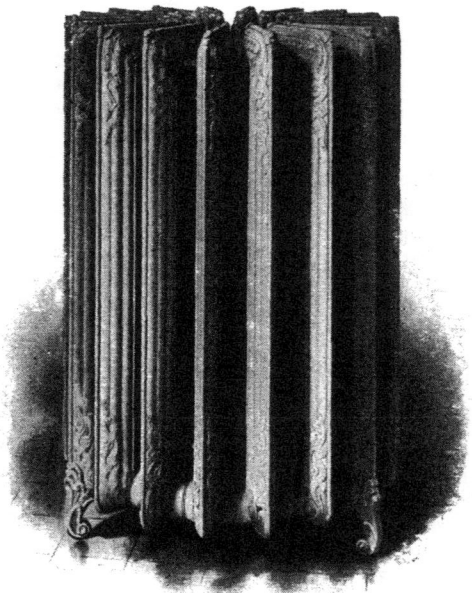

DIMENSIONS AND PRICES.

No.	Length in Inches	Heating Surface Square feet	Price for Water	Price for Steam
1	30	43½	$50 00	$46 00
2	35	54½	55 00	50 00
3	40	65½	60 00	54 00
4	45	76½	65 00	58 00
5	50	87½	70 00	62 00
6	55	98½	75 00	66 00
7	60	109½	80 00	70 00
8	65	120½	85 00	74 00
9	70	131½	90 00	78 00
10	75	142½	95 00	82 00

A useful device for the warming of plates, etc., and heating the room at the same time. Made in Three Column pattern only. Ovens are all the same size, 24x11x16 inches. Height, 38½ inches.

ROMAN CIRCULAR RADIATORS.

FOR STEAM OR WATER.

DIMENSIONS.

TWO COLUMN			THREE COLUMN		
No of Sec.	Inside Diameter at Legs	Outside Diameter at Legs	No. of Sec.	Inside Diameter at Legs	Outside Diameter at Legs
16	6½	23½	16	4½	25
18	8½	25½	18	6½	27
20	10¼	27¼	20	8¼	28¾
22	12¼	29¼	22	10¼	30¾
24	14½	31	24	11½	32½
26	15½	32½	26	12¾	33¼
28	17	34	28	14½	35
30	18½	35½	30	16¼	36¾
32	20	37	32	18	38½
34	21½	38½	34	19¾	40¼
36	22¼	39¼	36	21½	42
38	25	42	38	23¼	43¾
40	26½	43½			

This is one of our special patterns. Circular Radiators are made in all the heights of each pattern No less number of sections than given in list above can be used to form a complete circle. In ordering, always state whether Circular or if they are to fit around a Column, as Circular Radiators are generally made in one piece, but Column Radiators are made in two pieces; also state if wanted for marble top.

Column or Circular Radiators cannot be tapped larger than 1½ inch.

Louraine One Column Radiator

PLAIN

For Steam and Water

Width of sections, 5 inches.
Width across feet, 5⅝ inches.

Louraine One Column Radiator

PLAIN

For Steam and Water

DIMENSIONS AND CAPACITIES

Number Sections	Length Inches	Heating Surface—Square Feet					
		44 in. High	38 in. High	32 in. High	26 in. High	22 in. High	18 in. High
1	2½	3½	3	2½	2	1⅔	1⅓
2	5	7	6	5	4	3⅓	2⅔
3	7½	10½	9	7½	6	5	4
4	10	14	12	10	8	6⅔	5⅓
5	12½	17½	15	12½	10	8⅓	6⅔
6	15	21	18	15	12	10	8
7	17½	24½	21	17½	14	11⅔	9⅓
8	20	28	24	20	16	13⅓	10⅔
9	22½	31½	27	22½	18	15	12
10	25	35	30	25	20	16⅔	13⅓
11	27½	38½	33	27½	22	18⅓	14⅔
12	30	42	36	30	24	20	16
13	32½	45½	39	32½	26	21⅔	17⅓
14	35	49	42	35	28	23⅓	18⅔
15	37½	52½	45	37½	30	25	20
16	40	56	48	40	32	26⅔	21⅓
17	42½	59½	51	42½	34	28⅓	22⅔
18	45	63	54	45	36	30	24
19	47½	66½	57	47½	38	31⅔	25⅓
20	50	70	60	50	40	33⅓	26⅔
21	52½	73½	63	52½	42	35	28
22	55	77	66	55	44	36⅔	29⅓
23	57½	80½	69	57½	46	38⅓	30⅔
24	60	84	72	60	48	40	32
25	62½	87½	75	62½	50	41⅔	33⅓
26	65	91	78	65	52	43⅓	34⅔
27	67½	94½	81	67½	54	45	36
28	70	98	84	70	56	46⅔	37⅓
29	72½	101½	87	72½	58	48⅓	38⅔
30	75	105	90	75	60	50	40
31	77½	108½	93	77½	62	51⅔	41⅓
32	80	112	96	80	64	53⅓	42⅔
33	82½	115½	99	82½	66	55	44

State if for steam or water and whether for one or two-pipe work.

All radiators, unless otherwise specified, tapped two inches and plugged, or bushed to regular tappings. These bushings add about 1½ inches to the length of radiator with two-pipe tapping.

Louraine One Column Radiator

ORNAMENTED

For Steam and Water

Width of sections, 5 inches.
Width across feet, 5⅝ inches.

Louraine One Column Radiator

ORNAMENTED

For Steam and Water

DIMENSIONS AND CAPACITIES

Number Sections	Length Inches	Heating Surface—Square Feet					
		44 in. High	38 in. High	32 in. High	26 in. High	22 in. High	18 in. High
1	2½	3½	3	2½	2	1⅔	1⅓
2	5	7	6	5	4	3⅓	2⅔
3	7½	10½	9	7½	6	5	4
4	10	14	12	10	8	6⅔	5⅓
5	12½	17½	15	12½	10	8⅓	6⅔
6	15	21	18	15	12	10	8
7	17½	24½	21	17½	14	11⅔	9⅓
8	20	28	24	20	16	13⅓	10⅔
9	22½	31½	27	22½	18	15	12
10	25	35	30	25	20	16⅔	13⅓
11	27½	38½	33	27½	22	18⅓	14⅔
12	30	42	36	30	24	20	16
13	32½	45½	39	32½	26	21⅔	17⅓
14	35	49	42	35	28	23⅓	18⅔
15	37½	52½	45	37½	30	25	20
16	40	56	48	40	32	26⅔	21⅓
17	42½	59½	51	42½	34	28⅓	22⅔
18	45	63	54	45	36	30	24
19	47½	66½	57	47½	38	31⅔	25⅓
20	50	70	60	50	40	33⅓	26⅔
21	52½	73½	63	52½	42	35	28
22	55	77	66	55	44	36⅔	29⅓
23	57½	80½	69	57½	46	38⅓	30⅔
24	60	84	72	60	48	40	32
25	62½	87½	75	62½	50	41⅔	33⅓
26	65	91	78	65	52	43⅓	34⅔
27	67½	94½	81	67½	54	45	36
28	70	98	84	70	56	46⅔	37⅓
29	72½	101½	87	72½	58	48⅓	38⅔
30	75	105	90	75	60	50	40
31	77½	108½	93	77½	62	51⅔	41⅓
32	80	112	96	80	64	53⅓	42⅔
33	82½	115½	99	82½	66	55	44

State if for steam or water, and whether for one or two-pipe work.

All radiators, unless otherwise specified, tapped two inches and plugged, or bushed to regular tappings. These bushings add about 1½ inches to the length of radiator with two-pipe tapping.

Louraine Two Column Radiator

PLAIN

For Steam and Water

Width of sections, 7 3-16 inches.
Width across feet, 7¾ in.

Louraine Two Column Radiator

PLAIN

For Steam and Water

DIMENSIONS AND CAPACITIES

Number Sections	Length Inches	Heating Surface—Square Feet				
		45 in. High	38 in. High	32 in. High	26 in. High	20 in. High
1	2½	5	4	3⅓	2⅔	2
2	5	10	8	6⅔	5⅓	4
3	7½	15	12	10	8	6
4	10	20	16	13⅓	10⅔	8
5	12½	25	20	16⅔	13⅓	10
6	15	30	24	20	16	12
7	17½	35	28	23⅓	18⅔	14
8	20	40	32	26⅔	21⅓	16
9	22½	45	36	30	24	18
10	25	50	40	33⅓	26⅔	20
11	27½	55	44	36⅔	29⅓	22
12	30	60	48	40	32	24
13	32½	65	52	43⅓	34⅔	26
14	35	70	56	46⅔	37⅓	28
15	37½	75	60	50	40	30
16	40	80	64	53⅓	42⅔	32
17	42½	85	68	56⅔	45⅓	34
18	45	90	72	60	48	36
19	47½	95	76	63⅓	50⅔	38
20	50	100	80	66⅔	53⅓	40
21	52½	105	84	70	56	42
22	55	110	88	73⅓	58⅔	44
23	57½	115	92	76⅔	61⅓	46
24	60	120	96	80	64	48
25	62½	125	100	83⅓	66⅔	50
26	65	130	104	86⅔	69⅓	52
27	67½	135	108	90	72	54
28	70	140	112	93⅓	74⅔	56
29	72½	145	116	96⅔	77⅓	58
30	75	150	120	100	80	60
31	77½	155	124	103⅓	82⅔	62
32	80	160	128	106⅔	85⅓	64
33	82½	165	132	110	88	66

State if for steam or water, and whether for one or two-pipe work.

All radiators, unless otherwise specified, tapped two inches and plugged, or bushed to regular tappings. These bushings add about 1½ inches to the length of radiator with two-pipe tapping.

Louraine Two Column Radiator

ORNAMENTED

For Steam and Water

Width of sections, 7 3-16 inches.
Width across feet, 7¾ inches.

Louraine Two Column Radiator

ORNAMENTED

For Steam and Water

DIMENSIONS AND CAPACITIES

Number Sections	Length Inches	Heating Surface—Square Feet				
		45 in. High	38 in. High	32 in. High	26 in. High	20 in. High
1	2½	5	4	3⅓	2⅔	2
2	5	10	8	6⅔	5⅓	4
3	7½	15	12	10	8	6
4	10	20	16	13⅓	10⅔	8
5	12½	25	20	16⅔	13⅓	10
6	15	30	24	20	16	12
7	17½	35	28	23⅓	18⅔	14
8	20	40	32	26⅔	21⅓	16
9	22½	45	36	30	24	18
10	25	50	40	33⅓	26⅔	20
11	27½	55	44	36⅔	29⅓	22
12	30	60	48	40	32	24
13	32½	65	52	43⅓	34⅔	26
14	35	70	56	46⅔	37⅓	28
15	37½	75	60	50	40	30
16	40	80	64	53⅓	42⅔	32
17	42½	85	68	56⅔	45⅓	34
18	45	90	72	60	48	36
19	47½	95	76	63⅓	50⅔	38
20	50	100	80	66⅔	53⅓	40
21	52½	105	84	70	56	42
22	55	110	88	73⅓	58⅔	44
23	57½	115	92	76⅔	61⅓	46
24	60	120	96	80	64	48
25	62½	125	100	83⅓	66⅔	50
26	65	130	104	86⅔	69⅓	52
27	67½	135	108	90	72	54
28	70	140	112	93⅓	74⅔	56
29	72½	145	116	96⅔	77⅓	58
30	75	150	120	100	80	60
31	77½	155	124	103⅓	82⅔	62
32	80	160	128	106⅔	85⅓	64
33	82½	165	132	110	88	66

State if for steam or water, and whether for one or two-pipe work.

All radiators, unless otherwise specified, tapped two inches and plugged, or bushed to regular tappings. These bushings add about 1½ inches to the length of radiator with two-pipe tapping.

Louraine Three Column Radiator

PLAIN

For Steam and Water

Width of sections, 9 inches.
Width across feet, 9¼ inches.

Louraine Three Column Radiator

PLAIN

For Steam and Water

DIMENSIONS AND CAPACITIES

Number Sections	Length Inches	Heating Surface—Square Feet					
		44 in. High	38 in. High	32 in. High	26 in. High	22 in. High	18 in. High
1	2½	6	5	4½	3¾	3	2¼
2	5	12	10	9	7½	6	4½
3	7½	18	15	13½	11¼	9	6¾
4	10	24	20	18	15	12	9
5	12½	30	25	22½	18¾	15	11¼
6	15	36	30	27	22½	18	13½
7	17½	42	35	31½	26¼	21	15¾
8	20	48	40	36	30	24	18
9	22½	54	45	40½	33¾	27	20¼
10	25	60	50	45	37½	30	22½
11	27½	66	55	49½	41¼	33	24¾
12	30	72	60	54	45	36	27
13	32½	78	65	58½	48¾	39	29¼
14	35	84	70	63	52½	42	31½
15	37½	90	75	67½	56¼	45	33¾
16	40	96	80	72	60	48	36
17	42½	102	85	76½	63¾	51	38¼
18	45	108	90	81	67½	54	40½
19	47½	114	95	85½	71¼	57	42¾
20	50	120	100	90	75	60	45
21	52½	126	105	94½	78¾	63	47¼
22	55	132	110	99	82½	66	49½
23	57½	138	115	103½	86¼	69	51¾
24	60	144	120	108	90	72	54
25	62½	150	125	112½	93¾	75	56¼
26	65	156	130	117	97½	78	58½
27	67½	162	135	121½	101¼	81	60¾
28	70	168	140	126	105	84	63
29	72½	174	145	130½	108¾	87	65¼
30	75	180	150	135	112½	90	67½
31	77½	186	155	139½	116¼	93	69¾
32	80	192	160	144	120	96	72
33	82½	198	165	148½	123¾	99	74¼

State if for steam or water, and whether for one or two-pipe work.

All radiators, unless otherwise specified, tapped two inches and plugged, or bushed to regular tappings. These bushings add about 1½ inches to the length of radiator with two-pipe tapping.

Louraine Three Column Radiator

ORNAMENTED

For Steam and Water

Width of sections, 9 inches.

Width across feet, 9¼ inches.

See note regarding Tappings on page 76.

Louraine Three Column Radiator

ORNAMENTED

For Steam and Water

DIMENSIONS AND CAPACITIES

Number Sections	Length Inches	Heating Surface—Square Feet					
		44 in. High	38 in. High	32 in. High	26 in. High	22 in. High	18 in. High
1	2½	6	5	4½	3¾	3	2¼
2	5	12	10	9	7½	6	4½
3	7½	18	15	13½	11¼	9	6¾
4	10	24	20	18	15	12	9
5	12½	30	25	22½	18¾	15	11¼
6	15	36	30	27	22½	18	13½
7	17½	42	35	31½	26¼	21	15¾
8	20	48	40	36	30	24	18
9	22½	54	45	40½	33¾	27	20¼
10	25	60	50	45	37½	30	22½
11	27½	66	55	49½	41¼	33	24¾
12	30	72	60	54	45	36	37
13	32½	78	65	58½	48¾	39	29¼
14	35	84	70	63	52½	42	31½
15	37½	90	75	67½	56¼	45	33¾
16	40	96	80	72	60	48	36
17	42½	102	85	76½	63¾	51	38¼
18	45	108	90	81	67½	54	40½
19	47½	114	95	85½	71¼	57	42¾
20	50	120	100	90	75	60	45
21	52½	126	105	94½	78¾	63	47¼
22	55	132	110	99	82½	66	49½
23	57½	138	115	103½	86¼	69	51¾
24	60	144	120	108	90	72	54
25	62½	150	125	112½	93¾	75	56¼
26	65	156	130	117	97½	78	58½
27	67½	162	135	121½	101¼	81	60¾
28	70	168	140	126	105	84	63
29	72½	174	145	130½	108¾	87	65¼
30	75	180	150	135	112½	90	67½
31	77½	186	155	139½	116¼	93	69¾
32	80	192	160	144	120	96	72
33	82½	198	165	148½	123¾	99	74¼

State if for steam or water, and whether for one or two-pipe work.

All radiators, unless otherwise specified, tapped two inches and plugged or bushed to regular tappings. These bushings add about 1½ inches to the length of radiator with two-pipe tapping.

Louraine Four Column Radiator

PLAIN

For Steam and Water

Width of sections, 12 inches.
Width across feet, 12¼ inches.

Louraine Four Column Radiator

PLAIN

For Steam and Water

DIMENSIONS AND CAPACITIES

Number Sections	Length Inches	Heating Surface—Square Feet					
		44 in. High	38 in. High	32 in. High	26 in. High	22 in. High	18 in. High
1	2½	9	8	7	5⅔	4⅓	3½
2	5	18	16	14	11⅓	8⅔	7
3	7½	27	24	21	17	13	10½
4	10	36	32	28	22⅔	17⅓	14
5	12½	45	40	35	28⅓	21⅔	17½
6	15	54	48	42	34	26	21
7	17½	63	56	49	39⅔	30⅓	24½
8	20	72	64	56	45⅓	34⅔	28
9	22½	81	72	63	51	39	31½
10	25	90	80	70	56⅔	43⅓	35
11	27½	99	88	77	62⅓	47⅔	38½
12	30	108	96	84	68	52	42
13	32½	117	104	91	73⅔	56⅓	45½
14	35	126	112	98	79⅓	60⅔	49
15	37½	135	120	105	85	65	52½
16	40	144	128	112	90⅔	69⅓	56
17	42½	153	136	119	96⅓	73⅔	59½
18	45	162	144	126	102	78	63
19	47½	171	152	133	107⅔	82⅓	66½
20	50	180	160	140	113⅓	86⅔	70
21	52½	189	168	147	119	91	73½
22	55	198	176	154	124⅔	95⅓	77
23	57½	207	184	161	130⅓	99⅔	80½
24	60	216	192	168	136	104	84
25	62½	225	200	175	141⅔	108⅓	87½
26	65	234	208	182	147⅓	112⅔	91
27	67½	243	216	189	153	117	94½
28	70	252	224	196	158⅔	121⅓	98
29	72½	261	232	203	164⅓	125⅔	101½
30	75	270	240	210	170	130	105
31	77½	279	248	217	175⅔	134⅓	108½
32	80	288	256	224	181⅓	138⅔	112
33	82½	297	264	231	187	143	115½

State if for steam or water, and whether for one or two-pipe work.

All radiators, unless otherwise specified, tapped two inches and plugged, or bushed to regular tappings. These bushings add about 1½ inches to the length of radiator with two-pipe tapping.

Louraine Four Column Radiator

ORNAMENTED

For Steam and Water

Width of sections, 12 inches.
Width across feet, 12¼ inches.

Louraine Four Column Radiator

ORNAMENTED

For Steam and Water

DIMENSIONS AND CAPACITIES

Number Sections	Length Inches	Heating Surface—Square Feet					
		44 in. High	38 in. High	32 in. High	26 in. High	22 in. High	18 in. High
1	2½	9	8	7	5⅔	4⅓	3½
2	5	18	16	14	11⅓	8⅔	7
3	7½	27	24	21	17	13	10½
4	10	36	32	28	22⅔	17⅓	14
5	12½	45	40	35	28⅓	21⅔	17½
6	15	54	48	42	34	26	21
7	17½	63	56	49	39⅔	30⅓	24½
8	20	72	64	56	45⅓	34⅔	28
9	22½	81	72	63	51	39	31½
10	25	90	80	70	56⅔	43⅓	35
11	27½	99	88	77	62⅓	47⅔	38½
12	30	108	96	84	68	52	42
13	32½	117	104	91	73⅔	56⅓	45½
14	35	126	112	98	79⅓	60⅔	49
15	37½	135	120	105	85	65	52½
16	40	144	128	112	90⅔	69⅓	56
17	42½	153	136	119	96⅓	73⅔	59½
18	45	162	144	126	102	78	63
19	47½	171	152	133	107⅔	82⅓	66½
20	50	180	160	140	113⅓	86⅔	70
21	52½	189	168	147	119	91	73½
22	55	198	176	154	124⅔	95⅓	77
23	57½	207	184	161	130⅓	99⅔	80½
24	60	216	192	168	136	104	84
25	62½	225	200	175	141⅔	108⅓	87½
26	65	234	208	182	147⅓	112⅔	91
27	67½	243	216	189	153	117	94½
28	70	252	224	196	158⅔	121⅓	98
29	72½	261	232	203	164⅓	125⅔	101½
30	75	270	240	210	170	130	105
31	77½	279	248	217	175⅔	134⅓	108½
32	80	288	256	224	181⅓	138⅔	112
33	82½	297	264	231	187	143	115½

State if for steam or water, and whether for one or two-pipe work.

All radiators, unless otherwise specified, tapped two inches and plugged, or bushed to regular tappings. These bushings add about 1½ inches to the length of radiator with two-pipe tapping.

Louraine Window Radiator

PLAIN

For Steam and Water

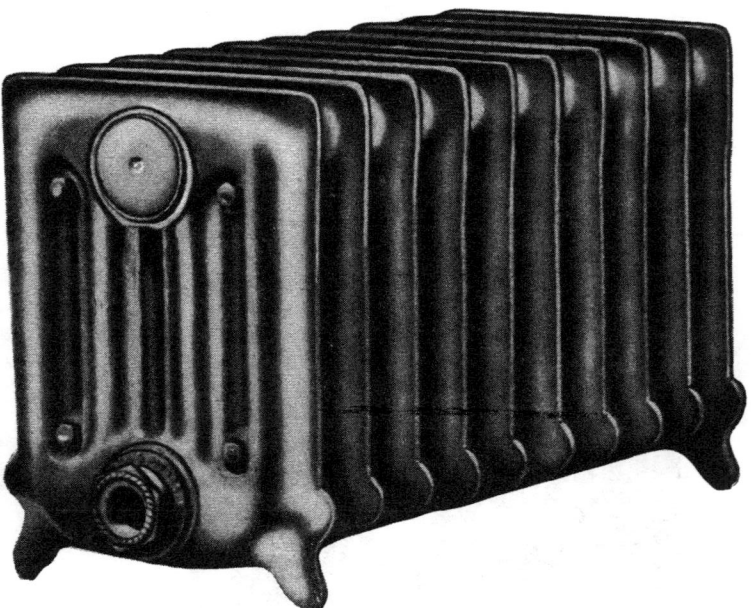

Width of sections, 12 inches.

Width across feet, 12¼ inches.

Louraine Window Radiator

PLAIN

For Steam and Water

DIMENSIONS AND CAPACITIES

Number Sections	Length Inches	Heating Surface—Square Feet						
		24 in. High	22 in. High	20 in. High	18 in. High	16 in. High	14 in. High	12 in. High
1	2½	5⅔	4⅓	4⅓	3½	3½	2¾	2¾
2	5	11⅓	8⅔	8⅔	7	7	5½	5½
3	7½	17	13	13	10½	10½	8¼	8¼
4	10	22⅔	17⅓	17⅓	14	14	11	11
5	12½	28⅓	21⅔	21⅔	17½	17½	13¾	13¾
6	15	34	26	26	21	21	16½	16½
7	17½	39⅔	30⅓	30⅓	24½	24½	19¼	19¼
8	20	45⅓	34⅔	34⅔	28	28	22	22
9	22½	51	39	39	31½	31½	24¾	24¾
10	25	56⅔	43⅓	43⅓	35	35	27½	27½
11	27½	62⅓	47⅔	47⅔	38½	38½	30¼	30¼
12	30	68	52	52	42	42	33	33
13	32½	73⅔	56⅓	56⅓	45½	45½	35¾	35¾
14	35	79⅓	60⅔	60⅔	49	49	38½	38½
15	37½	85	65	65	52½	52½	41¼	41¼
16	40	90⅔	69⅓	69⅓	56	56	44	44
17	42½	96⅓	73⅔	73⅔	59½	59½	46¾	46¾
18	45	102	78	78	63	63	49½	49½
19	47½	107⅔	82⅓	82⅓	66½	66½	52¼	52¼
20	50	113⅓	86⅔	86⅔	70	70	55	55
21	52½	119	91	91	73½	73½	57¾	57¾
22	55	124⅔	95⅓	95⅓	77	77	60½	60½
23	57½	130⅓	99⅔	99⅔	80½	80½	63¼	63¼
24	60	136	104	104	84	84	66	66
25	62½	141⅔	108⅓	108⅓	87½	87½	68¾	68¾
26	65	147⅓	112⅔	112⅔	91	91	71½	71½
27	67½	153	117	117	94½	94½	74¼	74¼
28	70	158⅔	121⅓	121⅓	98	98	77	77
29	72½	164⅓	125⅔	125⅔	101½	101½	79¾	79¾
30	75	170	130	130	105	105	82½	82½
31	77½	175⅔	134⅓	134⅓	108½	108½	85¼	85¼
32	80	181⅓	138⅔	138⅔	112	112	88	88
33	82½	187	143	143	115½	115½	90¾	90¾

State if for steam or water, and whether for one or two-pipe work.

All radiators, unless otherwise specified, tapped two inches and plugged or bushed to regular tappings. These bushings add about 1½ inches to the length of radiator with two-pipe tapping.

Louraine Window Radiator

ORNAMENTED

For Steam and Water

Width of sections, 12 inches.

Width across feet, 12¼ inches.

Louraine Window Radiator

ORNAMENTED

For Steam and Water

DIMENSIONS AND CAPACITIES

Number Sections	Length Inches	Heating Surface—Square Feet						
		24 in. High	22 in. High	20 in. High	18 in. High	16 in. High	14 in. High	12 in. High
1	2½	5⅔	4⅓	4⅓	3½	3½	2¾	2¾
2	5	11⅓	8⅔	8⅔	7	7	5½	5½
3	7½	17	13	13	10½	10½	8¼	8¼
4	10	22⅔	17⅓	17⅓	14	14	11	11
5	12½	28⅓	21⅔	21⅔	17½	17½	13¾	13¾
6	15	34	26	26	21	21	16½	16½
7	17½	39⅔	30⅓	30⅓	24½	24½	19¼	19¼
8	20	45⅓	34⅔	34⅔	28	28	22	22
9	22½	51	39	39	31½	31½	24¾	24¾
10	25	56⅔	43⅓	43⅓	35	35	27½	27½
11	27½	62⅓	47⅔	47⅔	38½	38½	30¼	30¼
12	30	68	52	52	42	42	33	33
13	32½	73⅔	56⅓	56⅓	45½	45½	35¾	35¾
14	35	79⅓	60⅔	60⅔	49	49	38½	38½
15	37½	85	65	65	52½	52½	41¼	41¼
16	40	90⅔	69⅓	69⅓	56	56	44	44
17	42½	96⅓	73⅔	73⅔	59½	59½	46¾	46¾
18	45	102	78	78	63	63	49½	49½
19	47½	107⅔	82⅓	82⅓	66½	66½	52¼	52¼
20	50	113⅓	86⅔	86⅔	70	70	55	55
21	52½	119	91	91	73½	73½	57¾	57¾
22	55	124⅔	95⅓	95⅓	77	77	60½	60½
23	57½	130⅓	99⅔	99⅔	80½	80½	63¼	63¼
24	60	136	104	104	84	84	66	66
25	62½	141⅔	108⅓	108⅓	87½	87½	68¾	68¾
26	65	147⅓	112⅔	112⅔	91	91	71½	71½
27	67½	153	117	117	94½	94½	74¼	74¼
28	70	158⅔	121⅓	121⅓	98	98	77	77
29	72½	164⅓	125⅔	125⅔	101½	101½	79¾	79¾
30	75	170	130	130	105	105	82½	82½
31	77½	175⅔	134⅓	134⅓	108½	108½	85¼	85¼
32	80	181⅓	138⅔	138⅔	112	112	88	88
33	82½	187	143	143	115½	115½	90¾	90¾

State if for steam or water, and whether for one or two-pipe work.

All radiators, unless otherwise specified, tapped two inches and plugged, or bushed to regular tappings. These bushings add about 1½ inches to the length of radiator with two-pipe tapping.

Louraine Dining Room Radiators

PLAIN OR ORNAMENTED

For Steam or Water

Made in 3 column, 44 inch height only.
Width of sections, 9 inches.

Louraine Dining Room Radiator

Plain or Ornamented

For Steam and Water

The "Louraine" Dining Room Radiator is of the ornamented or plain type. It is furnished with a capacious warming closet, surrounded on the bottom and both sides with direct heating surface. The closet is built with double doors and two shelves, 10½ inches wide by 17 inches long, which may be removed at any time if more space is desired.

No.	No. Sections.	Length Inches.	Surface Heating.	Price.
1	9	22½	43½	$ 53.00
2	11	27½	55½	58.00
3	13	32½	67½	63.00
4	15	37½	79½	73.00
5	17	42½	91½	83.00
6	19	47½	103½	93.00
7	21	52½	115½	103.00
8	23	57½	127½	113.00

State if for steam or water and whether for one or two pipe work.

All radiators, unless otherwise specified, tapped 2 inches and plugged or bushed to regular tappings. These bushings add about 1½ inches to the length of the radiator with two pipe tapping.

Pierce One-Column Radiator

PLAIN

For Steam and Water

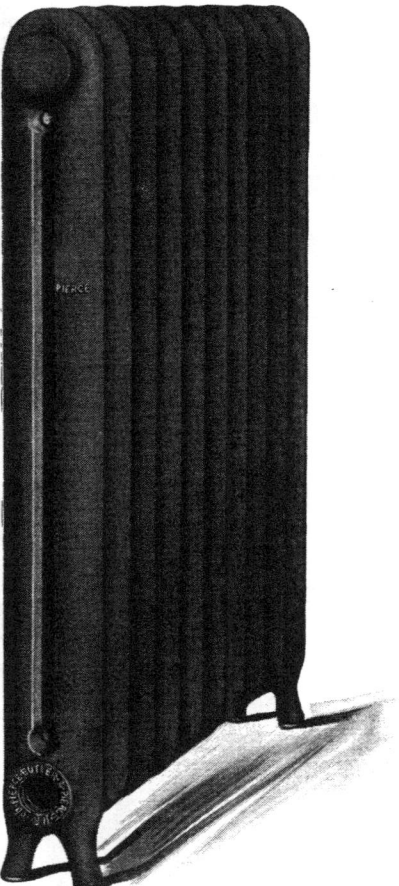

Width of Sections $4\frac{1}{2}$ inches.

See note regarding Tappings on page 71.

Pierce One-Column Radiator

PLAIN

For Steam and Water

List of Sizes and Heating Surfaces

Number of Sections	Length Inches	Heating Surface, Square Feet				
		38 Inches High 3 Square Feet per Section	32 Inches High 2½ Square Feet per Section	26 Inches High 2 Square Feet per Section	23 Inches High 1⅔ Square Feet per Section	20 Inches High 1½ Square Feet per Section
2	5	6	5	4	3⅓	3
3	7½	9	7½	6	5	4½
4	10	12	10	8	6⅔	6
5	12½	15	12½	10	8⅓	7½
6	15	18	15	12	10	9
7	17½	21	17½	14	11⅔	10½
8	20	24	20	16	13⅓	12
9	22½	27	22½	18	15	13½
10	25	30	25	20	16⅔	15
11	27½	33	27½	22	18⅓	16½
12	30	36	30	24	20	18
13	32½	39	32½	26	21⅔	19½
14	35	42	35	28	23⅓	21
15	37½	45	37½	30	25	22½
16	40	48	40	32	26⅔	24
17	42½	51	42½	34	28⅓	25½
18	45	54	45	36	30	27
19	47½	57	47½	38	31⅔	28½
20	50	60	50	40	33⅓	30
21	52½	63	52½	42	35	31½
22	55	66	55	44	36⅔	33
23	57½	69	57½	46	38⅓	34½
24	60	72	60	48	40	36
25	62½	75	62½	50	41⅔	37½
26	65	78	65	52	43⅓	39
27	67½	81	67½	54	45	40½
28	70	84	70	56	46⅔	42
29	72½	87	72½	58	48⅓	43½
30	75	90	75	60	50	45
31	77½	93	77½	62	51⅔	46½
32	80	96	80	64	53⅓	48

Width of section 4½ inches.

All radiators are regularly tapped 2 inches right-hand and bushed according to tapping list.

When top tapping is required it can be furnished 1½ inches and bushed any size smaller than 1½ inches.

Air vent tappings are regularly made ⅛ inch. Add ¾ inch for each bushing or plug to get total length measurement of radiator.

For tapping list and "roughing in" measurements see pages 71 to 74.

Pierce One-Column Radiator

ORNAMENTED

For Steam and Water

Width of sections, 4½ inches.

See note regarding tappings, page 71.

Pierce One-Column Radiator

ORNAMENTED

For Steam and Water

List of Sizes and Heating Surfaces

Number of Sections	Length Inches	Heating Surface, Square Feet				
		38 Inches High 3 Square Feet per Section	32 Inches High 2½ Square Feet per Section	26 Inches High 2 Square Feet per Section	23 Inches High 1⅔ Square Feet per Section	20 Inches High 1½ Square Feet per Section
2	5	6	5	4	3⅓	3
3	7½	9	7½	6	5	4½
4	10	12	10	8	6⅔	6
5	12½	15	12½	10	8⅓	7½
6	15	18	15	12	10	9
7	17½	21	17½	14	11⅔	10½
8	20	24	20	16	13⅓	12
9	22½	27	22½	18	15	13½
10	25	30	25	20	16⅔	15
11	27½	33	27½	22	18⅓	16½
12	30	36	30	24	20	18
13	32½	39	32½	26	21⅔	19½
14	35	42	35	28	23⅓	21
15	37½	45	37½	30	25	22½
16	40	48	40	32	26⅔	24
17	42½	51	42½	34	28⅓	25½
18	45	54	45	36	30	27
19	47½	57	47½	38	31⅔	28½
20	50	60	50	40	33⅓	30
21	52½	63	52½	42	35	31½
22	55	66	55	44	36⅔	33
23	57½	69	57½	46	38⅓	34½
24	60	72	60	48	40	36
25	62½	75	62½	50	41⅔	37½
26	65	78	65	52	43⅓	39
27	67½	81	67½	54	45	40½
28	70	84	70	56	46⅔	42
29	72½	87	72½	58	48⅓	43½
30	75	90	75	60	50	45
31	77½	93	77½	62	51⅔	46½
32	80	96	80	64	53⅓	48

Width of section 4½ inches.

All radiators are regularly tapped 2 inches right-hand and bushed according to tapping list.

When top tapping is required it can be furnished 1½ inches and bushed any size smaller than 1½ inches.

Air vent tappings are regularly made ⅛ inch. Add ¾ inch for each bushing or plug to get total length measurement of radiator.

For tapping list and "roughing-in" measurements see pages 71 to 74.

Pierce Two-Column Radiator

PLAIN

For Steam and Water

Width of sections, 7½ inches.

See note regarding tappings on page 71.

Pierce Two-Column Radiator

PLAIN

For Steam and Water

List of Sizes and Heating Surfaces

Number of Sections	Length Inches	Heating Surface, Square Feet					
		45 Inches High 5 Square Feet per Section	38 Inches High 4 Square Feet per Section	32 Inches High 3⅓ Square Feet per Section	26 Inches High 2⅔ Square Feet per Section	23 Inches High 2⅓ Square Feet per Section	20 Inches High 2 Square Feet per Section
2	5	10	8	6⅔	5⅓	4⅔	4
3	7½	15	12	10	8	7	6
4	10	20	16	13⅓	10⅔	9⅓	8
5	12½	25	20	16⅔	13⅓	11⅔	10
6	15	30	24	20	16	14	12
7	17½	35	28	23⅓	18⅔	16⅓	14
8	20	40	32	26⅔	21⅓	18⅔	16
9	22½	45	36	30	24	21	18
10	25	50	40	33⅓	26⅔	23⅓	20
11	27½	55	44	36⅔	29⅓	25⅔	22
12	30	60	48	40	32	28	24
13	32½	65	52	43⅓	34⅔	30⅓	26
14	35	70	56	46⅔	37⅓	32⅔	28
15	37½	75	60	50	40	35	30
16	40	80	64	53⅓	42⅔	37⅓	32
17	42½	85	68	56⅔	45⅓	39⅔	34
18	45	90	72	60	48	42	36
19	47½	95	76	63⅓	50⅔	44⅓	38
20	50	100	80	66⅔	53⅓	46⅔	40
21	52½	105	84	70	56	49	42
22	55	110	88	73⅓	58⅔	51⅓	44
23	57½	115	92	76⅔	61⅓	53⅔	46
24	60	120	96	80	64	56	48
25	62½	125	100	83⅓	66⅔	58⅓	50
26	65	130	104	86⅔	69⅓	60⅔	52
27	67½	135	108	90	72	63	54
28	70	140	112	93⅓	74⅔	65⅓	56
29	72½	145	116	96⅔	77⅓	67⅔	58
30	75	150	120	100	80	70	60
31	77½	155	124	103⅓	82⅔	72⅓	62
32	80	160	128	106⅔	85⅓	74⅔	64

Width of section 7½ inches.

All radiators are regularly tapped 2 inches right-hand and bushed according to tapping list.

When top tapping is required it can be furnished 1½ inches and bushed any size smaller than 1½ inches.

Air vent tappings are regularly made ⅛ inch. Add ¾ inch for each bushing or plug to get total length measurement of radiator.

For tapping list and "roughing-in" measurements see pages 71 and 74.

Pierce Two-Column Radiator

ORNAMENTED

For Steam and Water

Width of sections, $7\frac{1}{2}$ inches.

See note regarding tappings on page 71.

Pierce Two-Column Radiator

ORNAMENTED

For Steam and Water

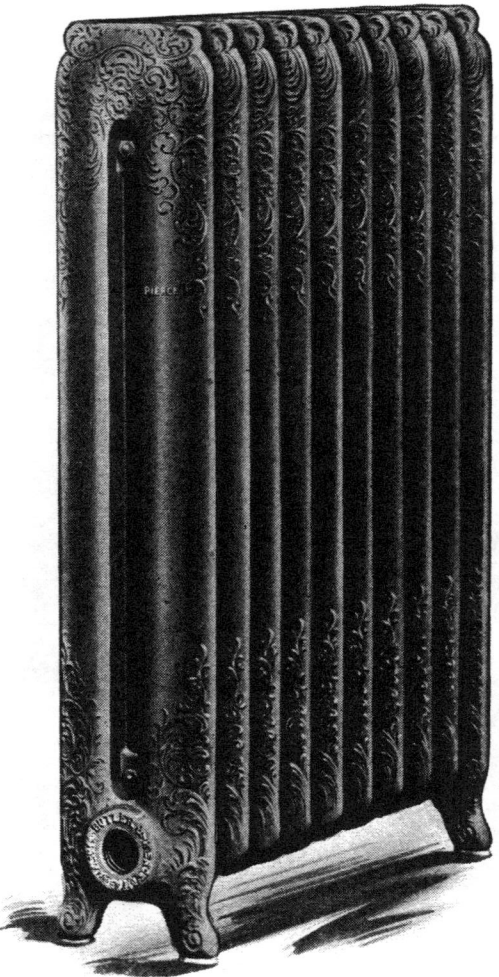

List of Sizes and Heating Surfaces

Number of Sections	Length Inches	Heating Surface, Square Feet					
		45 Inches High 5 Square Feet per Section	38 Inches High 4 Square Feet per Section	32 Inches High 3⅓ Square Feet per Section	26 Inches High 2⅔ Square Feet per Section	23 Inches High 2⅓ Square Feet per Section	20 Inches High 2 Square Feet per Section
2	5	10	8	6⅔	5⅓	4⅔	4
3	7½	15	12	10	8	7	6
4	10	20	16	13⅓	10⅔	9⅓	8
5	12½	25	20	16⅔	13⅓	11⅔	10
6	15	30	24	20	16	14	12
7	17½	35	28	23⅓	18⅔	16⅓	14
8	20	40	32	26⅔	21⅓	18⅔	16
9	22½	45	36	30	24	21	18
10	25	50	40	33⅓	26⅔	23⅓	20
11	27½	55	44	36⅔	29⅓	25⅔	22
12	30	60	48	40	32	28	24
13	32½	65	52	43⅓	34⅔	30⅓	26
14	35	70	56	46⅔	37⅓	32⅔	28
15	37½	75	60	50	40	35	30
16	40	80	64	53⅓	42⅔	37⅓	32
17	42½	85	68	56⅔	45⅓	39⅔	34
18	45	90	72	60	48	42	36
19	47½	95	76	63⅓	50⅔	44⅓	38
20	50	100	80	66⅔	53⅓	46⅔	40
21	52½	105	84	70	56	49	42
22	55	110	88	73⅓	58⅔	51⅓	44
23	57½	115	92	76⅔	61⅓	53⅔	46
24	60	120	96	80	64	56	48
25	62½	125	100	83⅓	66⅔	58⅓	50
26	65	130	104	86⅔	69⅓	60⅔	52
27	67½	135	108	90	72	63	54
28	70	140	112	93⅓	74⅔	65⅓	56
29	72½	145	116	96⅔	77⅓	67⅔	58
30	75	150	120	100	80	70	60
31	77½	155	124	103⅓	82⅔	72⅓	62
32	80	160	128	106⅔	85⅓	74⅔	64

Width of section 7½ inches.

All radiators are regularly tapped 2 inches right-hand and bushed according to tapping list.

When top tapping is required it can be furnished 1½ inches and bushed any size smaller than 1½ inches.

Air vent tappings are regularly made ⅛ inch. Add ¾ inch for each bushing or plug to get total length measurement of radiator.

For tapping list and "roughing-in" measurements see pages 71 to 74.

Pierce Three-Column Radiator

PLAIN

For Steam and Water

Width of sections, 9 inches.

See note regarding tappings on page 71.

Pierce Three-Column Radiator

PLAIN

For Steam and Water

List of Sizes and Heating Surfaces

Number of Sections	Length Inches	Heating Surface, Square Feet					
		45 Inches High 6 Square Feet per Section	38 Inches High 5 Square Feet per Section	32 Inches High 4½ Square Feet per Section	26 Inches High 3¾ Square Feet per Section	22 Inches High 3 Square Feet per Section	18 Inches High 2¼ Square Feet per Section
2	5	12	10	9	7½	6	4½
3	7½	18	15	13½	11¼	9	6¾
4	10	24	20	18	15	12	9
5	12½	30	25	22½	18¾	15	11¼
6	15	36	30	27	22½	18	13½
7	17½	42	35	31½	26¼	21	15¾
8	20	48	40	36	30	24	18
9	22½	54	45	40½	33¾	27	20¼
10	25	60	50	45	37½	30	22½
11	27½	66	55	49½	41¼	33	24¾
12	30	72	60	54	45	36	27
13	32½	78	65	58½	48¾	39	29¼
14	35	84	70	63	52½	42	31½
15	37½	90	75	67½	56¼	45	33¾
16	40	96	80	72	60	48	36
17	42½	102	85	76½	63¾	51	38¼
18	45	108	90	81	67½	54	40½
19	47½	114	95	85½	71¼	57	42¾
20	50	120	100	90	75	60	45
21	52½	126	105	94½	78¾	63	47¼
22	55	132	110	99	82½	66	49½
23	57½	138	115	103½	86¼	69	51¾
24	60	144	120	108	90	72	54
25	62½	150	125	112½	93¾	75	56¼
26	65	156	130	117	97½	78	58½
27	67½	162	135	121½	101¼	81	60¾
28	70	168	140	126	105	84	63
29	72½	174	145	130½	108¾	87	65¼
30	75	180	150	135	112½	90	67½
31	77½	186	155	139½	116¼	93	69¾
32	80	192	160	144	120	96	72

Width of section, 9 inches.

All radiators are regularly tapped 2 inches right-hand and bushed according to tapping list.

When top tapping is required it can be furnished 1½ inches and bushed any size smaller than 1½ inches.

Air vent tappings are regularly made ⅛ inch. Add ¾ inch for each bushing or plug to get total length measurement of radiator.

For tapping list and "roughing-in" measurements see pages 71 to 74.

Pierce Three-Column Radiator

ORNAMENTED

For Steam and Water

Width of sections, 9 inches.

See note regarding Tappings on page 71.

Pierce Three-Column Radiator

ORNAMENTED

For Steam and Water

List of Sizes and Heating Surfaces

Number of Sections	Length Inches	Heating Surface, Square Feet					
		45 Inches High 6 Square Feet per Section	38 Inches High 5 Square Feet per Section	32 Inches High 4½ Square Feet per Section	26 Inches High 3¾ Square Feet per Section	22 Inches High 3 Square Feet per Section	18 Inches High 2¼ Square Feet per Section
2	5	12	10	9	7½	6	4½
3	7½	18	15	13½	11¼	9	6¾
4	10	24	20	18	15	12	9
5	12½	30	25	22½	18¾	15	11¼
6	15	36	30	27	22½	18	13½
7	17½	42	35	31½	26¼	21	15¾
8	20	48	40	36	30	24	18
9	22½	54	45	40½	33¾	27	20¼
10	25	60	50	45	37½	30	22½
11	27½	66	55	49½	41¼	33	24¾
12	30	72	60	54	45	36	27
13	32½	78	65	58½	48¾	39	29¼
14	35	84	70	63	52½	42	31½
15	37½	90	75	67½	56¼	45	33¾
16	40	96	80	72	60	48	36
17	42½	102	85	76½	63¾	51	38¼
18	45	108	90	81	67½	54	40½
19	47½	114	95	85½	71¼	57	42¾
20	50	120	100	90	75	60	45
21	52½	126	105	94½	78¾	63	47¼
22	55	132	110	99	82½	66	49½
23	57½	138	115	103½	86¼	69	51¾
24	60	144	120	108	90	72	54
25	62½	150	125	112½	93¾	75	56¼
26	65	156	130	117	97½	78	58½
27	67½	162	135	121½	101¼	81	60¾
28	70	168	140	126	105	84	63
29	72½	174	145	130½	108¾	87	65¼
30	75	180	150	135	112½	90	67½
31	77½	186	155	139½	116¼	93	69¾
32	80	192	160	144	120	96	72

Width of section, 9 inches.

All radiators are regularly tapped 2 inches right-hand and bushed according to tapping list.

When top tapping is required it can be furnished 1½ inches and bushed any size smaller than 1½ inches.

Air vent tappings are regularly made ⅛ inch. Add ¾ inch for each bushing or plug to get total length measurement of radiator.

For tapping list and "roughing-in" measurements see pages 71 to 74.

Pierce Four-Column Radiator

PLAIN

For Steam and Water

Width of sections, $11\frac{1}{8}$ inches.

See note regarding tappings on page 71.

Pierce Four-Column Radiator

PLAIN

For Steam and Water

List of Sizes and Heating Surfaces

Number of Sections	Length Inches	Heating Surface, Square Feet					
		45 Inches High 10 Square Feet per Section	38 Inches High 8 Square Feet per Section	32 Inches High 6½ Square Feet per Section	26 Inches High 5 Square Feet per Section	22 Inches High 4 Square Feet per Section	18 Inches High 3 Square Feet per Section
2	6	20	16	13	10	8	6
3	9	30	24	19½	15	12	9
4	12	40	32	26	20	16	12
5	15	50	40	32½	25	20	15
6	18	60	48	39	30	24	18
7	21	70	56	45½	35	28	21
8	24	80	64	52	40	32	24
9	27	90	72	58½	45	36	27
10	30	100	80	65	50	40	30
11	33	110	88	71½	55	44	33
12	36	120	96	78	60	48	36
13	39	130	104	84½	65	52	39
14	42	140	112	91	70	56	42
15	45	150	120	97½	75	60	45
16	48	160	128	104	80	64	48
17	51	170	136	110½	85	68	51
18	54	180	144	117	90	72	54
19	57	190	152	123½	95	76	57
20	60	200	160	130	100	80	60
21	63	210	168	136½	105	84	63
22	66	220	176	143	110	88	66
23	69	230	184	149½	115	92	69
24	72	240	192	156	120	96	72
25	75	250	200	162½	125	100	75
26	78	260	208	169	130	104	78
27	81	270	216	175½	135	108	81
28	84	280	224	182	140	112	84
29	87	290	232	188½	145	116	87
30	90	300	240	195	150	120	90
31	93	310	248	201½	155	124	93
32	96	320	256	208	160	128	96

Width of section, 11⅛ inches.

All radiators are regularly tapped 2 inches right-hand and bushed according to tapping list.

When top tapping is required it can be furnished 1½ inches and bushed, any size smaller than 1½ inches.

Air vent tappings are regularly made ⅛ inch. Add ¾ inch for each bushing or plug to get total length measurement of radiator.

For tapping list and "roughing-in" measurements see pages 71 to 74.

Pierce Four-Column Radiator

ORNAMENTED

For Steam and Water

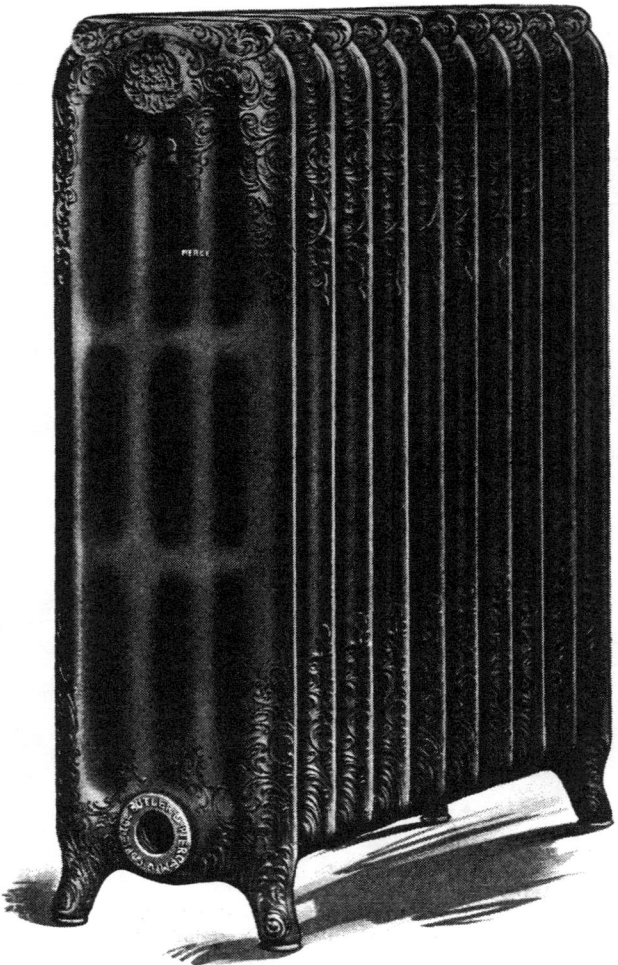

Width of sections, $11\frac{1}{8}$ inches.

See note regarding tappings on page 71.

Pierce Four-Column Radiator

ORNAMENTED

For Steam and Water

List of Sizes and Heating Surfaces

Number of Sections	Length Inches	Heating Surface, Square Feet					
		45 Inches High 10 Square Feet per Section	38 Inches High 8 Square Feet per Section	32 Inches High 6½ Square Feet per Section	26 Inches High 5 Square Feet per Section	22 Inches High 4 Square Feet per Section	18 Inches High 3 Square Feet per Section
2	6	20	16	13	10	8	6
3	9	30	24	19½	15	12	9
4	12	40	32	26	20	16	12
5	15	50	40	32½	25	20	15
6	18	60	48	39	30	24	18
7	21	70	56	45½	35	28	21
8	24	80	64	52	40	32	24
9	27	90	72	58½	45	36	27
10	30	100	80	65	50	40	30
11	33	110	88	71½	55	44	33
12	36	120	96	78	60	48	36
13	39	130	104	84½	65	52	39
14	42	140	112	91	70	56	42
15	45	150	120	97½	75	60	45
16	48	160	128	104	80	64	48
17	51	170	136	110½	85	68	51
18	54	180	144	117	90	72	54
19	57	190	152	123½	95	76	57
20	60	200	160	130	100	80	60
21	63	210	168	136½	105	84	63
22	66	220	176	143	110	88	66
23	69	230	184	149½	115	92	69
24	72	240	192	156	120	96	72
25	75	250	200	162½	125	100	75
26	78	260	208	169	130	104	78
27	81	270	216	175½	135	108	81
28	84	280	224	182	140	112	84
29	87	290	232	188½	145	116	87
30	90	300	240	195	150	120	90
31	93	310	248	201½	155	124	93
32	96	320	256	208	160	128	96

Width of Section, 11⅛ inches.

All radiators are regularly tapped 2 inches right-hand and bushed according to tapping list.

When top tapping is required it can be furnished 1½ inches and bushed, any size smaller than 1½ inches.

Air vent tappings are regularly made ⅛ inch. Add ¾ inch for each bushing or plug to get total length measurement of radiator.

For tapping list and "roughing-in" measurements see pages 71 to 74.

Pierce 6-Column Window Radiator

PLAIN ONLY

For Steam and Water

Width of sections, 12 inches.

See note regarding tappings, page 71.

Pierce Window Radiator

PLAIN ONLY

For Steam and Water

LIST OF SIZES AND HEATING SURFACES

Number of Sections	Length Inches	LIST OF SIZES AND HEATING SURFACES				
		20 Inches High 5 Square Feet per section	18 Inches High 4⅓ Square Feet per Section	16 Inches High 3¾ Square Feet per Section	14 Inches High 3 Square Feet per Section	13 Inches High 3 Square Feet per Section
2	6	10	8⅔	7½	6	6
3	9	15	13	11¼	9	9
4	12	20	17⅓	15	12	12
5	15	25	21⅔	18¾	15	15
6	18	30	26	22½	18	18
7	21	35	30⅓	26¼	21	21
8	24	40	34⅔	30	24	24
9	27	45	39	33¾	27	27
10	30	50	43⅓	37½	30	30
11	33	55	47⅔	41¼	33	33
12	36	60	52	45	36	36
13	39	65	56⅓	48¾	39	39
14	42	70	60⅔	52½	42	42
15	45	75	65	56¼	45	45
16	48	80	69⅓	60	48	48
17	51	85	73⅔	63¾	51	51
18	54	90	78	67½	54	54
19	57	95	82⅓	71¼	57	57
20	60	100	86½	75	60	60
21	63	105	91	78¾	63	63
22	66	110	95⅓	82½	66	66
23	69	115	99⅔	86¼	69	69
24	72	120	104	90	72	72
25	75	125	108⅓	93¾	75	75
26	78	130	112⅔	97½	78	78
27	81	135	117	101¼	81	81
28	84	140	121⅓	105	84	84
29	87	145	125⅔	108¾	87	87
30	90	150	130	112½	90	90
31	93	155	134⅓	116¼	93	93
32	96	160	138⅔	120	96	96

Width of legs, 13 inches; width of section 12 inches.

All radiators will be tapped 2 inches and bushed according to the tapping list. When top tapping is desired it can be furnished tapped 1½ inches and bushed to order, from factory.

All openings will be right-hand threaded, unless otherwise ordered.

Air valve tappings are regularly made ⅛ inch. Add ¾ inch for each bushing to get total length measurement of radiator.

For tapping list and "roughing-in" measurements see pages 71 to 74.

Pierce Dining Room Radiator

PLAIN PATTERN ONLY

For Steam and Water

Made in three column, 38 inch height only. Width of sections, 9 inches.

Pierce Dining Room Radiator

PLAIN PATTERN ONLY

For Steam and Water

The "Pierce" Dining Room Radiator is made in plain pattern only. It is furnished with a capacious warming closet, surrounded on the bottom and both sides with direct heating surface. The closet is built with double doors and one shelf, which may be removed at any time if more space is desired.

Built in 3 column, 38 inch height only.

No.	No. Sections	Length Inches	Surface Heating
1	13	32½	43
2	15	37½	53
3	17	42½	63
4	19	47½	73
5	21	52½	83
6	23	57½	93
7	25	62½	103
8	27	67½	113

State if for steam or water and whether for one or two pipe work.

All radiators, unless otherwise specified, tapped 2 inches and plugged or bushed to regular tappings. These bushings add about 1½ inches to the length of the radiator with two pipe tapping.

Rococo Single-Column Radiators

For Steam and Water

Each section is 4½ inches wide. Width of legs, 5½ inches.

These Radiators are made in special shapes as follows:—

Circular, Steam and Water ....see pages 93 to 95
Corner, Steam and Water ....see pages 96, 247 to 249
Curved, Steam and Water ....see page 97
Ventilating .... see pages 88 to 90
Legs, Extra High, for Steam and Water ....see page 102
Single-Foot Radiators, Steam and Water..............see page 101
Marble-Top Saddles for Steam and Water..............see page 101
Concealed Brackets, for Steam and Water ....see pages 98 to 100

Rococo Single-Column Radiators

For Steam and Water

No. of Sections	*Length 2½ in. per Sec.	Heating Surface—Square Feet				
		38-in. Height 3 Sq. Ft. per Sec.	32-in. Height 2½ Sq. Ft. per Sec.	26-in. Height 2 Sq. Ft. per Sec.	23-in. Height 1⅔ Sq. Ft. per Sec.	20-in. Height 1½ Sq. Ft. per Sec.
2	5	6	5	4	3⅓	3
3	7½	9	7½	6	5	4½
4	10	12	10	8	6⅔	6
5	12½	15	12½	10	8⅓	7½
6	15	18	15	12	10	9
7	17½	21	17½	14	11⅔	10½
8	20	24	20	16	13⅓	12
9	22½	27	22½	18	15	13½
10	25	30	25	20	16⅔	15
11	27½	33	27½	22	18⅓	16½
12	30	36	30	24	20	18
13	32½	39	32½	26	21⅔	19½
14	35	42	35	28	23⅓	21
15	37½	45	37½	30	25	22½
16	40	48	40	32	26⅔	24
17	42½	51	42½	34	28⅓	25½
18	45	54	45	36	30	27
19	47½	57	47½	38	31⅔	28½
20	50	60	50	40	33⅓	30
21	52½	63	52½	42	35	31½
22	55	66	55	44	36⅔	33
23	57½	69	57½	46	38⅓	34½
24	60	72	60	48	40	36
25	62½	75	62½	50	41⅔	37½
26	65	78	65	52	43⅓	39
27	67½	81	67½	54	45	40½
28	70	84	70	56	46⅔	42
29	72½	87	72½	58	48⅓	43½
30	75	90	75	60	50	45
31	77½	93	77½	62	51⅔	46½
32	80	96	80	64	53⅓	48

TAPPINGS: 2 inches and bushed as per list on page 59.

CONNECTIONS: **Water** — Extra-heavy right and left threaded nipples at top and bottom. **Steam** — right threaded, extra-heavy nipples at bottom only.

LOW DRIP HUBS: **One Pipe Steam** — on supply leg-section; **Two-Pipe Steam** — on return leg-section.

MEASUREMENTS: Center of tappings to floors, and between centers of upper and lower Water tappings, and between upper and ower concealed brackets, etc., see pages 242 to 246.

*Add ½ inch to length for each bushing.

Rococo Two-Column Radiators

For Steam and Water

Each section is 7⅜ inches wide. Width of legs, 8½ inches.

These Radiators are made in special shapes as follows:—

Circular, Steam and Water ....see pages 93 to 95
Corner, Steam and Water ....see pages 96, 247 to 249
Curved, Steam and Water ....see page 97
Ventilating....................................see pages 88 to 90
Legs, Extra High, for Steam and Water................see page 102
Single-Foot, Steam and Water ....see page 101
Marble-Top Saddles, for Steam and Water............see page 101
Marble-Top Lugs, for Steam and Water..............see page 101
Concealed Brackets, for Steam and Water......see pages 98 to 100

Rococo Two-Column Radiators

For Steam and Water

No. of Sections	* Length 2½ in. per Sec.	Heating Surface—Square Feet					
		45-in. Height 5 Sq.Ft. per Sec.	38-in. Height 4 Sq.Ft. per Sec.	32-in. Height 3⅓ Sq.Ft. per Sec.	26-in. Height 2⅔ Sq.Ft. per Sec.	23-in. Height 2⅓ Sq.Ft. per Sec.	20-in. Height. 2 Sq.Ft. per Sec.
2	5	10	8	6⅔	5⅓	4⅔	4
3	7½	15	12	10	8	7	6
4	10	20	16	13⅓	10⅔	9⅓	8
5	12½	25	20	16⅔	13⅓	11⅔	10
6	15	30	24	20	16	14	12
7	17½	35	28	23⅓	18⅔	16⅓	14
8	20	40	32	26⅔	21⅓	18⅔	16
9	22½	45	36	30	24	21	18
10	25	50	40	33⅓	26⅔	23⅓	20
11	27½	55	44	36⅔	29⅓	25⅔	22
12	30	60	48	40	32	28	24
13	32½	65	52	43⅓	34⅔	30⅓	26
14	35	70	56	46⅔	37⅓	32⅔	28
15	37½	75	60	50	40	35	30
16	40	80	64	53⅓	42⅔	37⅓	32
17	42½	85	68	56⅔	45⅓	39⅔	34
18	45	90	72	60	48	42	36
19	47½	95	76	63⅓	50⅔	44⅓	38
20	50	100	80	66⅔	53⅓	46⅔	40
21	52½	105	84	70	56	49	42
22	55	110	88	73⅓	58⅔	51⅓	44
23	57½	115	92	76⅔	61⅓	53⅔	46
24	60	120	96	80	64	56	48
25	62½	125	100	83⅓	66⅔	58⅓	50
26	65	130	104	86⅔	69⅓	60⅔	52
27	67½	135	108	90	72	63	54
28	70	140	112	93⅓	74⅔	65⅓	56
29	72½	145	116	96⅔	77⅓	67⅔	58
30	75	150	120	100	80	70	60
31	77½	155	124	103⅓	82⅔	72⅓	62
32	80	160	128	106⅔	85⅓	74⅔	64

TAPPINGS: 2 inches and bushed as per list on page 59.

CONNECTIONS: Water — Extra-heavy right and left threaded nipples top and bottom — all Plants. **Steam** — Extra-heavy right threaded nipples at bottom only at Pierce and Titusville, and with right and left-threaded nipples at bottom only, at all other Plants.

LOW DRIP HUBS: One Pipe Steam — on supply leg-section; **Two Pipe Steam** — on return leg-section.

MEASUREMENTS: Center of tappings to floors, and between centers of upper and lower Water tappings, and between upper and lower concealed brackets, etc., see pages 242 to 246.

***Add ½ inch to length for each bushing.**

Rococo Three-Column Radiators

For Steam and Water

Each section is 9¼ inches wide. Width of legs, 10 inches.

These Radiators are made in special shapes as follows:—

Circular, for Steam and Water.................see pages 93 to 95
Corner, for Steam and Water..............see pages 96, 247 to 249
Curved, for Steam and Water......................see page 97
Hot Closet, for Steam and Water....................see page 91
Ventilating...................................see pages 88 to 90
Legs, Extra High, Steam and Water..................see page 102
Single-Foot, Steam and Water......................see page 101
Marble-Top Lugs, for Steam and Water.............see page 101
Marble-Top Saddles, for Steam and Water...........see page 101
Concealed Brackets, Steam and Water......see pages 98 to 100

Rococo Three-Column Radiators

For Steam and Water

No. of Sections	* Length 2½ in. per Sec.	Heating Surface — Square Feet					
		45-in. Height 6 sq. ft. per Sec.	38-in. Height 5 sq. ft. per Sec.	32-in. Height 4½ sq. ft. per Sec.	26-in. Height 3¾ sq. ft. per Sec.	22-in. Height 3 sq. ft. per Sec.	18-in. Height 2¼ sq. ft. per Sec.
2	5	12	10	9	7½	6	4½
3	7½	18	15	13½	11¼	9	6¾
4	10	24	20	18	15	12	9
5	12½	30	25	22½	18¾	15	11¼
6	15	36	30	27	22½	18	13½
7	17½	42	35	31½	26¼	21	15¾
8	20	48	40	36	30	24	18
9	22½	54	45	40½	33¾	27	20¼
10	25	60	50	45	37½	30	22½
11	27½	66	55	49½	41¼	33	24¾
12	30	72	60	54	45	36	27
13	32½	78	65	58½	48¾	39	29¼
14	35	84	70	63	52½	42	31½
15	37½	90	75	67½	56¼	45	33¾
16	40	96	80	72	60	48	36
17	42½	102	85	76½	63¾	51	38¼
18	45	108	90	81	67½	54	40½
19	47½	114	95	85½	71¼	57	42¾
20	50	120	100	90	75	60	45
21	52½	126	105	94½	78¾	63	47¼
22	55	132	110	99	82½	66	49½
23	57½	138	115	103½	86¼	69	51¾
24	60	144	120	108	90	72	54
25	62½	150	125	112½	93¾	75	56¼
26	65	156	130	117	97½	78	58½
27	67½	162	135	121½	101¼	81	60¾
28	70	168	140	126	105	84	63
29	72½	174	145	130½	108¾	87	65¼
30	75	180	150	135	112½	90	67½
31	77½	186	155	139½	116¼	93	69¾
32	80	192	160	144	120	96	72

TAPPINGS: 2 inches and bushed as per list on page 59.

CONNECTIONS: Water — extra-heavy right and left threaded nipples at top and bottom — all Plants. **Steam** — with extra-heavy right threaded nipples at bottom only at Pierce and Titusville Plants, and with right and left threaded nipples at bottom only, at all other plants.

LOW DRIP HUBS: One Pipe Steam — on supply leg-section; **Two Pipe Steam** — on return leg-section.

MEASUREMENTS: Center of tappings to floors, and between centers of upper and lower Water tappings, and between upper and lower concealed brackets, etc., see pages 242 to 246.

*Add ½ inch to length for each bushing.

Rococo Four-Column Radiators

For Steam or Water

Each section is 10½ inches wide. Width of legs, 11¼ inches.

These Radiators are not made in special shapes but can be equipped as follows:—

Single-Foot, Steam and Water .... see page 101
Ventilating .... see pages 88 to 90
Marble-Top Saddles, for Steam and Water ..... see page 101
Concealed Brackets, for Steam and Water see pages 98 to 100

Rococo Four-Column Radiators

For Steam or Water

No. of Sections	* Length 3 in. per Sec.	Heating Surface — Square Feet					
		45-in. Height 10 sq. ft. per Sec.	38-in. Height 8 sq. ft. per Sec.	32-in. Height 6½ sq. ft. per Sec.	26-in. Height 5 sq. ft. per Sec.	22-in. Height 4 sq. ft. per Sec.	18-in. Height 3 sq. ft. per Sec.
2	6	20	16	13	10	8	6
3	9	30	24	19½	15	12	9
4	12	40	32	26	20	16	12
5	15	50	40	32½	25	20	15
6	18	60	48	39	30	24	18
7	21	70	56	45½	35	28	21
8	24	80	64	52	40	32	24
9	27	90	72	58½	45	36	27
10	30	100	80	65	50	40	30
11	33	110	88	71½	55	44	33
12	36	120	96	78	60	48	36
13	39	130	104	84½	65	52	39
14	42	140	112	91	70	56	42
15	45	150	120	97½	75	60	45
16	48	160	128	104	80	64	48
17	51	170	136	110½	85	68	51
18	54	180	144	117	90	72	54
19	57	190	152	123½	95	76	57
20	60	200	160	130	100	80	60
21	63	210	168	136½	105	84	63
22	66	220	176	143	110	88	66
23	69	230	184	149½	115	92	69
24	72	240	192	156	120	96	72
25	75	250	200	162½	125	100	75
26	78	260	208	169	130	104	78
27	81	270	216	175½	135	108	81
28	84	280	224	182	140	112	84
29	87	290	232	188½	145	116	87
30	90	300	240	195	150	120	90
31	93	310	248	201½	155	124	93
32	96	320	256	208	160	128	96

TAPPINGS: 2 inches and bushed as per list on page 59.

CONNECTIONS: Both **Water** and **Steam** — Extra-heavy right and left threaded nipples at top and bottom.

MEASUREMENTS: Center of tappings to floors, and between centers of upper and lower Water tappings, and between upper and lower concealed brackets, etc., see pages 242 to 246.

*Add ½ inch to length for each bushing.

Peerless Single-Column Radiators

For Steam and Water

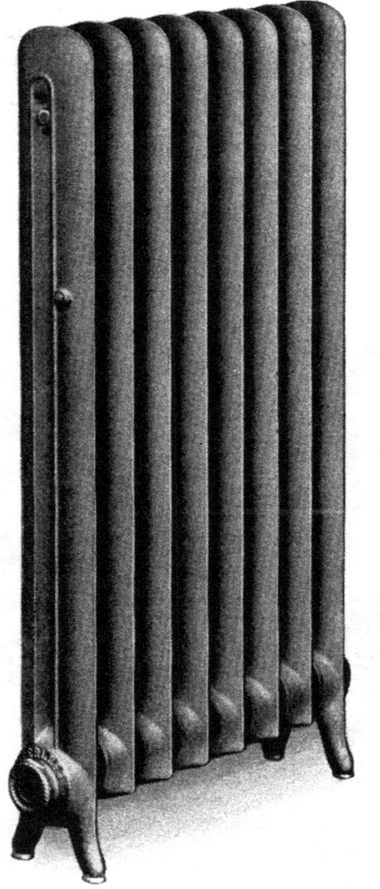

Each section is 4½ inches wide. Width of legs, 5½ inches.

These Radiators are made in special shapes as follows:—

Circular, for Steam and Water....................see pages 93 to 95
Corner, for Steam and Water.............see pages 96, 247 to 249
Curved, for Steam and Water..........................see page 97
Ventilating......................................see pages 88 to 90
Legs, Extra High, for Steam and Water..............see page 102
Single-Foot, Steam and Water.......................see page 101
Marble-Top Saddles, for Steam and Water..........see page 101
Concealed Brackets, for Steam and Water......see pages 98 to 100

Peerless Single-Column Radiators

For Steam and Water

No. of Sec-tions	* Length 2½ in. per Sec.	HEATING SURFACE — SQUARE FEET				
		38-in. Height 3 sq. ft. per Sec.	32-in. Height 2½ sq. ft. per Sec.	26-in. Height 2 sq. ft. per Sec.	23-in. Height 1⅔ sq. ft. per Sec.	20-in. Height 1½ sq. ft per Sec.
2	5	6	5	4	3⅓	3
3	7½	9	7½	6	5	4½
4	10	12	10	8	6⅔	6
5	12½	15	12½	10	8⅓	7½
6	15	18	15	12	10	9
7	17½	21	17½	14	11⅔	10½
8	20	24	20	16	13⅓	12
9	22½	27	22½	18	15	13½
10	25	30	25	20	16⅔	15
11	27½	33	27½	22	18⅓	16½
12	30	36	30	24	20	18
13	32½	39	32½	26	21⅔	19½
14	35	42	35	28	23⅓	21
15	37½	45	37½	30	25	22½
16	40	48	40	32	26⅔	24
17	42½	51	42½	34	28⅓	25½
18	45	54	45	36	30	27
19	47½	57	47½	38	31⅔	28½
20	50	60	50	40	33⅓	30
21	52½	63	52½	42	35	31½
22	55	66	55	44	36⅔	33
23	57½	69	57½	46	38⅓	34½
24	60	72	60	48	40	36
25	62½	75	62½	50	41⅔	37½
26	65	78	65	52	43⅓	39
27	67½	81	67½	54	45	40½
28	70	84	70	56	46⅔	42
29	72½	87	72½	58	48⅓	43½
30	75	90	75	60	50	45
31	77½	93	77½	62	51⅔	46½
32	80	96	80	64	53⅓	48

TAPPINGS: 2 inches and bushed as per list on page 59.

CONNECTIONS: Water — extra-heavy right and left threaded nipples at top and bottom. **Steam** — extra-heavy right threaded nipples at bottom only.

LOW DRIP HUBS: One Pipe Steam — on supply leg-section; **Two Pipe Steam** — on return leg-section.

MEASUREMENTS: Center of tappings to floors, and between centers of upper and lower Water tappings, and between upper and lower concealed brackets, etc., see pages 242 to 246.

*Add ½ inch to length for each bushing.

Peerless Two-Column Radiators

For Steam and Water

Each section is 7⅜ inches wide. Width of legs, 8½ inches.

These Radiators are made in special shapes as follows:—

Circular, for Steam and Water..................see pages 93 to 95
Corner, for Steam and Water............see pages 96, 247 to 249
Curved, for Steam and Water......................see page 97
Ventilating...................................see pages 88 to 90
Legs, Extra High, for Steam and Water..............see page 102
Single Foot, Steam and Water......................see page 101
Marble-Top Saddles, for Steam and Water............see page 101
Concealed Brackets, for Steam and Water......see pages 98 to 100

Peerless Two-Column Radiators

For Steam and Water

No. of Sec-tions	* Length 2½ in. per Sec.	Heating Surface — Square Feet					
		45-in. Height 5 sq. ft. per Sec.	38-in. Height 4 sq. ft. per Sec.	32-in. Height 3⅓ sq. ft. per Sec.	26-in. Height 2⅔ sq. ft. per Sec.	23-in. Height 2⅓ sq. ft. per Sec.	20-in. Height 2 sq. ft. per Sec.
2	5	10	8	6⅔	5⅓	4⅔	4
3	7½	15	12	10	8	7	6
4	10	20	16	13⅓	10⅔	9⅓	8
5	12½	25	20	16⅔	13⅓	11⅔	10
6	15	30	24	20	16	14	12
7	17½	35	28	23⅓	18⅔	16⅓	14
8	20	40	32	26⅔	21⅓	18⅔	16
9	22½	45	36	30	24	21	18
10	25	50	40	33⅓	26⅔	23⅓	20
11	27½	55	44	36⅔	29⅓	25⅔	22
12	30	60	48	40	32	28	24
13	32½	65	52	43⅓	34⅔	30⅓	26
14	35	70	56	46⅔	37⅓	32⅔	28
15	37½	75	60	50	40	35	30
16	40	80	64	53⅓	42⅔	37⅓	32
17	42½	85	68	56⅔	45⅓	39⅔	34
18	45	90	72	60	48	42	36
19	47½	95	76	63⅓	50⅔	44⅓	38
20	50	100	80	66⅔	53⅓	46⅔	40
21	52½	105	84	70	56	49	42
22	55	110	88	73⅓	58⅔	51⅓	44
23	57½	115	92	76⅔	61⅓	53⅔	46
24	60	120	96	80	64	56	48
25	62½	125	100	83⅓	66⅔	58⅓	50
26	65	130	104	86⅔	69⅓	60⅔	52
27	67½	135	108	90	72	63	54
28	70	140	112	93⅓	74⅔	65⅓	56
29	72½	145	116	96⅔	77⅓	67⅔	58
30	75	150	120	100	80	70	60
31	77½	155	124	103⅓	82⅔	72⅓	62
32	80	160	128	106⅔	85⅓	74⅔	64

TAPPINGS: 2 inches and bushed as per list on page 59.

CONNECTIONS: **Water** — extra-heavy right and left threaded nipples at top and bottom — all Plants. **Steam** — extra-heavy right threaded nipples at bottom (Pierce Plant); and with extra-heavy right and left threaded nipples at bottom (Detroit, Kansas City and Birmingham Plants).

LOW DRIP HUBS: **One Pipe Steam** — on supply leg-section; **Two Pipe Steam** — on return leg-section.

MEASUREMENTS: Center of tappings to floors and between centers of upper and lower Water tappings, and between upper and lower concealed brackets, etc., see pages 242 to 246.

*Add ½ inch to length for each bushing.

Peerless Three-Column Radiators

For Steam and Water

Each section is 9 inches wide. Width of legs, 10 inches.

These Radiators are made in special shapes as follows:—

Circular, for Steam and Water..................see pages 93 to 95
Corner, for Steam and Water................see pages 96, 247 to 249
Curved, for Steam and Water.....................see page 97
Ventilating.................................see pages 88 to 90
Legs, Extra High, for Steam and Water................see page 102
Single Foot, Steam and Water......................see page 101
Marble-Top Saddles, for Steam and Water............see page 101
Concealed Brackets, for Steam and Water........see pages 98 to 100

Peerless Three-Column Radiators

For Steam and Water

No. of Sections	* Length $2\frac{1}{2}$ in. per Sec.	Heating Surface — Square Feet					
		45-in. Height 6 sq. ft. per Sec.	38-in. Height 5 sq. ft. per Sec.	32-in. Height $4\frac{1}{2}$ sq. ft. per Sec.	26-in. Height $3\frac{3}{4}$ sq. ft. per Sec.	22-in. Height 3 sq. ft. per Sec.	18-in. Height $2\frac{1}{4}$ sq. ft. per Sec.
2	5	12	10	9	$7\frac{1}{2}$	6	$4\frac{1}{2}$
3	$7\frac{1}{2}$	18	15	$13\frac{1}{2}$	$11\frac{1}{4}$	9	$6\frac{3}{4}$
4	10	24	20	18	15	12	9
5	$12\frac{1}{2}$	30	25	$22\frac{1}{2}$	$18\frac{3}{4}$	15	$11\frac{1}{4}$
6	15	36	30	27	$22\frac{1}{2}$	18	$13\frac{1}{2}$
7	$17\frac{1}{2}$	42	35	$31\frac{1}{2}$	$26\frac{1}{4}$	21	$15\frac{3}{4}$
8	20	48	40	36	30	24	18
9	$22\frac{1}{2}$	54	45	$40\frac{1}{2}$	$33\frac{3}{4}$	27	$20\frac{1}{4}$
10	25	60	50	45	$37\frac{1}{2}$	30	$22\frac{1}{2}$
11	$27\frac{1}{2}$	66	55	$49\frac{1}{2}$	$41\frac{1}{4}$	33	$24\frac{3}{4}$
12	30	72	60	54	45	36	27
13	$32\frac{1}{2}$	78	65	$58\frac{1}{2}$	$48\frac{3}{4}$	39	$29\frac{1}{4}$
14	35	84	70	63	$52\frac{1}{2}$	42	$31\frac{1}{2}$
15	$37\frac{1}{2}$	90	75	$67\frac{1}{2}$	$56\frac{1}{4}$	45	$33\frac{3}{4}$
16	40	96	80	72	60	48	36
17	$42\frac{1}{2}$	102	85	$76\frac{1}{2}$	$63\frac{3}{4}$	51	$38\frac{1}{4}$
18	45	108	90	81	$67\frac{1}{2}$	54	$40\frac{1}{2}$
19	$47\frac{1}{2}$	114	95	$85\frac{1}{2}$	$71\frac{1}{4}$	57	$42\frac{3}{4}$
20	50	120	100	90	75	60	45
21	$52\frac{1}{2}$	126	105	$94\frac{1}{2}$	$78\frac{3}{4}$	63	$47\frac{1}{4}$
22	55	132	110	99	$82\frac{1}{2}$	66	$49\frac{1}{2}$
23	$57\frac{1}{2}$	138	115	$103\frac{1}{2}$	$86\frac{1}{4}$	69	$51\frac{3}{4}$
24	60	144	120	108	90	72	54
25	$62\frac{1}{2}$	150	125	$112\frac{1}{2}$	$93\frac{3}{4}$	75	$56\frac{1}{4}$
26	65	156	130	117	$97\frac{1}{2}$	78	$58\frac{1}{2}$
27	$67\frac{1}{2}$	162	135	$121\frac{1}{2}$	$101\frac{1}{4}$	81	$60\frac{3}{4}$
28	70	168	140	126	105	84	63
29	$72\frac{1}{2}$	174	145	$130\frac{1}{2}$	$108\frac{3}{4}$	87	$65\frac{1}{4}$
30	75	180	150	135	$112\frac{1}{2}$	90	$67\frac{1}{2}$
31	$77\frac{1}{2}$	186	155	$139\frac{1}{2}$	$116\frac{1}{4}$	93	$69\frac{3}{4}$
32	80	192	160	144	120	96	72

TAPPINGS: 2 inches and bushed as per list on page 59.

CONNECTIONS: Water — extra-heavy right and left threaded nipples at top and bottom. **Steam** — with extra-heavy right and left threaded nipples at bottom only.

LOW DRIP HUBS: One Pipe Steam — on supply leg-section **Two Pipe Steam** — on return leg-section.

MEASUREMENTS: Center of tappings to floors and between centers of upper and lower Water tappings, and between upper and lower concealed brackets, etc., see pages 242 to 246.

*Add ½ inch to length for each bushing.

Peerless Four-Column Radiators

For Steam or Water

Each section is 10½ inches wide. Width of legs, 11¼ inches.

These Radiators are not made in special shapes but can be equipped as follows:—

Single Foot, Steam and Water....................see page 101
Ventilating..................................see pages 88 to 90
Marble-Top Saddles, for Steam and Water............see page 101
Concealed Brackets, for Steam and Water........see pages 98 to 100

Peerless Four-Column Radiators

For Steam or Water

No. of Sections	* Length 3 in. per Sec.	Heating Surface — Square Feet					
		45-in. Height 10 sq. ft. per Sec.	38-in. Height 8 sq. ft. per Sec.	32-in. Height 6½ sq. ft. per Sec.	26-in. Height 5 sq. ft. per Sec.	22-in. Height 4 sq. ft. per Sec.	18-in. Height 3 sq. ft. per Sec.
2	6	20	16	13	10	8	6
3	9	30	24	19½	15	12	9
4	12	40	32	26	20	16	12
5	15	50	40	32½	25	20	15
6	18	60	48	39	30	24	18
7	21	70	56	45½	35	28	21
8	24	80	64	52	40	32	24
9	27	90	72	58½	45	36	27
10	30	100	80	65	50	40	30
11	33	110	88	71½	55	44	33
12	36	120	96	78	60	48	36
13	39	130	104	84½	65	52	39
14	42	140	112	91	70	56	42
15	45	150	120	97½	75	60	45
16	48	160	128	104	80	64	48
17	51	170	136	110½	85	68	51
18	54	180	144	117	90	72	54
19	57	190	152	123½	95	76	57
20	60	200	160	130	100	80	60
21	63	210	168	136½	105	84	63
22	66	220	176	143	110	88	66
23	69	230	184	149½	115	92	69
24	72	240	192	156	120	96	72
25	75	250	200	162½	125	100	75
26	78	260	208	169	130	104	78
27	81	270	216	175½	135	108	81
28	84	280	224	182	140	112	84
29	87	290	232	188½	145	116	87
30	90	300	240	195	150	120	90
31	93	310	248	201½	155	124	93
32	96	320	256	208	160	128	96

TAPPINGS: 2 inches and bushed as per list on page 59.

CONNECTIONS: Both **Steam** and **Water** — extra-heavy right and left threaded nipples at top and bottom.

MEASUREMENTS: Center of tappings to floors, and between centers of upper and lower Water tappings, and between upper and lower concealed brackets, etc. see pages 242 to 246.

*Add ½ inch to length for each bushing.

Rococo Window Radiators

For Steam or Water

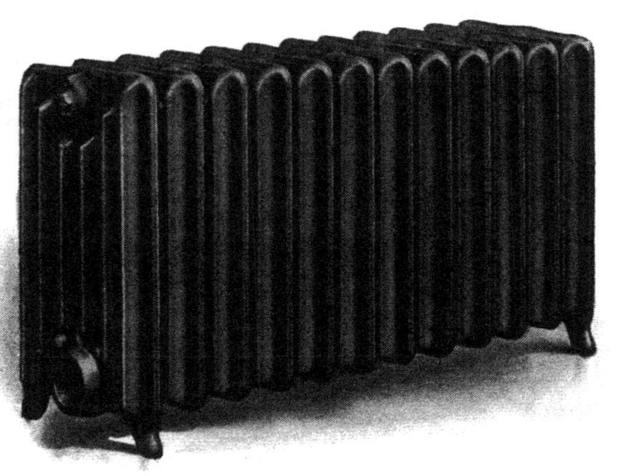

No. of Sections	* Length 3 Inches per Section	Heating Surface — Square Feet 20-in. Height 5 sq. ft. per Section	16-in. Height 3¾ sq. ft. per Section	13-in. Height 3 sq. ft. per Section
2	6	10	7½	6
3	9	15	11¼	9
4	12	20	15	12
5	15	25	18¾	15
6	18	30	22½	18
7	21	35	26¼	21
8	24	40	30	24
9	27	45	33¾	27
10	30	50	37½	30

Can be built up like all AMERICAN Radiators to any practical greater number of sections.

Each section is 12½ inches wide.

TAPPINGS: 2 inches and bushed as per list on page 59.

CONNECTIONS: Extra-heavy right and left threaded nipples at top and bottom.

MEASUREMENTS: Center of tappings to floors, and between centers of upper and lower Water Tappings, see pages 242 to 244.

For Rococo Window Radiators in Curved shape, see page 97; Corner, see pages 96, 247 to 249; and with Removable Lugs for Marble Tops, see page 101.

*Add ½ inch to length for each bushing.

Aetna Flue Window Radiators

For Steam or Water

No. of Sec-tions	* Length 3 inches per Sec.	Heating Surface—Square Feet. 20-in. Height 6 sq. ft. per Sec.	18-in. Height 5⅓ sq. ft. per Sec.	16-in. Height 4⅔ sq. ft. per Sec.	14-in. Height 4 sq. ft. per Sec.	13-in. Height 3⅔ sq. ft. per Sec.
2	6	12	10⅔	9⅓	8	7⅓
3	9	18	16	14	12	11
4	12	24	21⅓	18⅔	16	14⅔
5	15	30	26⅔	23⅓	20	18⅓
6	18	36	32	28	24	22
7	21	42	37⅓	32⅔	28	25⅔
8	24	48	42⅔	37⅓	32	29⅓
9	27	54	48	42	36	33
10	30	60	53⅓	46⅔	40	36⅔

Can be built up, like all AMERICAN Radiators, to any practical greater number of sections.

Each section is 12½ inches wide.

TAPPINGS: 2 inches and bushed as per list on page 59.

CONNECTIONS: Extra-heavy right and left threaded nipples at top and bottom.

MEASUREMENTS: Center of tappings to floors, and between centers of upper and lower Water Tappings, see pages 242 to 244.

For Aetna Curved and Corner Radiators, see pages 96, 97, 247 and 249. Can be furnished, on special order, with Detachable High Legs (see page 102) and with Removable Lugs for Marble Top (see page 101).

*Add ½ inch to length for each bushing.

Verona Ornamental Radiators

For Steam and Water

Each section is 8 inches wide. Width of legs, 8½ inches.

These Radiators are made in special shapes as follows:—

Curved, for Steam and Water .... see page 97
Corner, for Steam and Water .... see pages 96, 247 and 248
Legs, Detachable High, for Steam and Water .... see page 102
Marble-Top Lugs, for Steam and Water .... see page 101

Verona Ornamental Radiators

For Steam and Water

No. of Sec-tions	* Length 2½ in. per Sec.	Heating Surface—Square Feet			
		38-in. Height 4 sq. ft. per Sec.	32-in. Height 3⅓ sq. ft. per Sec.	26-in. Height 2⅔ sq. ft. per Sec.	20-in. Height 2 sq. ft. per Sec.
2	5	8	6⅔	5⅓	4
3	7½	12	10	8	6
4	10	16	13⅓	10⅔	8
5	12½	20	16⅔	13⅓	10
6	15	24	20	16	12
7	17½	28	23⅓	18⅔	14
8	20	32	26⅔	21⅓	16
9	22½	36	30	24	18
10	25	40	33⅓	26⅔	20
11	27½	44	36⅔	29⅓	22
12	30	48	40	32	24
13	32½	52	43⅓	34⅔	26
14	35	56	46⅔	37⅓	28
15	37½	60	50	40	30
16	40	64	53⅓	42⅔	32
17	42½	68	56⅔	45⅓	34
18	45	72	60	48	36
19	47½	76	63⅓	50⅔	38
20	50	80	66⅔	53⅓	40
21	52½	84	70	56	42
22	55	88	73⅓	58⅔	44
23	57½	92	76⅔	61⅓	46
24	60	96	80	64	48
25	62½	100	83⅓	66⅔	50
26	65	104	86⅔	69⅓	52
27	67½	108	90	72	54
28	70	112	93⅓	74⅔	56
29	72½	116	96⅔	77⅓	58
30	75	120	100	80	60
31	77½	124	103⅓	82⅔	62
32	80	128	106⅔	85⅓	64

TAPPINGS: 2 inches and bushed as per list on page 59.

CONNECTIONS: Water — with extra-heavy right and left threaded nipples at top and bottom. **Steam** — with extra-heavy right and left threaded nipples at bottom only.

LOW DRIP HUBS: One Pipe Steam — on supply leg-section; **Two Pipe Steam** — on return leg-section.

MEASUREMENTS: Center of tappings to floors, and between centers of upper and lower Water tappings, see pages 242 to 244.

*Add ½ inch to length for each bushing.

Italian Flue Ornamental Radiators

For Steam and Water

Each section is 8½ inches wide. Width of legs, 8½ inches.

These Radiators are made in special shapes as follows:—

Corner, for Steam and Water............ see pages 96, 247 and 248
Curved, for Steam and Water........................ see page 97
Legs, Detachable High, for Steam and Water.......... see page 102
Marble-Top Lugs, for Steam and Water.............. see page 101

Italian Flue Ornamental Radiators

For Steam and Water

No. of Sections	* Length 3 in. per Sec.	Heating Surface—Square Feet: 38-in. Height 7 sq. ft. per Sec.	32-in. Height 5¾ sq. ft. per Sec.	26-in. Height 4½ sq. ft. per Sec.	20-in. Height 3¼ sq. ft. per Sec.
2	6	14	11½	9	6½
3	9	21	17¼	13½	9¾
4	12	28	23	18	13
5	15	35	28¾	22½	16¼
6	18	42	34½	27	19½
7	21	49	40¼	31½	22¾
8	24	56	46	36	26
9	27	63	51¾	40½	29¼
10	30	70	57½	45	32½
11	33	77	63¼	49½	35¾
12	36	84	69	54	39
13	39	91	74¾	58½	42¼
14	42	98	80½	63	45½
15	45	105	86¼	67½	48¾
16	48	112	92	72	52
17	51	119	97¾	76½	55¼
18	54	126	103½	81	58½
19	57	133	109¼	85½	61¾
20	60	140	115	90	65
21	63	147	120¾	94½	68¼
22	66	154	126½	99	71½
23	69	161	132¼	103½	74¾
24	72	168	138	108	78
25	75	175	143¾	112½	81¼
26	78	182	149½	117	84½
27	81	189	155¼	121½	87¾
28	84	196	161	126	91
29	87	203	166¾	130½	94¼
30	90	210	172½	135	97½
31	93	217	178¼	139½	100¾
32	96	224	184	144	104

TAPPINGS: 2 inches and bushed as per list on page 59.

CONNECTIONS: Water — with extra-heavy right and left threaded nipples at top and bottom. **Steam** — with extra-heavy right and left threaded nipples at bottom only.

LOW DRIP HUBS: One Pipe Steam — on supply leg-section; **Two Pipe Steam** — on return leg-section.

MEASUREMENTS: Center of tappings to floors, and between centers of upper and lower Water tappings, see pages 242 to 244.

*Add ½ inch to length for each bushing.

Peerless Hospital Radiators

Made in Two-Column only

For Steam or Water

Made specially for hospitals, sanitariums, and all buildings where a Radiator having separated sections, easily cleaned, supplies the need for a heating surface which meets all the sanitary demands of such institutions.

Each section is 7⅜ inches wide. Width of legs, 8½ inches.

These Radiators are not made in special shapes but can be equipped as follows:—

Legs, Extra High . . . . see page 102
Concealed Brackets . . . . see pages 98 to 100

Peerless Hospital Radiators

Made in Two-Column only

For Steam or Water

No. of Sec- tions	* Length 3 in. per Sec.	Heating Surface—Square Feet					
		45-in. Height 5 sq. ft. per Sec.	38-in. Height 4 sq. ft. per Sec.	32-in. Height 3⅓ sq. ft. per Sec.	26-in. Height 2⅔ sq. ft. per Sec.	23-in. Height 2⅓ sq. ft. per Sec.	20-in. Height 2 sq. ft. per Sec.
2	6	10	8	6⅔	5⅓	4⅔	4
3	9	15	12	10	8	7	6
4	12	20	16	13⅓	10⅔	9⅓	8
5	15	25	20	16⅔	13⅓	11⅔	10
6	18	30	24	20	16	14	12
7	21	35	28	23⅓	18⅔	16⅓	14
8	24	40	32	26⅔	21⅓	18⅔	16
9	27	45	36	30	24	21	18
10	30	50	40	33⅓	26⅔	23⅓	20
11	33	55	44	36⅔	29⅓	25⅔	22
12	36	60	48	40	32	28	24
13	39	65	52	43⅓	34⅔	30⅓	26
14	42	70	56	46⅔	37⅓	32⅔	28
15	45	75	60	50	40	35	30
16	48	80	64	53⅓	42⅔	37⅓	32
17	51	85	68	56⅔	45⅓	39⅔	34
18	54	90	72	60	48	42	36
19	57	95	76	63⅓	50⅔	44⅓	38
20	60	100	80	66⅔	53⅓	46⅔	40
21	63	105	84	70	56	49	42
22	66	110	88	73⅓	58⅔	51⅓	44
23	69	115	92	76⅔	61⅓	53⅔	46
24	72	120	96	80	64	56	48
25	75	125	100	83⅓	66⅔	58⅓	50
26	78	130	104	86⅔	69⅓	60⅔	52
27	81	135	108	90	72	63	54
28	84	140	112	93⅓	74⅔	65⅓	56
29	87	145	116	96⅔	77⅓	67⅔	58
30	90	150	120	100	80	70	60
31	93	155	124	103⅓	82⅔	72⅓	62
32	96	160	128	106⅔	85⅓	74⅔	64

TAPPINGS: 2 inches and bushed as per list on page 59.

CONNECTIONS: Extra-heavy right and left threaded nipples at top and bottom; not made with bottom connection only.

MEASUREMENTS: Center of tappings to floors, and between centers of upper and lower Water tappings, see pages 242 to 246.

*Add ½ inch to length for each bushing.

Italian Flue Orna. Ventilating Radiators

For Steam and Water

Each section is 8½ inches wide.

This pattern of Radiator is not made in any special or odd shape, as the Box-Bases can only be made in straight form.

See page 86 for illustrations and data of the adjustable Box-Bases.

In ordering please state whether back or bottom inlet is required.

Italian Flue Orna. Ventilating Radiators

For Steam and Water

No. of Sections	* Length 3 inches per Sec.	Heating Surface—Square Feet 39½-in. Height 7 sq. ft. per Sec.	33½-in. Height 5¾ sq. ft. per Sec.	27½-in. Height 4½ sq. ft. per Sec.	21½-in. Height 3¼ sq. ft. per Sec.
2	6	14	11½	9	6½
3	9	21	17¼	13½	9¾
4	12	28	23	18	13
5	15	35	28¾	22½	16¼
6	18	42	34½	27	19½
7	21	49	40¼	31½	22¾
8	24	56	46	36	26
9	27	63	51¾	40½	29¼
10	30	70	57½	45	32½
11	33	77	63¼	49½	35¾
12	36	84	69	54	39
13	39	91	74¾	58½	42¼
14	42	98	80½	63	45½
15	45	105	86¼	67½	48¾
16	48	112	92	72	52
17	51	119	97¾	76½	55¼
18	54	126	103½	81	58½
19	57	133	109¼	85½	61¾
20	60	140	115	90	65
21	63	147	120¾	94½	68¼
22	66	154	126½	99	71½
23	69	161	132¼	103½	74¾
24	72	168	138	108	78
25	75	175	143¾	112½	81¼

TAPPINGS: 2 inches and bushed as per list on page 59.

CONNECTIONS: **Water** — with extra heavy right and left threaded nipples at top and bottom. **Steam** — with extra-heavy right and left threaded nipples at bottom only.

LOW DRIP HUBS: **One Pipe Steam** — on supply leg-section. **Two Pipe Steam** — on return leg-section.

MEASUREMENTS: Center of tappings to floors, and between centers of upper and lower Water Tappings, see pages 242 to 244.

*Add ½ inch to length for each bushing.

American Hot-Closet Radiators

Made in 38-In. Rococo 3-Column Only, Steam and Water

Number	*L'gth Inches	Heating Surface Square Feet	Number	*L'gth Inches	Heating Surface Square Feet
2	37½	53	6	57½	93
3	42½	63	7	62½	103
4	47½	73	8	67½	113
5	52½	83	Made larger on special order		

Doors are stenciled "R" for Right; "L" for Left — for correct assembling.

TAPPINGS: 2 inches and bushed as per list on page 59.

MEASUREMENTS: Oven has two shelves 26½ inches long, 12½ inches wide, with 7 inches space between.

The outside width of oven is 14 inches, and this fact should be borne in mind by fitters when arranging for connections, so that distance from center of tapping to wall shall not be less than 9 inches to make clearance from wall 2 inches.

*Add ½ inch to length for each bushing.

Rococo Pantry Radiators

For Steam or Water

This Radiator and Plate-warmer combined is made up from Rococo Wall Sections (7-foot only)—for Steam or Water.

It is not only very handy for residence pantries, but in extended constructions this warmer will be found most adaptable to the needs of hotel and restaurant kitchens wherein it is necessary to keep a large number of plates and other dishes warm and ready for service. It can be made up in various heights. It is shipped made up.

Sizes and Measurements

No.	Heights Inches	Lengths Inches	Widths Inches	Heating Surface
2	17	23	13¼	15 sq. ft.
3	27	23	13¼	23 "
4	37	23	13¼	31 "
5	47	23	13¼	39 "

Height, floor to bottom of lower section.............. 4 inches
Distance from floor to center of tapping on bottom section. 5¾ inches

TAPPINGS: Tapped regularly 1½ inches and bushed. In ordering, state whether for Steam or Water, and what size tapping is required; also in specifying locations of tappings, note same by alphabetical designations shown in illustration, and state what section is to be tapped. "B" and "F" are the regular tappings on each section; the others are special cast solid.

Circular Radiators

Rococo Two-Column Circular Radiator

Made in all heights of following patterns in steam and water:—

Rococo One-Column.	**Peerless One-Column.**
Rococo Two-Column.	**Peerless Two-Column.**
Rococo Three-Column.	**Peerless Three-Column.**

Radiators above listed are all made at Pierce and Detroit Plants except the twelve section, which is made at Detroit Plant only.

Rococo Two-Column Circular Steam Radiators, in 38-inch height only, are carried in stock at Detroit Plant, as per list on page 94.

All other patterns of Circular Radiators made on special order only.

For measurements, see page 95.

Rococo Wall Radiators

Rococo Wall Radiators should always be assembled with bars vertical to secure greatest heating efficiency. The 7- and 9-foot Sections are, therefore, made in two Styles: Nos. 7-A and 9-A have bars running crosswise of the Section and are regularly tapped for connecting end to end as illustrated. Nos. 7-B and 9-B have bars running lengthwise of the Section and are regularly tapped for connecting side by side as illustrated.

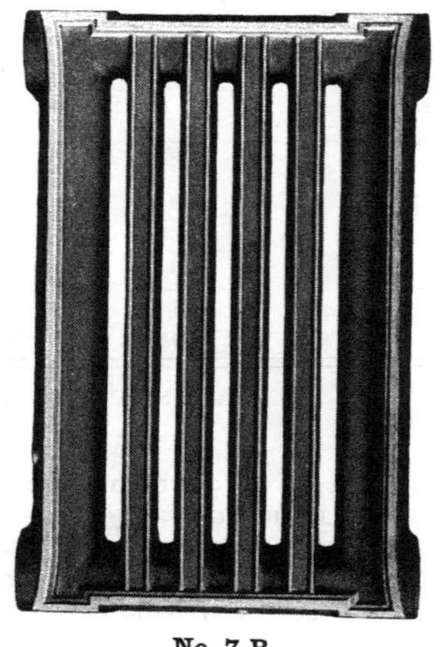

No. 7-B

No. 9-B

No. 5-A is made with bars running crosswise of the Section only and is regularly tapped for connecting end to end. On special order, however, the No. 5-A Sections can be furnished with tappings at 30, 40, 70, and 80 as illustrated.

For Ratings and Measurements of Sections, see page 106.

For additional Measurements and Methods of Assembling, see pages 250 to 258 inclusive.

For Tappings, Connections, Directions for Ordering, and Shipping Conditions, see page 241.

Rococo Wall Radiators—Continued

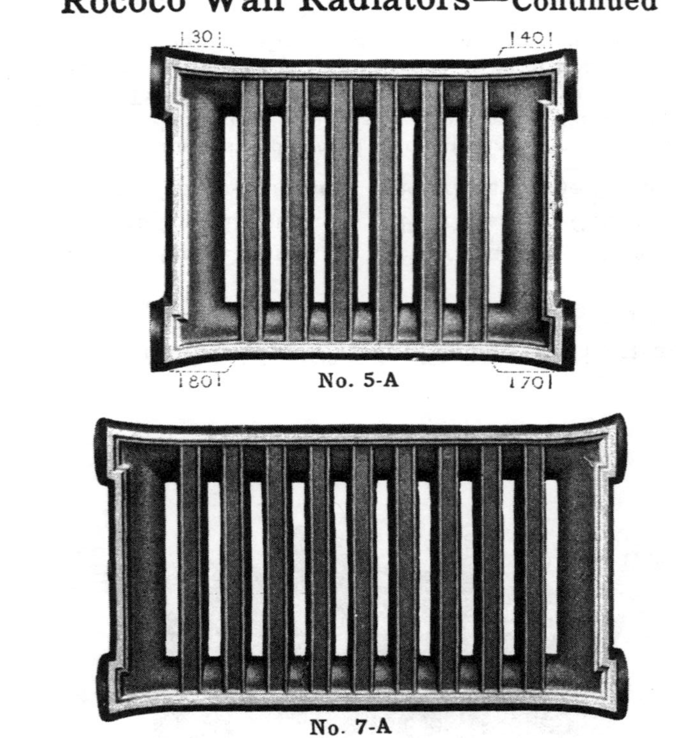

No. 5-A

No. 7-A

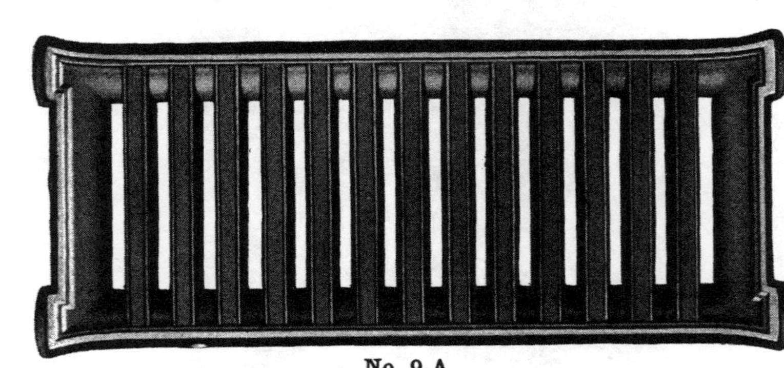

No. 9-A

Rating and Measurement of Sections

Sections Number	Height inches	Length or Width Inches	Thickness Inches	Thickness (with bracket) Inches	Heating Surface Sq. Ft.
5-A	13 5/16	16 5/8	2 7/8	3 1/2	5
7-A	13 5/16	21 7/8	2 7/8	3 1/2	7
7-B	21 7/8	13 5/16	3 1/16	3 11/16	7
9-A	13 5/16	29 1/16	2 7/8	3 1/2	9
9-B	29 1/16	13 5/16	3 1/16	3 11/16	9

Vento Cast-Iron Heaters

For Fan and Blower Work
(Patented December 15, 1903)

Regular Section **Cross Section** **Narrow Section**

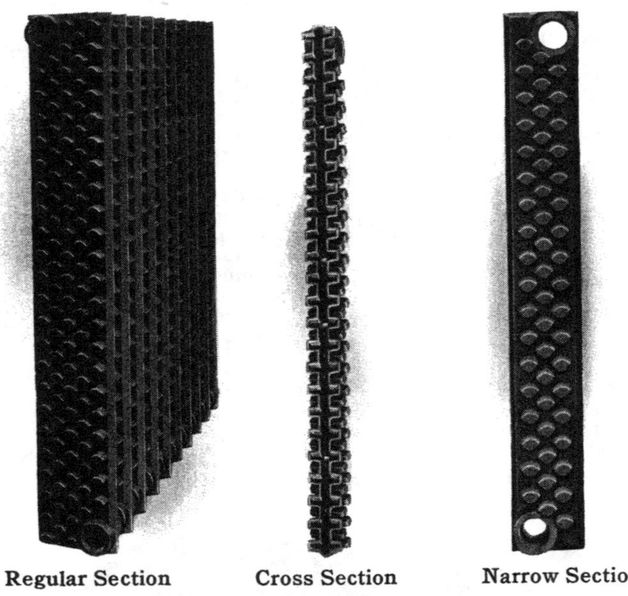

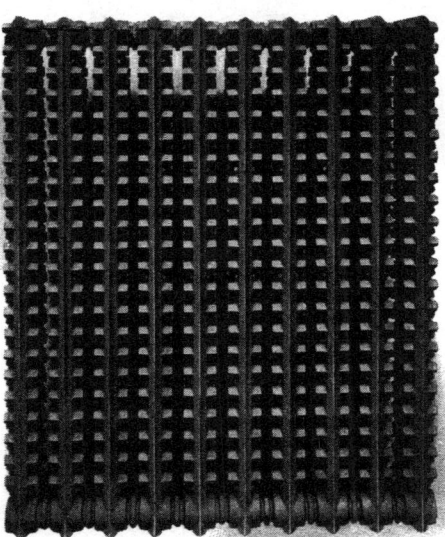

Front View of Ten-Section Stack

Made for Steam or Water, in 30-, 40-, 50-, 60-, and 72-inch Regular Sections, and in 40-, 50-, and 60-inch Narrow Sections. A great improvement over pipe coils for heating and ventilating work; also for drying work in lumber kilns, laundries, hotels, factories, mills, etc.

Vento Cast-Iron Heaters

The extended tables and large charts necessary to show the elaborate tests of VENTO Hot Blast Heaters make it quite impossible to condense the data and charts in the limited size pages of this pocket volume. Hence, please ask for special catalog: *"Engineers' Data on Vento Heaters."*

This special catalog (**free on request**) **embraces the following principal subjects:**

- Vento Tests and Pressures
- Tiering, Housing, etc.
- Circulation Principles
- Assembling and Supporting
- Examples in Estimating Surfaces
- Air Washing and Humidifying
- Water Heating and Cooling Data
- Constants for Heat Transmission
- Heat Transference Tables
- Allowable Velocities of Air, etc.
- Volume and Density of Dry Air
- Tables of Double Tiering
- Friction of Air through Heaters
- Final Temperature and Condensation Tables
- Condensation and Temperature Charts
- Air Vent Piping Diagrams, etc.

Sections are easily handled and transported and may be carried through doors or windows of any building, and can then be assembled in compact, complete heaters. The equivalent pipe coil stacks are cumbersome and difficult to handle and transport.

Perfection Pin Indirect Radiator

For Steam and Water — Threaded Nipple Connections

"Standard" Size, Water End Section

MEASUREMENTS: Heating surface, 10 square feet. Length, 36¼ inches. Height, 7½ inches—at connecting point 9$\frac{13}{16}$ inches. Width in stack, 2¾ inches. On **Special Order** we furnish nipples to make distance center to center of sections in stack, 3, 3¼, 3½, or 3¾ inches.

"Extra Large" Size, Steam End Section

MEASUREMENTS: Heating surface, 15 square feet. Length, 36¼ inches. Height, 11½ inches — at connecting point 14 inches. Width in stack, 2⅞ inches. On **Special Order** we furnish nipples to make distance center to center of sections in stack, 3⅛, 3⅜, 3⅝, or 3⅞ inches.

Both Sizes

CONSTRUCTION: Both "Standard" and "Extra-Large" sections are made in distinctive patterns for Steam and Water. The Steam patterns have one connection or passageway for Steam — the Water patterns have two connections or waterways.

TAPPINGS: 2 inches right-hand on one side, left-hand on other side. Unless otherwise ordered the inside tappings in bushings will be right-hand. **Air Valve Tap**—⅜-inch.

SPECIAL TAPPINGS: If other than regular tappings ("A" and "B" for water and "B" only for steam) are desired, we can furnish on the Standard size section special tappings 1¼-inches or smaller, at "C," "F," "D," and "E," and for steam section 2-inches or smaller at "A." On the Extra Large section, can furnish special tappings 2-inches or smaller at "B," "C," "D," and "F," and at "A" on the steam section.

CONNECTIONS: Extra-heavy 2-inch right and left threaded nipples with hexagon nut in center.

SHIPMENTS: Water sections separate unless ordered assembled in stacks of 5 or 6 sections; steam sections cannot be safely shipped assembled and are therefore shipped knocked down. Sufficient nipples are shipped to assemble.

See page 260 for Free Areas and Distance between Centers.

Perfection Pin Indirect Radiators

For Steam or Water—Flange and Bolt Connections

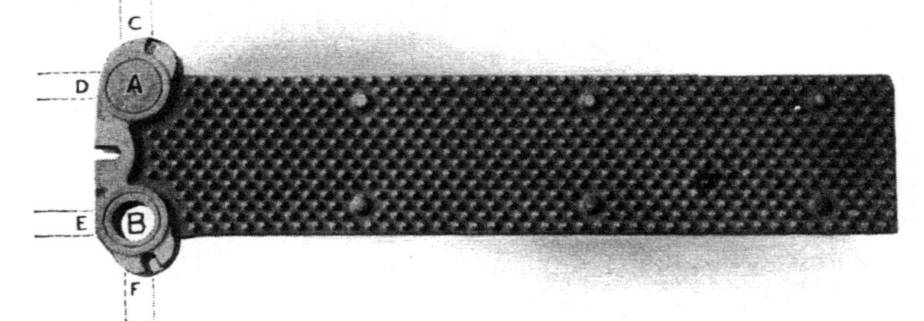

"Standard" Size Steam End Section

MEASUREMENTS: Standard Size — Heating surface, 10 square feet. Length, 36¼ inches. Height, 7½ inches — at connecting point 11½ inches. Width in stack, 2¾ inches.

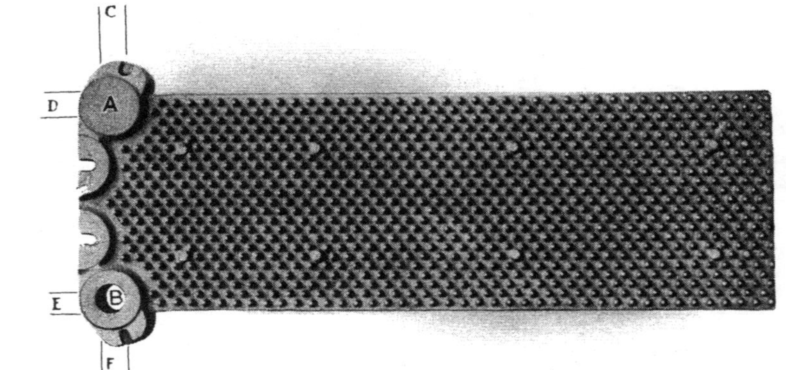

"Extra Large" Size Steam End Section

MEASUREMENTS: Extra Large Size — Heating surface, 15 square feet. Length, 36¼ inches. Height, 11½ inches — at connecting point, 15½ inches. Width in stack, 2⅞ inches.

Both Sizes

CONSTRUCTION: Made in one type for either steam or water — with openings at both top and bottom.

TAPPINGS: 2 inches, right-hand threads, unless otherwise ordered.

Air Valve Tap — ⅜-inch.

SPECIAL TAPPINGS: If other than regular tappings ("A" and "B" on water, and "B" only on steam) are desired, we can furnish special tappings 1¼ inches or smaller at "C," or "F," "D" and "E," and for steam 2 inches or smaller at "A."

SHIPMENTS: Always separately; cannot be shipped assembled Sufficient bolts are sent to assemble.

See page 260 for Free Areas and Distances between Centers.

Excelsior Indirect Radiators

For Steam and Water

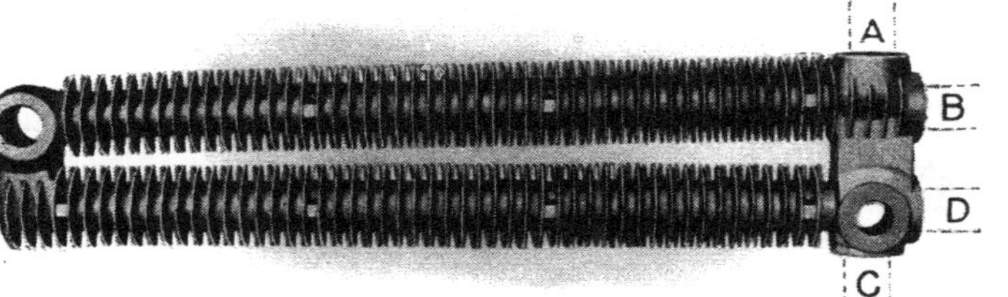

Water End Section

MEASUREMENTS: Heating surface, 12 square feet. Length, **Steam** section, 36 inches; **Water,** 36¾ inches. Height, 8 inches. Width in stack, 3⅝ inches; on **Special Order** we can furnish nipples to make distances from center to center of sections in stack—3⅞, 4⅛, or 4⅜ inches.

TAPPINGS: 1½ inches right threaded on supply; left threaded on return. If smaller opening is required for **Steam** use a 1½-inch nipple and reducing ell, instead of bushing — to avoid interfering with diaphragm opening. We do not furnish any bushings. **Air Valve Tap** — ⅜-inch. The supply pipe should be attached to the *right-hand side* of stack, and return pipe to the left-hand side.

SPECIAL TAPPINGS: If other tappings than regular are required we can furnish at "A," "B," "C," or "D" — 1½ inches or smaller.

CONNECTIONS: Extra-heavy 1½-inch right and left threaded nipples, with hexagon nut in center.

SHIPMENTS: Separate sections, unless ordered in stacks of five or six sections. Sufficient nipples are sent to assemble.

Excelsior Junior Indirect Radiators

For Steam and Water

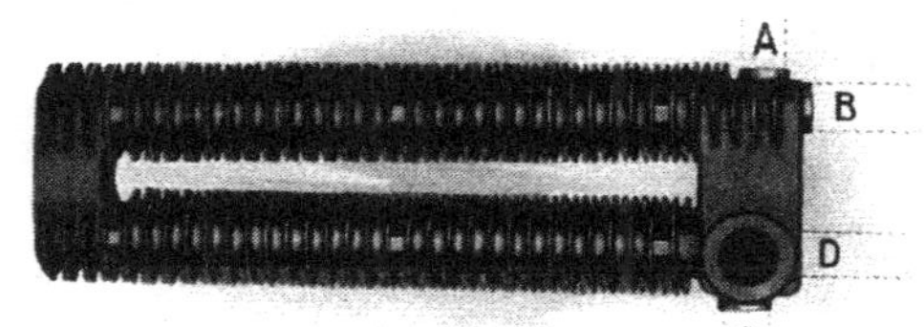

Steam End Section

MEASUREMENTS: Heating surface, 8 square feet. Length, **Steam** section, 23¾ inches; **Water** section, 22 inches. Height, 8 inches. Width in stack, 3⅝ inches. On **Special Order** we can furnish extra nipples to make distances from center to center of sections in stack, 3⅞, 4⅛, 4⅜ inches.

TAPPINGS: 1½ inches right-hand thread, on supply; left-hand on return. If smaller opening is required, use a 1½-inch nipple and reducing ell instead of a bushing — to avoid interfering with diaphragm opening. We do not supply any bushings. **Air Valve Tap** — ⅜-inch.

SPECIAL TAPPINGS: If other tapping than regular is desired, we can furnish at "A," "B," "C," or "D" — 1½-inch or smaller.

CONNECTIONS: Extra-heavy 1½-inch right and left threaded, with hexagon nut at center.

SHIPMENTS: Separate sections, unless ordered in stacks of five or six sections. Sufficient nipples are sent to assemble.

See page 260 for Free Areas and Distances between Centers.
See page 261 for Directions for Setting, and other Data.

Sterling Indirect Radiators

For Water Only

Single Section

MEASUREMENTS: Heating surface, 20 square feet. Length 36¾ inches. Height, 15¾ inches. Width — each section in stack, 3½ inches. On **Special Order** we furnish extra long nipples to make center to center of sections in stack, 3¾, 4, 4¼, or 4½ inches.

TAPPINGS: 2 inches, right threaded on supply; left threaded on return — unless otherwise ordered. When bushed down, the tapping inside the bushing is right-hand, unless otherwise ordered. **Air Valve Tap** — ⅜-inch.

SPECIAL TAPPINGS: If desired we can furnish special tappings at "E," "F," "G," or "H" — 2 inches or smaller.

CONNECTIONS: Extra-heavy 2-inch right and left threaded nipples, with hexagon nuts in center.

SHIPMENTS: Separate sections — unless specially ordered in stacks of five or six sections. Sufficient nipples are sent to assemble.

Cardinal Indirect Radiators

For Steam or Water

Single Section—Steam or Water

MEASUREMENTS: Heating surface, 15 square feet. Length, 37¼ inches; height, at connecting end, 11¼ inches; at opposite end, 9¼ inches. Width — in stack, 3½ inches. On **Special Order** we furnish extra long nipples to make distance center to center of sections in stack 3¼, 3½, 3¾, 4, 4¼ inches.

TAPPINGS: 2 inches, right threaded on supply; left threaded on return — unless otherwise ordered. When bushed down, the thread inside the bushing is right-hand, unless otherwise ordered. **Air Valve Tap** — ⅜-inch.

SPECIAL TAPPINGS: If tapping other than regular is desired, we can furnish special tappings at "A," or "B," 1½-inch or smaller.

CONNECTIONS: Extra-heavy 2-inch right and left threaded nipples, with hexagon nut in center.

SHIPMENTS: Separate sections, unless ordered assembled in stacks of five or six sections. Sufficient nipples are sent to assemble

See page 260 for Free Areas and Distances between Centers.

Sanitary School Pin Indirect Radiators

For Steam and Water

C D E F

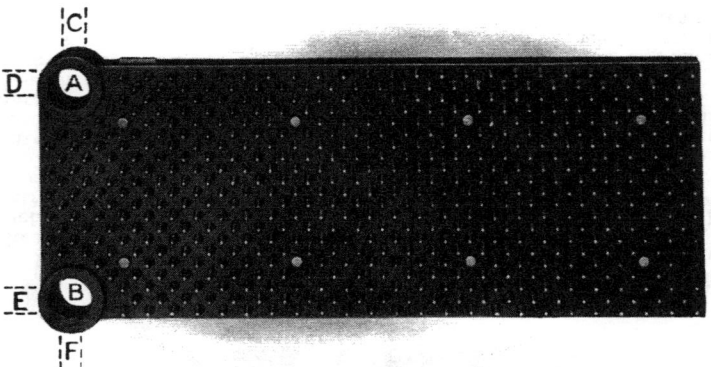

Section for Water

CONSTRUCTION: These sections are made in distinctive patterns for Steam and Water. The Steam patterns have one connection passageway for steam. The Water pattern has two connections or waterways.

MEASUREMENTS: Heating surface, 20 square feet. Length with regular tappings, 36⅛ inches — when tapping is at "D" or "E," 36⅜ inches; height, 13⅞ inches; height at connecting point with regular tappings, 15¼ inches — with special tappings at "C" or "F," 15½ inches. Width — each section in stack, 4 inches. On **Special Order,** we furnish nipples to make distances center to center in stack 3¾, 4¼, or 4½ inches.

TAPPINGS: 2 inches, right-hand on supply end; left-hand on return end. Unless otherwise ordered the inside tappings of bushings will be right-hand. **Air Valve Tap** — ⅜-inch.

CONNECTIONS: Extra-heavy 2-inch right and left threaded nipples with hexagon nut at center.

SHIPMENTS: Steam sections always separate; Water sections separate, but when so specified Water sections can be shipped in five or six section stacks. Sufficient nipples are sent to assemble.

C F

Section for Steam

NOTE, Special Tappings: If other than regular tappings ("A" and "B" on water section and "B" only on steam section) are desired, we can furnish special tappings 2 inches or smaller, at "C," "D," "E," and "F," and also at "A" on the steam section.

Data on Indirect Radiators

All AMERICAN Indirect Radiators are shipped with sufficient nipples to put the stack together on the job.

If the sections are assembled at our Plants an extra charge is made for the work.

All indirect air-valve tappings are regularly made ⅜ inch.

Measurements

Length of Section	Extreme Height	Pattern Name	Heating Surface	Width Each Section Occupies in Stack †Inches	Regular Tapping
23¾	8	Excelsior Junior Steam	8	3⅝	‡1½
36	8	Excelsior Steam	12	3⅝	‡1½
36¾	8	Excelsior Water	12	3⅝	‡1½
36¼	11½	Perfection Flange and Bolt, Standard size, Steam or Water	10	2¾	*2
36¼	15½	Perfection Flange and Bolt, extra-large size, Steam or Water	15	2⅞	*2
36¼	9 13/16	Perfection Right & Left Threaded, standard size, Steam or Water	10	2¾	*2
36¼	14	Perfection Right & Left Threaded, extra-large size, Steam or Water	15	2⅞	*2
37¼	11¼	Cardinal, Steam or Water	15	3½	*2
36¾	15¾	Sterling, Steam or Water	20	3½	*2
36⅛	15¼	Sanitary School Pin, Steam or Water	20	4	*2

*These Radiators are all regularly tapped 2 inches and bushed according to the size specified in order.

†When greater air space is desired between the sections we can so furnish on special order.

‡Bushing reduction cannot be made.

Princess

Single-Column

Steam or Water

Note.—Steam Radiators have semi-circular extension flanges between sections at top. These conceal the connecting rod.

REGULAR TAPPING, See Page 110

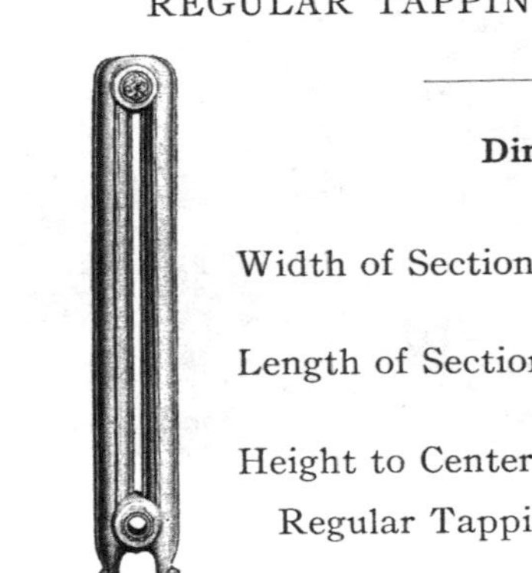

Single-Column

Dimensions

Width of Section	5¼ inches
Length of Section	3 "
Height to Center of Regular Tapping	4⅝ "

Princess

Single-Column

Radiating Surface in Feet

Sections	Total Length Ft.	In.	HEIGHT 45″	37″	31″	25″	19″
Feet per Section			4½	3½	3	2½	2
3	0	10	13½	10½	9	7½	6
4	1	1	18	14	12	10	8
5	1	4	22½	17½	15	12½	10
6	1	7	27	21	18	15	12
7	1	10	31½	24½	21	17½	14
8	2	1	36	28	24	20	16
9	2	4	40½	31½	27	22½	18
10	2	7	45	35	30	25	20
11	2	10	49½	38½	33	27½	22
12	3	1	54	42	36	30	24
13	3	4	58½	45½	39	32½	26
14	3	7	63	49	42	35	28
15	3	10	67½	52½	45	37½	30
16	4	1	72	56	48	40	32
17	4	4	76½	59½	51	42½	34
18	4	7	81	63	54	45	36
19	4	10	85½	66½	57	47½	38
20	5	1	90	70	60	50	40
21	5	4	94½	73½	63	52½	42
22	5	7	99	77	66	55	44
23	5	10	103½	80½	69	57½	46
24	6	1	108	84	72	60	48
25	6	4	112½	87½	75	62½	50

Princess

Two-Column

Steam or Water

Note.—Steam Radiators have semi-circular extension flanges between sections at top. These conceal the connecting rod.

REGULAR TAPPING, See Page 110

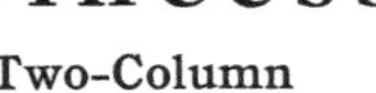

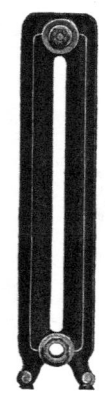

Two-Column

Dimensions

Width of Section	7	inches
Length of Section	3	"
Height to Center of Regular Tapping	4⅝	"

Princess

Two-Column

Radiating Surface in Feet

Sections	Total Length Ft.	Total Length In.	HEIGHT 45″	37″	31″	25″	19″
Feet per Section			5	4	3½	3	2¼
3	0	10	15	12	10½	9	6¾
4	1	1	20	16	14	12	9
5	1	4	25	20	17½	15	11¼
6	1	7	30	24	21	18	13½
7	1	10	35	28	24½	21	15¾
8	2	1	40	32	28	24	18
9	2	4	45	36	31½	27	20¼
10	2	7	50	40	35	30	22½
11	2	10	55	44	38½	33	24¾
12	3	1	60	48	42	36	27
13	3	4	65	52	45½	39	29¼
14	3	7	70	56	49	42	31½
15	3	10	75	60	52½	45	33¾
16	4	1	80	64	56	48	36
17	4	4	85	68	59½	51	38¼
18	4	7	90	72	63	54	40½
19	4	10	95	76	66½	57	42¾
20	5	1	100	80	70	60	45
21	5	4	105	84	73½	63	47¼
22	5	7	110	88	77	66	49½
23	5	10	115	92	80½	69	51¾
24	6	1	120	96	84	72	54
25	6	4	125	100	87½	75	56¼

Princess

Three-Column

Steam or Water

NOTE.—Steam Radiators have semi-circular extension flanges between sections at top. These conceal the connecting rod.

REGULAR TAPPING, See Page 110

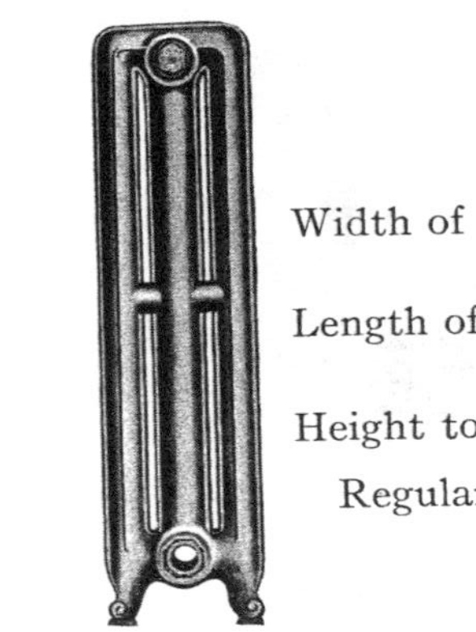

Three-Column

Dimensions

Width of Section	9	inches
Length of Section	3¼	"
Height to Center of Regular Tapping	4⅝	"

Princess

Three-Column

Radiating Surface in Feet

Sections	Total Length Ft.	Total Length In.	HEIGHT 45″	37″	31″	25″	19″
Feet per Section			8	6½	5½	4½	3½
3	0	10¾	24	19½	16½	13½	10½
4	1	2	32	26	22	18	14
5	1	5¼	40	32½	27½	22½	17½
6	1	8½	48	39	33	27	21
7	1	11¾	56	45½	38½	31½	24½
8	2	3	64	52	44	36	28
9	2	6¼	72	58½	49½	40½	31½
10	2	9½	80	65	55	45	35
11	3	¾	88	71½	60½	49½	38½
12	3	4	96	78	66	54	42
13	3	7¼	104	84½	71½	58½	45½
14	3	10½	112	91	77	63	49
15	4	1¾	120	97½	82½	67½	52½
16	4	5	128	104	88	72	56
17	4	8¼	136	110½	93½	76½	59½
18	4	11½	144	117	99	81	63
19	5	2¾	152	123½	104½	85½	66½
20	5	6	160	130	110	90	70
21	5	9¼	168	136½	115½	94½	73½
22	6	½	176	143	121	99	77
23	6	3¾	184	149½	126½	103½	80½
24	6	7	192	156	132	108	84
25	6	10¼	200	162½	137½	112½	87½

Princess

Five-Column

Steam and Water

REGULAR TAPPING, See Page 110

Dimensions

Width of Section	12	inches
Length of Section	3¼	"
Height to Center of Regular Tapping	4⅝	"

Five-Column

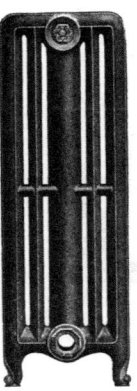

Princess

Five-Column

Radiating Surface in Feet

Sections	Total Length Ft.	Total Length In.	HEIGHT 37″	HEIGHT 25″
Feet per Section			10	7
3	0	10¾	30	21
4	1	2	40	28
5	1	5¼	50	35
6	1	8½	60	42
7	1	11¾	70	49
8	2	3	80	56
9	2	6¼	90	63
10	2	9½	100	70
11	3	¾	110	77
12	3	4	120	84
13	3	7¼	130	91
14	3	10½	140	98
15	4	1¾	150	105
16	4	5	160	112
17	4	8¼	170	119
18	4	11½	180	126
19	5	2¾	190	133
20	5	6	200	140
21	5	9¼	210	147
22	6	½	220	154
23	6	3¾	230	161
24	6	7	240	168
25	6	10¼	250	175

Princess

Five-Column

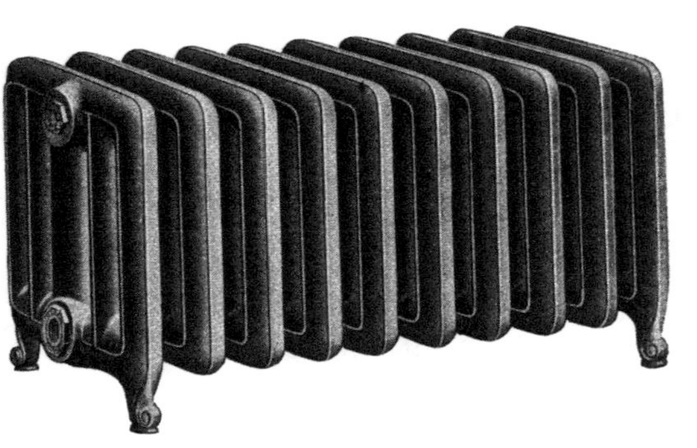

(Window Radiator)

Steam and Water

REGULAR TAPPING, See Page 110

Dimensions

Five-Column

Width of Section	12	inches
Length of Section	3¼	"
Height to Center of Regular Tapping	3	"

Princess

Five-Column

(Window Radiator)

Radiating Surface in Feet

Sections	Total Length Ft.	Total Length In.	HEIGHT 16″	HEIGHT 14″	HEIGHT 12″
Feet per Section			4⅔	4	3⅓
3	0	10¾	14	12	10
4	1	2	18⅔	16	13⅓
5	1	5¼	23⅓	20	16⅔
6	1	8½	28	24	20
7	1	11¾	32⅔	28	23⅓
8	2	3	37⅓	32	26⅔
9	2	6¼	42	36	30
10	2	9½	46⅔	40	33⅓
11	3	¾	51⅓	44	36⅔
12	3	4	56	48	40
13	3	7¼	60⅔	52	43⅓
14	3	10½	65⅓	56	46⅔
15	4	1¾	70	60	50
16	4	5	74⅔	64	53⅓
17	4	8¼	79⅓	68	56⅔
18	4	11½	84	72	60
19	5	2¾	88⅔	76	63⅓
20	5	6	93⅓	80	66⅔
21	5	9¼	98	84	70
22	6	½	102⅔	88	73⅓
23	6	3¾	107⅓	92	76⅔
24	6	7	112	96	80
25	6	10¼	116⅔	100	83⅓

Imperial

Single-Column

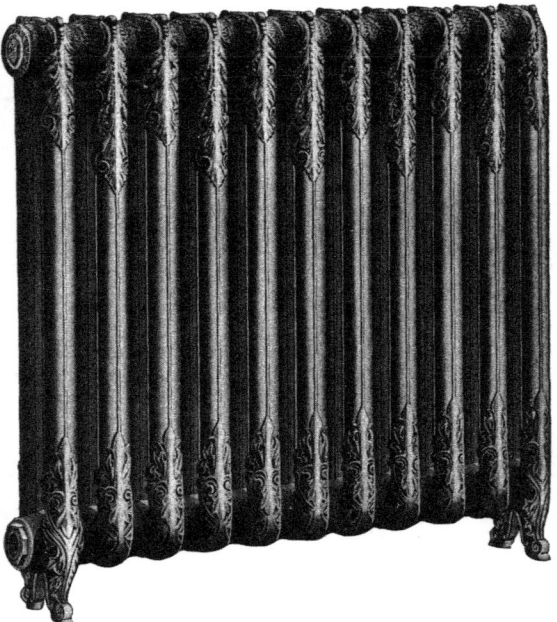

Steam and Water

REGULAR TAPPING, See Page 110

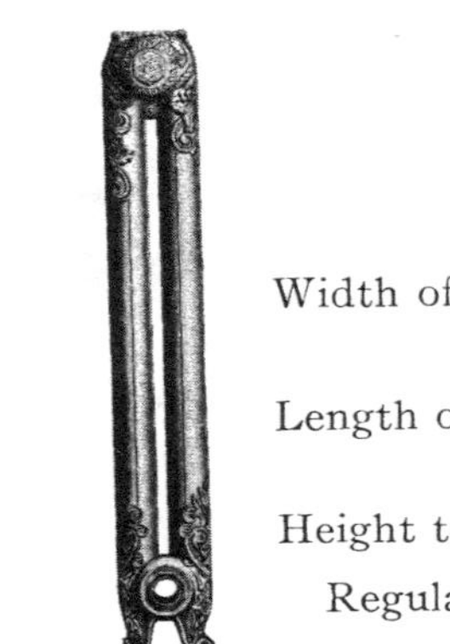
Single-Column

Dimensions

Width of Section	5¼ inches
Length of Section	3 "
Height to Center of Regular Tapping	4⅝ "

Imperial

Single-Column

Radiating Surface in Feet

Sections	Total Length Ft.	Total Length In.	HEIGHT 45″	37″	31″	25″	19″
Feet per Section			4½	3½	3	2½	2
3	0	10	13½	10½	9	7½	6
4	1	1	18	14	12	10	8
5	1	4	22½	17½	15	12½	10
6	1	7	27	21	18	15	12
7	1	10	31½	24½	21	17½	14
8	2	1	36	28	24	20	16
9	2	4	40½	31½	27	22½	18
10	2	7	45	35	30	25	20
11	2	10	49½	38½	33	27½	22
12	3	1	54	42	36	30	24
13	3	4	58½	45½	39	32½	26
14	3	7	63	49	42	35	28
15	3	10	67½	52½	45	37½	30
16	4	1	72	56	48	40	32
17	4	4	76½	59½	51	42½	34
18	4	7	81	63	54	45	36
19	4	10	85½	66½	57	47½	38
20	5	1	90	70	60	50	40
21	5	4	94½	73½	63	52½	42
22	5	7	99	77	66	55	44
23	5	10	103½	80½	69	57½	46
24	6	1	108	84	72	60	48
25	6	4	112½	87½	75	62½	50

Imperial

Two-Column

Steam or Water

Note.—Steam Radiators have semi-circular extension flanges between sections at top. These conceal the connecting rod.

REGULAR TAPPING, See Page 110

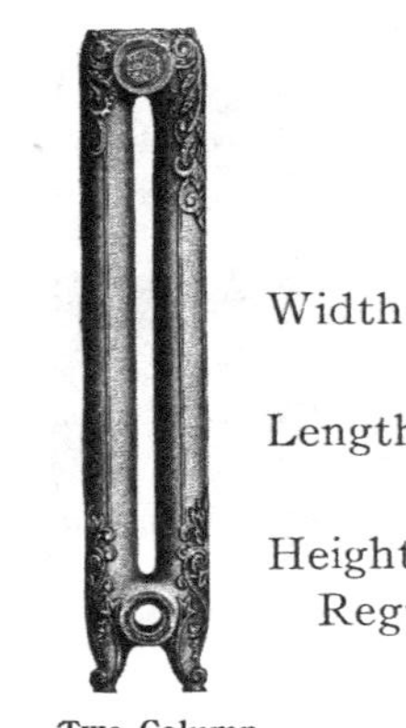

Two-Column

Dimensions

Width of Section	7	inches
Length of Section	3	"
Height to Center of Regular Tapping	4⅝	"

Imperial

Two-Column

Radiating Surface in Feet

Sec-tions	Total Length Ft.	Total Length In.	HEIGHT 45″	37″	31″	25″	19″
Feet per Section			5	4	3½	3	2¼
3	0	10	15	12	10½	9	6¾
4	1	1	20	16	14	12	9
5	1	4	25	20	17½	15	11¼
6	1	7	30	24	21	18	13½
7	1	10	35	28	24½	21	15¾
8	2	1	40	32	28	24	18
9	2	4	45	36	31½	27	20¼
10	2	7	50	40	35	30	22½
11	2	10	55	44	38½	33	24¾
12	3	1	60	48	42	36	27
13	3	4	65	52	45½	39	29¼
14	3	7	70	56	49	42	31½
15	3	10	75	60	52½	45	33¾
16	4	1	80	64	56	48	36
17	4	4	85	68	59½	51	38¼
18	4	7	90	72	63	54	40½
19	4	10	95	76	66½	57	42¾
20	5	1	100	80	70	60	45
21	5	4	105	84	73½	63	47¼
22	5	7	110	88	77	66	49½
23	5	10	115	92	80½	69	51¾
24	6	1	120	96	84	72	54
25	6	4	125	100	87½	75	56¼

Imperial

Three-Column

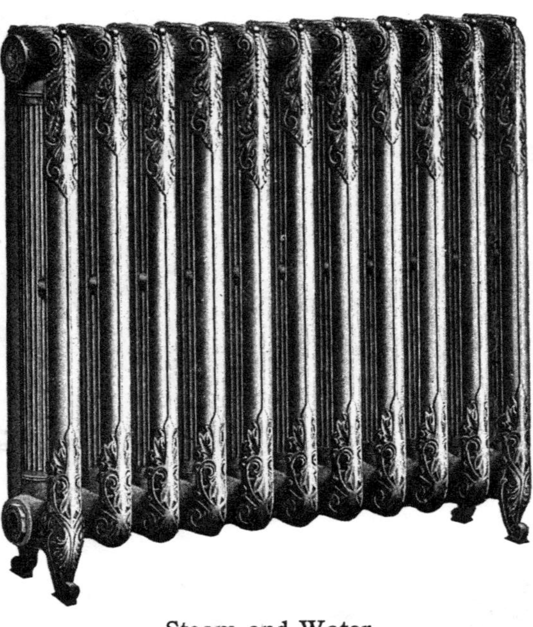

Steam and Water

REGULAR TAPPING, See Page 110

Three-Column

Dimensions

Width of Section	9	inches
Length of Section	3¼	"
Height to Center of Regular Tapping	4⅝	"

Imperial

Three-Column

Radiating Surface in Feet

Sections	Total Length Ft.	Total Length In.	HEIGHT 45″	37″	31″	25″	19″
Feet per Section			8	6½	5½	4½	3½
3	0	10¾	24	19½	16½	13½	10½
4	1	2	32	26	22	18	14
5	1	5¼	40	32½	27½	22½	17½
6	1	8½	48	39	33	27	21
7	1	11¾	56	45½	38½	31½	24½
8	2	3	64	52	44	36	28
9	2	6¼	72	58½	49½	40½	31½
10	2	9½	80	65	55	45	35
11	3	¾	88	71½	60½	49½	38½
12	3	4	96	78	66	54	42
13	3	7¼	104	84½	71½	58½	45½
14	3	10½	112	91	77	63	49
15	4	1¾	120	97½	82½	67½	52½
16	4	5	128	104	88	72	56
17	4	8¼	136	110½	93½	76½	59½
18	4	11½	144	117	99	81	63
19	5	2¾	152	123½	104½	85½	66½
20	5	6	160	130	110	90	70
21	5	9¼	168	136½	115½	94½	73½
22	6	½	176	143	121	99	77
23	6	3¾	184	149½	126½	103½	80½
24	6	7	192	156	132	108	84
25	6	10¼	200	162½	137½	112½	87½

Royal Union

Three-Column

Steam or Water

REGULAR TAPPING, See Page 110

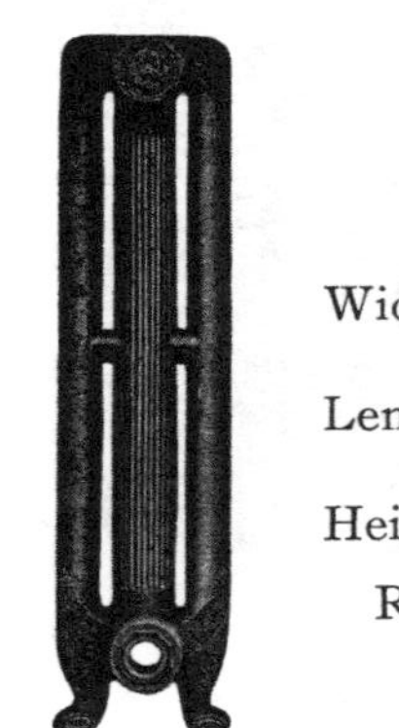

Three-Column

Dimensions

Width of Section	$8\frac{5}{8}$ inches
Length of Section	3 "
Height to Center of Regular Tapping	$4\frac{5}{8}$ "

Royal Union

Three-Column

Radiating Surface in Feet

Sections	Total Length Ft.	Total Length In.	HEIGHT 44″	38″	30″	24″	18″
Feet per Section			6	5	4	3	2
3	0	10	18	15	12	9	6
4	1	1	24	20	16	12	8
5	1	4	30	25	20	15	10
6	1	7	36	30	24	18	12
7	1	10	42	35	28	21	14
8	2	1	48	40	32	24	16
9	2	4	54	45	36	27	18
10	2	7	60	50	40	30	20
11	2	10	66	55	44	33	22
12	3	1	72	60	48	36	24
13	3	4	78	65	52	39	26
14	3	7	84	70	56	42	28
15	3	10	90	75	60	45	30
16	4	1	96	80	64	48	32
17	4	4	102	85	68	51	34
18	4	7	108	90	72	54	36
19	4	10	114	95	76	57	38
20	5	1	120	100	80	60	40
21	5	4	126	105	84	63	42
22	5	7	132	110	88	66	44
23	5	10	138	115	92	69	46
24	6	1	144	120	96	72	48
25	6	4	150	125	100	75	50

Sovereign

Three-Column—Flue Construction
Ornamental

Steam or Water

This radiator can be furnished without ornamentation.

REGULAR TAPPING, See Page 110

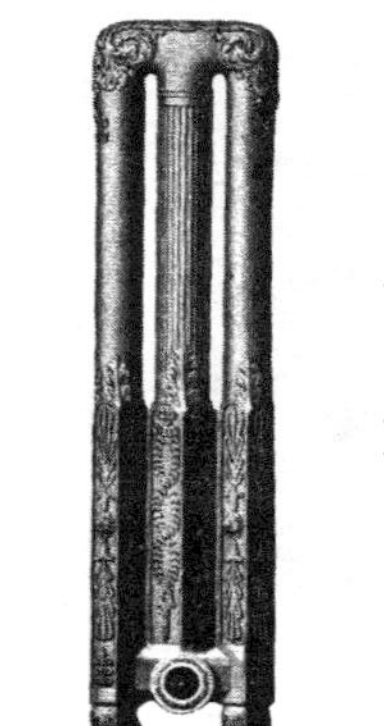

Three-Column Ornamental

Dimensions

Width of Section 8½ inches

Length of Section $2\frac{11}{16}$ "

Height to Center of Regular Tapping 5 "

Sovereign

Three-Column—Flue Construction

Radiating Surface in Feet

Sections	Total Length Ft.	In.	HEIGHT 37″	31″	25″
Feet per Section			6	5	4
3	0	$9\frac{1}{16}$	18	15	12
4	0	11¾	24	20	16
5	1	$2\frac{7}{16}$	30	25	20
6	1	5⅛	36	30	24
7	1	$7\frac{13}{16}$	42	35	28
8	1	10½	48	40	32
9	2	$1\frac{3}{16}$	54	45	36
10	2	3⅞	60	50	40
11	2	$6\frac{9}{16}$	66	55	44
12	2	9¼	72	60	48
13	2	$11\frac{15}{16}$	78	65	52
14	3	2⅝	84	70	56
15	3	$5\frac{5}{16}$	90	75	60
16	3	8	96	80	64
17	3	$10\frac{11}{16}$	102	85	68
18	4	1⅜	108	90	72
19	4	$4\frac{1}{16}$	114	95	76
20	4	6¾	120	100	80
21	4	$9\frac{7}{16}$	126	105	84
22	5	⅛	132	110	88
23	5	$2\frac{13}{16}$	138	115	92
24	5	5½	144	120	96
25	5	$8\frac{3}{16}$	150	125	100

X-Ray

WALL RADIATOR

1 x 3—5 Foot
5 Feet Per Section
No. 1 Legs

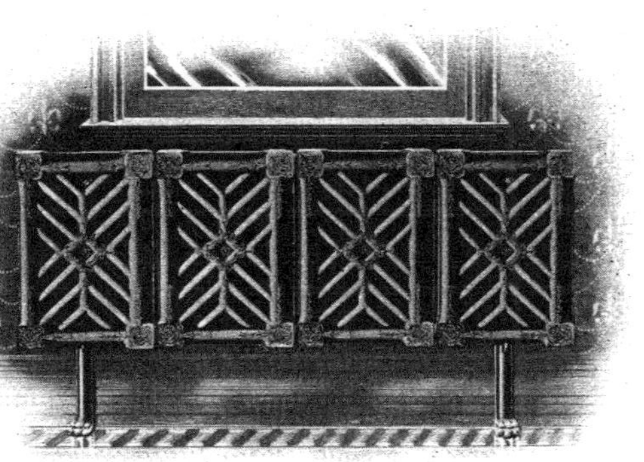

1 x 4—8 Foot Vertical
8 Feet Per Section
No. 1 Legs
REGULAR TAPPINGS, See Page 110

X-Ray

WALL RADIATOR

2 x 4—8 Foot—5 Foot
8 Feet Per Section
5 Feet Per Section
No. 3 Brackets
No. 1 Legs

1 x 3—8 Foot Horizontal
8 Feet Per Section
REGULAR TAPPING, See Page 110

X-Ray
WALL RADIATOR

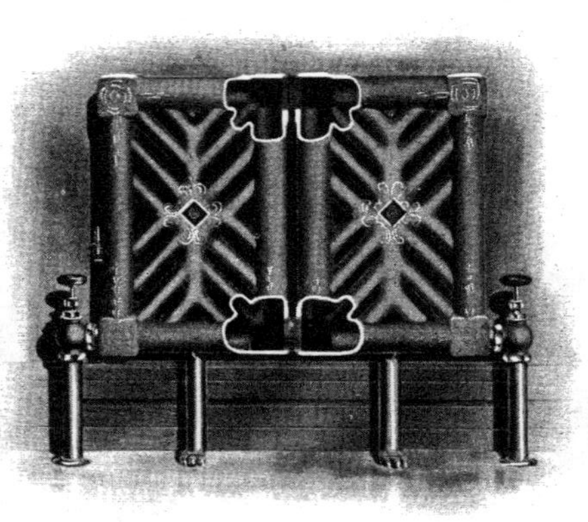

STEAM RADIATOR
1 x 2—8 Foot Vertical
8 Feet Per Section
No. 1 Leg

WATER RADIATOR
1 x 2—8 Foot Vertical
8 Feet Per Section
No. 1 Leg
REGULAR TAPPING, See Page 110

X-Ray

WALL RADIATOR

Dimensions

No. of Sections	5-FOOT X-RAY		8-FOOT X-RAY Vertical		8-FOOT X-RAY Horizontal	
Height Length	Feet of Surface	LENGTH Feet Inches	Feet of Surface	LENGTH Feet Inches	Feet of Surface	LENGTH Feet Inches
1x1	**5**	1— 2 5/16	**8**	1— 2 5/16	**8**	1— 9 3/4
1x2	**10**	2— 5 3/8	**16**	2— 5 5/8	**16**	3— 8 1/4
1x3	**15**	3— 8 7/16	**24**	3— 8 7/16	**24**	5— 6 3/4
1x4	**20**	4—11 1/2	**32**	4—11 1/2	**32**	7— 5 1/4
1x5	**25**	6— 2 9/16	**40**	6— 2 9/16	**40**	9— 3 3/4
1x6	**30**	7— 5 5/8	**48**	7— 7 5/8	**48**	11— 2 1/4
1x7	**35**	8— 8 11/16	**56**	8— 8 11/16	**56**	13— 3/4
1x8	**40**	9—11 3/4	**64**	9—11 3/4	**64**	14—11 1/4
	Height 1′ 2 5/16″		Height 1′ 9 3/4″		Height 1′ 2 5/16″	
2x1	**10**	1— 2 5/16	**16**	1— 2 5/16	**16**	1— 9 3/4
2x2	**20**	2— 5 3/8	**32**	2— 5 3/8	**32**	3— 8 1/4
2x3	**30**	3— 8 7/16	**48**	3— 8 7/16	**48**	5— 6 3/4
2x4	**40**	4—11 1/2	**64**	4—11 1/2	**64**	7— 5 1/4
2x5	**50**	6— 2 9/16	**80**	6— 2 9/16	**80**	9— 3 3/4
2x6	**60**	7— 5 5/8	**96**	7— 5 5/8	**96**	11— 2 1/4
2x7	**70**	8— 8 11/16	**112**	8— 8 11/16	**112**	13— 3/4
2x8	**80**	9—11 3/4	**128**	9—11 3/4	**128**	14—11 1/4
	Height 2′ 5 3/8″		Height 3′ 8 1/4″		Height 2′ 5 3/8″	
3x1	**15**	1— 2 5/16	**24**	1— 2 5/16	**24**	1— 9 3/4
3x2	**30**	2— 5 3/8	**48**	2— 5 3/8	**48**	3— 8 1/4
3x3	**45**	3— 8 7/16	**72**	3— 8 7/16	**72**	5— 6 3/4
3x4	**60**	4—11 1/2	**96**	4—11 1/2	**96**	7— 5 1/4
3x5	**75**	6— 2 9/16	**120**	6— 2 9/16	**120**	9— 3 3/4
3x6	**90**	7— 5 5/8	**144**	7— 5 5/8	**144**	11— 2 1/4
3x7	**105**	8— 8 11/16	**168**	8— 8 11/16	**168**	13— 3/4
3x8	**120**	9—11 3/4	**192**	9—11 3/4	**192**	14—11 1/4
	Height 3′ 8 7/16″		Height 5′ 6 3/4″		Height 3′ 8 7/16″	

X-Ray

PLATE WARMER RADIATOR

for

Steam or Water

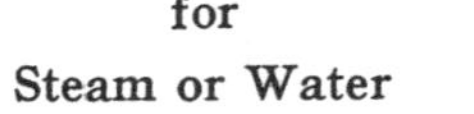

Assembled with 8 foot sections

Dimensions in Inches

No. of Sections high	Feet of Surface	Total Height	Total Length	Total Width
1	8	8	21¾	14 5/16
2	17	18	21¾	14 5/16
3	26	28	21¾	14 5/16
4	35	38	21¾	14 5/16
5	44	48	21¾	14 5/16

Shipped made up unless otherwise ordered.
Specify required tapping.

Circular Radiator

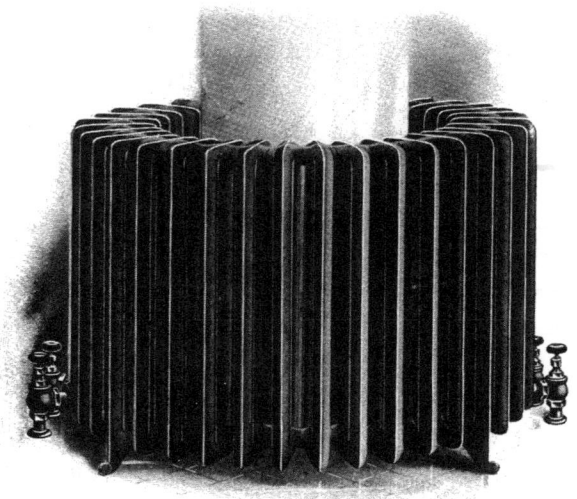

Three-Column Circular Radiator In Halves (Two Radiators) To Encircle Column

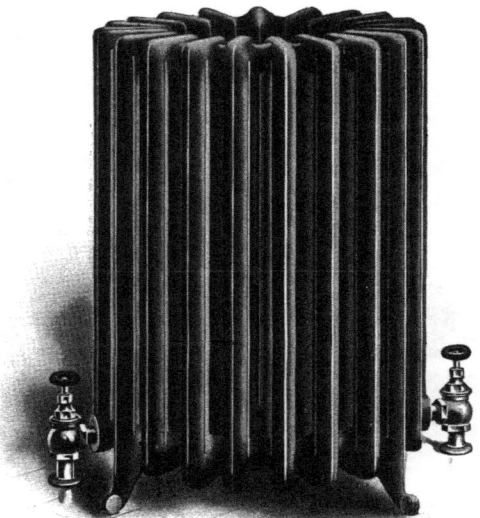

Two-Column Circular Radiator

Circular Radiator

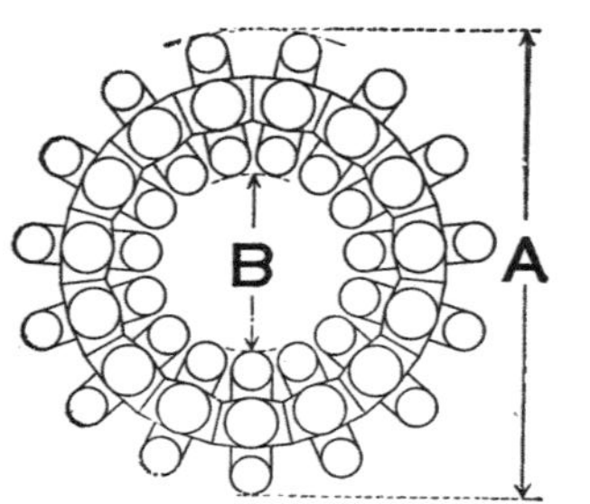

Circular Radiators may be assembled as one whole Radiator, or they may be assembled in halves for the purpose of encircling columns.

When Circular Radiators are in halves, each half becomes an independent Radiator. In ordering state which method of assembling is desired.

Imperial and Princess

Dimensions in Inches

Sections	Single Column Imperial and Princess		Two Column Imperial and Princess		Three Column Imperial and Princess		Five Column Princess	
	A	B	A	B	A	B	A	B
9	14 3/4	4 1/4	18 1/4	4 1/4	22	4	....	....
10	15 9/16	5 1/16	19	5	22 11/16	4 11/16	....	....
11	16 1/4	5 3/4	19 3/4	5 3/4	23 3/8	5 3/8	....	....
12	17 1/16	6 9/16	20 7/16	6 7/16	24 1/8	6 1/8	30 5/8	6 5/8
13	17 5/8	7 1/8	21 1/8	7 1/8	24 7/8	6 7/8	31 7/16	7 7/16
14	18 9/16	8 1/16	21 3/4	7 3/4	25 9/16	7 9/16	32 5/16	8 5/16
15	19 1/4	8 3/4	22 11/16	8 11/16	26 3/8	8 3/8	33 1/16	9 1/16
16	20	9 1/2	23 3/8	9 3/8	27	9	33 11/16	9 11/16
18	21 7/16	10 15/16	24 7/8	10 7/8	28 1/8	10 1/8	35 1/4	11 1/4
20	22 15/16	12 7/16	26 7/16	12 7/16	29 9/16	11 9/16	36 7/8	12 7/8
22	24 3/8	13 7/8	27 13/16	13 13/16	31 1/16	13 1/16	38 1/8	14 1/8
24	26	15 1/2	29 1/4	15 1/4	32 3/8	14 3/8	39 15/16	15 15/16
26	27 1/4	16 3/4	30 9/16	16 9/16	33 13/16	15 13/16	41 1/4	17 1/4
28	28 15/16	18 7/16	32 1/4	18 1/4	35 13/16	17 13/16	43	19
30	30 5/16	19 13/16	33 13/16	19 13/16	37 5/8	19 5/8	44 1/2	20 1/2
32	31 3/4	21 1/4	35 1/8	21 1/8	39 9/16	21 9/16	45 3/4	21 3/4
34	33 3/8	22 7/8	37 1/8	23 1/8	41 3/8	23 3/8	47 7/16	23 7/16
36	34 7/8	24 3/8	38 1/2	24 1/2	43 5/16	25 5/16	49 3/16	25 3/16
38	36 1/4	25 3/4	39 15/16	25 15/16	45 3/8	27 3/8	51 3/8	27 3/8
40	37 7/8	27 3/8	41 3/8	27 3/8	47 13/16	29 13/16	52 3/8	28 3/8
45	41 1/4	30 3/4	44 7/16	30 7/16	51 5/8	33 5/8	55 3/4	31 3/4
50	45 1/8	34 5/8	49	35	56 7/8	38 7/8	60 1/8	36 1/8

Aerial

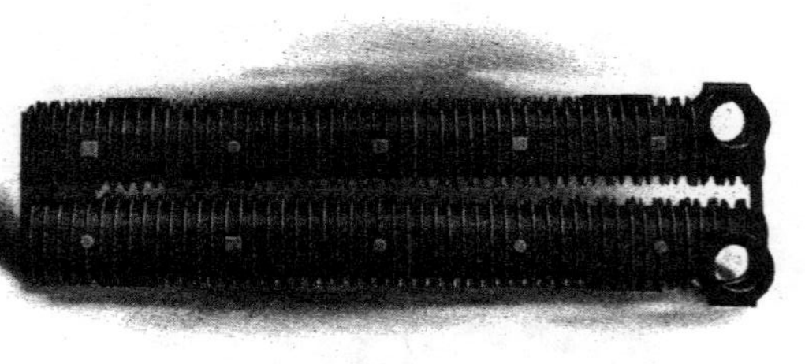

15-Foot Horizontal

STEAM OR WATER

15 Feet per Section

Dimensions of Section

	Inches
Distance between centers of Sections........	3 1/2
Distance between body of Sections.........	1 1/2
Length of Extended Surface...............	9/16
Height of Section........................	11
Length of Section........................	37
Height of Section........................	9 1/4
Size of R. and L. Nipple,....................	2

Regular Tapping

Supply.... 2″ R. H. Return..........2″ L. H.

Air Valve....... 3/8″

When Radiators are ordered tapped smaller than the above (2″) the female threads in bushings will be R. H.

Aerial

20-Foot Horizontal

STEAM OR WATER

20 Feet per Section

Dimensions of Section

	Inches
Distance between centers of Sections	3½
Distance between body of Sections	1½
Length of Extended Surface	$\frac{9}{16}$
Height of Section	$15\frac{13}{32}$
Length of Section	36¾
Height of Section	$14\frac{5}{16}$
Size of R. and L. Nipple,	2

Regular Tapping

Supply.... 2″ R. H. Return............2″ L.H.
Air Valve...... ⅜″

When Radiators are ordered tapped smaller than the above (2″) the female threads in bushings will be R. H.

Aerial

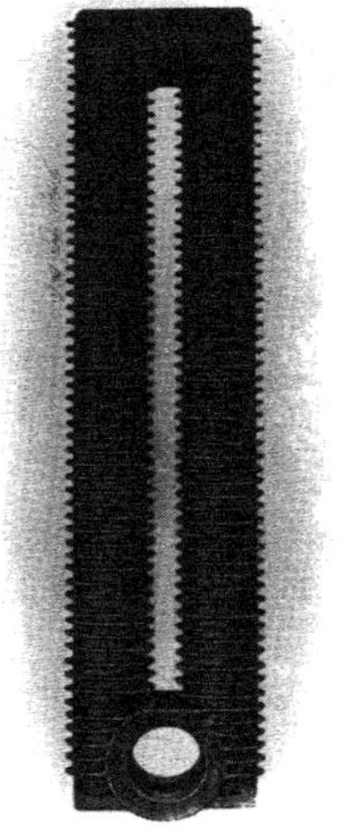

12½-Foot and 15-Foot Vertical

STEAM ONLY

12½ and 15 Feet per Section

To be used Vertically only

Feet per Section	**12½ Ft.**	**15 Ft.**
	Inches	
Distance from center to center	4½	4½
Distance between ends of Extended Surface	1¾	1¾
Length of Extended Surface	⅜	⅜
Width at Extended Surface	8⅝	8⅝
Height of Section	30	37¼
Width at Base	8⅛	8⅛
Thickness at Base	2¾	2¾
Thickness at Extended Base	2¾	2¾
Size of R. and L. Nipples,	3	3

REGULAR TAPPING

Supply.... 3″ R. H. Return........3″ R. H.
Air Valve........⅜″

If Radiators are to be tapped less than the above (3″) specify sizes on order and the Supply and Return Sections will be tapped Special.

Twelve-foot R. and L. Nipple Gold Pin

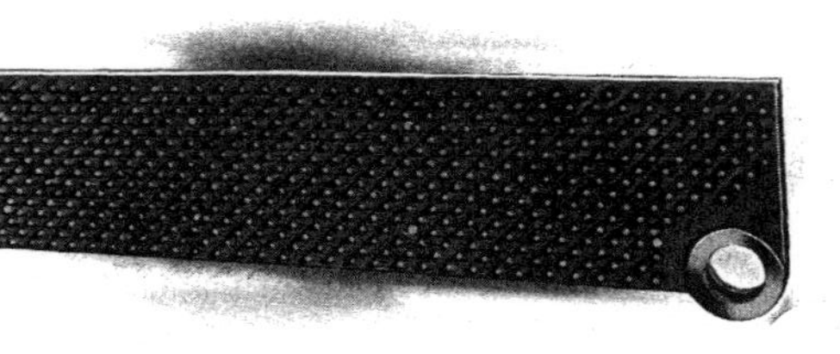

Intermediate Section

Steam Only

12 Feet Per Section

DIMENSIONS OF SECTION

Distance from center to center.......	3¼	inches
Distance between ends of Pins.......	¼	"
Length of Pin.......................	¾	"
Height of Section..................	9	"
Length of Section..................	36	"
Size of Right and Left Nipple.......	2	"

Shipping weight, per Section, 62 lbs.

Supply or Head Section is tapped L. H. for R. & L. Nipple

Return or Drain Section is tapped R. H. for R. & L. Nipple

REGULAR TAPPING

Supply.... 1½ inches   Return.... 1½ inches
Air Valve...... ⅜ inch

R. and L. Nipple Gold Pin

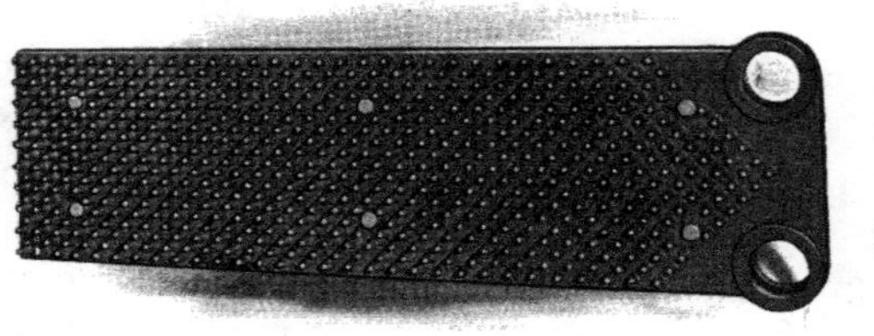

Intermediate Section
Steam or Water

15-Foot R. & L. Nipple Gold Pin

Height of Section.................... 11½ inches
Shipping weight, per Section, 77 lbs.

15 Feet Per Section

20-Foot R. & L. Nipple Gold Pin

Height of Section.................. 15½ inches
Shipping weight, per Section, 106 lbs.

20 Feet Per Section

DIMENSIONS COMMON TO BOTH

Distance from center to center.......	3¼	inches
Distance between ends of Pins.......	¼	"
Length of Pin......................	¾	"
Length of Section..................	36	"
Size of Right and Left Nipple........	2	"

REGULAR TAPPING

Supply.... 2 inches   Return.... 2 inches
Air Valve...... ⅜ inch

Supply or Head Section is tapped L. H. for R. & L. Nipple

Return or Drain Section is tapped R. H. for R. & L. Nipple

School Pin

Supply and Return End Section

Steam or Water

15-Foot School Pin

Height of Section.................. 11½ inches
Shipping weight, per Section, 82 lbs.
15 Feet Per Section

20-Foot School Pin

Height of Section.................. 15½ inches
Shipping weight, per Section, 115 lbs.
20 Feet Per Section

DIMENSIONS COMMON TO BOTH

Distance from center to center........	4	inches
Distance between ends of Pins.......	½	"
Length of Pin.....................	1	"
Length of Section..................	36	"
Size of Right and Left Nipple.......	2	"

REGULAR TAPPING

Supply.... 2 inches Return.... 2 inches
Air Valve...... ⅜ inch

Supply or Head Section is tapped L. H. for R. & L. Nipple

Return or Drain Section is tapped R. H. for R. & L. Nipple

Regular Pattern Gold Pin

Intermediate Section

Steam or Water

10 Feet Per Section

DIMENSIONS OF SECTION

Distance from center to center.......	3¼	inches
Distance between ends of Pins.......	¼	"
Length of Pin......................	¾	"
Height of Flange..................	10¾	"
Length of Section..................	40½	"
Height of Section..................	7¼	"

Shipping weight, per Section, 70 lbs.

REGULAR TAPPING

Supply.... 1¼ inches Return.... 1¼ inches
Air Valve...... ⅜ inch

Ten-inch Flange Gold Pin

Intermediate Section

Steam or Water

15 Feet Per Section

DIMENSIONS OF SECTION

Distance from center to center.......	3¼	inches
Distance between ends of Pins.......	¼	"
Length of Pin......................	¾	"
Length of Section..................	40½	"
Height of Section..................	10¾	"

Shipping weight, per Section, 108 lbs.

THATCHER

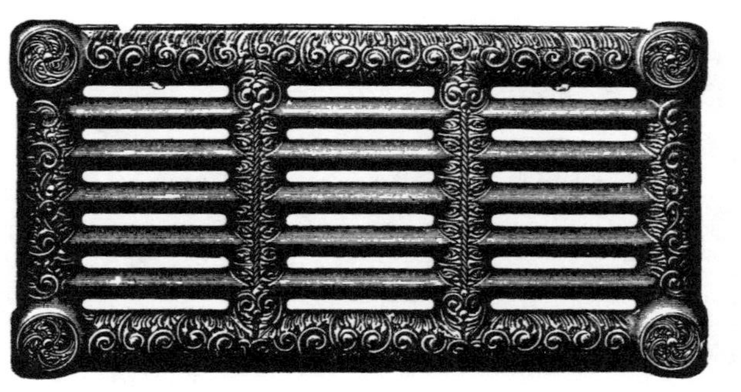

WALL RADIATORS

Dimensions of Fowler & Wolff Wall Radiators

	Width	Length	Thickness
3¾ ft. Sections	9½ inches	17 inches	3 inches
5 ft. Sections	12½ inches	17 inches	3 inches
6 ft. Sections	12½ inches	21 inches	3 inches
7 ft. Sections	12½ inches	24 inches	3 inches
9 ft. Sections	13 inches	24 inches	3¼ inches

Made in Horizontal and Vertical Sections for Steam or Water

ORDERING WALL RADIATORS

Give number of 7 or 9 foot sections in each radiator.
How assembled, horizontal or vertical.
Give location of supply and return tappings.
Specify size of tappings.
State whether for water or for one or two pipe steam.
Number and kind of brackets.
Send sketch showing how it is desired they be assembled.

ASSEMBLING

Wall Radiators are assembled with specially made screw nipples and shipped as follows:

Seven and nine feet horizontal sections are not assembled in radiators over three sections each.

Seven and nine foot vertical sections are not assembled in radiators over **six** sections each.

When **longer radiators** than above are ordered they will be shipped in units to make size and connected on the job with right and left hand threaded hexagon center nipples, which we furnish.

SINGLE-COLUMN RADIATOR

Plain Steam or Hot Water Radiator.

Assembled with Malleable Cast Iron Nipples.

THATCHER

SINGLE-COLUMN PLAIN OR ORNAMENTAL RADIATORS

Section	Length 2½ Ins. per Section	38 Ins. High 3 Feet per Section	32 Ins. High 2½ Feet per Section	26 Ins. High 2 Feet per Section	23 Ins. High 12/3 Feet per Section	20 Ins. High 1½ Feet per Section
2	5	6	5	4	3⅓	3
3	7½	9	7½	6	5	4½
4	10	12	10	8	6⅔	6
5	12½	15	12½	10	8⅓	7½
6	15	18	15	12	10	9
7	17½	21	17½	14	11⅔	10½
8	20	24	20	16	13⅓	12
9	22½	27	22½	18	15	13½
10	25	30	25	20	16⅔	15
11	27½	33	27½	22	18⅓	16½
12	30	36	30	24	20	18
13	32½	39	32½	26	21⅔	19½
14	35	42	35	28	23⅓	21
15	37½	45	37½	30	25	22½
16	40	48	40	32	26⅔	24
17	42½	51	42½	34	28⅓	25½
18	45	54	45	36	30	27
19	47½	57	47½	38	31⅔	28½
20	50	60	50	40	33⅓	30
21	52½	63	52½	42	35	31½
22	55	66	55	44	36⅔	33
23	57½	69	57½	46	38⅓	34½
24	60	72	60	48	40	36
25	62½	75	62½	50	41⅔	37½
26	65	78	65	52	43⅓	39
27	67½	81	67½	54	45	40½
28	70	84	70	56	46⅔	42
29	72½	87	72½	58	48⅓	43½
30	75	90	75	60	50	45
31	77½	93	77½	62	51⅔	46½
32	80	96	80	64	53⅓	48

SOLID TAPPINGS—Distance from floor to center of tapping for water or feed end of two-pipe steam, 5 inches. From floor to bottom of opening for one-pipe steam and return end of two-pipe steam, 4 inches. Width of radiator, 4⅜ inches. Width of legs, 5½ inches.

BUSHED TAPPINGS—Supplied if desired, without extra charge.

THATCHER

TWO-COLUMN RADIATOR

Plain Steam or Hot Water Radiator.

Assembled with Malleable Cast Iron Nipples.

THATCHER

TWO-COLUMN PLAIN OR ORNAMENTAL RADIATORS

Sections	Length 2½ Ins. per Section	45 Ins. High 5 Feet per Section	38 Ins. High 4 Feet per Section	32 Ins. High 3 1/3 Feet per Section	26 Ins. High 2 2/3 Feet per Section	23 Ins. High 2 1/3 Feet per Section	20 Ins. High 2 Feet per Section
2	5	10	8	6⅔	5⅓	4⅔	4
3	7½	15	12	10	8	7	6
4	10	20	16	13⅓	10⅔	9⅓	8
5	12½	25	20	16⅓	13⅓	11⅔	10
6	15	30	24	20	16	14	12
7	17½	35	28	23⅓	18⅔	16⅓	14
8	20	40	32	26⅔	21⅓	18⅔	16
9	22½	45	36	30	24	21	18
10	25	50	40	33⅓	26⅔	23⅓	20
11	27½	55	44	36⅔	29⅓	26⅔	22
12	30	60	48	40	32	28	24
13	32½	65	52	43⅓	34⅔	30⅓	26
14	35	70	56	46⅔	37⅓	32⅔	28
15	37½	75	60	60	40	35	30
16	40	80	64	53⅓	42⅔	37⅓	32
17	42½	85	68	56⅔	45⅓	39⅔	34
18	46	90	72	60	48	42	36
19	47½	95	76	63⅓	50⅔	44⅓	38
20	50	100	80	66⅔	53⅓	46⅔	40
21	52½	105	84	70	56	49	42
22	55	110	88	73⅓	58⅔	51⅓	44
23	57½	115	92	76⅔	61	53⅔	46
24	60	120	96	80	64⅔	56	48
25	62½	125	100	83⅓	66⅓	58⅓	50
26	65	130	104	86⅔	69⅓	60⅔	52
27	67½	135	108	90	72	63	54
28	70	140	112	93⅓	74⅔	65⅓	56
29	72½	145	116	96⅔	77⅓	67⅔	58
30	75	150	120	100	80	70	60
31	77½	155	124	103⅓	82⅔	72⅓	62
32	80	160	128	106⅔	85⅓	74⅔	64

SOLID TAPPINGS—Distance from floor to center of tapping for water or feed of two-pipe steam, 5 inches. From floor to bottom of opening for one-pipe steam or return end of two-pipe steam, 4 inches. Width of radiator over all, 8 inches.

BUSHED TAPPINGS—Supplied if desired, without extra charge.

THREE-COLUMN RADIATOR

Plain Steam or Hot Water Radiator.

Assembled with Malleable Cast Iron Nipples.

THREE-COLUMN PLAIN OR ORNAMENTAL RADIATORS

Section	Length 2½ Ins. per Section	45 Ins. High 6 Feet per Section	38 Ins. High 5 Feet per Section	32 Ins. High 4½ Feet per Section	26 Ins. High 3¾ Feet per Section	23 Ins. High 3¼ Feet per Section	20 Ins. High 2¾ Feet per Section
2	5	12	10	9	7½	6½	5½
3	7½	18	15	13½	11¼	9¾	8¼
4	10	24	20	18	15	14	11
5	12½	30	25	22½	18¾	16¼	13¾
6	15	36	30	27	22½	19½	16½
7	17½	42	35	31½	26¼	22¾	19¼
8	20	48	40	36	30	26	22
9	22½	54	45	40½	33¾	29¼	24¾
10	25	60	50	45	37½	32½	27½
11	27½	66	55	49½	41¼	35¾	30¼
12	30	72	60	54	45	39	33
13	32½	78	65	58½	48¾	42¼	35¾
14	35	84	70	63	52½	45½	38½
15	37½	90	75	67½	56¼	48¾	41¼
16	40	96	80	72	60	52	44
17	42½	102	85	76½	63¾	55¼	46¾
18	45	108	90	81	67½	58½	49½
19	47½	114	95	85½	71¼	62¾	52¼
20	50	120	100	90	75	65	55
21	52½	126	105	94½	78¾	68¼	57¾
22	55	132	110	99	82½	71½	60½
23	57½	138	115	103½	86¼	74¾	63¼
24	60	144	120	108	90	78	66
25	62½	150	125	112½	93¾	81¼	68¾
26	65	156	130	117	97½	84½	71½
27	67½	162	135	121½	101¼	87¾	74¼
28	70	168	140	126	105	91	77
29	72½	174	145	130½	108¾	94¼	79¾
30	75	180	150	135	112½	97½	82½
31	77½	186	155	139½	116¼	100¾	85¼
32	80	192	160	144	120	104	88

SOLID TAPPINGS—Distance from floor to centre of tapping for water or feed end of two-pipe steam, 5 inches. From floor to bottom of opening for one, pipe steam or return end of two-pipe steam, 4 inches. Width of radiator over all, 10¼ inches.

BUSHED TAPPINGS—Supplied, if desired, without extra charge.

THATCHER

FIVE-COLUMN RADIATOR

Plain Steam or Hot Water Radiator.

Assembled with Malleable Cast Iron Nipples

THATCHER

FIVE-COLUMN PLAIN OR ORNAMENTAL RADIATORS

Section	Length 2½ Inches per Section	38 Inches High 8 Feet per Section	32 Inches High 7 Feet per Section	26 Inches High 6 Feet per Section	22 Inches High 5 Feet per Section
2	5	16	14	12	10
3	7½	24	21	18	15
4	10	32	28	24	20
5	12½	40	35	30	25
6	15	48	42	36	30
7	17½	56	49	42	35
8	20	64	56	48	40
9	22½	72	63	54	45
10	25	80	70	60	50
11	27½	88	77	66	55
12	30	96	84	72	60
13	32½	104	91	78	65
14	35	112	98	84	70
15	37½	120	105	90	75
16	40	128	112	96	80
17	42½	136	119	102	85
18	45	144	126	108	90
19	47½	152	133	114	95
20	50	160	140	120	100
21	52½	168	147	126	105
22	55	176	154	132	110
23	57½	184	161	138	115
24	60	192	168	144	120
25	62½	200	175	150	125
26	65	208	182	156	130
27	67½	216	189	162	135
28	70	224	196	168	140
29	72½	232	203	174	145
30	75	240	210	180	150
31	77½	248	217	186	155
32	80	256	224	192	160

SOLID TAPPINGS—Distance from floor to center of tapping for water or feed end of two-pipe steam, 5 inches. From floor to bottom of opening for one-pipe steam or return end of two-pipe steam, 4 inches. Width of radiator over all, 13 inches.

BUSHED TAPPINGS—Supplied, if desired, without extra charge.

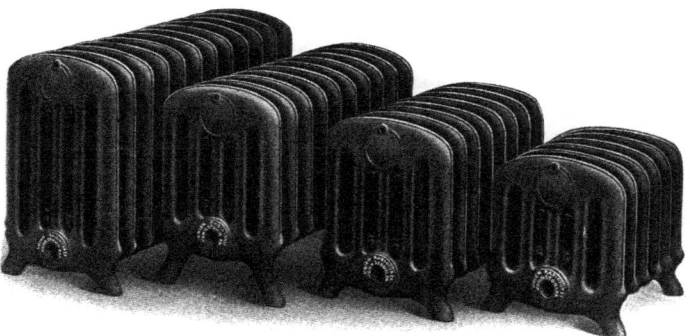

20″ 18″ 16″ 14″

FIVE-COLUMN PLAIN WINDOW RADIATOR

The "THATCHER" Five-Column Window Radiators are complete in all sizes, ornamental or plain.

Assembled with Malleable Cast Iron Nipples.

FIVE-COLUMN WINDOW, PLAIN OR ORNAMENTAL RADIATORS

Section	Length 2½ Ins. per Section	20 Ins. High 5 Feet per Section	18 Ins. High 4 Feet per Section	16 Ins. High 4 Feet per Section	16 Ins. High 3 Feet per Section	14 Ins. High 3 Feet per Section	12 Ins. High 2½ Feet per Section
2	5	10	8	8	6	6	5
3	7½	15	12	12	9	9	7½
4	10	20	16	16	12	12	10
5	12½	25	20	20	15	15	12½
6	15	30	24	24	18	18	15
7	17½	35	28	28	21	21	17½
8	20	40	32	32	24	24	20
9	22½	45	36	36	27	27	22½
10	25	50	40	40	30	30	25
11	27½	55	44	44	33	33	27½
12	30	60	48	48	36	36	30
13	32½	65	52	52	39	39	32½
14	35	70	56	56	42	42	35
15	37½	75	60	60	45	45	37½
16	40	80	64	64	48	48	40
17	42½	85	68	68	51	51	42½
18	45	90	72	72	54	54	45
19	47½	95	76	76	57	57	47½
20	50	100	80	80	60	60	50
21	52½	105	84	84	63	63	52½
22	55	110	88	88	66	66	55
23	57½	115	92	92	69	69	57½
24	60	120	96	96	72	72	60
25	62½	125	100	100	75	75	62½
26	65	130	104	104	78	78	65
27	67½	135	108	108	81	81	67½
28	70	140	112	112	84	84	70
29	72½	145	116	116	87	87	72½
30	75	150	120	120	90	90	75
31	77½	155	124	124	93	93	77½
32	80	160	128	128	96	96	80

SOLID TAPPINGS—20-inch, 16-inch with 4 feet to section, 14-inch and 12-inch, measure, from floor to center for water or feed end of two-pipe steam, 3 inches. From floor to bottom of opening for one-pipe steam or return end of two-pipe steam, 2 inches.

18-inch and 16-inch with 3 feet to section, measure, from floor to center for water or feed end of two-pipe steam, 5 inches. From floor to bottom of opening for one-pipe steam or return end of two-pipe steam, 4 inches.

Width of radiator over all, 13 inches.

BUSHED TAPPINGS—Supplied, if desired, without extra charge.

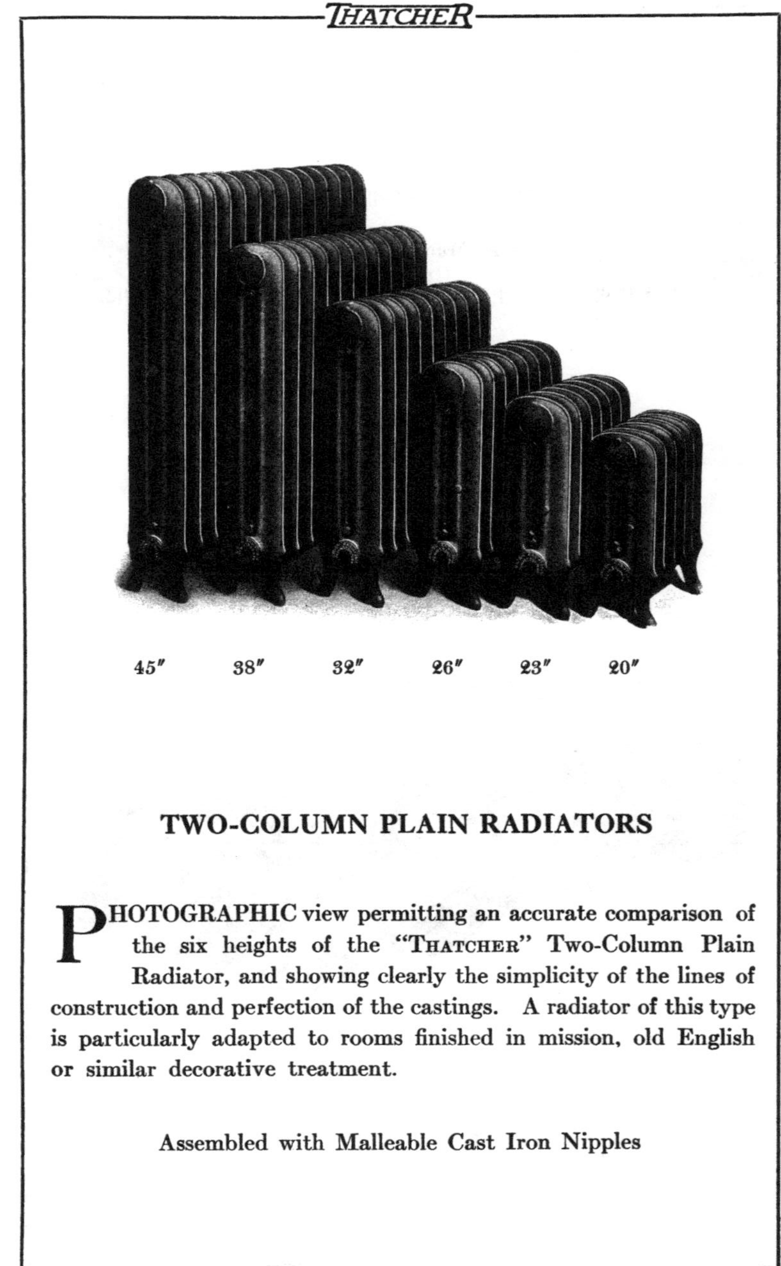

TWO-COLUMN PLAIN RADIATORS

PHOTOGRAPHIC view permitting an accurate comparison of the six heights of the "THATCHER" Two-Column Plain Radiator, and showing clearly the simplicity of the lines of construction and perfection of the castings. A radiator of this type is particularly adapted to rooms finished in mission, old English or similar decorative treatment.

Assembled with Malleable Cast Iron Nipples

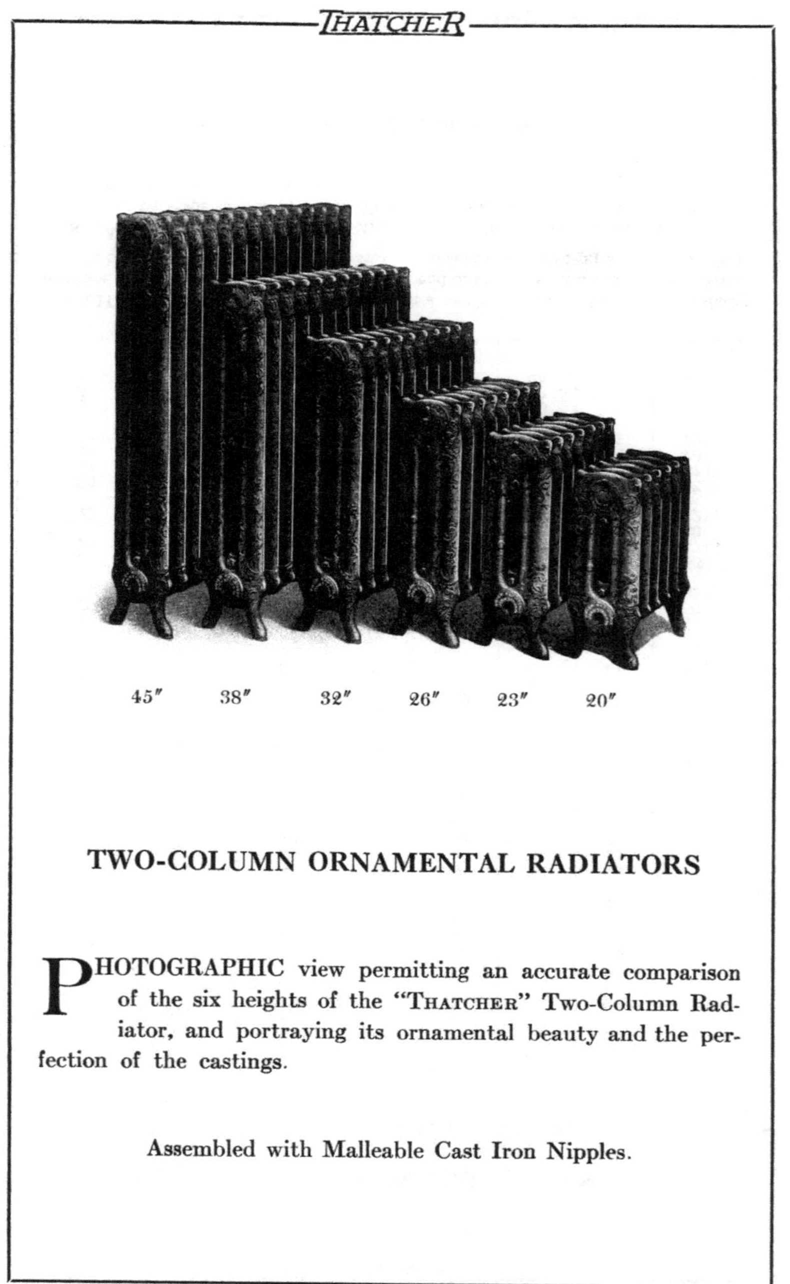

TWO-COLUMN ORNAMENTAL RADIATORS

PHOTOGRAPHIC view permitting an accurate comparison of the six heights of the "THATCHER" Two-Column Radiator, and portraying its ornamental beauty and the perfection of the castings.

Assembled with Malleable Cast Iron Nipples.

Gothic Three Tube Radiators

The graceful slenderness of this model makes it especially adapted for halls, bathrooms and other small rooms in apartments, homes or schools where floor space must be conserved. In the smaller heights it can be readily placed as a wall radiator

THE THATCHER COMPANY

Three-Tube Radiators

HEATING SURFACE—SQUARE FEET

No. of Sections	*Length 2½ Inches per Section	38-Inch 3½ Square Feet per Section	32-Inch 3 Square Feet per Section	26-Inch 2⅓ Square Feet per Section	20-Inch 1¾ Square Feet per Section
2	5	7	6	4⅔	3½
3	7½	10½	9	7	5¼
4	10	14	12	9⅓	7
5	12½	17½	15	11⅔	8¾
6	15	21	18	14	10½
7	17½	24½	21	16⅓	12¼
8	20	28	24	18⅔	14
9	22½	31½	27	21	15¾
10	25	35	30	23⅓	17½
11	27½	38½	33	25⅔	19¼
12	30	42	36	28	21
13	32½	45½	39	30⅓	22¾
14	35	49	42	32⅔	24½
15	37½	52½	45	35	26¼
16	40	56	48	37⅓	28
17	42½	59½	51	39⅔	29¾
18	45	63	54	42	31½
19	47½	66½	57	44⅓	33¼
20	50	70	60	46⅔	35
21	52½	73½	63	49	36¾
22	55	77	66	51⅓	38½
23	57½	80½	69	53⅔	40¼
24	60	84	72	56	42
25	62½	87½	75	58⅓	43¾
26	65	91	78	60⅔	45½
27	67½	94½	81	63	47¼
28	70	98	84	65⅓	49
29	72½	101½	87	67⅔	50¾
30	75	105	90	70	52½
31	77½	108½	93	72⅓	54¼
32	80	112	96	74⅔	56

*Add ½ inch to length for each bushing.

Thatcher Gothic Three Tube Radiators are tapped 1½ inches, both ends, and may be bushed to sizes required.

Width of feet 4½ inches; Width of section 4½ inches.

Height from floor to center of lower tapping, both feed and return for steam and water, 4½ inches.

THE THATCHER COMPANY

Gothic Four Tube Radiators

Having a little greater capacity than the three tube, this type is especially suited for your installations in private homes. You will find many other places too where it is more convenient than the larger sizes.

THE THATCHER COMPANY

Four-Tube Radiators

HEATING SURFACE—SQUARE FEET

No. of Sections	*Length 2½ Inches per Section	38-Inch 4¼ Square Feet per Section	32-Inch 3½ Square Feet per Section	26-Inch 2¾ Square Feet per Section	20-Inch 2¼ Square Feet per Section
2	5	8½	7	5½	4½
3	7½	12¾	10½	8¼	6¾
4	10	17	14	11	9
5	12½	21¼	17½	13¾	11¼
6	15	25½	21	16½	13½
7	17½	29¾	24½	19¼	15¾
8	20	34	28	22	18
9	22½	38¼	31½	24¾	20¼
10	25	42½	35	27½	22½
11	27½	46¾	38½	30¼	24¾
12	30	51	42	33	27
13	32½	55¼	45½	35¾	29¼
14	35	59½	49	38½	31½
15	37½	63¾	52½	41¼	33¾
16	40	68	56	44	36
17	42½	72¼	59½	46¾	38¼
18	45	76½	63	49½	40½
19	47½	80¾	66½	52¼	42¾
20	50	85	70	55	45
21	52½	89¼	73½	57¾	47¼
22	55	93½	77	60½	49½
23	57½	97¾	80½	63¼	51¾
24	60	102	84	66	54
25	62½	106¼	87½	68¾	56¼
26	65	110½	91	71½	58½
27	67½	114¾	94½	74¼	60¾
28	70	119	98	77	63
29	72½	123¼	101½	79¾	65¼
30	75	127½	105	82½	67½
31	77½	131¾	108½	85¼	69¾
32	80	136	112	88	72

*Add ½ inch to length for each bushing.

Thatcher Gothic Four Tube Radiators are tapped 1½ inches, both ends, and may be bushed to sizes required.

Width of feet 6¼ inches; Width of section 6¼ inches.

Height from floor to center of lower tapping, both feed and return for steam and water, 4½ inches.

Gothic Five Tube Radiators

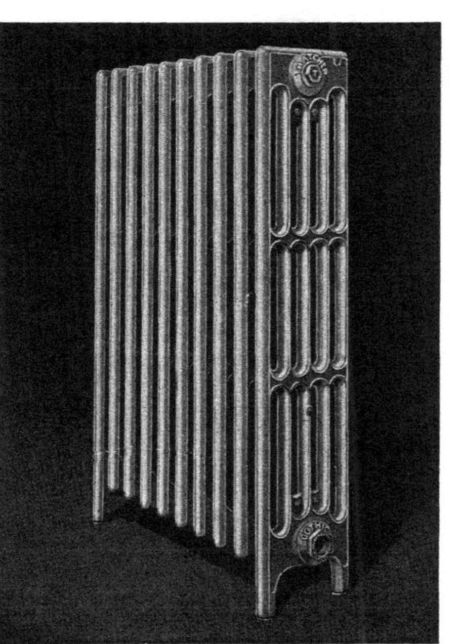

With the same gracefulness as the three and four tube radiators, this type has a heating capacity adequate for all purposes. It is probably used more universally than any other model, since it nearly always seems to fit the job.

Five-Tube Radiators

HEATING SURFACE—SQUARE FEET

No. of Sections	*Length 2½ Inches per Section	38-Inch 5 Square Feet per Section	32-Inch 4⅓ Square Feet per Section	26-Inch 3½ Square Feet per Section	23-Inch 3 Square Feet per Section	20-Inch 2⅔ Square Feet per Section
2	5	10	8⅔	7	6	5⅓
3	7½	15	13	10½	9	8
4	10	20	17⅓	14	12	10⅔
5	12½	25	21⅔	17½	15	13⅓
6	15	30	26	21	18	16
7	17½	35	30⅓	24½	21	18⅔
8	20	40	34⅔	28	24	21⅓
9	22½	45	39	31½	27	24
10	25	50	43⅓	35	30	26⅔
11	27½	55	47⅔	38½	33	29⅓
12	30	60	52	42	36	32
13	32½	65	56⅓	45½	39	34⅔
14	35	70	60⅔	49	42	37⅓
15	37½	75	65	52½	45	40
16	40	80	69⅓	56	48	42⅔
17	42½	85	73⅔	59½	51	45⅓
18	45	90	78	63	54	48
19	47½	95	82⅓	66½	57	50⅔
20	50	100	86⅔	70	60	53⅓
21	52½	105	91	73½	63	56
22	55	110	95⅓	77	66	58⅔
23	57½	115	99⅔	80½	69	61⅓
24	60	120	104	84	72	64
25	62½	125	108⅓	87½	75	66⅔
26	65	130	112⅔	91	78	69⅓
27	67½	135	117	94½	81	72
28	70	140	121⅓	98	84	74⅔
29	72½	145	125⅔	101½	87	77⅓
30	75	150	130	105	90	80
31	77½	155	134⅓	108½	93	82⅔
32	80	160	138⅔	112	96	85⅓

*Add ½ inch to length for each bushing.

Thatcher Gothic Five Tube Radiators are tapped 1½ inches, both ends, and may be bushed to sizes required.

Width of feet 8 inches; Width of section 8 inches.

Height from floor to center of lower tapping, both feed and return for steam and water, 4½ inches.

Gothic Six Tube Radiators

The width and heating capacity of this radiator suit it for all types of large rooms, where a great deal of heat is desired. In the smaller heights it is very popular for sunparlors and similar places where the windows are unusually low.

THE THATCHER COMPANY

Six-Tube Radiators

HEATING SURFACE—SQUARE FEET

No. of Sections	*Length 2½ Inches per Section	38-Inch 6 Square Feet per Section	32-Inch 5 Square Feet per Section	26-Inch 4 Square Feet per Section	20-Inch 3 Square Feet per Section	18-Inch 2¾ Square Feet per Section	14-Inch 2 Square Feet per Section
2	5	12	10	8	6	5½	4
3	7½	18	15	12	9	8¼	6
4	10	24	20	16	12	11	8
5	12½	30	25	20	15	13¾	10
6	15	36	30	24	18	16½	12
7	17½	42	35	28	21	19¼	14
8	20	48	40	32	24	22	16
9	22½	54	45	36	27	24¾	18
10	25	60	50	40	30	27½	20
11	27½	66	55	44	33	30¼	22
12	30	72	60	48	36	33	24
13	32½	78	65	52	39	35¾	26
14	35	84	70	56	42	38½	28
15	37½	90	75	60	45	41¼	30
16	40	96	80	64	48	44	32
17	42½	102	85	68	51	46¾	34
18	45	108	90	72	54	49½	36
19	47½	114	95	76	57	52¼	38
20	50	120	100	80	60	55	40
21	52½	126	105	84	63	57¾	42
22	55	132	110	88	66	60½	44
23	57½	138	115	92	69	63¼	46
24	60	144	120	96	72	66	48
25	62½	150	125	100	75	68¾	50
26	65	156	130	104	78	71½	52
27	67½	162	135	108	81	74¼	54
28	70	168	140	112	84	77	56
29	72½	174	145	116	87	79¾	58
30	75	180	150	120	90	82½	60
31	77½	186	155	124	93	85¼	62
32	80	192	160	128	96	88	64

*Add ½ inch to length for each bushing.

Thatcher Gothic Six Tube Radiators are tapped 1½ inches, both ends, and may be bushed to sizes required.

Width of feet 9¾ inches; Width of section 9¾ inches.

Height from floor to center of lower tapping, both feed and return for steam and water, 4½ inches.

THE THATCHER COMPANY

Seven-Tube Radiators

HEATING SURFACE—SQUARE FEET

Number of Sections	20-Inch 3⅔ Square Feet per Section	17-Inch 3 Square Feet per Section	14-Inch 2½ Square Feet per Section	Number of Sections	20-Inch 3⅔ Square Feet per Section	17-Inch 3 Square Feet per Section	14-Inch 2½ Square Feet per Section
2	7⅓	6	5	17	62⅓	51	42½
3	11	9	7½	18	66	54	45
4	14⅔	12	10	19	69⅔	57	47½
5	18⅓	15	12½	20	73⅓	60	50
6	22	18	15	21	77	63	52½
7	25⅔	21	17½	22	80⅔	66	55
8	29⅓	24	20	23	84⅓	69	57½
9	33	27	22½	24	88	72	60
10	36⅔	30	25	25	91⅔	75	62½
11	40⅓	33	27½	26	95⅓	78	65
12	44	36	30	27	99	81	67½
13	47⅔	39	32½	28	102⅔	84	70
14	51⅓	42	35	29	106⅓	87	72½
15	55	45	37½	30	110	90	75
16	58⅔	48	40	31	113⅔	93	77½

Length of above 2½ inches per section. Add ½ inch to length for each bushing.

Thatcher Gothic Seven Tube Radiators are tapped 1½ inches, both ends, and may be bushed to sizes required.

Width of feet 11⅜ inches; Width of section 11⅜ inches.

Height from floor to center of lower tapping, both feed and return for steam and water, 4½ inches.

Thatcher Wall Radiators

No. of Sec.	Height, Inches	Length or Width, Inches	Thickness, Inches	Thickness With Brackets, Inches	Heating Surface, Square Feet
7A	13⅞	22	3	3¾	7
7B	21¼	14	3	3¾	7
9A	13⅞	28	3	3¾	9
9B	27⅛	14	3	3¾	9

THE THATCHER COMPANY

Thatcher Concealed Radiators

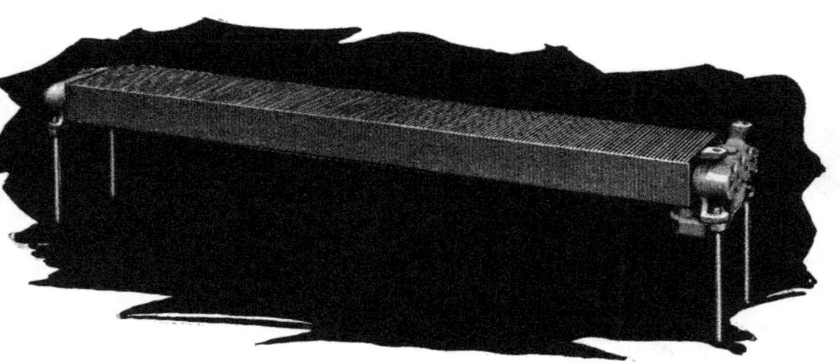

As usual, The Thatcher Company is one of the pioneers in the development of the Concealed Fin Type Radiator, which they have tested to prove its unusual qualities of efficiency and durability.

The edges of the fins of the Thatcher Concealed Radiator form a right angle so that each fin is in contact with the next. Greater convection is obtained by this design. The fins are made of extra heavy twenty gauge galvanized Armco Ingot iron and inside flanges provide greater contact and hence greater thermal conductivity between the fins and the tubes, which are designed with the maximum tube area.

The materials used in Thatcher Concealed Radiators have been carefully selected for durability. The headers are of cast iron and the tubes of copper; neither of which metals is affected by steam corrosion. The Armco Ingot iron fins will resist air corrosion indefinitely, due to the absence of impurities. As a further safeguard, however, the fins are galvanized with a thick coating of zinc. To make the Thatcher Concealed Radiator more rigid the copper tubes are fitted into the headers by a special process, using an expanded, tapered ferrule. Another support is the sturdy tie rod connecting the two headers.

THE THATCHER COMPANY

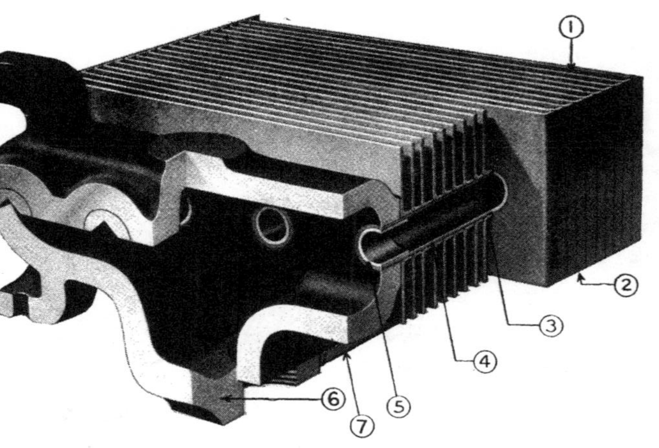

Features of the Thatcher Concealed Radiator

1. Amco Ingot Iron Fins, heavily galvanized give greater strength and durability and unusual thermal conductivity.
2. Outside flanges bring ends of fins into contact, making radiator more rigid and increasing heat convection.
3. Inside flanges provide greater contact between copper tubes and galvanized fins. Promote efficiency.
4. Pure copper tubes are not affected in any way by steam corrosion. Are of ample size to prevent clogging and provide maximum tube area.
5. Expanded brass ferrules secure copper tubes in cast iron headers forming a permanent and tight connection.
6. Cast iron headers are not affected by steam corrosion. Smooth, heavy castings are easily machined.
7. Tie rod. Unique Thatcher feature which adds greatly to the strength and durability of the entire radiator.

Types of Installations of Thatcher Concealed Radiators

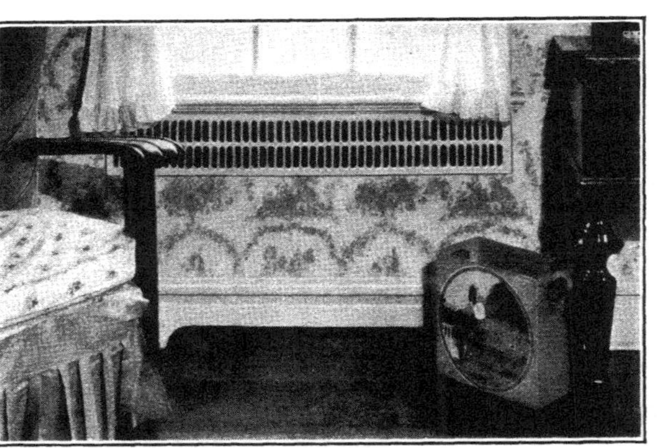

Built-In Type

This type, also called plastered-in-type, is a favorite because the decorative scheme can be carried out over the enclosure. The upper grille is of ornamental iron and easily removed. The sanitary opening is cut out of the base board, which is also removable.

Double Grille Type

In this type the two grilles and front panel are in one piece, which can be decorated to harmonize with the walls. It has the advantage of being easily removed, so that the radiator and lining can be cleaned and, if necessary, the valves and traps serviced.

Types of Installations of Thatcher Concealed Radiators

Sanitary Opening Type

Here the sanitary opening in the bottom of the front panel replaces the bottom grille in the double grille type. The panel fits flush and can easily be removed if desired. In this type the cold air is drawn directly off the floor.

Cabinet Type

When new heating plants are installed in old homes, the cabinet type, illustrated above, is some times preferable since it is not necessary to cut into the walls. The cabinet has all the advantages of a radiator cover and is more economical in first cost and more efficient in operation.

THE THATCHER COMPANY

The size and number of tubes selected by Thatcher engineers for this concealed radiator were chosen to secure the maximum flue area, the contact with the fins at several points to produce the highest thermal conductivity, and to assure a large enough tube to prevent it from clogging.

It will readily be seen that the heavy fins, expanded tubes, inside and outside flanges and tie rod contribute toward making the Thatcher Concealed Radiator most durable and rigid. The large tube area, the inside flanges, the flue construction and the materials used give the Thatcher Concealed Radiator an unusually high degree of efficiency.

3½″ Wide—3 Tube Series

Front Outlet

Heater Length	Stack Height in Inches							
	12	16	20	24	28	32	36	40
14″	5.6	6.8	7.5	8.1	8.5	8.8	9.1	9.3
18″	7.7	9.3	10.4	11.1	11.8	12.2	12.6	12.8
22″	9.8	11.9	13.3	14.2	15.0	15.6	16.1	16.3
26″	11.9	14.4	16.1	17.2	18.2	18.9	19.5	19.9
30″	14.0	17.0	19.0	20.3	21.5	22.3	23.0	23.4
36″	17.2	20.8	23.3	24.9	26.4	27.4	28.2	28.7
42″	20.4	24.7	27.6	29.5	31.2	32.4	33.4	34.0
48″	23.5	28.6	31.9	34.1	36.1	37.4	38.6	39.3
54″	26.7	32.4	36.2	38.7	41.0	42.5	43.9	44.6
60″	29.9	36.2	40.5	43.2	45.9	47.5	49.0	49.9

3½″ Wide—3 Tube Series

Top Outlet

Heater Length	Stack Height in Inches							
	12	16	20	24	28	32	36	40
14″	7.8	8.5	9.0	9.3	9.6	9.8	10.0	10.1
18″	10.7	11.7	12.4	12.9	13.2	13.6	13.8	13.9
22″	13.6	14.9	15.8	16.5	16.9	17.3	17.6	17.7
26″	16.6	18.2	19.2	20.0	20.6	21.1	21.4	21.6
30″	19.5	21.4	22.6	23.6	24.2	24.8	25.2	25.4
36″	23.9	26.2	27.8	29.0	29.7	30.4	30.9	31.2
42″	28.3	31.2	32.8	34.3	35.2	36.0	36.6	36.9
48″	32.8	36.0	37.9	39.6	40.6	41.6	42.3	42.6
54″	37.2	40.8	43.1	45.0	46.1	47.4	48.0	48.5
60″	41.6	45.6	48.1	50.4	51.5	52.9	53.6	54.1

THE THATCHER COMPANY

Top Outlet

A—Heater Length. B—Stack Height.

The thickness of the wall determines the width of the radiator to be used. In most cases the 5½″ series can be used in all outside walls up to 8″ thick. In walls over 8″ the 7½″ series can be used. In interior walls the 3½″ series is preferable. These figures apply to ordinary construction practices. Special types of construction must be figured individually.

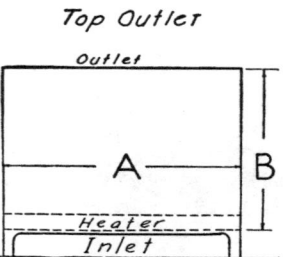

5½″ Wide—4 Tube Series

Front Outlet

Heater Length	Stack Height in Inches							
	12	16	20	24	28	32	36	40
14″	8.8	10.5	11.9	12.9	13.6	14.2	14.6	14.9
18″	12.1	14.5	16.4	17.8	18.7	19.6	20.2	20.5
22″	15.4	18.5	21.0	22.8	23.9	25.0	25.7	26.2
26″	18.7	22.5	25.5	27.6	29.0	30.4	31.2	31.9
30″	22.0	26.5	30.0	32.6	34.2	35.8	36.8	37.5
36″	27.0	32.5	36.8	40.0	42.0	43.9	45.1	46.0
42″	32.0	38.5	43.6	47.4	49.6	52.0	53.5	54.5
48″	37.0	44.5	50.4	54.8	57.5	60.1	61.9	63.0
54″	42.0	50.5	57.2	62.1	65.2	68.4	70.2	71.5
60″	47.0	56.5	64.0	69.5	73.0	76.4	78.5	80.0

5½″ Wide—4 Tube Series

Top Outlet

Heater Length	Stack Height in Inches							
	12	16	20	24	28	32	36	40
14″	12.6	13.6	14.3	14.7	15.2	15.5	15.7	15.9
18″	17.4	18.7	19.7	20.4	21.0	21.4	21.7	21.9
22″	22.2	23.9	25.2	26.0	26.8	27.3	27.7	28.0
26″	27.0	29.1	30.6	31.6	32.6	33.2	33.7	34.0
30″	31.8	34.2	36.0	37.2	38.3	39.1	39.7	40.0
36″	39.0	42.0	44.1	45.5	47.0	48.0	48.6	49.0
42″	46.3	49.7	52.3	54.0	55.6	56.8	57.6	58.1
48″	53.5	57.5	60.5	62.5	64.4	65.6	66.7	67.2
54″	60.6	65.3	68.6	71.0	73.0	74.5	75.8	76.4
60″	67.9	73.0	76.8	79.4	81.7	83.5	84.6	85.4

THE THATCHER COMPANY

The stack height is figured from the top of the outlet grille to the bottom of the fins. The top of the outlet grille is 1″ from the top of the cabinet and the bottom of the radiator 6″ from the bottom of the cabinet. Allowing 1″ for the pitch of the radiator unit the stack height is 8″ less than the height of the cabinet.

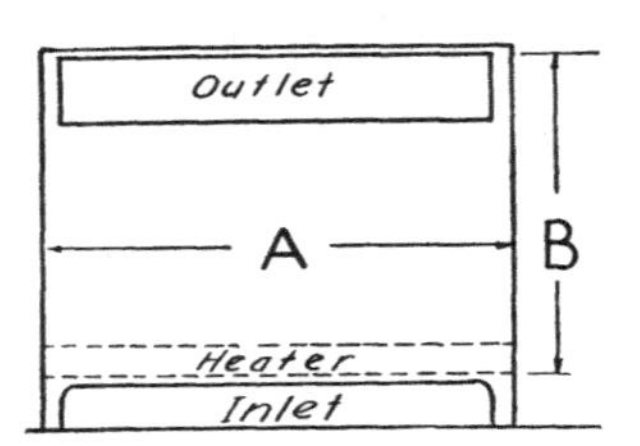

A—Heater Length. B—Stack Height.

7½″ Wide—5 Tube Series
Front Outlet

Heater Length	Stack Height in Inches							
	12	16	20	24	28	32	36	40
14″	10.3	12.5	14.0	15.8	16.7	17.4	17.9	18.4
18″	14.2	17.2	19.8	21.8	23.1	24.1	24.8	25.4
22″	18.2	21.9	25.3	27.8	29.5	30.7	31.6	32.4
26″	22.1	26.7	30.7	33.8	35.8	37.4	38.4	39.4
30″	26.0	31.4	36.2	39.8	42.2	44.0	45.3	46.4
36″	31.9	38.5	44.4	48.9	51.8	54.0	55.5	56.9
42″	37.8	45.6	52.6	57.9	61.4	64.0	65.8	67.4
48″	43.7	52.7	60.9	66.9	71.0	74.0	76.0	78.0
54″	49.6	59.8	69.0	75.9	80.5	83.9	86.4	88.4
60″	55.5	67.0	77.0	84.9	90.1	93.9	96.5	98.9

7½″ Wide—5 Tube Series
Top Outlet

Heater Length	Stack Height in Inches							
	12	16	20	24	28	32	36	40
14″	14.7	16.3	17.4	18.2	18.7	19.0	19.3	19.5
18″	20.3	22.4	24.1	25.2	25.8	26.3	26.7	27.0
22″	25.9	28.6	30.7	32.1	33.0	33.5	34.0	34.4
26″	31.5	34.8	37.4	39.0	40.1	40.8	41.4	41.8
30″	37.0	41.0	44.0	46.0	47.3	48.0	48.8	49.3
36″	45.5	50.4	54.0	56.4	58.0	58.9	59.9	60.4
42″	53.8	59.5	64.0	66.9	68.6	69.8	70.9	71.6
48″	62.3	68.9	74.0	77.4	79.5	80.7	82.0	82.8
54″	70.5	78.3	83.9	87.6	90.0	91.5	92.9	93.9
60″	79.0	87.5	93.8	98.0	101.0	102.2	104.0	105.0

THE H. B. SMITH CO.

IMPERIAL UNION—STEAM and WATER

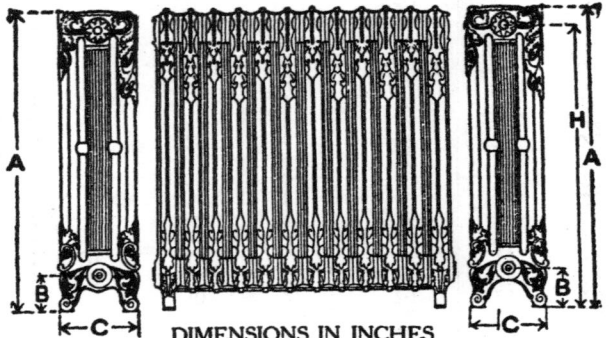

DIMENSIONS IN INCHES

A	Height of Radiator......	45	37	31	25	19
H	Height of Top Tapping..	43	35 1/16	29 1/16	23	17 3/16

B Height of Regular Tapping .... 4⅝ inches
C Width of Section.......................9 "

LIST OF SIZES

Number of Sections	Total Length		RADIATING SURFACE (Square Feet)				
	Feet	Inches	45 in. High	37 in. High	31 in. High	25 in. High	19 in. High
3	0	10¾	24	19½	16½	13½	10½
4	1	2	32	26	22	18	14
5	1	5¼	40	32½	27½	22½	17½
6	1	8½	48	39	33	27	21
7	1	11¾	56	45½	38½	31½	24½
8	2	3	64	52	44	36	28
9	2	6¼	72	58½	49½	40½	31½
10	2	9½	80	65	55	45	35
11	3	¾	88	71½	60½	49½	38½
12	3	4	96	78	66	54	42
13	3	7¼	104	84½	71½	58½	45½
14	3	10½	112	91	77	63	49
15	4	1¾	120	97½	82½	67½	52½
16	4	5	128	104	88	72	56
17	4	8¼	136	110½	93½	76½	59½
18	4	11½	144	117	99	81	63
19	5	2¾	152	123½	104½	85½	66½
20	5	6	160	130	110	90	70
21	5	9¼	168	136½	115½	94½	73½
22	6	½	176	143	121	99	77
23	6	3¾	184	149½	126½	103½	80½
24	6	7	192	156	132	108	84
25	6	10¼	200	162½	137½	112½	87½
List Price in Cents per Square Foot			41	42	46	50	57

H.B. Smith Co. – *circa 1910*

PRINCESS UNION—STEAM and WATER

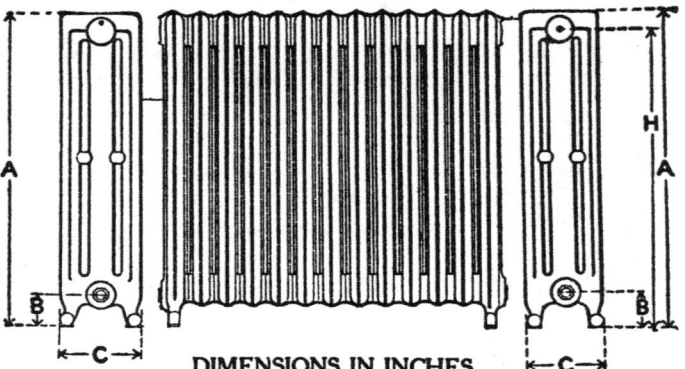

DIMENSIONS IN INCHES

A	Height of Radiator	45	37	31	25	19
H	Height of Top Tapping .	43	35 1/16	29 1/16	23	17 3/16

B Height of Regular Tapping............4⅝ inches
C Width of Section.......................9 "

LIST OF SIZES

Number of Sections	Total Length Feet	Total Length Inches	Radiating Surface (Square Feet) 45 in. High	37 in. High	31 in. High	25 in. High	19in. High
3	0	10¾	24	19½	16½	13½	10½
4	1	2	32	26	22	18	14
5	1	5¼	40	32½	27½	22½	17½
6	1	8½	48	39	33	27	21
7	1	11¾	56	45½	38½	31½	24½
8	2	3	64	52	44	36	28
9	2	6¼	72	58½	49½	40½	31½
10	2	9½	80	65	55	45	35
11	3	¾	88	71½	60½	49½	38½
12	3	4	96	78	66	54	42
13	3	7¼	104	84½	71½	58½	45½
14	3	10½	112	91	77	63	49
15	4	1¾	120	97½	82½	67½	52½
16	4	5	128	104	88	72	56
17	4	8¼	136	110½	93½	76½	59½
18	4	11½	144	117	99	81	63
19	5	2¾	152	123½	104½	85½	66½
20	5	6	160	130	110	90	70
21	5	9¼	168	136½	115½	94½	73½
22	6	½	176	143	121	99	77
23	6	3¾	184	149½	126½	103½	80½
24	6	7	192	156	132	108	84
25	6	10¼	200	162½	137½	112½	87½
List Price in Cents per Square Foot			41	42	46	50	57

ROYAL UNION—STEAM or WATER

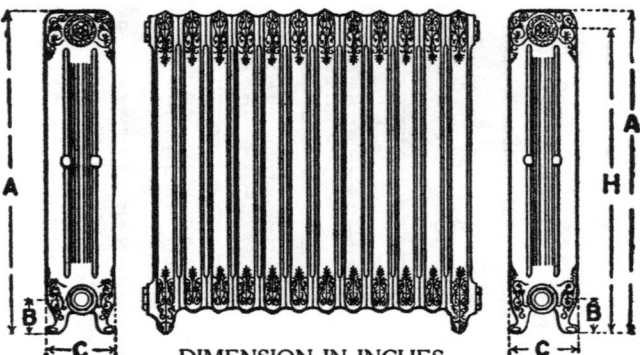

DIMENSION IN INCHES

A	Height of Radiator	44	38	30	24	18
H	Height of Top Tapping .	41 15/16	35 7/16	27 15/16	21 ¾	15 ⅞

B Height of Regular Tapping....................4⅝ inches
C Width of Section..................................8⅝ "

LIST OF SIZES

Number of Sections	Total Length Feet	Total Length Inches	Radiating Surface (Square Feet) 44 in. High	38 in. High	30 in. High	24 in. High	18 in. High
3	0	10	18	15	12	9	6
4	1	1	24	20	16	12	8
5	1	4	30	25	20	15	10
6	1	7	36	30	24	18	12
7	1	10	42	35	28	21	14
8	2	1	48	40	32	24	16
9	2	4	54	45	36	27	18
10	2	7	60	50	40	30	20
11	2	10	66	55	44	33	22
12	3	1	72	60	48	36	24
13	3	4	78	65	52	39	26
14	3	7	84	70	56	42	28
15	3	10	90	75	60	45	30
16	4	1	96	80	64	48	32
17	4	4	102	85	68	51	34
18	4	7	108	90	72	54	36
19	4	10	114	95	76	57	38
20	5	1	120	100	80	60	40
21	5	4	126	105	84	63	42
22	5	7	132	110	88	66	44
23	5	10	138	115	92	69	46
24	6	1	144	120	96	72	48
25	6	4	150	125	100	75	50
List Price in Cents per Square Foot			41	42	46	50	58

SCEPTER—STEAM ONLY

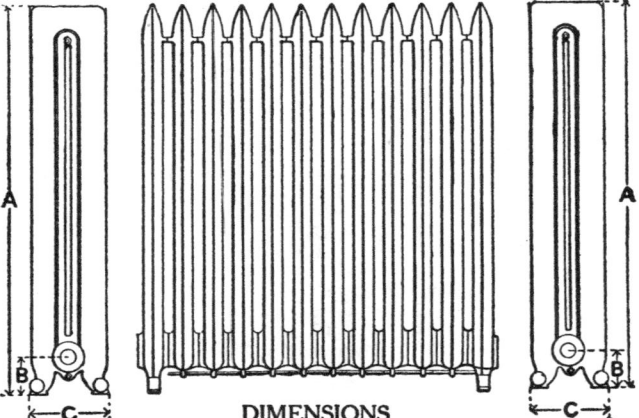

DIMENSIONS

A Height of Radiator ....(See table below)
B Height of Regular Tapping...............5 inches
C Width of Section ....7 "

LIST OF SIZES

Number of Sections	Total Length Feet	Total Length Inches	RADIATING SURFACE (Square Feet) 44 in. High	38 in. High	30 in. High	24 in. High	18 in. High
3	0	8⅛	14¼	12	9	7	5
4	0	10½	19	16	12	9⅓	6⅔
5	1	⅞	23¾	20	15	11⅔	8⅓
6	1	3¼	28½	24	18	14	10
7	1	5⅝	33¼	28	21	16⅓	11⅔
8	1	8	38	32	24	18⅔	13⅓
9	1	10⅜	42¾	36	27	21	15
10	2	¾	47½	40	30	23⅓	16⅔
11	2	3⅛	52¼	44	33	25⅔	18⅓
12	2	5½	57	48	36	28	20
13	2	7⅞	61¾	52	39	30⅓	21⅔
14	2	10¼	66½	56	42	32⅔	23⅓
15	3	⅝	71¼	60	45	35	25
16	3	3	76	64	48	37⅓	26⅔
17	3	5⅜	80¾	68	51	39⅔	28⅓
18	3	7¾	85½	72	54	42	30
19	3	10⅛	90¼	76	57	44⅓	31⅔
20	4	½	95	80	60	46⅔	33⅓
21	4	2⅞	99¾	84	63	49	35
22	4	5¼	104½	88	66	51⅓	36⅔
23	4	7⅝	109¼	92	69	53⅔	38⅓
24	4	10	114	96	72	56	40
25	5	⅜	118¾	100	75	58⅓	41⅔
List Price in Cents per Square Foot			41	42	46	50	58

THE H. B. SMITH CO.

CORONET—STEAM and WATER

SINGLE COLUMN

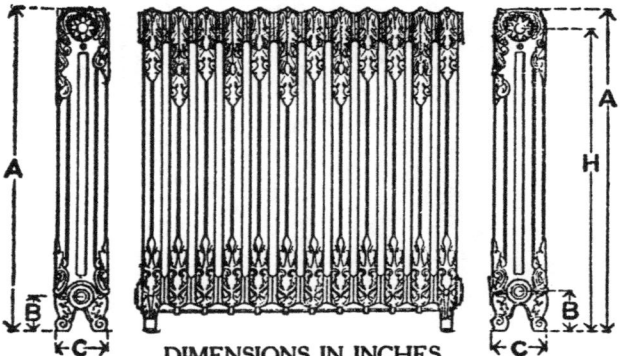

DIMENSIONS IN INCHES

A	Height of Radiator.....	45	37	31	25	19
H	Height of Top Tapping..	43 3/16	34 11/16	28 15/16	23 1/16	17⅛

B Height of Regular Tapping............4⅝ inches
C Width of Section.......................5¼ "

LIST OF SIZES

Number of Sections	Total Length Feet	Total Length Inches	RADIATING SURFACE (Square Feet) 45 in. High	37 in. High	31 in. High	25 in. High	19 in. High
3	0	10	13½	10½	9	7½	6
4	1	1	18	14	12	10	8
5	1	4	22½	17½	15	12½	10
6	1	7	27	21	18	15	12
7	1	10	31½	24½	21	17½	14
8	2	1	36	28	24	20	16
9	2	4	40½	31½	27	22½	18
10	2	7	45	35	30	25	20
11	2	10	49½	38½	33	27½	22
12	3	1	54	42	36	30	24
13	3	4	58½	45½	39	32½	26
14	3	7	63	49	42	35	28
15	3	10	67½	52½	45	37½	30
16	4	1	72	56	48	40	32
17	4	4	76½	59½	51	42½	34
18	4	7	81	63	54	45	36
19	4	10	85½	66½	57	47½	38
20	5	1	90	70	60	50	40
21	5	4	94½	73½	63	52½	42
22	5	7	99	77	66	55	44
23	5	10	103½	80½	69	57½	46
24	6	1	108	84	72	60	48
25	6	4	112½	87½	75	62½	50
List Price in Cents per Square Foot			41	42	46	50	57

DIADEM—STEAM and WATER

SINGLE COLUMN

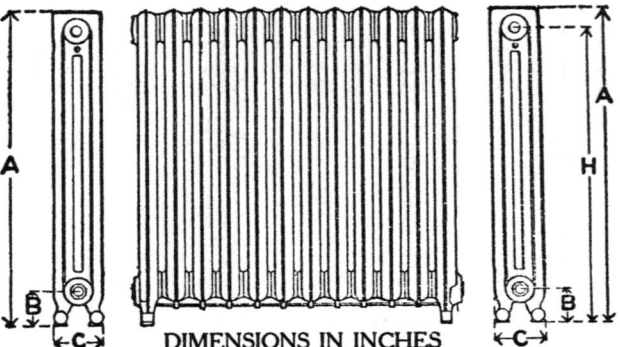

DIMENSIONS IN INCHES

A	Height of Radiator	45	37	31	25	19
H	Height of Top Tapping. .	$43\frac{3}{16}$	$34\frac{11}{16}$	$28\frac{15}{16}$	$23\frac{1}{16}$	$17\frac{1}{8}$

B Height of Regular Tapping............ 4⅝ inches
C Width of Section .... 5¼ "

LIST OF SIZES

Number of Sections	Total Length		RADIATING SURFACE (Square Feet)				
	Feet	Inches	45 in. High	37 in. High	31 in. High	25 in. High	19 in. High
3	0	10	13½	10½	9	7½	6
4	1	1	18	14	12	10	8
5	1	4	22½	17½	15	12½	10
6	1	7	27	21	18	15	12
7	1	10	31½	24½	21	17½	14
8	2	1	36	28	24	20	16
9	2	4	40½	31½	27	22½	18
10	2	7	45	35	30	25	20
11	2	10	49½	38½	33	27½	22
12	3	1	54	42	36	30	24
13	3	4	58½	45½	39	32½	26
14	3	7	63	49	42	35	28
15	3	10	67½	52½	45	37½	30
16	4	1	72	56	48	40	32
17	4	4	76½	59½	51	42½	34
18	4	7	81	63	54	45	36
19	4	10	85½	66½	57	47½	38
20	5	1	90	70	60	50	40
21	5	4	94½	73½	63	52½	42
22	5	7	99	77	66	55	44
23	5	10	103½	80½	69	57½	46
24	6	1	108	84	72	60	48
25	6	4	112½	87½	75	62½	50
List Price in Cents per Square Feet			41	42	46	50	57

SOVEREIGN UNION—STEAM or WATER

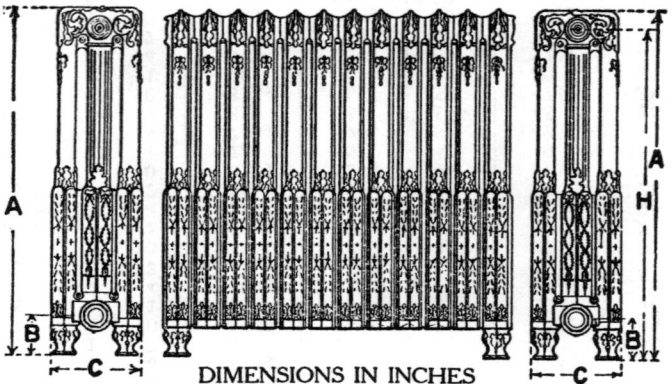

DIMENSIONS IN INCHES

A	Height of Radiator.......	37	31	25
H	Height of Top Tapping. . .	$35\frac{3}{8}$	$29\frac{9}{16}$	$23\frac{7}{8}$

B Height of Regular Tapping.................5 inches
C Width of Section.... ....8½ "

LIST OF SIZES

Number of Sections	Total Length		RADIATING SURFACE (Square Feet)		
	Feet	Inches	37 in. High	31 in. High	25 in. High
3	0	$9\frac{1}{16}$	18	15	12
4	0	11¾	24	20	16
5	1	$2\frac{7}{16}$	30	25	20
6	1	5⅛	36	30	24
7	1	$7\frac{13}{16}$	42	35	28
8	1	10½	48	40	32
9	2	$1\frac{3}{16}$	54	45	36
10	2	3⅞	60	50	40
11	2	$6\frac{9}{16}$	66	55	44
12	2	9¼	72	60	48
13	2	$11\frac{15}{16}$	78	65	52
14	3	2⅝	84	70	56
15	3	$5\frac{5}{16}$	90	75	60
16	3	8	96	80	64
17	3	$10\frac{11}{16}$	102	85	68
18	4	1⅜	108	90	72
19	4	$4\frac{1}{16}$	114	95	76
20	4	6¾	120	100	80
21	4	$9\frac{7}{16}$	126	105	84
22	5	⅛	132	110	88
23	5	$2\frac{13}{16}$	138	115	92
24	5	5½	144	120	96
25	5	$8\frac{3}{16}$	150	125	100
List Price in Cents per Square Foot			42	46	50

FIVE-COLUMN PRINCESS

(Window Radiator)

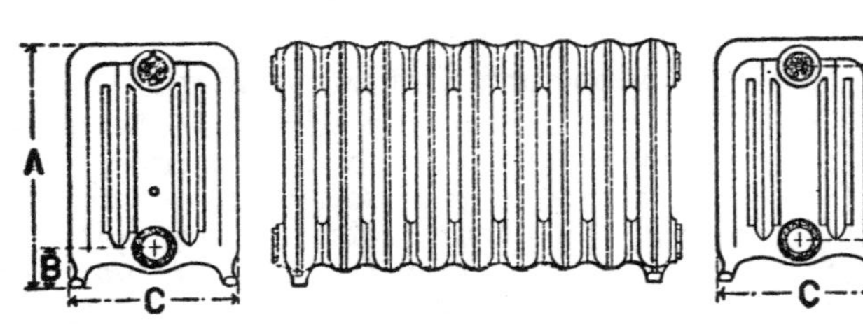

DIMENSIONS IN INCHES

A	Height of Radiator	16	14	12
H	Height of Top Tapping	14	12	10
B	Height of Regular Tapping	3 inches		
C	Width of Section	12 "		

LIST OF SIZES

Number of Sections	Total Length Feet	Total Length Inches	Radiating Surface (Square Feet) 12 ~~16~~ in. High	14 in. High	16 ~~12~~ in. High
3	0	10¾	10	12	14
4	1	2	13⅓	16	18⅔
5	1	5¼	16⅔	20	23⅓
6	1	8½	20	24	28
7	1	11¾	23⅓	28	32⅔
8	2	3	26⅔	32	37⅓
9	2	6¼	30	36	42
10	2	9½	33⅓	40	46⅔
11	3	0¾	36⅔	44	51⅓
12	3	4	40	48	56
13	3	7¼	43⅓	52	60⅔
14	3	10½	46⅔	56	65⅓
15	4	1¾	50	60	70
16	4	5	53⅓	64	74⅔
17	4	8¼	56⅔	68	79⅓
18	4	11½	60	72	84
19	5	2¾	63⅓	76	88⅔
20	5	6	66⅔	80	93⅓
21	5	9¼	70	84	98
22	6	0½	73⅓	88	102⅔
23	6	3¾	76⅔	92	107⅓
24	6	7	80	96	112
25	6	10¼	83⅓	100	116⅔
List Price in Cents per Square Foot			68 ~~60~~	64	60 ~~60~~

THE H. B. SMITH CO.

CIRCULAR RADIATOR

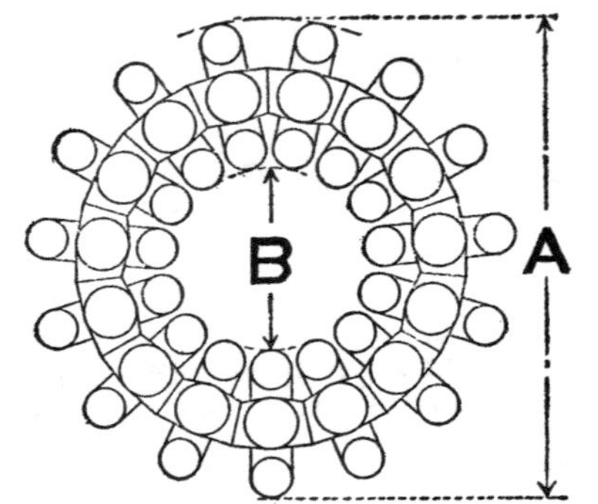

CIRCULAR RADIATORS can be assembled as one whole Radiator, or they can be assembled in halves for the purpose of encircling columns.

When Circular Radiators are in halves, each half becomes an independent Radiator. In ordering specify which method of assembling is desired.

Circular Radiators are made only in the styles and sizes indicated below:

DIMENSIONS IN INCHES

Number of Sections	IMPERIAL UNION and PRINCESS UNION: A Outside Diameter	B Inside Diameter	CORONET and DIADEM: A Outside Diameter	B Inside Diameter
9	24½ In.	4½ In.	18¾ In.	6¼ In.
12	27 "	7 "	20¾ "	8¼ "
15	29 "	9 "	22¾ "	10¼ "
18	30½ "	10½ "	24¾ "	12¼ "
20	32¾ "	12¾ "	25¾ "	13¼ "
24	35¼ "	15¼ "	28 "	15½ "
30	40¼ "	20¼ "	32¾ "	20¼ "
36	44¼ "	24¼ "	35¼ "	22¾ "
40	47½ "	27½ "	39¼ "	26¾ "
45	51¼ "	31¼ "	43¼ "	30¾ "

PRICE: Add $0.60 NET per Section to regular price

REGULAR PATTERN GOLD PIN

STEAM OR WATER

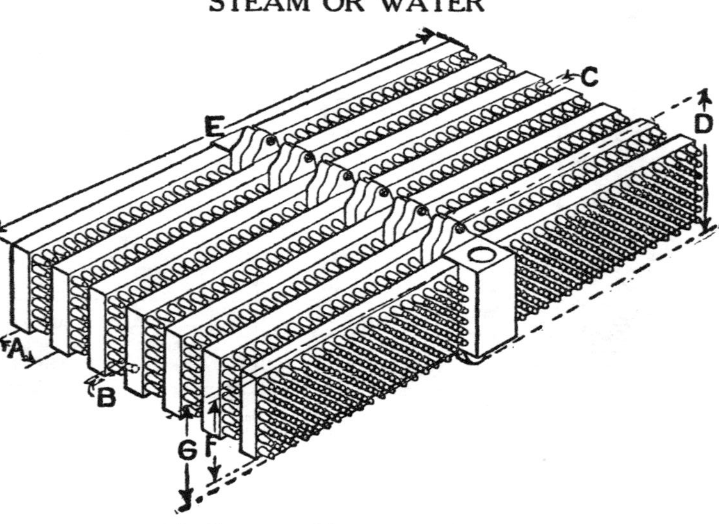

10 Square Feet per Section

DIMENSIONS OF SECTION

A	Distance from center to center	3¼″
B	Distance between ends of Pins	¼″
C	Length of Pin	¾″
D	Height of Flange	10¾″
E	Length of Section	40½″
F	Height of Section at end	6½″
G	Height of Section at center	7¼″

Shipping weight, per Section, 70 lbs.

REGULAR TAPPING

Supply........... 1¼″ Return........... 1¼″

Air Valve........... ⅜″

Price $0.27 per Square Foot

THE H. B. SMITH CO.

TEN-INCH FLANGE GOLD PIN

STEAM OR WATER

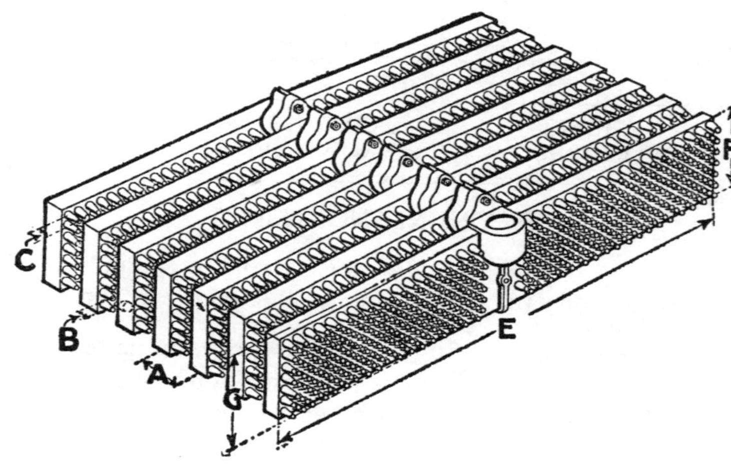

15 Square Feet per Section

DIMENSIONS OF SECTION

A	Distance from center to center	3¼″
B	Distance between ends of Pins	¼″
C	Length of Pin	¾″
E	Length of Section	40½″
F	Height of Section at end	10¼″
G	Height of Section at center	10¾″

Shipping weight, per Section, 108 lbs.

REGULAR TAPPING

Supply........... 1½″ Return........... 1½″

Air Valve........... ⅜″

Price $0.27 per Square Foot

12-FOOT R. & L. NIPPLE GOLD PIN

STEAM ONLY

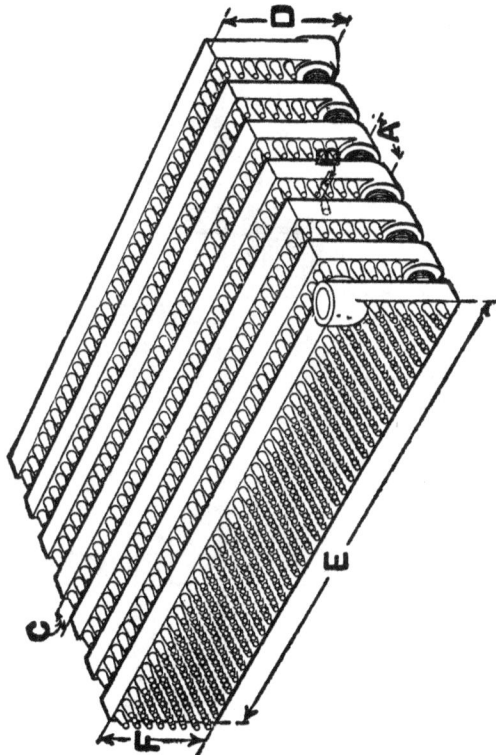

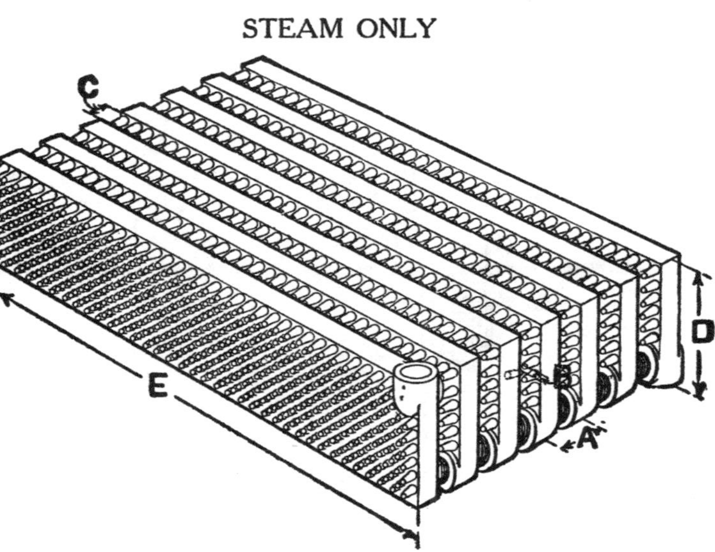

12 Square Feet per Section

DIMENSIONS OF SECTION

A	Distance from center to center	3¼″
B	Distance between ends of Pins	¼″
C	Length of Pin	¾″
D	Height of Section	9″
E	Length of Section	36″
F	Height of Section	8½″
	Size of Right and Left Nipple	2″

Shipping weight, per Section, 62 lbs.

Supply or Head Section is tapped L. H. for R. & L. Nipple
Return or Drain Section is tapped R. H. for R. & L. Nipple

REGULAR TAPPING

Supply............1¼″ Return............1¼″
Air Valve............⅜″

Price $0.27 per Square Foot

THE H. B. SMITH CO.

RIGHT AND LEFT NIPPLE GOLD PIN

STEAM OR WATER

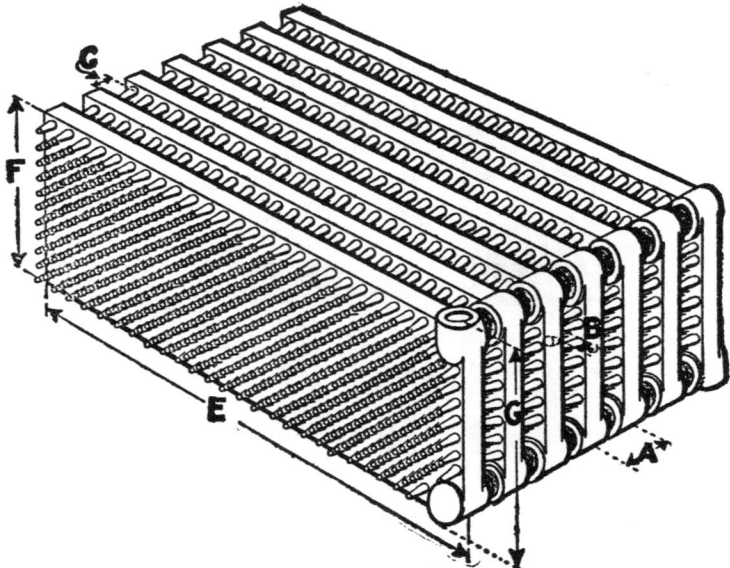

15-FOOT R. & L. NIPPLE GOLD PIN

F	Height of Section	10″
G	Height of Section	11½″

Shipping weight, per Section, 77 lbs.

15 Square Feet per Section

20-FOOT R. & L. NIPPLE GOLD PIN

F	Height of Section	14″
G	Height of Section	15½″

Shipping weight, per Section, 106 lbs.

20 Square Feet per Section

DIMENSIONS COMMON TO BOTH

A	Distance from center to center	3¼″
B	Distance between ends of Pins	¼″
C	Length of Pin	¾″
E	Length of Section	36″
	Size of R. & L. Nipple	2″

REGULAR TAPPING

Supply............1½″ Return............1½″
Air Valves............⅜″

Supply or Head Section is tapped L. H. for R. & L. Nipple
Return or Drain Section is tapped R. H. for R. &. L. Nipple

Price $0.27 per Square Foot

THE H. B. SMITH CO.

SCHOOL PIN

Section A-B

As used for warming and ventilating schoolhouses

THE H. B. SMITH CO.

SCHOOL PIN

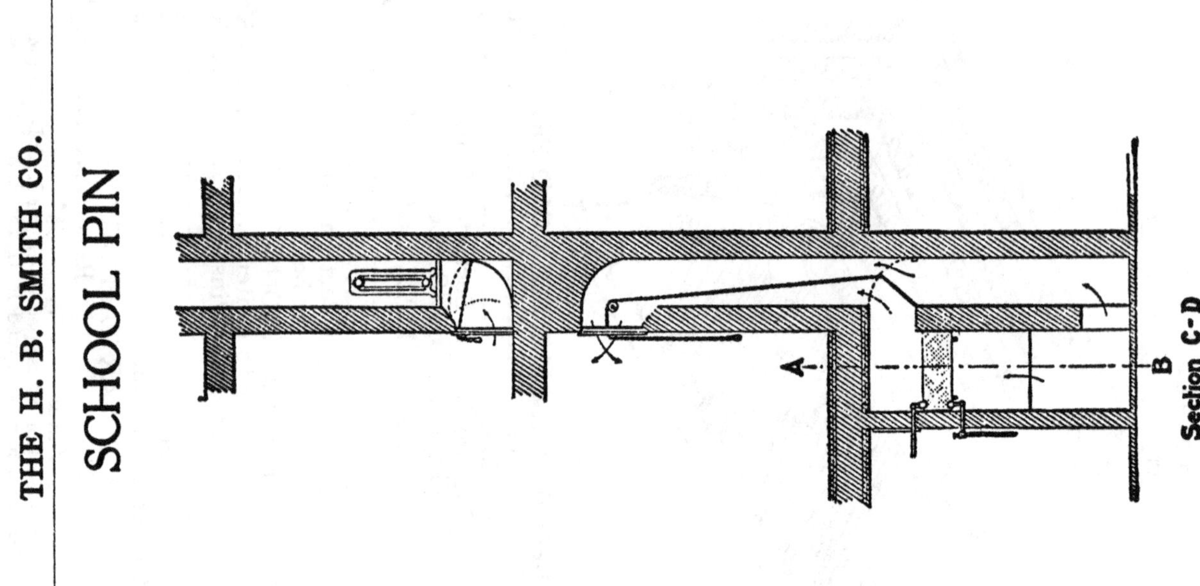

Section C-D

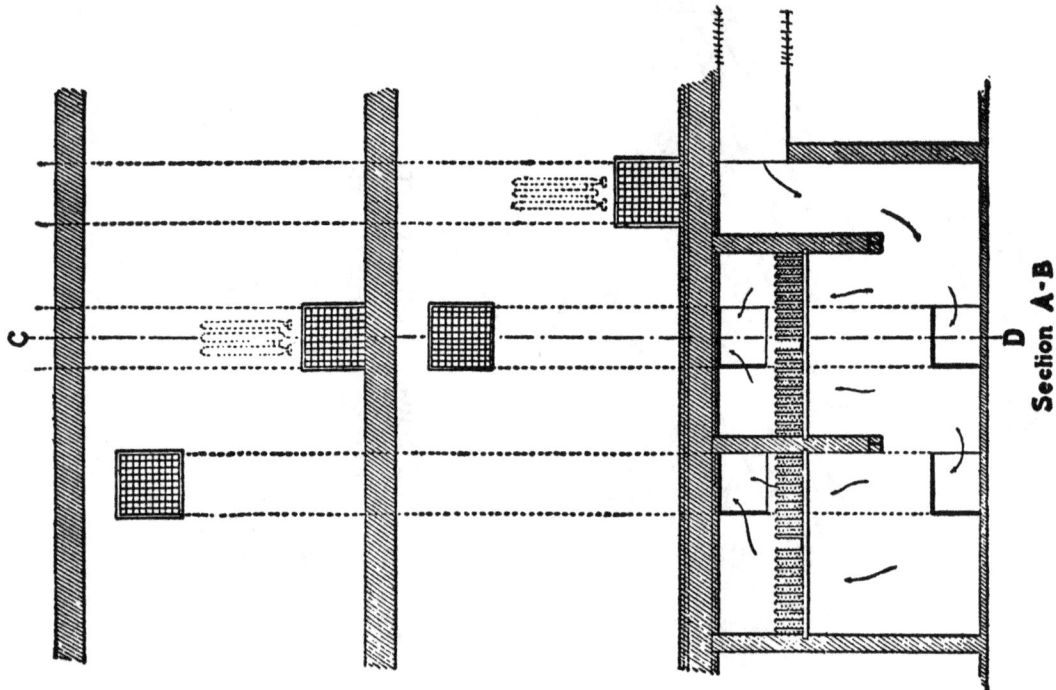

As used for warming and ventilating schoolhouses

SCHOOL PIN

STEAM OR WATER

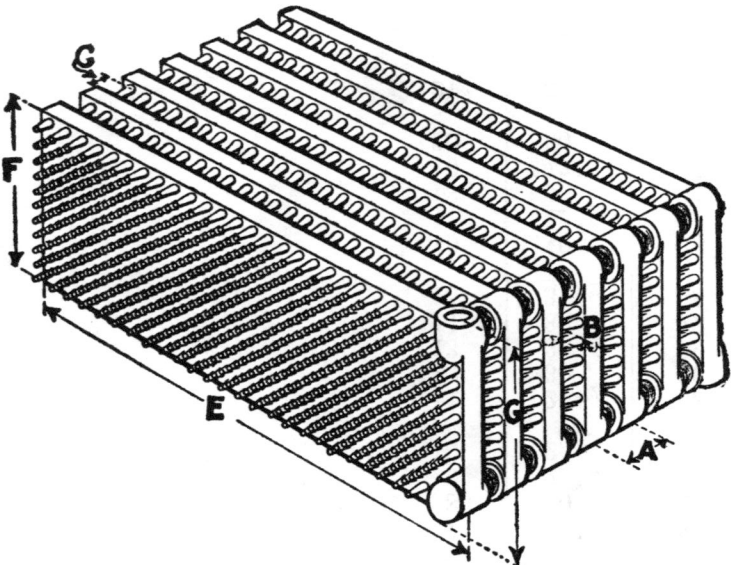

15-FOOT SCHOOL PIN

F	Height of Section	10″
G	Height of Section	11½″

Shipping weight, per Section, 82 lbs.
15 Square Feet per Section

20-FOOT SCHOOL PIN

F	Height of Section	14″
G	Height of Section	15½″

Shipping weight, per Section, 115 lbs.
20 Square Feet per Section

DIMENSIONS COMMON TO BOTH

A	Distance from center to center	4″
B	Distance between ends of Pins	½″
C	Length of Pin	1″
E	Length of Section	36″
	Size of R. & L. Nipple	2″

REGULAR TAPPING

Supply............2″ **Return**............2″

Air Valve............⅜″

Supply or Head Section is tapped L. H. for R. & L. Nipple
Return or Drain Section is tapped R. H. for R. & L. Nipple

Price $0.27 per Square Foot

Triton One-Column Radiators

For Steam and Water

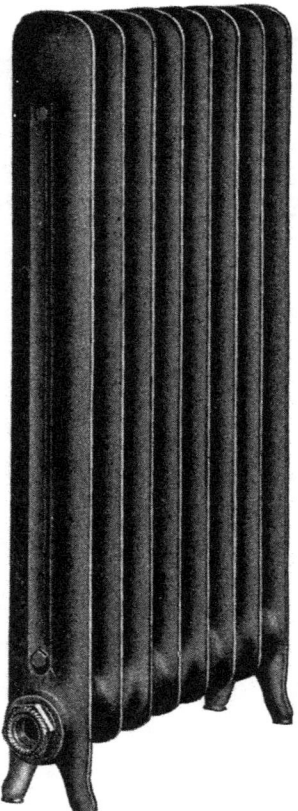

Each section is 4½ inches wide. Width of legs, 5 1/32 inches.

MADE in the following special forms: Side Wall for Concealed Brackets, steam and water, page 72; Legs extra high, solid, for steam and water, page 73.

Direct-Indirect, for steam or water, page 64.

Corner, curved and circular, for steam and water, pages 68 and 69

Triton One-Column Radiators

List of Sizes

Number of Sections	*Length Inches	Heating Surface				
		38 Inch Height 3 Square Feet per Section	32 Inch Height 2½ Square Feet per Section	26 Inch Height 2 Square Feet per Section	22 Inch Height 1⅔ Square Feet per Section	20 Inch Height 1½ Square Feet per Section
2	5	6	5	4	3⅓	3
3	7½	9	7½	6	5	4½
4	10	12	10	8	6⅔	6
5	12½	15	12½	10	8⅓	7½
6	15	18	15	12	10	9
7	17½	21	17½	14	11⅔	10½
8	20	24	20	16	13⅓	12
9	22½	27	22½	18	15	13½
10	25	30	25	20	16⅔	15
11	27½	33	27½	22	18⅓	16½
12	30	36	30	24	20	18
13	32½	39	32½	26	21⅔	19½
14	35	42	35	28	23⅓	21
15	37½	45	37½	30	25	22½
16	40	48	40	32	26⅔	24
17	42½	51	42½	34	28⅓	25½
18	45	54	45	36	30	27
19	47½	57	47½	38	31⅔	28½
20	50	60	50	40	33⅓	30
21	52½	63	52½	42	35	31½
22	55	66	55	44	36⅔	33
23	57½	69	57½	46	38⅓	34½
24	60	72	60	48	40	36
25	62½	75	62½	50	41⅔	37½

Above radiators are tapped and bushed as per list on page 150.

Distance from floor to center of tapping, see page 151.

***Allow ½ inch for each bushing in estimating length of radiators.**

See list prices, page 149.

Triton Two-Column Radiators

For Steam and Water

Each section is 7⅛ inches wide. Width of legs, 7 13/32 inches.

MADE in the following special forms: Side Wall for Concealed Brackets, steam and water, page 72; Legs extra high, solid (excepting 45-inch height), for steam and water, page 73; Direct-Indirect, for steam and water, page 64; and Hospital pattern, page 62.

Corner, curved and circular, for steam and water, pages 68 and 69.

Triton Two-Column Radiators

List of Sizes

No. of Sections	*Length Inches	Heating Surface: 45 Inch Height 5 Square Feet per Section	38 Inch Height 4 Square Feet per Section	32 Inch Height 3⅓ Square Feet per Section	26 Inch Height 2⅔ Square Feet per Section	22 Inch Height 2¼ Square Feet per Section	20 Inch Height 2 Square Feet per Section	15 Inch Height 1½ Square Feet per Section
2	5	10	8	6⅔	5⅓	4½	4	3
3	7½	15	12	10	8	6¾	6	4½
4	10	20	16	13⅓	10⅔	9	8	6
5	12½	25	20	16⅔	13⅓	11¼	10	7½
6	15	30	24	20	16	13½	12	9
7	17½	35	28	23⅓	18⅔	15¾	14	10½
8	20	40	32	26⅔	21⅓	18	16	12
9	22½	45	36	30	24	20¼	18	13½
10	25	50	40	33⅓	26⅔	22½	20	15
11	27½	55	44	36⅔	29⅓	24¾	22	16½
12	30	60	48	40	32	27	24	18
13	32½	65	52	43⅓	34⅔	29¼	26	19½
14	35	70	56	46⅔	37⅓	31½	28	21
15	37½	75	60	50	40	33¾	30	22½
16	40	80	64	53⅓	42⅔	36	32	24
17	42½	85	68	56⅔	45⅓	38¼	34	25½
18	45	90	72	60	48	40½	36	27
19	47½	95	76	63⅓	50⅔	42¾	38	28½
20	50	100	80	66⅔	53⅓	45	40	30
21	52½	105	84	70	56	47¼	42	31½
22	55	110	88	73⅓	58⅔	49½	44	33
23	57½	115	92	76⅔	61⅓	51¾	46	34½
24	60	120	96	80	64	54	48	36
25	62½	125	100	83⅓	66⅔	56¼	50	37½

Above radiators tapped and bushed, as per list on page 150.

Distance from floor to center of tapping, see page 151.

*Allow ½ inch for each bushing in estimating length of radiators.

See list prices, page 149.

CAPITOL BOILERS AND

Triton Three-Column Radiators

For Steam and Water

Each section is 9 inches wide. Width of legs, 9 5/16 inches.

MADE in the following special forms: Side Wall for Concealed Brackets, steam and water, page 72; Legs extra high, solid (excepting 45-inch height), for steam and water, page 73; Direct-Indirect, for steam and water, page 64; Corner, curved and circular, for steam and water, pages 68 and 69.

UNITED STATES RADIATORS

Triton Three-Column Radiators

List of Sizes

No. of Sections	*Length Inches	Heating Surface					
		45 Inch Height 6 Square Feet per Section	38 Inch Height 5 Square Feet per Section	32 Inch Height 4½ Square Feet per Section	26 Inch Height 3¾ Square Feet per Section	22 Inch Height 3 Square Feet per Section	18 Inch Height 2¼ Square Feet per Section
2	5	12	10	9	7½	6	4½
3	7½	18	15	13½	11¼	9	6¾
4	10	24	20	18	15	12	9
5	12½	30	25	22½	18¾	15	11¼
6	15	36	30	27	22½	18	13½
7	17½	42	35	31½	26¼	21	15¾
8	20	48	40	36	30	24	18
9	22½	54	45	40½	33¾	27	20¼
10	25	60	50	45	37½	30	22½
11	27½	66	55	49½	41¼	33	24¾
12	30	72	60	54	45	36	27
13	32½	78	65	58½	48¾	39	29¼
14	35	84	70	63	52½	42	31½
15	37½	90	75	67½	56¼	45	33¾
16	40	96	80	72	60	48	36
17	42½	102	85	76½	63¾	51	38¼
18	45	108	90	81	67½	54	40½
19	47½	114	95	85½	71¼	57	42¾
20	50	120	100	90	75	60	45
21	52½	126	105	94½	78¾	63	47¼
22	55	132	110	99	82½	66	49½
23	57½	138	115	103½	86¼	69	51¾
24	60	144	120	108	90	72	54
25	62½	150	125	112½	93¾	75	56¼

Above radiators tapped and bushed, as per list on page 150.

Distance from floor to center of tapping, see page 151.

*Allow ½ inch for each bushing in estimating length of radiators.

See list prices, page 149.

Triton Four-Column Radiators

For Steam or Water

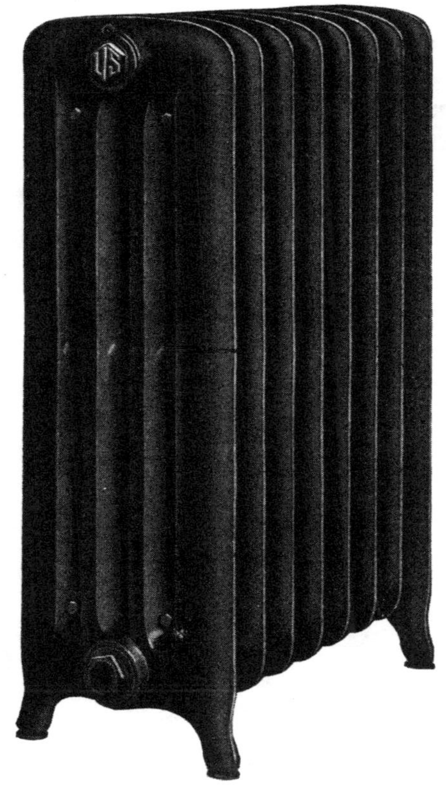

Each section is 12½ inches wide. Width of legs, 12$\frac{13}{16}$ inches.

MADE in the following special forms: Side Wall for Concealed Brackets, steam or water, page 72; Legs extra high, solid (excepting 44-inch height), for steam or water, page 73; Direct-Indirect, for steam or water, page 64.

Triton Four-Column Radiators

List of Sizes

No. of Sections	*Length Inches	Heating Surface					
		44 Inch Height 10 Square Feet per Section	38 Inch Height 8 Square Feet per Section	32 Inch Height 6½ Square Feet per Section	26 Inch Height 5 Square Feet per Section	22 Inch Height 4 Square Feet per Section	18 Inch Height 3 Square Feet per Section
2	6	20	16	13	10	8	6
3	9	30	24	19½	15	12	9
4	12	40	32	26	20	16	12
5	15	50	40	32½	25	20	15
6	18	60	48	39	30	24	18
7	21	70	56	45½	35	28	21
8	24	80	64	52	40	32	24
9	27	90	72	58½	45	36	27
10	30	100	80	65	50	40	30
11	33	110	88	71½	55	44	33
12	36	120	96	78	60	48	36
13	39	130	104	84½	65	52	39
14	42	140	112	91	70	56	42
15	45	150	120	97½	75	60	45
16	48	160	128	104	80	64	48
17	51	170	136	110½	85	68	51
18	54	180	144	117	90	72	54
19	57	190	152	123½	95	76	57
20	60	200	160	130	100	80	60
21	63	210	168	136½	105	84	63
22	66	220	176	143	110	88	66
23	69	230	184	149½	115	92	69
24	72	240	192	156	120	96	72
25	75	250	200	162½	125	100	75

Above radiators are tapped and bushed, as per list on page 150.

Distance from floor to center of tapping, see page 151.

*Allow ½ inch for each bushing in estimating length of radiators.

See list prices, page 149.

Triton Five-Column Window Radiators

For Steam or Water

Each section is 13 inches wide. Width of legs, 13 inches.

MADE in the following special forms: Legs extra high, solid, fo steam or water, page 73; corner and curved, for steam or water, page 68.

Triton Five-Column Window Radiators

List of Sizes

Number of Sections	*Length Inches	Heating Surface		
		20 Inch Height 5½ Square Feet per Section	17 Inch Height 4¾ Square Feet per Section	14 Inch Height 4 Square Feet per Section
2	6	11	9½	8
3	9	16½	14¼	12
4	12	22	19	16
5	15	27½	23¾	20
6	18	33	28½	24
7	21	38½	33¼	28
8	24	44	38	32
9	27	49½	42¾	36
10	30	55	47½	40
11	33	60½	52¼	44
12	36	66	57	48
13	39	71½	61¾	52
14	42	77	66½	56
15	45	82½	71¼	60
16	48	88	76	64
17	51	93½	80¾	68
18	54	99	85½	72
19	57	104½	90¼	76
20	60	110	95	80
21	63	115½	99¾	84
22	66	121	104½	88
23	69	126½	109¼	92
24	72	132	114	96
25	75	137½	118¾	100

Above radiators are tapped and bushed, as per list on page 150.

Distance from floor to center of tapping, see page 151.

*Allow ½ inch for each bushing in estimating length of radiators.

See list prices, page 149.

Florentine One-Column Radiators

For Steam and Water

Each section is $4\frac{1}{2}$ inches wide. Width of legs, $5\frac{1}{32}$ inches.

MADE in the following special forms: Side Wall for Concealed Brackets, steam and water, page 72. Legs extra high, solid, for steam and water, page 73.

Direct-Indirect, for steam or water, page 64.

Florentine One-Column Radiators

List of Sizes

Number of Sections	*Length Inches	Heating Surface				
		38 Inch Height 3 Square Feet per Section	32 Inch Height $2\frac{1}{2}$ Square Feet per Section	26 Inch Height 2 Square Feet per Section	22 Inch Height $1\frac{2}{3}$ Square Feet per Section	20 Inch Height $1\frac{1}{2}$ Square Feet per Section
2	5	6	5	4	$3\frac{1}{3}$	3
3	$7\frac{1}{2}$	9	$7\frac{1}{2}$	6	5	$4\frac{1}{2}$
4	10	12	10	8	$6\frac{2}{3}$	6
5	$12\frac{1}{2}$	15	$12\frac{1}{2}$	10	$8\frac{1}{3}$	$7\frac{1}{2}$
6	15	18	15	12	10	9
7	$17\frac{1}{2}$	21	$17\frac{1}{2}$	14	$11\frac{2}{3}$	$10\frac{1}{2}$
8	20	24	20	16	$13\frac{1}{3}$	12
9	$22\frac{1}{2}$	27	$22\frac{1}{2}$	18	15	$13\frac{1}{2}$
10	25	30	25	20	$16\frac{2}{3}$	15
11	$27\frac{1}{2}$	33	$27\frac{1}{2}$	22	$18\frac{1}{3}$	$16\frac{1}{2}$
12	30	36	30	24	20	18
13	$32\frac{1}{2}$	39	$32\frac{1}{2}$	26	$21\frac{2}{3}$	$19\frac{1}{2}$
14	35	42	35	28	$23\frac{1}{3}$	21
15	$37\frac{1}{2}$	45	$37\frac{1}{2}$	30	25	$22\frac{1}{2}$
16	40	48	40	32	$26\frac{2}{3}$	24
17	$42\frac{1}{2}$	51	$42\frac{1}{2}$	34	$28\frac{1}{3}$	$25\frac{1}{2}$
18	45	54	45	36	30	27
19	$47\frac{1}{2}$	57	$47\frac{1}{2}$	38	$31\frac{2}{3}$	$28\frac{1}{2}$
20	50	60	50	40	$33\frac{1}{3}$	30
21	$52\frac{1}{2}$	63	$52\frac{1}{2}$	42	35	$31\frac{1}{2}$
22	55	66	55	44	$36\frac{2}{3}$	33
23	$57\frac{1}{2}$	69	$57\frac{1}{2}$	46	$38\frac{1}{3}$	$34\frac{1}{2}$
24	60	72	60	48	40	36
25	$62\frac{1}{2}$	75	$62\frac{1}{2}$	50	$41\frac{2}{3}$	$37\frac{1}{2}$

Above radiators are tapped and bushed, as per list on page 150.

Distance from floor to center of tapping, see page 151.

*Allow $\frac{1}{2}$ inch for each bushing in estimating length of radiators.

See list prices, page 149.

CAPITOL BOILERS AND

Florentine Two-Column Radiators

For Steam and Water

Each section is 7⅛ inches wide. Width of legs, 7 13/32 inches.

MADE in the following special forms: Side Wall for Concealed Brackets, steam and water, page 72; Legs extra high, solid (excepting 45-inch height), for steam and water, page 73; Direct-Indirect, for steam and water, page 64.

UNITED STATES RADIATORS

Florentine Two-Column Radiators

List of Sizes

No. of Sections	*Length Inches	Heating Surface					
		45 Inch Height 5 Square Feet per Section	38 Inch Height 4 Square Feet per Section	32 Inch Height 3⅓ Square Feet per Section	26 Inch Height 2⅔ Square Feet per Section	22 Inch Height 2¼ Square Feet per Section	2) Inch Height 2 Square Feet per Section
2	5	10	8	6⅔	5⅓	4½	4
3	7½	15	12	10	8	6¾	6
4	10	20	16	13⅓	10⅔	9	8
5	12½	25	20	16⅔	13⅓	11¼	10
6	15	30	24	20	16	13½	12
7	17½	35	28	23⅓	18⅔	15¾	14
8	20	40	32	26⅔	21⅓	18	16
9	22½	45	36	30	24	20¼	18
10	25	50	40	33⅓	26⅔	22½	20
11	27½	55	44	36⅔	29⅓	24¾	22
12	30	60	48	40	32	27	24
13	32½	65	52	43⅓	34⅔	29¼	26
14	35	70	56	46⅔	37⅓	31½	28
15	37½	75	60	50	40	33¾	30
16	40	80	64	53⅓	42⅔	36	32
17	42½	85	68	56⅔	45⅓	38¼	34
18	45	90	72	60	48	40½	36
19	47½	95	76	63⅓	50⅔	42¾	38
20	50	100	80	66⅔	53⅓	45	40
21	52½	105	84	70	56	47¼	42
22	55	110	88	73⅓	58⅔	49½	44
23	57½	115	92	76⅔	61⅓	51¾	46
24	60	120	96	80	64	54	48
25	62½	125	100	83⅓	66⅔	56¼	50

Above radiators are tapped and bushed, as per list on page 150.

Distance from floor to center of tapping, see page 151.

*Allow ½ inch for each bushing in estimating length of radiators.

See list prices, page 149.

Florentine Three-Column Radiators

For Steam and Water

Each section is 9 inches wide. Width of legs, 9 5/16 inches.

MADE in the following special forms: Side Wall for Concealed Brackets, steam and water, page 72; Legs extra high, solid (excepting 45-inch height), for steam and water, page 73; Direct-Indirect, for steam and water, page 64.

Florentine Three-Column Radiators

List of Sizes

No. of Sections	*Length Inches	Heating Surface					
		45 Inch Height 6 Square Feet per Section	38 Inch Height 5 Square Feet per Section	32 Inch Height 4½ Square Feet per Section	26 Inch Height 3¾ Square Feet per Section	22 Inch Height 3 Square Feet per Section	18 Inch Height 2¼ Square Feet per Section
2	5	12	10	9	7½	6	4½
3	7½	18	15	13½	11¼	9	6¾
4	10	24	20	18	15	12	9
5	12½	30	25	22½	18¾	15	11¼
6	15	36	30	27	22½	18	13½
7	17½	42	35	31½	26¼	21	15¾
8	20	48	40	36	30	24	18
9	22½	54	45	40½	33¾	27	20¼
10	25	60	50	45	37½	30	22½
11	27½	66	55	49½	41¼	33	24¾
12	30	72	60	54	45	36	27
13	32½	78	65	58½	48¾	39	29¼
14	35	84	70	63	52½	42	31½
15	37½	90	75	67½	56¼	45	33¾
16	40	96	80	72	60	48	36
17	42½	102	85	76½	63¾	51	38¼
18	45	108	90	81	67½	54	40½
19	47½	114	95	85½	71¼	57	42¾
20	50	120	100	90	75	60	45
21	52½	126	105	94½	78¾	63	47¼
22	55	132	110	99	82½	66	49½
23	57½	138	115	103½	86¼	69	51¾
24	60	144	120	108	90	72	54
25	62½	150	125	112½	93¾	75	56¼

Above radiators tapped and bushed, as per list on page 150.

Distance from floor to center of tapping, see page 151.

*Allow ½ inch for each bushing in estimating length of radiators.

See list prices, page 149.

Capitol Boilers and

Florentine Four-Column Radiators

For Steam or Water

Each section is 12½ inches wide. Width of legs, 12 13/16 inches.

MADE in the following special forms: Side Wall for Concealed Brackets, steam or water, page 72; Legs extra high, solid (excepting 44-inch height), for steam or water, page 73; Direct-Indirect, for steam or water, page 64.

United States Radiators

Florentine Four-Column Radiators

List of Sizes

No. of Sections	*Length Inches	Heating Surface					
		44 Inch Height 10 Square Feet per Section	38 Inch Height 8 Square Feet per Section	32 Inch Height 6½ Square Feet per Section	26 Inch Height 5 Square Feet per Section	22 Inch Height 4 Square Feet per Section	18 Inch Height 3 Square Feet per Section
2	6	20	16	13	10	8	6
3	9	30	24	19½	15	12	9
4	12	40	32	26	20	16	12
5	15	50	40	32½	25	20	15
6	18	60	48	39	30	24	18
7	21	70	56	45½	35	28	21
8	24	80	64	52	40	32	24
9	27	90	72	58½	45	36	27
10	30	100	80	65	50	40	30
11	33	110	88	71½	55	44	33
12	36	120	96	78	60	48	36
13	39	130	104	84½	65	52	39
14	42	140	112	91	70	56	42
15	45	150	120	97½	75	60	45
16	48	160	128	104	80	64	48
17	51	170	136	110½	85	68	51
18	54	180	144	117	90	72	54
19	57	190	152	123½	95	76	57
20	60	200	160	130	100	80	60
21	63	210	168	136½	105	84	63
22	66	220	176	143	110	88	66
23	69	230	184	149½	115	92	69
24	72	240	192	156	120	96	72
25	75	250	200	162½	125	100	75

Above radiators are tapped and bushed, as per list on page 150.

Distance from floor to center of tapping, see page 151.

*Allow ½ inch for each bushing in estimating length of radiators.

See list prices, page 149.

Triton Hospital Radiators

For Steam or Water

One column section 4½ inches wide. Width of legs, 5 1/32 inches.
Two column section 7⅛ inches wide. Width of legs, 7 13/32 inches.
Three column section 9 inches wide. Width of legs, 9 5/16 inches.

Not made in special forms

RADIATORS specially designed for hospitals. The extra large spacings between sections allow easy cleaning. Triton Hospital Radiators are made in one, two and three column patterns, with three inch centers.

Triton Two-Column Hospital Radiators

List of Sizes

No. of Sections	*Length Inches	Heating Surface					
		45 Inch Height 5 Square Feet per Section	38 Inch Height 4 Square Feet per Section	32 Inch Height 3⅓ Square Feet per Section	26 Inch Height 2⅔ Square Feet per Section	22 Inch Height 2¼ Square Feet per Section	20 Inch Height 2 Square Feet per Section
2	6	10	8	6⅔	5⅓	4½	4
3	9	15	12	10	8	6¾	6
4	12	20	16	13⅓	10⅔	9	8
5	15	25	20	16⅔	13⅓	11¼	10
6	18	30	24	20	16	13½	12
7	21	35	28	23⅓	18⅔	15¾	14
8	24	40	32	26⅔	21⅓	18	16
9	27	45	36	30	24	20¼	18
10	30	50	40	33⅓	26⅔	22½	20
11	33	55	44	36⅔	29⅓	24¾	22
12	36	60	48	40	32	27	24
13	39	65	52	43⅓	34⅔	29¼	26
14	42	70	56	46⅔	37⅓	31½	28
15	45	75	60	50	40	33¾	30
16	48	80	64	53⅓	42⅔	36	32
17	51	85	68	56⅔	45⅓	38¼	34
18	54	90	72	60	48	40½	36
19	57	95	76	63⅓	50⅔	42¾	38
20	60	100	80	66⅔	53⅓	45	40
21	63	105	84	70	56	47¼	42
22	66	110	88	73⅓	58⅔	49½	44
23	69	115	92	76⅔	61⅓	51¾	46
24	72	120	96	80	64	54	48
25	75	125	100	83⅓	66⅔	56¼	50

Above radiators tapped and bushed, as per list on page 150.

Distance from floor to center of tapping, page 151.

*Allow ½ inch for each bushing in estimating length of radiator.

See list prices, page 149.

NOTE—Lengths of one and three column radiators are the same as for two column. Heating surfaces are the same as for regular Triton pattern.

United States Radiator Co. – *circa 1920*

Dining-Room Radiators

For Steam and Water

Number	*Length in Inches	Heating Surface Square Feet	Price for Steam	Price for Water
1	32½	43	$ 92.00	$104.00
2	37½	53	100.00	114.00
3	42½	63	108.00	123.00
4	47½	73	116.00	132.00
5	52½	83	124.00	141.00
6	57½	93	132.00	150.00
7	62½	103	140.00	159.00
8	67½	113	148.00	168.00
9	72½	123	156.00	180.00
10	77½	133	164.00	190.00

Made in Triton Three-Column pattern only. See page 49. Ovens are all the same size, inside dimensions, 27 x 13¼ x 15½ inches. Height of radiator complete, 38¼ inches.

Distance from back of oven to center of radiator tappings, 7 inches.

*Allow ½ inch for each bushing in estimating length of radiator.

Triton and Florentine Circular Radiators

Diameter in Inches

No. of Sections in Stack	1 Column		2 Column		3 Column	
	Inside Diam. at Legs	Outside Diam. at Legs	Inside Diam. at Legs	Outside Diam. at Legs	Inside Diam. at Legs	Outside Diam. at Legs
12	8⅜	18½	6	20⅞	4⅛	22¾
14	9¾	19⅞	7⅜	22¼	5½	24⅛
16	11⅛	21¼	8¾	23⅝	6⅞	25½
18	12½	22⅝	10⅛	25	8¼	26⅞
20	14⅛	24⅛	11¾	26½	9¾	28½
22	15½	25½	13⅛	27⅞	11⅛	29⅞
24	17⅛	27¼	15	29¾	13	31¾
26	18¼	28¼	15⅞	30⅝	13⅞	32⅝
28	19⅞	30	17½	32⅜	15⅝	34¼
30	21	31⅛	19⅝	33½	16¾	35⅜
32	22⅝	32¾	20¼	35⅛	18⅜	37
34	23⅞	33⅞	21½	36¼	19½	38¼
36	25⅜	35⅜	23	37¾	21	39¾
38	26⅝	36⅝	24¼	39	22¼	41
40	28	38⅛	25⅝	40½	23¾	42⅜
42	29⅜	39½	27	41⅞	25⅛	43¾
44	30⅞	41	28½	43⅜	26⅝	45¼
46	32½	42⅝	30⅛	45	28¼	46⅞
48	34⅜	44⅜	32	46¾	30	48¾
50	34⅞	45	32½	47⅜	30⅝	49¼
52	36⅛	46¼	33¾	48⅝	31⅞	50½
54	38	48⅛	35⅝	50½	33¾	52⅜
56	39	49⅛	36⅝	51½	34¾	53⅜
58	41	51	39⅝	53⅝	36⅝	55⅜
60	42¾	52¾	40⅜	55⅛	38⅜	57⅛

Circular Radiators may be ordered assembled in one piece or disconnected in halves to be assembled at the job. Or they may be built in halves to be installed as two separate radiators.

Marble Tops can be furnished if desired.

Pantry Radiator

For Steam or Water

THIS radiator is useful for pantries, restaurants, dining rooms and any place where heat is required, and the additional service of plate warming needed. It is made up from seven-foot sections only. All openings on lower shelf are tapped.

The radiator may be constructed from one to five sections high as follows:

Number	Height Inches	Heating Surface Feet	List Price
1	7	7	$16.00
2	17	15	30.00
3	27	23	44.00
4	37	31	58.00
5	47	39	72.00

Length 24¼ inches. Width 13¼ inches.
Tapping, see page 150.

United States Radiators

Triton Fractional Radiators

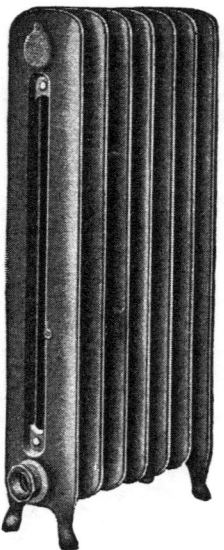

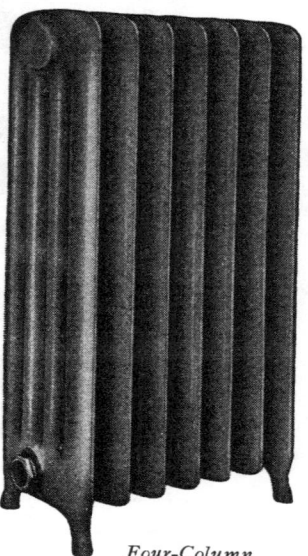

DESIGNED to meet the growing demand for regulation on one pipe steam installations.

The above arrangement of special recessed section and U. S. R. control air valve permits the operation of all or part of radiator as the occasion demands.

Furnished in various sizes, requires no special roughing in and shipped complete with vents.

Booklet explaining complete operation mailed on request.

LINCOLN RADIATORS

One-Column

Two-Column

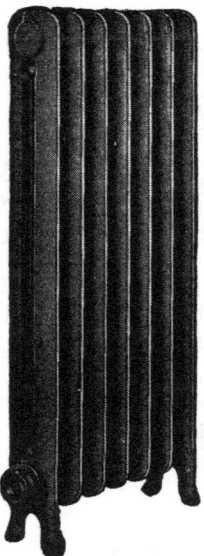

Three-Column

Four-Column

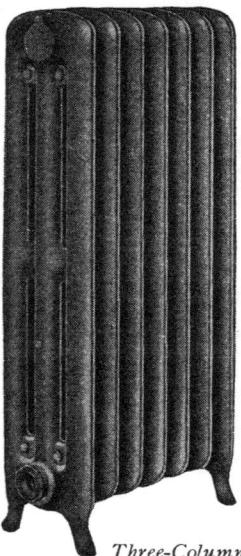

LINCOLN RADIATORS

ONE-COLUMN

Made in

38″, 32″, 26″, 20″

No. of Sections	†Length 2½ Inches Per Section	HEATING SURFACE			
		38-Inch 3 Sq. Ft. Per Section	32-Inch 2½ Sq. Ft. Per Section	26-Inch 2 Sq. Ft. Per Section	20-Inch 1½ Sq. Ft. Per Section
2	5	6	5	4	3
3	7½	9	7½	6	4½
4	10	12	10	8	6
5	12½	15	12½	10	7½
6	15	18	15	12	9
7	17½	21	17½	14	10½
8	20	24	20	16	12
9	22½	27	22½	18	13½
10	25	30	25	20	15
11	27½	33	27½	22	16½
12	30	36	30	24	18
13	32½	39	32½	26	19½
14	35	42	35	28	21
15	37½	45	37½	30	22½
16	40	48	40	32	24
17	42½	51	42½	34	25½
18	45	54	45	36	27
19	47½	57	47½	38	28½
20	50	60	50	40	30
*Distance from floor to center of upper tappings, in.		35¾	30¼	23⅞	18
Distance from floor to center of bottom tappings, in......		4½	4½	4½	4½
Width, in.......		4½	4½	4½	4½
Width at legs, in.		5	5	5	5

Radiators tapped 2 inches and bushed to specified sizes.

*Upper tappings furnished only when specified.

†Allow ½ inch for each bushing in estimating length of radiators.

LINCOLN RADIATORS

TWO-COLUMN

Made in

38″, 32″, 26″, 23″, 20″

No. of Sections	†Length 2½ Inches Per Section	HEATING SURFACE				
		38-Inch 4 Sq. Ft. Per Section	32-Inch 3⅓ Sq. Ft. Per Section	26-Inch 2⅔ Sq. Ft. Per Section	23-Inch 2⅓ Sq. Ft. Per Section	20-Inch 2 Sq. Ft. Per Section
2	5	8	6⅔	5⅓	4⅔	4
3	7½	12	10	8	7	6
4	10	16	13⅓	10⅔	9⅓	8
5	12½	20	16⅔	13⅓	11⅔	10
6	15	24	20	16	14	12
7	17½	28	23⅓	18⅔	16⅓	14
8	20	32	26⅔	21⅓	18⅔	16
9	22½	36	30	24	21	18
10	25	40	33⅓	26⅔	23⅓	20
11	27½	44	36⅔	29⅓	25⅔	22
12	30	48	40	32	28	24
13	32½	52	43⅓	34⅔	30⅓	26
14	35	56	46⅔	37⅓	32⅔	28
15	37½	60	50	40	35	30
16	40	64	53⅓	42⅔	37⅓	32
17	42½	68	56⅔	45⅓	39⅔	34
18	45	72	60	48	42	36
19	47½	76	63⅓	50⅔	44⅓	38
20	50	80	66⅔	53⅓	46⅔	40
*Distance from floor to center of upper tappings, in.....		35¼	29	23⅛	20⅜	17¼
Distance from floor to center of bottom tappings, in.....		4½	4½	4½	4½	4½
Width, in.....		7⅛	7⅛	7⅛	7⅛	7⅛
Width at legs, in......		7⅛	7⅛	7⅛	7⅛	7⅛

Radiators tapped 2 inches and bushed to specified sizes.

*Upper tappings furnished only when specified.

†Allow ½ inch for each bushing in estimating length of radiators.

LINCOLN RADIATORS

THREE-COLUMN

Made in

38″, 32″, 26″, 22″, 18″

No. of Sections	†Length 2½ Inches Per Section	HEATING SURFACE: 38-Inch 5 Sq. Ft. Per Section	32-Inch 4½ Sq. Ft. Per Section	26-Inch 3¾ Sq. Ft. Per Section	22-Inch 3 Sq. Ft. Per Section	18-Inch 2¼ Sq. Ft. Per Section
2	5	10	9	7½	6	4½
3	7½	15	13½	11¼	9	6¾
4	10	20	18	15	12	9
5	12½	25	22½	18¾	15	11¼
6	15	30	27	22½	18	13½
7	17½	35	31½	26¼	21	15¾
8	20	40	36	30	24	18
9	22½	45	40½	33¾	27	20¼
10	25	50	45	37½	30	22½
11	27½	55	49½	41¼	33	24¾
12	30	60	54	45	36	27
13	32½	65	58½	48¾	39	29¼
14	35	70	63	52½	42	31½
15	37½	75	67½	56¼	45	33¾
16	40	80	72	60	48	36
17	42½	85	76½	63¾	51	38¼
18	45	90	81	67½	54	40½
19	47½	95	85½	71¼	57	42¾
20	50	100	90	75	60	45
*Distance from floor to center of upper tappings, in.....		35⅜	29⅝	23½	19½	15⅛
Distance from floor to center of bottom tappings, in.....		4½	4½	4½	4½	4½
Width, in.....		9	9	9	9	9
Width at legs, in......		9	9	9	9	9

Radiators tapped 2 inches and bushed to specified sizes.

*Upper tappings furnished only when specified.

†Allow ½ inch for each bushing in estimating length of radiators.

LINCOLN RADIATORS

FOUR-COLUMN

Made in

38″, 32″, 26″, 22″, 18″

No. of Sections	Length 3 Inches Per Section	HEATING SURFACE: 38-Inch 8 Sq. Ft. Per Section	32-Inch 6½ Sq. Ft. Per Section	26-Inch 5 Sq. Ft. Per Section	22-Inch 4 Sq. Ft. Per Section	18-Inch 3 Sq. Ft. Per Section
2	6	16	13	10	8	6
3	9	24	19½	15	12	9
4	12	32	26	20	16	12
5	15	40	32½	25	20	15
6	18	48	39	30	24	18
7	21	56	45½	35	28	21
8	24	64	52	40	32	24
9	27	72	58½	45	36	27
10	30	80	65	50	40	30
11	33	88	71½	55	44	33
12	36	96	78	60	48	36
13	39	104	84½	65	52	39
14	42	112	91	70	56	42
15	45	120	97½	75	60	45
16	48	128	104	80	64	48
17	51	136	110½	85	68	51
18	54	144	117	90	72	54
19	57	152	123½	95	76	57
20	60	160	130	100	80	60
Distance from floor to center of upper tappings, in.....		35 1/16	29 1/16	23 1/16	19 3/16	15 3/16
Distance from floor to center of bottom tappings, in.....		4½	4½	4½	4½	4½
Width, in..		11 5/16	11 5/16	11 5/16	11 5/16	11 5/16
Width at legs, in...		11 5/16	11 5/16	11 5/16	11 5/16	11 5/16

Radiators tapped 2 inches and bushed to regular list sizes.

Allow ½ inch for each bushing in estimating length of radiators.

FIVE-COLUMN LINCOLN RADIATORS

Made in 22″, 18″, 14″

No. of Sections	†Length 3 Inches Per Section	HEATING SURFACE 22-Inch 6 Sq. Ft. Per Section	18-Inch 5 Sq. Ft. Per Section	14-Inch 4 Sq. Ft. Per Section
2	6	12	10	8
3	9	18	15	12
4	12	24	20	16
5	15	30	25	20
6	18	36	30	24
7	21	42	35	28
8	24	48	40	32
9	27	54	45	36
10	30	60	50	40
11	33	66	55	44
12	36	72	60	48
13	39	78	65	52
14	42	84	70	56
15	45	90	75	60
16	48	96	80	64
17	51	102	85	68
18	54	108	90	72
19	57	114	95	76
20	60	120	100	80
*Distance from floor to center of upper tappings, in.		20	16	12
Distance from floor to center of bottom tappings, in.		3½	3½	3½
Width, in.		13⅛	13⅛	13⅛
Width at legs, in.		13⅛	13⅛	13⅛

Radiators tapped 2 inches and bushed to specified sizes.

*Upper tappings furnished only when specified.

†Allow ½ inch for each bushing in estimating length of radiators.

LINCOLN WALL RADIATORS

Made in 7-B, 9-B

Section Numbers	Height Inches	Width Inches	Distance Center to Center of Tappings	Heating Surface Sq. Ft.
7–B	22	12	19″	7
9–B	29	12	25 15/16″	9

Thickness without brackets, 3 inches; thickness with brackets, 3½ inches.

All steam radiators have a 2-inch tapping on each end at bottom only.

On each end of water and vapor radiators, at the bottom only, there is a 2-inch tapping, and at the top there is 1½ inch tapping.

All tappings are bushed in accordance with the schedule on this sheet, unless otherwise specified.

When the length of radiators is estimated, ½ inch for each bushing should be added.

SCHEDULE OF RADIATOR TAPPINGS

One Pipe Steam

0 to 24 sq. ft.—1″ and plug
25 to 60 sq. ft.—1¼″ and plug
61 to 100 sq. ft.—1½″ and plug
100 sq. ft. and up—2″ and plug

Two Pipe Steam

0 to 48 sq. ft.—1″ x¾″
49 to 96 sq. ft.—1¼″x1″
97 sq. ft. and up—1½″x1¼″

Regular Water

0 to 40 sq. ft.—1″ x1″
41 to 72 sq. ft.—1¼″x1¼″
73 sq. ft. and up—1½″x1½″

Vapor

0 to 30 sq. ft.— ½″x½″ eccentric
31 to 60 sq. ft.— ¾″x½″ eccentric
61 to 125 sq. ft.—1″ x½″ eccentric
126 to 175 sq. ft.—1¼″x½″ eccentric

LINCOLN WALL RADIATORS

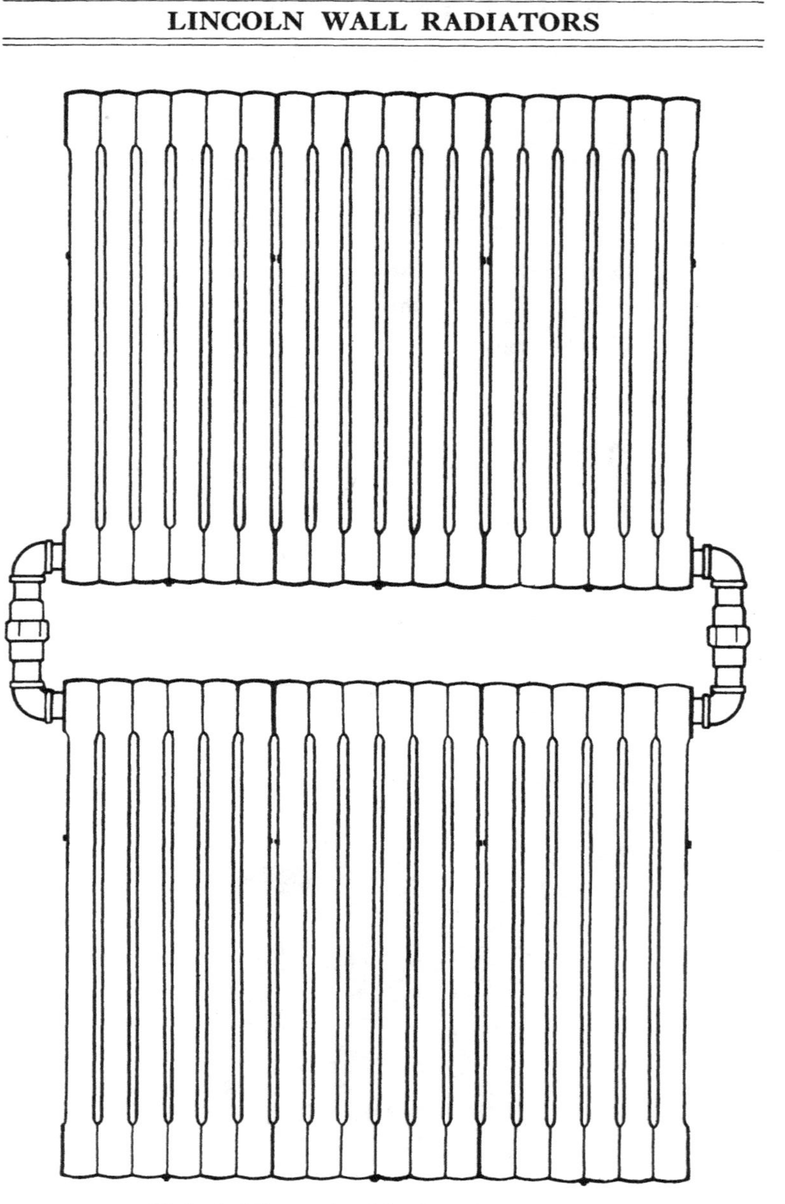

Method of Connecting Lincoln Wall Radiation when assembled vertically

(Assembled two tiers of 3 sections each)

LINCOLN LEGLESS COLUMN RADIATORS

One Column without Legs used as Wall Radiation

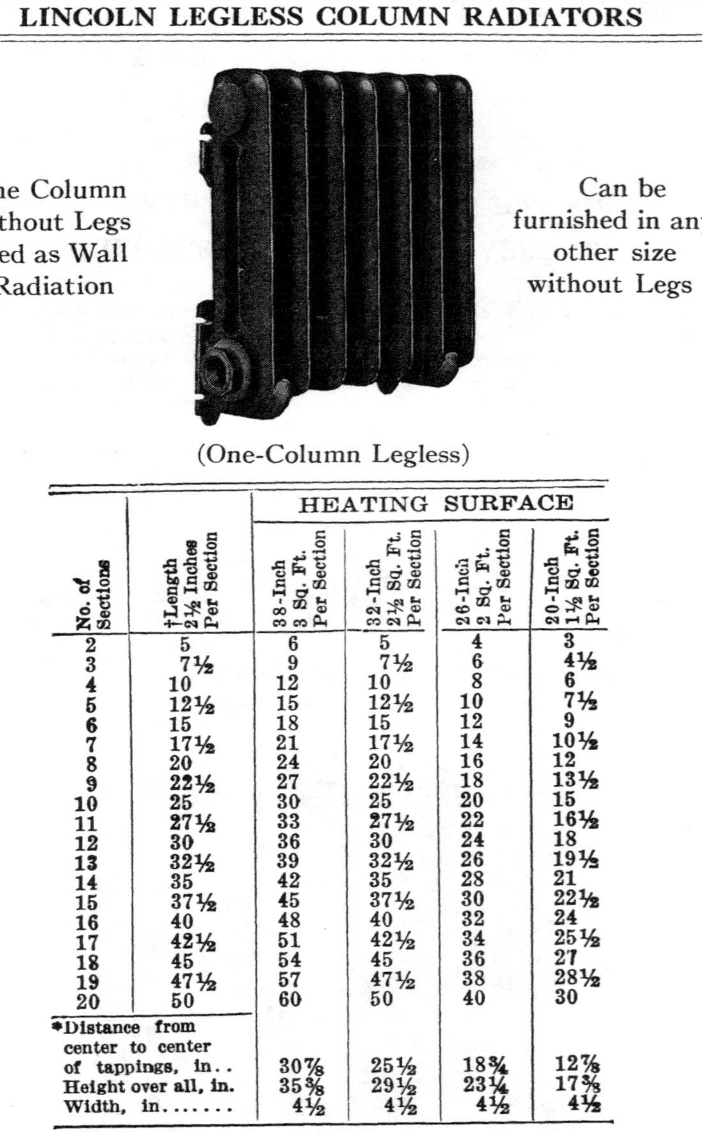

Can be furnished in any other size without Legs

(One-Column Legless)

No. of Sections	†Length 2½ Inches Per Section	HEATING SURFACE 38-Inch 3 Sq. Ft. Per Section	32-Inch 2½ Sq. Ft. Per Section	26-Inch 2 Sq. Ft. Per Section	20-Inch 1½ Sq. Ft. Per Section
2	5	6	5	4	3
3	7½	9	7½	6	4½
4	10	12	10	8	6
5	12½	15	12½	10	7½
6	15	18	15	12	9
7	17½	21	17½	14	10½
8	20	24	20	16	12
9	22½	27	22½	18	13½
10	25	30	25	20	15
11	27½	33	27½	22	16½
12	30	36	30	24	18
13	32½	39	32½	26	19½
14	35	42	35	28	21
15	37½	45	37½	30	22½
16	40	48	40	32	24
17	42½	51	42½	34	25½
18	45	54	45	36	27
19	47½	57	47½	38	28½
20	50	60	50	40	30
*Distance from center to center of tappings, in..		30⅞	25½	18¾	12⅞
Height over all, in.		35⅜	29½	23¼	17⅜
Width, in.......		4½	4½	4½	4½

Radiators tapped 2 inches and bushed to specified sizes.

Wall Brackets furnished upon order.

*Upper tappings furnished only when specified.

†Allow ⅛ inch for each bushing in estimating length of radiators.

For Steam and Water

These Radiators are specially designed for hospitals and all buildings where sanitary demands require surfaces that can be easily cleaned.

Hospital Radiators are furnished in either 4½″ (standard) or 6″ legs without extra charge. Manufactured in one-column, two-column and three-column sizes. Widths of sections are the same as those of standard radiators of the same number of columns.

LINCOLN HOSPITAL RADIATORS

TWO-COLUMN

For Steam and Water

Number of Sections	*Length, 3 In. per Section	Heating Surface—Square Feet					
		45 In. Height 5 Sq. Ft. per Sec.	38 In. Height 4 Sq. Ft. per Sec.	32 In. Height 3⅓ Sq. Ft. per Sec.	26 In. Height 2⅔ Sq. Ft. per Sec.	23 In. Height 2⅓ Sq. Ft. per Sec.	20 In. Height 2 Sq. Ft. per Sec.
2	6	10	8	6⅔	5⅓	4⅔	4
3	9	15	12	10	8	7	6
4	12	20	16	13⅓	10⅔	9⅓	8
5	15	25	20	16⅔	13⅓	11⅔	10
6	18	30	24	20	16	14	12
7	21	35	28	23⅓	18⅔	16⅓	14
8	24	40	32	26⅔	21⅓	18⅔	16
9	27	45	36	30	24	21	18
10	30	50	40	33⅓	26⅔	23⅓	20
11	33	55	44	36⅔	29⅓	25⅔	22
12	36	60	48	40	32	28	24
13	39	65	52	43⅓	34⅔	30⅓	26
14	42	70	56	46⅔	37⅓	32⅔	28
15	45	75	60	50	40	35	30
16	48	80	64	53⅓	42⅔	37⅓	32
17	51	85	68	56⅔	45⅓	39⅔	34
18	54	90	72	60	48	42	36
19	57	95	76	63⅓	50⅔	44⅓	38
20	60	100	80	66⅔	53⅓	46⅔	40
21	63	105	84	70	56	49	42
22	66	110	88	73⅓	58⅔	51⅓	44
23	69	115	92	76⅔	61⅓	53⅔	46
24	72	120	96	80	64	56	48
25	75	125	100	83⅓	66⅔	58⅓	50

*This length is net; allow ½″ for each bushing.

All of the above radiators are tapped and bushed as per list on page 123.

NOTE—Lengths of one and three-column radiators are the same as for two-column. Heating surfaces are the same as for regular radiators.

"American" Corto Radiators

Three-Tube

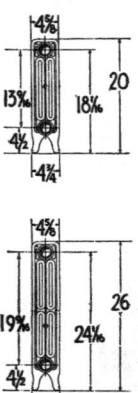

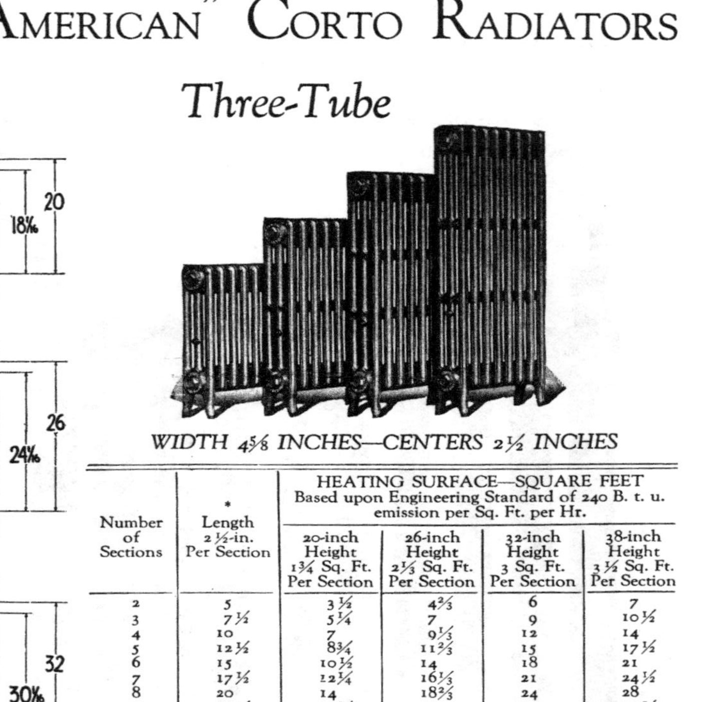

WIDTH 4⅝ INCHES—CENTERS 2½ INCHES

Number of Sections	* Length 2½-in. Per Section	HEATING SURFACE—SQUARE FEET Based upon Engineering Standard of 240 B. t. u. emission per Sq. Ft. per Hr.			
		20-inch Height 1¾ Sq. Ft. Per Section	26-inch Height 2⅓ Sq. Ft. Per Section	32-inch Height 3 Sq. Ft. Per Section	38-inch Height 3½ Sq. Ft. Per Section
2	5	3½	4⅔	6	7
3	7½	5¼	7	9	10½
4	10	7	9⅓	12	14
5	12½	8¾	11⅔	15	17½
6	15	10½	14	18	21
7	17½	12¼	16⅓	21	24½
8	20	14	18⅔	24	28
9	22½	15¾	21	27	31½
10	25	17½	23⅓	30	35
11	27½	19¼	25⅔	33	38½
12	30	21	28	36	42
13	32½	22¾	30⅓	39	45½
14	35	24½	32⅔	42	49
15	37½	26¼	35	45	52½
16	40	28	37⅓	48	56
17	42½	29¾	39⅔	51	59½
18	45	31½	42	54	63
19	47½	33¼	44⅓	57	66½
20	50	35	46⅔	60	70
21	52½	36¾	49	63	73½
22	55	38½	51⅓	66	77
23	57½	40¼	53⅔	69	80½
24	60	42	56	72	84
25	62½	43¾	58⅓	75	87½
26	65	45½	60⅔	78	91
27	67½	47¼	63	81	94½
28	70	49	65⅓	84	98
29	72½	50¾	67⅔	87	101½
30	75	52½	70	90	105

TAPPINGS—1½" top and bottom. Bushed for steam or water as per specifications.

CONNECTIONS—Both steam and water—extra heavy 1½" right and left threaded nipples at top and bottom.

*Add ½" to length for each bushing.

"American" Corto Radiators

Four-Tube

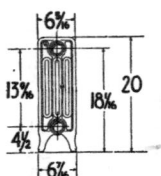

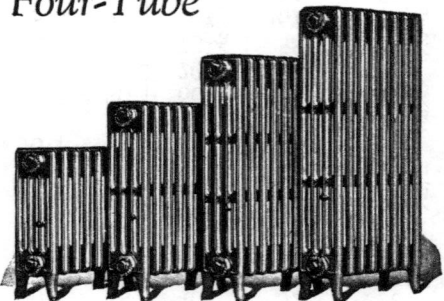

WIDTH 6$\frac{5}{16}$ INCHES—CENTERS 2½ INCHES

Number of Sections	* Length 2½-in. Per Section	HEATING SURFACE—SQUARE FEET Based upon Engineering Standard of 240 B. t. u. emission per Sq. Ft. per Hr.			
		20-inch Height 2¼ Sq. Ft. Per Section	26-inch Height 2¾ Sq. Ft. Per Section	32-inch Height 3½ Sq. Ft. Per Section	38-inch Height 4¼ Sq. Ft. Per Section
2	5	4½	5½	7	8½
3	7½	6¾	8¼	10½	12¾
4	10	9	11	14	17
5	12½	11¼	13¾	17½	21¼
6	15	13½	16½	21	25½
7	17½	15¾	19¼	24½	29¾
8	20	18	22	28	34
9	22½	20¼	24¾	31½	38¼
10	25	22½	27½	35	42½
11	27½	24¾	30¼	38½	46¾
12	30	27	33	42	51
13	32½	29¼	35¾	45½	55¼
14	35	31½	38½	49	59½
15	37½	33¾	41¼	52½	63¾
16	40	36	44	56	68
17	42½	38¼	46¾	59½	72¼
18	45	40½	49½	63	76½
19	47½	42¾	52¼	66½	80¾
20	50	45	55	70	85
21	52½	47¼	57¾	73½	89¼
22	55	49½	60½	77	93½
23	57½	51¾	63¼	80½	97¾
24	60	54	66	84	102
25	62½	56¼	68¾	87½	106¼
26	65	58½	71½	91	110½
27	67½	60¾	74¼	94½	114¾
28	70	63	77	98	119
29	72½	65¼	79¾	101½	123¼
30	75	67½	82½	105	127½

TAPPINGS—1½" top and bottom. Bushed for steam or water as per specifications.

CONNECTIONS—Both steam and water—extra heavy 1½" right and left threaded nipples at top and bottom.

*Add ½" to length for each bushing.

"American" Corto Radiators

Five-Tube

WIDTH 8 INCHES—CENTERS 2½ INCHES

Number of Sections	* Length 2½-in. Per Section	HEATING SURFACE—SQUARE FEET Based upon Engineering Standard of 240 B. t. u. emission per Sq. Ft. per Hr. — 20-inch Height 2⅔ Sq. Ft. Per Section	26-inch Height 3½ Sq. Ft. Per Section	32-inch Height 4⅓ Sq. Ft. Per Section	38-inch Height 5 Sq. Ft. Per Section
2	5	5⅓	7	8⅔	10
3	7½	8	10½	13	15
4	10	10⅔	14	17⅓	20
5	12½	13⅓	17½	21⅔	25
6	15	16	21	26	30
7	17½	18⅔	24½	30⅓	35
8	20	21⅓	28	34⅔	40
9	22½	24	31½	39	45
10	25	26⅔	35	43⅓	50
11	27½	29⅓	38½	47⅔	55
12	30	32	42	52	60
13	32½	34⅔	45½	56⅓	65
14	35	37⅓	49	60⅔	70
15	37½	40	52½	65	75
16	40	42⅔	56	69⅓	80
17	42½	45⅓	59½	73⅔	85
18	45	48	63	78	90
19	47½	50⅔	66½	82⅓	95
20	50	53⅓	70	86⅔	100
21	52½	56	73½	91	105
22	55	58⅔	77	95⅓	110
23	57½	61⅓	80½	99⅔	115
24	60	64	84	104	120
25	62½	66⅔	87½	108⅓	125
26	65	69⅓	91	112⅔	130
27	67½	72	94½	117	135
28	70	74⅔	98	121⅓	140
29	72½	77⅓	101½	125⅔	145
30	75	80	105	130	150

TAPPINGS—1½" top and bottom. Bushed for steam or water as per specifications.

CONNECTIONS—Both steam and water—extra heavy 1½" right and left threaded nipples at top and bottom.

*Add ½" to length for each bushing.

"American" Corto Radiators

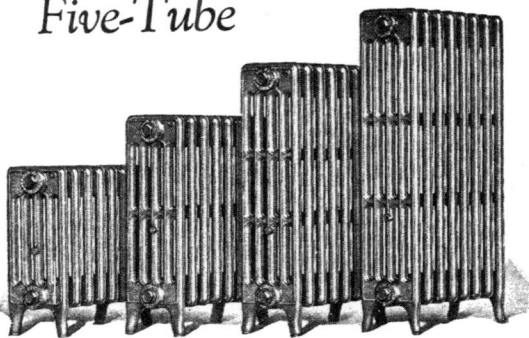

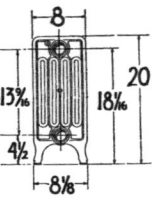

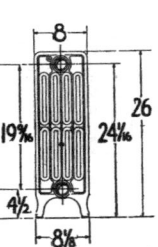

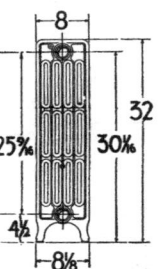

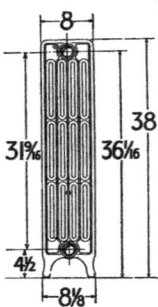

Six-Tube

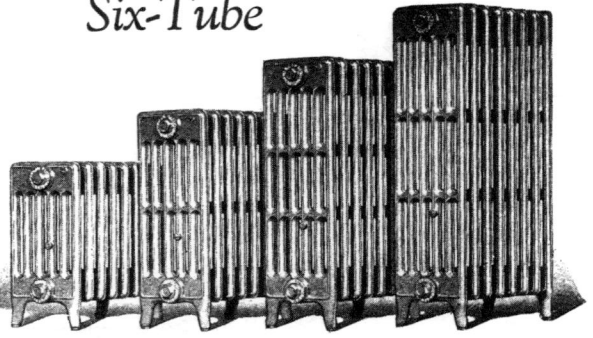

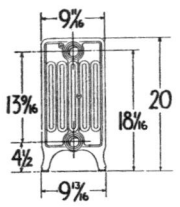

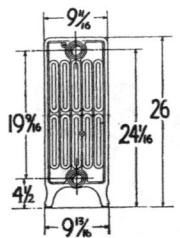

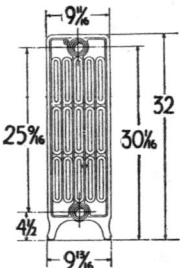

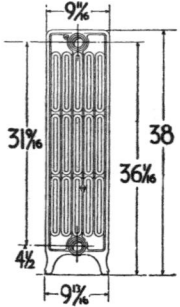

WIDTH 9 11/16 INCHES—CENTERS 2½ INCHES

Number of Sections	* Length 2½-in. Per Section	HEATING SURFACE—SQUARE FEET Based upon Engineering Standard of 240 B. t. u. emission per Sq. Ft. per Hr. — 20-inch Height 3 Sq. Ft. Per Section	26-inch Height 4 Sq. Ft. Per Section	32-inch Height 5 Sq. Ft. Per Section	38-inch Height 6 Sq. Ft. Per Section
2	5	6	8	10	12
3	7½	9	12	15	18
4	10	12	16	20	24
5	12½	15	20	25	30
6	15	18	24	30	36
7	17½	21	28	35	42
8	20	24	32	40	48
9	22½	27	36	45	54
10	25	30	40	50	60
11	27½	33	44	55	66
12	30	36	48	60	72
13	32½	39	52	65	78
14	35	42	56	70	84
15	37½	45	60	75	90
16	40	48	64	80	96
17	42½	51	68	85	102
18	45	54	72	90	108
19	47½	57	76	95	114
20	50	60	80	100	120
21	52½	63	84	105	126
22	55	66	88	110	132
23	57½	69	92	115	138
24	60	72	96	120	144
25	62½	75	100	125	150
26	65	78	104	130	156
27	67½	81	108	135	162
28	70	84	112	140	168
29	72½	87	116	145	174
30	75	90	120	150	180

TAPPINGS—1½" top and bottom. Bushed for steam or water as per specifications.

CONNECTIONS—Both steam and water—extra heavy 1½" right and left threaded nipples at top and bottom.

*Add ½" to length for each bushing.

"American" Corto Window Radiators

Seven-Tube

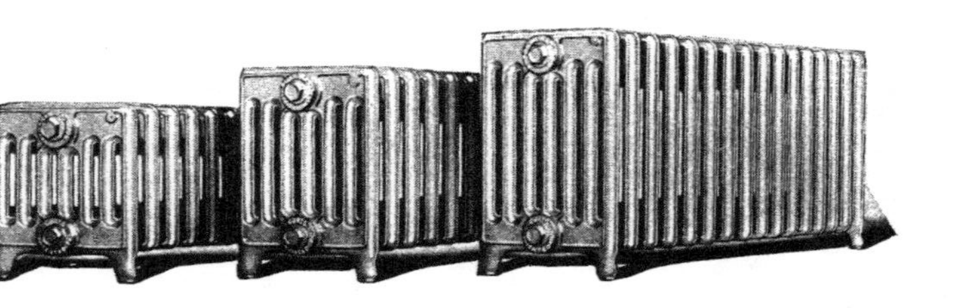

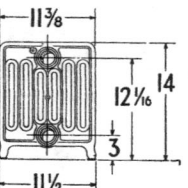

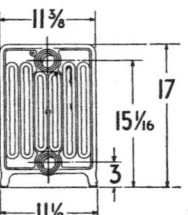

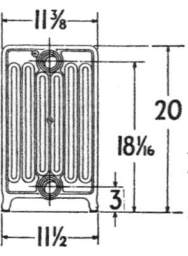

WIDTH 11⅜ INCHES—CENTERS 2½ INCHES

Number of Sections	* Length 2½ in. Per Section	HEATING SURFACE—SQUARE FEET Based upon Engineering Standard of 240 B. t. u. emission per Sq. Ft. per Hr.		
		14-inch Height 2½ Sq. Ft. Per Section	17-inch Height 3 Sq. Ft. Per Section	20-inch Height 3⅔ Sq. Ft. Per Section
2	5	5	6	7⅓
3	7½	7½	9	11
4	10	10	12	14⅔
5	12½	12½	15	18⅓
6	15	15	18	22
7	17½	17½	21	25⅔
8	20	20	24	29⅓
9	22½	22½	27	33
10	25	25	30	36⅔
11	27½	27½	33	40⅓
12	30	30	36	44
13	32½	32½	39	47⅔
14	35	35	42	51⅓
15	37½	37½	45	55
16	40	40	48	58⅔
17	42½	42½	51	62⅓
18	45	45	54	66
19	47½	47½	57	69⅔
20	50	50	60	73⅓
21	52½	52½	63	77
22	55	55	66	80⅔
23	57½	57½	69	84⅓
24	60	60	72	88
25	62½	62½	75	91⅔
26	65	65	78	95⅓
27	67½	67½	81	99
28	70	70	84	102⅔
29	72½	72½	87	106⅓
30	75	75	90	110

TAPPINGS—1½″ top and bottom. Bushed for steam or water as per specifications.

CONNECTIONS—Both steam and water—extra heavy 1½″ right and left threaded nipples at top and bottom.

*Add ½″ to length for each bushing.

WALL RADIATORS

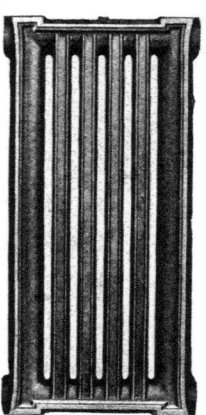

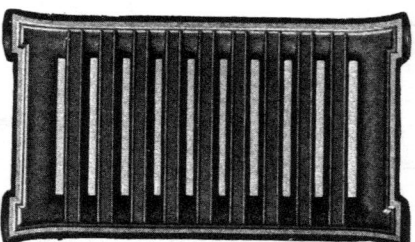

WHEREVER conditions demand maximum heating results from radiators confined in a limited space, as in factory work shops, loft buildings, storehouses, garages, lobbies, corridors, stairways, bath rooms, etc., etc., American Peerless Wall Radiators will render especially desirable service.

These radiators are made up of sections in a wide variety of sizes, with provisions for numerous groupings; and may therefore be assembled to meet any structural condition, fitting into restricted spaces of practically any size or shape, under windows or between them, on walls, ceilings or in skylights.

RATING AND MEASUREMENT OF SECTIONS

Number of Sections	Height Inches	Length or Width Inches	Thickness Inches	Thickness (with bracket) Inches	Heating Surface Sq. Ft.
5-A	13 5/16	16⅝	2⅞	3½	5
7-A	13 5/16	21⅞	2⅞	3½	7
7-B	21⅞	13 5/16	3 1/16	3 11/16	7
9-A	13 5/16	29 1/16	2⅞	3½	9
9-B	29 1/16	13 5/16	3 1/16	3 11/16	9

RADIANTRIM - model 8
dimensions

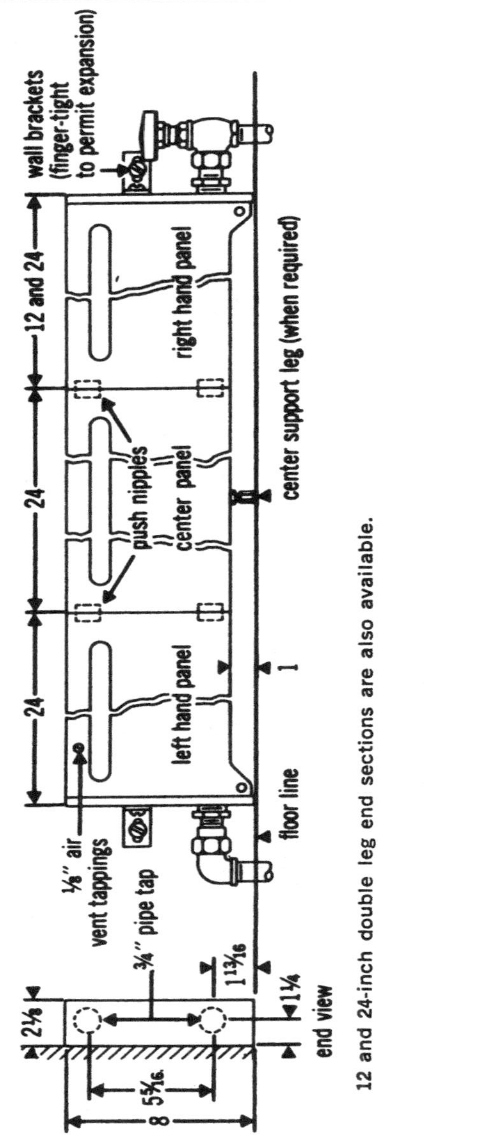

12 and 24-inch double leg end sections are also available.

RADIANTRIM - model 8
ratings and data

panel length * number of lineal feet	output in sq ft water or steam (215°) †	capacities—Mbh—thousand Btu per hour								
		hot water—average water temperature—°F.								steam
		150°	160°	170°	180°	190°	200°	210°	220°	215°F
		heat emission Btu per sq ft for above temperatures								
		108	127	147	166	188	206	228	252	240
1	2.6	.3	.3	.4	.4	.5	.5	.6	.7	.6
2	5.1	.6	.7	.8	.9	1.0	1.1	1.2	1.3	1.2
3	7.7	.8	1.0	1.1	1.3	1.4	1.6	1.8	1.9	1.8
4	10.2	1.1	1.3	1.5	1.7	1.9	2.1	2.3	2.6	2.5
5	12.8	1.4	1.6	1.9	2.1	2.4	2.6	2.9	3.2	3.1
6	15.4	1.7	2.0	2.3	2.5	2.9	3.2	3.5	3.9	3.7
7	17.9	1.9	2.3	2.6	3.0	3.4	3.7	4.1	4.6	4.3
8	20.5	2.2	2.6	3.0	3.4	3.8	4.2	4.7	5.2	4.9
9	23.0	2.5	2.9	3.4	3.8	4.3	4.8	5.3	5.8	5.5
10	25.6	2.8	3.3	3.8	4.2	4.8	5.3	5.8	6.5	6.1
11	28.2	3.0	3.6	4.1	4.7	5.3	5.8	6.4	7.1	6.8
12	30.7	3.3	3.9	4.5	5.1	5.8	6.3	7.0	7.7	7.4
13	33.3	3.6	4.2	4.9	5.5	6.2	6.9	7.6	8.4	8.0
14	35.8	3.9	4.6	5.3	5.9	6.7	7.4	8.2	9.0	8.6
15	38.4	4.1	4.9	5.6	6.4	7.2	7.9	8.8	9.7	9.2
16	41.0	4.4	5.2	6.0	6.8	7.7	8.5	9.3	10.3	9.8
17	43.5	4.7	5.5	6.4	7.2	8.1	9.0	9.9	11.0	10.4
18	46.1	5.0	5.9	6.8	7.6	8.6	9.5	10.5	11.6	11.1
19	48.6	5.2	6.2	7.1	8.1	9.1	10.0	11.1	12.3	11.7
20	51.2	5.5	6.5	7.5	8.5	9.6	10.6	11.7	12.9	12.3
21	53.8	5.8	6.8	7.9	8.9	10.1	11.1	12.3	13.6	12.9
22	56.3	6.1	7.2	8.3	9.3	10.5	11.6	12.8	14.2	13.5
23	58.9	6.4	7.5	8.6	9.8	11.0	12.1	13.4	14.8	14.1
24	61.4	6.6	7.8	9.0	10.2	11.5	12.7	14.0	15.5	14.7
25	64.0	6.9	8.1	9.4	10.6	12.0	13.2	14.6	16.1	15.4
26	66.6	7.2	8.5	9.8	11.0	12.5	13.7	15.2	16.8	16.0
27	69.1	7.5	8.8	10.1	11.5	12.9	14.3	15.7	17.4	16.6
28	71.7	7.7	9.1	10.5	11.9	13.4	14.8	16.3	18.1	17.2
29	74.2	8.0	9.4	10.9	12.3	13.9	15.3	16.9	18.7	17.8
30	76.8	8.3	9.8	11.3	12.7	14.4	15.8	17.5	19.4	18.4

*Add 1/2 inch to length for each bushing. Also, add 5½ inches to length for each valve enclosure, 4¼ inches for each inverted corner cover and 1¾ inches for each projecting cover.
†Ratings are 2.56 sq. ft. per lineal ft., based on 240 Btu emission per square foot per hour for steam or average hot water temp of 215°F.

NOTE:
Ratings are shown in Btu to permit easy selection of Radiantrim Panels. The following simple formula applies: First calculate the heat loss of the room in Btu's, using any recognized and approved method. Then locate the heat loss in vertical column under desired "Average Water Temperatures" or "Steam" in rating table above. Following a line horizontally to left, find the number of lineal feet in first vertical column. For example, determine the number of panels for a job, assuming the heat loss of room to be 5000 Btu, with an average water temperature of 180° to be maintained. In the table locate 5.1 (5100 Btu expressed in Mbh) in the column under 180°. On the same line, note the figure in first column (Panel Length) at left. It is 12, indicating 12 lineal feet of panels are required. If the average water temperature is to be 200°, 10 lineal feet will be needed.

SUNRAD radiators dimensions

with legs

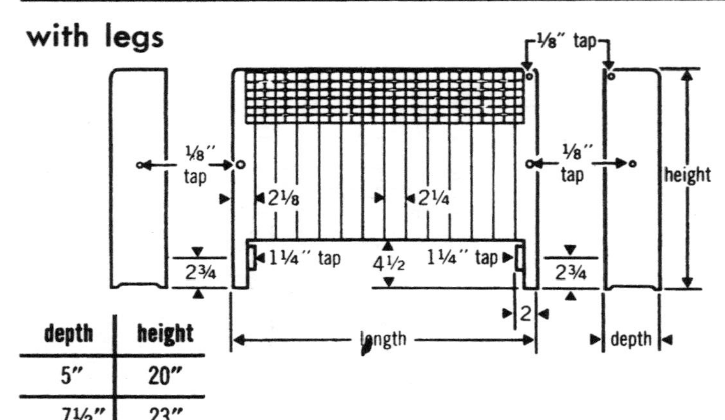

depth	height
5″	20″
7½″	23″

CONNECTIONS—Both steam and water extra heavy 1″ [on 5″ x 20″] and 1¼″ [on 7½″ x 23″] malleable nipples at top and bottom. End sections regularly supplied with 1¼″ inside bottom tappings, and on special order 1½″ outside bottom and 1¼″ outside top tappings, bushed if so specified. Order must specify right or left supply.

without legs

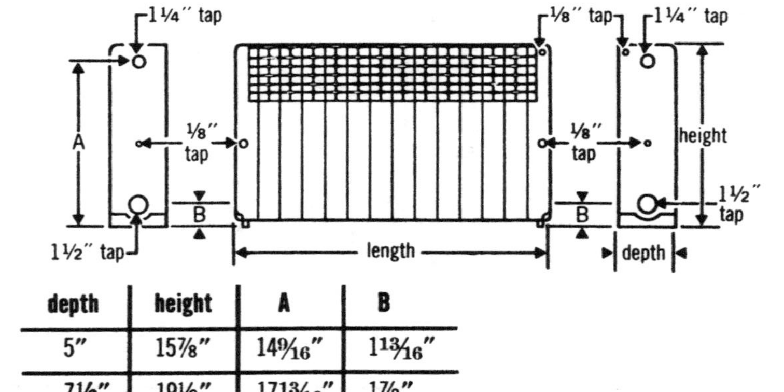

depth	height	A	B
5″	15⅞″	14⁹⁄₁₆″	1¹³⁄₁₆″
7½″	19⅛″	17¹³⁄₁₆″	1⅞″

CONNECTIONS—Both steam and water extra heavy 1″ [on 5″ x 20″] and 1¼″ [on 7½″ x 23″] malleable nipples at top and bottom. End sections regularly supplied with 1½″ outside bottom and 1¼″ outside top tappings, bushed if so specified.

SUNRAD radiators ratings

Number of Sections	Radiator Length (inches)●	Type M5 x 20 2.25 sq ft per section ■	Type M7½ x 23 3.4 sq ft per section ■
4	8¾	9.0	13.6
6	13¼	13.5	20.4
8	17¾	18.0	27.2
10	22¼	22.5	34.0
12	26¾	27.0	40.8
14	31¼	31.5	47.6
16	35¾	36.0	54.4
18	40¼	40.5	61.2
20	44¾	45.0	68.0
22	49¼	49.5	74.8
24	53¾	54.0	81.6
26	58¼	58.5	88.4
28	62¾	63.0	95.2
30	67¼	67.5	102.0
31	69½	69.75	105.4
33	74	74.25	112.2
35	78½	78.75	119.0
37	83	83.25	125.8
39	87½	87.75	132.6
41	92	92.25	139.4
43	96½	96.75	146.2
45	101	101.25	153.0

● Add approximately ¼″ to overall length due to slightly heavier end sections and to provide for expansion when recessed.

■ Ratings shown are for free standing and wall-hung radiation. For recessed installations, before selecting Sunrad, add 5% to room radiation requirements if radiator will have ¾″ air space on top and sides, and ½″ at back; and 15% if radiator will be tightly recessed, without any clearance on top and sides, but with ½″ space at back.

Sunrad Radiators are sold only in even number of sections up to a maximum of 30 sections, and in an odd number of sections from 31 to 45 sections.

For Sunrad Radiators larger than 30 sections, a center leg section will be installed on center line of assembly.

average water temperature in radiator	220	215	210	200	190	180	170	160	150
heat emission Btu per sq ft	230	220	210	195	180	160	145	128	112

AMERICAN RADIATORS

NEW MURRAY RADIATORS

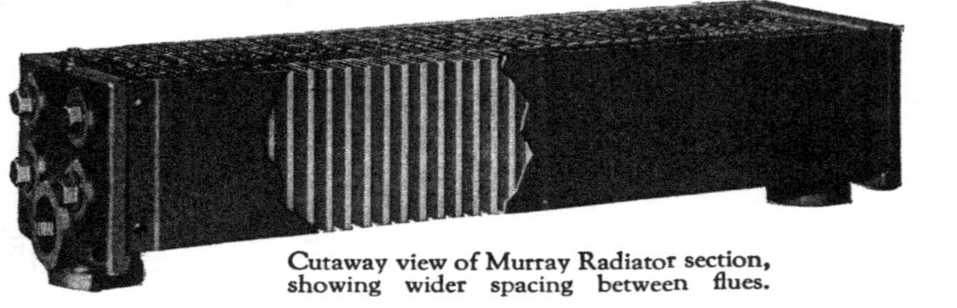
Cutaway view of Murray Radiator section, showing wider spacing between flues.

In the field of non-ferrous type radiation, the New Murray Radiator has achieved outstanding success. Years of designing and testing in our laboratories have placed it on a high level of service in point of efficient and hygienic operation.

The New Murray Radiator is made in six widths — No. 2, 2⅜″ wide; No. 3, 3¾″ wide; No. 5, 5″ wide; No. 6, 6⅜″ wide; No. 7, 7¾″ wide; and No. 10, 10⅜″ wide.

It is equally well adapted for one or two pipe steam, vapor or hot water systems and, when installed with Arco Enclosures, combines high heating efficiency with attractive appearance.

Arco Enclosures similar to those shown for the Arco Convector on pages 44-59, are made specially for New Murray Radiators. Correctly designed and proportioned, they assure ease of installation and utmost efficiency.

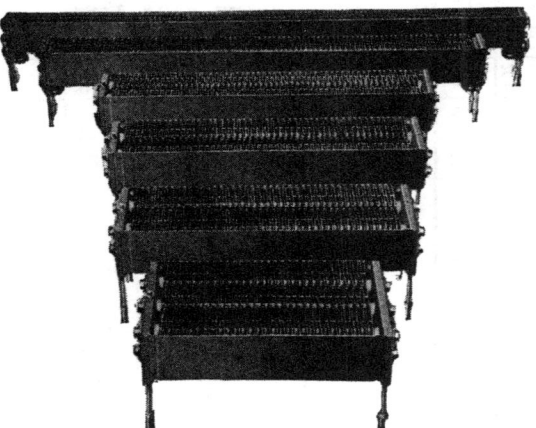

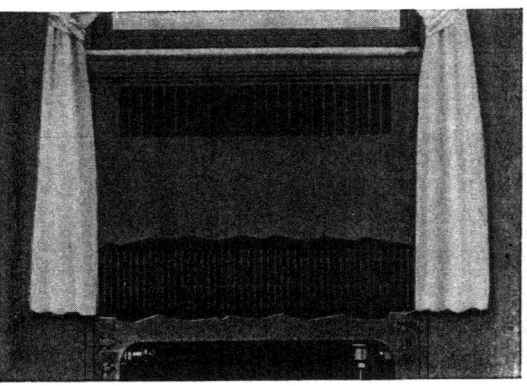

AMERICAN RADIATORS

NEW MURRAY RADIATOR

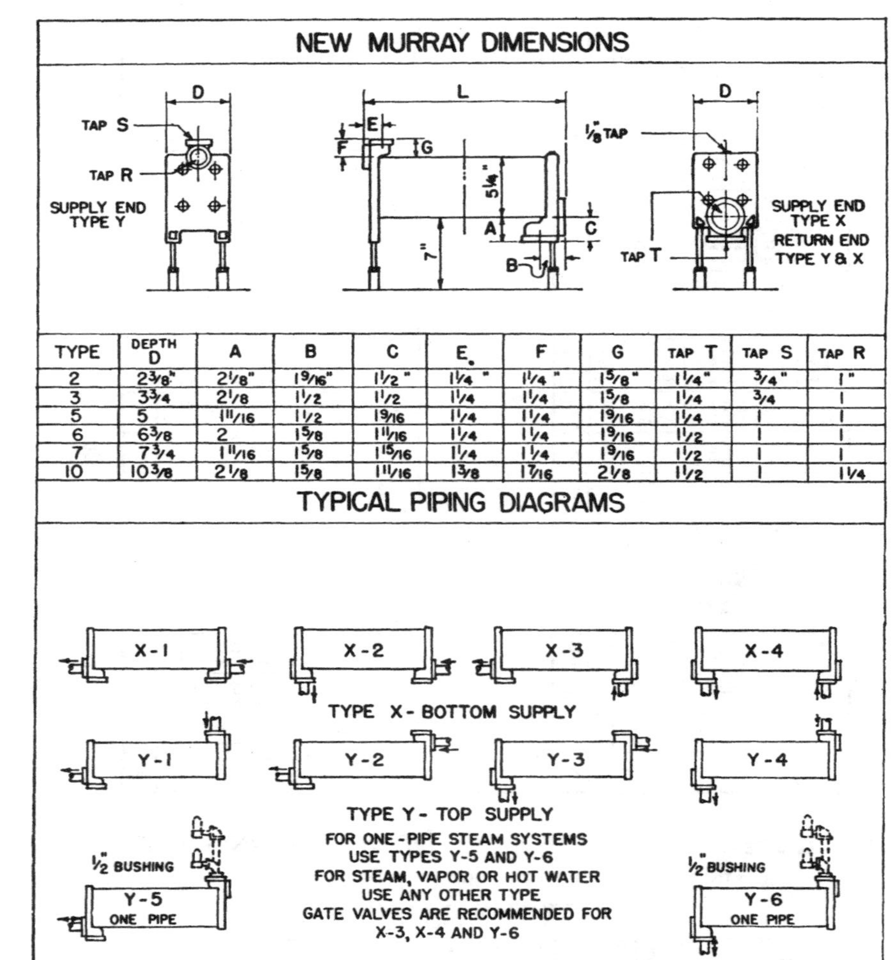

TYPE	DEPTH D	A	B	C	E	F	G	TAP T	TAP S	TAP R
2	2⅜″	2⅛″	1 9/16″	1½″	1¼″	1¼″	1⅝″	1¼″	¾″	1″
3	3¾	2⅛	1½	1½	1¼	1¼	1⅝	1¼	¾	1
5	5	1 11/16	1½	1 9/16	1¼	1¼	1 9/16	1¼	1	1
6	6⅜	2	1⅝	1 11/16	1¼	1¼	1 9/16	1½	1	1
7	7¾	1 11/16	1⅝	1 15/16	1¼	1¼	1 9/16	1½	1	1
10	10⅜	2⅛	1⅝	1 11/16	1⅜	1 7/16	2⅛	1½	1	1¼

Add ½″ to "L" for each plug or bushing as hexagon head plugs are furnished in side tappings.

AMERICAN RADIATORS

NEW MURRAY STEAM AND WATER RADIATOR RATINGS

*Output in Sq. Ft. Equivalent Direct Radiation

Radiator No. 2 ($2\frac{3}{8}''$ Wide)

Length in Inches	Unit No.	18	20	22	24	26	29	32	35	38	42	47	57	67
Enclosure Height Type "W"		13	15	17	19	21	24	27	30	33				
12½	212	5.9	6.1	6.3	6.4	6.6	6.8	6.9	7.1	7.2	7.3	7.4	7.6	7.7
15	215	7.2	7.5	7.7	7.8	8.0	8.3	8.5	8.6	8.8	8.9	9.0	9.2	9.3
17½	217	8.5	8.8	9.1	9.3	9.5	9.8	10.0	10.2	10.4	10.5	10.7	10.9	11.0
20	220	9.9	10.2	10.5	10.7	11.0	11.3	11.6	11.8	12.0	12.2	12.3	12.5	12.7
22½	222	11.2	11.6	11.9	12.2	12.4	12.8	13.1	13.3	13.5	13.8	14.0	14.2	14.4
25	225	12.5	13.0	13.3	13.6	13.9	14.3	14.6	15.0	15.2	15.4	15.6	16.0	16.3
27½	227	13.9	14.3	14.7	15.1	15.4	15.8	16.2	16.5	16.8	17.1	17.3	17.6	17.8
30	230	15.2	15.7	16.2	16.5	16.8	17.3	17.7	18.0	18.4	18.7	18.9	19.3	19.5
32½	232	16.5	17.1	17.6	18.0	18.3	18.8	19.3	19.6	20.0	20.3	20.6	21.0	21.2
35	235	17.8	18.4	18.9	19.4	19.7	20.2	20.8	21.2	21.6	21.9	22.2	22.7	22.9
37½	237	19.2	19.8	20.3	20.8	21.2	21.8	22.4	22.8	23.2	23.6	23.9	24.4	24.6
40	240	20.5	21.1	21.7	22.2	22.7	23.3	23.9	24.3	24.8	25.2	25.5	26.0	26.3
42½	242	21.8	22.5	23.1	23.7	24.2	24.8	25.5	25.9	26.4	26.8	27.2	27.7	28.0
45	245	23.1	23.8	24.4	25.1	25.6	26.3	27.0	27.5	27.9	28.4	28.8	29.4	29.7
47½	247	24.4	25.2	25.9	26.5	27.1	27.8	28.5	29.1	29.5	30.1	30.5	31.1	31.4
50	250	25.7	26.5	27.3	27.9	28.5	29.3	30.0	30.6	31.1	31.7	32.1	32.7	33.1
52½	252	27.1	27.9	28.7	29.4	30.0	30.9	31.6	32.2	32.7	33.4	33.8	34.4	34.8
55	255	28.4	29.3	30.0	30.8	31.5	32.4	33.1	33.8	34.3	35.0	35.4	36.1	36.4
57½	257	29.7	30.6	31.4	32.2	33.0	33.9	34.7	35.4	36.0	36.6	37.1	37.8	38.1
60	260	31.0	31.9	32.8	33.6	34.4	35.3	36.2	37.0	37.6	38.2	38.7	39.4	39.8

(Column heads 18–67: Enclosure Height Except Type "W".)

Radiator No. 3 ($3\frac{3}{4}''$ Wide)

Length in Inches	Unit No.	18	20	22	24	26	29	32	35	38	42	47	57	67
Enclosure Height Type "W"		13	15	17	19	21	24	27	30	33				
12½	312	8.0	8.3	8.4	8.6	8.8	8.9	9.1	9.3	9.4	9.6	9.7	9.9	10.0
15	315	9.8	10.1	10.3	10.5	10.7	10.9	11.1	11.3	11.6	11.8	11.9	12.1	12.2
17½	317	11.6	11.9	12.2	12.4	12.7	13.0	13.2	13.4	13.6	13.9	14.1	14.3	14.4
20	320	13.4	13.8	14.1	14.4	14.6	15.0	15.3	15.5	15.7	16.0	16.2	16.5	16.6
22½	322	15.2	15.6	16.0	16.3	16.6	16.9	17.3	17.6	17.8	18.0	18.3	18.7	18.9
25	325	16.9	17.4	17.8	18.2	18.5	18.9	19.3	19.6	19.9	20.2	20.5	20.9	21.1
27½	327	18.8	19.3	19.7	20.1	20.5	20.9	21.4	21.7	22.0	22.3	22.7	23.1	23.3
30	330	20.6	21.1	21.6	22.0	22.4	22.9	23.3	23.8	24.1	24.5	24.9	25.3	25.5
32½	332	22.4	23.0	23.5	24.0	24.4	24.9	25.4	25.9	26.3	26.7	27.1	27.5	27.8
35	335	24.2	24.9	25.4	25.9	26.3	26.8	27.4	27.9	28.4	28.8	29.2	29.7	30.0
37½	337	26.0	26.7	27.3	27.8	28.3	28.9	29.5	30.0	30.5	31.0	31.4	31.9	32.2
40	340	27.8	28.5	29.2	29.7	30.3	30.9	31.5	32.0	32.6	33.1	33.6	34.1	34.4
42½	342	29.7	30.4	31.1	31.7	32.2	32.9	33.5	34.1	34.7	35.3	35.7	36.4	36.7
45	345	31.5	32.2	32.9	33.6	34.1	34.9	35.5	36.2	36.8	37.4	37.8	38.6	38.9
47½	347	33.3	34.1	34.8	35.5	36.1	36.9	37.6	38.3	38.9	39.5	40.0	40.8	41.1
50	350	35.1	35.9	36.6	37.4	38.1	38.8	39.6	40.3	40.9	41.6	42.2	43.0	43.3
52½	352	36.9	37.8	38.6	39.5	40.1	40.9	41.7	42.4	43.0	43.8	44.4	45.2	45.6
55	355	38.6	39.6	40.5	41.6	42.0	42.9	43.7	44.4	45.1	45.9	46.5	47.4	47.9
57½	357	40.5	41.5	42.4	43.4	44.0	44.9	45.7	46.5	47.3	48.1	48.7	49.6	50.2
60	360	42.3	43.3	44.2	45.1	45.9	46.9	47.7	48.6	49.5	50.2	50.9	51.8	52.4

(Column heads 18–67: Enclosure Height Except Type "W".)

Radiator Lengths are shown. Standard Enclosures are 1½″ longer.

Above ratings based on front outlet enclosures. For top outlet rating see table on page 43.

*To determine size of radiator divide total heat loss in B.t.u. by 240 for steam at 215°, or by 150 B.t.u. for water at 170°. For other water temperatures, see page 70.

AMERICAN RADIATORS

NEW MURRAY STEAM AND WATER RADIATOR RATINGS

*Output in Sq. Ft. Equivalent Direct Radiation

Radiator No. 5 (5″ Wide)

Length in Inches	Unit No.	18	20	22	24	26	29	32	35	38	42	47	57	67
Enclosure Height Type "W"		13	15	17	19	21	24	27	30	33				
12½	512	11.0	11.2	11.4	11.7	11.9	12.1	12.3	12.5	12.8	12.9	13.1	13.4	13.6
15	515	13.5	13.9	14.1	14.4	14.6	14.9	15.2	15.4	15.6	15.8	16.1	16.4	16.7
17½	517	16.0	16.4	16.7	17.1	17.3	17.6	17.9	18.3	18.5	18.7	19.0	19.6	19.8
20	520	18.5	18.9	19.4	19.7	20.0	20.4	20.7	21.0	21.4	21.7	22.0	22.4	22.9
22½	522	21.0	21.5	21.9	22.3	22.7	23.1	23.5	23.9	24.2	24.5	24.9	25.4	26.0
25	525	23.4	24.0	24.5	25.0	25.4	25.9	26.3	26.7	27.1	27.4	27.8	28.4	29.0
27½	527	26.0	26.6	27.2	27.6	28.2	28.8	29.1	29.6	29.9	30.4	30.8	31.4	32.1
30	530	28.4	29.2	29.7	30.3	30.8	31.5	31.9	32.4	32.8	33.2	33.8	34.5	35.2
32½	532	30.9	31.7	32.4	32.9	33.5	34.2	34.7	35.2	35.7	36.1	36.7	37.6	38.3
35	535	33.4	34.2	35.0	35.5	36.2	36.9	37.5	38.0	38.5	39.0	39.6	40.6	41.4
37½	537	36.0	36.8	37.7	38.3	38.9	39.7	40.3	40.8	41.4	42.0	42.6	43.6	44.5
40	540	38.5	39.4	40.3	41.0	41.6	42.4	43.0	43.6	44.2	44.9	45.5	46.5	47.5
42½	542	41.1	42.0	42.9	43.6	44.3	45.2	45.8	46.5	47.1	47.8	48.5	49.5	50.6
45	545	43.6	44.6	45.4	46.2	47.0	47.9	48.6	49.3	50.0	50.6	51.5	52.5	53.6
47½	547	46.1	47.1	48.0	48.9	49.7	50.7	51.4	52.2	52.9	53.5	54.4	55.6	56.7
50	550	48.5	49.6	50.6	51.5	52.4	53.4	54.2	55.0	55.8	56.4	57.3	58.6	59.8
52½	552	51.0	52.2	53.2	54.2	55.1	56.2	57.0	57.8	58.7	59.4	60.2	61.7	62.9
55	555	53.5	54.7	55.8	56.8	57.8	58.9	59.7	60.6	61.5	62.3	63.1	64.7	66.0
57½	557	56.0	57.2	58.4	59.4	60.5	61.7	62.5	63.5	64.4	65.2	66.1	67.7	69.1
60	560	58.5	59.7	61.0	62.0	63.1	64.4	65.3	66.3	67.2	68.0	69.0	70.7	72.2

(Column heads 18–67: Enclosure Height Except Type "W".)

Radiator No. 6 ($6\frac{3}{8}''$ Wide)

Length in Inches	Unit No.	18	20	22	24	26	29	32	35	38	42	47	57	67
Enclosure Height Type "W"		13	15	17	19	21	24	27	30	33				
12½	612	13.3	13.6	13.9	14.1	14.3	14.5	14.7	15.0	15.2	15.4	15.6	16.1	16.3
15	615	16.3	16.7	17.1	17.3	17.5	17.8	18.2	18.4	18.6	18.8	19.1	19.7	19.9
17½	617	19.3	19.8	20.1	20.5	20.7	21.1	21.5	21.8	22.0	22.3	22.7	23.2	23.7
20	620	22.4	22.9	23.3	23.7	24.0	24.4	24.9	25.2	25.5	25.9	26.2	26.8	27.3
22½	622	25.5	26.0	26.4	26.8	27.2	27.7	28.2	28.6	28.8	29.3	29.7	30.5	31.0
25	625	28.5	29.0	29.6	30.0	30.5	31.0	31.5	32.0	32.4	32.8	33.2	34.1	34.6
27½	627	31.6	32.2	32.7	33.2	33.7	34.3	35.0	35.3	35.8	36.2	36.7	37.8	38.4
30	630	34.7	35.3	35.8	36.4	37.0	37.6	38.1	38.8	39.2	39.7	40.4	41.4	42.1
32½	632	37.7	38.4	39.0	39.6	40.2	40.9	41.5	42.2	42.7	43.2	43.9	45.0	45.8
35	635	40.7	41.5	42.1	42.8	43.4	44.2	44.9	45.5	46.1	46.6	47.3	48.5	49.5
37½	637	43.7	44.6	45.3	46.0	46.7	47.5	48.4	49.0	49.6	50.1	50.8	52.1	53.2
40	640	46.7	47.6	48.4	49.2	49.9	50.8	51.6	52.4	53.0	53.6	54.3	55.7	56.9
42½	642	49.8	50.7	51.6	52.4	53.1	54.1	55.0	55.8	56.4	57.1	57.9	59.4	60.6
45	645	52.8	53.8	54.7	55.6	56.3	57.4	58.3	59.2	59.8	60.5	61.4	63.0	64.2
47½	647	55.9	56.9	57.9	58.8	59.6	60.7	61.7	62.6	63.3	64.0	65.0	66.6	67.9
50	650	59.0	60.0	61.0	62.0	62.8	64.0	65.0	65.9	66.7	67.5	68.5	70.2	71.6
52½	652	62.0	63.1	64.1	65.2	66.1	67.3	68.4	69.3	70.2	71.0	72.0	73.8	75.3
55	655	65.0	66.2	67.2	68.3	69.3	70.5	71.7	72.7	73.6	74.5	75.5	77.4	78.9
57½	657	68.1	69.3	70.4	71.5	72.5	73.8	75.0	76.1	77.0	78.0	79.1	81.0	82.7
60	660	71.1	72.4	73.5	74.6	75.7	77.1	78.3	79.4	80.4	81.4	82.6	84.5	86.4

(Column heads 18–67: Enclosure Height Except Type "W".)

Above ratings based on front outlet enclosures. For top outlet rating see table on page 43.

*To determine size of radiator divide total heat loss in B.t.u. by 240 for steam at 215° or by 150 B.t.u. for water at 170°. For other water temperatures, see page 70.

AMERICAN RADIATORS

NEW MURRAY STEAM AND WATER RADIATOR RATINGS

*Output in Sq. Ft. Equivalent Direct Radiation

Radiator No. 7 ($7\frac{3}{4}''$ Wide)

Type "W" Enclosure Height	Enclosure Height Except Type "W"	12½	15	17½	20	22½	25	27½	30	32½	35	37½	40	42½	45	47½	50	52½	55	57½	60
	Unit No.	712	715	717	720	722	725	727	730	732	735	737	740	742	745	747	750	752	755	757	760
15	20	15.3	18.8	22.2	25.7	29.3	32.7	36.2	39.7	43.2	46.6	50.1	53.6	57.1	60.5	64.0	67.4	70.9	74.4	77.9	81.4
17	22	15.6	19.1	22.6	26.3	29.9	33.3	36.9	40.4	44.0	47.5	51.1	54.6	58.1	61.6	65.2	68.8	72.3	75.8	79.4	83.0
19	24	16.0	19.5	23.1	26.7	30.3	33.9	37.5	41.0	44.7	48.3	51.9	55.4	59.0	62.6	66.3	69.9	73.5	77.0	80.7	84.3
21	26	16.2	19.8	23.4	27.1	30.7	34.3	38.1	41.7	45.4	49.0	52.6	56.2	59.9	63.6	67.2	70.8	74.5	78.1	81.8	85.5
24	29	16.5	20.2	23.9	27.6	31.4	35.1	38.8	42.5	46.3	50.0	53.7	57.3	61.1	64.8	68.8	72.7	76.2	79.6	83.4	87.1
27	32	16.7	20.6	24.3	28.2	31.9	35.8	39.5	43.2	47.0	50.8	54.6	58.4	62.2	65.9	69.7	73.5	77.3	81.1	84.9	88.6
30	35	17.1	20.9	24.8	28.6	32.5	36.3	40.2	44.0	47.9	51.7	55.6	59.4	63.2	67.0	70.9	74.7	78.6	82.4	86.2	90.0
33	38	17.3	21.2	25.1	28.9	32.9	36.9	40.7	44.6	48.5	52.4	56.3	60.2	64.1	68.0	71.9	75.8	79.7	83.6	87.5	91.4
—	42	17.6	21.6	25.5	29.5	33.4	37.4	41.4	45.3	49.3	53.3	57.3	61.2	65.2	69.1	73.1	77.1	81.1	85.0	89.0	93.0
—	47	17.9	22.0	26.0	30.0	34.1	38.1	42.2	46.2	50.2	54.2	58.2	62.2	66.4	70.5	74.5	78.5	82.6	86.7	90.7	94.7
—	57	18.5	22.6	26.8	31.0	35.1	39.3	43.5	47.6	51.8	56.0	60.2	64.4	68.6	72.7	77.1	81.5	85.4	89.3	93.5	97.7
—	67	18.8	23.1	27.4	31.7	35.9	40.2	44.4	48.7	53.0	57.2	61.5	65.8	70.1	74.4	78.6	82.8	87.4	92.0	96.0	100.0

Radiator No. 10 ($10\frac{3}{8}''$ Wide)

Type "W" Enclosure Height	Enclosure Height Except Type "W"	12½	15	17½	20	22½	25	27½	30	32½	35	37½	40	42½	45	47½	50	52½	55	57½	60
	Unit No.	1012	1015	1017	1020	1022	1025	1027	1030	1032	1035	1037	1040	1042	1045	1047	1050	1052	1055	1057	1060
17	22	21.0	25.7	30.5	35.2	39.9	44.6	49.5	54.2	59.0	63.8	68.6	73.3	78.1	82.8	87.6	92.3	97.1	101.9	106.6	111.3
19	24	21.2	25.9	30.7	35.4	40.3	45.0	49.8	54.6	59.4	64.2	69.0	73.7	78.5	83.3	88.1	92.8	97.6	102.4	107.2	112.0
21	26	21.3	26.1	30.8	35.6	40.5	45.3	50.2	54.9	59.7	64.5	69.3	74.1	78.9	83.7	88.6	93.4	98.2	103.0	107.9	112.7
24	29	21.5	26.3	31.2	36.0	40.8	45.8	50.6	55.4	60.2	65.0	69.9	74.8	79.7	84.5	89.4	94.2	99.0	103.8	108.7	113.5
27	32	21.7	26.5	31.5	36.3	41.2	46.1	51.0	55.9	60.8	65.7	70.6	75.5	80.4	85.2	90.1	94.9	99.8	104.7	109.6	114.4
30	35	21.9	26.7	31.7	36.6	41.5	46.4	51.3	56.2	61.2	66.1	71.0	75.9	80.8	85.7	90.7	95.6	100.5	105.4	110.3	115.2
33	38	22.0	27.0	31.9	36.8	41.7	46.6	51.6	56.5	61.5	66.4	71.4	76.3	81.3	86.2	91.2	96.1	101.1	105.9	110.8	115.7
—	42	22.2	27.2	32.1	37.1	42.0	47.0	52.0	57.0	62.0	67.0	72.0	76.9	81.9	86.9	91.9	96.8	101.8	106.7	111.7	116.6
—	47	22.4	27.4	32.4	37.4	42.3	47.4	52.5	57.5	62.5	67.5	72.6	77.6	82.6	87.6	92.6	97.6	102.6	107.5	112.5	117.5
—	57	22.7	27.7	32.8	37.8	42.9	48.0	53.0	58.1	63.2	68.2	73.3	78.3	83.4	88.4	93.6	98.7	103.7	108.7	113.8	118.8
—	67	22.8	27.9	33.0	38.1	43.2	48.2	53.4	58.4	63.5	68.6	73.5	78.8	83.9	88.9	94.0	99.1	104.3	109.4	114.5	119.6

Radiator Lengths are shown. Standard Enclosures are 1½″ longer.

Above ratings based on front outlet enclosures. For top outlet rating see table on **page 43.**

*To determine size of radiator divide total heat loss in B.t.u. by 240 for steam at 215°, or by 150 B.t.u. for water at 170°. For other water temperatures, see page 70

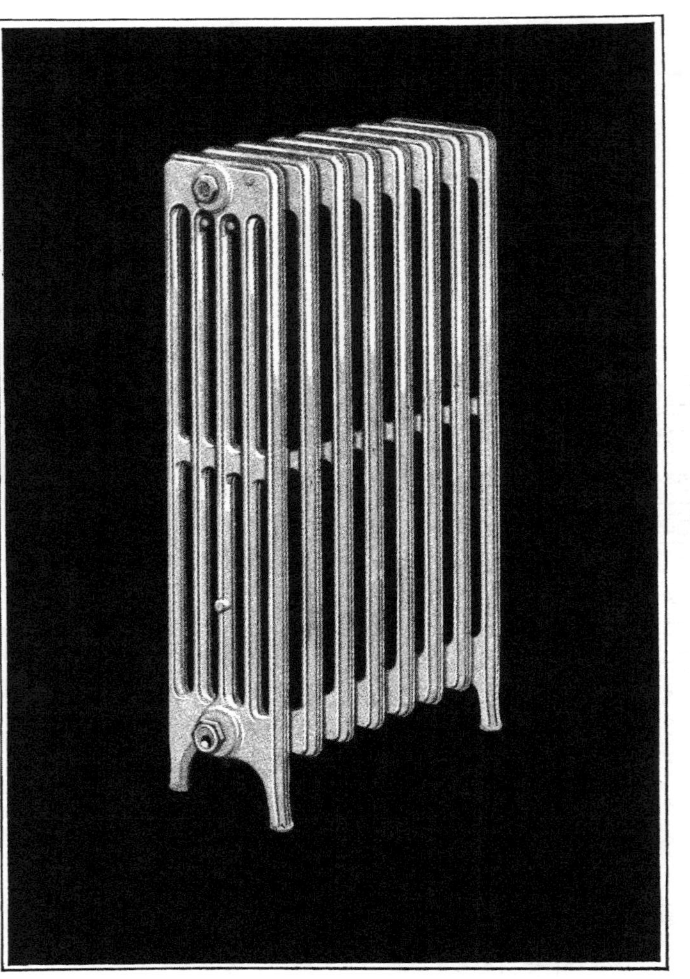

THE CAPITOL

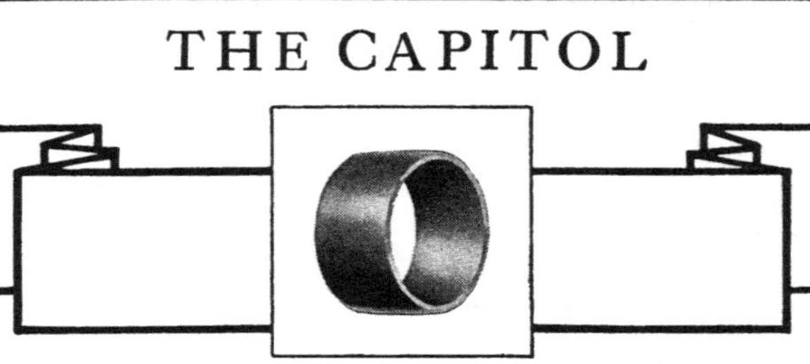

The Radiator Masterpiece

WHAT won for the Capitol such universal acclaim as the Radiator masterpiece?

Its classic beauty and harmonious grace that instantly impressed all observers. Its strength that was the perfected result of unhurried experiment and careful development. Its notable heating ability, approved as superior in tests made by the engineering laboratories of a great university.

Its instant success was a foregone conclusion. For never has heating efficiency been clothed with greater symmetry. In profile or in full view it equally exhibits its classic beauty. Lines that melt in grace, contours of flawless perfection; every detail aids its capacity, not merely for more speedy transmission of heat, but for blending into the decorative scheme of any home without unduly accenting itself.

It has the added advantage of the most approved type of assembly. Extra heavy malleable cast iron push nipples, machined with hair-breadth precision, form a perfect, tight iron-to-iron joint. They need no gaskets, have no threads to rust, are taken apart and assembled with the greatest ease. Unobtrusive connecting rods truss them like a steel bridge into a sturdy unit that cannot be wrenched loose by rack or strain.

Finally, the *standardized* radiator ratings on the following pages fit any standard set of specifications, offering the greater beauty, efficiency, and value of Capitol Radiators without the necessity of refiguring the job.

CAPITOL THREE TUBE

LONG research and study preceded each step in the design of the Capitol radiator. No enthusiasm was permitted to hurry out an immature radiator that might require changing later. Every detail was checked for strength, every line scrutinized for beauty. Extreme narrowness with unusual stability on its feet is the outstanding feature of the Capitol three tube radiator.

CAPITOL THREE TUBE RADIATORS

FOR STEAM OR WATER

No. of Sections	*Length Inches	HEATING SURFACE—SQUARE FEET				
		36-inch Height 3½ Sq. Ft. Per Section	30-inch Height 3 Sq. Ft. Per Section	26-inch Height 2⅓ Sq. Ft. Per Section	23-inch Height 2 Sq. Ft. Per Section	20-inch Height 1¾ Sq. Ft. Per Section
2	5	7	6	4⅔	4	3½
3	7½	10½	9	7	6	5¼
4	10	14	12	9⅓	8	7
5	12½	17½	15	11⅔	10	8¾
6	15	21	18	14	12	10½
7	17½	24½	21	16⅓	14	12¼
8	20	28	24	18⅔	16	14
9	22½	31½	27	21	18	15¾
10	25	35	30	23⅓	20	17½
11	27½	38½	33	25⅔	22	19¼
12	30	42	36	28	24	21
13	32½	45½	39	30⅓	26	22¾
14	35	49	42	32⅔	28	24½
15	37½	52½	45	35	30	26¼
16	40	56	48	37⅓	32	28
17	42½	59½	51	39⅔	34	29¾
18	45	63	54	42	36	31½
19	47½	66½	57	44⅓	38	33¼
20	50	70	60	46⅔	40	35
21	52½	73½	63	49	42	36¾
22	55	77	66	51⅓	44	38½
23	57½	80½	69	53⅔	46	40¼
24	60	84	72	56	48	42
25	62½	87½	75	58⅓	50	43¾

*Allow ½ inch for each bushing in estimating length of radiators. Tappings 1½ inches, top and bottom, bushed as per list on page 16, unless otherwise specified. Furnished with 6 inch legs on special order, or without legs as illustrated on page 12. Special shapes shown on page 14.

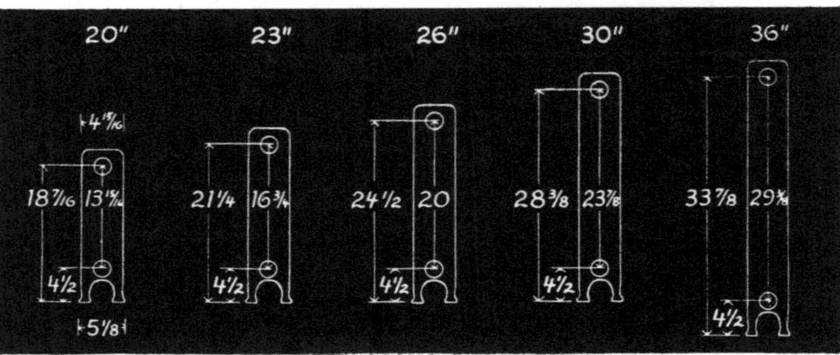

CAPITOL FOUR TUBE

DECORATORS with a feeling for lovely line, engineers who understand heating, both acclaim the new Capitol as the radiator masterpiece. Never has heating efficiency been clothed with greater symmetry. Capitol four tube radiators meet the demand for a maximum of footage where conditions of installation require narrow radiation in a limited wall space.

CAPITOL FOUR TUBE RADIATORS

FOR STEAM OR WATER

No. of Sections	*Length Inches	HEATING SURFACE—SQUARE FEET				
		37-inch Height 4¼ Sq. Ft. Per Section	32-inch Height 3½ Sq. Ft. Per Section	26-inch Height 2¾ Sq. Ft. Per Section	23-inch Height 2½ Sq. Ft. Per Section	20-inch Height 2¼ Sq. Ft. Per Section
2	5	8½	7	5½	5	4½
3	7½	12¾	10½	8¼	7½	6¾
4	10	17	14	11	10	9
5	12½	21¼	17½	13¾	12½	11¼
6	15	25½	21	16½	15	13½
7	17½	29¾	24½	19¼	17½	15¾
8	20	34	28	22	20	18
9	22½	38¼	31½	24¾	22½	20¼
10	25	42½	35	27½	25	22½
11	27½	46¾	38½	30¼	27½	24¾
12	30	51	42	33	30	27
13	32½	55¼	45½	35¾	32½	29¼
14	35	59½	49	38½	35	31½
15	37½	63¾	52½	41¼	37½	33¾
16	40	68	56	44	40	36
17	42½	72¼	59½	46¾	42½	38¼
18	45	76½	63	49½	45	40½
19	47½	80¾	66½	52¼	47½	42¾
20	50	85	70	55	50	45
21	52½	89¼	73½	57¾	52½	47¼
22	55	93½	77	60½	55	49½
23	57½	97¾	80½	63¼	57½	51¾
24	60	102	84	66	60	54
25	62½	106¼	87½	68¾	62½	56¼

*Allow ½ inch for each bushing in estimating length of radiators. Tappings 1½ inches, top and bottom, bushed as per list on page 16, unless otherwise specified. Furnished with 6 inch legs on special order, or without legs as illustrated on page 12. Special shapes shown on page 14.

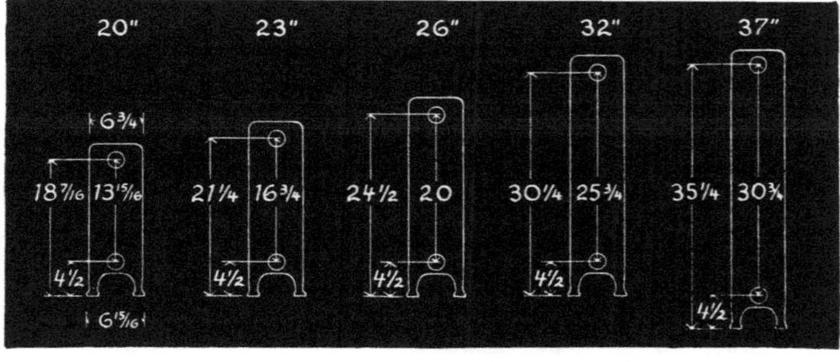

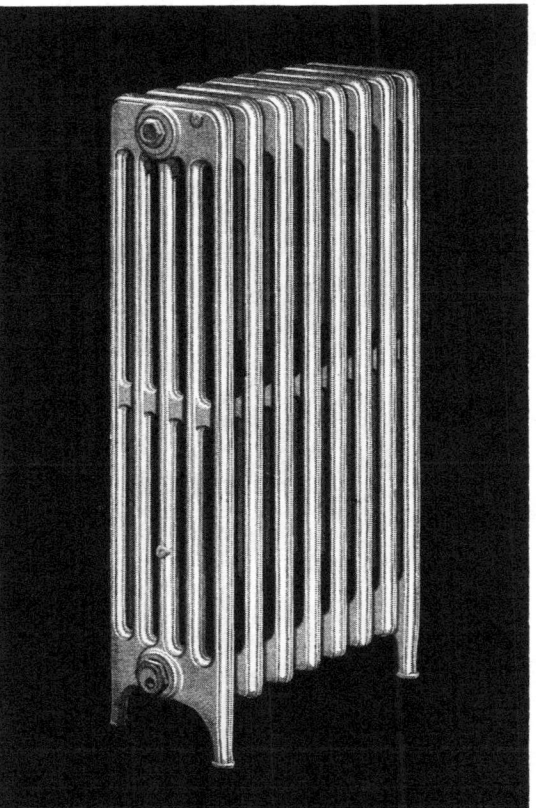

CAPITOL FIVE TUBE

IN our judgment, the Capitol is considered by far the finest and most efficient radiator that we have ever produced. The prime feature of the five tube is the unusual amount of surface per section. This extra surface is obtained without sacrificing efficiency by reducing air passages. Uniform ample air passages are maintained in all Capitol patterns.

CAPITOL FIVE TUBE RADIATORS

FOR STEAM OR WATER

No. of Sections	*Length Inches	HEATING SURFACE—SQUARE FEET				
		37-inch Height 5 Sq. Ft. Per Section	32-inch Height 4⅓ Sq. Ft. Per Section	26-inch Height 3½ Sq. Ft. Per Section	23-inch Height 3 Sq. Ft. Per Section	20-inch Height 2⅔ Sq. Ft. Per Section
2	5	10	8⅔	7	6	5⅓
3	7½	15	13	10½	9	8
4	10	20	17⅓	14	12	10⅔
5	12½	25	21⅔	17½	15	13⅓
6	15	30	26	21	18	16
7	17½	35	30⅓	24½	21	18⅔
8	20	40	34⅔	28	24	21⅓
9	22½	45	39	31½	27	24
10	25	50	43⅓	35	30	26⅔
11	27½	55	47⅔	38½	33	29⅓
12	30	60	52	42	36	32
13	32½	65	56⅓	45½	39	34⅔
14	35	70	60⅔	49	42	37⅓
15	37½	75	65	52½	45	40
16	40	80	69⅓	56	48	42⅔
17	42½	85	73⅔	59½	51	45⅓
18	45	90	78	63	54	48
19	47½	95	82⅓	66½	57	50⅔
20	50	100	86⅔	70	60	53⅓
21	52½	105	91	73½	63	56
22	55	110	95⅓	77	66	58⅔
23	57½	115	99⅔	80½	69	61⅓
24	60	120	104	84	72	64
25	62½	125	108⅓	87½	75	66⅔

*Allow ½ inch for each bushing in estimating length of radiators. Tappings 1½ inches, top and bottom, bushed as per list on page 16, unless otherwise specified. Furnished with 6 inch legs on special order, or without legs as illustrated on page 12. Special shapes shown on page 14.

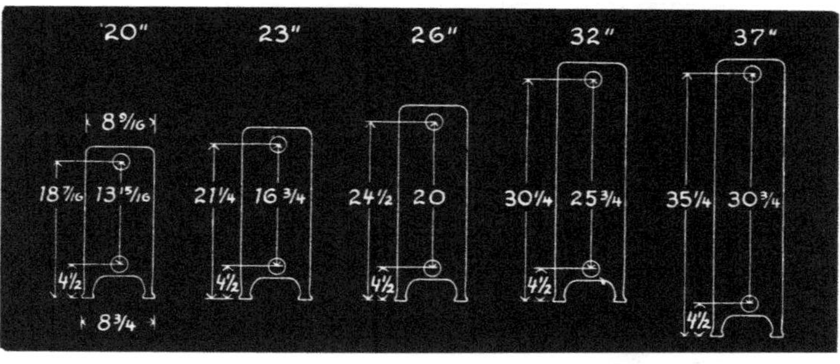

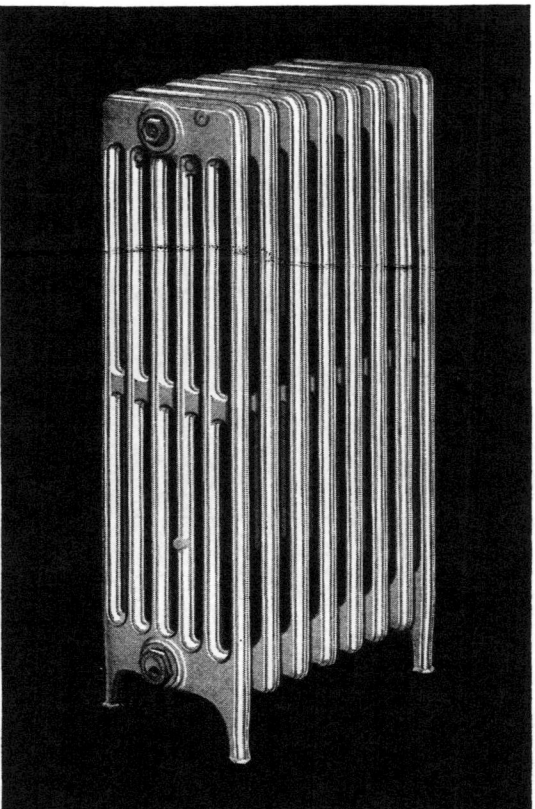

CAPITOL SIX TUBE

THESE attributes of the Capitol radiator: the clearly defined verticals, the play of lights and shadows on the delicate modeling, the lines of simple grace that somehow express a staunch strength beneath, all set a new standard of radiator beauty. This is maintained even in the six and seven tube patterns which meet the demand for mass radiation.

CAPITOL SIX TUBE RADIATORS

FOR STEAM OR WATER

No. of Sec-tions	*Length Inches	HEATING SURFACE—SQUARE FEET				
		37-inch Height 6 Sq. Ft. Per Section	32-inch Height 5 Sq. Ft. Per Section	26-inch Height 4 Sq. Ft. Per Section	23-inch Height 3½ Sq. Ft. Per Section	20-inch Height 3 Sq. Ft. Per Section
2	5	12	10	8	7	6
3	7½	18	15	12	10½	9
4	10	24	20	16	14	12
5	12½	30	25	20	17½	15
6	15	36	30	24	21	18
7	17½	42	35	23	24½	21
8	20	48	40	32	28	24
9	22½	54	45	35	31½	27
10	25	60	50	40	35	30
11	27½	66	55	44	38½	33
12	30	72	60	48	42	36
13	32½	78	65	52	45½	39
14	35	84	70	55	49	42
15	37½	90	75	60	52½	45
16	40	96	80	64	56	48
17	42½	102	85	68	59½	51
18	45	108	90	72	63	54
19	47½	114	95	76	66½	57
20	50	120	100	80	70	60
21	52½	126	105	84	73½	63
22	55	132	110	88	77	66
23	57½	138	115	92	80½	69
24	60	144	120	95	84	72
25	62½	150	125	100	87½	75

*Allow ½ inch for each bushing in estimating length of radiators. Tappings 1½ inches, top and bottom, bushed as per list on page 16, unless otherwise specified. Furnished with 6 inch legs on special order, or without legs as illustrated on page 12. Special shapes shown on page 14.

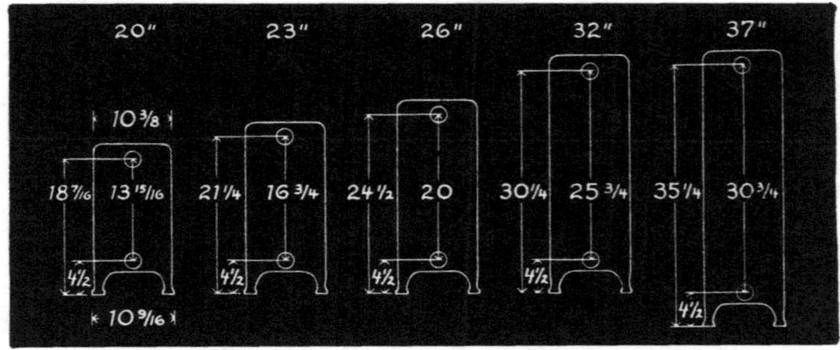

CAPITOL SEVEN TUBE

NEITHER the slender tube effect nor the grace of the Capitol has been sacrificed in the seven tube model. There is hardly a window sill built too low for the thirteen inch height. The laboratory attests to the exceptionally high efficiency of low radiators and especially of the Capitol seven tube.

CAPITOL SEVEN TUBE WINDOW RADIATORS

FOR STEAM OR WATER

No. of Sec-tions	*Length Inches	HEATING SURFACE—SQUARE FEET		
		20-inch Height 4¼ Sq. Ft. Per Section	16½-inch Height 3½ Sq. Ft. Per Section	13-inch Height 2¾ Sq. Ft. Per Section
2	5	8½	7	5½
3	7½	12¾	10½	8¼
4	10	17	14	11
5	12½	21¼	17½	13¾
6	15	25½	21	16½
7	17½	29¾	24½	19¼
8	20	34	28	22
9	22½	38¼	31½	24¾
10	25	42½	35	27½
11	27½	46¾	38½	30¼
12	30	51	42	33
13	32½	55¼	45½	35¾
14	35	59½	49	38½
15	37½	63¾	52½	41¼
16	40	68	56	44
17	42½	72¼	59½	46¾
18	45	76½	63	49½
19	47½	80¾	66½	52¼
20	50	85	70	55
21	52½	89¼	73½	57¾
22	55	93½	77	60½
23	57½	97¾	80½	63¼
24	60	102	84	66
25	62½	106¼	87½	68¾

*Allow ½ inch for each bushing in estimating length of radiators. Tappings 1½ inches, top and bottom, bushed as per list on page 16, unless otherwise specified. Furnished with 4½ inch legs on special order, or without legs as illustrated on page 12. Special shapes shown on page 14.

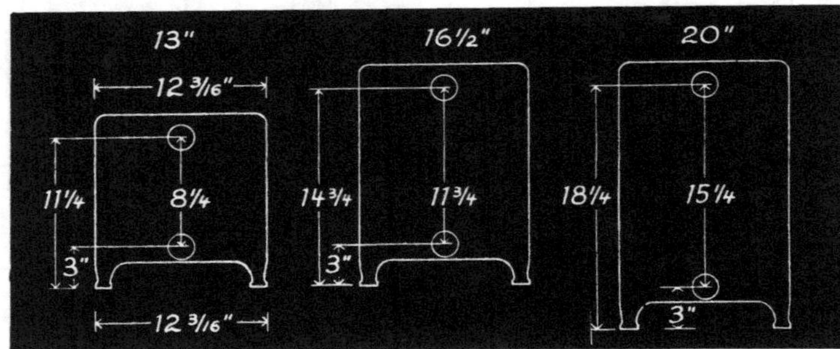

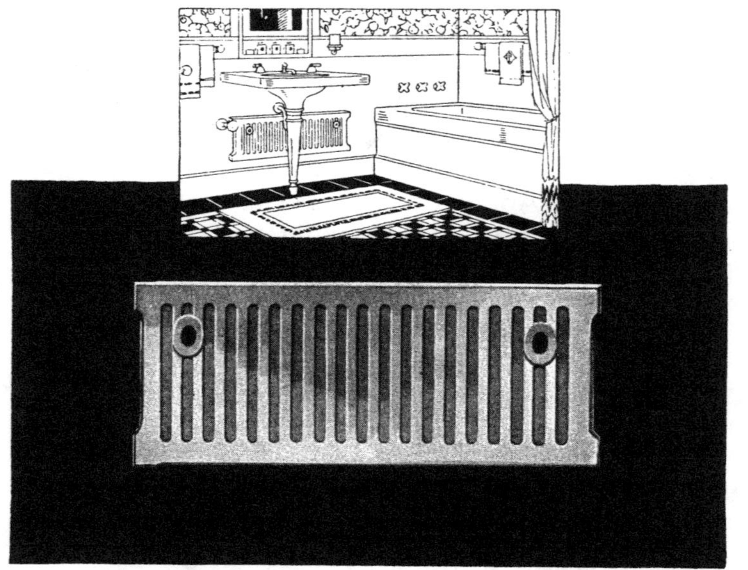

TRITON BATHROOM WALL RADIATOR

FITS under the lavatory, saving valuable space in modern bathrooms of limited dimensions. Attached with plain lag screws or hooks. Can be supplied in a new enamel finish, as immaculately white as the bathroom fixtures, that will neither chip, check, nor discolor.

Number	Height Inches	Length Inches	Thickness Inches	Nominal Surface Sq. Ft.
3A	8	16½	1½	3
3½A	8	20½	1½	3½

Above radiators tapped ½ inch.

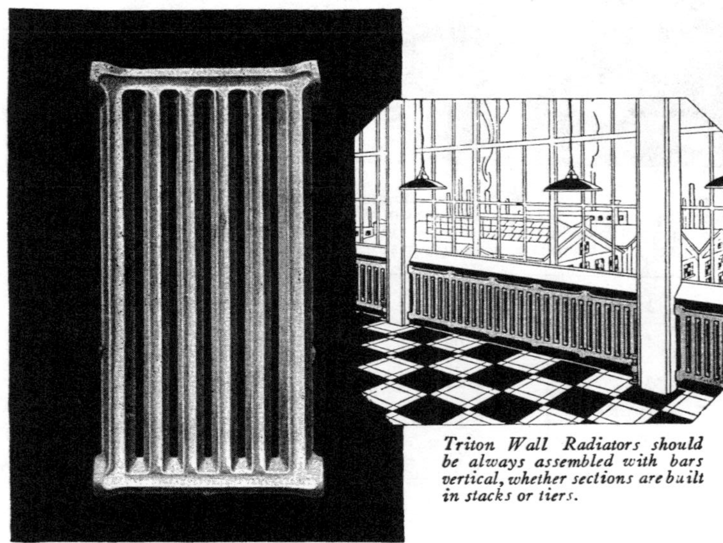

No. 9-B for side to side assembly

Triton Wall Radiators should be always assembled with bars vertical, whether sections are built in stacks or tiers.

FOR factories, storage houses, corridors, stairways, lobbies, and wherever the utmost radiating surface is needed in limited space, Triton Wall Radiators are unexcelled.

The wide variety of sizes adaptable to either tier or stack arrangement permits adapting their installation to any wall space available.

Sections may be added at any time should the building be enlarged. Steam or water may be confined to any number of the units during mild weather, assuring uniform temperatures with maximum economy. Condensed steam or exhaust steam often available in industrial installations may be utilized with the greatest efficiency.

No wall radiators are built that are more efficient, adaptable, or durable.

TRITON WALL RADIATORS

No. 9-A for end to end assembly

No. 5-A for end to end assembly

No. 7-B for side by side assembly

No. 7-A for end to end assembly

Section Numbers	Height Inches	Length or Width Inches	Thickness Inches	Thickness With Brkts. Inches	Heating Surface Sq. Ft.
5A	14 1/8	16 1/2	3	3 1/2	5
7A	14 1/8	22 7/8	3	3 1/2	7
9A	14 1/8	29 1/4	3	3 1/2	9
7B	22 7/8	14 1/8	3	3 1/2	7
9B	29 1/4	14 1/8	3	3 1/2	9

Above radiators are tapped 1 1/2 inches

Blends with walls and draperies, like a mural decoration.

AS HARMONIOUS AS A MURAL DECORATION . . .

AGAIN the United States Radiator Corporation paces progress in heating . . . the Capitol Mural Radiator is here. Appropriate is its name, for installed under a window or recessed in the wall, it blends with the interior as beautifully as a mural painting.

Behind its solid sculptured front, the tubes act as flues, speeding the circulation of warmed air. The extra face surface increases heat radiation through the lower part of the room. Warmer floors and cooler ceilings result.

The Capitol Mural Radiator occupies less space than other types. Its design and strength are the perfected result of unhurried experiment and careful development. It is in every way worthy to carry the Capitol name.

CAPITOL MURAL RADIATORS

ONE TUBE

With adjustable wall bracket — *With sheet metal sill bracket*

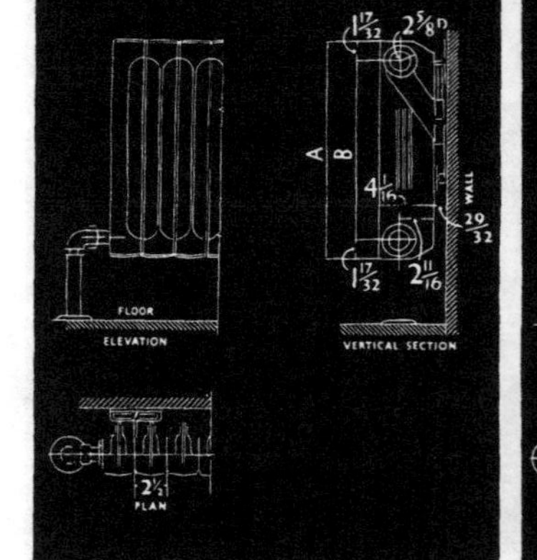

17-INCH HEIGHT, MEASUREMENT A, $17\frac{1}{16}$"; B, $13\frac{15}{16}$"
23-INCH HEIGHT, MEASUREMENT A, $22\frac{13}{16}$"; B, $19\frac{11}{16}$"

Number of Sections	*Length Inches	** 17-inch Height 1¾ Square Feet Per Section	** 23-inch Height 2¼ Square Feet Per Section
2	4½	3½	4½
3	7	5¼	6¾
4	9½	7	9
5	12	8¾	11¼
6	14½	10½	13½
7	17	12¼	15¾
8	19½	14	18
9	22	15¾	20¼
10	24½	17½	22½
11	27	19¼	24¾
12	29½	21	27
13	32	22¾	29¼
14	34½	24½	31½
15	37	26¼	33¾
16	39½	28	36
17	42	29¾	38¼
18	44½	31½	40½
19	47	33¼	42¾
20	49½	35	45
21	52	36¾	47¼
22	54½	38½	49½
23	57	40¼	51¾
24	59½	42	54
25	62	43¾	56¼

*Allow ½ inch for each bushing in estimating length of radiators.

**Based on Engineering Standards of 215 degrees Fahrenheit steam temperature, 70 degrees room temperature and 240 B. t. u. per square foot per hour.

TAPPINGS—1¼" top and bottom. Bushed for steam or water as per specifications.

CONNECTIONS—Both steam and water—extra heavy 1¼" right and left threaded nipples at top and bottom.

CAPITOL MURAL RADIATORS

TWO TUBE

With adjustable wall bracket *With sheet metal sill bracket*

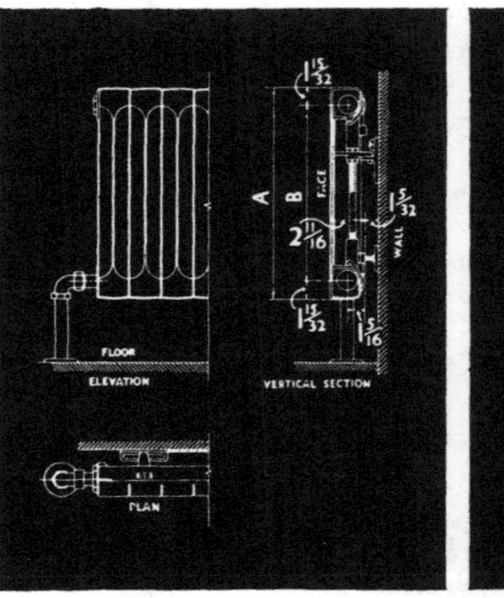

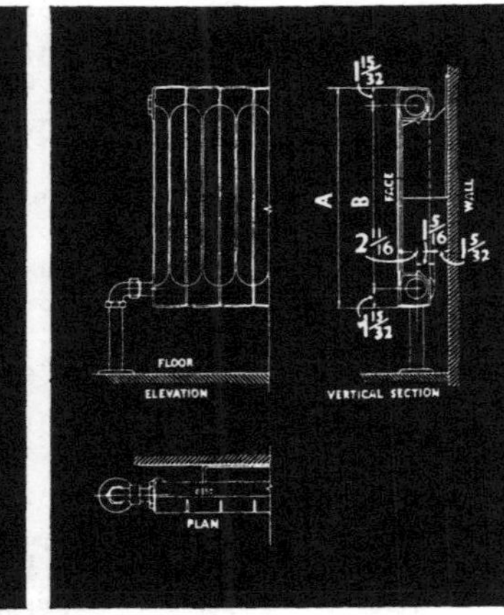

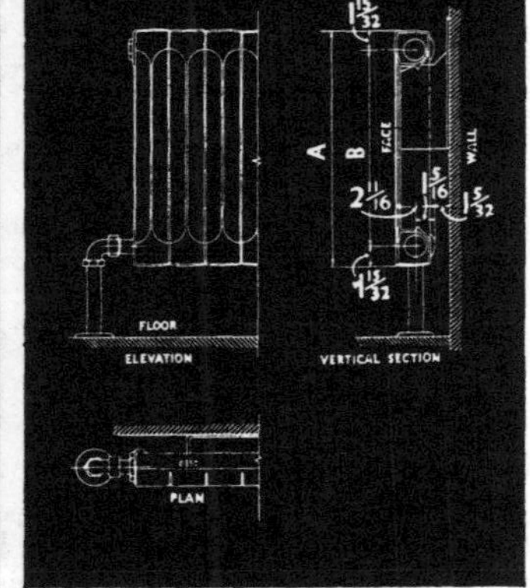

17-Inch Height, Measurement A, 17"; B, 14"
20-Inch Height, Measurement A, 19¾"; B, 16⅞"
23-Inch Height, Measurement A, 22¾"; B, 19¾"

Assembly Number	*Length Inches	**17-inch Height 3⅓ Sq. Ft. Per Succeeding Assembly Number	**20-inch Height 3¾ Sq. Ft. Per Succeeding Assembly Number	**23-inch Height 4¼ Sq. Ft. Per Succeeding Assembly Number
2	12½	6⅔	7½	8½
3	17½	10	11¼	12¾
4	25	13⅓	15	17
5	30	16⅔	18¾	21¼
6	37½	20	22½	25½
7	42½	23⅓	26¼	29¾
8	50	26⅔	30	34
9	52½	30	33¾	38¼
10	62½	33⅓	37½	42½
11	67½	36⅔	41¼	46¾
12	75	40	45	51
13	77½	43⅓	48¾	55¼
14	87½	46⅔	52½	59½
15	92½	50	56¼	63¾
16	100	53⅓	60	68

*Allow ½ inch for each bushing in estimating length of radiators.
**Based on Engineering Standards of 215 degrees Fahrenheit steam temperature, 70 degrees room temperature and 240 B. t. u. per square foot per hour.

Tappings—1¼" top and bottom. Bushed for steam or water as per specifications.

Connections—Both steam and water—extra heavy 1¼" right and left threaded nipples at top and bottom.

Note—Two Tube Mural Radiators used for water systems are to be vented through tapped Top Plug provided on specification.

CAPITOL MURAL RADIATORS

THREE TUBE

With adjustable wall bracket *With sheet metal sill bracket*

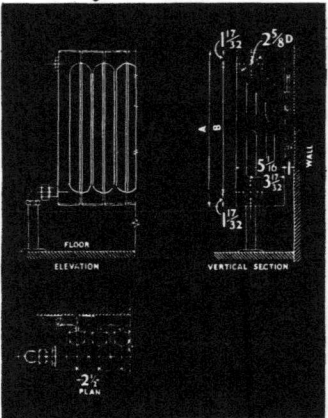

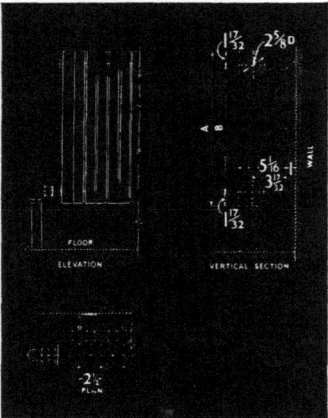

17-Inch Height, Measurement A, 17"; B, 13$\frac{15}{16}$"
20-Inch Height, Measurement A, 20"; B, 16$\frac{15}{16}$"
23-Inch Height, Measurement A, 22¾"; B 19$\frac{11}{16}$"

Number of Sections	*Length Inches	**17-inch Height 2 Sq. Ft. Per Section	**20-inch Height 2⅓ Sq. Ft. Per Section	**23-inch Height 2⅔ Sq. Ft. Per Section
2	4½	4	4⅔	5⅓
3	7	6	7	8
4	9½	8	9⅓	10⅔
5	12	10	11⅔	13⅓
6	14½	12	14	16
7	17	14	16⅓	18⅔
8	19½	16	18⅔	21⅓
9	22	18	21	24
10	24½	20	23⅓	26⅔
11	27	22	25⅔	29⅓
12	29½	24	28	32
13	32	26	30⅓	34⅔
14	34½	28	32⅔	37⅓
15	37	30	35	40
16	39½	32	37⅓	42⅔
17	42	34	39⅔	45⅓
18	44½	36	42	48
19	47	38	44⅓	50⅔
20	49½	40	46⅔	53⅓
21	52	42	49	56
22	54½	44	51⅓	58⅔
23	57	46	53⅔	61⅓
24	59½	48	56	64
25	62	50	58⅓	66⅔

*Allow ½ inch for each bushing in estimating length of radiators.
**Based on Engineering Standards of 215 degrees Fahrenheit steam temperature, 70 degrees room temperature and 240 B. t. u. per square foot per hour.

Tappings—1¼" top and bottom. Bushed for steam or water as per specifications.

Connections—Both steam and water—extra heavy 1¼" right and left threaded nipples at top and bottom.

CAPITOL MURAL RADIATORS

FOUR TUBE

With adjustable wall bracket — *With sheet metal sill bracket*

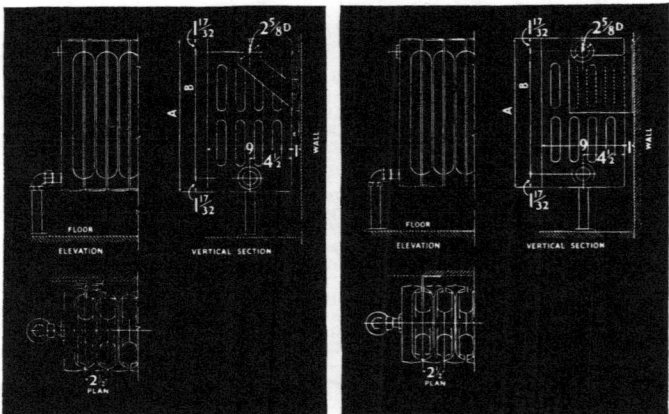

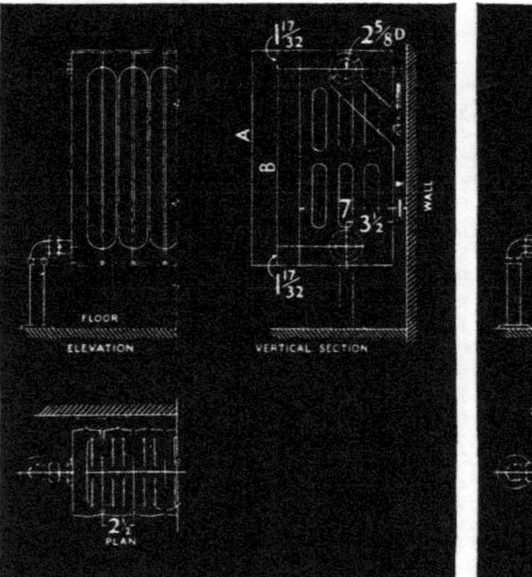

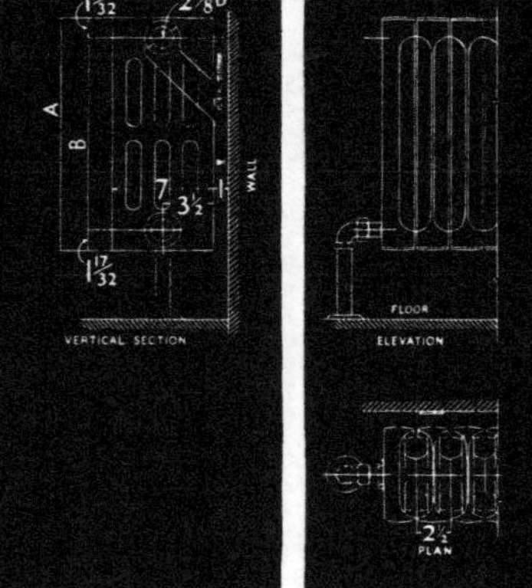

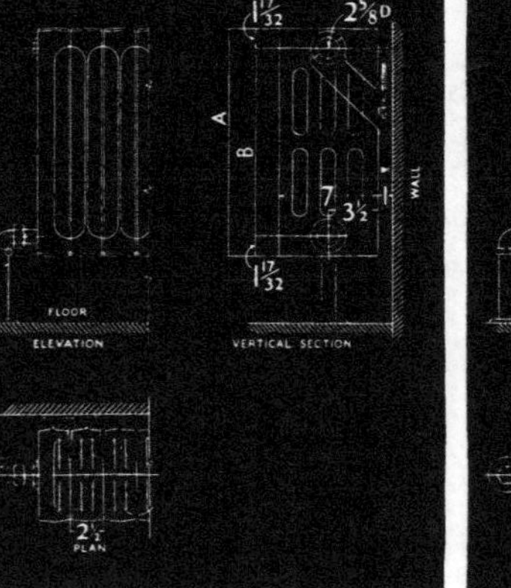

17-Inch Height, Measurement A, 17"; B, 13 15/16"
20-Inch Height, Measurement A, 20"; B, 16 15/16"
23-Inch Height, Measurement A, 22¾"; B, 19 11/16"

Number of Sections	*Length Inches	**17-inch Height 2⅔ Sq. Ft. Per Section	**20-inch Height 3 Sq. Ft. Per Section	**23-inch Height 3⅓ Sq. Ft. Per Section
2	4½	5⅓	6	6⅔
3	7	8	9	10
4	9½	10⅔	12	13⅓
5	12	13⅓	15	16⅔
6	14½	16	18	20
7	17	18⅔	21	23⅓
8	19½	21⅓	24	26⅔
9	22	24	27	30
10	24½	26⅔	30	33⅓
11	27	29⅓	33	36⅔
12	29½	32	36	40
13	32	34⅔	39	43⅓
14	34½	37⅓	42	46⅔
15	37	40	45	50
16	39½	42⅔	48	53⅓
17	42	45⅓	51	56⅔
18	44½	48	54	60
19	47	50⅔	57	63⅓
20	49½	53⅓	60	66⅔
21	52	56	63	70
22	54½	58⅔	66	73⅓
23	57	61⅓	69	76⅔
24	59½	64	72	80
25	62	66⅔	75	83⅓

*Allow ½ inch for each bushing in estimating length of radiators.
**Based on Engineering Standards of 215 degrees Fahrenheit steam temperature, 70 degrees room temperature and 240 B. t. u. per square foot per hour.

Tappings—1¼" top and bottom. Bushed for steam or water as per specifications.

Connections—Both steam and water—extra heavy 1¼" right and left threaded nipples at top and bottom.

CAPITOL MURAL RADIATORS

FIVE TUBE

With adjustable wall bracket — *With sheet metal sill bracket*

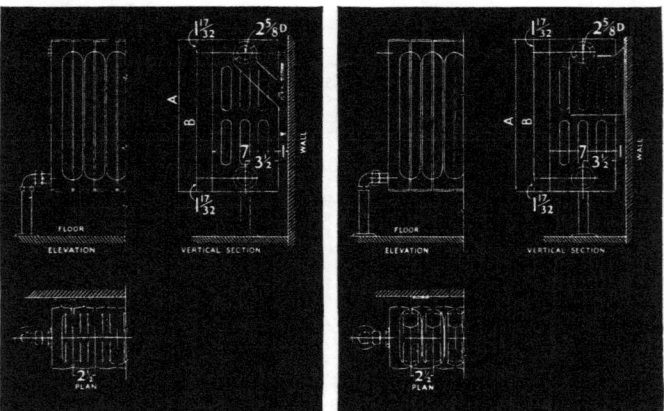

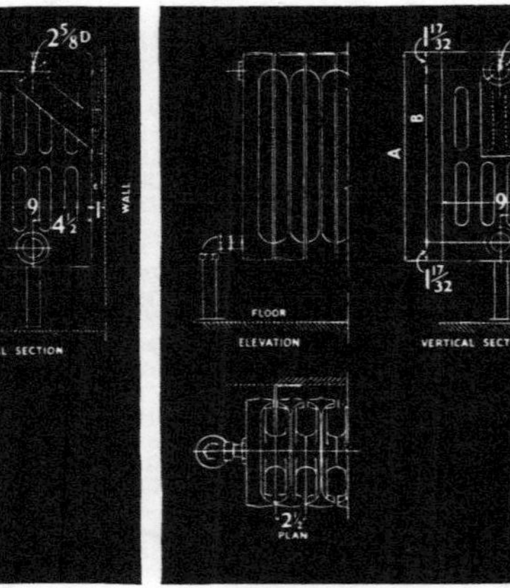

17-Inch Height, Measurement A, 17"; B, 13 15/16"
23-Inch Height, Measurement A, 22¾"; B, 19 11/16"

Number of Sections	*Length Inches	**17-inch Height 3¼ Sq. Ft. Per Section	**23-inch Height 4 Sq. Ft. Per Section
2	4½	6½	8
3	7	9¾	12
4	9½	13	16
5	12	16¼	20
6	14½	19½	24
7	17	22¾	28
8	19½	26	32
9	22	29¼	36
10	24½	32½	40
11	27	35¾	44
12	29½	39	48
13	32	42¼	52
14	34½	45½	56
15	37	48¾	60
16	39½	52	64
17	42	55¼	68
18	44½	58½	72
19	47	61¾	76
20	49½	65	80
21	52	68¼	84
22	54½	71½	88
23	57	74¾	92
24	59½	78	96
25	62	81¼	100

*Allow ½ inch for each bushing in estimating length of radiators.
**Based on Engineering Standards of 215 degrees Fahrenheit steam temperature, 70 degrees room temperature and 240 B. t. u. per square foot per hour.

Tappings—1½" top and bottom. Bushed for steam or water as per specifications.

Connections—Both steam and water—extra heavy 1¼" right and left threaded nipples at top and bottom.

Graceful and pleasing, this slender model is particularly adapted to narrow corridors, and rooms where space is at a premium.

NATIONAL AERO THREE TUBE RADIATION

Three Tube Sizes and Ratings

Number of Sections	*Length 2½ in. Per Sec.	Square Feet Per Section				
		36-in. Height 3½ Sq. Ft. Per Sec.	30-in. Height 3 Sq. Ft. Per Sec.	26-in. Height 2⅓ Sq. Ft. Per Sec.	23-in. Height 2 Sq. Ft. Per Sec.	20-in. Height 1¾ Sq. Ft. Per Sec.
2	5	7	6	4⅔	4	3½
3	7½	10½	9	7	6	5¼
4	10	14	12	9⅓	8	7
5	12½	17½	15	11⅔	10	8¾
6	15	21	18	14	12	10½
7	17½	24½	21	16⅓	14	12¼
8	20	28	24	18⅔	16	14
9	22½	31½	27	21	18	15¾
10	25	35	30	23⅓	20	17½
11	27½	38½	33	25⅔	22	19¼
12	30	42	36	28	24	21
13	32½	45½	39	30⅓	26	22¾
14	35	49	42	32⅔	28	24½
15	37½	52½	45	35	30	26¼
16	40	56	48	37⅓	32	28
17	42½	59½	51	39⅔	34	29¾
18	45	63	54	42	36	31½
19	47½	66½	57	44⅓	38	33¼
20	50	70	60	46⅔	40	35
21	52½	73½	63	49	42	36¾
22	55	77	66	51⅓	44	38½
23	57½	80½	69	53⅔	46	40¼
24	60	84	72	56	48	42
25	62½	87½	75	58⅓	50	43¾
Distance from floor to center of top tapping.		33 13/16	27 27/32	23 13/16	20 53/64	17 27/32
Distance from floor to center of bottom tapping.		4½	4½	4½	4½	4½

Detailed measurements are given on page 20.

*Add ½-inch to length for each bushing.

Width of feet, 5⅛ inches. Width of section, 5⅛ inches.

Tapped 1½ inches top and bottom both ends and bushed to sizes required.

National Aero Radiators are furnished legless or with legs 6 inches from floor to center of tapping boss when ordered.

To determine the overall height of 3-tube legless radiators, deduct 2⅛ inches from the standard heights shown for this type. See pages 16, 20 for legless data.

Assembled with extra heavy malleable iron push nipples, top and bottom.

The slender tubes which contribute to the Aero Radiator's charm are responsible for its efficiency; they provide the scientifically correct ratio of air space to heating area

Four Tube Sizes and Ratings

Number of Sections	*Length 2½ in. Per Sec.	Square Feet Per Section				
		36-in. Height 4¼ Sq. Ft. Per Sec.	30-in. Height 3½ Sq. Ft. Per Sec.	26-in. Height 2¾ Sq. Ft. Per Sec.	23-in. Height 2½ Sq. Ft. Per Section	20-in. Height 2¼ Sq. Ft. Per Sec.
2	5	8½	7	5½	5	4½
3	7½	12¾	10½	8¼	7½	6¾
4	10	17	14	11	10	9
5	12½	21¼	17½	13¾	12½	11¼
6	15	25½	21	16½	15	13½
7	17½	29¾	24½	19¼	17½	15¾
8	20	34	28	22	20	18
9	22½	38¼	31½	24¾	22½	20¼
10	25	42½	35	27½	25	22½
11	27½	46¾	38½	30¼	27½	24¾
12	30	51	42	33	30	27
13	32½	55¼	45½	35¾	32½	29¼
14	35	59½	49	38½	35	31½
15	37½	63¾	52½	41¼	37½	33¾
16	40	68	56	44	40	36
17	42½	72¼	59½	46¾	42½	38¼
18	45	76½	63	49½	45	40½
19	47½	80¾	66½	52¼	47½	42¾
20	50	85	70	55	50	45
21	52½	89¼	73½	57¾	52½	47¼
22	55	93½	77	60½	55	49½
23	57½	97¾	80½	63¼	57½	51¾
24	60	102	84	66	60	54
25	62½	106¼	87½	68¾	62½	56¼
Distance from floor to center of top tapping.		33 13/16	27 27/32	23 13/16	20 53/64	17 27/32
Distance from floor to center of bottom tapping.		4½	4½	4½	4½	4½

Detailed measurements are given on page 20.

*Add ½-inch to length for each bushing.

Width of feet, 6 13/16 inches. Width of section, 6 13/16 inches.

Tapped 1½ inches top and bottom both ends and bushed to sizes required.

National Aero Radiators are furnished legless or with legs 6 inches from floor to center of tapping boss when ordered.

To determine the overall height of 4-tube legless radiators deduct 2⅛ inches from the standard heights shown for this type. See pages 16, 20 for legless data.

Assembled with extra heavy malleable iron push nipples, top and bottom.

This model finds its field in all general applications: homes, schools and everywhere.

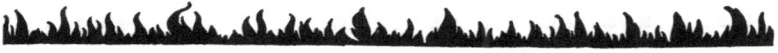

NATIONAL AERO FIVE TUBE RADIATION

Five Tube Sizes and Ratings

Number of Sections	*Length 2½ in. Per Sec.	Square Feet Per Section				
		36-in. Height 5 Sq. Ft. Per Sec.	30-in. Height 4⅓ Sq. Ft. Per Sec.	26-in. Height 3½ Sq. Ft. Per Sec.	23-in. Height 3 Sq. Ft. Per Sec.	20-in. Height 2⅔ Sq. Ft. Per Sec.
2	5	10	8⅔	7	6	5⅓
3	7½	15	13	10½	9	8
4	10	20	17⅓	14	12	10⅔
5	12½	25	21⅔	17½	15	13⅓
6	15	30	26	21	18	16
7	17½	35	30⅓	24½	21	18⅔
8	20	40	34⅔	28	24	21⅓
9	22½	45	39	31½	27	24
10	25	50	43⅓	35	30	26⅔
11	27½	55	47⅔	38½	33	29⅓
12	30	60	52	42	36	32
13	32½	65	56⅓	45½	39	34⅔
14	35	70	60⅔	49	42	37⅓
15	37½	75	65	52½	45	40
16	40	80	69⅓	56	48	42⅔
17	42½	85	73⅔	59½	51	45⅓
18	45	90	78	63	54	48
19	47½	95	82⅓	66½	57	50⅔
20	50	100	86⅔	70	60	53⅓
21	52½	105	91	73½	63	56
22	55	110	95⅓	77	66	58⅔
23	57½	115	99⅔	80½	69	61⅓
24	60	120	104	84	72	64
25	62½	125	108⅓	87½	75	66⅔
Distance from floor to center of top tapping.		33 13/16	27 27/32	23 13/16	20 53/64	17 27/32
Distance from floor to center of bottom tapping.		4½	4½	4½	4½	4½

Detailed measurements are given on page 20.

*Add ½-inch to length for each bushing.

Width of feet, 8 13/32 inches. Width of sections, 8 13/32 inches.

Tapped 1½ inches top and bottom both ends and bushed to sizes required.

National Aero Radiators are furnished legless or with legs 6 inches from floor to center of tapping boss when ordered.

To determine the overall height of 5 tube legless radiators deduct 2⅛ inches from the standard heights shown for this type. See pages 16, 20 for legless data.

Assembled with extra heavy malleable iron push nipples, top and bottom.

The six tube type provides an unusual amount of radiating surface, but being only nine inches wide takes up very little space

NATIONAL AERO SIX TUBE RADIATION

Six Tube Sizes and Ratings

Number of Sections	*Length 2½-in. Per Sec.	Square Feet Per Section				
		38-in. Height 6 Sq. Ft. Per Sec.	32-in. Height 5 Sq. Ft. Per Sec.	26-in. Height 4 Sq. Ft. Per Sec.	23-in. Height 3½ Sq. Ft. Per Sec.	20-in. Height 3 Sq. Ft. Per Sec.
2	5	12	10	8	7	6
3	7½	18	15	12	10½	9
4	10	24	20	16	14	12
5	12½	30	25	20	17½	15
6	15	36	30	24	21	18
7	17½	42	35	28	24½	21
8	20	48	40	32	28	24
9	22½	54	45	36	31½	27
10	25	60	50	40	35	30
11	27½	66	55	44	38½	33
12	30	72	60	48	42	36
13	32½	78	65	52	45½	39
14	35	84	70	56	49	42
15	37½	90	75	60	52½	45
16	40	96	80	64	56	48
17	42½	102	85	68	59½	51
18	45	108	90	72	63	54
19	47½	114	95	76	66½	57
20	50	120	100	80	70	60
21	52½	126	105	84	73½	63
22	55	132	110	88	77	66
23	57½	138	115	92	80½	69
24	60	144	120	96	84	72
25	62½	150	125	100	87½	75
Distance from floor to center of top tapping.		35⅞	29⅞	23⅞	20⅝	17⅞
Distance from floor to center of bottom tapping.		4½	4½	4½	4½	4½

Detailed measurements are given on page 20.

*Add ½ inch to length for each bushing.

Width of feet, 9 inches. Width of section, 9 inches.

Tapped 1½ inches top and bottom both ends and bushed to size required.

National Aero Radiators are furnished legless or with legs 6 inches from floor to center of tapping boss when ordered.

To determine the overall height of 6-tube legless radiators deduct 2½ inches from the standard heights shown for this type. See pages **16, 20** for legless data.

Assembled with extra heavy malleable iron push nipples.

A unit with tremendous warming capacity. The low heights fit nicely under windows, applying the heat where needed. The 36, 30 and 26 inch heights are used where space limitations will not permit a long radiator.

National Aero Radiator Pedestals

Where additional clearance beneath any Aero Radiator is desired cast iron Aero Radiator Pedestals should be used. Heights available are ½″, 1″, 1½″, 2″, 2½″, 3″, and 4″.

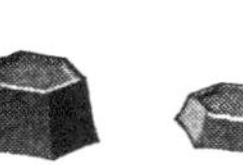

NATIONAL AERO SEVEN TUBE RADIATION

Seven Tube Sizes and Ratings

Number of Sections	*Length 2½-in. Per Sec.	Square Feet Per Section					
		36-in. Height 6¾ Sq. Ft. Per Sec.	30-in. Height 5½ Sq. Ft. Per Sec.	26-in. Height 4¾ Sq. Ft. Per Sec.	20-in. Height 3⅔Sq.Ft. Per Sec.	16½-in. Height 3Sq. Ft. Per Sec.	13½-in. Height 2½Sq.Ft. Per Sec.
2	5	13½	11	9½	7⅓	6	5
3	7½	20¼	16½	14¼	11	9	7½
4	10	27	22	19	14⅔	12	10
5	12½	33¾	27½	23¾	18⅓	15	12½
6	15	40½	33	28½	22	18	15
7	17½	47¼	38½	33¼	25⅔	21	17½
8	20	54	44	38	29⅓	24	20
9	22½	60¾	49½	42¾	33	27	22½
10	25	67½	55	47½	36⅔	30	25
11	27½	74¼	60½	52¼	40⅓	33	27½
12	30	81	66	57	44	36	30
13	32½	87¾	71½	61¾	47⅔	39	32½
14	35	94½	77	66½	51⅓	42	35
15	37½	101¼	82½	71¼	55	45	37½
16	40	108	88	76	58⅔	48	40
17	42½	114¾	93½	80¾	62⅓	51	42½
18	45	121½	99	85½	66	54	45
19	47½	128¼	104½	90¼	69⅔	57	47½
20	50	135	110	95	73⅓	60	50
21	52½	141¾	115½	99¾	77	63	52½
22	55	148½	121	104½	80⅔	66	55
23	57½	155¼	126½	109¼	84⅓	69	57½
24	60	162	132	114	88	72	60
25	62½	168¾	137½	118¾	91⅔	75	62½
Distance from floor to center of top tapping.		33 13/16	27 27/32	23 13/16	17 27/32	14 11/32	11⅜
Distance from floor to center of bottom tapping.		4½	4½	4½	4½	3	3

Detailed measurements are given on page 20.

*Add ½-inch to length for each bushing.

Width of feet, 12 inches. Width of section, 12 inches.

Tapped 1½ inches top and bottom both ends and bushed to sizes required.

Can be furnished legless or with 6 inch high legs on all six heights also 4½ inch high legs on 16½ inch and 13½ inch heights.

To determine the overall height of the 7-tube legless radiators deduct 2⅛ inches from the standard height except on the 13½ inch and 16½ inch heights in which case ¾ of an inch should be deducted. See page 16, 20 for legless data.

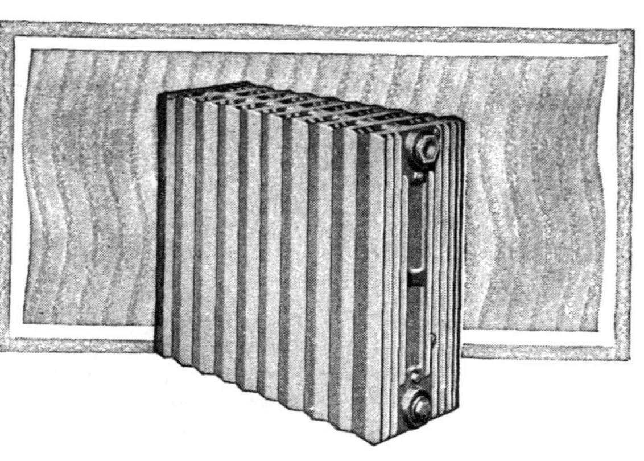

National Panel Radiation (5-Tube)

IN designing Panel-Rad (Registered Trade Mark) the National Radiator Corporation successfully coordinated three divergent and desirable qualities, to produce a unit that meets every requirement.

National Panel Radiation is unobtrusive; only its pleasingly smooth face is visible.

National Panel Radiation is space saving; when fully recessed it occupies no floor space whatever, leaves the room clear for furniture and fittings.

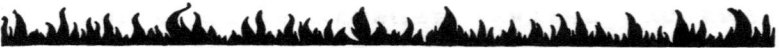

National Panel Radiation is highly efficient; the convection air currents progress unimpeded and at high velocity through specially designed flues which present a maximum of heating surface, and promote quick and continuous heat transfer. There is also a large percentage of radiated heat.

Efficient . . .

space saving unobtrusive

NATIONAL Panel-Rad (registered trade-mark name) finds its particular field in large buildings, where every foot of space is valuable and every means of saving space must be utilized. It is likewise of value for homes and hospitals. High efficiency, a high percentage of radiated heat which warms the lower portion of the room rapidly, and the decorative effect presented by the solid metal panel recommend it for all applications.

One advantage of National Panel-Rad is found in the fact that its closed end sections permit it to be recessed or wall mounted, without the necessity of entirely enclosing the unit. The radiation may be fully enclosed in a sheet metal casing with a grill at the bottom and the top, or the grill at the bottom may be omitted, or no casing need be used at all. When the radiator is recessed it is advisable to insulate the recess with asbestos or cork board.

National Panel-Rad owes its attractiveness to the fact that front faces of the sections come together, making an uninterrupted, iron-to-iron contact, and presenting therefore a uniform and pleasing appearance. This is made possible through National's use of push nipples, permitting the sections to be assembled tightly and permanently and without the use of gaskets.

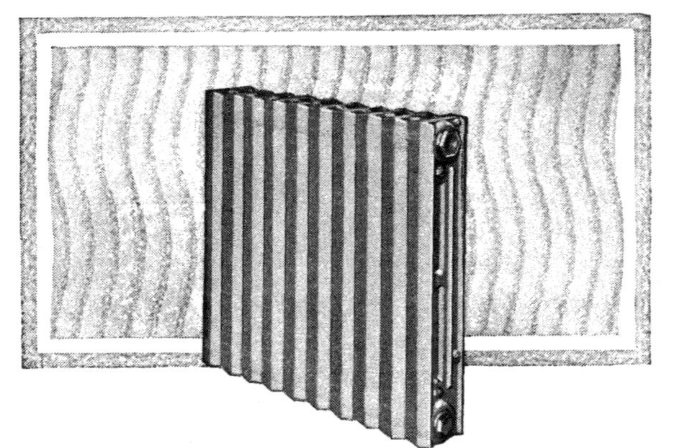

One Tube Panel Radiation—Sizes and Ratings

Number of Sections	Length Overall Inches	17-Inch Height 1¾ Square Feet Per Section	23-Inch Height 2¼ Square Feet Per Section
2	4½	3½	4½
3	7	5¼	6¾
4	9½	7	9
5	12	8¾	11¼
6	14½	10½	13½
7	17	12¼	15¾
8	19½	14	18
9	22	15¾	20¼
10	24½	17½	22½
11	27	19¼	24¾
12	29½	21	27
13	32	22¾	29¼
14	34½	24½	31½
15	37	26¼	33¾
16	39½	28	36
17	42	29¾	38¼
18	44½	31½	40½
19	47	33¼	42¾
20	49½	35	45
21	52	36¾	47¼
22	54½	38½	49½
23	57	40¼	51¾
24	59½	42	54
25	62	43¾	56¼

One Tube Panel Radiation

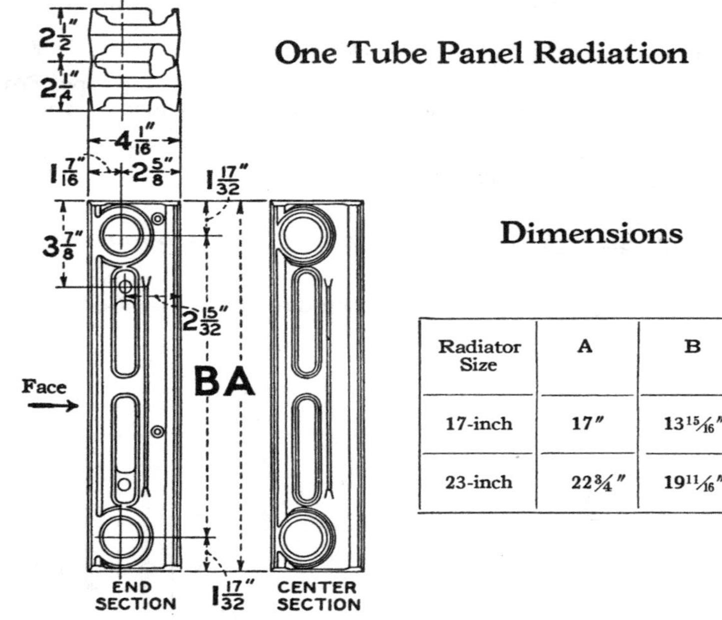

Dimensions

Radiator Size	A	B
17-inch	17″	13 15/16″
23-inch	22¾″	19 11/16″

Tappings—1½ inch top and bottom both ends. Bushed to meet requirements.

Connections—Assembled with extra heavy Malleable Iron Push Nipples.

Vents—All Panel Radiators regularly furnished with Steam and Water Vents.

Note: Distance from top of radiator to center of ½ inch diameter top rod hole—3⅞ inches. Rod hole is 5/32″ off center line of nipple opening.

Add ½ inch to length for each bushing.

Guaranteed Heat Emission of 240 B. T. U. per Square Foot listed rating in room temperature of 70° F. with Steam at 215° F.

Interchangeable for Steam or Water.

Detail of hangers furnished on request.

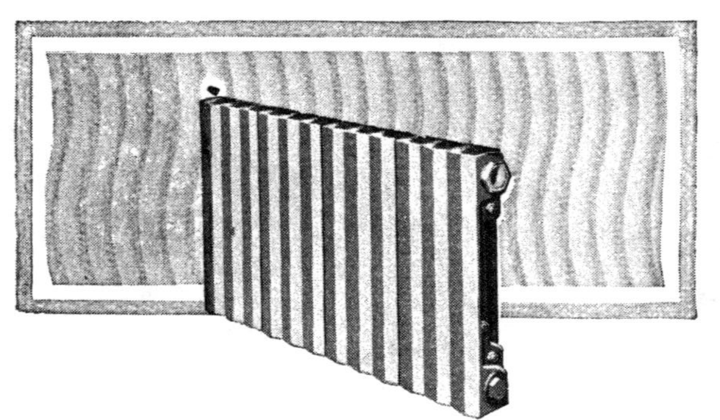

Two Tube Panel Radiation—Sizes and Ratings

Number of Sections	Length Overall Inches	17-Inch Height 3⅓ Square Feet Per Section	23-Inch Height 4¼ Square Feet Per Section
2	15	6⅔	8½
3	22½	10	12¾
4	30	13⅓	17
5	37½	16⅔	21¼
6	45	20	25½
7	52½	23⅓	29¾
8	60	26⅔	34
9	67½	30	38¼
10	75	33⅓	42½
11	82½	36⅔	46¾
12	90	40	51
13	97½	43⅓	55¼
14	105	46⅔	59½
15	112½	50	63¾
16	120	53⅓	68

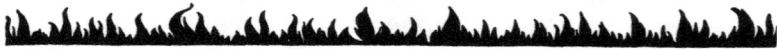

Two Tube Panel Radiation

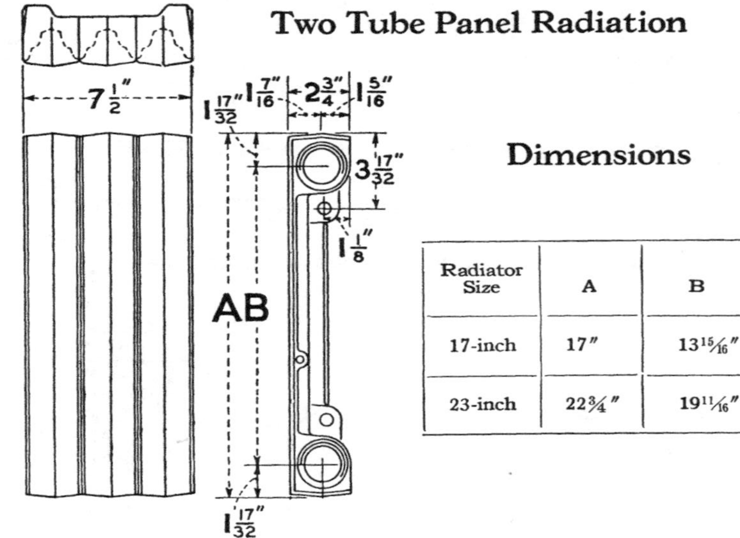

Dimensions

Radiator Size	A	B
17-inch	17"	13 15/16"
23-inch	22¾"	19 11/16"

Tappings—1½ inch top and bottom both ends. Bushed to meet requirements.

Connections—Assembled with extra heavy Malleable Iron Push Nipples.

Vents—All Panel Radiators regularly furnished with Steam and Water Vents.

Note: Distance from top of radiator to center of ½ inch diameter top rod hole—3 17/32 inches.

Add ½ inch to length for each bushing.

Guaranteed Heat Emission of 240 B. T. U. per Square Foot listed rating in room temperature of 70° F. with Steam at 215° F.

Interchangeable for Steam or Water.

Detail of hangers furnished on request.

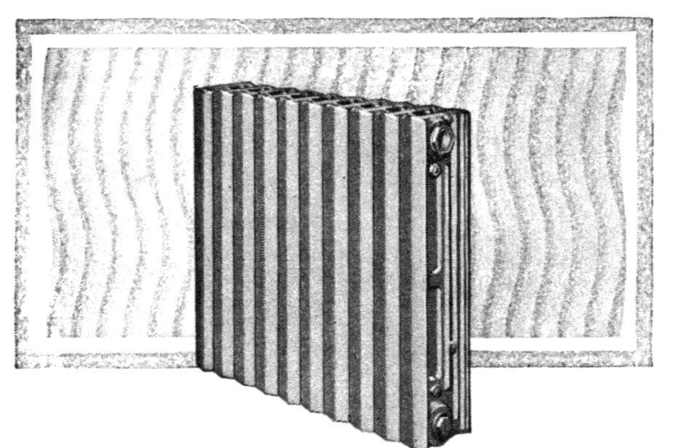

Three Tube Panel Radiation—Sizes and Ratings

Number of Sections	Length Overall Inches	17-Inch Height 2 Square Feet Per Section	20-Inch Height 2⅓ Square Feet Per Section	23-Inch Height 2⅔ Square Feet Per Section
2	4½	4	4⅔	5⅓
3	7	6	7	8
4	9½	8	9⅓	10⅔
5	12	10	11⅔	13⅓
6	14½	12	14	16
7	17	14	16⅓	18⅔
8	19½	16	18⅔	21⅓
9	22	18	21	24
10	24½	20	23⅓	26⅔
11	27	22	25⅔	29⅓
12	29½	24	28	32
13	32	26	30⅓	34⅔
14	34½	28	32⅔	37⅓
15	37	30	35	40
16	39½	32	37⅓	42⅔
17	42	34	39⅔	45⅓
18	44½	36	42	48
19	47	38	44⅓	50⅔
20	49½	40	46⅔	53⅓
21	52	42	49	56
22	54½	44	51⅓	58⅔
23	57	46	53⅔	61⅓
24	59½	48	56	64
25	62	50	58⅓	66⅔

NATIONAL PANEL RADIATION

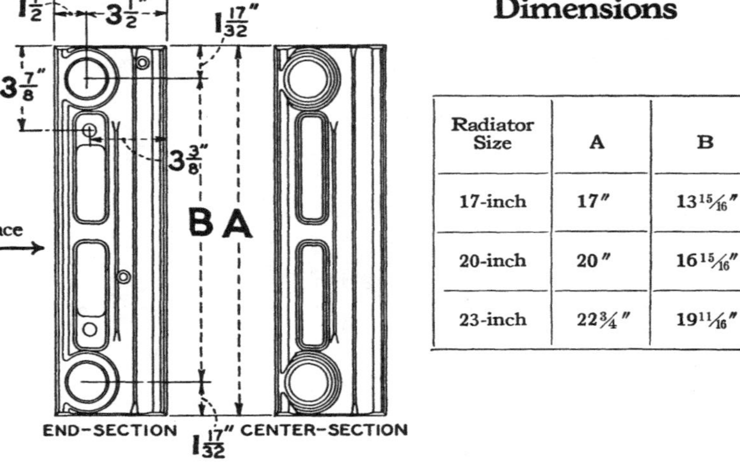

Three Tube Panel Radiation

Dimensions

Radiator Size	A	B
17-inch	17″	$13\frac{15}{16}''$
20-inch	20″	$16\frac{15}{16}''$
23-inch	22¾″	$19\frac{11}{16}''$

Tappings—1½ inch top and bottom both ends. Bushed to meet requirements.

Connections—Assembled with extra heavy Malleable Iron Push Nipples.

Vents—All Panel Radiators regularly furnished with Steam and Water Vents.

Note: Distance from top of radiator to center of ½ inch diameter top rod hole—3⅞ inches. Rod hole is ⅛″ off center line of nipple opening.

Add ½ inch to length for each bushing.

Guaranteed Heat Emission of 240 B. T. U. per Square Foot listed rating in room temperature of 70° F. with Steam at 215° F.

Interchangeable for Steam or Water.

Detail of hangers furnished on request.

NATIONAL ***MADE-TO-MEASURE*** HEATING SYSTEMS

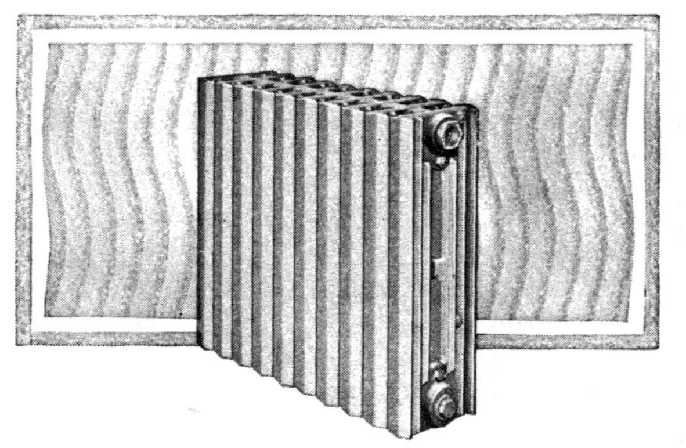

Four Tube Panel Radiation—Sizes and Ratings

Number of Sections	Length Overall Inches	17-Inch Height 2⅔ Square Feet Per Section	20-Inch Height 3 Square Feet Per Section	23-Inch Height 3⅓ Square Feet Per Section
2	4½	5⅓	6	6⅔
3	7	8	9	10
4	9½	10⅔	12	13⅓
5	12	13⅓	15	16⅔
6	14½	16	18	20
7	17	18⅔	21	23⅓
8	19½	21⅓	24	26⅔
9	22	24	27	30
10	24½	26⅔	30	33⅓
11	27	29⅓	33	36⅔
12	29½	32	36	40
13	32	34⅔	39	43⅓
14	34½	37⅓	42	46⅔
15	37	40	45	50
16	39½	43⅔	48	53⅓
17	42	45⅓	51	56⅔
18	44½	48	54	60
19	47	50⅔	57	63⅓
20	49½	53⅓	60	66⅔
21	52	56	63	70
22	54½	58⅔	66	73⅓
23	57	61⅓	69	76⅔
24	59½	64	72	80
25	62	66⅔	75	83⅓

Four Tube Panel Radiation

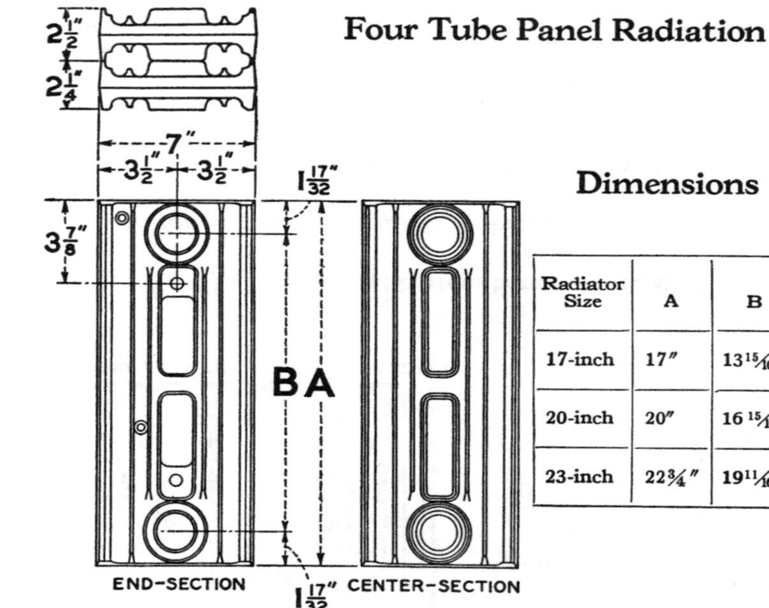

Dimensions

Radiator Size	A	B
17-inch	17″	13 15/16″
20-inch	20″	16 15/16″
23-inch	22¾″	19 11/16″

Tappings—1½ inch top and bottom both ends. Bushed to meet requirements.

Connections—Assembled with extra heavy Malleable Iron Push Nipples.

Vents—All Panel Radiators regularly furnished with Steam and Water Vents.

Note: Distance from top of radiator to center of ½ inch diameter top rod hole—3⅞ inches.

Add ½ inch to length for each bushing.

Guaranteed Heat Emission of 240 B. T. U. per Square Foot listed rating in room temperature of 70° F. with Steam at 215° F.

Interchangeable for Steam or Water.

Detail of hangers furnished on request.

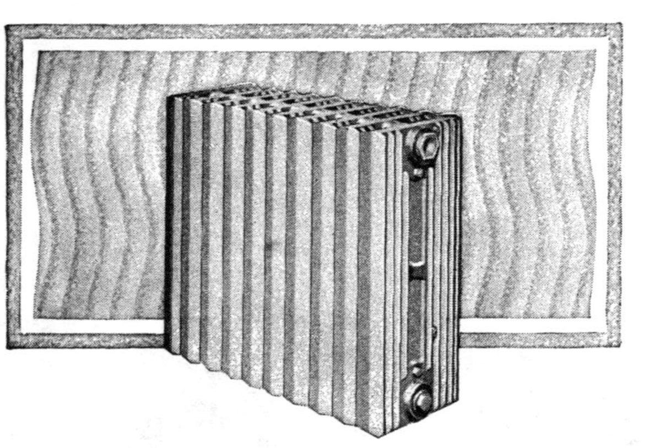

Five Tube Panel Radiation—Sizes and Ratings

Number of Sections	Length Overall Inches	17-Inch Height 3¼ Square Feet Per Section	23-Inch Height 4 Square Feet Per Section
2	4½	6½	8
3	7	9¾	12
4	9½	13	16
5	12	16¼	20
6	14½	19½	24
7	17	22¾	28
8	19½	26	32
9	22	29¼	36
10	24½	32½	40
11	27	35¾	44
12	29½	39	48
13	32	42¼	52
14	34½	45½	56
15	37	48¾	60
16	39½	52	64
17	42	55¼	68
18	44½	58½	72
19	47	61¾	76
20	49½	65	80
21	52	68¼	84
22	54½	71½	88
23	57	74¾	92
24	59½	78	96
25	62	81¼	100

NATIONAL PANEL RADIATION

Five Tube Panel Radiation

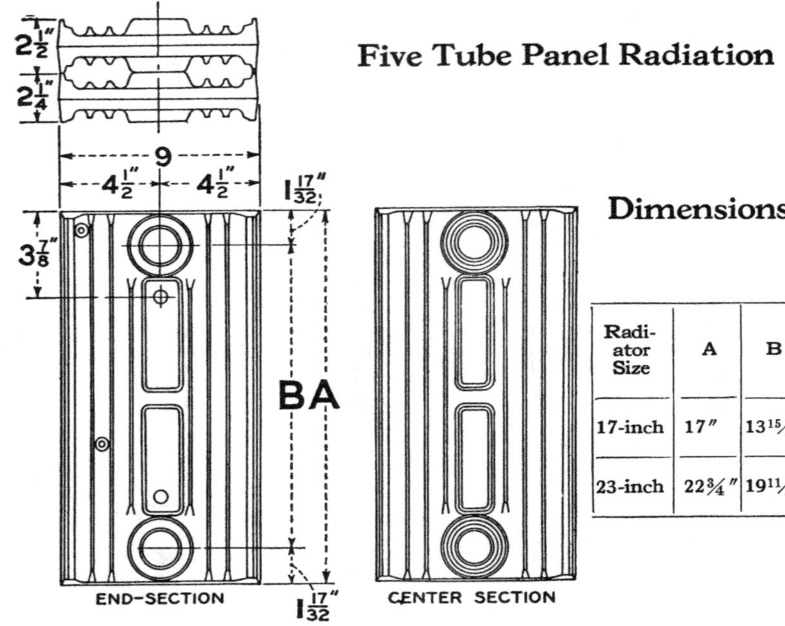

Dimensions

Radiator Size	A	B
17-inch	17″	13 15/16″
23-inch	22¾″	19 11/16″

Tappings—1½ inch top and bottom both ends. Bushed to meet requirements.

Connections—Assembled with extra heavy Malleable Iron Push Nipples.

Vents—All Panel Radiators regularly furnished with Steam and Water Vents.

Note: Distance from top of radiator to center of ½ inch diameter top rod hole—3⅞ inches.

Add ½ inch to length for each bushing.

Guaranteed Heat Emission of 240 B. T. U. per Square Foot listed rating in room temperature of 70° F. with Steam at 215° F.

Interchangeable for Steam or Water.

Detail of hangers furnished on request.

NATIONAL ***MADE-TO-MEASURE*** HEATING SYSTEMS

Richardson New Two-Tube Wall Radiators

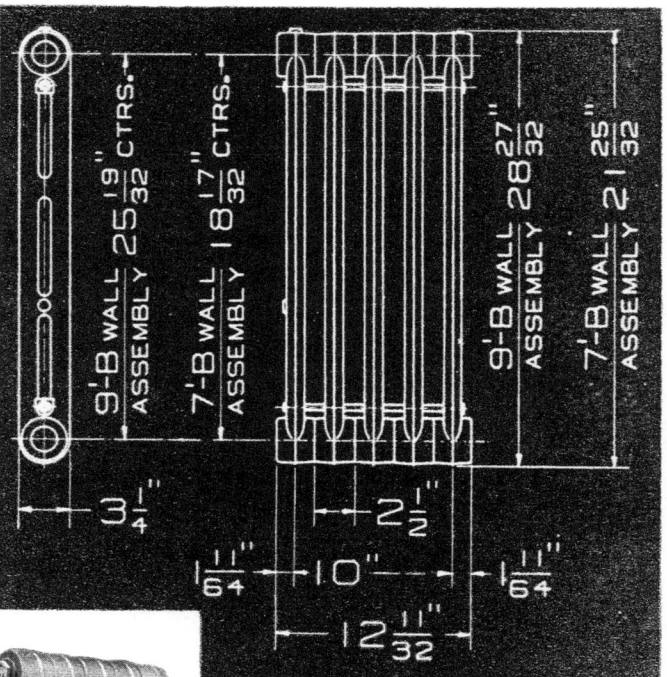

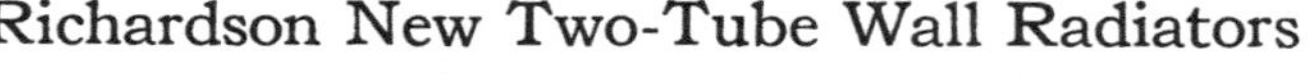

A Wall Radiator in the new and lighter tube style, procurable in exact footage requirement.

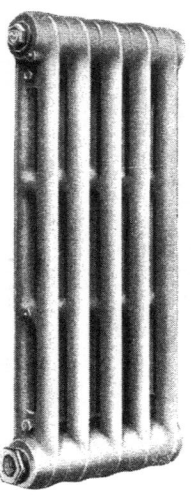

Richardson Wall and Two-Tube Radiators

2-Tube Wall Radiators

For Steam and Water

Section Numbers	Height Inches	Width	Distance Center to Center of Tappings	Heating Surface Sq. Ft.
7-B	21 25/32	12 7/20	18 17/32	7
9-B	28 27/32	12 7/20	25 19/32	9

Thickness without brackets, 3¼ inches; thickness with brackets, 3¾ inches.

All tappings right hand thread unless ordered otherwise on special order.

2-Tube Wall Radiators

For Steam and Water

Number of Sections	Length 2½ In. Per Section	7-B Type 1⅖ Sq. Ft. Per Section	9-B Type 1⅘ Sq. Ft. Per Section
2	5	2⅘	3⅗
3	7½	4⅕	5⅖
4	10	5⅗	7⅕
5	12½	7	9
6	15	8⅖	10⅘
7	17½	9⅘	12⅗
8	20	11⅕	14⅖
9	22½	12⅗	16⅕
10	25	14	18
11	27½	15⅖	19⅘
12	30	16⅘	21⅗
13	32½	18⅕	23⅖
14	35	19⅗	25⅕
15	37½	21	27
16	40	22⅖	28⅘
17	42½	23⅘	30⅗
18	45	25⅕	32⅖
19	47½	26⅗	34⅕
20	50	28	36
21	52½	29⅖	37⅘
22	55	30⅘	39⅗
23	57½	32⅕	41⅖
24	60	33⅗	43⅕
25	62½	35	45
Distance from center of top tappings to center of bottom tappings, inches		18 17/32	25 19/32
Width, inches		3¼	3¼

Radiators tapped 1½ inches, top and bottom both ends.
Allow ⅛ inch for each bushing in estimating length of radiators.
Furnished with standard 4½-inch legs on special order at no extra charge.

Richardson Three-Tube Radiators

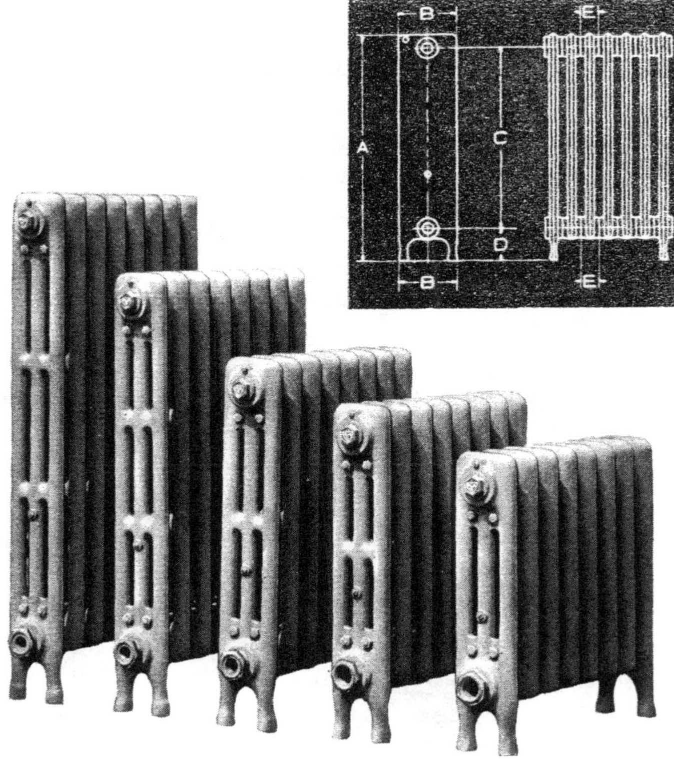

A Radiator of high efficiency and limited space-demand for use where a narrow radiator is required, as in halls and bathrooms.

Three-Tube

Height A	Width B	C	D	E	Sq. Ft. Per Sec.
38"	4 5/8"	31 1/32"	4 1/2"	2 1/2"	3 1/2
32"	4 5/8"	25 5/32"	4 1/2"	2 1/2"	3
26"	4 5/8"	19 5/64"	4 1/2"	2 1/2"	2 1/3
23"	4 5/8"	16 5/32"	4 1/2"	2 1/2"	2
20"	4 5/8"	13 3/32"	4 1/2"	2 1/2"	1 3/4

RICHARDSON AND BOYNTON CO.

Richardson Three-Tube Radiators

3-Tube Radiators

For Steam and Water

Number of Sections	Length 2 1/2 Inches Per Section	38-Inch 3 1/2 Sq. Ft. Per Section	32-Inch 3 Sq. Ft. Per Section	26-Inch 2 1/3 Sq. Ft. Per Section	23-Inch 2 Sq. Ft. Per Section	20-Inch 1 3/4 Sq. Ft. Per Section
2	5	7	6	4 2/3	4	3 1/2
3	7 1/2	10 1/2	9	7	6	5 1/4
4	10	14	12	9 1/3	8	7
5	12 1/2	17 1/2	15	11 2/3	10	8 3/4
6	15	21	18	14	12	10 1/2
7	17 1/2	24 1/2	21	16 1/3	14	12 1/4
8	20	28	24	18 2/3	16	14
9	22 1/2	31 1/2	27	21	18	15 3/4
10	25	35	30	23 1/3	20	17 1/2
11	27 1/2	38 1/2	33	25 2/3	22	19 1/4
12	30	42	36	28	24	21
13	32 1/2	45 1/2	39	30 1/3	26	22 3/4
14	35	49	42	32 2/3	28	24 1/2
15	37 1/2	52 1/2	45	35	30	26 1/4
16	40	56	48	37 1/3	32	28
17	42 1/2	59 1/2	51	39 2/3	34	29 3/4
18	45	63	54	42	36	31 1/2
19	47 1/2	66 1/2	57	44 1/3	38	33 1/4
20	50	70	60	46 2/3	40	35
21	52 1/2	73 1/2	63	49	42	36 3/4
22	55	77	66	51 1/3	44	38 1/2
23	57 1/2	80 1/2	69	53 2/3	46	40 1/4
24	60	84	72	56	48	42
25	62 1/2	87 1/2	75	58 1/3	50	43 3/4
Distance from floor to center of upper tappings, inches		35 17/32	29 21/32	23 37/64	20 21/32	17 19/32
Distance from floor to center of bottom tappings, inches		4 1/2	4 1/2	4 1/2	4 1/2	4 1/2
Width, inches		4 5/8	4 5/8	4 5/8	4 5/8	4 5/8
Width at legs, inches		4 5/8	4 5/8	4 5/8	4 5/8	4 5/8

Radiators tapped 1 1/2 inches, top and bottom both ends.
Allow 1/2 inch for each bushing in estimating length of radiators.
Furnished with 6-inch legs or without legs on special order.

Richardson & Boynton Co. – *circa 1931*

Richardson Four-Tube Radiators

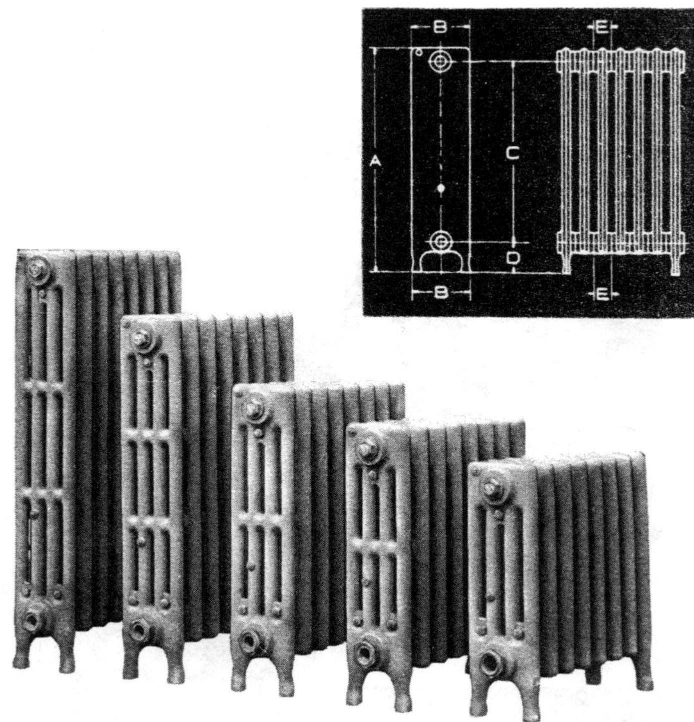

The Four-Tube Radiator, particularly the lower heights, is favored for bedrooms, where unobtrusive harmony with the furnishings is so necessary.

Four-Tube

Height A	Width B	C	D	E	Sq. Ft. Per Sec.
38″	6 5/16″	31 15/32″	4 1/2″	2 1/2″	4 1/4
32″	6 5/16″	25 9/16″	4 1/2″	2 1/2″	3 1/2
26″	6 5/16″	19 9/16″	4 1/2″	2 1/2″	2 3/4
23″	6 5/16″	16 17/32″	4 1/2″	2 1/2″	2 1/2
20″	6 5/16″	13 9/16″	4 1/2″	2 1/2″	2 1/4

RICHARDSON AND BOYNTON CO.

Richardson Four-Tube Radiators

4-Tube Radiators

For Steam and Water

Number of Sections	Length 2 1/2 Inches Per Section	38-Inch 4 1/4 Sq. Ft. Per Section	32-Inch 3 1/2 Sq. Ft. Per Section	26-Inch 2 3/4 Sq. Ft. Per Section	23-Inch 2 1/2 Sq. Ft. Per Section	20-Inch 2 1/4 Sq. Ft. Per Section
2	5	8 1/2	7	5 1/2	5	4 1/2
3	7 1/2	12 3/4	10 1/2	8 1/4	7 1/2	6 3/4
4	10	17	14	11	10	9
5	12 1/2	21 1/4	17 1/2	13 3/4	12 1/2	11 1/4
6	15	25 1/2	21	16 1/2	15	13 1/2
7	17 1/2	29 3/4	24 1/2	19 1/4	17 1/2	15 3/4
8	20	34	28	22	20	18
9	22 1/2	38 1/4	31 1/2	24 3/4	22 1/2	20 1/4
10	25	42 1/2	35	27 1/2	25	22 1/2
11	27 1/2	46 3/4	38 1/2	30 1/4	27 1/2	24 3/4
12	30	51	42	33	30	27
13	32 1/2	55 1/4	45 1/2	35 3/4	32 1/2	29 1/4
14	35	59 1/2	49	38 1/2	35	31 1/2
15	37 1/2	63 3/4	52 1/2	41 1/4	37 1/2	33 3/4
16	40	68	56	44	40	36
17	42 1/2	72 1/4	59 1/2	46 3/4	42 1/2	38 1/4
18	45	76 1/2	63	49 1/2	45	40 1/2
19	47 1/2	80 3/4	66 1/2	52 1/4	47 1/2	42 3/4
20	50	85	70	55	50	45
21	52 1/2	89 1/4	73 1/2	57 3/4	52 1/2	47 1/4
22	55	93 1/2	77	60 1/2	55	49 1/2
23	57 1/2	97 3/4	80 1/2	63 1/4	57 1/2	51 3/4
24	60	102	84	66	60	54
25	62 1/2	106 1/4	87 1/2	68 3/4	62 1/2	56 1/4
Distance from floor to center of upper tappings, inches		35 31/32	30 1/16	24 1/16	21 1/32	18 1/16
Distance from floor to center of bottom tappings, inches		4 1/2	4 1/2	4 1/2	4 1/2	4 1/2
Width, inches		6 5/16	6 5/16	6 5/16	6 5/16	6 5/16
Width at legs, inches		6 5/16	6 5/16	6 5/16	6 5/16	6 5/16

Radiators tapped 1 1/2 inches, top and bottom both ends.
Allow 1/2 inch for each bushing in estimating length of radiators.
Furnished with 6-inch legs or without legs on special order.

Richardson Five-Tube Radiators

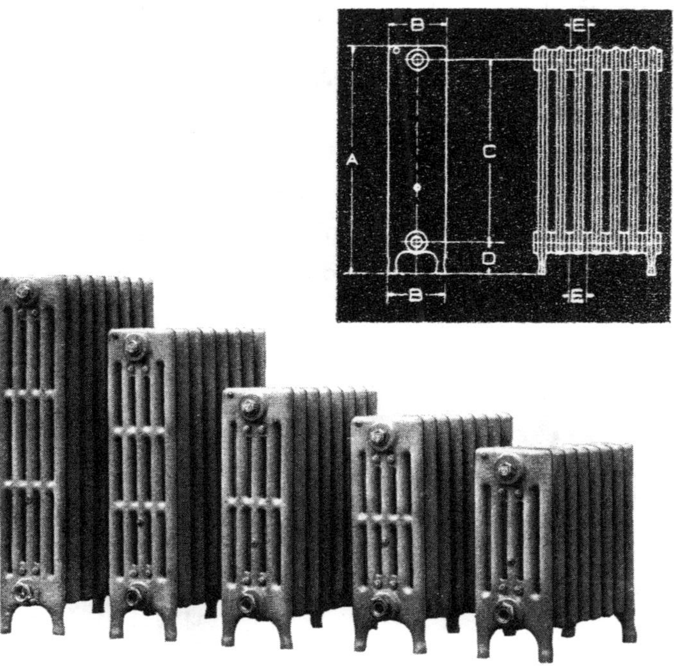

The most popular size of all, adaptable for almost every heating requirement, in a style and effect that is appreciated by discriminating architects and builders.

Five-Tube

Height A	Width B	C	D	E	Sq. Ft. Per Sec.
38″	8″	31 15/32″	4 1/2″	2 1/2″	5
32″	8″	25 9/16″	4 1/2″	2 1/2″	4 1/3
26″	8″	19 9/16″	4 1/2″	2 1/2″	3 1/2
23″	8″	16 17/32″	4 1/2″	2 1/2″	3
20″	8″	13 9/16″	4 1/2″	2 1/2″	2 2/3

Richardson Five-Tube Radiators

5-Tube Radiators

For Steam and Water

Number of Sections	Length 2 1/2 Inches Per Section	38-Inch 5 Sq. Ft. Per Section	32-Inch 4 1/3 Sq. Ft. Per Section	26-Inch 3 1/2 Sq. Ft. Per Section	23-Inch 3 Sq. Ft. Per Section	20-Inch 2 2/3 Sq. Ft. Per Section
2	5	10	8 2/3	7	6	5 1/3
3	7 1/2	15	13	10 1/2	9	8
4	10	20	17 1/3	14	12	10 2/3
5	12 1/2	25	21 2/3	17 1/2	15	13 1/3
6	15	30	26	21	18	16
7	17 1/2	35	30 1/3	24 1/2	21	18 2/3
8	20	40	34 2/3	28	24	21 1/3
9	22 1/2	45	39	31 1/2	27	24
10	25	50	43 1/3	35	30	26 2/3
11	27 1/2	55	47 2/3	38 1/2	33	29 1/3
12	30	60	52	42	36	32
13	32 1/2	65	56 1/3	45 1/2	39	34 2/3
14	35	70	60 2/3	49	42	37 1/3
15	37 1/2	75	65	52 1/2	45	40
16	40	80	69 1/3	56	48	42 2/3
17	42 1/2	85	73 2/3	59 1/2	51	45 1/3
18	45	90	78	63	54	48
19	47 1/2	95	82 1/3	66 1/2	57	50 2/3
20	50	100	86 2/3	70	60	53 1/3
21	52 1/2	105	91	73 1/2	63	56
22	55	110	95 1/3	77	66	58 2/3
23	57 1/2	115	99 2/3	80 1/2	69	61 1/3
24	60	120	104	84	72	64
25	62 1/2	125	108 1/3	87 1/2	75	66 2/3
Distance from floor to center of upper tappings, inches		35 31/32	30 1/16	24 1/16	21 1/32	18 1/16
Distance from floor to center of bottom tappings, inches		4 1/2	4 1/2	4 1/2	4 1/2	4 1/2
Width, inches		8	8	8	8	8
Width at legs, inches		8	8	8	8	8

Radiators tapped 1 1/2 inches, top and bottom both ends.
Allow 1/2 inch for each bushing in estimating length of radiators.
Furnished with 6-inch legs or without legs on special order.

Richardson Six-Tube Radiators

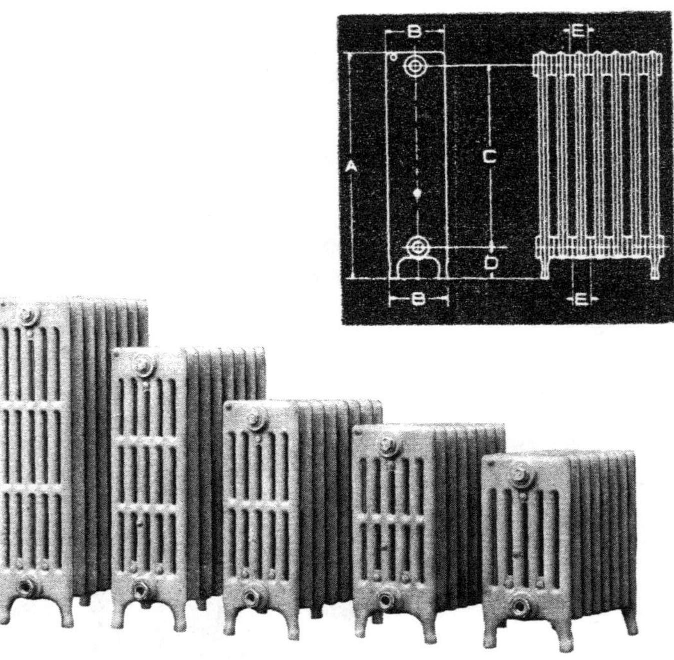

Where heat in large volume is required and little wall space is available, the Richardson Six-tube radiator will be found unusually valuable.

Six-Tube

Height A	Width B	C	D	E	Sq. Ft. Per Sec.
38″	9 11/16″	31 15/32″	4 1/2″	2 1/2″	6
32″	9 11/16″	25 9/16″	4 1/2″	2 1/2″	5
26″	9 11/16″	19 9/16″	4 1/2″	2 1/2″	4
23″	9 11/16″	16 17/32″	4 1/2″	2 1/2″	3 1/2
20″	9 11/16″	13 9/16″	4 1/2″	2 1/2″	3

RICHARDSON AND BOYNTON CO.

Richardson Six-Tube Radiators

6-Tube Radiators

For Steam and Water

Number of Sections	Length 2 1/2 Inches Per Section	38-Inch 6 Sq. Ft. Per Section	32-Inch 5 Sq. Ft. Per Section	26-Inch 4 Sq. Ft. Per Section	23-Inch 3 1/2 Sq. Ft. Per Section	20-Inch 3 Sq. Ft. Per Section
2	5	12	10	8	7	6
3	7 1/2	18	15	12	10 1/2	9
4	10	24	20	16	14	12
5	12 1/2	30	25	20	17 1/2	15
6	15	36	30	24	21	18
7	17 1/2	42	35	28	24 1/2	21
8	20	48	40	32	28	24
9	22 1/2	54	45	36	31 1/2	27
10	25	60	50	40	35	30
11	27 1/2	66	55	44	38 1/2	33
12	30	72	60	48	42	36
13	32 1/2	78	65	52	45 1/2	39
14	35	84	70	56	49	42
15	37 1/2	90	75	60	52 1/2	45
16	40	96	80	64	56	48
17	42 1/2	102	85	68	59 1/2	51
18	45	108	90	72	63	54
19	47 1/2	114	95	76	66 1/2	57
20	50	120	100	80	70	60
21	52 1/2	126	105	84	73 1/2	63
22	55	132	110	88	77	66
23	57 1/2	138	115	92	80 1/2	69
24	60	144	120	96	84	72
25	62 1/2	150	125	100	87 1/2	75
Distance from floor to center of upper tappings, inches		35 31/32	30 1/16	24 1/16	21 1/32	18 1/16
Distance from floor to center of bottom tappings, inches		4 1/2	4 1/2	4 1/2	4 1/2	4 1/2
Width, inches		9 11/16	9 11/16	9 11/16	9 11/16	9 11/16
Width at legs, inches		9 11/16	9 11/16	9 11/16	9 11/16	9 11/16

Radiators tapped 1 1/2 inches, top and bottom both ends.
Allow 1/2 inch for each bushing in estimating length of radiators.
Furnished with 6-inch legs or without legs on special order.

Richardson Seven-Tube Radiators

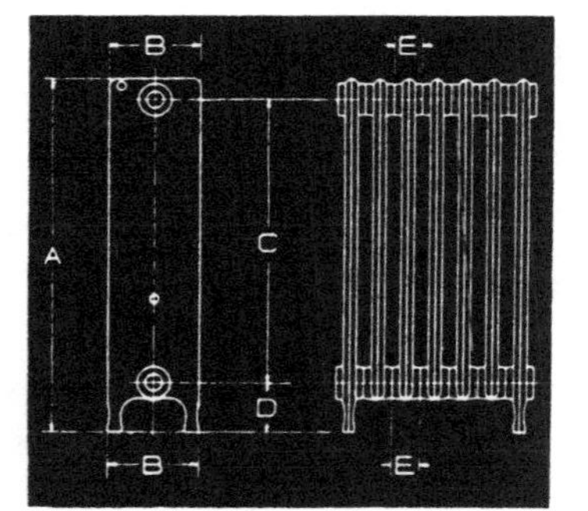

Where a radiator is required to fit under window sills and still give a maximum of heat, the Richardson Window Radiator meets both demands most effectively.

Seven-Tube

Height A	Width B	C	D	E	Sq. Ft. Per Sec.
20″	11⅜″	15 1/16″	3″	2½″	3⅔
17″	11⅜″	12 1/16″	3″	2½″	3
14″	11⅜″	9 1/16″	3″	2½″	2½

RICHARDSON AND BOYNTON CO.

Richardson Window Radiators

7-Tube Window Radiators

For Steam and Water

Number of Sections	Length 2½ Inches Per Section	20-Inch 3⅔ Sq. Ft. Per Section	17-Inch 3 Sq. Ft. Per Section	14-Inch 2½ Sq. Ft. Per Section
2	5	7⅓	6	5
3	7½	11	9	7½
4	10	14⅔	12	10
5	12½	18⅓	15	12½
6	15	22	18	15
7	17½	25⅔	21	17½
8	20	29⅓	24	20
9	22½	33	27	22½
10	25	36⅔	30	25
11	27½	40⅓	33	27½
12	30	44	36	30
13	32½	47⅔	39	32½
14	35	51⅓	42	35
15	37½	55	45	37½
16	40	58⅔	48	40
17	42½	62⅓	51	42½
18	45	66	54	45
19	47½	69⅔	57	47½
20	50	73⅓	60	50
21	52½	77	63	52½
22	55	80⅔	66	55
23	57½	84⅓	69	57½
24	60	88	72	60
25	62½	91⅔	75	62½
Distance from floor to center of upper tappings, inches		18 1/16	15 1/16	12 1/16
Distance from floor to center of bottom tappings, inches		3	3	3
Width, inches		11⅜	11⅜	11⅜
Width at legs, inches		11⅜	11⅜	11⅜

Radiators tapped 1½ inches, top and bottom both ends.
Allow ½ inch for each bushing in estimating length of radiators.
Furnished with 4½-inch legs or without legs on special order.

Pressed Metal Radiator Co. – *circa 1920*

"Kinnear"
Improved
Pressed
Radiators
for
Steam and
Hot Water
Heating

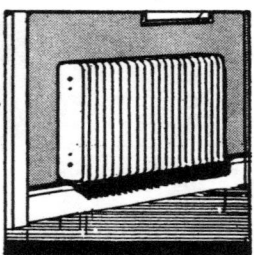

On the Wall
Off the Floor
Out of the Way

Made
Exclusively by the
PRESSED METAL RADIATOR CO.
General Offices
BAILEY-FARREL BLDG. PITTSBURGH Pa.

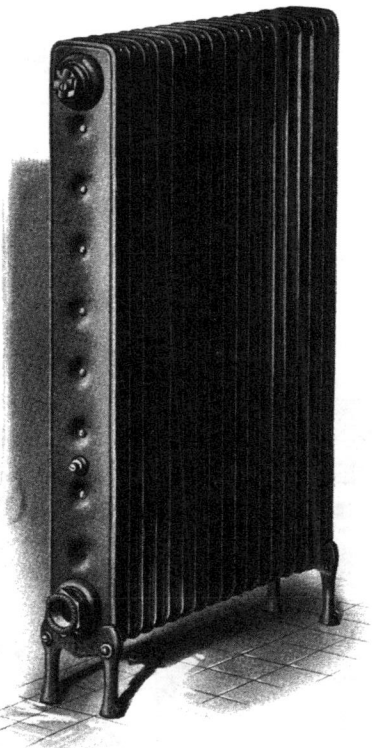

FLOOR OR WALL RADIATOR

BEAVER

For Steam or Water

Each Section is 4 inches wide. Leg spread 5 inches.

See opposite page for table of sizes and ratings.

BEAVER

FLOOR OR WALL RADIATOR

For Steam or Water

Each Section is 4 inches wide. Leg spread 5 inches.

No. of Sections	* Length 1⅛″ per Section	HEATING SURFACE—SQUARE FEET			
		32″ high	26″ high	20″ high	14″ high
		2 sq. ft. per Section	1⅔ sq. ft. per Section	1⅓ sq. ft. per Section	1 sq. ft. per Section
4	5	8	6⅔	5⅓	4
5	6⅛	10	8⅓	6⅔	5
6	7¼	12	10	8	6
7	8⅜	14	11⅔	9⅓	7
8	9½	16	13⅓	10⅔	8
9	10⅝	18	15	12	9
10	11¾	20	16⅔	13⅓	10
11	12⅞	22	18⅓	14⅔	11
12	14	24	20	16	12
13	15⅛	26	21⅔	17⅓	13
14	16¼	28	23⅓	18⅔	14
15	17⅜	30	25	20	15
16	18½	32	26⅔	21⅓	16
17	19⅝	34	28⅓	22⅔	17
18	20¾	36	30	24	18
19	21⅞	38	31⅔	25⅓	19
20	23	40	33⅓	26⅔	20
21	24⅛	42	35	28	21
22	25¼	44	36⅔	29⅓	22
23	26⅜	46	38⅓	30⅔	23
24	27½	48	40	32	24
25	28⅝	50	41⅔	33⅓	25
26	29¾	52	43⅓	34⅔	26
27	30⅞	54	45	36	27
28	32	56	46⅔	37⅓	28
29	33⅛	58	48⅓	38⅔	29
30	34¼	60	50	40	30
31	35⅜	62	51⅔	41⅓	31
32	36½	64	53⅓	42⅔	32
33	37⅝	66	55	44	33
34	38¾	68	56⅔	45⅓	34
35	39⅞	70	58⅓	46⅔	35
List Price per square foot		46c	50c	57c	64c

*Length of radiator overall including malleable iron hubs. Add ¾-in. for each bushing.

Legs are detachable and can be applied to any section.

Above radiators are tapped 1½ in. and bushed as per list on page 36.

For complete dimensions and "roughing in" measurements see page 30.

For Legs, Ceiling and Adjustable Wall Brackets see pages 24 and 25.

Price list see page 37.

FLOOR OR WALL RADIATOR

INVINCIBLE

For Steam or Water

Each section is 7⅝ inches wide. Leg spread 8½ inches.

See opposite page for table of sizes and ratings.

INVINCIBLE

FLOOR OR WALL RADIATOR

For Steam or Water

Each section is 7⅝ inches wide. Leg spread 8½ inches.

No. of Sec-tions	* Length 2″ per Section	HEATING SURFACE—SQUARE FEET					
		38″ high	32″ high	26″ high	23″ high	20″ high	14″ high
		4 sq. ft. per Section	3⅓ sq. ft. per Section	2⅔ sq. ft. per Section	2⅓ sq. ft. per Section	2 sq. ft. per Section	1⅓ sq. ft. per Section
4	8	16	13⅓	10⅔	9⅓	8	5⅓
5	10	20	16⅔	13⅓	11⅔	10	6⅔
6	12	24	20	16	14	12	8
7	14	28	23⅓	18⅔	16⅓	14	9⅓
8	16	32	26⅔	21⅓	18⅔	16	10⅔
9	18	36	30	24	21	18	12
10	20	40	33⅓	26⅔	23⅓	20	13⅓
11	22	44	36⅔	29⅓	25⅔	22	14⅔
12	24	48	40	32	28	24	16
13	26	52	43⅓	34⅔	30⅓	26	17⅓
14	28	56	46⅔	37⅓	32⅔	28	18⅔
15	30	60	50	40	35	30	20
16	32	64	53⅓	42⅔	37⅓	32	21⅓
17	34	68	56⅔	45⅓	39⅔	34	22⅔
18	36	72	60	48	42	36	24
19	38	76	63⅓	50⅔	44⅓	38	25⅓
20	40	80	66⅔	53⅓	46⅔	40	26⅔
21	42	84	70	56	49	42	28
22	44	88	73⅓	58⅔	51⅓	44	29⅓
23	46	92	76⅔	61⅓	53⅔	46	30⅔
24	48	96	80	64	56	48	32
25	50	100	83⅓	66⅔	58⅓	50	33⅓
26	52	104	86⅔	69⅓	60⅔	52	34⅔
27	54	108	90	72	63	54	36
28	56	112	93⅓	74⅔	65⅓	56	37⅓
29	58	116	96⅔	77⅓	67⅔	58	38⅔
30	60	120	100	80	70	60	40
31	62	124	103⅓	82⅔	72⅓	62	41⅓
32	64	128	106⅔	85⅓	74⅔	64	42⅔
33	66	132	110	88	77	66	44
34	68	136	113⅓	90⅔	79⅓	68	45⅓
35	70	140	116⅔	93⅓	81⅔	70	46⅔
List Price per sq. ft.		42c	46c	50c	53c	57c	64c

* Length of radiator overall including malleable iron hubs. Add ¾-inch for each Bushing.

Legs are detachable and can be applied to any section.

Above radiators are tapped 2 in. and bushed as per list on page 36.

For complete dimensions and "roughing in" measurements see page 31.

For Legs, Ceiling and Adjustable Wall Brackets see pages 24 and 25.

Price List see page 37.

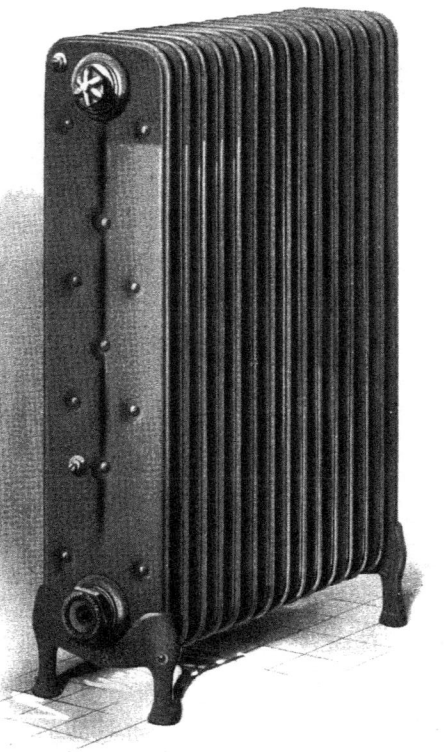

FLOOR OR WALL RADIATOR

HECLA

For Steam or Water

Each section is 7⅝ inches wide. Leg spread 8½ inches.

See opposite page for table of sizes and ratings

HECLA

FLOOR OR WALL RADIATOR

For Steam or Water

Each Section is 7⅝ inches wide. Leg spread 8½ inches.

No. of Sections	* Length 1½" per Section	HEATING SURFACE—SQUARE FEET					
		38" high	32" high	26" high	23" high	20" high	14" high
		4 sq. ft. per Section	3⅓ sq. ft. per Section	2⅔ sq. ft. per Section	2⅓ sq. ft. per Section	2 sq. ft. per Section	1⅓ sq. ft. per Section
4	6½	16	13⅓	10⅔	9⅓	8	5⅓
5	8	20	16⅔	13⅓	11⅔	10	6⅔
6	9½	24	20	16	14	12	8
7	11	28	23⅓	18⅔	16⅓	14	9⅓
8	12½	32	26⅔	21⅓	18⅔	16	10⅔
9	14	36	30	24	21	18	12
10	15½	40	33⅓	26⅔	23⅓	20	13⅓
11	17	44	36⅔	29⅓	25⅔	22	14⅔
12	18½	48	40	32	28	24	16
13	20	52	43⅓	34⅔	30⅓	26	17⅓
14	21½	56	46⅔	37⅓	32⅔	28	18⅔
15	23	60	50	40	35	30	20
16	24½	64	53⅓	42⅔	37⅓	32	21⅓
17	26	68	56⅔	45⅓	39⅔	34	22⅔
18	27½	72	60	48	42	36	24
19	29	76	63⅓	50⅔	44⅓	38	25⅓
20	30½	80	66⅔	53⅓	46⅔	40	26⅔
21	32	84	70	56	49	42	28
22	33½	88	73⅓	58⅔	51⅓	44	29⅓
23	35	92	76⅔	61⅓	53⅔	46	30⅔
24	36½	96	80	64	56	48	32
25	38	100	83⅓	66⅔	58⅓	50	33⅓
26	39½	104	86⅔	69⅓	60⅔	52	34⅔
27	41	108	90	72	63	54	36
28	42½	112	93⅓	74⅔	65⅓	56	37⅓
29	44	116	96⅔	77⅓	67⅔	58	38⅔
30	45½	120	100	80	70	60	40
31	47	124	103⅓	82⅔	72⅓	62	41⅓
32	48½	128	106⅔	85⅓	74⅔	64	42⅔
33	50	132	110	88	77	66	44
34	51½	136	113⅓	90⅔	79⅓	68	45⅓
35	53	140	116⅔	93⅓	81⅔	70	46⅔
List Price per sq. ft.		42c	46c	50c	53c	57c	64c

* Length of radiator overall including malleable iron hubs. Add ¾-inch for each Bushing.

Legs are detachable and can be applied to any section.

Above radiators are tapped 2 inches and bushed as per list on page 36.

For complete dimensions and "roughing in" measurements see page 32.

For Legs, Ceiling and Adjustable Wall Brackets see pages 24 and 25.

Price list see page 37.

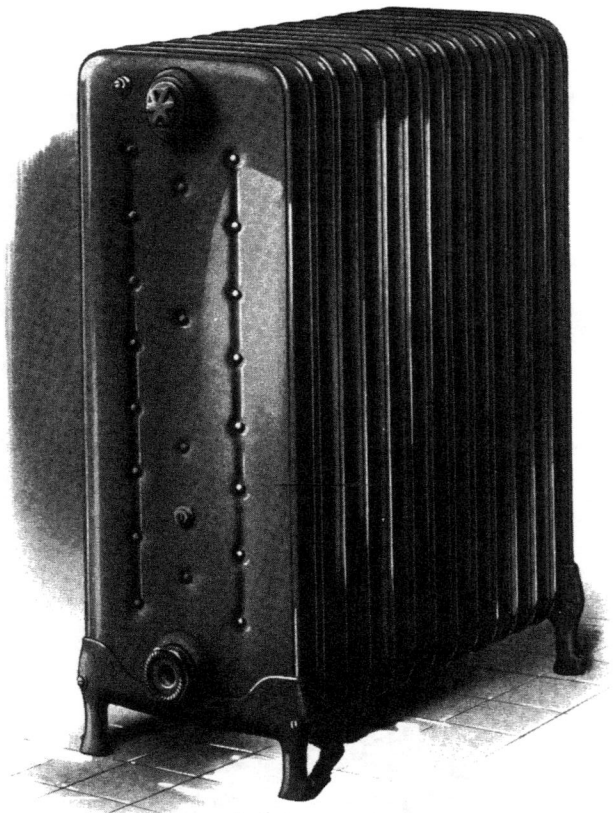

FLOOR OR WALL RADIATOR

EUREKA

For Steam or Water

Each section is 12½ inches wide. Leg spread 13¼ inches.

See opposite page for table of sizes and ratings.

EUREKA

FLOOR OR WALL RADIATOR

For Steam or Water

Each Section is 12½ inches wide. Leg spread 13¼ inches.

No. of Sections	* Length 1¾″ per Section	HEATING SURFACE—SQUARE FEET				
		32″ high	26″ high	20″ high	17½″ high	14″ high
		6 sq. ft. per Section	5 sq. ft. per Section	4 sq. ft. per Section	3⅓ sq. ft. per Section	2⅔ sq. ft. per Section
4	7¼	24	20	16	13⅓	10⅔
5	9	30	25	20	16⅔	13⅓
6	10¾	36	30	24	20	16
7	12½	42	35	28	23⅓	18⅔
8	14¼	48	40	32	26⅔	21⅓
9	16	54	45	36	30	24
10	17¾	60	50	40	33⅓	26⅔
11	19½	66	55	44	36⅔	29⅓
12	21¼	72	60	48	40	32
13	23	78	65	52	43⅓	34⅔
14	24¾	84	70	56	46⅔	37⅓
15	26½	90	75	60	50	40
16	28¼	96	80	64	53⅓	42⅔
17	30	102	85	68	56⅔	45⅓
18	31¾	108	90	72	60	48
19	33½	114	95	76	63⅓	50⅔
20	35¼	120	100	80	66⅔	53⅓
21	37	126	105	84	70	56
22	38¾	132	110	88	73⅓	58⅔
23	40½	138	115	92	76⅔	61⅓
24	42¼	144	120	96	80	64
25	44	150	125	100	83⅓	66⅔
26	45¾	156	130	104	86⅔	69⅓
27	47½	162	135	108	90	72
28	49¼	168	140	112	93⅓	74⅔
29	51	174	145	116	96⅔	77⅓
30	52¾	180	150	120	100	80
31	54½	186	155	124	103⅓	82⅔
32	56¼	192	160	128	106⅔	85⅓
33	58	198	165	132	110	88
34	59¾	204	170	136	113⅓	90⅔
35	61½	210	175	140	116⅔	93⅓
List Price per square foot		46c	50c	57c	60c	64c

* Length of radiator overall including malleable iron hubs. Add ¾-inch for each Bushing.

Legs are detachable and can be applied to any section.

Above radiators are tapped 2 inches and bushed as per list on page 36.

For complete dimensions and "roughing in" measurements see page 33.

For Legs, Ceiling and Adjustable Wall Brackets see pages 24 and 25.

Price List see page 37.

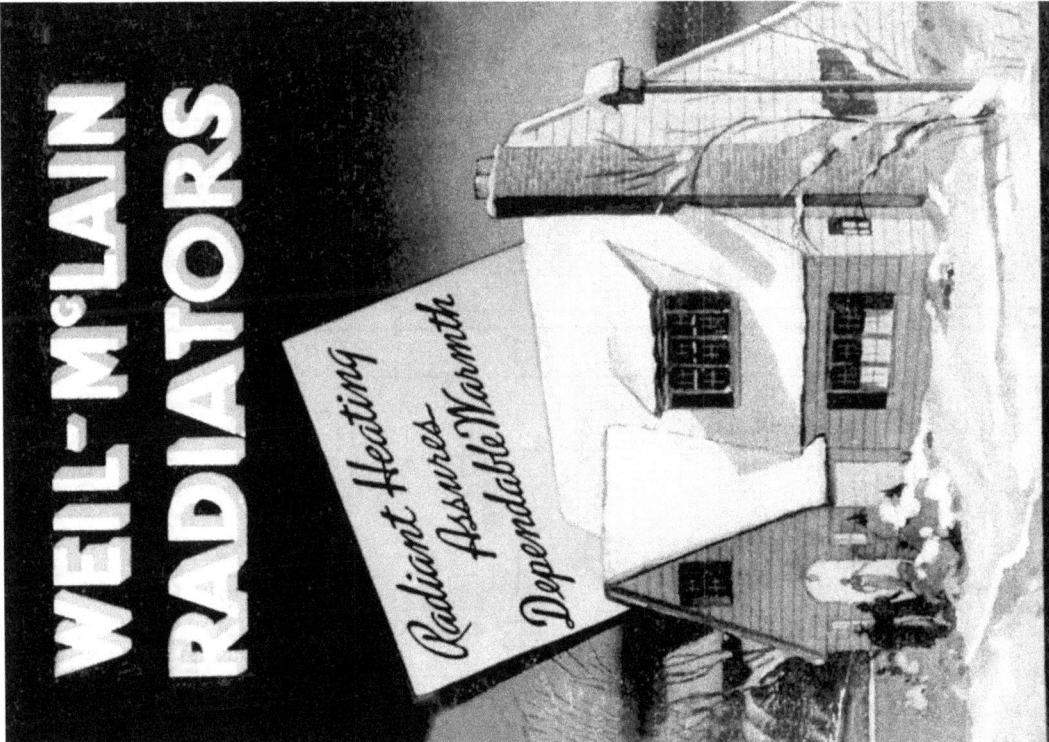

WEIL-McLAIN RADIATORS

Radiant Heating Assures Dependable Warmth

W. G. SHAFER CO, Inc.
100 N. State St.
Syracuse, N. Y.

BOOKLET H-52

Radiator Heat PAYS DIVIDENDS IN BETTER HEALTH . . . GREATER COMFORT AND LOWER HEATING COSTS . . . .

An important advantage of steam, vapor or hot water heating is that it provides the best and most practicable foundation for modern air conditioning. Since the factor of heating is at least eighty per cent of good air conditioning home owners should be sure they have an efficient and positive heating plant. All the supplementary phases of complete air conditioning may be added to dependable radiator heating at any time.

Radiator heat is economical heat because its circulation can be controlled and the heat sent to points where it is needed. Absence of periodic repairs is an added economy.

With radiator heat, room temperatures are not affected by varying winds. Steam, vapor or hot water circulating in a piping system, in contrast with heat circulating through ducts, cannot be influenced by outside wind pressures.

With radiator heat an abundant supply of Domestic Hot Water for the bath, laundry and kitchen can be economically heated in winter or the year around by the water in the heating boiler.

The basement space occupied by a modern boiler is negligible. The piping of hot water and steam or vapor systems is comparatively small and hung close to the ceiling—out of the way.

The Weil-McLain line of Raydiant and Cameo Radiators with ratings, sizes, etc. are shown on the following pages.

Weil-McLain Company
(Radiator Division)
Erie, Pa.

Meet Cold Where Cold Comes in

The chief source of cold in any room is the window. When heat is placed beneath the window the cold air is warmed as it enters—cold does not reach the floor. Illustration below shows how to meet cold where cold comes in. Note that Weil-McLain Radiators supply *both convected and radiant heat* to produce the most comforting and dependable warmth obtainable.

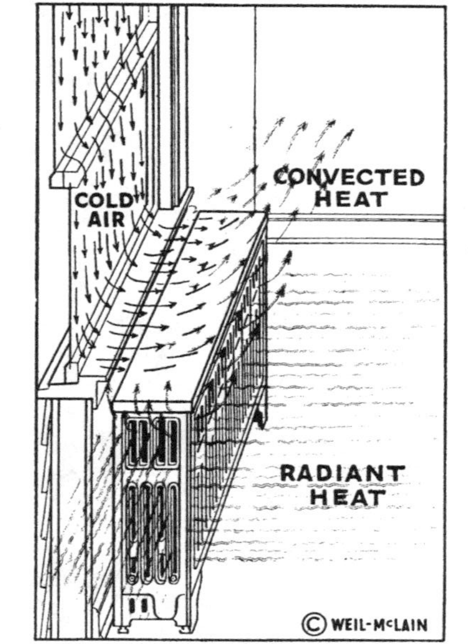

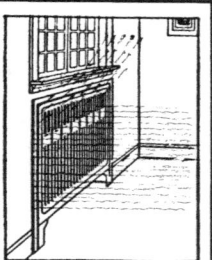

Concealed Raydiant.

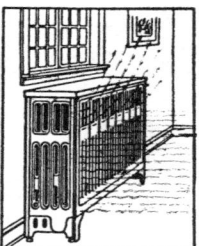

Cabinet Raydiant.

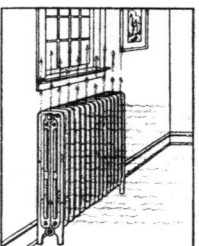

Cameo Junior.

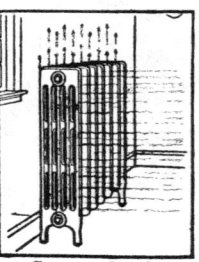

Cameo Senior

Avoid Cold Air and Cold Drafts at Floor Levels with Modern Radiator Heat

Weil-McLain Raydiant Concealed Radiator

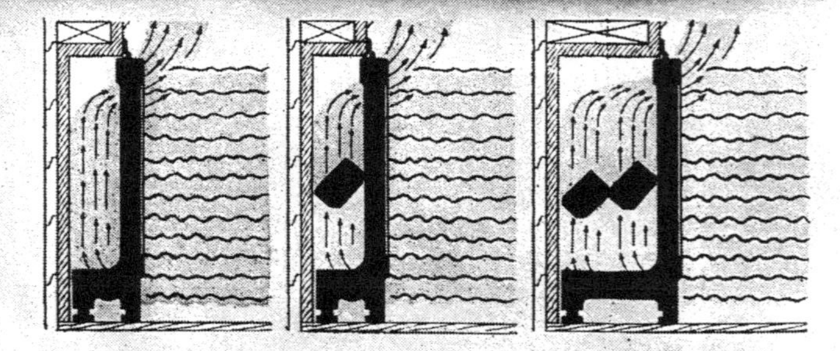

Panels only Single Vectant Double Vectant

Illustrations show the three types of "Concealed" Raydiant. Note the heat action of the "vectants" and the "live" front.

4

Construction Details

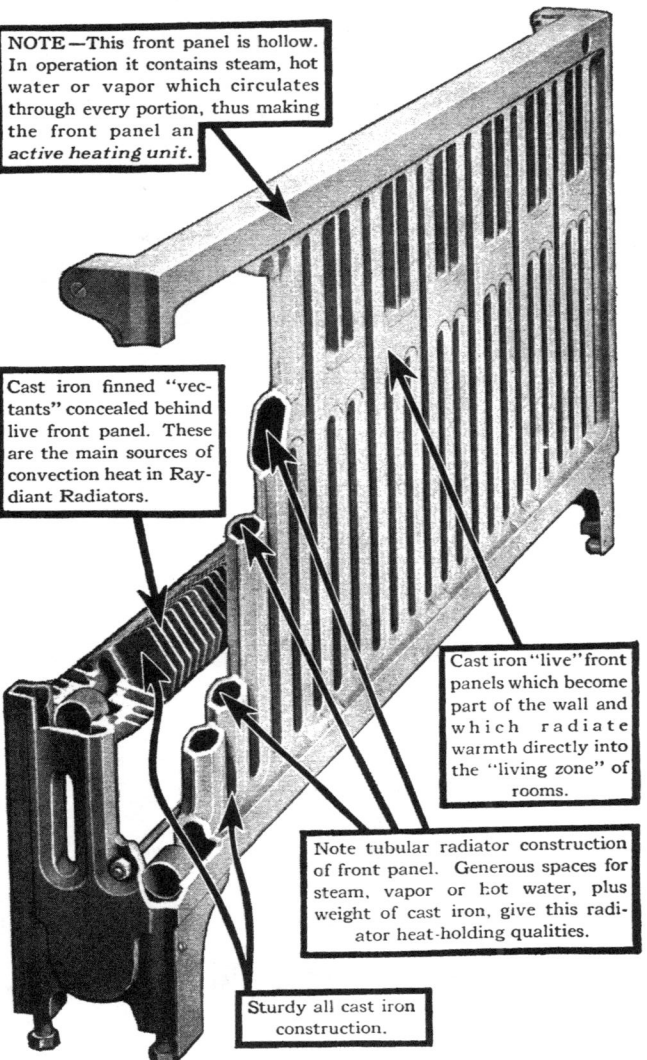

NOTE—This front panel is hollow. In operation it contains steam, hot water or vapor which circulates through every portion, thus making the front panel an *active heating unit.*

Cast iron finned "vectants" concealed behind live front panel. These are the main sources of convection heat in Raydiant Radiators.

Cast iron "live" front panels which become part of the wall and which radiate warmth directly into the "living zone" of rooms.

Note tubular radiator construction of front panel. Generous spaces for steam, vapor or hot water, plus weight of cast iron, give this radiator heat-holding qualities.

Sturdy all cast iron construction.

Weil-McLain Raydiant Concealed Radiators

Panels only—For 4⅛″ Recess

Sizes, Ratings, Heights, etc.

No.	Recess Length "RL" Inches	RECESS HEIGHTS—INCHES 20½	23½	26½	29½
		Ratings (E. D. R. sq. ft.)			
100	13¼	8	9	10	11
105	18	9¾	11¼	12½	14
200	22¾	11¾	13½	15¼	17
205	27½	13¾	15½	18	20
300	32¼	15½	18	20½	23
305	37	17¼	20¼	23	26
400	41¾	19¼	22½	25¾	29
405	46¾	21	24½	28½	32
500	51½	23	27	31	35
505	56¼	24¾	29¼	33½	38
600	61	26¾	31½	36¼	41
605	65¾	28½	33½	39	44
700	70½	30½	36	41½	47
705	75¼	32½	38¼	44	50
800	80	34¼	40½	46¾	53
805	85	36	42½	49½	56
900	89¾	38	45	52	59
905	94½	40	47	54½	62
1000	99¼	42	49½	57	65

Recess Dimensions

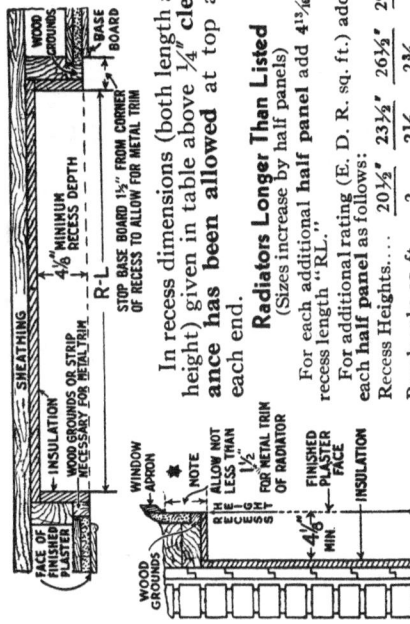

In recess dimensions (both length and height) given in table above ¼″ **clearance has been allowed** at top and each end.

Radiators Longer Than Listed

(Sizes increase by half panels)

For each additional **half panel** add 4$^{13}/_{16}$″ to recess length "RL."

For additional rating (E. D. R. sq. ft.) add for each **half panel** as follows:

Recess Heights....	20½″	23½″	26½″	29½″
Panels only, sq. ft..	2	2½	2¾	3

Weil-McLain Raydiant Concealed Radiators

Single Vectant—For 4⅛″ Recess

Sizes, Ratings, Heights, etc.

No.	Recess Length "RL" Inches	RECESS HEIGHTS—INCHES 20½	23½	26½	29½
		Ratings (E. D. R. sq. ft.)			
100	13¼	10	11¼	12½	13¾
105	18	12¾	14½	16¼	18
200	22¾	15¾	18	20¼	22½
205	27½	18½	21¼	24	27
300	32¼	21½	24¾	28	31
305	37	24¼	28	32	35½
400	41¾	27¼	31½	35½	40
405	46¾	30	35	39½	44½
500	51½	33	38	43½	49
505	56¼	36	41½	47½	53
600	61	39	45	51	57½
605	65¾	−41½	48½	55	62
700	70½	44½	51½	59	66
705	75¼	47½	55	63	70½
800	80	50	58½	67	75
805	85	53	62	70½	79
900	89¾	56	65	74½	84
905	94½	59	68½	78½	88
1000	99¼	62	72	82	92½

Recess Dimensions

SHEATHING
FACE OF FINISHED PLASTER
INSULATION
WOOD GROUNDS OR STRIP NECESSARY FOR METAL TRIM
4⅛″ MINIMUM RECESS DEPTH
WOOD GROUNDS
R-L
BASE BOARD
STOP BASE BOARD 1½″ FROM CORNER OF RECESS TO ALLOW FOR METAL TRIM
WOOD GROUNDS
WINDOW APRON
NOTE
ALLOW NOT LESS THAN 1½″ FOR METAL TRIM OF RADIATOR
RECESS HEIGHT
4⅛″ MIN
FINISHED PLASTER FACE
INSULATION

In recess dimensions (both length and height) given in table above ¼″ **clearance has been allowed** at top and each end.

Radiators Longer Than Listed

(Sizes increase by half panels)

For each additional **half panel** add 4$\frac{13}{16}$″ to recess length "RL."

For additional rating (E. D. R. sq. ft.) add for each **half panel** as follows:

Recess Heights. . .	20½″	23½″	26½″	29½″
SingleVectant,sq.ft	3	3½	4	4½

Weil-McLain Raydiant Concealed Radiators

Double Vectant—For 7¾″ Recess

Sizes, Ratings, Heights — Recess Dimensions

No.	Recess Length "RL" Inches	RECESS HEIGHTS—INCHES 20½	23½	26½	29½
		Ratings (E. D. R. sq. ft.)			
100	13¼	11	13	15	16¾
105	18	15	17½	20	22¼
200	22¾	19	22	25	27¾
205	27½	23	26½	30	33½
300	32¼	27	31	35	39
305	37	31	35½	40	44½
400	41¾	35	40	45	50
405	46¾	39	44½	50	55½
500	51½	43	49	55	61
505	56¼	47	53½	60	66½
600	61	51	58	65	72
605	65¾	55	62½	70	77½
700	70½	59	67	75	83
705	75¼	63	71½	80	88½
800	80	67	76	85	94
805	85	71	80½	90	99½
900	89¾	75	85	95	105
905	94½	79	89½	100	110½
1000	99¼	83	94	105	116

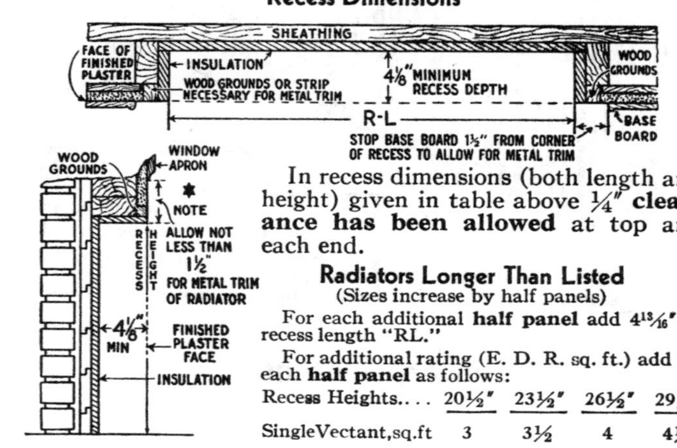

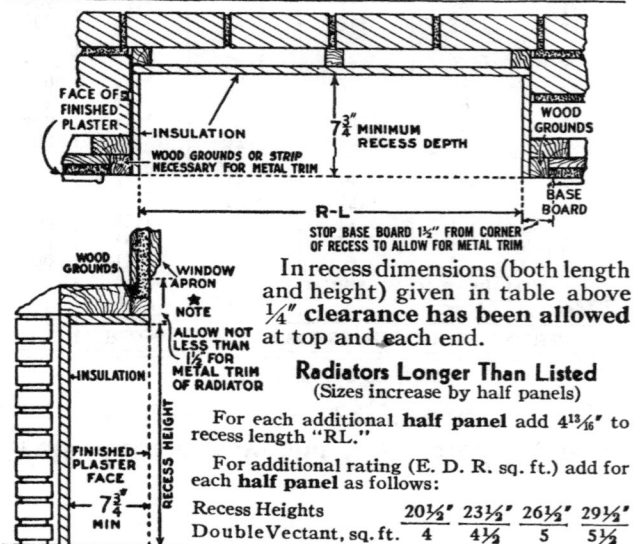

In recess dimensions (both length and height) given in table above ¼″ **clearance has been allowed** at top and each end.

Radiators Longer Than Listed

(Sizes increase by half panels)

For each additional **half panel** add 4$\frac{13}{16}$″ to recess length "RL."

For additional rating (E. D. R. sq. ft.) add for each **half panel** as follows:

Recess Heights	20½″	23½″	26½″	29½″
DoubleVectant, sq. ft.	4	4½	5	5½

Roughing Dimensions For Concealed Raydiant

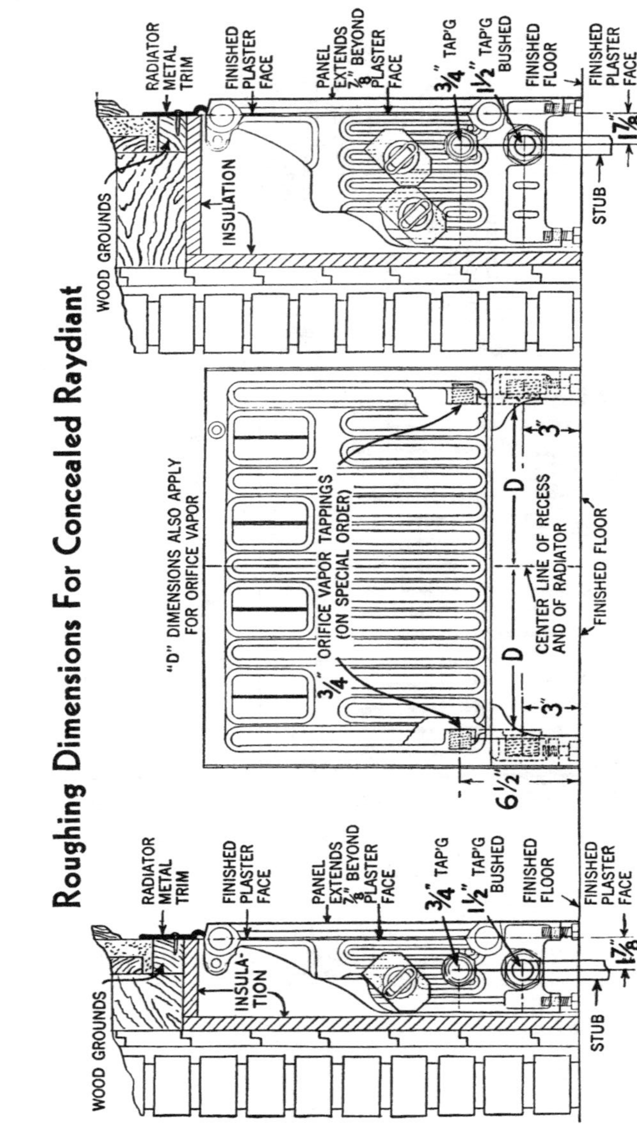

See preceding page for "D" Dimension Table

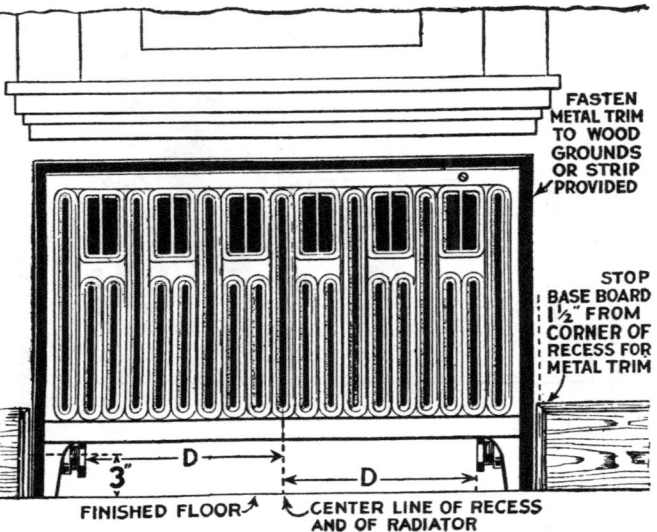

Concealed Radiator Dimension Center to Face of either Bushing

FASTEN METAL TRIM TO WOOD GROUNDS OR STRIP PROVIDED

STOP BASE BOARD 1½" FROM CORNER OF RECESS FOR METAL TRIM

3" D D

FINISHED FLOOR

CENTER LINE OF RECESS AND OF RADIATOR

IMPORTANT. "D" measurement is from the center of radiator to face of either bushing and radiator should be set exactly to this center which is the center of recess also. Therefore, stub holes in two pipe installations should be laid out from the center of the recess for the supply end and also from the center of the recess for the return end. Likewise, distance should be measured from the center for one pipe installation.

Dimension "D"

Center of radiator to face of either bushing as indicated above. Also applies to face of special ¾" tapped boss. For orifice and optional vapor (see dimensional cut on following page).

Size of Radiator	"D" Inches	Size of Radiator	"D" Inches
No. 100	4¼	No. 600	28¼
No. 105	6⅝	No. 605	30⅝
No. 200	9	No. 700	33
No. 205	11½	No. 705	35⅜
No. 300	13⅞	No. 800	37¾
No. 305	16¼	No. 805	40⅛
No. 400	18⅝	No. 900	42½
No. 405	21	No. 905	44⅞
No. 500	23⅜	No. 1000	47¼
No. 505	25¾		

For longer radiators, add per **half panel,** 2⅜".

Cabinet Radiator Dimensions

NOTE: All tapping lengths are from center of radiator.

Lower Tappings (inside and outside) are 1½". Dimensions given include ½" allowance for bushings.

Upper Tappings (inside and outside) are ¾". Dimensions given for upper tappings are without allowance for bushing.

For "D" Dimension of Radiators see tables pages 14 and 15

Inside Valve Hook-up For Concealed or Cabinet Raydiant Radiation

Valve Hook-up
For Water, Steam or Vapor

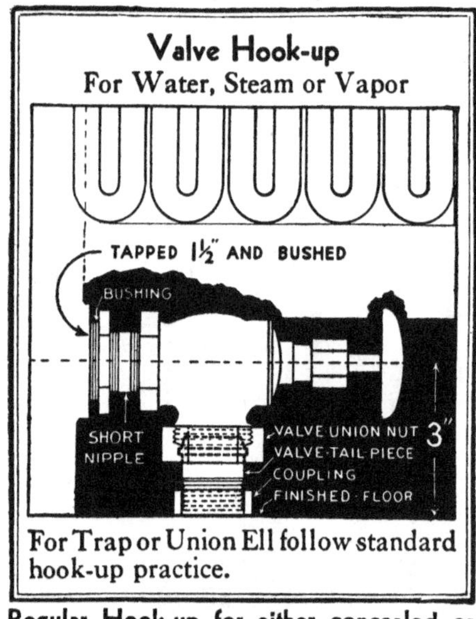

For Trap or Union Ell follow standard hook-up practice.

Regular Hook-up for either concealed or cabinet radiators.

Orifice Vapor Hook-up
Optional for Ordinary Vapor

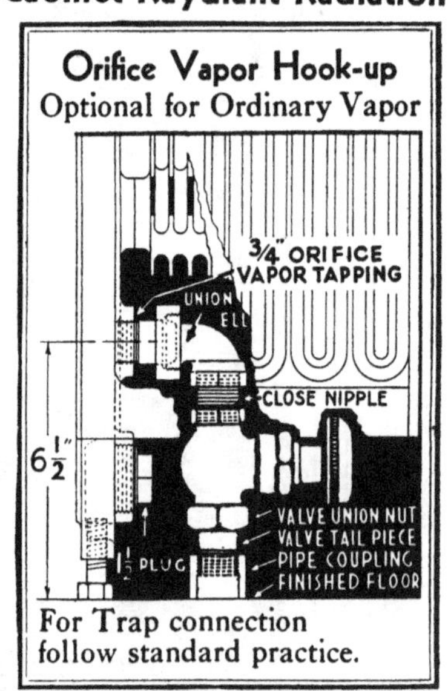

For Trap connection follow standard practice.

Furnished on special order only for concealed or cabinet radiators.

Weil-McLain Raydiant Cabinet Radiator

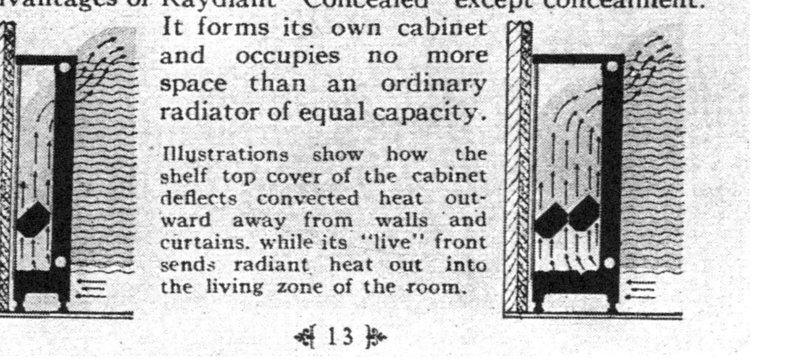

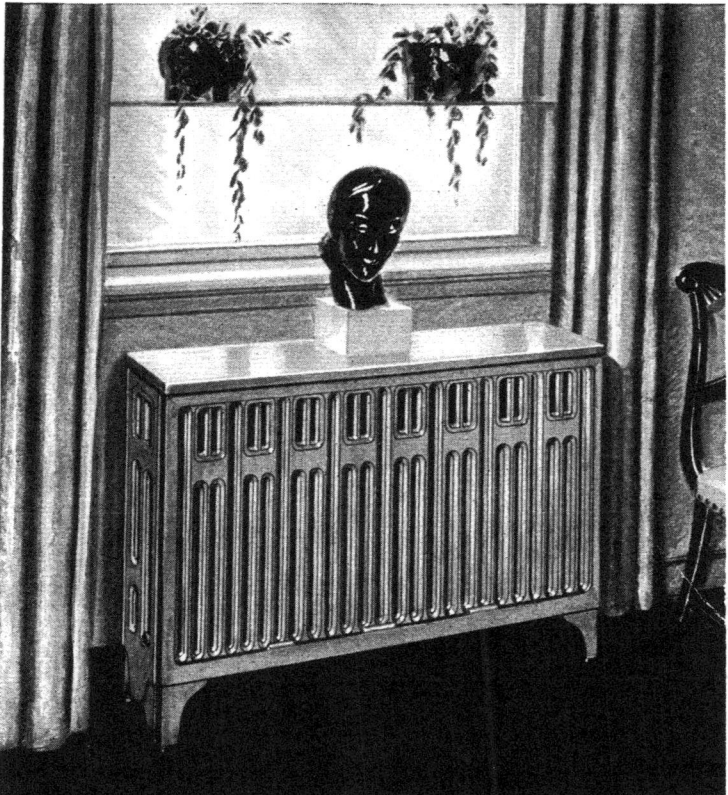

The Raydiant Cabinet Radiator offers all the heating advantages of Raydiant "Concealed" except concealment. It forms its own cabinet and occupies no more space than an ordinary radiator of equal capacity.

Illustrations show how the shelf top cover of the cabinet deflects convected heat outward away from walls and curtains, while its "live" front sends radiant heat out into the living zone of the room.

Weil-McLain Cabinet Raydiant 5" Deep

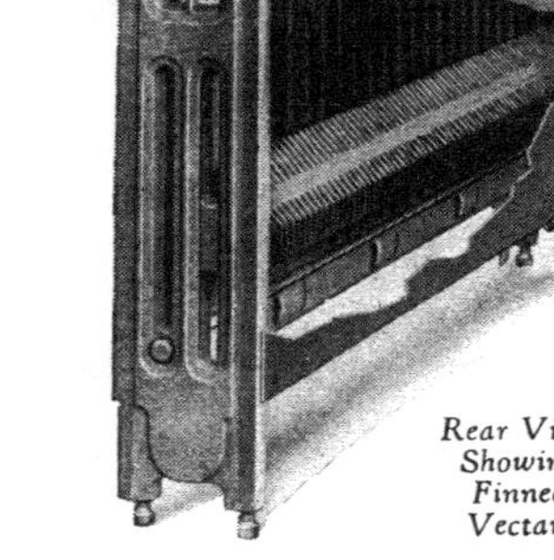

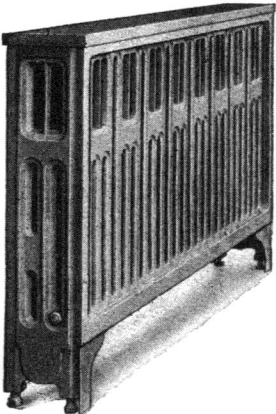

Rear View Showing Finned Vectant

Single Vectant Cabinet Radiator

No.	Cabinet Top Length Inches	CABINET HEIGHTS—INCHES 20	23	26	29	* Dimen "D" Inches For Rgh'g
		Ratings (E. D. R. sq. ft.)				
100	12¾	11	12¼	13½	15	4¼
105	17½	13¾	15½	17½	19¼	6⅝
200	22⅜	16½	19	21¼	23¾	9
205	27⅛	19½	22¼	25¼	28	11½
300	31⅞	22½	25¾	29	32½	13⅞
305	36⅝	25	29	33	37	16¼
400	41½	28	32½	37	41	18⅝
405	46¼	31	36	41	45½	21
500	51	34	39	44½	50	23⅜
505	55¾	37	42½	48½	54½	25¾
600	60⅝	39½	46	52½	59	28¼
605	65⅜	42½	49½	56	63	30⅝
700	70⅛	45½	53	60	67½	33
705	74⅞	48	56	64	72	35⅜
800	79¾	51	59½	68	76	37¾
805	84½	54	63	72	80½	40⅛
900	89¼	57	66	75½	85	42½
905	94	60	69½	79½	89½	44⅞
1000	98⅞	62½	73	83½	94	47¼

For Longer Radiators Add per Half Panel

	4 13/16	3	3½	4	4½	2⅜

*See page 12 for complete Cabinet Radiator Dimensions.

Weil-McLain Cabinet Raydiant 8¼″ Deep

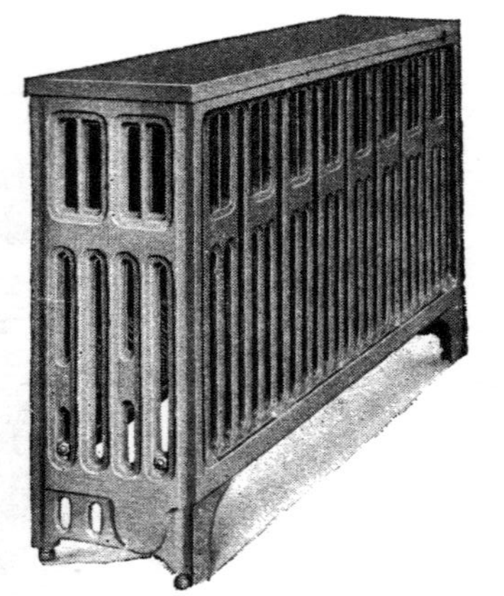

Double Vectant Cabinet Radiator

No.	Cabinet Top Length Inches	CABINET HEIGHTS—INCHES 20	23	25	29	* Dimen. "D" Inches For Rgh'g
		Ratings (E. D. R. sq. ft.)				
100	12¾	14	16	18	20	4¼
105	17½	18	20½	23	25½	6⅝
200	22⅜	22	25	28	31	9
205	27⅛	26	29½	33	36½	11½
300	31⅞	30	34	38	42	13⅞
305	36⅝	34	38½	43	47½	16¼
400	41½	38	43	48	53	18⅝
405	46¼	42	47½	53	58½	21
500	51	46	52	58	64	23⅜
505	55¾	50	56½	63	69½	25¾
600	60⅝	54	61	68	75	28¼
605	65⅜	58	65½	73	80½	30⅝
700	70⅛	62	70	78	86	33
705	74⅞	66	74½	83	91½	35⅜
800	79¾	70	79	88	97	37¾
805	84½	74	83½	93	102½	40⅛
900	89¼	78	88	98	108	42½
905	94	82	92½	103	113½	44⅞
1000	98⅞	86	97	108	119	47¼

For Longer Radiators Add per Half Panel

	4 13/16	4	4½	5	5½	2⅜

*See page 12 for complete Cabinet Radiator Dimensions.

Weil-McLain Junior Cameo Radiators

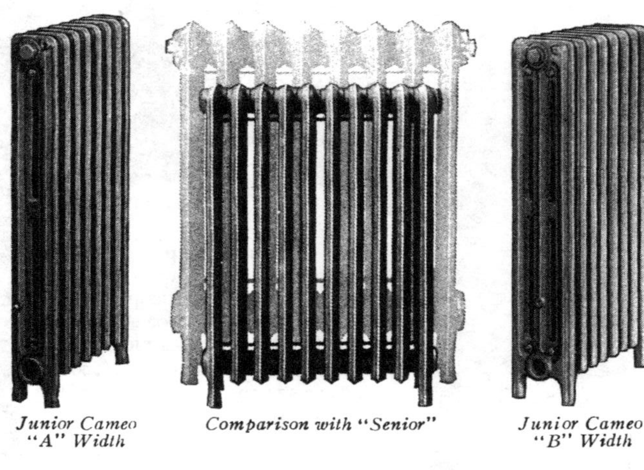

Junior Cameo "A" Width — *Comparison with "Senior"* — *Junior Cameo "B" Width*

Cameo Jr. Radiators require less floor and less room space than do senior size radiators of equivalent capacity, yet they will actually heat as much and heat more quickly.

The comparison made in illustration above shows the space saving possibilities when Cameo Jr. Radiators are used instead of the Senior.

Cameo Jr. Radiators are made in two widths: 3½ and 4¾ inches, and three heights: 19, 22 and 25 inches.

Tables containing complete data will be found on opposite page.

Junior Cameo Measurements

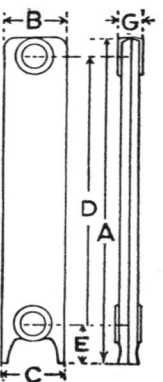

DIMENSIONS

	Jr. A and Jr. B				Jr. A	Jr. B
Hgt.	A	D	E	G	B&C	B&C
25-in.	25	21½	2½	1½	3½	4¾
22-in.	22	18½	2½	1½	3½	4¾
19-in.	19	15½	2½	1½	3½	4¾

Weil-McLain Junior Cameo Radiators

No. of Sec.	* Length 1½ inch per Sec.	Junior "A" Htg. Surface—Sq. Ft. 25-in. Height 1½ sq. ft. per Sec.	Junior "A" 22-in. Height 1.3 sq. ft. per Sec.	Junior "A" 19-in. Height 1.1 sq. ft. per Sec.	Junior "B" Htg. Surface—Sq. Ft. 25-in. Height 1.8 sq. ft. per Sec.	Junior "B" 22-in. Height 1.6 sq. ft. per Sec.	Junior "B" 19-in. Height 1.4 sq. ft. per Sec.
1	1½	1.5	1.3	1.1	1.8	1.6	1.4
2	3	3	2.6	2.2	3.6	3.2	2.8
3	4½	4.5	3.9	3.3	5.4	4.8	4.2
4	6	6	5.2	4.4	7.2	6.4	5.6
5	7½	7.5	6.5	5.5	9	8	7
6	9	9	7.8	6.6	10.8	9.6	8.4
7	10½	10.5	9.1	7.7	12.6	11.2	9.8
8	12	12	10.4	8.8	14.4	12.8	11.2
9	13½	13.5	11.7	9.9	16.2	14.4	12.6
10	15	15	13	11	18	16	14
11	16½	16.5	14.3	12.1	19.8	17.6	15.4
12	18	18	15.6	13.2	21.6	19.2	16.8
13	19½	19.5	16.9	14.3	23.4	20.8	18.2
14	21	21	18.2	15.4	25.2	22.4	19.6
15	22½	22.5	19.5	16.5	27	24	21
16	24	24	20.8	17.6	28.8	25.6	22.4
17	25½	25.5	22.1	18.7	30.6	27.2	23.8
18	27	27	23.4	19.8	32.4	28.8	25.2
19	28½	28.5	24.7	20.9	34.2	30.4	26.6
20	30	30	26	22	36	32	28
21	31½	31.5	27.3	23.1	37.8	33.6	29.4
22	33	33	28.6	24.2	39.6	35.2	30.8
23	34½	34.5	29.9	25.3	41.4	36.8	32.2
24	36	36	31.2	26.4	43.2	38.4	33.6
25	37½	37.5	32.5	27.5	45	40	35
26	39	39	33.8	28.6	46.8	41.6	36.4
27	40½	40.5	35.1	29.7	48.6	43.2	37.8
28	42	42	36.4	30.8	50.4	44.8	39.2
29	43½	43.5	37.7	31.9	52.2	46.4	40.6
30	45	45	39	33	54	48	42
31	46½	46.5	40.3	34.1	55.8	49.6	43.4
32	48	48	41.6	35.2	57.6	51.2	44.8
33	49½	49.5	42.9	36.3	59.4	52.8	46.2
34	51	51	44.2	37.4	61.2	54.4	47.6
35	52½	52.5	45.5	38.5	63	56	49
36	54	54	46.8	39.6	64.8	57.6	50.4
37	55½	55.5	48.1	40.7	66.6	59.2	51.8
38	57	57	49.4	41.8	68.4	60.8	53.2
39	58½	58.5	50.7	42.9	70.2	62.4	54.6
40	60	60	52	44	72	64	56

*Allow ½" for each bushing in estimating length of radiators.
Above radiators tapped 1 inch at top and bottom. Bushed for steam or water as per specifications.
Distance from floor to center of lower tapping, 2½ inches.

CAMEO
WEIL-McLAIN RADIATORS
Weil-McLain "Cameo" Radiators are made in a complete range of sizes, heights and widths, for every place and purpose in modern homes and buildings. Besides the regular floor type, Weil-McLain also make other types of "Cameo" such as the Junior floor type radiator, "Cameo" wall and bath room types. The complete line of "Cameo" radiators is briefly described on the following pages together with tables of sizes and dimensions.

Weil-McLain Three-Tube Cameo Radiator

No. of Sections	* Length 2½ in. per Sec.	Heating Surface—Square Feet				
		38-in. Height 3½ sq. ft. per Sec.	32-in. Height 3 sq. ft. per Sec.	26-in. Height 2⅓ sq. ft. per Sec.	23-in. Height 2 sq. ft. per Sec.	20-in. Height 1¾ sq. ft. per Sec.
2	5	7	6	4⅔	4	3½
3	7½	10½	9	7	6	5¼
4	10	14	12	9⅓	8	7
5	12½	17½	15	11⅔	10	8¾
6	15	21	18	14	12	10½
7	17½	24½	21	16⅓	14	12¼
8	20	28	24	18⅔	16	14
9	22½	31½	27	21	18	15¾
10	25	35	30	23⅓	20	17½
11	27½	38½	33	25⅔	22	19¼
12	30	42	36	28	24	21
13	32½	45½	39	30⅓	26	22¾
14	35	49	42	32⅔	28	24½
15	37½	52½	45	35	30	26¼
16	40	56	48	37⅓	32	28
17	42½	59½	51	39⅔	34	29¾
18	45	63	54	42	36	31½
19	47½	66½	57	44⅓	38	33¼
20	50	70	60	46⅔	40	35
21	52½	73½	63	49	42	36¾
22	55	77	66	51⅓	44	38½
23	57½	80½	69	53⅔	46	40¼
24	60	84	72	56	48	42
25	62½	87½	75	58⅓	50	43¾
26	65	91	78	60⅔	52	45½
27	67½	94½	81	63	54	47¼
28	70	98	84	65⅓	56	49
29	72½	101½	87	67⅔	58	50¾
30	75	105	90	70	60	52½
Distance from floor to center of Upper Tapping, inches. .		36 1/16	30 1/16	24 1/16	21 1/16	18 1/16

Distance from floor to center of lower tapping, 4½ inches.

*Allow ½" for each bushing in estimating length of radiators.

Above radiators tapped 1½ inches at top and bottom. Bushed for steam or water as per specifications.

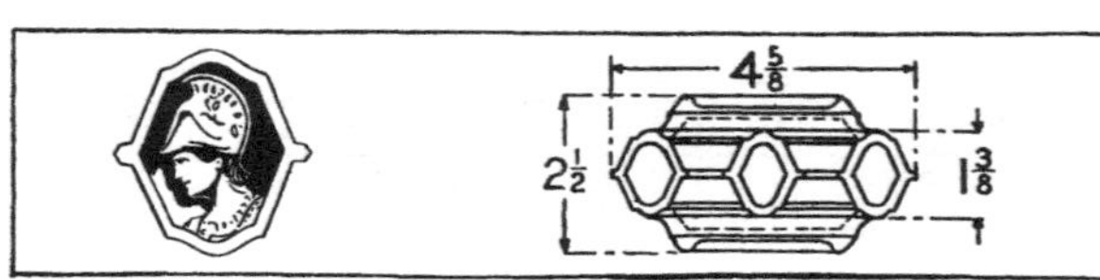
4⅝
2½
1⅜

Weil-McLain Four-Tube Cameo Radiator

No. of Sections	* Length, 2½ in. per Sec.	Heating Surface—Square Feet				
		38-in. Height 4¼ sq. ft. per Sec.	32-in. Height 3½ sq. ft. per Sec.	26-in. Height 2¾ sq. ft. per Sec.	23-in. Height 2½ sq. ft. per Sec.	20-in. Height 2¼ sq. ft. per Sec.
2	5	8½	7	5½	5	4½
3	7½	12¾	10½	8¼	7½	6¾
4	10	17	14	11	10	9
5	12½	21¼	17½	13¾	12½	11¼
6	15	25½	21	16½	15	13½
7	17½	29¾	24½	19¼	17½	15¾
8	20	34	28	22	20	18
9	22½	38¼	31½	24¾	22½	20¼
10	25	42½	35	27½	25	22½
11	27½	46¾	38½	30¼	27½	24¾
12	30	51	42	33	30	27
13	32½	55¼	45½	35¾	32½	29¼
14	35	59½	49	38½	35	31½
15	37½	63¾	52½	41¼	37½	33¾
16	40	68	56	44	40	36
17	42½	72¼	59½	46¾	42½	38¼
18	45	76½	63	49½	45	40½
19	47½	80¾	66½	52¼	47½	42¾
20	50	85	70	55	50	45
21	52½	89¼	73½	57¾	52½	47¼
22	55	93½	77	60½	55	49½
23	57½	97¾	80½	63¼	57½	51¾
24	60	102	84	66	60	54
25	62½	106¼	87½	68¾	62½	56¼
26	65	110½	91	71½	65	58½
27	67½	114¾	94½	74¼	67½	60¾
28	70	119	98	77	70	63
29	72½	123¼	101½	79¾	72½	65¼
30	75	127½	105	82½	75	67½
Distance from floor to center of upper tapping, inches...		36¹⁄₁₆	30¹⁄₁₆	24¹⁄₁₆	21¹⁄₁₆	18¹⁄₁₆

Distance from floor to center of lower tapping, 4½ inches.
*Allow ½" for each bushing in estimating length of radiators.
Above radiators tapped 1½" at top and bottom. Bushed for steam or water as per specifications.

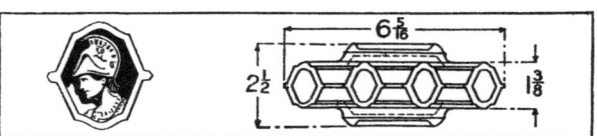

Weil-McLain Five-Tube Cameo Radiator

No. of Sections	* Length, 2½ in. per Sec.	Heating Surface—Square Feet				
		38-in. Height 5 sq. ft. per Sec.	32-in. Height 4⅓ sq. ft. per Sec.	26-in. Height 3½ sq. ft. per Sec.	23-in. Height 3 sq. ft. per Sec.	20-in. Height 2⅔ sq. ft. per Sec.
2	5	10	8⅔	7	6	5⅓
3	7½	15	13	10½	9	8
4	10	20	17⅓	14	12	10⅔
5	12½	25	21⅔	17½	15	13⅓
6	15	30	26	21	18	16
7	17½	35	30⅓	24½	21	18⅔
8	20	40	34⅔	28	24	21⅓
9	22½	45	39	31½	27	24
10	25	50	43⅓	35	30	26⅔
11	27½	55	47⅔	38½	33	29⅓
12	30	60	52	42	36	32
13	32½	65	56⅓	45½	39	34⅔
14	35	70	60⅔	49	42	37⅓
15	37½	75	65	52½	45	40
16	40	80	69⅓	56	48	42⅔
17	42½	85	73⅔	59½	51	45⅓
18	45	90	78	63	54	48
19	47½	95	82⅓	66½	57	50⅔
20	50	100	86⅔	70	60	53⅓
21	52½	105	91	73½	63	56
22	55	110	95⅓	77	66	58⅔
23	57½	115	99⅔	80½	69	61⅓
24	60	120	104	84	72	64
25	62½	125	108⅓	87½	75	66⅔
26	65	130	112⅔	91	78	69⅓
27	67½	135	117	94½	81	72
28	70	140	121⅓	98	84	74⅔
29	72½	145	125⅔	101½	87	77⅓
30	75	150	130	105	90	80
Distance from floor to center of upper tapping, inches...		36¹⁄₁₆	30¹⁄₁₆	24¹⁄₁₆	21¹⁄₁₆	18¹⁄₁₆

Distance from floor to center of lower tapping, 4½ inches.
*Allow ½" for each bushing in estimating length of radiators.
Above radiators tapped 1½" at top and bottom. Bushed for steam or water as per specifications.

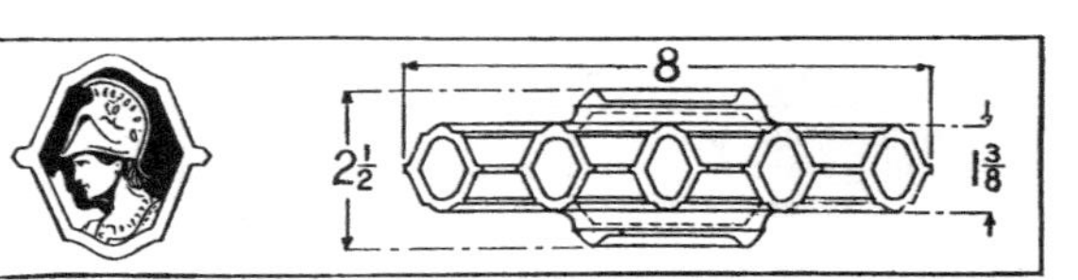
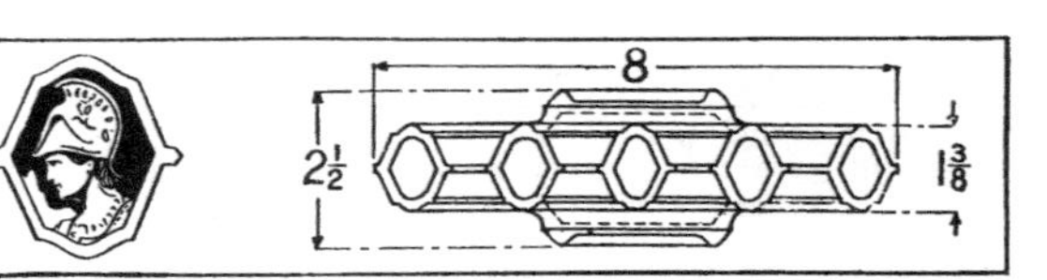

Weil-McLain Six-Tube Cameo Radiator

No. of Sections	* Length, 2½ in. per Sec.	Heating Surface—Square Feet				
		38-in. Height 6 sq. ft. per Sec.	32-in. Height 5 sq. ft. per Sec.	26-in. Height 4 sq. ft. per Sec.	23-in. Height 3½ sq. ft. per Sec.	20-in. Height 3 sq. ft. per Sec.
2	5	12	10	8	7	6
3	7½	18	15	12	10½	9
4	10	24	20	16	14	12
5	12½	30	25	20	17½	15
6	15	36	30	24	21	18
7	17½	42	35	28	24½	21
8	20	48	40	32	28	24
9	22½	54	45	36	31½	27
10	25	60	50	40	35	30
11	27½	66	55	44	38½	33
12	30	72	60	48	42	36
13	32½	78	65	52	45½	39
14	35	84	70	56	49	42
15	37½	90	75	60	52½	45
16	40	96	80	64	56	48
17	42½	102	85	68	59½	51
18	45	108	90	72	63	54
19	47½	114	95	76	66½	57
20	50	120	100	80	70	60
21	52½	126	105	84	73½	63
22	55	132	110	88	77	66
23	57½	138	115	92	80½	69
24	60	144	120	96	84	72
25	62½	150	125	100	87½	75
26	65	156	130	104	91	78
27	67½	162	135	108	94½	81
28	70	168	140	112	98	84
29	72½	174	145	116	101½	87
30	75	180	150	120	105	90
Distance from floor to center of upper tapping, inches		36 1/16	30 1/16	24 1/16	21 1/16	18 1/16

Distance from floor to center of lower tapping, 4½ inches.

*Allow ½" for each bushing in estimating lengths of radiators.

Above radiators tapped 1½ inches at top and bottom. Bushed for steam or water as per specifications.

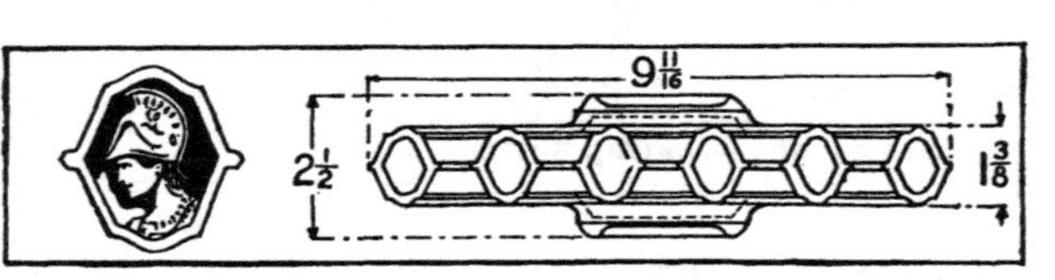

Weil-McLain "Window" Cameo Radiator

No. of Sections	Length 2½-in. per Sec.	Window (4½-in. Legs) Htg. Surface Sq. Ft.			Window (3-in. Legs) Htg. Surface Sq. Ft.		
		21½-in. Height 3⅔ sq. ft. per Sec.	18½-in Height 3 sq. ft. per Sec.	15½-in. Height 2½ sq. ft. per Sec.	20-in. Height 3⅔ sq. ft. per Sec.	17-in. Height 3 sq. ft. per Sec.	14-in. Height 2½ sq. ft. per Sec.
2	5	7⅓	6	5	7⅓	6	5
3	7½	11	9	7½	11	9	7½
4	10	14⅔	12	10	14⅔	12	10
5	12½	18⅓	15	12½	18⅓	15	12½
6	15	22	18	15	22	18	15
7	17½	25⅔	21	17½	25⅔	21	17½
8	20	29⅓	24	20	29⅓	24	20
9	22½	33	27	22½	33	27	22½
10	25	36⅔	30	25	36⅔	30	25
11	27½	40⅓	33	27½	40⅓	33	27½
12	30	44	36	30	44	36	30
13	32½	47⅔	39	32½	47⅔	39	32½
14	35	51⅓	42	35	51⅓	42	35
15	37½	55	45	37½	55	45	37½
16	40	58⅔	48	40	58⅔	48	40
17	42½	62⅓	51	42½	62⅓	51	42½
18	45	66	54	45	66	54	45
19	47½	69⅔	57	47½	69⅔	57	47½
20	50	73⅓	60	50	73⅓	60	50
21	52½	77	63	52½	77	63	52½
22	55	80⅔	66	55	80⅔	66	55
23	57½	84⅓	69	57½	84⅓	69	57½
24	60	88	72	60	88	72	60
25	62½	91⅔	75	62½	91⅔	75	62½
26	65	95⅓	78	65	95⅓	78	65
27	67½	99	81	67½	99	81	67½
28	70	102⅔	84	70	102⅔	84	70
29	72½	106⅓	87	72½	106⅓	87	72½
30	75	110	90	75	110	90	75
Distance from floor to center of upper tapping, inches		19 9/16	16 9/16	13 9/16	18 1/16	15 1/16	12 1/16

Floor to center of lower tapping same as leg heights.

*Allow ½" for each bushing in estimating length of radiators.

Above radiators tapped 1½ inches at top and bottom. Bushed for steam or water as per specifications.

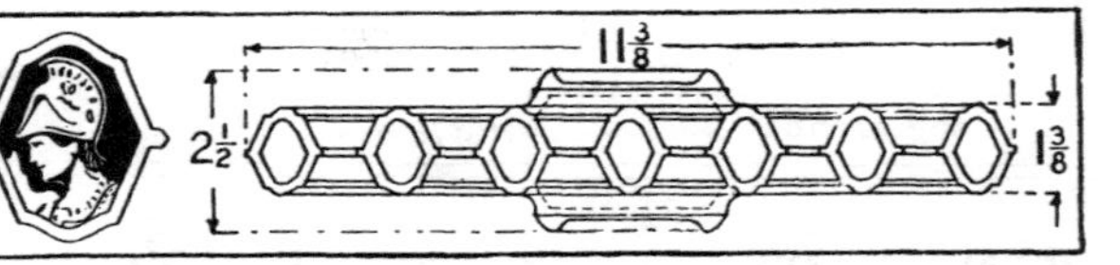

Weil-McLain Cameo Wall Radiation

Cameo wall is a two tube wall radiator pleasing in appearance and harmonizing with regular Cameo Tube Radiation.

Made in two sizes; 1 1/2 sq. ft. per section and 2 sq. ft. per section.

Cameo Wall with its pleasing appearance is suitable for particular applications in homes and apartments, such as corridors, sun parlors, breakfast nooks, *as well* as shops, factories, store houses, garages and similar buildings where wall radiators in the past have had their greatest use. In fact its pleasing appearance makes it more desirable wherever wall radiation is regarded the most practical type of radiation.

Cameo Wall is assembled in multiples of 1 1/2 ft. sections and 2 ft. sections, making possible the selection of a wall radiator more nearly to the size required.

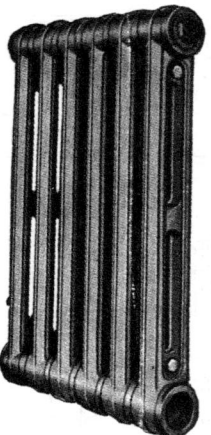

Dimensions: 1 1/2 sq. ft. and 2 sq. ft. sizes.

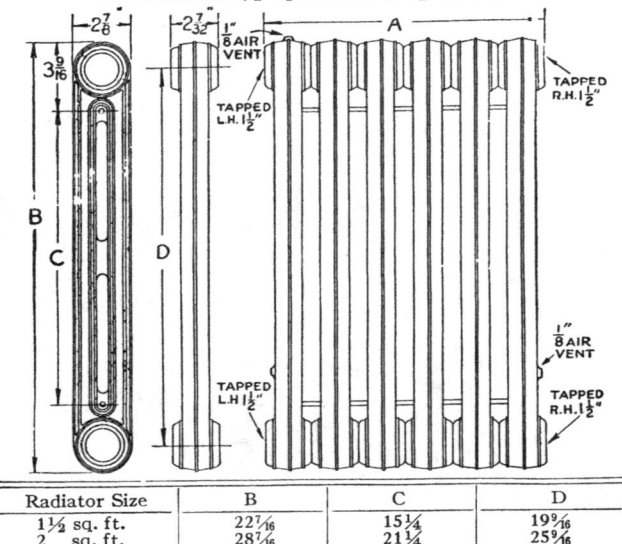

Radiator Size	B	C	D
1 1/2 sq. ft.	22 7/16	15 1/4	19 9/16
2 sq. ft.	28 7/16	21 1/4	25 9/16

For wall brackets, see page 29.

Weil-McLain Cameo Wall Radiation

1 1/2 Sq. Ft. per Section			2 Sq. Ft. per Section		
No. of Sections	Length "A" Inches	Heating Surface Sq. Ft.	No. of Sections	Length "A" Inches	Heating Surface Sq. Ft.
3	6 5/8	4 1/2	3	6 5/8	6
4	8 7/8	6	4	8 7/8	8
5	11 1/8	7 1/2	5	11 1/8	10
6	13 5/16	9	6	13 5/16	12
7	15 1/2	10 1/2	7	15 1/2	14
8	17 3/4	12	8	17 3/4	16
9	20	13 1/2	9	20	18
10	22 1/4	15	10	22 1/4	20
11	24 3/8	16 1/2	11	24 3/8	22
12	26 5/8	18	12	26 5/8	24
13	28 3/4	19 1/2	13	28 3/4	26
14	31	21	14	31	28
15	33 1/4	22 1/2	15	33 1/4	30
16	35 7/16	24	16	35 7/16	32
17	37 5/8	25 1/2	17	37 5/8	34
18	39 15/16	27	18	39 15/16	36
19	42 1/8	28 1/2	19	42 1/8	38
20	44 5/16	30	20	44 5/16	40
21	46 1/2	31 1/2	21	46 1/2	42
22	48 3/4	33	22	48 3/4	44
23	51	34 1/2	23	51	46
24	53 1/4	36	24	53 1/4	48
25	55 3/8	37 1/2	25	55 3/8	50
26	57 5/8	39	26	57 5/8	52
27	59 7/8	40 1/2	27	59 7/8	54
28	62	42	28	62	56
29	64 1/4	43 1/2	29	64 1/4	58
30	66 9/16	45	30	66 9/16	60
31	68 3/4	46 1/2	31	68 3/4	62
32	71	48	32	71	64
33	73 1/4	49 1/2	33	73 1/4	66
34	75 7/16	51	34	75 7/16	68
35	77 5/8	52 1/2	35	77 5/8	70
36	79 7/8	54	36	79 7/8	72
37	82 1/8	55 1/2	37	82 1/8	74
38	84 5/16	57	38	84 5/16	76
39	86 1/2	58 1/2	39	86 1/2	78
40	88 3/4	60	40	88 3/4	80
41	91	61 1/2	41	91	82
42	93 3/16	63	42	93 3/16	84
43	95 7/16	64 1/2	43	95 7/16	86
44	97 5/8	66	44	97 5/8	88
45	99 7/8	67 1/2	45	99 7/8	90
46	102	69	46	102	92
47	104 1/4	70 1/2	47	104 1/4	94
48	106 1/2	72	48	106 1/2	96

Add 1 1/8 inch to length for each R. & L. Hexagon nipple when long radiators are furnished in more than one unit. Allow 1/2 inch for each bushing in estimating length of radiator.

For wall brackets, see page 29.

Weil-McLain Raydiant Wall Radiation

Here is a modern attractive wall radiator that literally "hugs the wall." It is only 1¾ inches thick as compared to the 2⅞ inch thickness in conventional types. Because of this extreme thinness, the Raydiant Wall Type Radiator does not extend obtrusively out from the wall.

Its Raydiant design lends this radiator a pleasing appearance; hence it is often the choice over other radiators where a wall type of radiator is needed or desired.

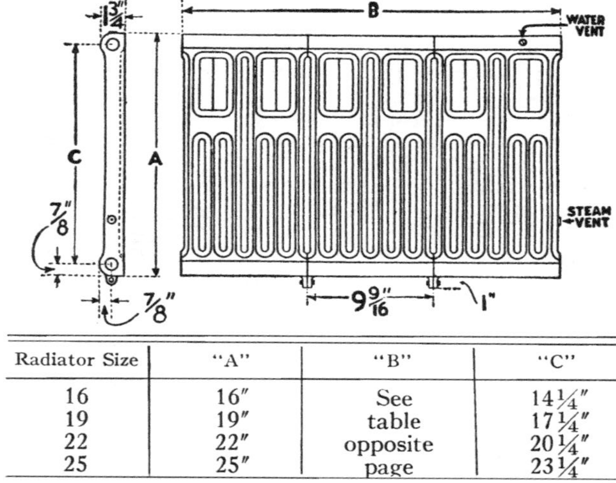

Radiator Size	"A"	"B"	"C"
16	16″	See table opposite page	14¼″
19	19″		17¼″
22	22″		20¼″
25	25″		23¼″

For Raydiant Wall Brackets, see page 28.

Weil-McLain Raydiant Wall Radiation

Heights A		16″	19″	22″	25″
		Ratings (E. D. R. sq. ft.)			
No. of Panels	Length "B" Inches	3½ Ft. per Panel	4 Ft. per Panel	4½ Ft. per Panel	5 Ft. per Panel
1	9½	3½	4	4½	5
1½	14⅜	5¼	6	6¾	7½
2	19⅛	7	8	9	10
2½	23⅞	8¾	10	11¼	12½
3	28⅝	10½	12	13½	15
3½	33½	12¼	14	15¾	17½
4	38¼	14	16	18	20
4½	43	15¾	18	20¼	22½
5	47¾	17½	20	22½	25
5½	52⅝	19¼	22	24¾	27½
6	57⅜	21	24	27	30
6½	62⅛	22¾	26	29¼	32½
7	66⅞	24½	28	31½	35
7½	71¾	26¼	30	33¾	37½
8	76½	28	32	36	40
8½	81¼	29¾	34	38¼	42½
9	86	31½	36	40½	45
9½	90⅞	33¼	38	42¾	47½
10	95⅝	35	40	45	50
10½	100⅜	36¾	42	47¼	52½
11	105⅛	38½	44	49½	55
11½	110	40¼	46	51¾	57½
12	114¾	42	48	54	60
12½	119½	43¾	50	56¼	62½
13	124¼	45½	52	58½	65
13½	129	47¼	54	60¾	67½
14	133⅞	49	56	63	70
14½	138⅝	50¾	58	65¼	72½
15	143⅜	52½	60	67½	75

Tapped 1″ top and bottom, and bushed to smaller sizes. Allow ½″ for each bushing.

For Raydiant Wall Brackets, see page 28.

Combination Top and Bottom Bracket for Raydiant Wall

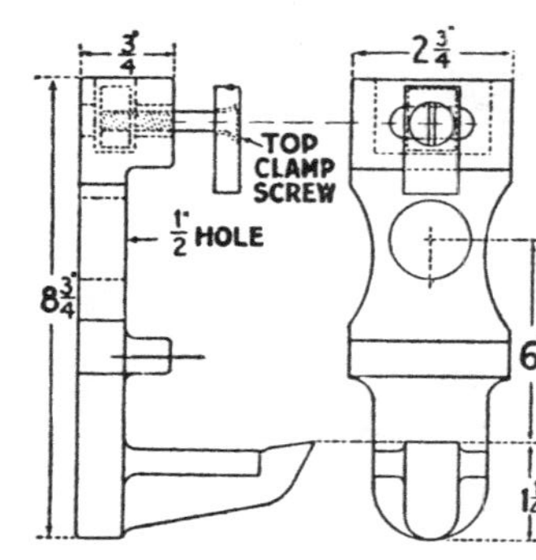

Elongated horizontal slot provides for side adjustment and therefore bracket may be located at most convenient point: over stud in wall, for instance; and top bracket screw can be moved sidewise to meet opening between tubes.

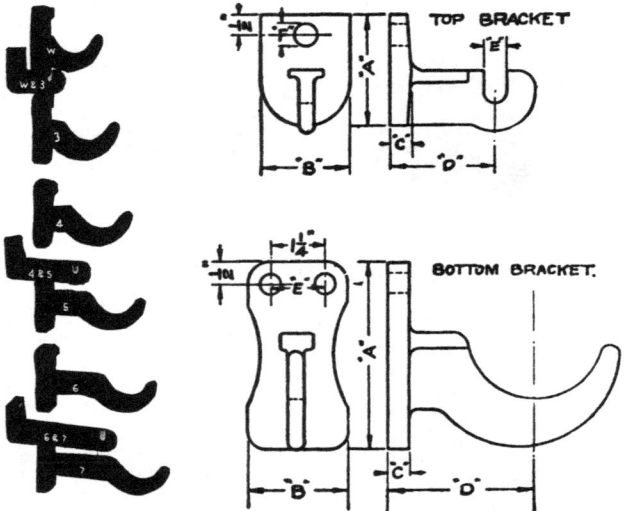

Junior Cameo Rigid Brackets

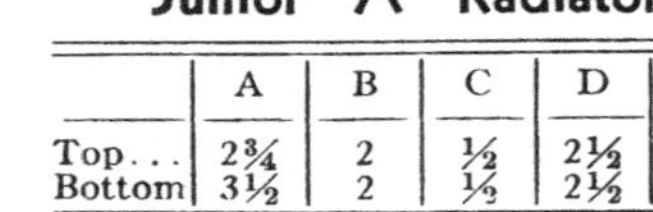

Junior "A" Radiator

	A	B	C	D	E
Top...	2¾	2	½	2½	7/16
Bottom	3½	2	½	2½	7/16

Junior "B" Radiator

	A	B	C	D	E
Top...	2¾	2	½	2 5/16	7/16
Bottom	3½	2	½	3⅛	7/16

Radiator hangs ¾ in. from wall on above brackets.

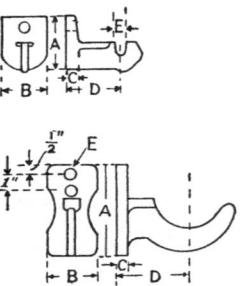

Cast Iron Radiator Pedestals

Cast iron pedestals can be furnished to provide additional clearance beneath Cameo Radiators when desired. They are made in the following heights: ½, 1, 1½, 2, 2½, 3, 3½ and 4 inches.

Cameo Rigid Brackets

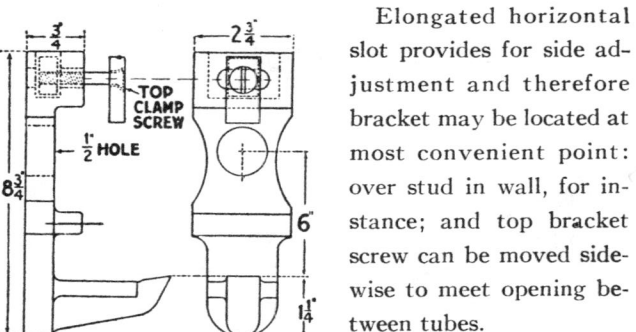

TOP BRACKET

BOTTOM BRACKET

Brackets for Cameo Wall Radiators

Type	A	B	C	D	E	F
Top	2¾"	2"	½"	2 7/16"	½"	7/16"
Bottom	4⅜"	2¼"	½"	2 7/16"	7/16"	.....

Top Brackets for Cameo Legless Radiators

Type	A	B	C	D	E	F
3-Tube	2¾"	2"	½"	2 7/16"	½"	7/16"
4 and 5-Tube	2¾"	2"	½"	4⅛"	½"	7/16"
6 and 7-Tube	2¾"	2"	½"	5⅞"	½"	7/16"

Bottom Brackets for Cameo Legless Radiators

Type	A	B	C	D	E
3-Tube	4⅜"	2¼"	½"	3 5/16"	7/16"
4-Tube	4⅜"	2¼"	½"	4⅛"	7/16"
5-Tube	4⅜"	2¼"	½"	5"	7/16"
6-Tube	4⅜"	2¼"	½"	5⅞"	7/16"
7-Tube	4⅜"	2¼"	½"	6¾"	7/16"

Radiator hangs 1" from wall on above Brackets.

Weil-McLain Special Cameo Radiators

Curved—Angle—Corner

WEIL-MCLAIN Cameo Radiators, all patterns, can be furnished in curved angle and corner types on special order. A plan sketch with complete information and necessary dimensions should accompany order.

CURVED RADIATORS

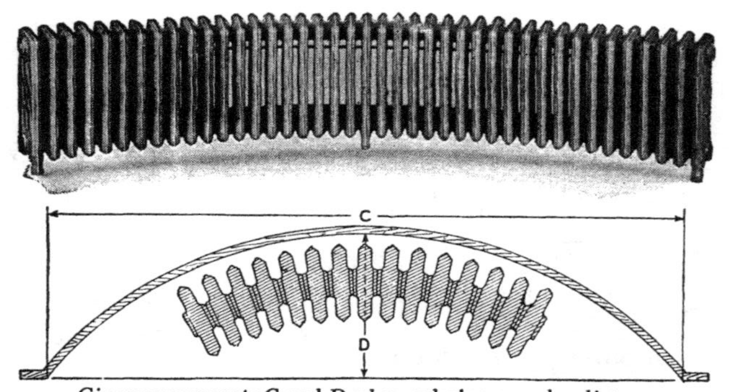

Give measurements C and D when ordering curved radiators.

ANGLE RADIATORS

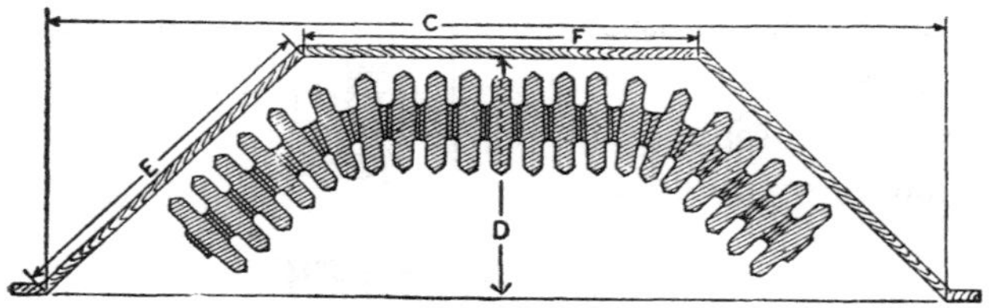

Give measurements C, D, E and F when ordering angle radiators.

Automatic Humidifying Radiator

[Supplied in Double Vectant Radiators Only, in Cabinet or "Concealed" Type, 26″ and 29″ Heights]

The Weil-McLain Automatic Humidifying Radiator is a combination of a Raydiant Radiator and a Heat-Chambered Humidifying unit. In the assembly the humidifier becomes part of the radiator, and whenever there is heat in the radiator and water in the humidifying unit evaporation takes place. Because of its heat-chambered construction the evaporating capacity of the unit is greater than that of ordinary pans.

Water is automatically supplied to the evaporating unit and is held at a fixed level by a float regulated valve. An overflow is provided to drain off surplus water should the valve at any time fail to hold the water at proper level.

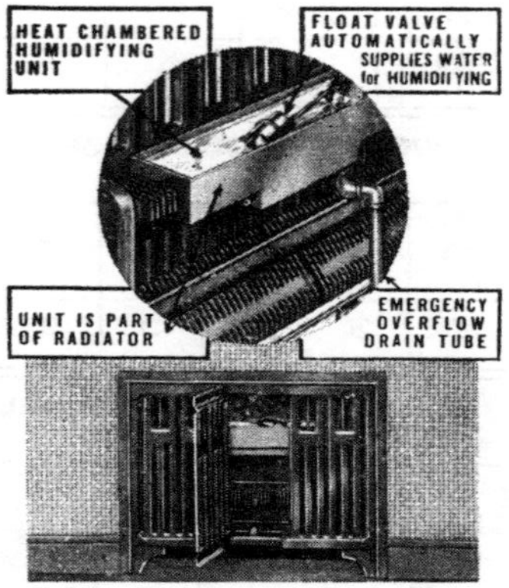

Illustration shows assembly of automatic humidifying unit in the Raydiant concealed type radiator. Assembly is the same in the cabinet type.

The Weil-McLain Raydiant Automatic Humidifying Radiator is a humidifier of moderate capacity. Under ordinary conditions a single unit will provide practicable humidification for the average six to eight room house.

Evaporating Capacity with steam heat is 2½ pints of water per hour under average conditions—evaporation will be relatively less with hot water heat or with lower temperature in the radiator.

The Heating Capacities, sizes and dimensions of the Humidifying Raydiant Radiators are the same as those given for the corresponding "CONCEALED" or CABINET Raydiant Radiators shown elsewhere in this booklet.

Aluminum Hand-Fill Humidifying Pans

for Raydiant Cabinet Radiators

Pans are supplied for all heights of both single and double vectant Raydiant Cabinet Radiators. These pans provide during the winter months, when the natural relative humidity of heated air is low, an inexpensive means for increasing the moisture content of the air and relieving excessive air dryness.

Pan is filled from front of radiator through convenient trough that extends from pan to grille opening or by lifting top cover of radiator. Pan is removable for occasional cleaning.

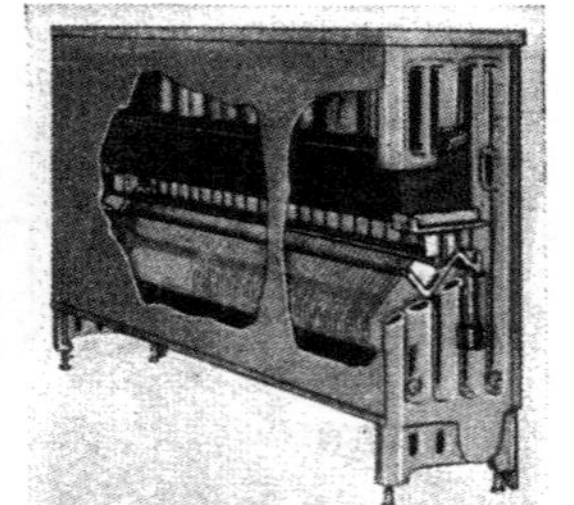

Cut-away view of Cabinet Raydiant Radiator showing Pan

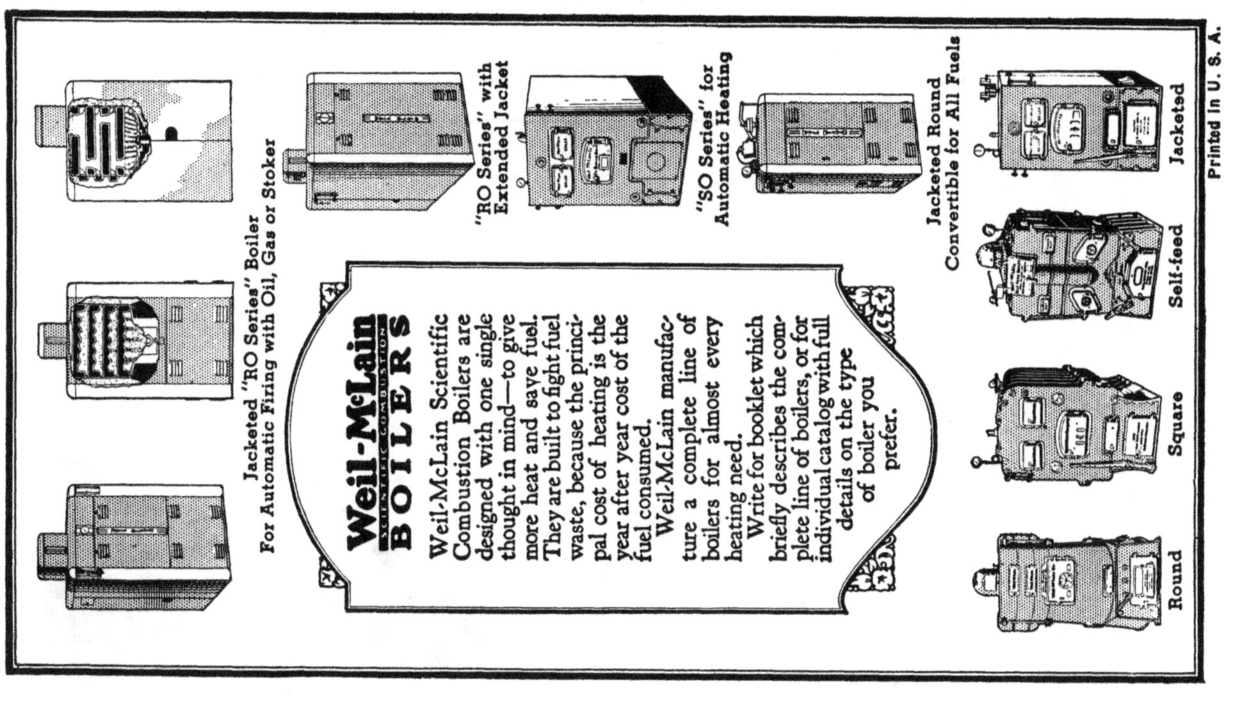
Jacketed "RO Series" Boiler
For Automatic Firing with Oil, Gas or Stoker
"RO Series" with
Extended Jacket
"SO Series" for
Automatic Heating
Weil-McLain
SCIENTIFIC COMBUSTION
BOILERS
Weil-McLain Scientific Combustion Boilers are designed with one single thought in mind—to give more heat and save fuel. They are built to fight fuel waste, because the principal cost of heating is the year after year cost of the fuel consumed.
Weil-McLain manufacture a complete line of boilers for almost every heating need.
Write for booklet which briefly describes the complete line of boilers, or for individual catalog with full details on the type of boiler you prefer.
Jacketed Round
Convertible for All Fuels
Round
Square
Self-feed
Jacketed
Printed in U. S. A.

Smith "144" Radiator

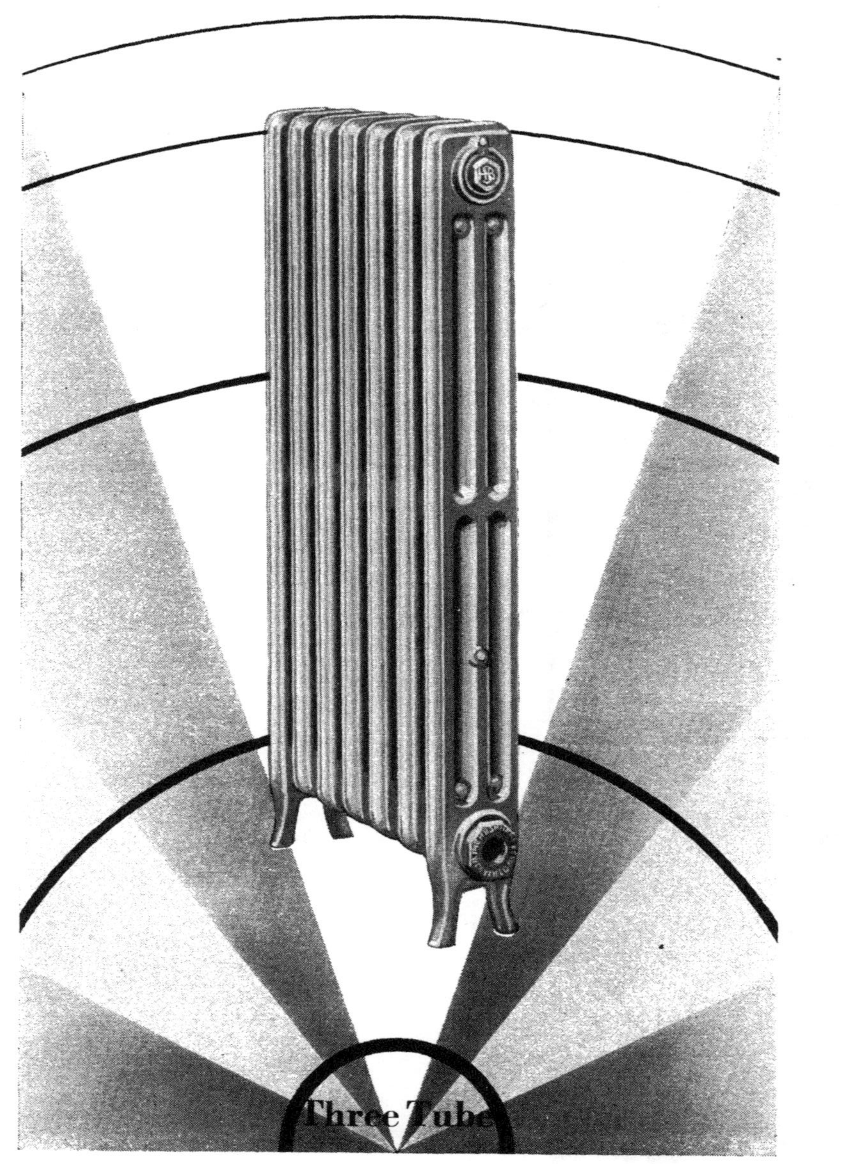

Smith "144" Radiator

Three Tube

Steam or Water

Radiating Surface in Feet

Sections	Total* Length ft.	–	in.	HEIGHT 37″ 3 ft. per sec.	32″ 2½ ft. per sec.	25″ 2 ft. per sec.	21″ 1½ ft. per sec.
3	0	–	7½	9	7½	6	4½
4	0	–	10	12	10	8	6
5	1	–	½	15	12½	10	7½
6	1	–	3	18	15	12	9
7	1	–	5½	21	17½	14	10½
8	1	–	8	24	20	16	12
9	1	–	10½	27	22½	18	13½
10	2	–	1	30	25	20	15
11	2	–	3½	33	27½	22	16½
12	2	–	6	36	30	24	18
13	2	–	8½	39	32½	26	19½
14	2	–	11	42	35	28	21
15	3	–	1½	45	37½	30	22½
16	3	–	4	48	40	32	24
17	3	–	6½	51	42½	34	25½
18	3	–	9	54	45	36	27
19	3	–	11½	57	47½	38	28½
20	4	–	2	60	50	40	30
21	4	–	4½	63	52½	42	31½
22	4	–	7	66	55	44	33
23	4	–	9½	69	57½	46	34½
24	5	–	0	72	60	48	36
25	5	–	2½	75	62½	50	37½
26	5	–	5	78	65	52	39
27	5	–	7½	81	67½	54	40½
28	5	–	10	84	70	56	42
29	6	–	½	87	72½	58	43½
30	6	–	3	90	75	60	45

For Dimension Table see page 18

***Add ½ inch for each bushing**

Smith "144" Radiator

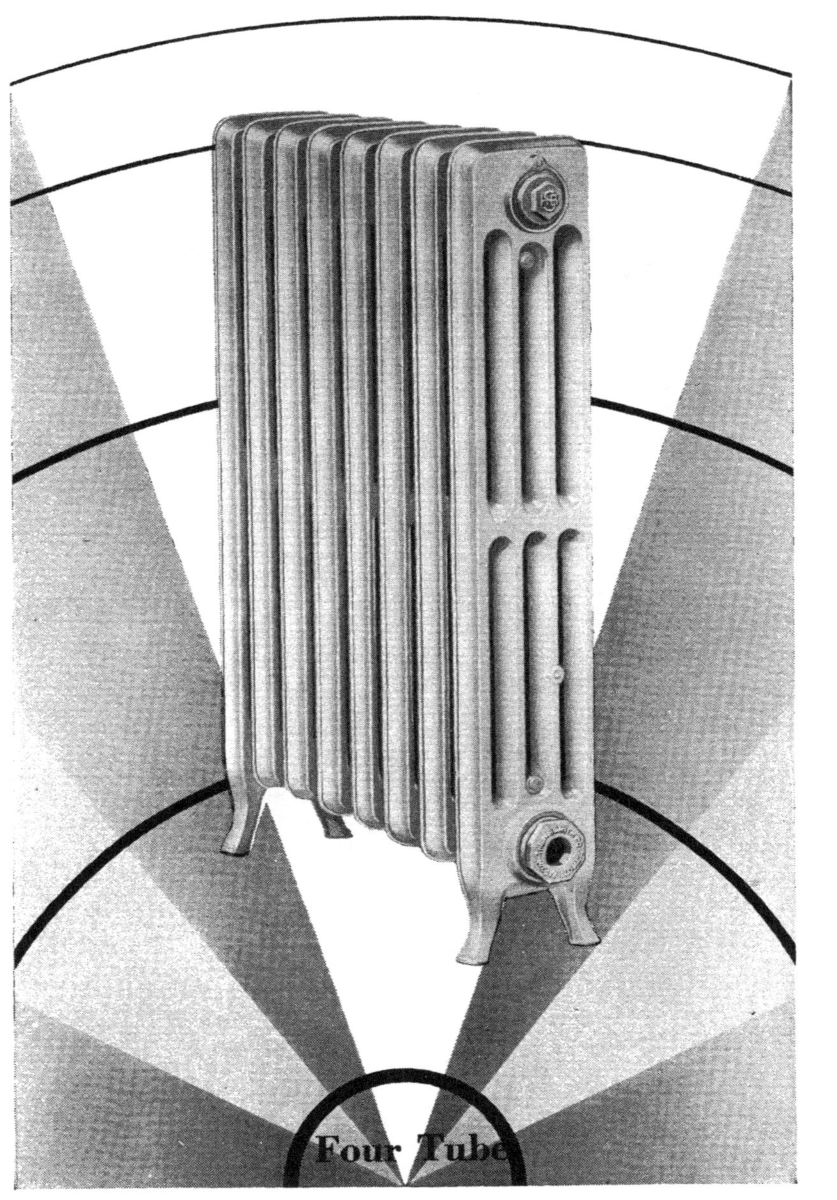

Smith "144" Radiator

Four Tube

Steam or Water

Radiating Surface in Feet

Sections	Total* Length ft. – in.	HEIGHT 37″ 4 ft. per sec.	32″ 3⅓ ft. per sec.	25″ 2½ ft. per sec.	21″ 2 ft. per sec.
3	0 – 7½	12	10	7½	6
4	0 – 10	16	13⅓	10	8
5	1 – ½	20	16⅔	12½	10
6	1 – 3	24	20	15	12
7	1 – 5½	28	23⅓	17½	14
8	1 – 8	32	26⅔	20	16
9	1 – 10½	36	30	22½	18
10	2 – 1	40	33⅓	25	20
11	2 – 3½	44	36⅔	27½	22
12	2 – 6	48	40	30	24
13	2 – 8½	52	43⅓	32½	26
14	2 – 11	56	46⅔	35	28
15	3 – 1½	60	50	37½	30
16	3 – 4	64	53⅓	40	32
17	3 – 6½	68	56⅔	42½	34
18	3 – 9	72	60	45	36
19	3 – 11½	76	63⅓	47½	38
20	4 – 2	80	66⅔	50	40
21	4 – 4½	84	70	52½	42
22	4 – 7	88	73⅓	55	44
23	4 – 9½	92	76⅔	57½	46
24	5 – 0	96	80	60	48
25	5 – 2½	100	83⅓	62½	50
26	5 – 5	104	86⅔	65	52
27	5 – 7½	108	90	67½	54
28	5 – 10	112	93⅓	70	56
29	6 – ½	116	96⅔	72½	58
30	6 – 3	120	100	75	60

For Dimension Table see page 18

*Add ½ inch for each bushing

Smith "144" Radiator

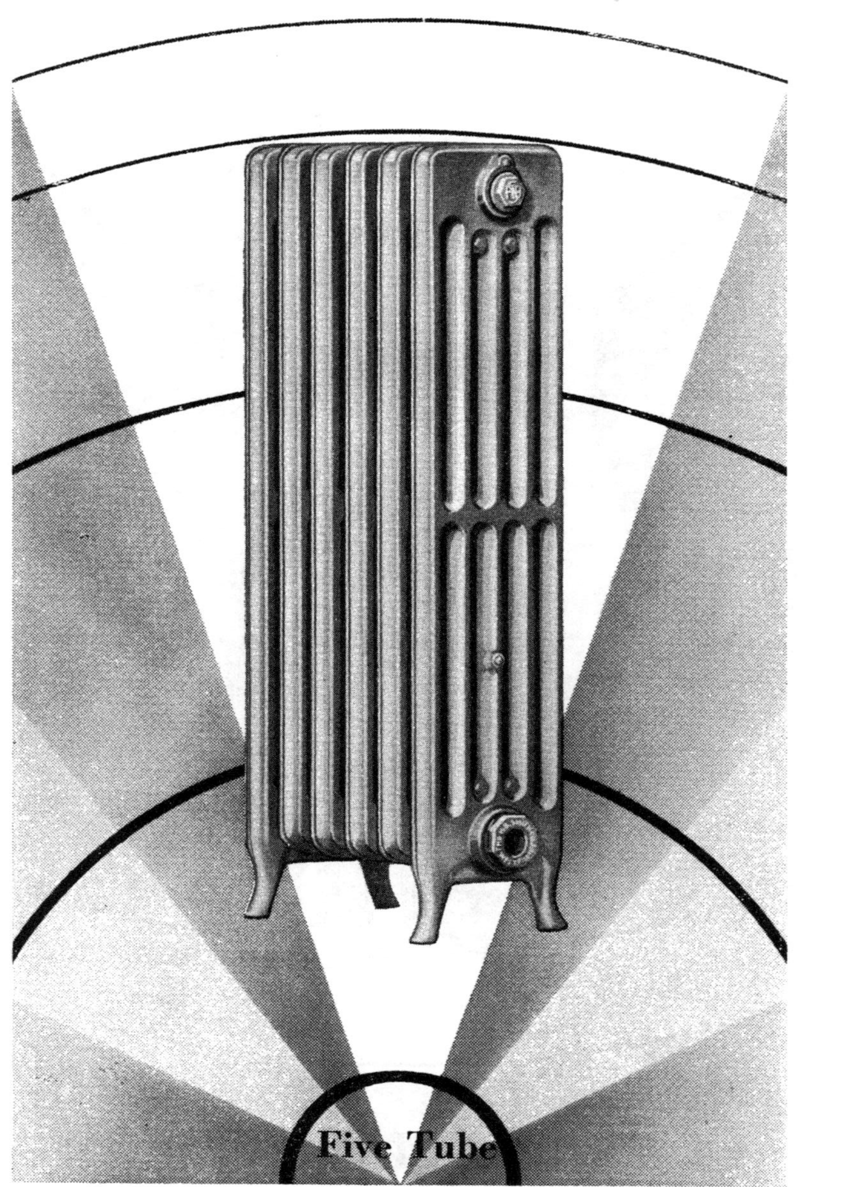

Smith "144" Radiator

Five Tube

Steam or Water

Radiating Surface in Feet

Sections	Total* Length	HEIGHT			
		37″	32″	25″	21″
	ft. – in.	5⅛ ft. per sec.	4¼ ft. per sec.	3¼ ft. per sec.	2½ ft. per sec.
3	0 – 7½	15⅜	12¾	9¾	7½
4	0 – 10	20½	17	13	10
5	1 – ½	25⅝	21¼	16¼	12½
6	1 – 3	30¾	25½	19½	15
7	1 – 5½	35⅞	29¾	22¾	17½
8	1 – 8	41	34	26	20
9	1 – 10½	46⅛	38¼	29¼	22½
10	2 – 1	51¼	42½	32½	25
11	2 – 3½	56⅜	46¾	35¾	27½
12	2 – 6	61½	51	39	30
13	2 – 8½	66⅝	55¼	42¼	32½
14	2 – 11	71¾	59½	45½	35
15	3 – 1½	76⅞	63¾	48¾	37½
16	3 – 4	82	68	52	40
17	3 – 6½	87⅛	72¼	55¼	42½
18	3 – 9	92¼	76½	58½	45
19	3 – 11½	97⅜	80¾	61¾	47½
20	4 – 2	102½	85	65	50
21	4 – 4½	107⅝	89¼	68¼	52½
22	4 – 7	112¾	93½	71½	55
23	4 – 9½	117⅞	97¾	74¾	57½
24	5 – 0	123	102	78	60
25	5 – 2½	128⅛	106¼	81¼	62½
26	5 – 5	133¼	110½	84½	65
27	5 – 7½	138⅜	114¾	87¾	67½
28	5 – 10	143½	119	91	70
29	6 – ½	148⅝	123¼	94¼	72½
30	6 – 3	153¾	127½	97½	75

For Dimension Table see page 18

*Add ½ inch for each bushing

Smith "144" Radiator

Six Tube

Smith "144" Radiator

Six Tube

Steam or Water

Radiating Surface in Feet

Sections	Total Length *	HEIGHT				
		37″	**32″**	**25″**	**21″**	**14″**
	ft. – in.	**6 ft.** per sec.	**5 ft.** per sec.	**3¾ ft.** per sec.	**3 ft.** per sec.	**2 ft.** per sec.
3	0 – 7½	18	15	11¼	9	6
4	0 – 10	24	20	15	12	8
5	1 – ½	30	25	18¾	15	10
6	1 – 3	36	30	22½	18	12
7	1 – 5½	42	35	26¼	21	14
8	1 – 8	48	40	30	24	16
9	1 – 10½	54	45	33¾	27	18
10	2 – 1	60	50	37½	30	20
11	2 – 3½	66	55	41¼	33	22
12	2 – 6	72	60	45	36	24
13	2 – 8½	78	65	48¾	39	26
14	2 – 11	84	70	52½	42	28
15	3 – 1½	90	75	56¼	45	30
16	3 – 4	96	80	60	48	32
17	3 – 6½	102	85	63¾	51	34
18	3 – 9	108	90	67½	54	36
19	3 – 11½	114	95	71¼	57	38
20	4 – 2	120	100	75	60	40
21	4 – 4½	126	105	78¾	63	42
22	4 – 7	132	110	82½	66	44
23	4 – 9½	138	115	86¼	69	46
24	5 – 0	144	120	90	72	48
25	5 – 2½	150	125	93¾	75	50
26	5 – 5	156	130	97½	78	52
27	5 – 7½	162	135	101¼	81	54
28	5 – 10	168	140	105	84	56
29	6 – ½	174	145	108¾	87	58
30	6 – 3	180	150	112½	90	60

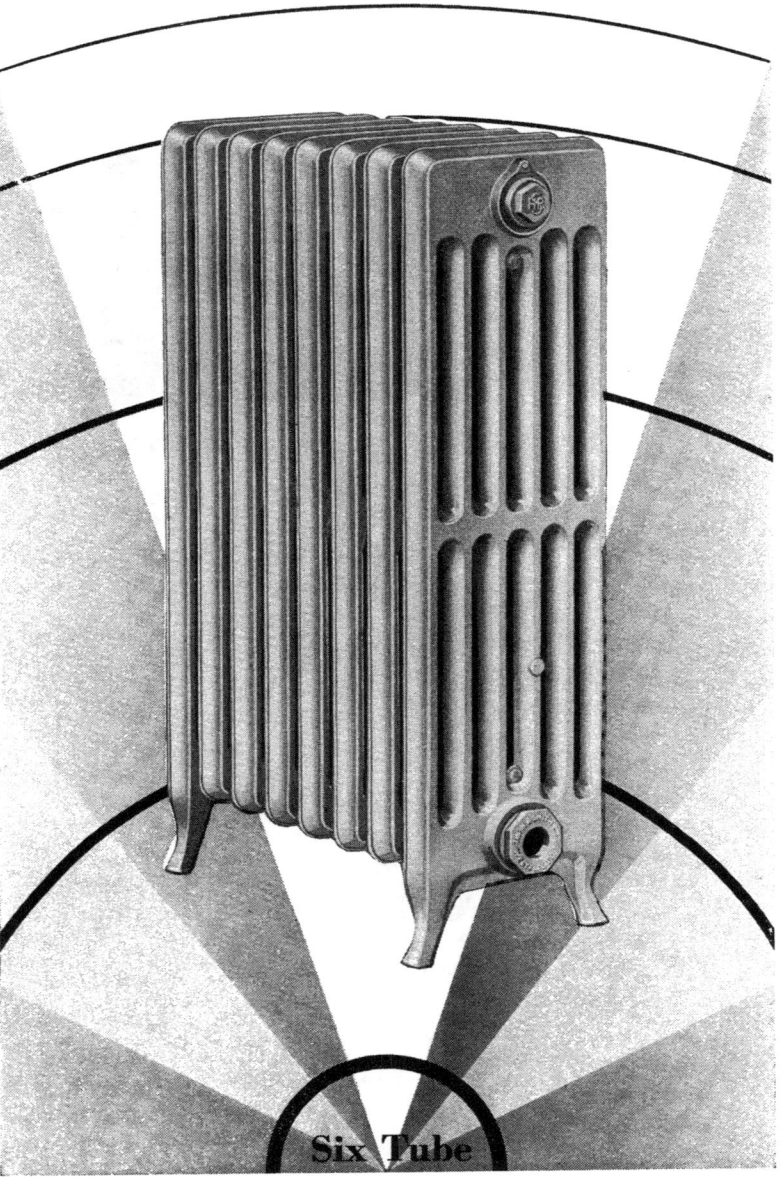

For Dimension Table see page 18

*Add ½ inch for each bushing

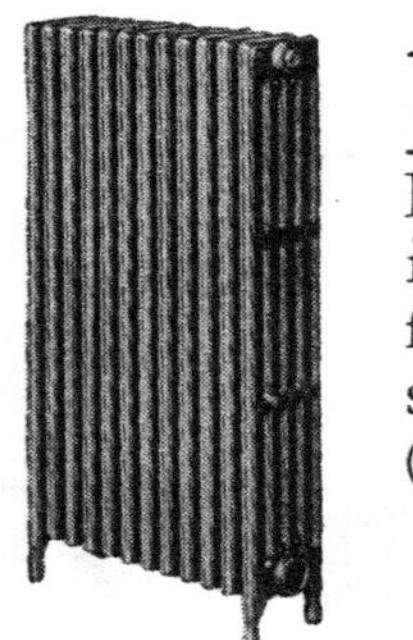

BURNHAM Slenderized Radiators are outstanding in appearance, space saving features (occupy 40% less space) and performance (heat 40% faster).

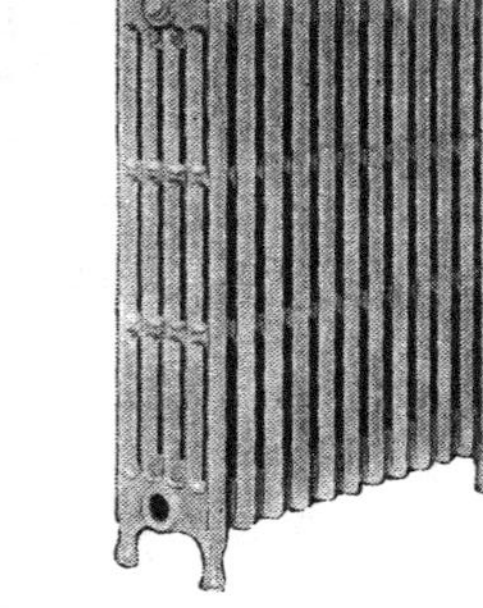

FERO Tube Radiators are of the conventional tube type design. They are neat and clean in appearance and made in all standard sizes.

RATINGS—Based upon the Standard Heat Emission of 240 B.T.U. Per Square Foot Per Hour

CONCEALED TREATMENT

BURNHAM Slenderized Radiators can be furnished with Radiant Front Panels for recessing. Please note that the radiator is exposed to the room. This permits the radiator to give off its healthful radiant heat and also eliminates floor drafts.

Burnham
SLENDERIZED RADIATOR

THREE-TUBE 3¼″ WIDE

Number of Sections	* Length 1½ Inches Per Section	19-inch Height — 1.1 Sq. Ft. Per Section	22-Inch Height — 1.3 Sq. Ft. Per Section	25-Inch Height — 1.5 Sq. Ft. Per Section
		0.733 Sq. Ft. Per Lineal Inch	0.867 Sq. Ft. Per Lineal Inch	1.000 Sq. Ft. Per Lineal Inch
2	3	2.2	2.6	3
4	6	4.4	5.2	6
6	9	6.6	7.8	9
8	12	8.8	10.4	12
10	15	11.0	13.0	15
12	18	13.2	15.6	18
14	21	15.4	18.2	21
16	24	17.6	20.8	24
18	27	19.8	23.4	27
20	30	22.0	26.0	30
22	33	24.2	28.6	33
24	36	26.4	31.2	36
26	39	28.6	33.8	39
28	42	30.8	36.4	42
30	45	33.0	39.0	45
32	48	35.2	41.6	48
34	51	37.4	44.2	51
36	54	39.6	46.8	54
38	57	41.8	49.4	57
40	60	44.0	52.0	60
42	63	46.2	54.6	63
44	66	48.4	57.2	66
46	69	50.6	59.8	69
48	72	52.8	62.4	72
50	75	55.0	65.0	75

*Add ½″ to length for each bushing.

Tapped—Top, 1″ both ends—Bottom, 1¼″ both ends.

Regularly furnished with legs measuring 2½″ from floor to center of bottom tapping, but on special order can be furnished with 4½″ legs or legless.

For detail dimensions, see page 14.

Burnham
SLENDERIZED RADIATOR

FOUR-TUBE 4 7/16″ WIDE

Number of Sections	* Length 1½ Inches Per Section	19-Inch Height — 1.4 Sq. Ft. Per Section	22-Inch Height — 1.6 Sq. Ft. Per Section	25-Inch Height — 1.8 Sq. Ft. Per Section
		0.933 Sq. Ft. Per Lineal Inch	1.067 Sq. Ft. Per Lineal Inch	1.200 Sq. Ft. Per Lineal Inch
2	3	2.8	3.2	3.6
4	6	5.6	6.4	7.2
6	9	8.4	9.6	10.8
8	12	11.2	12.8	14.4
10	15	14.0	16.0	18.0
12	18	16.8	19.2	21.6
14	21	19.6	22.4	25.2
16	24	22.4	25.6	28.8
18	27	25.2	28.8	32.4
20	30	28.0	32.0	36.0
22	33	30.8	35.2	39.6
24	36	33.6	38.4	43.2
26	39	36.4	41.6	46.8
28	42	39.2	44.8	50.4
30	45	42.0	48.0	54.0
32	48	44.8	51.2	57.6
34	51	47.6	54.4	61.2
36	54	50.4	57.6	64.8
38	57	53.2	60.8	68.4
40	60	56.0	64.0	72.0
42	63	58.8	67.2	75.6
44	66	61.6	70.4	79.2
46	69	64.4	73.6	82.8
48	72	67.2	76.8	86.4
50	75	70.0	80.0	90.0

*Add ½″ to length for each bushing.

Tapped—Top, 1″ both ends—Bottom, 1¼″ both ends.

Regularly furnished with legs measuring 2½″ from floor to center of bottom tapping, but on special order can be furnished with 4½″ legs or legless.

For detail dimensions, see page 14.

Burnham
SLENDERIZED RADIATOR

FIVE-TUBE 5 11/16″ WIDE

Number of Sections	* Length 1½ Inches Per Section	20-In. Height — 1 8 Sq. Ft. Per Section	23-In. Height — 2.1 Sq. Ft. Per Section	26-In. Height — 2.4 Sq. Ft. Per Section	32-In. Height — 3.0 Sq. Ft. Per Section
		1.200 Sq. Ft. Per Lineal Inch	1.400 Sq. Ft. Per Lineal Inch	1.600 Sq. Ft. Per Lineal Inch	2.000 Sq. Ft. Per Lineal Inch
2	3	3.6	4.2	4.8	6
4	6	7.2	8.4	9.6	12
6	9	10.8	12.6	14.4	18
8	12	14.4	16.8	19.2	24
10	15	18.0	21.0	24.0	30
12	18	21.6	25.2	28.8	36
14	21	25.2	29.4	33.6	42
16	24	28.8	33.6	38.4	48
18	27	32.4	37.8	43.2	54
20	30	36.0	42.0	48.0	60
22	33	39.6	46.2	52.8	66
24	36	43.2	50.4	57.6	72
26	39	46.8	54.6	62.4	78
28	42	50.4	58.8	67.2	84
30	45	54.0	63.0	72.0	90
32	48	57.6	67.2	76.8	96
34	51	61.2	71.4	81.6	102
36	54	64.8	75.6	86.4	108
38	57	68.4	79.8	91.2	114
40	60	72.0	84.0	96.0	120
42	63	75.6	88.2	100.8	126
44	66	79.2	92.4	105.6	132
46	69	82.8	96.6	110.4	138
48	72	86.4	100.8	115.2	144
50	75	90.0	105.0	120.0	150

*Add ½″ to length for each bushing.

Tapped—Top, 1″ both ends—Bottom, 1¼″ both ends.

Regularly furnished with legs measuring 3½″ from floor to center of bottom tapping, but on special order can be furnished with 4½″ legs or legless.

For detail dimensions, see page 14.

Burnham

SLENDERIZED RADIATOR

SIX-TUBE $6\frac{15}{16}''$ WIDE

Number of Sections	* Length 1½ Inches Per Section	14-Inch Height: 1.5 Sq. Ft. Per Section / 1 Sq. Ft. Per Lineal Inch	17-Inch Height: 1.8 Sq. Ft. Per Section / 1.2 Sq. Ft. Per Lineal Inch	20-Inch Height: 2.2 Sq. Ft. Per Section / 1.47 Sq. Ft. Per Lineal Inch	26-Inch Height: 2.9 Sq. Ft. Per Section / 1.93 Sq. Ft. Per Lineal Inch
2	3	3.0	3.6	4.4	5.8
4	6	6.0	7.2	8.8	11.6
6	9	9.0	10.8	13.2	17.4
8	12	12.0	14.4	17.6	23.2
10	15	15.0	18.0	22.0	29.0
12	18	18.0	21.6	26.4	34.8
14	21	21.0	25.2	30.8	40.6
16	24	24.0	28.8	35.2	46.4
18	27	27.0	32.4	39.6	52.2
20	30	30.0	36.0	44.0	58.0
22	33	33.0	39.6	48.4	63.8
24	36	36.0	43.2	52.8	69.6
26	39	39.0	46.8	57.2	75.4
28	42	42.0	50.4	61.6	81.2
30	45	45.0	54.0	66.0	87.0
32	48	48.0	57.6	70.4	92.8
34	51	51.0	61.2	74.8	98.6
36	54	54.0	64.8	79.2	104.4
38	57	57.0	68.4	83.6	110.2
40	60	60.0	72.0	88.0	116.0
42	63	63.0	75.6	92.4	121.8
44	66	66.0	79.2	96.8	127.6
46	69	69.0	82.8	101.2	133.4
48	72	72.0	86.4	105.6	139.2
50	75	75.0	90.0	110.0	145.0

*Add ½″ to length for each bushing.

Tapped—Top, 1″ both ends—Bottom, 1¼″ both ends.

Regularly furnished with legs measuring 3½″ from floor to center of bottom tapping, but on special order can be furnished with 4½″ legs or legless.

For detail dimensions, see page 14.

Slenderized

WALL RADIATOR

THE new Slenderized Wall Radiator has numerous advantages over the present heavy type wall radiator.

It is lighter, easier to handle, occupies less space and costs less. Furthermore, being made up of 1½ inch sections, it can be furnished to meet nearly all requirements.

It is not however recommended to be used on a ceiling.

No.	Sq. Ft.	Size Legless Radiator	Length	Height	Depth
6A	6.6	6 Sec.—19-3	9″	17½″	3¼″
11A	11.0	10 Sec.—19-3	15″	17½″	3¼″
6B	6.	4 Sec.—25-3	6″	23½″	3¼″
9B	9.	6 Sec.—25-3	9″	23½″	3¼″
12B	12.	8 Sec.—25-3	12″	23½″	3¼″

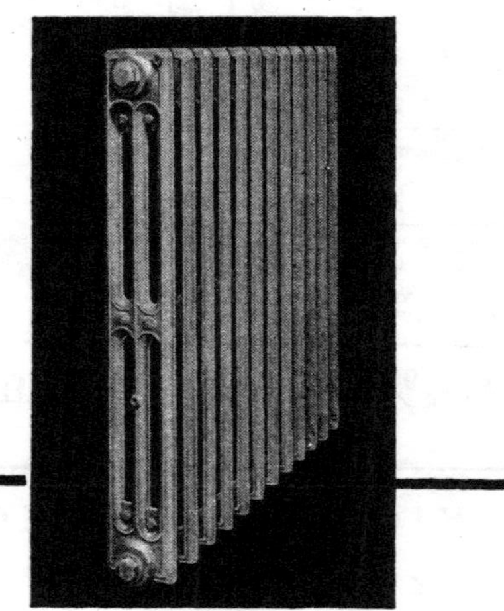

Fero
TUBE RADIATOR

THREE-TUBE — 5¼″ WIDE

Number of Sections	* Length 2½-Inch per Section	38-Inch Height (Square Feet) 3½ Sq. Ft. per Section	31-Inch Height (Square Feet) 3 Sq. Ft. per Section	27-Inch Height (Square Feet) 2⅓ Sq. Ft. per Section	23-Inch Height (Square Feet) 2 Sq. Ft. per Section	20-Inch Height (Square Feet) 1¾ Sq. Ft. per Section
2	5	7	6	4⅔	4	3½
3	7½	10½	9	7	6	5¼
4	10	14	12	9⅓	8	7
5	12½	17½	15	11⅔	10	8¾
6	15	21	18	14	12	10½
7	17½	24½	21	16⅓	14	12¼
8	20	28	24	18⅔	16	14
9	22½	31½	27	21	18	15¾
10	25	35	30	23⅓	20	17½
11	27½	38½	33	25⅔	22	19¼
12	30	42	36	28	24	21
13	32½	45½	39	30⅓	26	22¾
14	35	49	42	32⅔	28	24½
15	37½	52½	45	35	30	26¼
16	40	56	48	37⅓	32	28
17	42½	59½	51	39⅔	34	29¾
18	45	63	54	42	36	31½
19	47½	66½	57	44⅓	38	33¼
20	50	70	60	46⅔	40	35
21	52½	73½	63	49	42	36¾
22	55	77	66	51⅓	44	38½
23	57½	80½	69	53⅔	46	40¼
24	60	84	72	56	48	42
25	62½	87½	75	58⅓	50	43¾
26	65	91	78	60⅔	52	45½
27	67½	94½	81	63	54	47¼
28	70	98	84	65⅓	56	49
29	72½	101½	87	67⅔	58	50¾
30	75	105	90	70	60	52½
31	77½	108½	93	72⅓	62	54¼
32	80	112	96	74⅔	64	56

*Add ½″ to length for each bushing.
Tapped 1½″ Top and Bottom both ends.
Regularly furnished with legs measuring 4½″ from floor to center of bottom tapping, but on special order can be furnished with 6″ legs or legless.
For detail dimensions, see page 14.

Fero
TUBE RADIATOR

FOUR-TUBE — 6⅝″ WIDE

Number of Sections	* Length 2½-Inch per Section	38-Inch Height (Square Feet) 4¼ Sq. Ft. per Section	32-Inch Height (Square Feet) 3½ Sq. Ft. per Section	26-Inch Height (Square Feet) 2¾ Sq. Ft. per Section	23-Inch Height (Square Feet) 2½ Sq. Ft. per Section	20-Inch Height (Square Feet) 2¼ Sq. Ft. per Section
2	5	8½	7	5½	5	4½
3	7½	12¾	10½	8¼	7½	6¾
4	10	17	14	11	10	9
5	12½	21¼	17½	13¾	12½	11¼
6	15	25½	21	16½	15	13½
7	17½	29¾	24½	19¼	17½	15¾
8	20	34	28	22	20	18
9	22½	38¼	31½	24¾	22½	20¼
10	25	42½	35	27½	25	22½
11	27½	46¾	38½	30¼	27½	24¾
12	30	51	42	33	30	27
13	32½	55¼	45½	35¾	32½	29¼
14	35	59½	49	38½	35	31½
15	37½	63¾	52½	41¼	37½	33¾
16	40	68	56	44	40	36
17	42½	72¼	59½	46¾	42½	38¼
18	45	76½	63	49½	45	40½
19	47½	80¾	66½	52¼	47½	42¾
20	50	85	70	55	50	45
21	52½	89¼	73½	57¾	52½	47¼
22	55	93½	77	60½	55	49½
23	57½	97¾	80½	63¼	57½	51¾
24	60	102	84	66	60	54
25	62½	106¼	87½	68¾	62½	56¼
26	65	110½	91	71½	65	58½
27	67½	114¾	94½	74¼	67½	60¾
28	70	119	98	77	70	63
29	72½	123¼	101½	79¾	72½	65¼
30	75	127½	105	82½	75	67½
31	77½	131¾	108½	85¼	77½	69¾
32	80	136	112	88	80	72

*Add ½″ to length for each bushing.
Tapped 1½″ Top and Bottom both ends.
Regularly furnished with legs measuring 4½″ from floor to center of bottom tapping, but on special order can be furnished with 6″ legs or legless.
For detail dimensions, see page 14.

Fero

TUBE RADIATOR

FIVE-TUBE — 8½″ WIDE

Number of Sections	* Length 2½-Inch per Section	Square Feet: 38-Inch Height — 5 Sq. Ft. per Section	32-Inch Height — 4⅓ Sq. Ft. per Section	26-Inch Height — 3½ Sq. Ft. per Section	23-Inch Height — 3 Sq. Ft. per Section	20-Inch Height — 2⅔ Sq. Ft. per Section
2	5	10	8⅔	7	6	5⅓
3	7½	15	13	10½	9	8
4	10	20	17⅓	14	12	10⅔
5	12½	25	21⅔	17½	15	13⅓
6	15	30	26	21	18	16
7	17½	35	30⅓	24½	21	18⅔
8	20	40	34⅔	28	24	21⅓
9	22½	45	39	31½	27	24
10	25	50	43⅓	35	30	26⅔
11	27½	55	47⅔	38½	33	29⅓
12	30	60	52	42	36	32
13	32½	65	56⅓	45½	39	34⅔
14	35	70	60⅔	49	42	37⅓
15	37½	75	65	52½	45	40
16	40	80	69⅓	56	48	42⅔
17	42½	85	73⅔	59½	51	45⅓
18	45	90	78	63	54	48
19	47½	95	82⅓	66½	57	50⅔
20	50	100	86⅔	70	60	53⅓
21	52½	105	91	73½	63	56
22	55	110	95⅓	77	66	58⅔
23	57½	115	99⅔	80½	69	61⅓
24	60	120	104	84	72	64
25	62½	125	108⅓	87½	75	66⅔
26	65	130	112⅔	91	78	69⅓
27	67½	135	117	94½	81	72
28	70	140	121⅓	98	84	74⅔
29	72½	145	125⅔	101½	87	77⅓
30	75	150	130	105	90	80
31	77½	155	134⅓	108½	93	82⅔
32	80	160	138⅔	112	96	85⅓

*Add ½″ to length for each bushing.
Tapped 1½″ Top and Bottom both ends.
Regularly furnished with legs measuring 4½″ from floor to center of bottom tapping, but on special order can be furnished with 6″ legs or legless.
For detail dimensions, see page 14.

Fero

TUBE RADIATOR

SIX-TUBE — 10$\frac{5}{16}$″ WIDE

Number of Sections	* Length 2½-Inch per Section	Square Feet: 38-Inch Height — 6 Sq. Ft. per Section	32-Inch Height — 5 Sq. Ft. per Section	26-Inch Height — 4 Sq. Ft. per Section	23-Inch Height — 3½ Sq. Ft. per Section	20-Inch Height — 3 Sq. Ft. per Section
2	5	12	10	8	7	6
3	7½	18	15	12	10½	9
4	10	24	20	16	14	12
5	12½	30	25	20	17½	15
6	15	36	30	24	21	18
7	17½	42	35	28	24½	21
8	20	48	40	32	28	24
9	22½	54	45	36	31½	27
10	25	60	50	40	35	30
11	27½	66	55	44	38½	33
12	30	72	60	48	42	36
13	32½	78	65	52	45½	39
14	35	84	70	56	49	42
15	37½	90	75	60	52½	45
16	40	96	80	64	56	48
17	42½	102	85	68	59½	51
18	45	108	90	72	63	54
19	47½	114	95	76	66½	57
20	50	120	100	80	70	60
21	52½	126	105	84	73½	63
22	55	132	110	88	77	66
23	57½	138	115	92	80½	69
24	60	144	120	96	84	72
25	62½	150	125	100	87½	75
26	65	156	130	104	91	78
27	67½	162	135	108	94½	81
28	70	168	140	112	98	84
29	72½	174	145	116	101½	87
30	75	180	150	120	105	90
31	77½	186	155	124	108½	93
32	80	192	160	128	112	96

*Add ½″ to length for each bushing.
Tapped 1½″ Top and Bottom both ends.
Regularly furnished with legs measuring 4½″ from floor to center of bottom tapping, but on special order can be furnished with 6″ legs or legless.
For detail dimensions, see page 14.

Fero

TUBE RADIATOR

SEVEN-TUBE 12⅛″ WIDE

Number of Sections	* Length 2½-In. per Section	Square Feet: 20-Inch Height — 3⅔ Sq. Ft. per Section	Square Feet: 17-Inch Height — 3¼ Sq. Ft. per Section	Square Feet: 14-Inch Height — 2⅔ Sq. Ft. per Section
2	5	7⅓	6½	5⅓
3	7½	11	9¾	8
4	10	14⅔	13	10⅔
5	12½	18⅓	16¼	13⅓
6	15	22	19½	16
7	17½	25⅔	22¾	18⅔
8	20	29⅓	26	21⅓
9	22½	33	29¼	24
10	25	36⅔	32½	26⅔
11	27½	40⅓	35¾	29⅓
12	30	44	39	32
13	32½	47⅔	42¼	34⅔
14	35	51⅓	45½	37⅓
15	37½	55	48¾	40
16	40	58⅔	52	42⅔
17	42½	62⅓	55¼	45⅓
18	45	66	58½	48
19	47½	69⅔	61¾	50⅔
20	50	73⅓	65	53⅓
21	52½	77	68¼	56
22	55	80⅔	71½	58⅔
23	57½	84⅓	74¾	61⅓
24	60	88	78	64
25	62½	91⅔	81¼	66⅔
26	65	95⅓	84½	69⅓
27	67½	99	87¾	72
28	70	102⅔	91	74⅔
29	72½	106⅓	94¼	77⅓
30	75	110	97½	80
31	77½	113⅔	100¾	82⅔
32	80	117⅓	104	85⅓

*Add ½″ to length for each bushing.
Tapped 1½″ Top and Bottom both ends.
Regularly furnished with legs measuring 3″ from floor to center of bottom tapping, but on special order can be furnished with 6″ legs or legless.
For detail dimensions, see page 14.

AMERICAN - STANDARD

Arco Convectors

Cast Iron

American Radiator and Standard Sanitary Corp.
Pittsburgh 30, Pa.

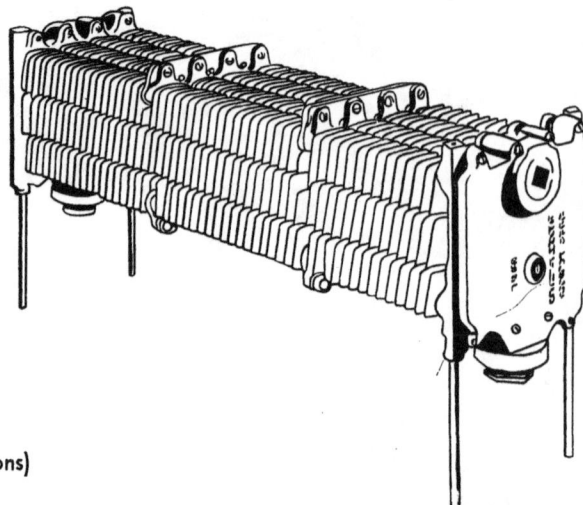

Enclosure Types
and Measuring Instructions

(Note: Ratings on facing page are based on element dimensions)

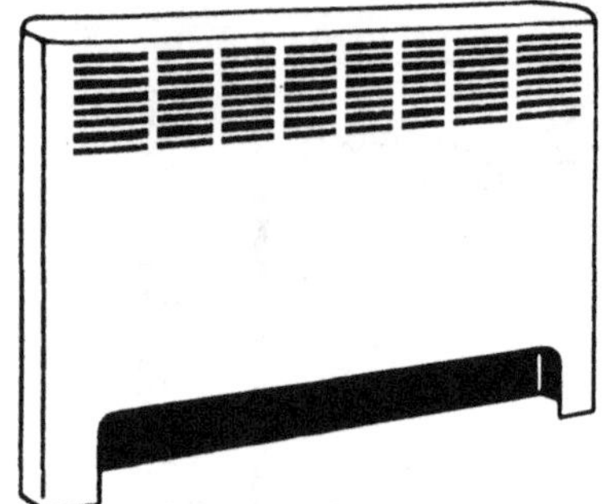

Free Standing Enclosure—L—Actual; H—Actual; D—Actual, less ⅞ in. to 1 in.

Semi-Recessel Enclosure—L—Actual, less 1½ in.; H—Actual; D—Actual, less ⅞ in. to 1 in.

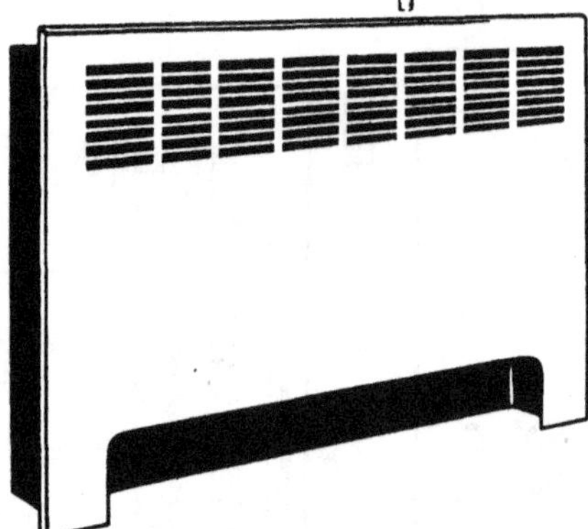

Recessed Enclosure—L—Actual, less 2½ in.; H—Actual; D—Actual, less ⅝ in.

Plaster Front—L—Grille length + 3½ in.; H—Actual; D—Actual, less 1 in.

Wall Hung—Flat Top—Type "W"—L—Actual, less 1½ in.; H—Actual—Use; D—Actual, less 1 in. h.w. column.

Wall Hung—Sloping Top—L—Actual, less 1½ in.; H—Actual—Use; D—Actual, less 1 in.

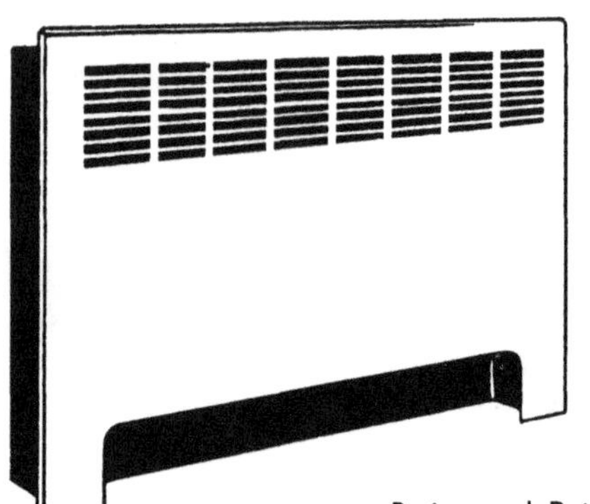

Left: Flush Front Panel—L—Actual, less 5 in.; H—Actual; D—Measure element.

Right: Extended Front Panel—Actual, less 5 in.; H—Actual; D—Measure element.

Ratings and Data Shown in Effect on May 15, 1951

RATINGS FOR ARCO CAST IRON CONVECTORS

(Sq. ft. EDR based on 215 deg. steam, 240 Btu)

	"L" Length, Inches		▲18	▲23	▲28	▲33	▲38	▲43	▲48	▲53	▲63
	Unit No.		518	523	528	533	538	543	548	553	563
WIDTH OF ELEMENT 5⅝″	Type "W" Enclosure Hgt.	Enclosure Hgt. Except Type "W"									
	16	▲20	13.5	17.4	21.3	25.2	29.2	33.1	37.0	40.9	48.7
	20	▲24	15.4	19.9	24.4	28.9	33.4	37.9	42.4	46.8	55.8
	28	▲32	17.5	22.6	27.7	32.9	38.0	43.1	48.1	53.3	63.5

SEE FACING PAGE FOR MEASURING INSTRUCTIONS

	"L" Length, Inches		28	▲33	▲38	▲43	▲48	▲53	▲63
	Unit No.		728	733	738	743	748	753	763
WIDTH OF ELEMENT 7⅜″	Type "W" Enclosure Height	Enclosure Hgt. Except Type "W"							
	16	▲20	27.2	32.2	37.2	42.3	47.3	52.3	62.3
	20	▲24	30.7	36.4	42.1	47.8	53.5	59.2	70.6
	28	▲32	35.7	42.3	48.9	55.5	62.0	68.6	81.8

SEE FACING PAGE FOR MEASURING INSTRUCTIONS

	"L" Length, Inches		33	▲38	▲43	▲48	▲53	▲63
	Unit No.		933	938	943	948	953	963
WIDTH OF ELEMENT 9½″	Type "W" Enclosure Height	Enclosure Height Except Type "W"						
	16	▲20	38.9	45.0	51.1	57.2	63.3	75.5
	20	▲24	44.2	51.1	58.0	64.9	71.8	85.6
	28	▲32	51.4	59.5	67.5	75.6	83.6	99.7

AMERICAN STANDARD*

Arco Multifin Convectors

*American Radiator and Standard Sanitary Corp., Pittsburgh 30, Pa.

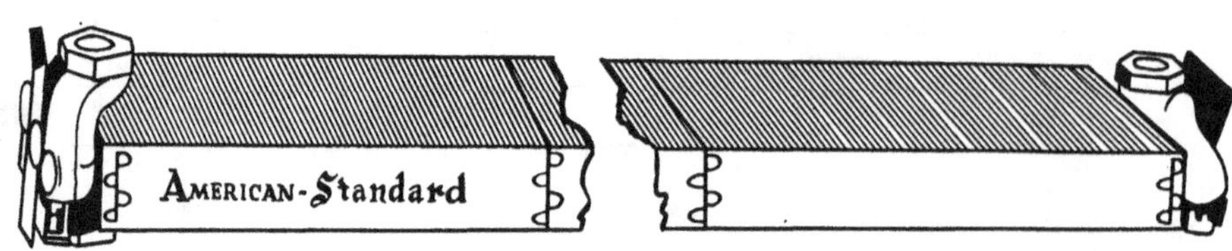

Enclosure Types and Measuring Instructions
(Note: Ratings on facing page are based on element dimensions)

Free Standing Enclosure—L—Actual; H—Actual; D—Actual, less 7/8 in. to 1 in.

Semi-Recessed Enclosure—L—Actual, less 1 1/2 in.; H—Actual; D—Actual, less 7/8 in. to 1 in.

Recessed Enclosure—L—Actual, less 2 1/2 in.; H—Actual; D—Actual, less 5/8 in.

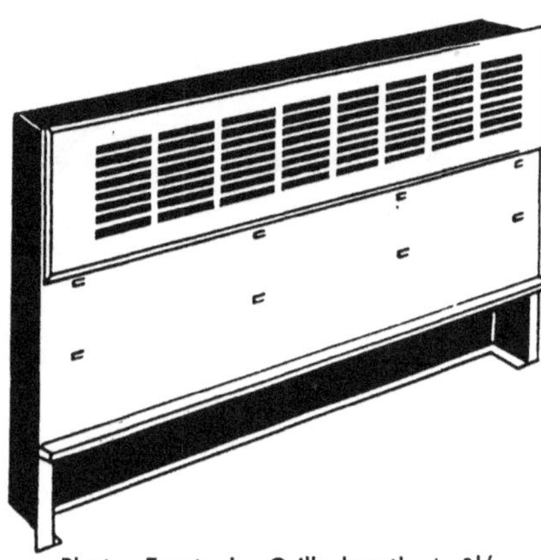

Plaster Front—L—Grille length + 3 1/2 in.; H—Actual; D—Actual, less 1 in.

Wall Hung—Flat Top—Type "W"—L—Actual, less 1 1/2 in.; H—Actual—Use; D—Actual, less 1 in. h.w. column.

Wall Hung—Sloping Top—L—Actual, less 1 1/2 in.; H—Actual—Use; D—Actual, less 1 in.

Left: Flush Front Panel—L—Actual, less 5 in.; H—Actual; D—Measure element.

Right: Extended Front Panel—Actual, less 5 in.; H—Actual; D—Measure element.

NEW MULTIFIN CONVECTORS

Sloping Top outlet enclosures, Square Foot Rating (Steam 215°) 240 BTU

Nominal Length		20	24	28	32	36	40	44	48	56	64
Enclosure Length		20½	24½	28½	32½	36½	40½	44½	48½	56½	64½
	Enclosure Height (Inches)										
ELEMENT WIDTH 3⅜"	18	10.9	13.4	16.0	18.5	21.0	23.6	26.1	28.6	33.7	38.8
	20	11.4	14.1	16.7	19.4	22.0	24.7	27.3	29.8	34.9	40.0
	24	13.2	16.2	19.2	22.2	25.2	28.3	31.3	34.3	40.3	46.4
	26	13.4	16.4	19.5	22.6	25.6	28.7	31.7	34.8	40.9	47.0
	32	14.0	17.2	20.4	23.6	26.8	30.0	33.2	36.4	42.8	49.2
	38	14.6	18.0	21.3	24.6	28.0	31.3	34.7	38.0	44.7	51.4
ELEMENT WIDTH 5⅜"	18	16.3	20.0	23.8	27.5	31.3	35.1	38.7	42.5	50.0	57.5
	20	17.0	20.9	24.9	28.8	32.7	36.6	40.5	44.5	52.3	60.1
	24	18.5	22.7	27.0	31.2	35.5	39.7	44.0	48.2	56.7	65.2
	26	18.8	23.1	27.4	31.7	36.0	40.3	44.6	48.9	57.5	66.2
	32	19.7	24.2	28.7	33.2	37.8	42.3	46.8	51.4	60.4	69.5
	38	20.7	25.4	30.2	34.9	39.7	44.4	49.2	53.9	63.4	72.9
ELEMENT WIDTH 7⅜"	18	20.8	25.6	30.4	35.2	40.0	44.8	49.6	54.4	64.0	73.6
	20	21.8	26.9	31.9	36.9	42.0	47.0	52.1	57.1	67.2	77.3
	24	24.1	29.6	35.2	40.8	46.3	51.9	57.4	63.0	74.1	85.2
	26	24.4	30.1	35.7	41.3	47.0	52.6	58.3	63.9	75.2	86.5
	32	25.4	31.3	37.2	43.1	49.0	54.8	60.7	66.6	78.4	90.1
	38	26.5	32.6	38.7	44.8	50.9	57.0	63.1	69.3	81.5	93.7
ELEMENT WIDTH 9⅜"	18	23.5	28.9	34.4	39.8	45.2	50.7	56.1	61.5	72.4	83.2
	20	25.0	30.8	36.6	42.3	48.1	53.9	59.7	65.5	77.0	88.6
	24	28.1	34.6	41.1	47.6	54.1	60.6	67.0	73.5	86.5	99.5
	26	28.6	35.2	41.8	48.4	55.0	61.7	68.3	74.9	88.1	101.3
	32	30.2	37.2	44.2	51.1	58.1	65.1	72.1	79.1	93.0	107.0
	38	31.6	38.9	46.2	53.5	60.8	68.1	75.4	82.7	97.3	111.9

The above enclosure heights are for floor type enclosures and are the heights from the floor to the highest point, measured at the back. Wall hung enclosures are 4" less in height, and for installation not less than 4" above the floor.

NEW MULTIFIN CONVECTOR RATINGS

Face outlet enclosure, Square Foot Rating (Steam 215°) 240 BTU

Nominal Length		20	24	28	32	36	40	44	48	56	64
Enclosure Length		20½	24½	28½	32½	36½	40½	44½	48½	56½	64½
	Enclosure Height (Inches)										
ELEMENT WIDTH 3⅜"	18	10.5	12.9	15.2	17.6	20.0	22.4	24.8	27.2	32.0	36.8
	20	11.3	13.9	16.5	19.1	21.7	24.3	26.9	29.5	34.7	39.9
	24	13.2	16.2	19.2	22.2	25.2	28.3	31.3	34.3	40.3	46.4
	26	13.4	16.4	19.5	22.6	25.6	28.7	31.7	34.8	40.9	47.0
	32	14.0	17.2	20.4	23.6	26.8	30.0	33.2	36.4	42.8	49.2
	38	14.6	18.0	21.3	24.6	28.0	31.3	34.7	38.0	44.7	51.4
ELEMENT WIDTH 5⅜"	18	15.2	18.7	22.2	25.7	29.2	32.7	36.2	39.7	46.7	53.7
	20	16.3	20.0	23.8	27.5	31.3	35.0	38.8	42.5	50.0	57.5
	24	18.5	22.7	27.0	31.2	35.5	39.7	44.0	48.2	56.7	65.2
	26	18.8	23.1	27.4	31.7	36.0	40.3	44.6	48.9	57.5	66.2
	32	19.7	24.2	28.7	33.2	37.8	42.3	46.8	51.4	60.4	69.5
	38	20.7	25.4	30.2	34.9	39.7	44.4	49.2	53.9	63.4	72.9
ELEMENT WIDTH 7⅜"	18	18.6	22.9	27.1	31.4	35.7	39.9	44.2	48.5	57.0	65.6
	20	19.9	24.5	29.0	33.6	38.2	42.7	47.3	51.9	61.0	70.1
	24	22.5	27.7	32.8	38.0	43.2	48.3	53.5	58.7	69.0	79.4
	26	23.0	28.2	33.5	38.8	44.1	49.4	54.6	59.9	70.5	81.0
	32	24.4	30.1	35.7	41.3	46.9	52.5	58.2	63.8	75.0	86.2
	38	25.9	31.8	37.8	43.7	49.6	55.6	61.5	67.5	79.3	91.2
ELEMENT WIDTH 9⅜"	18	20.3	25.1	29.9	34.6	39.4	44.2	49.0	53.7	63.3	72.8
	20	22.0	27.2	32.4	37.5	42.7	47.9	53.0	58.2	68.5	78.9
	24	25.2	31.1	37.0	42.9	48.8	54.7	60.7	66.6	78.4	90.2
	26	25.8	31.8	37.8	43.9	49.9	56.0	62.0	68.0	80.1	92.2
	32	27.5	34.0	40.5	46.9	53.4	59.8	66.3	72.8	85.7	98.6
	38	29.2	36.1	43.0	49.8	56.7	63.5	70.4	77.3	91.0	104.7

The above enclosure heights are for floor type enclosures and are the heights from the floor to the highest point, measured at the back. Wall hung enclosures are 4" less in height, and for installation not less than 4" above the floor.

AIRTHERM MANUFACTURING COMPANY

700 South Spring Street, St. Louis 10, Mo.

Airtherm Copper Convectors

Enclosure Types and Measuring Instructions

IDENTIFICATION

To identify the convector as an Airtherm unit, check the inside of the enclosure. The name "AIRTHERM" will be found inside, on the center of the rear panel.

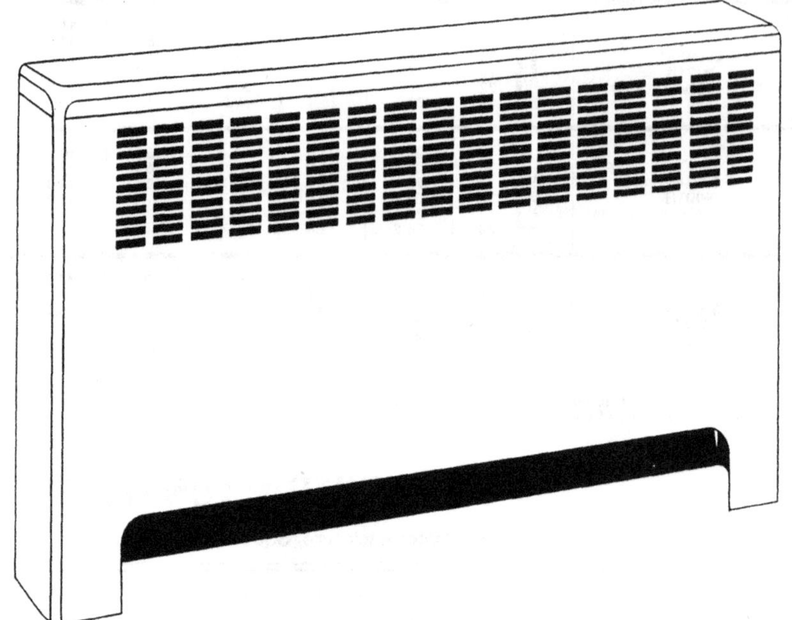

Above: Type "F" floor cabinet is designated by this drawing.

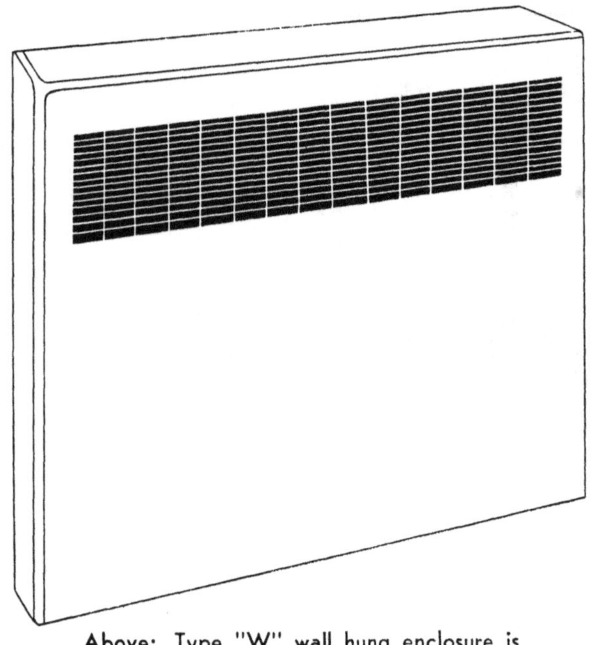

Above: Type "W" wall hung enclosure is illustrated.

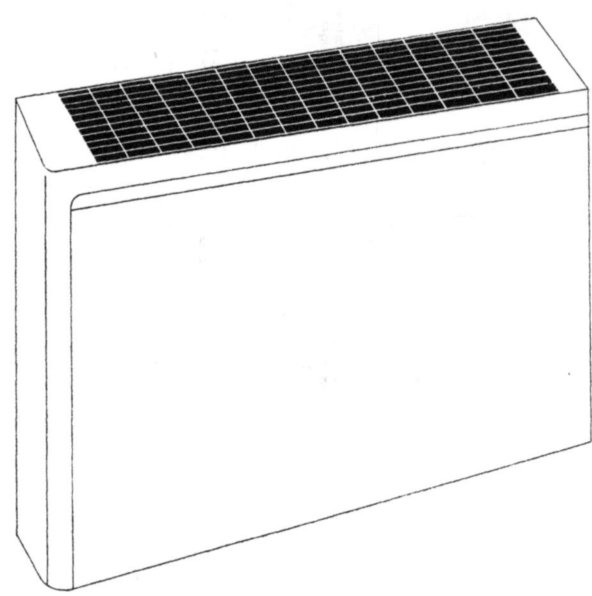

Above: Type "S" wall hung enclosure.

RATINGS FOR AIRTHERM COPPER CONVECTORS*

*(Note: Ratings are given in sq. ft. E.D.R., based on 215 deg steam, 240 Btu and 65 deg entering air temperature)

Types "F" and "W"

Enclosure Length	Height, Type W	Height, Type F	20″	24″	28″	32″	36″	40″	48″	56″	64″
WIDTH OF ELEMENT 5½″ ENCLOSURE DEPTH 5⅞″	15½″	20″	16.0	20.0	24.0	27.0	31.0	35.5	42.0	48.0	56.0
	19½″	24″	17.5	23.0	27.0	31.0	34.0	39.0	47.0	55.0	63.0
	27½″	32″	19.0	24.0	29.0	34.0	38.0	43.0	52.0	60.0	69.0
WIDTH OF ELEMENT 7⅝″ ENCLOSURE DEPTH 8″	15½″	20″				35.0	39.0	44.0	55.0	65.0	75.0
	19½″	24″				37.5	44.0	48.0	59.0	69.0	80.0
	27½″	32″				41.0	47.0	53.0	64.0	75.0	85.0
WIDTH OF ELEMENT 10¼″ ENCLOSURE DEPTH 10⅝″	15½″	20″					45.0	49.0	60.0	71.0	81.0
	19½″	24″					52.0	57.0	69.0	80.0	93.0
	27½″	32″					56.0	61.0	74.5	87.5	101.0

Type "S"

(Given in sq. ft. E.D.R., based on 215 deg steam, 240 Btu and 65 deg entering air)

Enclosure Length	Enclosure Height	20″	24″	28″	32″	36″	40″	48″	56″	64″
WIDTH OF ELEMENT 5½″ ENCLOSURE DEPTH 5⅞″	15½″	19.5	25.0	27.0	33.5	37.0	40.0	47.0	57.0	65.0
	19½″	21.0	26.0	30.0	35.0	38.0	42.0	52.0	62.0	72.0
	27½″	22.0	28.0	32.0	36.0	41.0	46.0	57.0	68.0	78.0
WIDTH OF ELEMENT 7⅝″ ENCLOSURE DEPTH 8″	15½″				40.0	45.0	51.0	62.0	72.0	82.0
	19½″				42.0	46.0	52.0	63.0	76.0	88.0
	27½″				44.0	51.0	58.0	68.0	82.0	97.0
WIDTH OF ELEMENT 10¼″ ENCLOSURE DEPTH 10⅝″	15½″					51.0	57.0	68.0	82.0	95.5
	19½″					58.0	62.0	75.0	88.0	102.0
	27½″					59.0	63.0	78.0	92.0	108.0

AMERICAN COILS COMPANY

360 Thomas Street, Newark 5, New Jersey

Amcoil Copper Convectors

Enclosure Types and Measuring Instructions

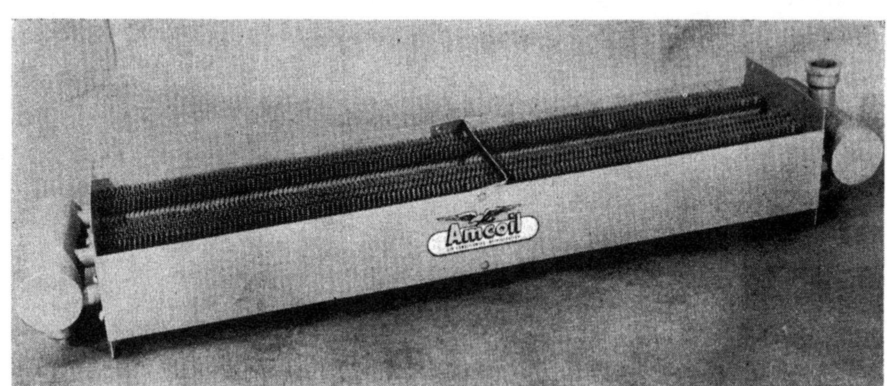

Convector element, showing the location of the trademark.

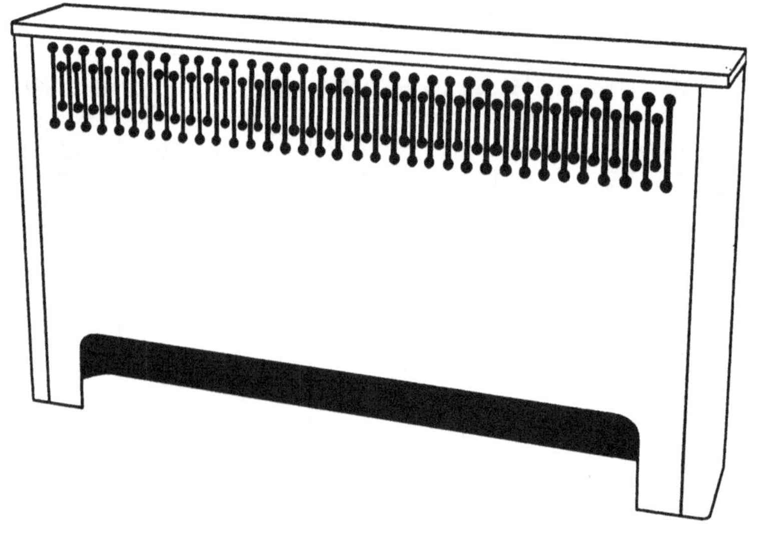

Left: This unit designates the Amcoil 24 inch high free standing enclosure.

RATINGS FOR AMCOIL 24 INCH HIGH FREE STANDING ENCLOSURES*

*(Note: Ratings are given in sq. ft. E.D.R., based on 215 deg steam and 65 deg entering air temperature)

Enclosure Depth	Enclosure Height	Enclosure Length	20½″	24½″	28½″	32½″	36½″	40½″	44½″	48½″	56½″	64½″
6⅜″	24″	sq. ft. E.D.R.	18.5	22.5	26.5	30.5	34.5	38.5	42.5	46.5	55.0	63.0

AMCOIL COPPER CONVECTOR RATINGS

The units shown in the three drawings below show enclosure styles for the Amcoil 21½ inch partially recessed enclosure. At left is the side view; center is shown convector element partially revealed; right drawing shows end view dimensions.

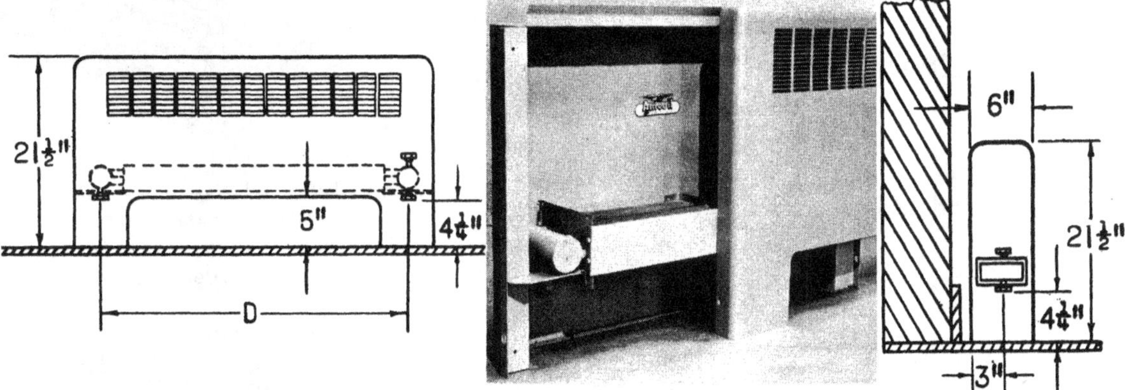

RATINGS FOR AMCOIL 21½ INCH PARTIALLY RECESSED ENCLOSURES*

*(Note: Ratings are given in sq. ft. E.D.R., based on 215 deg steam and 65 deg entering air temperature)

Enclosure Depth 6"	Front Panel Height 21½"	Front Panel Length	24½"	28½"	32½"	36½"	40½"	44½"	48½"	52½"	60½"	68½"
Recess Depth	Recess Height	Recess Length	20½"	24½"	28½"	32½"	36½"	40½"	44½"	48½"	56½"	64½"
4"	20"	sq.ft.E.D.R.	16.0	21.0	25.0	29.0	33.0	36.5	40.5	44.0	52.0	60.0

Units shown in drawings below are Amcoil 21½ inch free standing enclosure styles. At left is side view dimensions; center shows convector cabinet front removed, revealing element; at right is the end view giving dimensions.

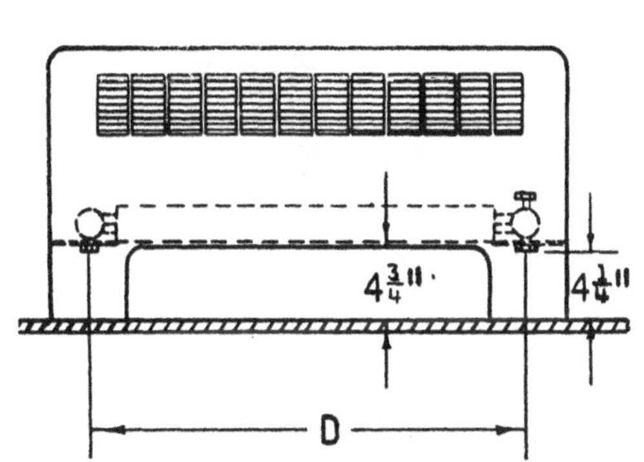

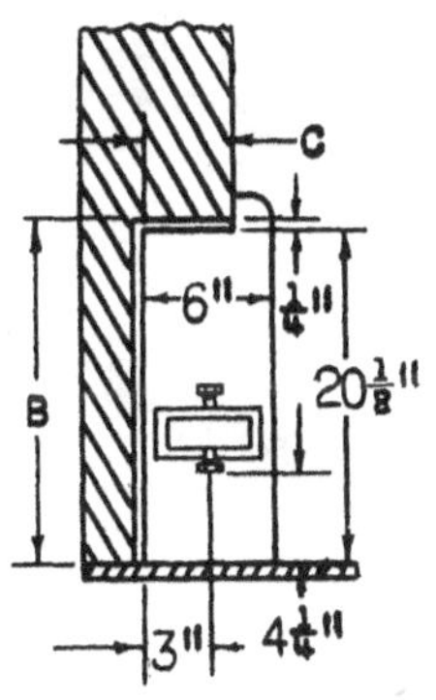

RATINGS FOR AMCOIL 21½ INCH HIGH FREE STANDING ENCLOSURES*

*(Note: Ratings are given in sq. ft. E.D.R., based on 215 deg steam and 65 deg entering air temperature)

Enclosure Depth	Enclosure Height	Enclosure Length	20½"	24½"	28½"	32½"	36½"	40½"	44½"	48½"	56½"	64½"
6⅜"	21½"	sq. ft. E.D.R.	18.0	22.0	26.0	30.0	34.0	38.0	42.0	46.0	55.0	63.0

CRANE CO.

836 S. Michigan Avenue, Chicago 5, Illinois

*Crane Cast Iron Convectors**

*(No longer manufactured)

Enclosure Types and Measuring Instructions

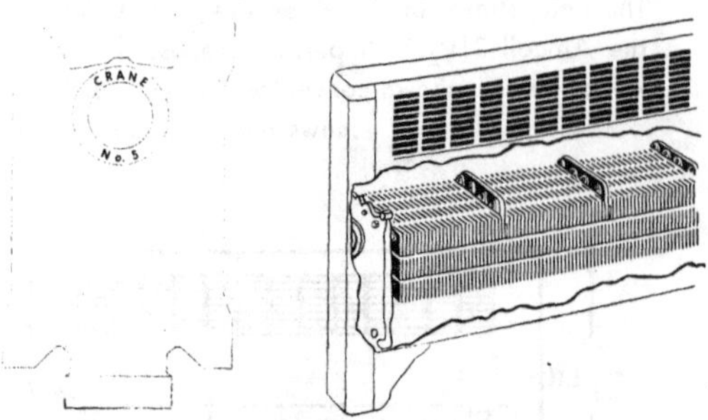

Above, Left: End view of header showing name of manufacturer.

Above, Right: Phantom view of the element and the deluxe enclosure.

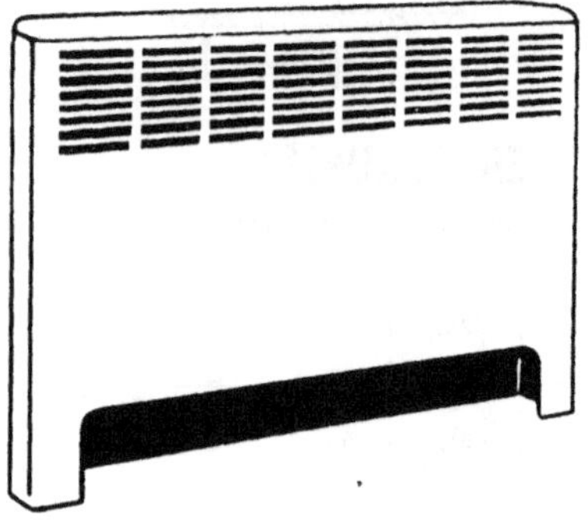

Free-standing complete enclosure. Use actual measurements.

Semi-recessed complete enclosure. Use actual measurements.

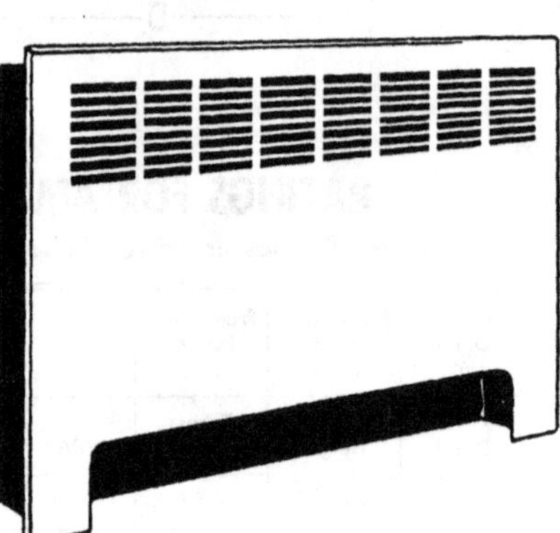

Fully recessed complete inclosure. Use actual measurements.

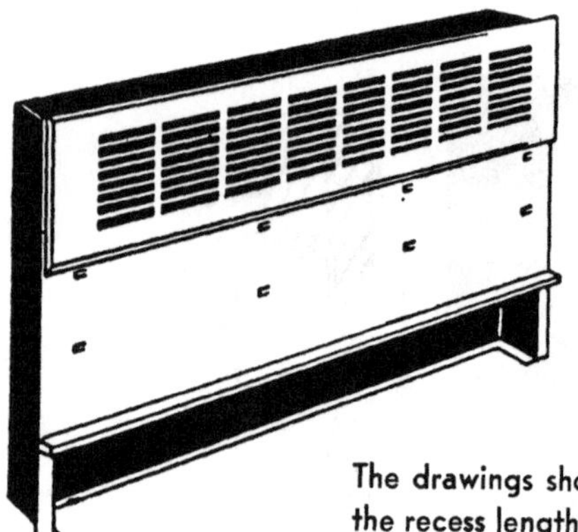

Left: Plaster front. Make actual measurements and deduct ¾ in. from the depth. Use actual height and length.

Right: Wall hung unit. Use actual measurements.

The drawings shown below illustrate various recess lengths used. Check the recess length against the element length to determine if short or long recess has been used.

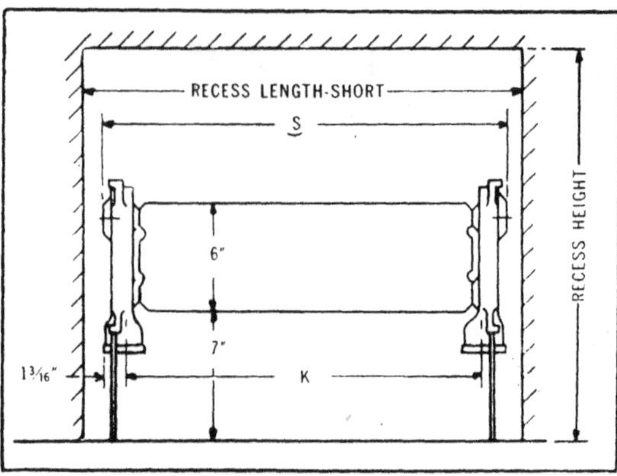

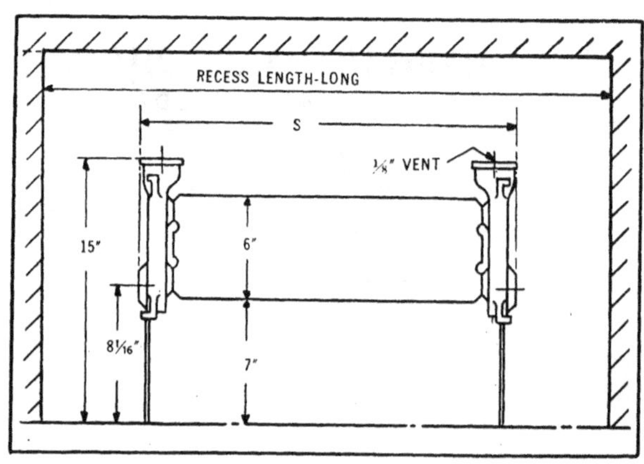

RATINGS FOR CRANE CAST IRON CONVECTORS*

*(Note: Ratings are given in sq. ft. E.D.R. for steam or water)

NUMBER 3 CRANE CONVECTORS

WIDTH OF ELEMENT 3¾″ — RECESS DEPTH 4⅜″ — See Note Under Plaster Front

Recess Length, Short	15″	20″	22½″	25″	27½″	30″	32½″	35″	37½″	40″	42½″	45″	47½″	50″	52½″	55″	57½″
Recess Length, Long	25″	30″	32½″	35″	37½″	40″	42½″	45″	47½″	50″	52½″	55″	57½″	60″	62½″	65″	67½″
Element Length (S)	13″	18″	20½″	23″	25½″	28″	30½″	33″	35½″	38″	40½″	43″	45½″	48″	50½″	53″	55½″
Enclosure Height	sq. ft.	sq. ft.	sq. ft.	sq. ft.	sq. ft.	sq. ft.	sq. ft.	sq. ft.	sq. ft.	sq. ft.	sq. ft.	sq. ft.	sq. ft.	sq. ft.	sq. ft.	sq. ft.	sq. ft.
18″	6.0	8.4	9.7	10.9	12.1	13.3	14.5	15.8	17.0	18.2	19.4	20.6	21.8	23.1	24.3	25.5	26.7
20″	6.5	9.1	10.5	11.8	13.1	14.4	15.7	17.1	18.4	19.7	21.0	22.3	23.6	25.0	26.3	27.6	28.9
22″	7.0	9.8	11.2	12.7	14.1	15.5	16.9	18.4	19.8	21.3	22.6	24.1	25.4	26.9	28.3	29.8	31.1
24″	7.5	10.5	12.0	13.5	15.0	16.5	18.1	19.7	21.1	22.7	24.2	25.7	27.2	28.7	30.2	31.8	33.3
26″	7.8	11.0	12.6	14.2	15.8	17.4	19.0	20.6	22.2	23.8	25.3	26.9	28.5	30.1	31.7	33.3	34.9
29″	8.2	11.5	13.1	14.8	16.4	18.1	19.8	21.5	23.1	24.8	26.4	28.1	29.7	31.4	33.0	34.7	36.3
32″	8.4	11.8	13.5	15.2	16.9	18.6	20.4	22.1	23.8	25.5	27.2	28.9	30.6	32.3	34.0	35.7	37.4
38″	8.8	12.3	14.1	15.9	17.6	19.4	21.2	23.0	24.7	26.5	28.3	30.1	31.8	33.6	35.4	37.2	38.9

Recess Length, Short	60″	62½″	65″	67½″	70″	72½″	75″	77½″	80″	82½″	85″	87½″	90″	92½″	95″	97½″	100″	102½″
Recess Length, Long	70″	72½″	75″	77½″	80″	82½″	85″	87½″	90″	92½″	95″	97½″	100″	102½″	105″	107½″	110″	112½″
Element Length (S)	58″	60½″	63″	65½″	68″	70½″	73″	75½″	78″	80½″	83″	85½″	88″	90½″	93″	95½″	98″	100½″
Enclosure Height	sq. ft.	sq. ft.	sq. ft.	sq. ft.	sq. ft.	sq. ft.	sq. ft.	sq. ft.	sq. ft.	sq. ft.	sq. ft.	sq. ft.	sq. ft.	sq. ft.	sq. ft.	sq. ft.	sq. ft.	sq. ft.
18″	28.0	29.2	30.5	31.7	33.0	34.2	35.5	36.7	38.0	39.2	40.5	41.7	43.0	44.2	45.5	46.7	48.0	49.2
20″	30.3	31.6	33.0	34.3	35.7	37.0	38.4	39.7	41.1	42.4	43.8	45.1	46.5	47.8	49.2	50.5	51.9	53.2
22″	32.6	34.0	35.5	36.9	38.4	39.8	41.3	42.7	44.2	45.6	47.1	48.5	50.0	51.4	52.9	54.3	55.8	57.2
24″	34.8	36.3	37.9	39.4	41.0	42.5	44.1	45.6	47.2	48.7	50.3	51.8	53.4	54.9	56.5	58.0	59.6	61.1
26″	36.5	38.1	39.7	41.3	42.9	44.5	46.1	47.7	49.3	50.9	52.5	54.1	55.7	57.3	58.9	60.5	62.1	63.7
29″	38.0	39.6	41.3	42.9	44.6	46.2	47.9	49.5	51.2	52.8	54.5	56.1	57.8	59.4	61.1	62.7	64.4	66.0
32″	39.1	40.8	42.5	44.2	45.9	47.6	49.3	51.0	52.7	54.4	56.1	57.8	59.5	61.2	62.9	64.6	66.3	68.0
38″	40.7	42.5	44.3	46.1	47.9	49.7	51.5	53.3	55.1	56.9	58.7	60.5	62.3	64.1	67.7	67.7	69.5	71.3

NUMBER 5 CRANE CONVECTORS

WIDTH OF ELEMENT 5⅝″ — RECESS DEPTH 6¼″ — See Note Under Plaster Front

Enclosure Height																	
18″	8.7	12.3	14.1	15.9	17.7	19.5	21.3	23.1	24.9	26.7	28.5	30.3	32.1	33.9	35.7	37.5	39.3
20″	9.5	13.5	15.4	17.4	19.3	21.3	23.2	25.2	27.2	29.2	31.1	33.1	35.0	37.0	38.9	40.9	42.8
22″	10.3	14.5	16.6	18.7	20.8	23.0	25.1	27.2	29.3	31.4	33.5	35.6	37.7	39.8	42.0	44.1	46.2
24″	10.9	15.4	17.6	19.9	22.2	24.4	26.6	28.9	31.1	33.4	35.6	37.9	40.1	42.4	44.6	46.8	49.0
26″	11.5	16.2	18.5	20.9	23.2	25.6	28.0	30.4	32.7	35.1	37.4	39.8	42.1	44.5	46.8	49.2	51.5
29″	12.0	17.0	19.4	21.9	24.4	26.9	29.3	31.8	34.3	36.8	39.2	41.7	44.2	46.7	49.1	51.6	54.0
32″	12.4	17.5	20.1	22.6	25.2	27.7	30.3	32.9	35.4	38.0	40.5	43.1	45.6	48.1	50.7	53.3	55.8
38″	12.9	18.2	20.8	23.5	26.1	28.8	31.4	34.1	36.7	39.4	42.0	44.7	47.3	50.0	52.6	55.3	57.9

Enclosure Height																		
18″	41.1	42.9	44.7	46.5	48.3	50.1	51.9	53.7	55.5	57.3	59.1	60.9	62.7	64.5	66.3	68.1	69.9	71.7
20″	44.8	46.7	48.7	50.6	52.6	54.5	56.5	58.4	60.4	62.3	64.3	66.2	68.2	70.1	72.1	74.0	76.0	77.9
22″	48.3	50.4	52.5	54.6	56.7	58.8	60.9	63.0	65.1	67.2	69.3	71.4	73.5	75.6	77.7	79.8	81.9	84.0
24″	51.3	53.5	55.8	58.0	60.3	62.5	64.8	67.0	69.3	71.5	73.8	76.0	78.3	80.5	82.8	85.0	87.3	89.5
26″	53.9	56.3	58.7	61.0	63.4	65.7	68.1	70.4	72.8	75.1	77.5	79.8	82.2	84.5	86.9	89.2	91.6	93.9
29″	56.5	59.0	61.5	63.9	66.4	68.8	71.3	73.7	76.2	78.6	81.1	83.5	86.0	88.4	90.9	93.3	95.8	98.2
32″	58.4	60.9	63.5	66.0	68.6	71.1	73.7	76.2	78.8	81.3	83.9	86.4	89.0	91.5	94.1	96.6	99.2	101.7
38″	60.6	63.2	65.9	68.5	71.2	73.8	76.5	79.1	81.8	84.4	87.1	89.7	92.4	95.0	97.7	100.3	103.0	105.6

NUMBER 7 CRANE CONVECTORS

WIDTH OF ELEMENT 7⅝″ — RECESS DEPTH 8¼″ — See Note Under Plaster Front

Recess Length, Short	15″	20″	22½″	25″	27½″	30″	32½″	35″	37½″	40″	42½″	45″	47½″	50″	52½″	55″	57½″
Recess Length, Long	25″	30″	32½″	35″	37½″	40″	42½″	45″	47½″	50″	52½″	55″	57½″	60″	62½″	65″	67½″
Element Length (S)	13″	18″	20½″	23″	25½″	28″	30½″	33″	35½″	38″	40½″	43″	45½″	48″	50½″	53″	55½″
Enclosure Height	sq. ft.	sq. ft.	sq. ft.	sq. ft.	sq. ft.	sq. ft.	sq. ft.	sq. ft.	sq. ft.	sq. ft.	sq. ft.	sq. ft.	sq. ft.	sq. ft.	sq. ft.	sq. ft.	sq. ft.
18″	11.3	16.0	18.4	20.8	23.1	25.4	27.7	30.0	32.4	34.7	37.1	39.6	41.9	44.2	46.5	48.8	51.2
20″	12.1	17.1	19.7	22.2	24.7	27.2	29.7	32.2	34.7	37.2	39.7	42.3	44.8	47.3	49.8	52.3	54.8
22″	12.9	18.3	21.0	23.6	26.3	29.0	31.7	34.4	37.0	39.7	42.3	45.0	47.7	50.4	53.1	55.8	58.4
24″	13.7	19.4	22.2	25.0	27.9	30.7	33.6	36.4	39.2	42.1	44.9	47.8	50.6	53.5	56.3	59.2	62.0
26″	14.4	20.4	23.4	26.4	29.4	32.4	35.4	38.4	41.3	44.3	47.3	50.3	53.3	56.3	59.3	62.3	65.3
29″	15.3	21.6	24.8	27.9	31.1	34.2	37.4	40.6	43.7	46.9	50.1	53.3	56.4	59.6	62.7	65.9	69.0
32″	15.9	22.5	25.8	29.1	32.4	35.7	39.0	42.3	45.6	48.9	52.2	55.5	58.7	62.0	65.3	68.6	71.9
38″	16.7	23.7	27.1	30.6	34.1	37.5	41.0	44.5	47.9	51.4	54.9	58.4	61.8	65.3	68.8	72.3	75.7

Recess Length, Short	60″	62½″	65″	67½″	70″	72½″	75″	77½″	80″	82½″	85″	87½″	90″	92½″	95″	97½″	100″	102½″
Recess Length, Long	70″	72½″	75″	77½″	80″	82½″	85″	87½″	90″	92½″	95″	97½″	100″	102½″	105″	107½″	110″	112½″
Element Length (S)	58″	60½″	63″	65½″	68″	70½″	73″	75½″	78″	80½″	83″	85½″	88″	90½″	93″	95½″	98″	100½″
Enclosure Height	sq. ft.	sq. ft.	sq. ft.	sq. ft.	sq. ft.	sq. ft.	sq. ft.	sq. ft.	sq. ft.	sq. ft.	sq. ft.	sq. ft.	sq. ft.	sq. ft.	sq. ft.	sq. ft.	sq. ft.	sq. ft.
18″	53.5	55.8	58.1	60.4	62.7	65.0	67.3	69.6	71.9	74.2	76.5	78.8	81.1	83.4	85.7	88.0	90.3	92.6
20″	57.3	59.8	62.3	64.8	67.3	69.8	72.3	74.8	77.3	79.8	82.3	84.8	87.3	89.8	92.3	94.8	97.3	99.8
22″	61.1	63.8	66.5	69.2	71.9	74.6	77.3	80.0	82.7	85.4	88.1	90.8	93.5	96.2	98.9	101.6	104.3	107.0
24″	64.9	67.7	70.6	73.4	76.3	79.1	82.0	84.8	87.7	90.5	93.4	96.2	99.1	101.9	104.8	107.6	110.5	113.3
26″	68.3	71.3	74.3	77.3	80.3	83.3	86.3	89.3	92.3	95.3	98.3	101.3	104.3	107.3	110.3	113.3	116.3	119.3
29″	72.2	75.4	78.6	81.7	84.9	88.0	91.2	94.3	97.5	100.6	103.8	106.9	110.1	113.2	116.4	119.5	122.7	125.8
32″	75.2	78.5	81.8	85.1	88.4	91.7	95.0	98.3	101.6	104.9	108.2	111.5	114.8	118.1	121.4	124.7	128.0	131.3
38″	79.2	82.6	86.1	89.5	93.0	96.4	99.9	103.3	106.8	110.2	113.7	117.1	120.6	124.0	127.5	130.9	134.4	137.8

NUMBER 9 CRANE CONVECTORS

WIDTH OF ELEMENT 9½″ — RECESS DEPTH 10⅛″ — See Note Under Plaster Front

Enclosure Height																	
18″	13.5	19.2	22.1	24.9	27.8	30.6	33.5	36.2	39.0	41.9	44.7	47.6	50.4	53.3	56.1	59.0	61.8
20″	14.5	20.6	23.7	26.7	29.8	32.8	35.9	38.9	41.9	45.0	48.0	51.1	54.1	57.2	60.2	63.3	66.3
22″	15.5	22.0	25.3	28.5	31.8	35.0	38.3	41.6	44.8	48.1	51.3	54.6	57.8	61.1	64.3	67.6	70.8
24″	16.5	23.4	26.9	30.3	33.8	37.2	40.7	44.2	47.6	51.1	54.5	58.0	61.4	64.9	68.3	71.8	75.2
26″	17.3	24.6	28.2	31.8	35.5	39.1	42.7	46.3	50.0	53.6	57.2	60.8	64.5	68.1	71.8	75.4	79.0
29″	18.4	26.1	29.9	33.7	37.6	41.4	45.3	49.2	53.0	56.8	60.6	64.5	68.3	72.2	76.0	79.9	83.7
32″	19.2	27.3	31.3	35.3	39.3	43.3	47.3	51.4	55.4	59.5	63.4	67.5	71.5	75.6	79.5	83.6	87.5
38″	20.3	28.8	33.0	37.2	41.4	45.7	49.9	54.2	58.8	62.7	66.9	71.2	75.3	79.6	83.8	88.1	92.3

Enclosure Height																		
18″	64.7	67.5	70.4	73.2	76.1	78.9	81.8	84.6	87.5	90.3	93.2	96.0	98.9	101.7	104.6	107.4	110.3	113.3
20″	69.4	72.4	75.5	78.5	81.6	84.6	87.7	90.7	93.8	96.8	99.9	102.9	106.0	109.0	112.1	115.1	118.2	121.3
22″	74.1	77.3	80.6	83.8	87.1	90.3	93.6	96.8	100.1	103.3	106.6	109.8	113.1	116.3	119.6	122.8	126.1	129.3
24″	78.7	82.1	85.6	89.0	92.5	95.9	99.4	102.8	106.3	109.7	113.2	116.6	120.1	123.5	127.0	130.4	133.9	137.3
26″	82.6	86.2	89.8	93.4	97.0	100.5	104.2	107.8	111.4	115.0	118.6	122.2	125.8	129.4	133.0	136.6	140.2	143.8
29″	87.6	91.4	95.3	99.1	103.0	106.8	110.7	114.5	118.4	122.2	126.1	129.9	133.8	137.6	141.5	143.3	149.2	153.0
32″	91.6	95.6	99.7	103.7	107.8	111.8	115.9	119.9	124.0	128.0	132.1	136.1	140.2	144.2	148.3	152.3	156.4	160.4
38″	96.6	100.8	105.1	109.3	113.6	117.8	122.1	126.3	130.6	134.8	139.1	143.3	147.6	151.8	156.1	160.3	164.6	168.8

C. A. DUNHAM COMPANY

400 W. Madison Street, Chicago, Ill.

Dunham Convectors

(Heating element consists of copper or aluminum fins on copper tubes, cast bronze headers.)

Enclosure Types and Measuring Instructions

See facing page for Dunham convector ratings

Right: There is no manufacturer's identification on either the element or the convector enclosure. Use these illustrations to identify Dunham convectors.

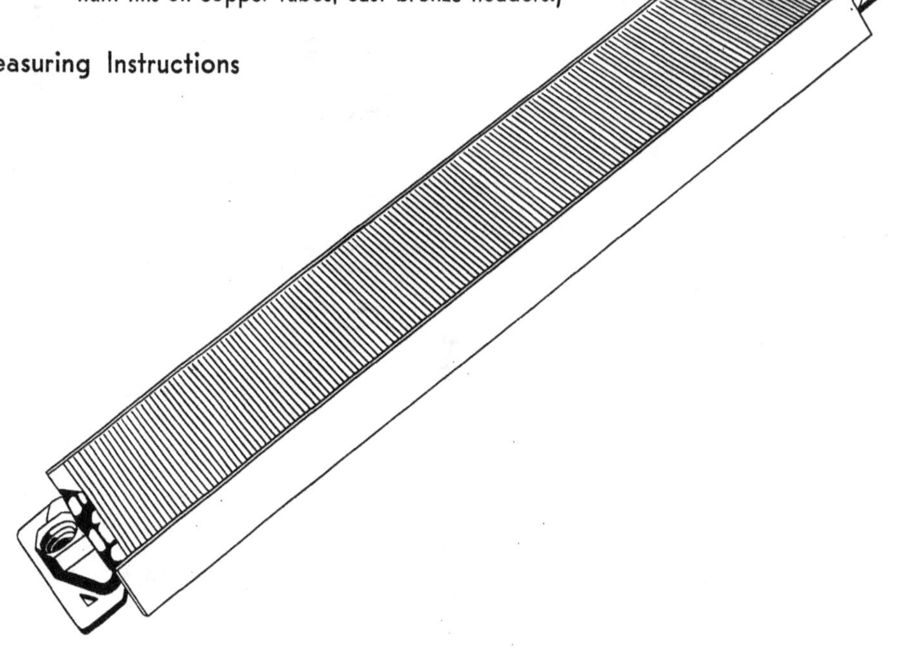

Left: Free standing enclosure. Use actual measurements of the unit.

Right: Semi-recessed unit. Use actual measurements. For size of recessed opening deduct 3 in. from actual length and 1½ in. from actual height.

Left: Fully recessed unit. Use actual depth. For size of recessed opening deduct 3 in. from actual length and 1½ in. from actual height.

Right: Wall hung, flat top convector. Use actual measurements.

DUNHAM CONVECTOR RATINGS

Left: Wall hung, sloping top convector. Use actual measurements. Measure height to rear of enclosure top. Ordering height includes 4 in. between floor and convector bottom.

Right: Free standing, sloping top convector. Use actual measurements. Measure height to rear of enclosure top.

RATINGS FOR DUNHAM CONVECTORS*

*(All ratings are given in output in sq. ft. of equivalent direct radiation, E.D.R.)

WIDTH OF ENCLOSURE	ENCLOSURE LENGTH		18"	20"	24"	28"	32"	40"	48"	56"	64"
	Enclosure Height Wall Cabinets**	Enclosure Height Floor Cabinets	sq. ft.	sq. ft.	sq. ft.	sq. ft.	sq. ft.	sq. ft.	sq. ft.	sq. ft.	sq. ft.
4"	16"	20"	12.0	13.5	16.5	19.5	22.5	28.0	33.5	37.5	41.5
	20"	24"	13.0	15.0	18.0	21.5	25.0	30.5	37.0	42.0	46.5
	28"	32"	14.0	16.5	20.0	23.5	27.0	33.5	40.0	46.0	50.5

**(Add 4 in. to actual height when ordering. Ex., for 16 in. height wall cabinet, order a unit 20 in. high.)

*(All ratings are given in output in sq. ft. of equivalent direct radiation, E.D.R.)

WIDTH OF ENCLOSURE	ENCLOSURE LENGTH		18"	20"	24"	28"	32"	40"	48"	56"	64"
	Enclosure Height Wall Cabinets**	Enclosure Height Floor Cabinets	sq. ft.	sq. ft.	sq. ft.	sq. ft.	sq. ft.	sq. ft.	sq. ft.	sq. ft.	sq. ft.
6"	16"	20"	....	19.5	23.5	27.0	31.5	39.5	47.0	54.0	60.0
	20"	24"	....	22.0	27.5	31.5	36.0	45.5	53.0	60.0	65.0
	28"	32"	....	23.0	28.5	34.0	39.0	48.5	57.5	65.0	71.0

**(Add 4 in. to actual height when ordering. Ex., for 16 in. height wall cabinet, order a unit 20 in. high.)

*(All ratings are given in output in sq. ft. of equivalent direct radiation, E.D.R.)

WIDTH OF ENCLOSURE	ENCLOSURE LENGTH		18"	20"	24"	28"	32"	40"	48"	56"	64"
	Enclosure Height Wall Cabinets**	Enclosure Height Floor Cabinets	sq. ft.	sq. ft.	sq. ft.	sq. ft.	sq. ft.	sq. ft.	sq. ft.	sq. ft.	sq. ft.
8"	16"	20"	....	....	....	....	40.5	51.0	61.5	72.0	80.5
	20"	24"	....	....	....	....	44.0	56.5	68.5	79.5	88.0
	28"	32"	....	....	....	....	47.0	60.0	72.5	84.0	94.0

**(Add 4 in. to actual height when ordering. Ex., for 16 in. height wall cabinet, order a unit 20 in. high.)

*(All ratings are given in output in sq. ft. of equivalent direct radiation, E.D.R.)

WIDTH OF ENCLOSURE	ENCLOSURE LENGTH		18"	20"	24"	28"	32"	40"	48"	56"	64"
	Enclosure Height Wall Cabinets**	Enclosure Height Floor Cabinets	sq. ft.	sq. ft.	sq. ft.	sq. ft.	sq. ft.	sq. ft.	sq. ft.	sq. ft.	sq. ft.
10"	16"	20"	....	....	....	....	....	55.5	68.0	81.0	92.5
	20"	24"	....	....	....	....	....	61.0	74.5	87.5	96.0
	28"	32"	....	....	....	....	....	66.0	80.5	94.0	108.0

**(Add 4 in. to actual height when ordering. Ex., for 16 in. height wall cabinet, order a unit 20 in. high.)

FEDDERS-QUIGAN CORPORATION

Buffalo 7, New York

Fedders-Quigan Copper Convectors

Enclosure Types and Convector Ratings

Fedders-Quigan convectors can be identified by the trade name shown on the front of the element.

This convector enclosure identifies the Fedders-Quigan copper convector, type F.

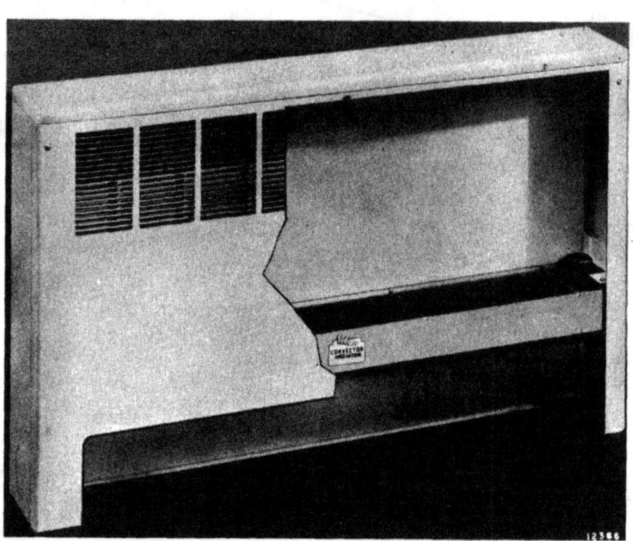

Right: Type "F" Fedders-Quigan enclosure, showing trade name location on the element, and element type.

RATINGS FOR FEDDERS-QUIGAN COPPER CONVECTORS, TYPE "F"

*(Note: Ratings are given in sq. ft. E.D.R., based on 215 deg steam and 65 deg entering air temperature)

ENCLOSURE LENGTH			20⅜"	24⅜"	28⅜"	32⅜"	36⅜"	40⅜"	44⅜"	48⅜"	56⅜"	64⅜"
			sq. ft.	sq. ft.	sq. ft.	sq. ft.	sq. ft.	sq. ft.	sq. ft.	sq. ft.	sq. ft.	sq. ft.
ENCLOSURE DEPTH 6"	Enclosure Height	20"	16.2	19.7	23.2	26.8	30.3	33.7	37.4	41.0	48.0	55.0
		24"	18.7	22.7	26.8	30.8	34.8	38.9	43.0	47.0	55.5	63.6
		32"	20.2	24.2	28.8	33.3	37.9	42.4	46.5	51.5	60.0	70.1

ENCLOSURE LENGTH			20⅜"	24⅜"	28⅜"	32⅜"	36⅜"	40⅜"	44⅜"	48⅜"	56⅜"	64⅜"
			sq. ft.	sq. ft.	sq. ft.	sq. ft.	sq. ft.	sq. ft.	sq. ft.	sq. ft.	sq. ft.	sq. ft.
ENCLOSURE DEPTH 8"	Enclosure Height	20"	....	....	....	35.9	41.0	46.0	....	55.5	65.1	74.7
		24"	....	....	....	38.9	44.4	49.5	....	59.6	70.2	80.8
		32"	....	....	....	41.4	47.0	52.5	....	63.6	74.7	85.8

ENCLOSURE LENGTH			20⅜"	24⅜"	28⅜"	32⅜"	36⅜"	40⅜"	44⅜"	48⅜"	56⅜"	64⅜"
			sq. ft.	sq. ft.	sq. ft.	sq. ft.	sq. ft.	sq. ft.	sq. ft.	sq. ft.	sq. ft.	sq. ft.
ENCLOSURE DEPTH 10"	Enclosure Height	20"	....	....	....	....	45.5	50.5	....	61.1	71.7	82.3
		24"	....	....	....	....	51.5	57.6	....	69.7	81.8	93.4
		32"	....	....	....	....	56.0	62.6	....	75.6	88.9	102.0

FEDDERS-QUIGAN TYPE "FE" AND "FB" CONVECTOR RATINGS

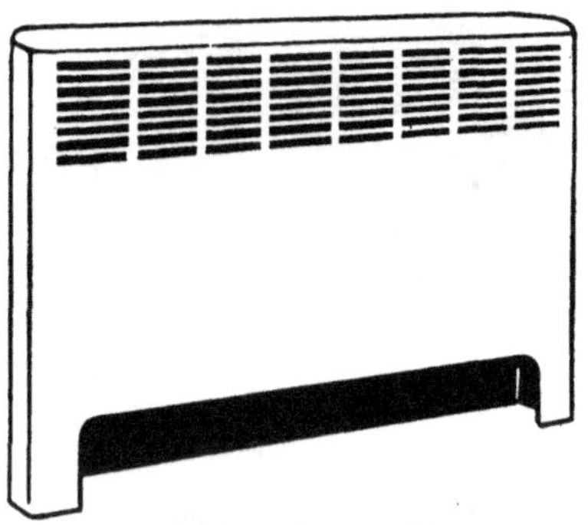

Left: This enclosure identifies Fedders-Quigan cabinet convector type "FE".

Right: Cabinet convector type "FB" is shown in this drawing of the enclosure.

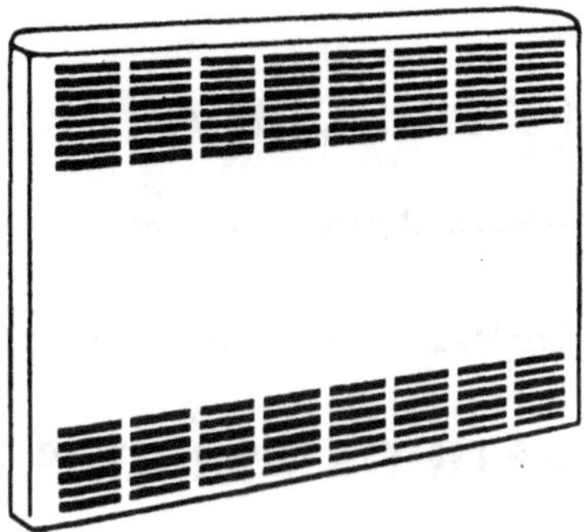

RATINGS FOR CONVECTOR TYPES "FE" AND "FB"*

*(Note: In sq. ft. E.D.R. based on steam at 215 deg, entering air at 65 deg.)

ENCLOSURE LENGTH	Enclosure Height	16⅜″	20⅜″	24⅜″	28⅜″	32⅜″	36⅜″	40⅜″	44⅜″	48⅜″	56⅜″	64⅜″
		sq. ft.	sq. ft.	sq. ft.	sq. ft.	sq. ft.	sq. ft.	sq. ft.	sq. ft.	sq. ft.	sq. ft.	sq. ft.
ENCLOSURE DEPTH 4″	18″	7.6	10.1	12.1	14.1	16.7	18.7	20.8	23.2	25.3	29.3	33.8
	20″	9.1	11.6	14.1	16.7	19.2	21.7	24.2	26.8	29.3	34.3	39.4
	24″	10.2	13.1	16.2	18.7	21.7	24.7	27.3	30.3	33.3	38.9	45.0
	26″	10.6	13.6	16.6	19.7	22.7	25.7	28.8	31.8	34.8	40.8	46.9
	32″	11.1	14.1	17.2	20.2	23.2	26.3	29.3	32.3	35.4	42.0	48.0
	38″	11.1	14.1	17.7	20.7	23.7	26.7	30.3	33.3	36.4	42.8	49.0

ENCLOSURE LENGTH	Enclosure Height	16⅜″	20⅜″	24⅜″	28⅜″	32⅜″	36⅜″	40⅜″	44⅜″	48⅜″	56⅜″	64⅜″
		sq. ft.	sq. ft.	sq. ft.	sq. ft.	sq. ft.	sq. ft.	sq. ft.	sq. ft.	sq. ft.	sq. ft.	sq. ft.
ENCLOSURE DEPTH 6″	18″	11.1	14.1	17.7	20.7	23.7	26.8	30.0	33.3	36.4	42.4	49.0
	20″	12.6	16.2	19.7	23.2	26.8	30.3	33.7	37.4	41.0	48.0	55.0
	24″	14.6	18.7	22.7	26.8	30.8	34.8	38.9	43.0	47.0	55.5	63.6
	26″	15.1	19.1	23.2	27.8	31.8	36.3	40.4	44.4	49.0	57.5	66.0
	32″	15.6	20.2	24.2	28.8	33.3	37.9	42.4	46.5	51.5	60.0	70.1
	38″	16.1	20.7	25.2	29.8	34.3	38.8	43.4	47.9	53.0	62.0	71.1

ENCLOSURE LENGTH	Enclosure Height	16⅜″	20⅜″	24⅜″	28⅜″	32⅜″	36⅜″	40⅜″	44⅜″	48⅜″	56⅜″	64⅜″
		sq. ft.	sq. ft.	sq. ft.	sq. ft.	sq. ft.	sq. ft.	sq. ft.	sq. ft.	sq. ft.	sq. ft.	sq. ft.
ENCLOSURE DEPTH 8″	18″	15.1	19.2	23.2	27.8	31.8	35.9	40.4	44.4	48.5	57.0	65.7
	20″	16.7	21.7	26.3	31.3	35.9	41.0	46.0	50.5	55.5	65.1	74.7
	24″	18.2	23.2	28.8	33.8	38.9	44.4	49.5	54.5	59.6	70.2	80.8
	26″	18.6	24.2	29.3	34.7	40.3	45.4	50.9	56.5	61.5	72.5	83.0
	32″	19.2	24.7	30.3	35.8	41.4	47.0	52.5	58.3	63.6	74.7	85.8
	38″	19.7	25.3	31.3	36.8	42.4	47.9	54.0	59.5	65.1	76.2	87.6

ENCLOSURE LENGTH	Enclosure Height	16⅜″	20⅜″	24⅜″	28⅜″	32⅜″	36⅜″	40⅜″	44⅜″	48⅜″	56⅜″	64⅜″
		sq. ft.	sq. ft.	sq. ft.	sq. ft.	sq. ft.	sq. ft.	sq. ft.	sq. ft.	sq. ft.	sq. ft.	sq. ft.
ENCLOSURE DEPTH 10″	18″	15.6	20.0	24.2	28.8	32.8	37.3	41.9	46.5	50.5	59.0	68.1
	20″	18.7	24.2	29.3	34.8	39.9	45.5	50.5	56.1	61.1	71.7	82.3
	24″	21.2	27.3	33.3	39.4	45.5	51.5	57.6	63.6	69.7	81.8	93.4
	26″	22.2	28.2	34.7	40.8	47.4	54.0	60.0	66.6	72.6	85.2	97.8
	32″	22.7	29.8	36.4	42.9	49.5	56.0	62.6	69.2	75.6	88.9	102.0
	38″	23.7	30.8	37.4	44.4	51.0	58.0	64.6	71.6	78.1	92.4	106.0

FEDDERS-QUIGAN CORPORATION

(Continued from previous page)

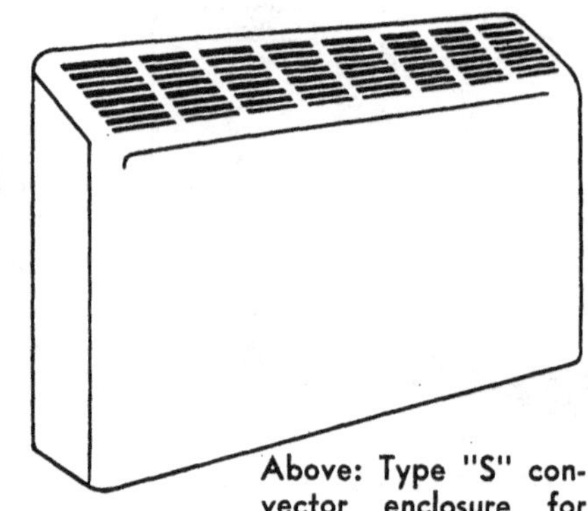

Above: Type "S" convector enclosure for Fedders-Quigan convectors.

Enclosure Types and Convector Ratings

RATINGS FOR TYPE "S" CONVECTOR*

*(Note: Ratings are given in sq. ft. E.D.R. based on 215 deg steam and 65 deg entering air temperature)

ENCLOSURE LENGTH			16⅜"	20⅜"	24⅜"	28⅜"	32⅜"	36⅜"	40⅜"	44⅜"	48⅜"	56⅜"	64"
			sq. ft.	sq. ft.	sq. ft.	sq. ft.	sq. ft.	sq. ft.	sq. ft.	sq. ft.	sq. ft.	sq. ft.	sq. ft.
ENCLOSURE DEPTH 4"	Enclosure Height	14"	10.1	12.6	15.6	18.2	20.7	23.7	26.3	29.3	31.7	37.3	42.8
		18"	10.6	13.6	16.6	19.2	22.2	25.2	27.7	30.8	33.8	39.8	46.9
		20"	10.6	13.6	16.7	19.7	22.7	25.7	28.7	31.8	34.8	40.8	47.0
		26"	11.1	14.1	17.2	20.2	23.2	26.2	29.2	32.3	35.3	41.8	48.8
		32"	11.1	14.1	17.7	20.7	23.7	26.7	30.3	33.3	36.4	42.8	49.0

ENCLOSURE LENGTH			16⅜"	20⅜"	24⅜"	28⅜"	32⅜"	36⅜"	40⅜"	44⅜"	48⅜"	56⅜"	64⅜"
			sq. ft.	sq. ft.	sq. ft.	sq. ft.	sq. ft.	sq. ft.	sq. ft.	sq. ft.	sq. ft.	sq. ft.	sq. ft.
ENCLOSURE DEPTH 6"	Enclosure Height	14"	17.2	22.3	26.9	31.4	37.3	41.0	46.0	50.5	56.0	65.5	74.7
		18"	18.2	22.8	27.8	33.0	38.0	42.6	47.8	52.8	58.0	68.0	78.0
		20"	18.7	23.2	28.3	33.8	38.8	43.9	48.9	54.0	59.6	69.6	80.2
		26"	18.7	23.8	28.9	34.0	39.5	45.0	50.5	55.2	61.0	71.0	81.8
		32"	20.7	26.7	32.8	38.4	44.4	50.5	56.0	62.1	68.6	80.2	91.8

ENCLOSURE LENGTH			16⅜"	20⅜"	24⅜"	28⅜"	32⅜"	36⅜"	40⅜"	44⅜"	48⅜"	56⅜"	64⅜"
			sq. ft.	sq. ft.	sq. ft.	sq. ft.	sq. ft.	sq. ft.	sq. ft.	sq. ft.	sq. ft.	sq. ft.	sq. ft.
ENCLOSURE DEPTH 8"	Enclosure Height	14"	21.7	27.8	33.8	40.5	46.6	52.8	59.2	64.6	71.5	83.8	96.2
		18"	22.2	28.3	34.8	41.0	47.2	53.8	60.0	65.7	72.0	85.0	97.2
		20"	22.7	29.3	35.3	41.4	47.8	54.0	60.6	67.6	73.7	87.7	99.5
		26"	23.2	29.8	36.4	43.0	50.2	57.0	63.2	69.7	77.0	90.2	103.5
		32"	24.3	31.3	38.9	45.4	52.5	59.5	67.1	73.6	80.2	94.5	109.0

ENCLOSURE LENGTH			16⅜"	20⅜"	24⅜"	28⅜"	32⅜"	36⅜"	40⅜"	44⅜"	48⅜"	56⅜"	64⅜"
			sq. ft.	sq. ft.	sq. ft.	sq. ft.	sq. ft.	sq. ft.	sq. ft.	sq. ft.	sq. ft.	sq. ft.	sq. ft.
ENCLOSURE DEPTH 10"	Enclosure Height	14"	24.7	32.3	38.9	46.0	52.5	60.5	67.0	73.7	81.2	95.0	108.5
		18"	26.3	33.8	41.4	49.0	56.6	64.0	71.6	78.8	87.0	102.0	116.5
		20"	27.3	34.8	42.8	50.5	58.6	66.6	73.6	81.8	89.2	105.0	121.5
		26"	28.3	37.4	45.5	53.5	61.6	70.0	78.8	86.4	95.0	111.5	128.0
		32"	30.3	39.4	48.0	56.5	65.2	74.0	82.1	91.8	100.0	118.0	135.2

FEDDERS-QUIGAN CONVECTOR RATINGS, TYPES "R", "RB", "RC", "RCB", "P", "PB"

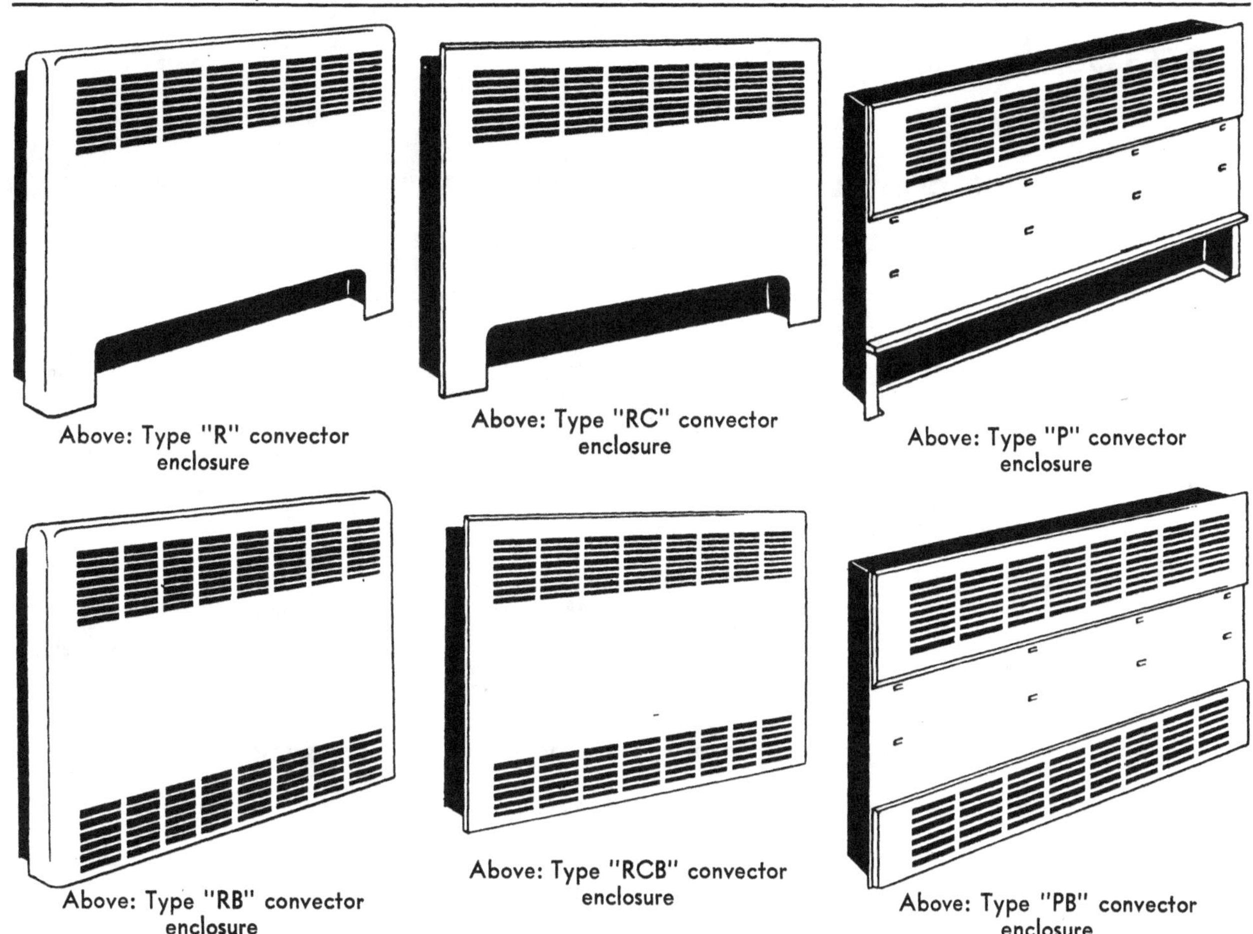

Above: Type "R" convector enclosure

Above: Type "RC" convector enclosure

Above: Type "P" convector enclosure

Above: Type "RB" convector enclosure

Above: Type "RCB" convector enclosure

Above: Type "PB" convector enclosure

RATINGS FOR FEDDERS-QUIGAN CONVECTORS, TYPES "R", "RB", "RC", "RCB", "P," "PB"*

(Note: Ratings are given in sq. ft. E.D.R., based on 215 deg steam and 65 deg entering air temperature)

		ENCLOSURE PANEL LENGTHS—TYPES R, RB, RC, RCB	19″	23″	27″	31″	35″	39″	43″	47″	51″	59″	67″
		ENCLOSURE PANEL LENGTHS—TYPES P, PB	18″	22″	26″	30″	34″	38″	42″	46″	50″	58″	66″
ENCLOSURE DEPTH	Enclosure Panel Height—Types R, RB, RC, RCB	Enclosure Panel Height—Types P and PB	sq. ft.	sq. ft.	sq. ft.	sq. ft.	sq. ft.	sq. ft.	sq. ft.	sq. ft.	sq. ft.	sq. ft.	sq. ft.
4″	19½″	19″	7.6	10.1	12.1	14.1	16.7	18.7	20.8	23.2	25.3	29.3	33.8
4″	21½″	21″	9.1	11.6	14.1	16.7	19.2	21.7	24.2	26.8	29.3	34.3	39.4
4″	25½″	25″	10.2	13.1	16.2	18.7	21.7	24.7	27.3	30.3	33.3	38.9	45.0
4″	27½″	27″	10.6	13.6	16.6	19.7	22.7	25.7	28.8	31.8	34.8	40.8	46.9
4″	33½″	33″	11.1	14.1	17.2	20.2	23.2	26.3	29.3	32.3	35.4	42.0	48.0
4″	39½″	39″	11.1	14.1	17.7	20.7	23.7	26.7	30.3	33.3	36.4	42.8	49.0

		ENCLOSURE PANEL LENGTHS—TYPES R, RB, RC, RCB	19″	23″	27″	31″	35″	39″	43″	47″	51″	59″	67″
		ENCLOSURE PANEL LENGTHS—TYPES P, PB	18″	22″	26″	30″	34″	38″	42″	46″	50″	58″	66″
ENCLOSURE DEPTH	Enclosure Panel Height—Types R, RB, RC, RCB	Enclosure Panel Height—Types P and PB	sq. ft.	sq. ft.	sq. ft.	sq. ft.	sq. ft.	sq. ft.	sq. ft.	sq. ft.	sq. ft.	sq. ft.	sq. ft.
6″	19½″	19″	11.1	14.1	17.7	20.7	23.7	26.8	20.0	33.3	36.4	42.4	49.0
6″	21½″	21″	12.6	16.2	19.7	23.2	26.8	30.3	33.7	37.4	41.0	48.0	55.0
6″	25½″	25″	14.6	18.7	22.7	26.8	30.8	34.8	38.9	43.0	47.0	55.5	63.6
6″	27½″	27″	15.1	19.1	23.2	27.8	31.8	36.3	40.4	44.4	49.0	57.5	66.0
6″	33½″	33″	15.6	20.2	24.2	28.8	33.3	37.9	42.4	46.5	51.5	60.0	70.1
6″	39½″	39″	16.1	20.7	25.2	29.8	34.3	38.8	43.4	47.9	53.0	62.0	71.1

FEDDERS-QUIGAN CORPORATION

(Continued from previous page)

RATINGS FOR CONVECTOR TYPES "R", "RB", "RC", "RCB", "P", "PB"*

*(Note: Ratings are given in sq. ft. E.D.R., based on 215 deg steam and 65 deg entering air temperature)

		ENCLOSURE PANEL LENGTHS—TYPES R, RB, RC, RCB	19"	23"	27"	31"	35"	39"	43"	47"	51"	59"	67"
		ENCLOSURE PANEL LENGTHS—TYPES P, PB	18"	22"	26"	30"	34"	38"	42"	46"	50"	58"	66"
	Enclosure Panel Height—Types R, RB, RC, RCB	Enclosure Panel Height—Types P and PB	sq. ft.	sq. ft.	sq. ft.	sq. ft.	sq. ft.	sq. ft.	sq. ft.	sq. ft.	sq. ft.	sq. ft.	sq. ft.
ENCLOSURE DEPTH 8"	19½"	19"	15.1	19.2	23.2	27.8	31.8	35.9	40.4	44.4	48.5	57.0	65.7
	21½"	21"	16.7	21.7	26.3	31.3	35.9	41.0	46.0	50.5	55.5	65.1	74.7
	25½"	25"	18.2	23.2	28.8	33.8	38.9	44.4	49.5	54.5	59.6	70.2	80.8
	27½"	27"	18.6	24.2	29.3	34.7	40.3	45.4	50.9	56.5	61.5	72.5	83.0
	33½"	33"	19.2	24.7	30.3	35.8	41.4	47.0	52.5	58.3	63.6	74.7	85.8
	39½"	39"	19.7	25.3	31.3	36.8	42.4	47.9	54.0	59.5	65.1	76.2	87.6

RATINGS FOR CONVECTOR TYPES "R", "RB", "RC", "RCB", "P", "PB"*

*(Note: Ratings are given in sq. ft. E.D.R., based on 215 deg steam and 65 deg entering air temperature)

		ENCLOSURE PANEL LENGTHS—TYPES R, RB, RC, RCB	19"	23"	27"	31"	35"	39"	43"	47"	51"	59"	67"
		ENCLOSURE PANEL LENGTHS—TYPES P, PB	18"	22"	26"	30"	34"	38"	42"	46"	50"	58"	66"
	Enclosure Panel Height—Types R, RB, RC, RCB	Enclosure Panel Height—Types P and PB	sq. ft.	sq. ft.	sq. ft.	sq. ft.	sq. ft.	sq. ft.	sq. ft.	sq. ft.	sq. ft.	sq. ft.	sq. ft.
ENCLOSURE DEPTH 10"	19½"	19"	15.6	20.0	24.2	28.8	32.8	37.3	41.9	46.5	50.5	59.0	68.1
	21½"	21"	18.7	24.2	29.3	34.8	39.9	45.5	50.5	56.1	61.1	71.7	82.3
	25½"	25"	21.2	27.3	33.3	39.4	45.5	51.5	57.6	63.6	69.7	81.8	93.4
	27½"	27"	22.2	28.2	34.7	40.8	47.4	54.0	60.0	66.6	72.6	85.2	97.8
	33½"	33"	22.7	29.8	36.4	42.9	49.5	56.0	62.6	69.2	75.6	88.9	102.0
	39½"	39"	23.7	30.8	37.4	44.4	51.0	58.0	64.6	71.6	78.1	92.4	106.0

RATINGS FOR CONVECTOR TYPES "SF" AND "SFB"

Enclosure Types Shown Below

See Facing Page for Convector Ratings

At left: This drawing shows the enclosure type used for Fedders-Quigan Type "SF" convectors.

At right: The enclosure type used with Fedders-Quigan Type "SFB" convectors is shown here.

RATINGS FOR FEDDERS-QUIGAN CONVECTORS, TYPES "SF" AND "SFB"*

***(Note: Ratings are given in sq. ft. E.D.R., based on 215 deg steam and 65 deg entering air temperature)**

ENCLOSURE LENGTH		16⅜"	20⅜"	24⅜"	28⅜"	32⅜"	36⅜"	40⅜"	44⅜"	48⅜"	56⅜"	64⅜"
	Enclosure Height	sq. ft.	sq. ft.	sq. ft.	sq. ft.	sq. ft.	sq. ft.	sq. ft.	sq. ft.	sq. ft.	sq. ft.	sq. ft.
ENCLOSURE DEPTH 4"	18"	9.1	11.6	14.1	16.7	19.2	21.7	24.2	26.8	29.3	33.9	38.9
	20"	10.1	12.6	15.6	18.2	20.7	23.7	26.3	29.3	31.7	37.3	42.8
	24"	10.6	13.6	16.6	19.2	22.2	25.2	27.7	30.8	33.8	39.8	46.9
	26"	10.6	13.6	16.7	19.7	22.7	25.7	28.7	31.8	34.8	40.8	47.0
	32"	11.1	14.1	17.2	20.2	23.2	26.2	29.2	32.3	35.3	41.8	48.0
	38"	11.1	14.1	17.7	20.7	23.7	26.7	30.3	33.3	36.4	42.8	49.0

ENCLOSURE LENGTH		16⅜"	20⅜"	24⅜"	28⅜"	32⅜"	36⅜"	40⅜"	44⅜"	48⅜"	56⅜"	64⅜"
	Enclosure Height	sq. ft.	sq. ft.	sq. ft.	sq. ft.	sq. ft.	sq. ft.	sq. ft.	sq. ft.	sq. ft.	sq. ft.	sq. ft.
ENCLOSURE DEPTH 6"	18"	16.7	21.2	26.3	30.8	35.9	39.4	43.9	50.0	53.8	62.6	72.2
	20"	17.2	22.3	26.9	31.4	37.3	41.0	46.0	50.5	56.0	65.5	74.7
	24"	18.2	22.8	27.8	33.0	38.0	42.6	47.8	52.8	58.0	68.0	78.0
	26"	18.7	23.2	28.3	33.8	38.8	43.9	48.9	54.0	59.6	69.6	80.2
	32"	18.7	23.8	28.9	34.0	39.5	45.0	50.5	55.2	61.0	71.0	81.8
	38"	20.7	26.7	32.8	38.4	44.4	50.5	56.0	62.1	68.6	80.2	91.8

ENCLOSURE LENGTH		16⅜"	20⅜"	24⅜"	28⅜"	32⅜"	36⅜"	40⅜"	44⅜"	48⅜"	56⅜"	64⅜"
	Enclosure Height	sq. ft.	sq. ft.	sq. ft.	sq. ft.	sq. ft.	sq. ft.	sq. ft.	sq. ft.	sq. ft.	sq. ft.	sq. ft.
ENCLOSURE DEPTH 8"	18"	21.2	27.3	32.8	38.9	44.4	50.5	56.6	62.1	68.2	79.8	91.9
	20"	21.7	27.8	33.8	40.5	46.6	52.8	59.2	64.6	71.5	83.8	96.2
	24"	22.2	28.3	34.8	41.0	47.2	53.8	60.0	65.7	72.0	85.0	97.2
	26"	22.7	29.3	35.3	41.4	47.8	54.0	60.6	67.6	73.7	87.7	99.5
	32"	23.2	29.8	36.4	43.0	50.2	57.0	63.2	69.7	77.0	90.2	103.5
	38"	24.3	31.3	38.9	45.4	52.5	59.5	67.1	73.6	80.2	94.5	109.0

ENCLOSURE LENGTH		16⅜"	20⅜"	24⅜"	28⅜"	32⅜"	36⅜"	40⅜"	44⅜"	48⅜"	56⅜"	64⅜"
	Enclosure Height	sq. ft.	sq. ft.	sq. ft.	sq. ft.	sq. ft.	sq. ft.	sq. ft.	sq. ft.	sq. ft.	sq. ft.	sq. ft.
ENCLOSURE DEPTH 10"	18"	22.2	28.8	35.9	40.4	45.5	53.0	59.6	66.2	71.7	83.8	97.0
	20"	24.7	32.3	38.9	46.0	52.5	60.5	67.0	73.7	81.2	95.0	108.5
	24"	26.3	33.8	41.4	49.0	56.6	64.0	71.6	78.8	87.0	102.0	116.5
	26"	27.3	34.8	42.8	50.5	58.6	66.6	73.6	81.8	89.2	105.0	121.0
	32"	28.3	37.4	45.5	53.5	61.6	70.0	78.8	86.4	95.0	111.5	128.0
	38"	30.3	39.4	48.0	56.5	65.2	74.0	82.8	91.8	100.0	118.0	135.2

FEDDERS-QUIGAN CORPORATION

(Continued from previous page)

RATINGS FOR CONVECTOR TYPE "W"*

Right: The enclosure used with Fedders-Quigan convector Type "W."

*(Note: Ratings are given in sq. ft. E.D.R., based on 215 deg steam and 65 deg entering air temperature)

ENCLOSURE LENGTH			16⅜"	20⅜"	24⅜"	28⅜"	32⅜"	36⅜"	40⅜"	44⅜"	48⅜"	56⅜"	64⅜"
			sq. ft.	sq. ft.	sq. ft.	sq. ft.	sq. ft.	sq. ft.	sq. ft.	sq. ft.	sq. ft.	sq. ft.	sq. ft.
ENCLOSURE DEPTH 4"	Enclosure Height	14"	9.1	11.6	14.1	16.6	19.2	21.7	24.2	26.8	29.3	34.3	39.4
		18"	10.1	13.1	16.1	18.7	21.7	24.7	27.3	30.3	33.3	38.4	44.9
		20"	10.6	13.6	16.7	19.7	22.7	25.7	28.7	31.8	34.8	40.8	47.0
		26"	11.1	14.1	17.2	20.2	23.2	26.2	29.2	32.3	35.3	41.8	48.0
		32"	11.1	14.1	17.7	20.7	23.7	26.7	30.3	33.3	36.4	42.8	49.0

ENCLOSURE LENGTH			16⅜"	20⅜"	24⅜"	28⅜"	32⅜"	36⅜"	40⅜"	44⅜"	48⅜"	56⅜"	64⅜"
			sq. ft.	sq. ft.	sq. ft.	sq. ft.	sq. ft.	sq. ft.	sq. ft.	sq. ft.	sq. ft.	sq. ft.	sq. ft.
ENCLOSURE DEPTH 6"	Enclosure Height	14"	12.6	16.2	19.8	23.0	26.8	30.4	34.0	37.5	41.0	48.2	55.2
		18"	14.6	18.7	22.8	27.0	31.0	35.0	39.0	43.2	47.2	56.0	64.0
		20"	15.1	19.2	23.2	27.8	31.7	36.4	40.4	44.4	49.0	57.5	66.0
		26"	15.6	20.2	24.2	28.8	33.5	38.0	42.6	46.4	51.8	60.4	69.5
		32"	16.1	20.7	25.2	29.8	34.3	38.8	43.4	47.9	53.0	62.0	71.1

ENCLOSURE LENGTH			16⅜"	20⅜"	24⅜"	28⅜"	32⅜"	36⅜"	40⅜"	44⅜"	48⅜"	56⅜"	64⅜"
			sq. ft.	sq. ft.	sq. ft.	sq. ft.	sq. ft.	sq. ft.	sq. ft.	sq. ft.	sq. ft.	sq. ft.	sq. ft.
ENCLOSURE DEPTH 8"	Enclosure Height	14"	16.7	21.7	26.3	31.3	36.0	41.0	46.0	50.5	56.2	65.5	75.0
		18"	18.2	23.2	28.8	33.8	39.0	44.6	49.6	54.5	60.0	70.5	81.2
		20"	18.7	24.2	29.3	34.8	40.4	45.5	51.0	56.5	61.6	72.6	83.2
		26"	19.2	24.7	30.3	35.8	41.6	47.2	53.2	58.3	64.0	75.0	86.0
		32"	19.7	25.3	31.3	36.8	42.4	47.9	54.0	59.5	65.1	76.2	87.6

ENCLOSURE LENGTH			16⅜"	20⅜"	24⅜"	28⅜"	32⅜"	36⅜"	40⅜"	44⅜"	48⅜"	56⅜"	64⅜"
			sq. ft.	sq. ft.	sq. ft.	sq. ft.	sq. ft.	sq. ft.	sq. ft.	sq. ft.	sq. ft.	sq. ft.	sq. ft.
ENCLOSURE DEPTH 10"	Enclosure Height	14"	18.7	24.2	29.3	34.8	39.9	45.6	50.8	56.1	61.5	72.0	82.8
		18"	21.2	27.3	33.3	39.4	45.5	51.8	58.0	63.6	70.0	82.0	93.8
		20"	22.2	28.3	34.8	40.8	47.5	54.0	60.0	66.6	72.7	85.2	98.0
		26"	22.7	29.8	36.4	42.9	49.5	56.2	63.0	69.2	76.2	89.2	102.0
		32"	23.7	30.8	37.4	44.4	51.0	58.0	64.6	71.6	78.1	92.4	106.0

GOVERNALE BROS. INC.

5518 Avenue "N", Brooklyn 34, N. Y.

International Convectors

ELEMENT TYPES AND CONVECTOR RATINGS

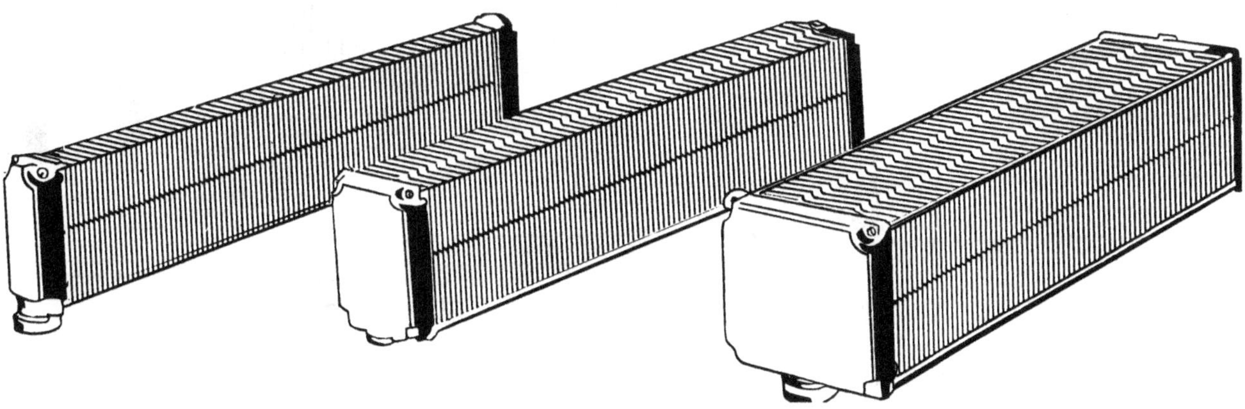

Above: The three drawings show construction of Governale Bros. Inc. element types for convector series 313-973. The convectors can be identified by the trade name "International," which is stamped on the header.

RATINGS FOR INTERNATIONAL CONVECTOR SERIES 313-973*

*(Note: Ratings are given in sq. ft. E.D.R. based on 215 deg steam and 65 deg entering air temperature)

ELEMENT LENGTH		13"	16"	22"	25"	28"	31"	34"	37"	40"	43"	46"	49"	52"	55"	58"	61"	64"	67"	70"	73"
CABINET LENGTH		15"	18"	24"	27"	30"	33"	36"	39"	42"	45"	48"	51"	54"	57"	60"	63"	66"	69"	72"	75"
	Cabinet Height	sq. ft.	sq. ft.	sq. ft.	sq. ft.	sq. ft.	sq. ft.	sq. ft.	sq. ft.	sq. ft.	sq. ft.	sq. ft.	sq. ft.	sq. ft.	sq. ft.	sq. ft.	sq. ft.	sq. ft.	sq. ft.	sq. ft.	sq. ft.
ELEMENT DEPTH 3⅛"	20"	5.5	7.0	10.5	11.5	13.5	15.0	16.5	18.0	19.5	21.0	22.5	24.0	25.5	27.0	28.5	29.5	30.0	31.5	33.0	34.5
	22"	5.5	7.0	10.0	11.5	13.5	14.5	16.5	18.0	19.5	21.0	22.5	24.0	26.0	27.5	28.5	30.5	32.0	33.0	35.0	36.5
	24"	6.0	7.0	10.5	12.0	13.5	15.0	17.0	18.0	19.5	21.5	23.0	24.5	26.5	28.0	29.0	31.0	32.5	34.0	35.5	37.0
	26"	6.0	7.5	10.5	12.0	14.0	15.5	17.0	18.5	20.0	22.0	23.5	25.0	27.0	28.5	30.0	31.5	33.0	34.5	36.5	37.5
CABINET DEPTH 3½"	29"	6.0	7.5	11.0	12.5	14.0	16.0	17.5	19.0	21.0	22.5	24.0	26.0	27.5	29.0	31.0	33.0	34.0	36.0	38.0	39.0
	32"	6.5	8.0	11.5	13.0	15.0	16.5	18.0	20.0	21.5	23.0	25.0	26.5	28.5	30.0	32.0	34.0	35.0	37.0	39.0	40.0
	35"	6.5	8.0	11.5	13.0	15.5	17.0	18.5	21.0	21.5	23.5	25.5	27.5	29.0	30.5	32.5	34.5	36.0	38.0	40.0	41.0

ELEMENT LENGTH		13"	16"	22"	25"	28"	31"	34"	37"	40"	43"	46"	49"	52"	55"	58"	61"	64"	67"	70"	73"
CABINET LENGTH		15"	18"	24"	27"	30"	33"	36"	39"	42"	45"	48"	51"	54"	57"	60"	63"	66"	69"	72"	75"
	Cabinet Height	sq. ft.	sq. ft.	sq. ft.	sq. ft.	sq. ft.	sq. ft.	sq. ft.	sq. ft.	sq. ft.	sq. ft.	sq. ft.	sq. ft.	sq. ft.	sq. ft.	sq. ft.	sq. ft.	sq. ft.	sq. ft.	sq. ft.	sq. ft.
ELEMENT DEPTH 6⅛"	20"	9.5	12.0	17.0	19.5	22.0	24.5	27.5	30.0	32.5	35.0	37.5	40.0	42.5	45.0	47.5	50.5	53.0	55.5	57.5	60.0
	22"	9.5	12.5	17.5	20.0	22.5	25.0	28.0	30.5	33.0	35.0	38.0	41.0	43.5	46.0	48.5	51.0	54.0	56.0	59.0	61.5
	24"	10.0	12.5	18.0	20.5	23.0	25.5	28.5	31.5	34.0	36.0	39.0	42.0	44.5	47.0	49.0	52.0	55.0	57.0	60.0	63.0
	26"	10.0	12.5	18.5	21.0	23.5	26.0	29.0	32.0	35.0	37.0	40.0	43.0	44.5	48.5	50.5	53.0	56.0	58.0	61.5	65.0
CABINET DEPTH 6½"	29"	10.0	13.0	19.0	21.5	24.5	27.0	30.0	33.0	36.0	38.0	41.0	44.0	47.0	50.0	52.0	55.5	58.0	60.0	64.0	67.0
	32"	10.5	13.5	19.5	22.0	25.0	27.5	31.0	34.0	37.0	39.0	42.0	45.0	48.0	51.0	53.5	56.5	59.0	62.0	65.0	68.0
	35"	11.0	14.0	20.0	23.0	26.0	28.5	31.5	35.0	38.0	40.0	43.0	46.0	49.0	52.0	55.0	57.5	61.0	64.0	66.5	69.5

ELEMENT LENGTH		13"	16"	22"	25"	28"	31"	34"	37"	40"	43"	46"	49"	52"	55"	58"	61"	64"	67"	70"	73"
CABINET LENGTH		15"	18"	24"	27"	30"	33"	36"	39"	42"	45"	48"	51"	54"	57"	60"	63"	66"	69"	72"	75"
	Cabinet Height	sq. ft.	sq. ft.	sq. ft.	sq. ft.	sq. ft.	sq. ft.	sq. ft.	sq. ft.	sq. ft.	sq. ft.	sq. ft.	sq. ft.	sq. ft.	sq. ft.	sq. ft.	sq. ft.	sq. ft.	sq. ft.	sq. ft.	sq. ft.
ELEMENT DEPTH 9⅛"	20"	13.0	16.5	23.5	27.0	30.5	34.0	37.0	41.0	45.0	48.0	51.0	54.5	58.5	61.5	65.5	68.5	72.0	76.0	79.0	83.0
	22"	13.5	17.0	24.0	28.0	31.0	34.5	38.5	42.0	45.5	49.0	52.5	56.0	59.5	63.0	67.0	70.5	74.0	78.0	81.0	85.0
	24"	14.0	17.0	24.5	28.5	31.5	35.5	39.0	42.5	46.5	50.0	53.5	57.0	61.0	64.5	68.5	72.0	76.0	79.0	83.0	87.0
	26"	14.5	17.5	25.0	29.0	32.0	36.0	40.0	43.5	47.0	51.0	54.5	58.0	62.0	65.5	69.5	73.0	77.0	81.0	84.0	88.5
CABINET DEPTH 9½"	29"	14.5	17.5	25.5	29.5	32.5	36.5	40.5	44.0	47.5	52.0	55.5	59.0	63.0	66.5	70.5	74.5	78.0	81.5	86.0	90.0
	32"	14.5	18.0	26.0	30.0	33.0	37.0	41.0	44.5	48.0	52.5	56.0	60.0	63.5	67.0	71.5	75.0	79.0	82.5	87.0	91.0
	35"	15.0	18.5	26.5	30.5	33.5	37.5	42.0	45.0	49.0	53.0	57.0	61.0	64.0	68.0	72.5	76.0	80.0	83.0	88.0	92.0

GOVERNALE BROS. INC.

(Continued from previous page)

Element Types and
Convector Ratings

RATINGS FOR INTERNATIONAL CONVECTORS SERIES 315-1060*

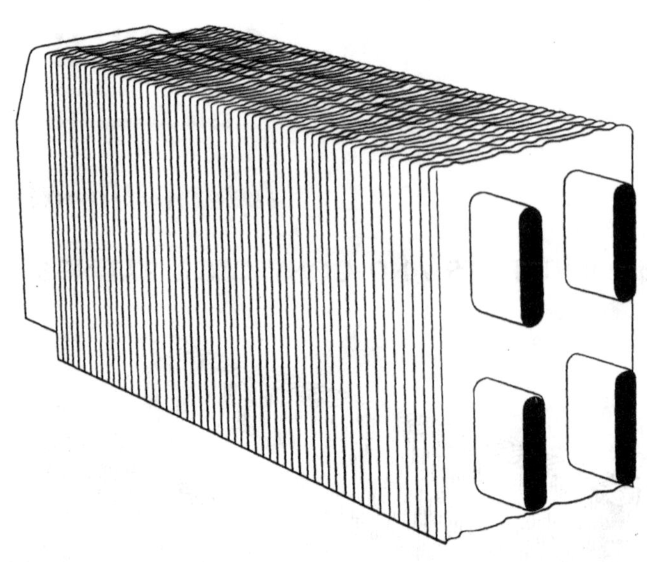

At right: This drawing illustrates the type of convector element used in Governale Bros. Inc. Series 315-1060 International convectors.

*(Note: Ratings are given in sq. ft. E.D.R. based on 215 deg steam and 65 deg entering air temperature)

ELEMENT LENGTH		15″	18″	21″	24″	27″	30″	33″	36″	39″	42″	45″	48″	51″	54″	57″	60″
CABINET LENGTH		17″	20″	23″	25″	29″	32″	35″	38″	41″	44″	47″	50″	53″	56″	59″	62″
	Cabinet Height	sq. ft.	sq. ft.	sq. ft.	sq. ft.	sq. ft.	sq. ft.	sq. ft.	sq. ft.	sq. ft.	sq. ft.	sq. ft.	sq. ft.	sq. ft.	sq. ft.	sq. ft.	sq. ft.
ELEMENT DEPTH 3⅞″	20″	7.0	9.0	11.0	13.5	15.5	17.5	20.0	22.0	24.0	26.0	28.0	30.5	32.5	34.5	36.5	39.0
	22″	7.5	9.5	11.5	14.0	16.0	18.5	21.0	23.0	25.0	27.5	29.5	32.0	34.5	36.5	38.5	41.0
	24″	8.0	10.0	12.0	14.5	16.5	19.0	21.5	24.0	26.0	28.5	30.5	33.0	35.0	37.5	40.0	42.0
	26″	8.5	10.5	12.5	15.0	17.0	19.5	22.0	24.5	26.5	29.0	31.5	34.0	36.0	38.5	41.0	43.0
CABINET DEPTH 3¾″	29″	9.0	11.0	13.0	15.5	18.0	20.0	23.5	26.0	27.5	30.0	32.0	35.0	37.0	39.5	41.5	43.5
	32″	9.5	11.5	13.5	16.0	18.5	22.0	25.0	27.0	28.5	31.0	33.0	36.0	38.0	40.0	42.0	44.5
	35″	10.0	12.0	14.0	16.5	19.0	22.5	25.5	27.5	29.5	31.5	34.0	37.0	39.0	41.0	43.0	45.5

ELEMENT LENGTH		15″	18″	21″	24″	27″	30″	33″	36″	39″	42″	45″	48″	51″	54″	57″	60″
CABINET LENGTH		17″	20″	23″	25″	29″	32″	35″	38″	41″	44″	47″	50″	53″	56″	59″	62″
	Cabinet Height	sq. ft.	sq. ft.	sq. ft.	sq. ft.	sq. ft.	sq. ft.	sq. ft.	sq. ft.	sq. ft.	sq. ft.	sq. ft.	sq. ft.	sq. ft.	sq. ft.	sq. ft.	sq. ft.
ELEMENT DEPTH 5⅞″	20″	9.5	12.5	15.0	18.0	21.5	24.5	27.5	30.5	33.5	36.5	39.5	42.5	45.5	48.5	51.5	54.0
	22″	10.0	13.0	16.0	19.0	22.5	25.5	28.5	32.0	35.0	38.5	41.5	44.5	47.5	50.5	53.5	56.0
	24″	10.5	13.5	16.5	19.5	23.5	26.5	29.5	33.0	36.0	39.5	43.0	45.5	49.0	52.0	55.5	58.0
	26″	11.0	14.0	17.0	20.0	24.0	27.0	30.5	34.0	37.0	40.5	44.0	47.0	50.0	53.5	57.0	60.0
CABINET DEPTH 5¾″	29″	11.5	14.5	17.5	20.5	24.5	27.5	31.0	35.0	38.0	41.0	45.5	48.5	51.5	55.0	58.0	62.0
	32″	12.0	15.0	18.0	21.0	25.0	28.0	32.0	36.0	39.0	42.0	46.5	49.5	52.5	56.0	59.5	63.5
	35″	12.5	15.5	18.5	21.5	25.5	28.5	32.5	36.5	39.5	43.0	47.0	50.0	53.5	57.0	60.5	65.0

ELEMENT LENGTH		15″	18″	21″	24″	27″	30″	33″	36″	39″	42″	45″	48″	51″	54″	57″	60″
CABINET LENGTH		17″	20″	23″	25″	29″	32″	35″	38″	41″	44″	47″	50″	53″	56″	59″	62″
	Cabinet Height	sq. ft.	sq. ft.	sq. ft.	sq. ft.	sq. ft.	sq. ft.	sq. ft.	sq. ft.	sq. ft.	sq. ft.	sq. ft.	sq. ft.	sq. ft.	sq. ft.	sq. ft.	sq. ft.
ELEMENT DEPTH 7⅞″	20″	11.0	14.5	18.0	22.0	25.5	29.0	33.0	36.5	40.0	43.5	47.5	51.0	54.5	58.0	61.5	65.0
	22″	11.5	15.5	19.0	23.0	27.0	30.5	34.0	38.0	42.0	45.5	49.5	53.0	56.5	60.5	64.0	68.0
	24″	12.0	16.0	19.5	23.5	27.5	31.5	35.0	39.0	43.0	46.5	50.5	54.0	58.0	62.0	66.0	69.5
	26″	12.5	16.5	20.0	24.0	28.0	32.0	36.0	40.0	44.0	48.0	52.0	55.5	59.5	63.5	67.5	71.0
CABINET DEPTH 7¾″	29″	13.0	17.0	20.5	25.0	29.5	33.5	37.0	40.5	45.0	49.0	53.0	57.0	61.0	65.0	68.5	72.5
	32″	13.5	18.0	21.5	25.5	30.5	34.0	38.0	41.5	46.0	50.0	54.0	58.0	62.0	66.0	69.5	74.0
	35″	14.0	18.5	22.5	26.5	31.0	35.0	39.0	42.5	47.0	51.0	55.0	59.0	63.0	67.0	71.0	75.0

ELEMENT LENGTH		15″	18″	21″	24″	27″	30″	33″	36″	39″	42″	45″	48″	51″	54″	57″	60″
CABINET LENGTH		17″	20″	23″	25″	29″	32″	35″	38″	41″	44″	47″	50″	53″	56″	59″	62″
	Cabinet Height	sq. ft.	sq. ft.	sq. ft.	sq. ft.	sq. ft.	sq. ft.	sq. ft.	sq. ft.	sq. ft.	sq. ft.	sq. ft.	sq. ft.	sq. ft.	sq. ft.	sq. ft.	sq. ft.
ELEMENT DEPTH 10¾″	20″	16.0	21.5	26.5	32.0	37.0	42.5	48.0	53.0	58.5	64.0	69.0	74.0	79.0	84.0	89.0	94.0
	22″	17.0	22.5	28.0	33.5	39.0	44.5	50.0	55.5	61.0	66.5	72.0	77.0	83.0	88.5	93.5	98.5
	24″	18.0	23.0	28.5	34.5	40.0	46.0	51.0	57.0	62.5	68.5	74.0	79.0	85.0	91.0	96.0	101.0
	26″	19.0	23.5	29.5	35.5	41.5	47.0	53.0	58.5	64.5	70.5	76.0	81.5	87.5	93.0	99.0	104.0
CABINET DEPTH 11¼″	29″	20.0	24.5	30.5	36.5	43.0	48.0	54.0	60.0	65.5	72.0	78.0	83.0	89.0	94.5	101.0	107.0
	32″	21.0	26.0	32.0	38.0	44.0	50.0	56.0	62.0	67.5	73.5	79.5	84.5	90.5	96.0	102.5	109.0
	35″	22.0	27.0	33.0	39.0	45.0	51.0	57.0	63.5	69.5	75.0	81.0	87.0	93.0	99.0	105.0	111.5

GOVERNALE COPPER CONVECTORS

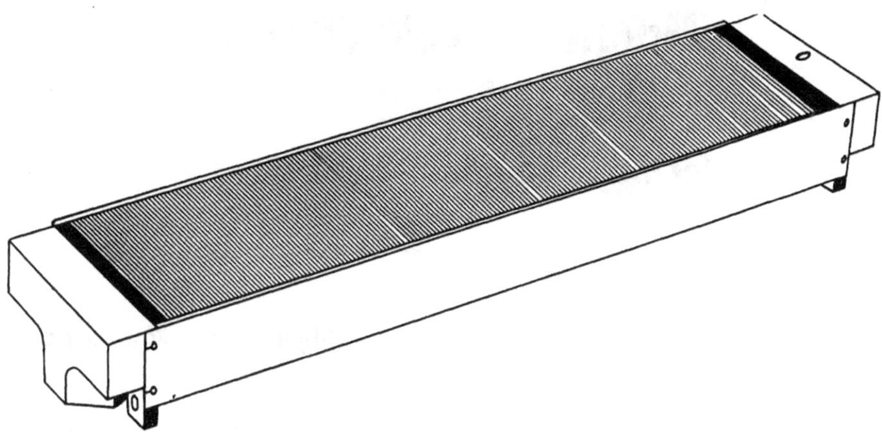

All cabinets are 6⅞" deep.

RATINGS FOR GOVERNALE COPPER CONVECTORS

Sq. ft. E.D.R. based on one pound of steam 215 deg operating pressure and 65 deg inlet air.

ELEMENT LENGTH			19¼"	23¼"	27¼"	31¼"	35¼"	39¼"	43¼"	47¼"	55¼"	63¼"
CABINET LENGTH			20"	24"	28"	32"	36"	40"	44"	48"	56"	64"
			sq. ft.	sq. ft.	sq. ft.	sq. ft.	sq. ft.	sq. ft.	sq. ft.	sq. ft.	sq. ft.	sq. ft.
ELEMENT DEPTH 00½"	Cabinet Height	20"	16.0	19.5	23.0	26.5	30.0	34.0	38.0	42.0	49.5	57.0
		24"	18.0	22.0	26.0	30.0	34.5	39.0	43.0	47.0	55.5	64.0
		26"	19.0	23.0	27.0	31.5	36.0	40.5	45.0	50.0	59.0	68.0
		32"	20.0	24.0	28.5	33.0	37.5	42.5	47.0	51.5	61.0	70.5

McQUAY, INCORPORATED

1600 Broadway, N.E., Minneapolis 13, Minn.

McQuay Copper Convectors

Enclosure Types and Convector Ratings

Ratings for Types "ET" and "WT" are given below and continued on following page

Right: Type "WT" McQuay copper convector enclosure. Use actual measurements.

Left: Type "ET" McQuay copper convector enclosure. Use actual measurements.

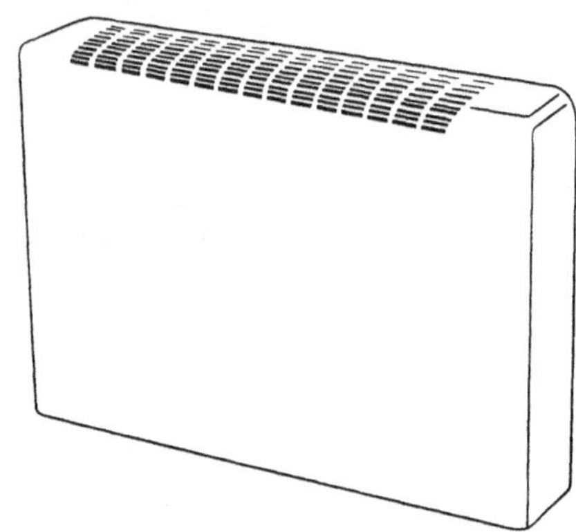

RATINGS FOR McQUAY COPPER CONVECTORS, TYPES "ET" and "WT"*

*(Note: Ratings given in sq. ft. E.D.R. for steam)

ENCLOSURE LENGTH	Height—Type WT	Height—Type ET	15″	17½″	20″	22½″	25″	30″	35″	40″	45″	50″	55″	60″	65″	70″
			sq. ft.	sq. ft.	sq. ft.	sq. ft.	sq. ft.	sq. ft.	sq. ft.	sq. ft.	sq. ft.	sq. ft.	sq. ft.	sq. ft.	sq. ft.	sq. ft.
ELEMENT WIDTH 3¼″ ENCLOSURE WIDTH 3⅝″	14½″	20″	9.0	10.5	12.0	13.5	15.0	18.0	21.0	24.5	27.5	30.5	33.5	36.0	39.0	42.0
	16½″	22″	9.5	11.0	12.5	14.0	15.5	19.0	22.0	25.5	29.0	31.5	35.0	38.0	41.0	44.5
	18½″	24″	9.8	11.5	13.0	14.5	16.5	19.7	23.0	26.3	30.3	32.8	36.3	39.5	42.3	46.3
	20½″	26″	10.0	12.0	13.5	15.0	17.0	20.5	24.0	27.0	30.5	34.0	37.5	41.0	44.5	48.0
	22½″	28″	10.3	12.3	13.8	15.5	17.3	21.0	24.5	27.8	31.5	35.0	38.5	42.0	45.8	49.3
	24½″	30″	10.5	12.5	14.0	16.0	17.5	21.5	25.0	28.5	32.5	36.0	39.5	43.0	47.0	50.5
	26½″	32″	10.8	12.8	14.3	16.5	18.0	22.0	25.5	29.3	33.3	36.3	40.5	44.3	48.0	51.8
	28½″	34″	11.0	13.0	14.5	17.0	18.5	22.5	26.0	30.0	34.0	37.5	41.5	45.5	49.0	53.0
	30½″	36″	11.4	13.4	14.9	17.5	19.0	23.0	27.0	31.1	34.8	38.3	42.5	46.5	50.0	54.0
	32½″	38″	12.0	14.0	15.5	18.0	19.5	24.0	28.0	32.0	35.7	39.0	43.5	47.5	51.0	55.0
	34½″	40″	12.6	14.6	16.1	18.5	20.0	25.0	29.0	33.0	36.6	39.8	44.0	48.5	52.0	56.0

ENCLOSURE LENGTH	Height—Type WT	Height—Type ET	15″	17½″	20″	22½″	25″	30″	35″	40″	45″	50″	55″	60″	65″	70″
			sq. ft.	sq. ft.	sq. ft.	sq. ft.	sq. ft.	sq. ft.	sq. ft.	sq. ft.	sq. ft.	sq. ft.	sq. ft.	sq. ft.	sq. ft.	sq. ft.
ELEMENT WIDTH 5⅜″ ENCLOSURE WIDTH 5¾″	14½″	20″	14.5	17.0	19.5	22.0	24.5	29.5	34.5	40.0	46.0	50.0	55.5	60.5	66.0	71.0
	16½″	22″	15.0	17.5	20.0	22.5	25.5	31.0	36.5	42.0	48.0	53.5	59.0	64.5	70.0	75.5
	18½″	24″	16.0	18.5	21.0	23.5	26.5	32.5	38.0	44.0	50.0	56.0	61.5	67.5	73.0	79.0
	20½″	26″	17.0	19.5	21.5	24.5	27.5	33.5	39.5	45.5	52.0	58.0	64.0	70.0	76.0	82.0
	22½″	28″	17.5	20.0	22.0	25.5	28.5	34.5	40.5	47.0	53.5	60.0	66.0	72.5	78.5	85.0
	24½″	30″	18.0	20.5	22.5	26.0	29.0	35.5	42.0	48.5	55.0	61.5	68.0	74.5	81.0	87.5
	26½″	32″	18.5	21.0	23.0	26.5	29.5	36.5	43.0	49.5	56.5	63.0	69.5	76.5	83.0	89.5
	28½″	34″	19.0	21.5	23.5	27.0	30.5	37.0	44.0	50.5	58.0	64.0	71.0	78.0	85.0	91.5
	30½″	36″	19.6	22.3	24.2	27.6	31.2	37.6	45.0	51.5	59.4	65.0	72.5	79.5	86.5	92.5
	32½″	38″	21.2	23.0	25.0	28.3	31.8	38.4	46.0	52.5	60.5	66.0	73.7	80.5	88.5	93.5
	34½″	40″	22.6	23.7	25.8	29.0	32.4	39.2	47.0	53.5	61.4	67.0	74.9	81.5	90.5	94.5

McQUAY, INCORPORATED

(Continued from previous page)

See previous pages for additional ratings and for enclosure types for McQuay convector types "ET" and "WT".

RATINGS FOR McQUAY CONVECTORS, TYPES "ET" and "WT"*

*(Note: Ratings given in sq. ft. E.D.R. for steam)

ENCLOSURE LENGTH			15"	17½"	20"	22½"	25"	30"	35"	40"	45"	50"	55"	60"	65"	70"
	Height—Type WT	Height—Type ET	sq. ft.	sq. ft.	sq. ft.	sq. ft.	sq. ft.	sq. ft.	sq. ft.	sq. ft.	sq. ft.	sq. ft.	sq. ft.	sq. ft.	sq. ft.	sq. ft.
ELEMENT WIDTH 8" ENCLOSURE WIDTH 8⅜"	14½"	20"	22.0	24.5	26.5	30.5	34.5	42.0	49.0	58.0	65.0	73.0	81.0	89.0	96.0	104.0
	16½"	22"	23.0	25.5	28.0	32.5	36.5	44.5	52.5	61.0	69.5	77.5	85.5	94.0	101.5	110.5
	18½"	24"	24.0	26.5	29.0	33.5	37.5	46.0	54.5	63.0	72.0	80.0	88.5	97.5	105.0	114.0
	20½"	26"	25.0	27.5	30.0	34.5	38.5	47.5	56.0	65.0	74.0	82.5	91.5	100.5	109.0	117.5
	22½"	28"	25.5	28.0	30.5	35.0	39.5	48.5	57.5	66.5	75.5	84.0	93.5	102.5	111.0	120.0
	24½"	30"	26.0	28.5	31.0	35.5	40.5	49.5	58.5	67.5	76.5	86.0	95.5	104.5	113.5	122.5
	26½"	32"	26.5	29.0	31.5	36.0	41.0	50.0	59.5	69.0	78.0	87.5	97.0	106.0	115.5	124.5
	28½"	34"	27.0	29.5	32.0	37.0	41.5	51.0	60.5	70.0	79.5	88.5	98.0	107.5	117.5	126.5
	30½"	36"	27.5	30.0	32.7	37.8	42.2	51.7	61.7	70.5	80.5	89.4	98.7	109.0	118.8	127.8
	32½"	38"	28.0	30.7	33.4	38.5	42.7	52.3	62.4	71.0	81.0	90.0	99.4	110.0	119.7	128.3
	34½"	40"	28.5	31.4	34.0	39.2	43.2	53.0	63.2	71.5	81.5	90.5	100.4	111.0	120.5	129.0

ENCLOSURE LENGTH			15"	17½"	20"	22½"	25"	30"	35"	40"	45"	50"	55"	60"	65"	70"
	Height—Type WT	Height—Type ET	sq. ft.	sq. ft.	sq. ft.	sq. ft.	sq. ft.	sq. ft.	sq. ft.	sq. ft.	sq. ft.	sq. ft.	sq. ft.	sq. ft.	sq. ft.	sq. ft.
ELEMENT WIDTH 10⅝" ENCLOSURE WIDTH 11"	14½"	20"	26.0	29.5	33.0	37.5	42.0	52.0	61.0	70.0	80.0	90.0	100.0	110.0	118.0	127.0
	16½"	22"	28.0	31.0	34.0	39.0	44.0	54.0	64.0	74.0	84.0	94.5	104.5	114.0	124.5	134.5
	18½"	24"	29.5	32.5	35.5	40.5	46.0	56.0	66.5	77.0	87.0	97.5	108.5	118.5	129.0	139.5
	20½"	26"	30.5	33.5	36.5	42.0	47.5	58.0	69.0	80.0	90.5	101.5	112.0	123.0	133.5	144.5
	22½"	28"	31.5	34.5	37.5	43.0	49.0	59.5	71.0	82.5	93.5	104.5	115.5	127.0	137.5	149.0
	24½"	30"	32.5	35.5	38.5	44.0	50.0	61.5	73.0	84.5	96.0	107.5	119.0	131.0	142.0	154.0
	26½"	32"	34.0	36.5	39.0	45.0	51.5	63.0	75.0	87.0	98.5	110.0	122.0	134.5	146.0	158.0
	28½"	34"	35.0	37.5	40.0	46.0	52.5	64.5	77.0	89.0	101.5	113.5	125.5	138.0	150.0	162.0
	30½"	36"	35.8	38.3	40.9	47.0	53.5	65.3	78.8	90.7	102.5	114.5	126.2	139.7	151.7	165.5
	32½"	38"	36.6	39.0	41.8	47.8	54.0	66.0	80.2	92.0	103.0	115.0	127.0	139.8	153.0	168.0
	34½"	40"	37.4	39.7	42.7	48.6	54.5	66.5	81.6	93.3	103.5	115.8	127.8	140.5	154.3	170.0

Enclosure Types and Measuring Instructions

McQuay Convectors, Types "WF", "EF", "PT", "PR", "EPT", "WPT", "H"

See Facing Page for Ratings

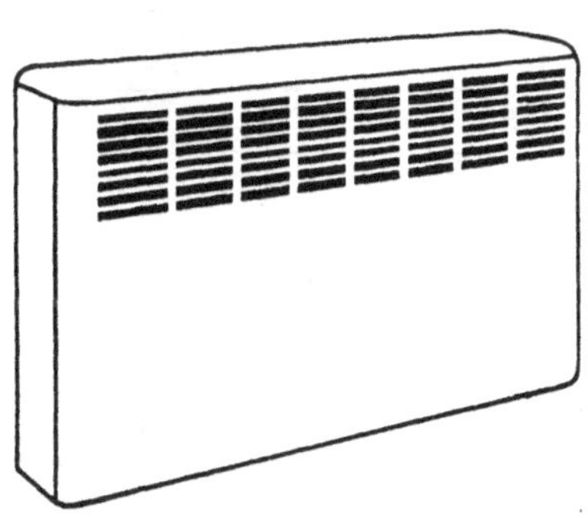

Left: This enclosure style is used with McQuay convectors "WR" and "WPT". Use actual measurements.

Right: Enclosure style used with McQuay copper convectors, type "EF". Use actual measurements.

Left: To identify McQuay convector type, check enclosure. This enclosure type is used with "PT" convectors. Use actual measurements less 2½ in., other measurements actual.

Right: Used with McQuay convector type "H", this enclosure is easy to identify. Use actual measurements on all sides, except deduct 2½ in. from height.

RATINGS FOR McQUAY COPPER CONVECTORS, TYPE "WF", "EF", "PT", "PR", "EPT", "WPT", "H"*

*(Note: Ratings given in sq. ft. E.D.R. based on 2 lb steam pressure and 65 deg entering air temperature)

	Height—Type WF	Height—Types EF, PT, PR, EPT, WPT, H	15"	17½"	20"	22½"	25"	30"	35"	40"	45"	50"	55"	60"	65"	70"
ENCLOSURE LENGTH			sq. ft.	sq. ft.	sq. ft.	sq. ft.	sq. ft.	sq. ft.	sq. ft.	sq. ft.	sq. ft.	sq. ft.	sq. ft.	sq. ft.	sq. ft.	sq. ft.
ELEMENT DEPTH 3¼" ENCLOSURE DEPTH 3⅝"	14½"	20"	8.0	9.5	10.5	12.0	13.0	15.5	18.0	20.5	23.0	25.5	28.0	30.5	33.0	35.5
	16½"	22"	8.3	9.8	11.0	12.5	13.8	16.5	19.0	22.0	24.5	27.5	30.0	32.0	35.0	37.5
	18½"	24"	8.5	10.0	11.5	13.0	14.5	17.5	20.0	23.0	26.0	29.0	31.5	34.5	37.0	40.0
	20½"	26"	9.0	10.5	12.0	13.5	15.0	18.0	21.0	24.5	27.5	30.5	33.5	36.0	39.0	42.0
	22½"	28"	9.5	11.0	12.5	14.0	15.5	19.0	22.0	25.5	29.0	31.5	35.0	38.0	41.0	44.5
	24½"	30"	9.8	11.5	13.0	14.5	16.7	19.8	23.0	26.3	30.3	32.8	36.3	39.5	42.3	46.3
	26½"	32"	10.0	12.0	13.5	15.0	17.0	20.5	24.0	27.0	30.5	34.0	37.5	41.0	44.5	48.0
	28½"	34"	10.3	12.3	13.8	15.5	17.3	21.0	24.5	27.8	31.5	35.0	38.5	42.0	45.8	49.3
	30½"	36"	10.5	12.5	14.0	16.0	17.5	21.5	25.0	28.5	32.5	36.0	39.5	43.0	47.0	50.5
	32½"	38"	10.8	12.8	14.3	16.5	18.0	22.0	25.5	29.3	33.3	36.8	40.5	44.3	48.0	51.8
	34½"	40"	11.0	13.0	14.5	17.0	18.5	22.5	26.0	30.0	34.0	37.5	41.5	45.5	49.0	53.0

	Height—Type WF	Height—Types EF, PT, PR, EPT, WPT, H	15"	17½"	20"	22½"	25"	30"	35"	40"	45"	50"	55"	60"	65"	70"
ENCLOSURE LENGTH			sq. ft.	sq. ft.	sq. ft.	sq. ft.	sq. ft.	sq. ft.	sq. ft.	sq. ft.	sq. ft.	sq. ft.	sq. ft.	sq. ft.	sq. ft.	sq. ft.
ELEMENT DEPTH 5⅜" ENCLOSURE DEPTH 5¾"	14½"	20"	11.0	13.0	15.0	17.0	19.0	22.5	26.5	30.0	34.0	38.0	41.5	45.5	49.0	53.0
	16½"	22"	12.5	14.5	17.5	18.5	21.0	25.0	29.5	34.0	38.0	42.5	46.5	51.0	55.5	60.0
		24"	14.0	16.0	18.5	20.5	23.0	28.0	32.5	37.5	42.5	47.0	52.0	56.5	61.5	66.5
	20½"	26"	14.5	17.0	19.5	22.0	24.5	29.5	34.5	40.0	46.0	50.0	55.5	60.5	66.0	71.0
	22½"	28"	15.0	17.5	20.0	22.5	25.5	31.0	36.5	42.0	48.0	53.5	59.0	64.5	70.0	75.5
	24½"	30"	16.0	18.5	21.0	23.5	26.5	32.5	38.0	44.0	50.0	56.0	61.5	67.5	73.0	79.0
	26½"	32"	17.0	19.5	21.5	24.5	27.5	33.5	39.5	45.5	52.0	58.0	64.0	70.0	76.0	82.0
	28½"	34"	17.5	20.0	22.0	25.5	28.5	34.5	40.5	47.0	53.5	60.0	66.0	72.5	78.5	85.0
	30½"	36"	18.0	20.5	22.5	26.0	29.0	35.5	42.0	48.5	55.0	61.5	68.0	74.5	81.0	87.5
	32½"	38"	18.5	21.0	23.0	26.5	29.5	36.5	43.0	49.5	56.5	63.0	69.5	76.5	83.0	89.5
	34½"	40"	19.0	21.5	23.5	27.0	30.5	37.0	44.0	50.5	58.0	64.0	71.0	78.0	85.0	91.5

	Height—Type WF	Height—Types EF, PT, PR, EPT, WPT, H	15"	17½"	20"	22½"	25"	30"	35"	40"	45"	50"	55"	60"	65"	70"
ENCLOSURE LENGTH			sq. ft.	sq. ft.	sq. ft.	sq. ft.	sq. ft.	sq. ft.	sq. ft.	sq. ft.	sq. ft.	sq. ft.	sq. ft.	sq. ft.	sq. ft.	sq. ft.
ELEMENT DEPTH 8" ENCLOSURE DEPTH 8⅜"	14½"	20"	16.0	19.0	22.0	25.0	28.0	34.0	40.0	46.0	52.5	58.5	64.5	70.5	76.5	82.5
	16½"	22"	17.5	20.5	23.5	27.0	30.5	36.0	43.5	50.0	57.5	64.0	70.5	77.0	84.0	90.0
	18½"	24"	19.5	22.5	25.5	29.5	33.0	40.0	47.5	54.5	62.0	69.5	76.5	84.0	91.0	98.5
	20½"	26"	22.0	24.5	26.5	30.5	34.5	42.0	49.0	58.0	65.0	73.0	81.0	89.0	96.0	104.0
	22½"	28"	23.0	25.5	28.0	32.5	36.5	44.5	52.5	61.0	69.5	77.5	85.5	94.0	101.5	110.5
	24½"	30"	24.0	26.5	29.0	33.5	37.5	46.0	54.5	63.0	72.0	80.0	88.5	97.5	105.0	114.0
	26½"	32"	25.0	27.5	30.0	34.5	38.5	47.5	56.0	65.0	74.0	82.5	91.5	100.5	109.0	117.5
	28½"	34"	25.5	28.0	30.5	35.0	39.5	48.5	57.5	66.5	75.5	84.0	93.5	102.5	111.0	120.0
	30½"	36"	26.0	28.5	31.0	35.5	40.5	49.5	58.5	67.5	76.5	86.0	95.5	104.5	113.5	122.5
	32½"	38"	26.5	29.0	31.5	36.0	41.0	50.0	59.5	69.0	78.0	87.5	97.0	106.0	115.5	124.5
	34½"	40"	27.0	29.5	32.0	37.0	41.5	51.0	60.5	70.0	79.5	88.5	98.0	107.5	117.5	126.5

	Height—Type WF	Height—Types EF, PT, PR, EPT, WPT, H	15"	17½"	20"	22½"	25"	30"	35"	40"	45"	50"	55"	60"	65"	70"
ENCLOSURE LENGTH			sq. ft.	sq. ft.	sq. ft.	sq. ft.	sq. ft.	sq. ft.	sq. ft.	sq. ft.	sq. ft.	sq. ft.	sq. ft.	sq. ft.	sq. ft.	sq. ft.
ELEMENT DEPTH 10⅝" ENCLOSURE DEPTH 11"	14½"	20"	20.0	23.4	27.0	31.0	34.5	42.0	50.0	57.5	65.5	73.0	80.5	88.5	96.0	103.5
	16½"	22"	22.0	25.5	29.0	33.0	37.0	45.0	54.0	62.0	71.0	79.0	87.5	96.0	104.0	112.0
	18½"	24"	24.5	28.0	31.5	36.0	40.5	49.5	58.5	67.5	76.5	85.5	95.0	104.0	113.0	122.0
	20½"	26"	26.0	29.5	33.0	37.5	42.0	52.0	61.0	70.0	80.0	90.0	100.0	110.0	118.0	127.0
	22½"	28"	28.0	31.0	34.0	39.0	44.0	54.0	64.0	74.0	84.0	94.0	104.5	114.0	124.5	134.5
	24½"	30"	29.5	32.5	35.5	40.5	46.0	56.0	66.0	77.0	87.0	97.5	108.5	118.5	129.0	139.5
	26½"	32"	30.5	33.5	36.5	42.0	47.5	58.0	69.0	80.0	90.5	101.5	112.0	123.0	133.5	144.5
	28½"	34"	31.5	34.5	37.5	43.0	49.0	59.5	71.0	82.5	93.5	104.5	115.5	127.0	137.5	149.0
	30½"	36"	32.5	35.5	38.5	44.0	50.0	61.5	73.0	84.5	96.0	107.5	119.0	131.0	142.0	154.0
	32½"	38"	34.0	36.5	39.0	45.0	51.5	63.0	75.0	87.0	98.5	110.0	122.0	134.5	146.0	158.0
	34½"	40"	35.0	37.5	40.0	46.0	52.5	64.5	77.0	89.0	101.5	113.5	125.5	138.0	150.0	162.0

McQUAY, INCORPORATED

(Continued from previous page)

Enclosure Types and Measuring Instructions

McQuay Copper Convectors

See Facing Page for Convector Ratings

Left: Convector enclosure used with McQuay Type "EPT" units. Use actual measurements.

Right: Enclosure used with McQuay type "PR" convectors. Use actual measurements except for length, from which $2\frac{1}{2}$ in. should be deducted.

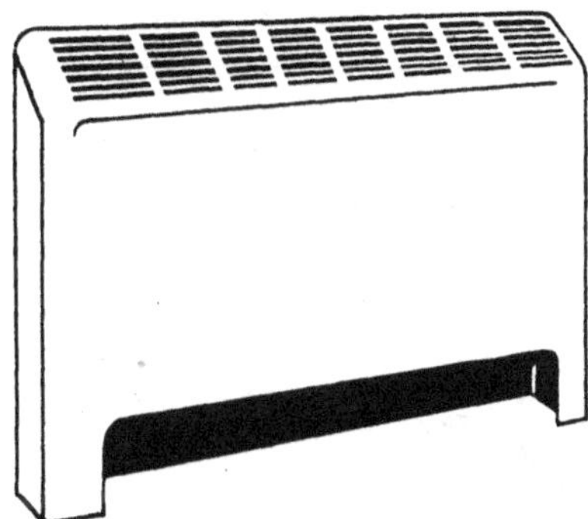

Left: Type "ES" convector enclosure. Use actual measurements.

Right: Enclosure used with McQuay type "WS" convectors. Use actual measurements in sizing and identifying.

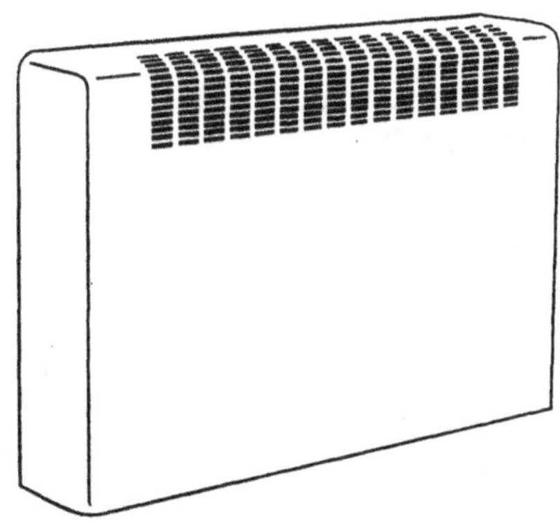

Left: McQuay convector enclosure for type "WR". Use actual measurements.

Right: Enclosure for McQuay convector type "ER." Use actual measurements.

RATINGS FOR McQUAY CONVECTORS, TYPES "WS", "WR", "ES" and "ER"*

*(Note: Ratings are given in sq. ft. E.D.R. based on steam)

ENCLOSURE LENGTH	Height—Types WS and WR	Height—Types ES and ER	15″	17½″	20″	22½″	25″	30″	35″	40″	45″	50″	55″	60″	65″	70″
			sq. ft.	sq. ft.	sq. ft.	sq. ft.	sq. ft.	sq. ft.	sq. ft.	sq. ft.	sq. ft.	sq. ft.	sq. ft.	sq. ft.	sq. ft.	sq. ft.
ELEMENT DEPTH 3¼″ ENCLOSURE DEPTH 3⅝″	14½″	20″	8.4	9.9	11.3	12.7	14.2	17.0	19.5	22.5	25.2	28.3	30.7	33.2	36.0	38.2
	16½″	22″	8.7	10.3	11.7	13.3	14.7	17.7	20.5	23.7	27.6	29.7	32.5	35.2	38.0	41.0
	18½″	24″	9.3	10.8	12.3	13.7	15.3	18.5	21.5	25.0	28.3	31.0	34.7	37.0	40.0	43.2
	20½″	26″	9.6	11.3	12.7	14.3	16.0	19.4	22.5	25.9	29.5	32.2	35.6	38.7	41.6	45.4
	22½″	28″	9.9	11.7	13.3	14.7	16.7	20.0	23.5	26.7	30.4	33.4	36.9	40.2	42.9	47.2
	24½″	30″	10.1	12.1	13.6	15.3	17.1	20.7	24.3	27.4	31.0	34.5	38.0	41.5	45.1	48.6
	26½″	32″	10.4	12.4	13.9	15.7	17.4	21.3	24.7	28.2	32.0	35.5	39.0	42.5	44.6	49.9
	28½″	34″	10.6	12.7	14.1	16.3	17.7	21.7	25.3	28.9	32.9	36.4	40.0	43.6	47.5	51.1
	30½″	36″	10.9	12.9	14.4	16.7	18.3	22.3	25.7	29.7	33.7	37.1	41.0	44.9	48.5	52.4
	32½″	38″	11.2	13.2	14.7	17.2	18.7	22.7	26.3	30.6	34.4	37.9	42.0	46.0	49.5	53.5
	34½″	40″	11.7	13.7	15.2	17.7	19.3	23.5	27.5	31.5	35.2	38.7	43.0	47.0	50.5	54.5

ENCLOSURE LENGTH	Height—Types WS and WR	Height—Types ES and ER	15″	17½″	20″	22½″	25″	30″	35″	40″	45″	50″	55″	60″	65″	70″
			sq. ft.	sq. ft.	sq. ft.	sq. ft.	sq. ft.	sq. ft.	sq. ft.	sq. ft.	sq. ft.	sq. ft.	sq. ft.	sq. ft.	sq. ft.	sq. ft.
ELEMENT DEPTH 5⅜″ ENCLOSURE DEPTH 5¾″	14½″	20″	13.2	15.2	18.0	19.5	22.0	26.5	31.0	35.7	40.2	44.8	49.7	53.7	58.5	63.2
	16½″	22″	14.3	16.5	19.0	21.3	23.7	28.7	33.5	38.7	44.3	48.5	53.7	58.5	63.2	68.7
	18½″	24″	14.7	17.3	19.7	22.3	25.0	30.2	35.5	41.0	47.0	50.7	57.2	62.5	68.0	73.3
	20½″	26″	15.5	18.0	20.5	23.0	26.0	31.7	37.2	43.0	49.0	54.7	59.7	66.0	71.5	76.7
	22½″	28″	16.5	19.0	21.3	24.0	27.0	32.0	38.7	44.7	51.0	57.0	62.3	68.7	74.5	80.5
	24½″	30″	17.3	19.7	21.7	25.0	27.0	34.0	39.0	46.2	52.7	59.0	65.0	71.7	77.3	83.5
	26½″	32″	17.7	20.3	22.3	25.7	28.7	35.0	41.3	47.7	54.3	60.7	67.0	73.5	79.8	86.3
	28½″	34″	18.3	20.7	22.7	26.2	29.3	36.0	42.5	49.0	55.7	62.3	68.7	75.5	82.0	88.5
	30½″	36″	18.7	21.3	23.3	26.7	29.7	36.7	43.5	50.0	57.2	63.5	70.2	77.2	84.0	90.5
	32½″	38″	19.3	21.8	23.8	27.3	30.8	37.3	44.5	51.0	58.7	64.5	71.8	78.7	85.7	92.0
	34½″	40″	19.9	22.7	24.6	28.0	31.5	38.0	45.5	52.0	60.0	65.5	73.2	80.0	87.7	93.0

ENCLOSURE LENGTH	Height—Types WS and WR	Height—Types ES and ER	15″	17½″	20″	22½″	25″	30″	35″	40″	45″	50″	55″	60″	65″	70″
			sq. ft.	sq. ft.	sq. ft.	sq. ft.	sq. ft.	sq. ft.	sq. ft.	sq. ft.	sq. ft.	sq. ft.	sq. ft.	sq. ft.	sq. ft.	sq. ft.
ELEMENT DEPTH 8″ ENCLOSURE DEPTH 8⅜″	14½″	20″	18.5	21.5	24.5	28.3	31.7	38.0	45.5	52.3	59.7	66.7	73.5	80.5	87.5	94.3
	16½″	22″	20.3	23.5	25.0	30.0	33.7	41.0	48.2	55.2	63.5	71.2	78.7	86.5	93.5	101.2
	18½″	24″	22.5	25.0	27.2	31.5	35.5	43.3	50.7	59.5	67.2	75.2	83.2	91.5	98.7	107.2
	20½″	26″	23.5	26.0	28.5	33.0	37.0	45.2	53.5	62.0	70.7	78.7	87.0	95.7	103.2	112.2
	22½″	28″	24.5	27.0	29.5	34.0	38.0	46.7	55.2	64.0	73.0	81.2	90.0	99.0	107.0	115.7
	24½″	30″	25.7	27.8	30.2	34.7	39.0	48.0	56.7	65.7	74.7	83.2	92.5	101.5	110.0	118.7
	26½″	32″	25.7	28.3	30.7	35.2	40.0	49.0	58.0	67.0	76.0	85.0	94.5	103.5	112.2	121.2
	28½″	34″	26.3	28.7	31.2	35.7	40.7	49.7	59.0	68.2	77.2	86.7	96.2	105.2	114.5	123.5
	30½″	36″	26.7	29.3	31.7	36.5	41.2	50.5	60.0	69.5	78.7	88.0	97.5	106.7	116.5	125.5
	32½″	38″	27.3	29.8	32.3	37.4	41.8	51.4	60.4	70.3	80.2	89.0	98.4	108.2	118.5	127.0
	34½″	40″	27.8	30.3	33.0	38.3	42.5	52.0	62.0	70.8	80.7	89.8	99.0	109.7	119.2	128.0

ENCLOSURE LENGTH	Height—Types WS and WR	Height—Types ES and ER	15″	17½″	20″	22½″	25″	30″	35″	40″	45″	50″	55″	60″	65″	70″
			sq. ft.	sq. ft.	sq. ft.	sq. ft.	sq. ft.	sq. ft.	sq. ft.	sq. ft.	sq. ft.	sq. ft.	sq. ft.	sq. ft.	sq. ft.	sq. ft.
ELEMENT DEPTH 10⅝″ ENCLOSURE DEPTH 11″	14½″	20″	23.2	26.7	29.7	34.5	38.7	47.2	56.2	64.7	73.7	82.2	91.2	100.0	108.5	117.0
	16½″	22″	25.2	28.7	32.2	36.7	41.2	50.2	59.7	68.7	78.2	87.7	97.5	107.0	115.5	124.5
	18½″	24″	27.0	30.2	33.5	38.2	43.0	53.0	62.5	72.0	82.0	92.2	102.2	112.0	121.2	130.7
	20½″	26″	28.7	31.7	34.7	39.7	45.0	55.0	65.2	75.5	85.5	96.0	106.0	116.2	126.2	137.0
	22½″	28″	30.0	33.0	36.0	41.2	46.7	57.0	67.7	78.5	88.7	99.5	110.2	120.7	131.2	142.0
	24½″	30″	31.0	34.0	37.0	42.5	48.2	58.7	70.0	81.2	92.0	103.0	113.2	125.0	135.0	146.7
	26½″	32″	32.0	35.0	38.0	43.5	49.5	60.5	72.0	83.5	94.7	106.0	117.2	129.0	139.7	151.5
	28½″	34″	33.2	36.0	38.7	44.5	50.7	62.2	74.0	85.7	97.2	108.2	120.5	132.7	144.0	156.0
	30½″	36″	34.5	37.0	39.5	45.5	52.0	63.7	76.0	88.0	100.0	111.7	123.7	135.7	148.0	160.0
	32½″	38″	35.4	37.9	40.5	46.5	53.0	64.9	78.0	90.0	102.0	113.8	125.8	138.5	151.0	164.0
	34½″	40″	36.2	38.7	41.4	47.4	53.8	65.8	79.7	91.5	102.8	114.5	126.6	139.4	152.5	167.0

MODINE MANUFACTURING COMPANY

Racine, Wisconsin

Modine Copper Convectors

Enclosure Types and Convector Ratings

Below: Modine convectors may be identified by the name plate on the top half of the unit, on the damper. This applies only to F and W units. Other types have the name Modine embossed on the lower right hand front of unit.

RATINGS FOR MODINE COPPER CONVECTORS, TYPE "S"*

*(Note: Ratings are based on sq. ft. EDR, at 215 degree steam and 65 degree entering air temperature)

ENCLOSURE LENGTH			20″	24″	28″	32″	36″	40″	44″	48″	56″	64″
			sq. ft.	sq. ft.	sq. ft.	sq. ft.	sq. ft.	sq. ft.	sq. ft.	sq. ft.	sq. ft.	sq. ft.
ENCLOSURE DEPTH 6″	Enclosure Height Actual Height 4½″	18″	....	....	....	....	....	....	....	....	....	....
		20″	16.0	21.0	26.0	30.0	35.0	40.0	44.0	49.0	58.0	68.0
		24″	18.0	22.0	28.0	33.0	38.0	43.0	48.0	53.0	63.0	73.0
		32″	18.0	24.0	29.0	34.0	40.0	45.0	50.0	55.0	66.0	76.0

ENCLOSURE LENGTH			20″	24″	28″	32″	36″	40″	44″	48″	56″	64″
			sq. ft.	sq. ft.	sq. ft.	sq. ft.	sq. ft.	sq. ft.	sq. ft.	sq. ft.	sq. ft.	sq. ft.
ENCLOSURE DEPTH 8″	Enclosure Height	18″	....	....	....	....	....	....	....	....	....	....
		20″	....	....	....	40.0	46.0	52.0	....	64.0	77.0	89.0
		24″	....	....	....	43.0	49.0	56.0	....	69.0	82.0	96.0
		32″	....	....	....	46.0	53.0	60.0	....	74.0	88.0	102.0

ENCLOSURE LENGTH			20″	24″	28″	32″	36″	40″	44″	48″	56″	64″
			sq. ft.	sq. ft.	sq. ft.	sq. ft.	sq. ft.	sq. ft.	sq. ft.	sq. ft.	sq. ft.	sq. ft.
ENCLOSURE DEPTH 10″	Enclosure Height	18″	....	....	....	....	....	....	....	....	....	....
		20″	....	....	....	....	54.0	61.0	....	76.0	90.0	104.0
		24″	....	....	....	....	59.0	67.0	....	83.0	99.0	114.0
		32″	....	....	....	....	65.0	74.0	....	91.0	108.0	126.0

Left: Modine type "F" copper convector identification. In checking size and rating, use actual measurements.

Right: Type "W" Modine copper convectors. Use actual measurements to check rating on tables below. Enclosure height equals actual height plus $4\frac{1}{2}$ in. from floor.

(Ratings continued on following page)

RATINGS FOR MODINE COPPER CONVECTORS, TYPES "F" and "W"*

*(Note: Ratings are based on sq. ft. EDR, at 215 degree steam and 65 degree entering air temperature)

ENCLOSURE LENGTH		20″	24″	28″	32″	36″	40″	44″	48″	56″	64″
	Enclosure Height	sq. ft.	sq. ft.	sq. ft.	sq. ft.	sq. ft.	sq. ft.	sq. ft.	sq. ft.	sq. ft.	sq. ft.
ENCLOSURE DEPTH 4″	18″	9.0	12.0	14.0	17.0	20.0	22.0	25.0	28.0	33.0	38.0
	20″	10.0	13.0	16.0	19.0	22.0	25.0	27.0	30.0	36.0	42.0
	24″	11.0	15.0	18.0	21.0	24.0	28.0	31.0	34.0	40.0	47.0
	32″	12.0	16.0	19.0	23.0	26.0	30.0	33.0	37.0	44.0	51.0

ENCLOSURE LENGTH		20″	24″	28″	32″	36″	40″	44″	48″	56″	64″
	Enclosure Height	sq. ft.	sq. ft.	sq. ft.	sq. ft.	sq. ft.	sq. ft.	sq. ft.	sq. ft.	sq. ft.	sq. ft.
ENCLOSURE DEPTH 6″	18″	14.0	18.0	21.0	25.0	29.0	33.0	37.0	41.0	49.0	56.0
	20″	15.0	19.0	23.0	27.0	32.0	36.0	40.0	44.0	53.0	61.0
	24″	17.0	22.0	26.0	31.0	36.0	41.0	45.0	50.0	60.0	69.0
	32″	18.0	23.0	28.0	33.0	39.0	44.0	49.0	54.0	64.0	75.0

ENCLOSURE LENGTH		20″	24″	28″	32″	36″	40″	44″	48″	56″	64″
	Enclosure Height	sq. ft.	sq. ft.	sq. ft.	sq. ft.	sq. ft.	sq. ft.	sq. ft.	sq. ft.	sq. ft.	sq. ft.
ENCLOSURE DEPTH 8″	18″	....	....	....	31.0	36.0	41.0	....	50.0	60.0	69.0
	20″	....	....	....	34.0	39.0	44.0	....	54.0	64.0	75.0
	24″	....	....	....	38.0	44.0	50.0	....	61.0	73.0	85.0
	32″	....	....	....	41.0	47.0	53.0	....	66.0	78.0	91.0

ENCLOSURE LENGTH		20″	24″	28″	32″	36″	40″	44″	48″	56″	64″
	Enclosure Height	sq. ft.	sq. ft.	sq. ft.	sq. ft.	sq. ft.	sq. ft.	sq. ft.	sq. ft.	sq. ft.	sq. ft.
ENCLOSURE DEPTH 10″	18″	....	....	....	....	41.0	46.0	....	57.0	68.0	79.0
	20″	....	....	....	....	44.0	50.0	....	61.0	73.0	84.0
	24″	....	....	....	....	50.0	56.0	....	69.0	83.0	96.0
	32″	....	....	....	....	53.0	60.0	....	74.0	88.0	103.0

MODINE MFG. COMPANY

(Continued from previous page)

Enclosure Styles and Convector Ratings for Types "IF" and "IW".

Modine Mfg. Company Type "IF" convector. Use actual dimensions.

Modine Mfg. Company's type "IW" convector. Use actual measurements. Height equals actual measurements plus 4½ in.

RATINGS FOR MODINE COPPER CONVECTORS, TYPES "IF" and "IW"*

*(Note: Ratings are given in sq. ft. EDR, based on 215 degree steam and 65 degree entering air temperature)

ENCLOSURE LENGTH			20″	24″	28″	32″	36″	40″	44″	48″	56″	64″
			sq. ft.	sq. ft.	sq. ft.	sq. ft.	sq. ft.	sq. ft.	sq. ft.	sq. ft.	sq. ft.	sq. ft.
ENCLOSURE DEPTH 4″	Enclosure Height	20″	10.0	13.0	16.0	18.0	21.0	24.0	27.0	30.0	35.0	41.0
		24″	11.0	14.0	17.0	21.0	24.0	27.0	30.0	33.0	39.0	46.0
		32″	12.0	16.0	19.0	23.0	26.0	30.0	33.0	37.0	44.0	51.0

ENCLOSURE LENGTH			20″	24″	28″	32″	36″	40″	44″	48″	56″	64″
			sq. ft.	sq. ft.	sq. ft.	sq. ft.	sq. ft.	sq. ft.	sq. ft.	sq. ft.	sq. ft.	sq. ft.
ENCLOSURE DEPTH 6″	Enclosure Height	20″	14.0	18.0	22.0	26.0	30.0	34.0	38.0	42.0	50.0	58.0
		24″	16.0	20.0	25.0	29.0	33.0	38.0	42.0	47.0	56.0	65.0
		32″	18.0	23.0	28.0	33.0	38.0	43.0	48.0	53.0	63.0	73.0

ENCLOSURE LENGTH			20″	24″	28″	32″	36″	40″	44″	48″	56″	64″
			sq. ft.	sq. ft.	sq. ft.	sq. ft.	sq. ft.	sq. ft.	sq. ft.	sq. ft.	sq. ft.	sq. ft.
ENCLOSURE DEPTH 8″	Enclosure Height	20″	....	....	....	31.0	35.0	40.0	....	50.0	59.0	68.0
		24″	....	....	....	35.0	40.0	46.0	....	56.0	67.0	78.0
		32″	....	....	....	39.0	45.0	51.0	....	64.0	76.0	88.0

ENCLOSURE LENGTH			20″	24″	28″	32″	36″	40″	44″	48″	56″	64″
			sq. ft.	sq. ft.	sq. ft.	sq. ft.	sq. ft.	sq. ft.	sq. ft.	sq. ft.	sq. ft.	sq. ft.
ENCLOSURE DEPTH 10″	Enclosure Height	20″	....	....	....	....	41.0	46.0	....	57.0	68.0	79.0
		24″	....	....	....	....	46.0	52.0	....	65.0	77.0	89.0
		32″	....	....	....	....	52.0	58.0	....	72.0	86.0	100.0

Right: Type "S" and "IS" Modine convector enclosure style. Please note that Modine Types "IF", "IW" and "IS" are institutional convectors, having heavy gage enclosures and close spacing between grille bars. Use actual measurements.

RATINGS FOR MODINE COPPER CONVECTORS, TYPE "IS"*

*(Note: Ratings are given in sq. ft. EDR, based on 215 degree steam and 65 degree entering air temperature)

ENCLOSURE LENGTH			20″	24″	28″	32″	36″	40″	44″	48″	56″	64″
			sq. ft.	sq. ft.	sq. ft.	sq. ft.	sq. ft.	sq. ft.	sq. ft.	sq. ft.	sq. ft.	sq. ft.
ENCLOSURE DEPTH 6″	Enclosure Height	20″	16.0	21.0	26.0	30.0	35.0	40.0	44.0	49.0	58.0	68.0
		24″	18.0	23.0	29.0	33.0	38.0	43.0	48.0	53.0	63.0	73.0
		32″	18.0	24.0	29.0	34.0	40.0	45.0	50.0	55.0	66.0	76.0

RATINGS FOR MODINE COPPER CONVECTORS, TYPE "IS"*

*(Note: Ratings are given in sq. ft. EDR, based on 215 degree steam and 65 degree entering air temperature)

ENCLOSURE LENGTH			20″	24″	28″	32″	36″	40″	44″	48″	56″	64″
			sq. ft.	sq. ft.	sq. ft.	sq. ft.	sq. ft.	sq. ft.	sq. ft.	sq. ft.	sq. ft.	sq. ft.
ENCLOSURE DEPTH 8″	Enclosure Height	20″	....	....	....	40.0	46.0	52.0	....	64.0	77.0	89.0
		24″	....	....	....	43.0	49.0	56.0	....	60.0	82.0	96.0
		32″	....	....	....	46.0	53.0	60.0	....	74.0	88.0	102.0

RATINGS FOR MODINE COPPER CONVECTORS, TYPE "IS"*

*(Note: Ratings are given in sq. ft. EDR, based on 215 degree steam and 65 degree entering air temperature)

ENCLOSURE LENGTH			20″	24″	28″	32″	36″	40″	44″	48″	56″	64″
			sq. ft.	sq. ft.	sq. ft.	sq. ft.	sq. ft.	sq. ft.	sq. ft.	sq. ft.	sq. ft.	sq. ft.
ENCLOSURE DEPTH 10″	Enclosure Height	20″	....	....	....	....	54.0	61.0	....	76.0	90.0	104.0
		24″	....	....	....	....	59.0	67.0	....	83.0	99.0	114.0
		32″	....	....	....	....	65.0	74.0	....	91.0	108.0	126.0

MODINE MANUFACTURING CO.

Racine, Wisconsin

"STANDARD," "HIFLO," "TURBOFLO" AND "RED CAP" CONVECTORS

(No longer manufactured)

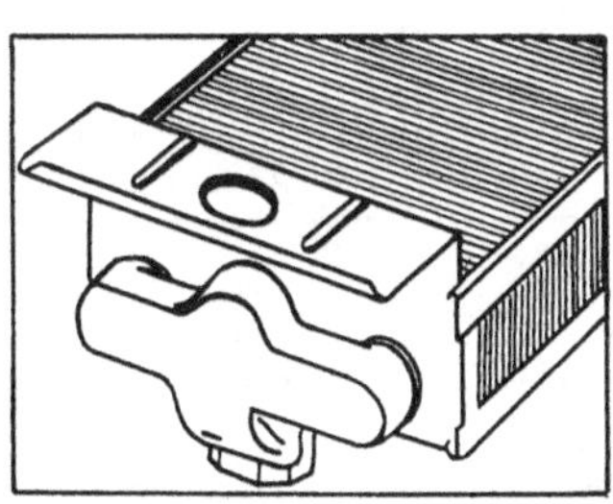

Standard, Hiflo and Turboflow convectors. Note header arrangement and mounting bracket.

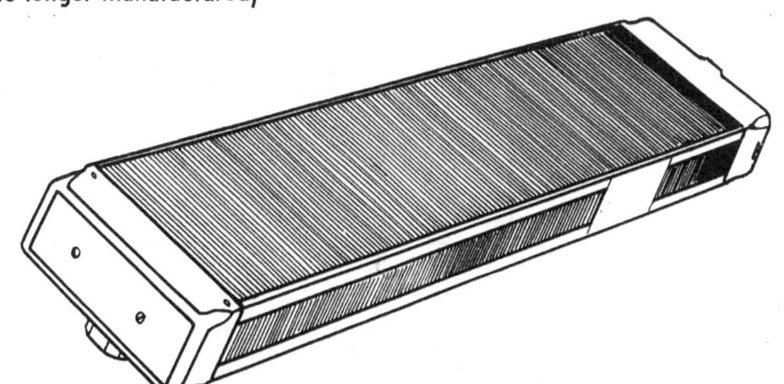

Red Cap Convector. Note red headers and nameplate on element side.

GRILLE TYPES AND MEASURING INSTRUMENTS

Free Standing Enclosure—Type FC—L—Actual; H—Actual; D—Actual—¼".

Semi-Recessed Enclosure—Type PR—L—Actual—2½"; H—Actual—1¼"; D—Actual—¼"

Recessed Enclosure—Type FR—L—Actual—2½"; H—Actual—1¼"; D—Actual—¼".

Plaster Front—Type C—L—Actual—2"; H—Actual—1"; D—Actual—¾"

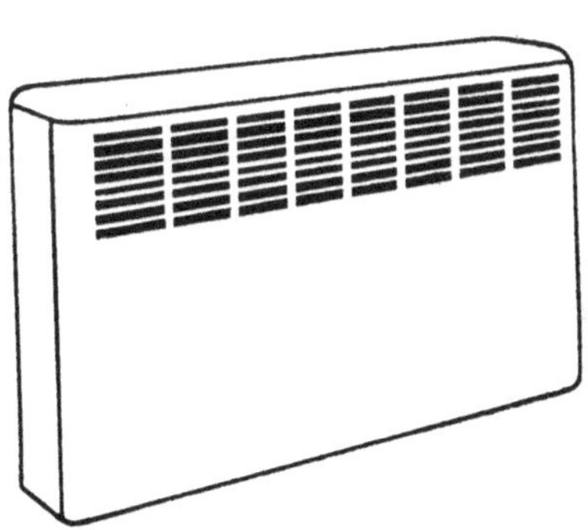

Wall Hung—Flat Top—Type RWC—L—Actual; H—Actual from floor; D—Actual—¼".

Wall Hung—Sloping Top—Type SWC—L—Actual; H—Actual from floor; D—Actual—¼".

NATIONAL CONVECTOR RATINGS, TYPE "S"

MODINE "STANDARD", "HIFLO", "TURBOFLO" AND "RED CAP" CONVECTORS

STEAM CAPACITIES★

Convector Manufacturers' Association Certified Ratings Based on Standard Code of A. S. H. & V. E.
At 240 Btu. per Sq. Ft. Based on 215° Steam, 65° Entering Air Guaranteed for maximum pressure 50 lbs. saturated steam.

D=Depth of heating unit in inches	†L=Length of enclosure in inches	H=Height of Enclosure in inches for Concealed, Recessed, Floor Cabinet													†L=Length of enclosure in inches
		18	20	22	24	26	28	30	32	36	40	44	50*	70*	
		H=Height of Enclosure in inches for Wall Cabinet													
		12¼	14¼	16¼	18¼	20¼	22¼	24¼	26¼	30¼	34¼	38¼			
		Sq. ft.	Sq. ft.	Sq. ft.	Sq. ft.	Sq. ft.	Sq. ft.	Sq. ft.	Sq. ft.	Sq. ft.	Sq. ft.	Sq. ft.	Sq. ft.	Sq. ft.	
3⅝	15	8.7	9.3	9.8	10.2	10.5	10.8	11.1	11.4	11.6	11.8	12.0	12.2	13.3	15
	17½	10.6	11.3	11.9	12.3	12.8	13.1	13.4	13.7	14.0	14.2	14.5	14.9	16.0	17½
	20	12.5	13.2	13.7	14.5	15.0	15.3	15.8	16.1	16.4	16.7	17.0	17.3	18.9	20
	22½	14.1	15.1	15.8	16.5	17.2	17.6	18.1	18.4	18.7	19.1	19.5	19.9	21.5	22½
	25	15.8	17.1	17.8	18.7	19.4	19.8	20.4	20.8	21.2	21.6	22.0	22.4	24.4	25
	30	19.6	21.0	21.8	22.8	23.8	24.4	25.0	25.4	26.1	26.4	26.9	27.6	29.9	30
	35	23.4	24.8	26.0	27.1	28.2	28.9	29.6	30.2	30.8	31.3	32.0	32.6	35.4	35
	40	26.9	28.7	30.0	31.4	32.6	33.4	34.2	34.9	35.6	36.2	36.8	37.8	41.0	40
	45	30.6	32.9	34.0	35.6	36.9	37.9	38.9	39.7	40.3	41.2	42.0	43.0	46.7	45
	50	34.3	36.5	38.2	39.9	41.5	42.5	43.5	44.4	45.3	46.0	46.9	48.0	52.1	50
	55	37.8	40.3	42.3	44.1	45.8	47.0	48.1	49.1	49.9	51.0	52.0	53.3	57.8	55
	60	41.5	44.3	46.4	48.4	50.2	51.4	52.6	53.8	54.9	56.1	56.9	58.2	63.4	60
5½	15	12.3	13.1	13.7	14.3	14.8	15.2	15.5	15.8	16.2	16.6	17.0	17.4	18.9	15
	17½	14.8	15.8	16.5	17.2	17.8	18.3	18.8	19.1	19.6	20.0	20.4	21.0	22.9	17½
	20	17.4	18.5	19.4	20.2	20.9	21.5	22.0	22.4	22.9	23.5	24.0	24.6	26.8	20
	22½	19.9	21.2	22.3	23.2	24.1	24.6	25.2	25.7	26.4	26.9	27.5	28.2	30.7	22½
	25	22.6	23.9	25.1	26.1	27.2	27.7	28.5	29.0	29.7	30.2	31.1	31.1	34.7	25
	30	27.7	29.5	30.8	32.0	33.3	34.1	35.0	35.6	36.4	37.2	38.2	39.1	42.6	30
	35	32.9	34.9	36.5	38.0	39.5	40.4	41.5	42.2	43.2	44.1	45.1	46.3	50.6	35
	40	37.4	40.4	42.2	43.9	45.6	46.7	48.0	48.8	49.9	51.0	52.2	53.6	58.4	40
	45	43.1	45.8	47.9	50.0	51.8	53.1	54.4	55.3	56.7	57.8	59.3	60.8	66.3	45
	50	48.2	51.2	53.6	55.7	58.1	59.3	60.8	62.0	63.3	64.8	66.2	68.1	74.3	50
	55	53.4	56.6	59.4	61.9	64.0	65.6	67.3	68.6	70.1	71.6	73.4	75.3	82.1	55
	60	58.4	62.1	65.0	67.7	70.4	72.1	73.8	75.1	76.9	78.5	80.5	82.6	90.1	60
7⅜	15	15.0	15.8	16.5	17.1	17.8	18.1	18.6	19.0	19.6	20.0	20.5	21.0	22.9	15
	17½	18.0	19.1	20.0	20.7	21.4	21.9	22.5	23.0	23.6	24.1	24.8	25.4	27.6	17½
	20	21.1	22.4	23.4	24.1	25.1	25.7	26.3	27.0	27.7	28.3	29.0	29.7	32.4	20
	22½	24.2	25.7	26.8	27.8	28.8	29.4	30.2	30.9	31.8	32.4	33.2	34.1	37.6	22½
	25	27.4	28.9	30.4	31.4	32.4	33.2	34.1	34.9	35.8	36.6	37.4	38.6	41.9	25
	30	33.5	35.5	37.3	38.4	39.8	40.7	41.9	42.8	44.0	44.9	46.0	47.3	51.4	30
	35	39.9	42.1	44.1	45.7	47.3	48.2	49.6	50.6	52.2	53.2	54.4	56.1	61.0	35
	40	46.1	48.7	50.9	52.8	54.6	55.8	57.4	58.6	60.2	61.5	63.0	64.7	70.5	40
	45	52.2	55.3	57.9	59.7	62.0	63.4	65.1	66.4	68.4	69.6	71.5	73.4	79.9	45
	50	58.5	61.8	64.8	66.0	69.3	70.8	72.8	74.4	76.5	78.0	79.8	82.2	89.5	50
	55	64.6	68.5	71.6	74.1	76.7	78.5	80.6	82.3	84.7	86.3	88.5	90.9	99.0	55
	60	70.9	75.0	78.5	81.2	84.0	86.0	88.2	90.2	92.6	94.5	97.0	99.5	108.8	60
9¼	15	17.2	18.2	19.0	19.6	20.3	20.8	21.4	21.8	22.5	23.1	23.6	24.3	26.6	15
	17½	20.7	21.8	22.9	23.7	24.4	25.2	26.0	26.4	27.1	27.8	28.6	29.2	32.1	17½
	20	24.3	25.7	26.7	27.7	28.7	29.4	30.2	31.0	31.8	32.7	33.4	34.4	37.6	20
	22½	27.9	29.4	30.7	31.8	32.9	33.7	34.6	35.4	36.4	37.4	38.4	39.4	43.1	22½
	25	31.4	33.2	34.6	35.9	37.2	38.0	39.0	40.0	41.1	42.2	43.3	44.4	48.6	25
	30	38.5	40.7	42.6	44.0	45.5	46.6	47.9	49.0	50.5	51.8	53.0	54.5	59.6	30
	35	45.7	48.3	50.4	52.2	54.0	55.3	56.7	58.1	59.8	61.4	62.9	64.7	70.7	35
	40	52.8	55.7	58.2	60.4	62.2	64.0	65.5	67.1	69.1	71.0	72.7	74.6	81.8	40
	45	60.0	63.4	66.1	68.5	70.8	72.4	74.3	76.1	78.4	80.6	82.6	84.7	92.7	45
	50	67.0	70.8	73.9	76.5	79.1	81.0	83.2	85.2	87.8	90.0	92.2	94.7	103.8	50
	55	74.2	78.5	81.9	84.6	87.5	89.7	92.0	94.3	97.2	99.7	102.1	104.7	114.7	55
	60	81.4	85.9	89.7	92.8	96.2	98.4	101.0	103.3	106.7	109.3	112.0	115.0	125.8	60
11⅛	15	19.5	20.7	21.4	22.2	22.9	23.4	24.0	24.5	25.1	25.7	26.5	27.3	29.6	15
	17½	23.6	24.9	25.9	26.8	27.7	28.2	28.9	29.6	30.4	31.0	32.0	32.9	35.7	17½
	20	27.6	29.2	30.3	31.4	32.5	33.2	33.9	34.6	35.5	36.4	37.4	38.4	41.9	20
	22½	31.6	33.4	34.8	36.0	37.1	37.9	38.8	39.6	40.6	41.7	42.8	44.1	47.9	22½
	25	35.6	37.6	39.2	40.6	41.9	43.0	43.9	44.8	46.0	47.0	48.3	49.8	54.1	25
	30	43.8	46.2	48.1	49.7	51.5	52.5	53.8	54.9	56.4	57.5	59.3	61.1	66.3	30
	35	51.7	54.9	57.0	59.0	61.0	62.3	63.6	65.0	66.6	68.2	70.2	72.3	78.5	35
	40	59.9	63.3	65.9	68.0	70.4	71.8	73.5	75.0	77.0	78.8	81.2	83.6	90.8	40
	45	67.9	71.8	74.8	77.3	79.9	81.6	83.5	85.1	87.5	89.5	92.3	94.9	102.8	45
	50	76.0	80.3	83.6	86.5	89.5	91.3	93.4	95.2	98.0	100.0	103.2	106.1	115.2	50
	55	84.0	88.9	92.5	95.7	98.9	100 8	103.3	105.3	108.2	110.8	114.0	117.3	128.2	55
	60	92.0	99.7	101.4	104.8	108.5	110.7	113.1	115.5	118.8	121.7	125.1	128.7	139.7	60

★NOTE: Net length of heating unit only is L-½".

THE NATIONAL RADIATOR COMPANY

Johnstown, Pennsylvania

National Non-Ferrous Convectors

Enclosure Types, Measuring Instructions and Convector Ratings

Left: Type "F" National non-ferrous convector is identified by this enclosure. Use actual measurements to obtain rating from the tables below.

Right: Type "S", wall hung, sloping top National non-ferrous convector enclosure. Use actual measurements for rating purposes.

RATINGS FOR NATIONAL CONVECTORS TYPE "F", "R", "O", "E" AND "P"*

*(Note: Ratings are given in sq. ft. steam)

ENCLOSURE LENGTH			20⅛″	24⅛″	28⅛″	32⅛″	36⅛″	40⅛″	44⅛″	48⅛″	56⅛″	64⅛″
	Enclosure Height Types	Enclosure Height All Other Types	sq. ft.	sq. ft.	sq. ft.	sq. ft.	sq. ft.	sq. ft.	sq. ft.	sq. ft.	sq. ft.	sq. ft.
ENCLOSURE DEPTH 4 3/16″	16″	20″	10.1	12.5	14.8	17.2	19.6	21.9	24.3	26.6	31.3	36.0
	20″	24″	11.9	14.7	17.4	20.2	22.9	25.7	28.5	31.2	36.8	42.3
	28″	32″	12.7	15.7	18.6	21.6	24.5	27.5	30.4	33.4	39.3	45.2

ENCLOSURE LENGTH			20⅛″	24⅛″	28⅛″	32⅛″	36⅛″	40⅛″	44⅛″	48⅛″	56⅛″	64⅛″
	Enclosure Height Types	Enclosure Height All Other Types	sq. ft.	sq. ft.	sq. ft.	sq. ft.	sq. ft.	sq. ft.	sq. ft.	sq. ft.	sq. ft.	sq. ft.
ENCLOSURE DEPTH 6 3/16″	16″	20″	14.3	17.8	21.4	25.0	28.5	32.1	35.6	39.3	46.3	53.4
	20″	24″	16.5	20.6	24.7	28.8	32.9	37.0	41.1	45.3	53.4	61.6
	28″	32″	17.7	22.1	26.5	30.9	35.4	39.8	44.2	48.6	57.4	66.2

ENCLOSURE LENGTH			20⅛″	24⅛″	28⅛″	32⅛″	36⅛″	40⅛″	44⅛″	48⅛″	56⅛″	64⅛″
	Enclosure Height Types	Enclosure Height All Other Types	sq. ft.	sq. ft.	sq. ft.	sq. ft.	sq. ft.	sq. ft.	sq. ft.	sq. ft.	sq. ft.	sq. ft.
ENCLOSURE DEPTH 8⅛″	16″	20″	......	......	......	33.1	37.9	42.6	......	52.1	61.6	71.0
	20″	24″	......	......	......	36.7	42.0	47.2	......	57.7	68.2	78.7
	28″	32″	......	......	......	39.2	44.8	50.4	......	61.6	72.8	83.9

ENCLOSURE LENGTH			20⅛″	24⅛″	28⅛″	32⅛″	36⅛″	40⅛″	44⅛″	44⅛″	56⅛″	64⅛″
	Enclosure Height Types	Enclosure Height All Other Types	sq. ft.	sq. ft.	sq. ft.	sq. ft.	sq. ft.	sq. ft.	sq. ft.	sq. ft.	sq. ft.	sq. ft.
ENCLOSURE DEPTH 10⅛″	16″	20″	......	......	......	......	44.5	50.1	......	61.2	72.4	83.5
	20″	24″	......	......	......	......	49.2	55.3	......	67.6	80.0	92.1
	28″	32″	......	......	......	......	52.6	59.2	......	72.4	85.4	98.6

NATIONAL CONVECTOR RATINGS, TYPE "S"

Types "R" and "D" National copper convectors are identified by this convector enclosure style. These units are fully recessed. For measuring, use the actual length and deduct 3 inches. Use the actual height and deduct 1 1/2 inches. Use the actual depth. Obtain rating for dimensions found from rating tables below.

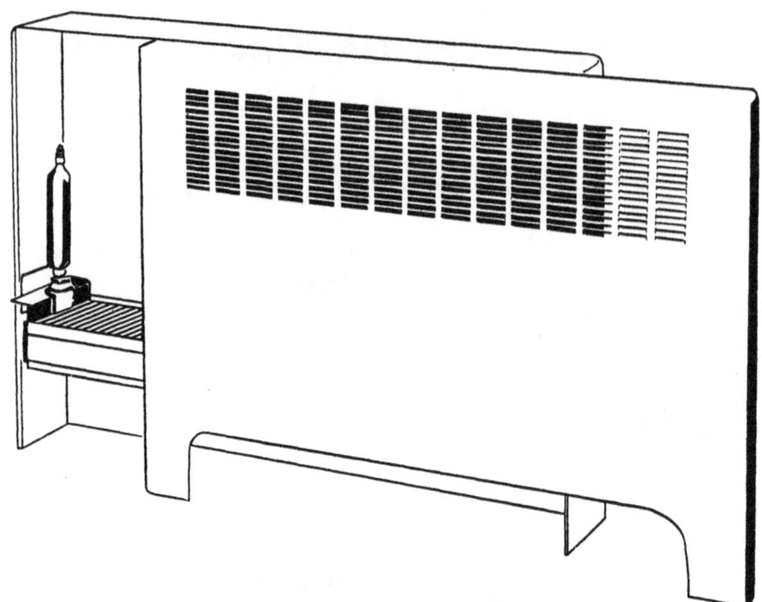

National copper convectors can generally be identified by checking the convector element set-up inside the enclosure, as shown in the drawing above. Ratings are the same for any convector regardless of convector enclosure or cabinet style.

RATINGS FOR NATIONAL CONVECTORS, TYPE "S"*

*(Ratings are given in sq. ft. E.D.R. for steam)

ENCLOSURE LENGTH	Enclosure Height	20 3/16″	24 3/16″	28 3/16″	32 3/16″	36 3/16″	40 3/16″	44 3/16″	48 3/16″	56 3/16″	64 3/16″
		sq. ft.	sq. ft.	sq. ft.	sq. ft.	sq. ft.	sq. ft.	sq. ft.	sq. ft.	sq. ft.	sq. ft.
ENCLOSURE DEPTH 6 3/16″	16″	16.4	20.5	24.6	28.7	32.7	36.8	40.9	45.0	53.2	61.3
	20″	17.8	22.2	26.7	31.1	35.6	40.0	44.4	48.8	57.7	66.6
	28″	19.3	24.1	28.9	33.7	38.5	43.3	48.2	53.0	62.6	72.2

ENCLOSURE LENGTH	Enclosure Height	20 3/16″	24 3/16″	28 3/16″	32 3/16″	36 3/16″	40 3/16″	44 3/16″	48 3/16″	56 3/16″	64 3/16″
		sq. ft.	sq. ft.	sq. ft.	sq. ft.	sq. ft.	sq. ft.	sq. ft.	sq. ft.	sq. ft.	sq. ft.
ENCLOSURE DEPTH 8 1/8″	16″	....	....	....	37.2	42.5	47.8	....	58.4	69.0	79.6
	20″	....	....	....	40.0	45.7	51.4	....	62.9	74.3	85.7
	28″	....	....	....	42.9	49.0	55.1	....	67.4	79.6	91.8

ENCLOSURE LENGTH	Enclosure Height	20 3/16″	24 3/16″	28 3/16″	32 3/16″	36 3/16″	40 3/16″	44 3/16″	48 3/16″	56 3/16″	64 3/16″
		sq. ft.	sq. ft.	sq. ft.	sq. ft.	sq. ft.	sq. ft.	sq. ft.	sq. ft.	sq. ft.	sq. ft.
ENCLOSURE DEPTH 10 1/8″	16″	....	....	....	....	50.4	56.6	....	69.2	81.8	94.4
	20″	....	....	....	....	54.2	61.0	....	74.6	88.0	101.6
	28″	....	....	....	....	56.9	64.0	....	78.3	92.4	106.7

THE NATIONAL RADIATOR COMPANY

Johnstown, Pennsylvania

National "Aero" Cast Iron Convectors

Enclosure Types and Measuring Instructions

Right: This convector element identifies National cast iron convectors of all types mentioned.

Type "RE" National convector, complete enclosure. For measuring and checking rating against the tables at right, use actual length, height and depth.

Type "OE" complete enclosure, recessed. For measurements use actual length less 1½ inches, actual height less ½ inch and actual depth.

Type "SW" National Convector, sloping top enclosure. Use actual dimensions of the unit, including length, height and depth.

Types "RF" and "EF", front panels only. For measurements, use actual length less 2 inches, actual height less 1 inch and actual depth.

RATINGS FOR NATIONAL "AERO" CAST IRON CONVECTORS*

*(Note: Ratings are given in sq. ft. for steam)

ELEMENT LENGTH		16"	18"	20"	22"	24"	26"	28"	30"	32"	34"	36"	38"	40"	42"	44"	46"	48"
ENCLOSURE LENGTH		19"	21"	23"	25"	27"	29"	31"	33"	35"	37"	39"	41"	43"	45"	47"	49"	51"
ENCLOSURE DEPTH 3¾" — Height of Enclosure	20"	10.0	11.0	12.0	14.0	15.0	16.0	17.0	18.0	20.0	21.0	22.0	23.0	25.0	26.0	27.0	28.0	29.0
	23"	11.0	12.0	13.0	15.0	16.0	17.0	18.0	20.0	21.0	22.0	24.0	25.0	26.0	28.0	29.0	30.0	32.0
	26"	11.0	12.0	14.0	15.0	17.0	18.0	19.0	21.0	22.0	24.0	25.0	26.0	28.0	29.0	31.0	32.0	33.0
	29"	12.0	13.0	14.0	16.0	17.0	19.0	20.0	22.0	23.0	25.0	26.0	27.0	29.0	30.0	32.0	33.0	35.0
	32"	12.0	13.0	15.0	16.0	18.0	19.0	21.0	22.0	24.0	25.0	27.0	28.0	30.0	31.0	33.0	34.0	36.0

ELEMENT LENGTH		50"	52"	54"	56"	58"	60"	62"	64"	66"	68"	70"	72"	74"	76"	78"	80"	82"
ENCLOSURE LENGTH		53"	55"	57"	59"	61"	63"	65"	67"	69"	71"	73"	75"	77"	79"	81"	82"	85"
ENCLOSURE DEPTH 3¾" — Height of Enclosure	20"	31.0	32.0	33.0	34.0	36.0	37.0	38.0	39.0	41.0	42.0	43.0	44.0	45.0	47.0	48.0	49.0	50.0
	23"	33.0	34.0	36.0	37.0	38.0	39.0	41.0	42.0	43.0	45.0	46.0	47.0	49.0	50.0	51.0	53.0	54.0
	26"	35.0	36.0	37.0	39.0	40.0	42.0	43.0	44.0	46.0	47.0	49.0	50.0	51.0	53.0	54.0	55.0	57.0
	29"	36.0	38.0	39.0	40.0	42.0	43.0	45.0	46.0	48.0	49.0	51.0	52.0	53.0	55.0	56.0	58.0	59.0
	32"	37.0	39.0	40.0	42.0	43.0	45.0	46.0	48.0	49.0	51.0	52.0	53.0	55.0	56.0	58.0	59.0	61.0

NATIONAL AERO CONVECTOR RATINGS (Note: Ratings are given in Sq. Ft. Steam)

ELEMENT LENGTH		16"	18"	20"	22"	24"	26"	28"	30"	32"	34"	36"	38"	40"	42"	44"	46"	48"	50"	52"	54"	56"	58"	60"	62"	64"	66"	68"	70"	72"	74"	76"	78"	80"	82"
ENCLOSURE LENGTH		19"	21"	23"	25"	27"	29"	31"	33"	35"	37"	39"	41"	43"	45"	47"	49"	51"	53"	55"	57"	59"	61"	63"	65"	67"	69"	71"	73"	75"	77"	79"	81"	82"	85"
ENCLOSURE DEPTH 4⅜"	Height of Enclosure 20"	10.0	11.0	13.0	14.0	15.0	16.0	18.0	19.0	20.0	21.0	23.0	24.0	25.0	26.0	28.0	29.0	30.0	31.0	33.0	34.0	35.0	36.0	38.0	39.0	40.0	41.0	42.0	44.0	45.0	46.0	47.0	49.0	50.0	51.0
	23"	11.0	13.0	14.0	15.0	17.0	18.0	19.0	21.0	22.0	24.0	25.0	26.0	28.0	29.0	31.0	32.0	33.0	35.0	36.0	38.0	39.0	40.0	42.0	43.0	44.0	46.0	47.0	49.0	50.0	51.0	53.0	54.0	56.0	57.0
	26"	12.0	13.0	15.0	16.0	18.0	19.0	21.0	22.0	24.0	25.0	27.0	28.0	30.0	31.0	33.0	34.0	35.0	37.0	38.0	40.0	41.0	43.0	44.0	46.0	47.0	49.0	50.0	52.0	53.0	55.0	56.0	58.0	59.0	60.0
	29"	12.0	14.0	15.0	17.0	18.0	20.0	21.0	23.0	24.0	26.0	27.0	29.0	30.0	32.0	33.0	35.0	36.0	38.0	39.0	41.0	42.0	44.0	45.0	47.0	48.0	50.0	51.0	53.0	54.0	56.0	57.0	59.0	60.0	62.0
	32"	13.0	14.0	16.0	17.0	19.0	20.0	22.0	23.0	25.0	27.0	28.0	30.0	31.0	33.0	34.0	36.0	38.0	39.0	41.0	42.0	44.0	45.0	47.0	48.0	50.0	52.0	53.0	55.0	56.0	58.0	59.0	61.0	63.0	64.0

ELEMENT LENGTH		16"	18"	20"	22"	24"	26"	28"	30"	32"	34"	36"	38"	40"	42"	44"	46"	48"	50"	52"	54"	56"	58"	60"	62"	64"	66"	68"	70"	72"	74"	76"	78"	80"	82"
ENCLOSURE LENGTH		19"	21"	23"	25"	27"	29"	31"	33"	35"	37"	39"	41"	43"	45"	47"	49"	51"	53"	55"	57"	59"	61"	63"	65"	67"	69"	71"	73"	75"	77"	79"	81"	82"	85"
ENCLOSURE DEPTH 5⅞"	Height of Enclosure 20"	11.0	13.0	14.0	16.0	17.0	19.0	20.0	21.0	23.0	24.0	26.0	27.0	28.0	30.0	31.0	33.0	34.0	36.0	37.0	38.0	40.0	41.0	43.0	44.0	46.0	47.0	48.0	50.0	51.0	53.0	54.0	55.0	57.0	58.0
	21"	13.0	14.0	16.0	18.0	19.0	21.0	22.0	24.0	26.0	27.0	29.0	30.0	32.0	34.0	35.0	37.0	38.0	40.0	42.0	43.0	45.0	46.0	48.0	50.0	51.0	53.0	54.0	56.0	58.0	59.0	61.0	62.0	64.0	66.0
	23"	14.0	15.0	17.0	19.0	20.0	22.0	24.0	26.0	27.0	29.0	31.0	32.0	34.0	36.0	37.0	39.0	41.0	43.0	44.0	46.0	48.0	49.0	51.0	53.0	54.0	56.0	58.0	60.0	61.0	63.0	65.0	66.0	68.0	70.0
	26"	15.0	17.0	19.0	20.0	22.0	24.0	26.0	28.0	30.0	32.0	33.0	35.0	37.0	39.0	41.0	43.0	45.0	46.0	48.0	50.0	52.0	54.0	56.0	58.0	59.0	61.0	63.0	65.0	67.0	69.0	71.0	72.0	74.0	76.0
	29"	16.0	18.0	20.0	22.0	24.0	26.0	28.0	30.0	32.0	33.0	35.0	37.0	39.0	41.0	43.0	45.0	47.0	49.0	51.0	53.0	55.0	57.0	59.0	61.0	63.0	65.0	67.0	69.0	71.0	73.0	75.0	77.0	79.0	81.0
	32"	16.0	18.0	20.0	22.0	24.0	26.0	28.0	31.0	33.0	35.0	37.0	39.0	41.0	43.0	45.0	47.0	49.0	51.0	53.0	55.0	57.0	59.0	61.0	63.0	65.0	67.0	69.0	71.0	73.0	75.0	77.0	79.0	81.0	83.0

ELEMENT LENGTH		16"	18"	20"	22"	24"	26"	28"	30"	32"	34"	36"	38"	40"	42"	44"	46"	48"	50"	52"	54"	56"	58"	60"	62"	64"	66"	68"	70"	72"	74"	76"	78"	80"	82"
ENCLOSURE LENGTH		19"	21"	23"	25"	27"	29"	31"	33"	35"	37"	39"	41"	43"	45"	47"	49"	51"	53"	55"	57"	59"	61"	63"	65"	67"	69"	71"	73"	75"	77"	79"	81"	82"	85"
ONE PIPE STEAM ONLY ENCLOSURE DEPTH 8"	Height of Enclosure 20"	15.0	17.0	19.0	21.0	23.0	24.0	26.0	28.0	30.0	32.0	34.0	36.0	38.0	39.0	41.0	43.0	45.0	47.0	49.0	51.0	53.0	54.0	56.0	58.0	60.0	62.0	64.0	66.0	68.0	69.0	71.0	73.0	75.0	77.0
	23"	16.0	19.0	21.0	23.0	25.0	27.0	29.0	31.0	33.0	35.0	37.0	39.0	41.0	43.0	45.0	47.0	49.0	51.0	53.0	55.0	57.0	59.0	62.0	64.0	66.0	68.0	70.0	72.0	74.0	76.0	78.0	80.0	82.0	84.0
	26"	18.0	20.0	22.0	24.0	26.0	28.0	31.0	33.0	35.0	37.0	39.0	42.0	44.0	46.0	48.0	50.0	52.0	55.0	57.0	59.0	61.0	63.0	66.0	68.0	70.0	72.0	74.0	76.0	79.0	81.0	83.0	85.0	87.0	90.0
	29"	18.0	21.0	23.0	25.0	27.0	30.0	32.0	34.0	36.0	39.0	41.0	43.0	46.0	48.0	50.0	52.0	55.0	57.0	59.0	62.0	64.0	66.0	68.0	71.0	73.0	75.0	77.0	80.0	82.0	84.0	87.0	89.0	91.0	93.0
	32"	19.0	21.0	23.0	26.0	28.0	30.0	33.0	35.0	37.0	40.0	42.0	45.0	47.0	49.0	52.0	54.0	56.0	59.0	61.0	63.0	66.0	68.0	70.0	73.0	75.0	77.0	80.0	82.0	84.0	87.0	89.0	91.0	94.0	96.0

ELEMENT LENGTH		16"	18"	20"	22"	24"	26"	28"	30"	32"	34"	36"	38"	40"	42"	44"	46"	48"	50"	52"	54"	56"	58"	60"	62"	64"	66"	68"	70"	72"	74"	76"	78"	80"	82"
ENCLOSURE LENGTH		19"	21"	23"	25"	27"	29"	31"	33"	35"	37"	39"	41"	43"	45"	47"	49"	51"	53"	55"	57"	59"	61"	63"	65"	67"	69"	71"	73"	75"	77"	79"	81"	82"	85"
WATER, VAPOR OR VACUUM ENCLOSURE DEPTH 8"	Height of Enclosure 20"	16.0	18.0	20.0	22.0	24.0	26.0	29.0	31.0	33.0	35.0	37.0	39.0	41.0	43.0	45.0	47.0	49.0	51.0	53.0	55.0	57.0	59.0	61.0	63.0	65.0	67.0	69.0	71.0	73.0	75.0	77.0	79.0	82.0	84.0
	23"	19.0	21.0	23.0	26.0	28.0	30.0	33.0	35.0	37.0	39.0	42.0	44.0	46.0	49.0	51.0	53.0	56.0	58.0	60.0	63.0	65.0	67.0	70.0	72.0	74.0	77.0	79.0	81.0	84.0	86.0	88.0	91.0	93.0	95.0
	26"	20.0	23.0	25.0	28.0	30.0	33.0	35.0	38.0	40.0	43.0	45.0	48.0	50.0	53.0	55.0	58.0	61.0	63.0	66.0	68.0	71.0	73.0	76.0	78.0	81.0	83.0	86.0	88.0	91.0	93.0	96.0	98.0	101.0	103.0
	29"	21.0	24.0	27.0	30.0	32.0	35.0	38.0	40.0	43.0	46.0	48.0	51.0	54.0	56.0	59.0	62.0	64.0	67.0	70.0	72.0	75.0	78.0	80.0	83.0	86.0	88.0	91.0	94.0	97.0	99.0	102.0	105.0	107.0	110.0
	32"	22.0	25.0	28.0	31.0	34.0	36.0	39.0	42.0	45.0	48.0	50.0	53.0	56.0	59.0	62.0	64.0	67.0	70.0	73.0	76.0	78.0	81.0	84.0	87.0	90.0	92.0	95.0	98.0	101.0	104.0	106.0	109.0	112.0	115.0

ELEMENT LENGTH		16"	18"	20"	22"	24"	26"	28"	30"	32"	34"	36"	38"	40"	42"	44"	46"	48"	50"	52"	54"	56"	58"	60"	62"	64"	66"	68"	70"	72"	74"	76"	78"	80"	82"
ENCLOSURE LENGTH		19"	21"	23"	25"	27"	29"	31"	33"	35"	37"	39"	41"	43"	45"	47"	49"	51"	53"	55"	57"	59"	61"	63"	65"	67"	69"	71"	73"	75"	77"	79"	81"	82"	85"
ENCLOSURE DEPTH 9½"	Height of Enclosure 21"	19.0	21.0	23.0	25.0	28.0	30.0	32.0	35.0	37.0	39.0	42.0	44.0	46.0	49.0	51.0	53.0	56.0	58.0	60.0	63.0	65.0	67.0	69.0	72.0	74.0	76.0	79.0	81.0	83.0	86.0	88.0	90.0	93.0	95.0
	23"	20.0	23.0	25.0	28.0	30.0	33.0	35.0	38.0	41.0	43.0	46.0	48.0	51.0	53.0	56.0	58.0	61.0	63.0	66.0	68.0	71.0	73.0	76.0	79.0	81.0	84.0	86.0	89.0	91.0	94.0	96.0	99.0	101.0	104.0
	26"	22.0	25.0	28.0	31.0	33.0	36.0	39.0	42.0	44.0	47.0	50.0	53.0	56.0	58.0	61.0	64.0	67.0	69.0	72.0	75.0	78.0	80.0	83.0	86.0	89.0	92.0	94.0	97.0	100.0	103.0	105.0	108.0	111.0	114.0
	29"	23.0	26.0	29.0	32.0	35.0	37.0	40.0	43.0	46.0	49.0	52.0	55.0	58.0	61.0	63.0	66.0	69.0	72.0	75.0	78.0	81.0	84.0	86.0	89.0	92.0	95.0	98.0	101.0	104.0	107.0	109.0	112.0	115.0	118.0
	32"	28.0	32.0	35.0	39.0	42.0	46.0	50.0	53.0	57.0	60.0	64.0	67.0	71.0	74.0	78.0	81.0	85.0	88.0	92.0	96.0	99.0	103.0	106.0	110.0	113.0	117.0	120.0	124.0	127.0	131.0	134.0	138.0	141.0	145.0

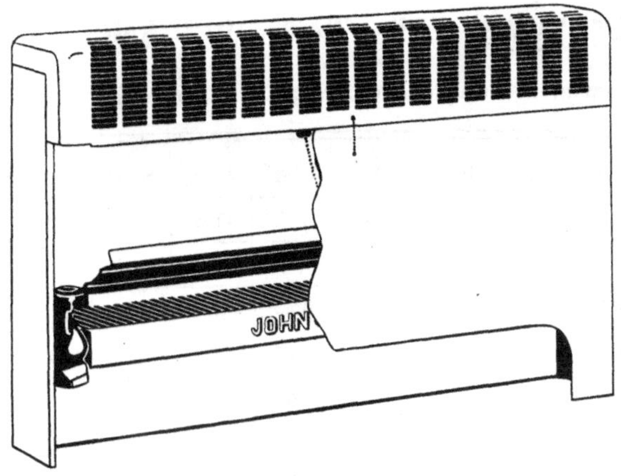

JOHN J. NESBITT, INC.

Philadelphia 36, Pa.

Enclosure Types and Ratings

Left: Convector enclosure type for Nesbitt Model "U" convector. Nesbitt convectors are made in this model only. Use actual dimensions.

Below: Element identifying Nesbitt Model "U" convector. Note that name is stamped on the side of the convector element.

RATINGS FOR NESBITT CONVECTOR "U"*

*(Note: Ratings are sq. ft. E.D.R., 215 deg steam, 65 deg entering air)

CABINET LENGTH			20"	24"	28"	32"	36"	40"	44"	48"	56"	64"
			sq. ft.	sq. ft.	sq. ft.	sq. ft.	sq. ft.	sq. ft.	sq. ft.	sq. ft.	sq. ft.	sq. ft.
ENCLOSURE DEPTH 6¼"	Enclosure Height	20"	18.5	22.5	26.0	30.0	34.0	38.0	42.0	46.0	53.5	61.5
		24"	21.0	25.5	30.0	34.5	39.5	44.0	48.5	53.0	62.0	71.0

THE RITTLING CORPORATION

1202 Rand Building, Buffalo 3, N. Y.

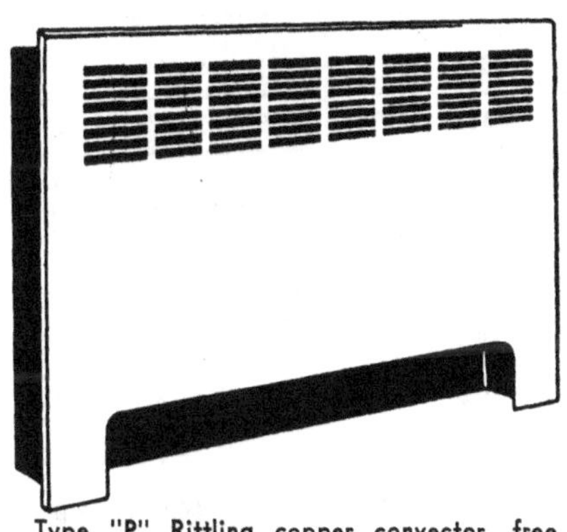

Type "P" Rittling copper convector, free standing. Measurements: Use actual length less ½ in.; actual height and actual depth less ⅛ in.

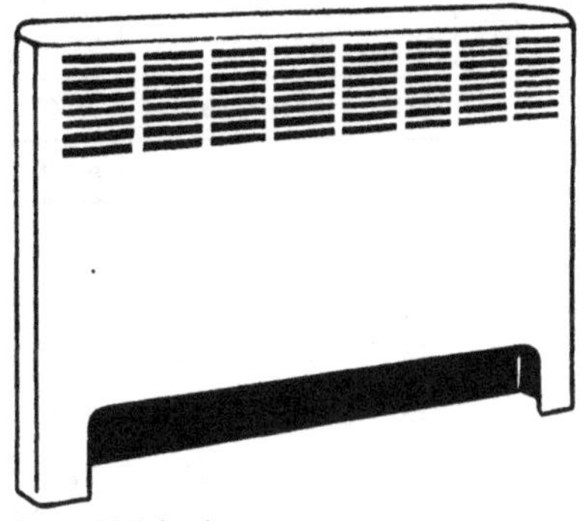

Type "R" Rittling copper convector, semi-recessed. Measurements: Length, use actual dimensions less 3½ in.; use actual height less ½ in. and use actual depth less ⅛ in.

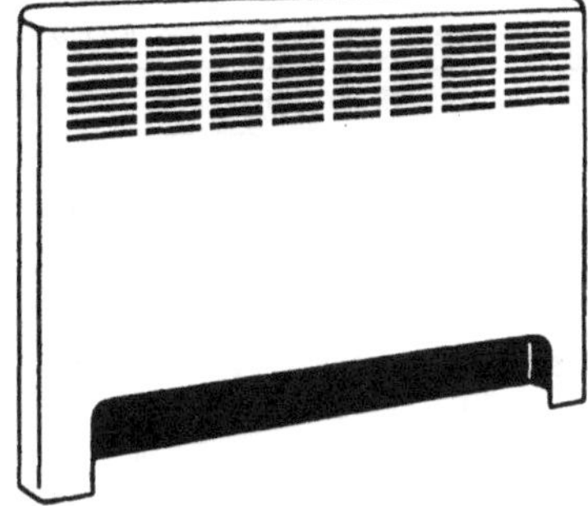

Type "F" Rittling convector, free standing. Measurements: Use actual length less ½ in.; actual height and actual depth less ⅛ in.

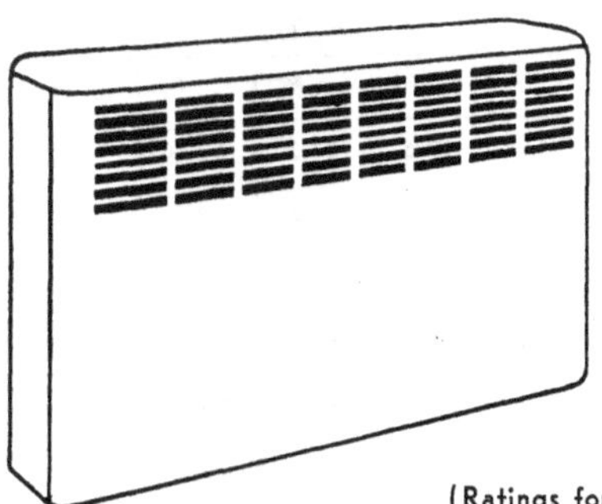

Type "W" Rittling copper convector, wall hung with face outlet. For measurements, use actual length less ½ in.; actual height and actual depth less ⅛ in.

Type "S" Rittling copper convector, wall hung, sloping top outlet. For measurements use actual length less ½ in.; actual height and actual depth less ⅛ in.

(Ratings for Type "S" Rittling convector are on page 41)

RATINGS FOR RITTLING COPPER CONVECTORS TYPES "R", "W", "P" AND "F"

***(Note: Ratings are given in sq. ft. E.D.R. based on steam at 215 deg and entering air at 65 deg)**

ENCLOSURE LENGTH—TYPES F AND W			16½″	20½″	24½″	28½″	32½″	36½″	40½″	44½″	48½″	56½″	64½″
ENCLOSURE LENGTH—TYPES P AND R			19½″	23½″	27½″	31½″	35½″	39½″	43½″	47½″	51½″	59½″	67½″
	Height of Wall Enclosures	Height of Floor Enclosures	sq. ft.	sq. ft.	sq. ft.	sq. ft.	sq. ft.	sq. ft.	sq. ft.	sq. ft.	sq. ft.	sq. ft.	sq. ft.
ENCLOSURE DEPTH 10⅛″	......	18″	15.3	19.8	23.8	28.2	32.2	36.6	41.1	45.5	49.5	57.9	66.8
	14″	20″	18.3	23.8	28.7	34.2	39.1	44.5	49.5	54.9	59.9	70.3	80.7
	18″	24″	20.8	26.7	32.7	38.6	44.5	50.5	56.3	62.4	68.3	80.2	91.6
	20″	26″	21.8	27.7	34.2	40.1	46.5	53.0	58.9	65.3	71.3	83.7	96.0
	26″	32″	22.3	29.2	35.6	42.1	48.5	54.9	61.4	67.8	74.2	87.1	100.0
	32″	38″	23.3	30.2	36.6	43.6	50.0	56.9	63.4	70.3	76.7	90.6	103.9

ENCLOSURE LENGTH—TYPES F AND W			16½″	20½″	24½″	28½″	32½″	36½″	40½″	44½″	48½″	56½″	64½″
ENCLOSURE LENGTH—TYPES P AND R			19½″	23½″	27½″	31½″	35½″	39½″	43½″	47½″	51½″	59½″	67½″
	Height of Wall Enclosures	Height of Floor Enclosures	sq. ft.	sq. ft.	sq. ft.	sq. ft.	sq. ft.	sq. ft.	sq. ft.	sq. ft.	sq. ft.	sq. ft.	sq. ft.
ENCLOSURE DEPTH 4⅛″	......	18″	7.4	9.9	11.9	13.9	16.3	18.3	20.4	22.8	24.8	28.7	33.2
	14″	20″	8.9	11.4	13.9	16.3	18.8	21.3	23.8	26.2	28.7	33.7	38.6
	18″	24″	9.9	12.9	15.8	18.3	21.3	24.3	26.7	29.7	32.7	38.1	44.1
	20″	26″	10.4	13.4	16.3	19.3	22.3	25.2	28.2	31.2	34.2	40.1	46.0
	26″	32″	10.9	13.9	16.8	19.8	22.8	25.7	28.7	31.7	34.6	41.1	47.0
	32″	38″	10.9	13.9	17.3	20.3	23.3	26.2	29.7	32.7	35.6	42.1	48.0

ENCLOSURE LENGTH—TYPES F AND W			16½″	20½″	24½″	28½″	32½″	36½″	40½″	44½″	48½″	56½″	64½″
ENCLOSURE LENGTH—TYPES P AND R			19½″	23½″	27½″	31½″	35½″	39½″	43½″	47½″	51½″	59½″	67½″
	Height of Wall Enclosures	Height of Floor Enclosures	sq. ft.	sq. ft.	sq. ft.	sq. ft.	sq. ft.	sq. ft.	sq. ft.	sq. ft.	sq. ft.	sq. ft.	sq. ft.
ENCLOSURE DEPTH 6⅛″	......	18″	10.9	13.9	17.3	20.3	23.3	26.2	29.2	32.7	35.6	41.6	48.0
	14″	20″	12.4	15.8	19.3	22.8	26.2	29.7	33.2	36.6	40.1	47.0	54.0
	18″	24″	14.4	18.3	22.3	26.2	30.2	34.2	38.1	42.1	46.0	54.4	62.4
	20″	26″	14.8	18.8	22.8	27.2	31.2	35.6	39.6	43.6	48.0	56.4	64.8
	26″	32″	15.3	19.8	23.8	28.2	32.7	37.1	41.6	45.5	50.5	58.9	67.8
	32″	38″	15.8	20.3	24.7	29.2	33.7	38.1	42.6	47.0	52.0	60.9	69.8

ENCLOSURE LENGTH—TYPES F AND W			16½″	20½″	24½″	28½″	32½″	36½″	40½″	44½″	48½″	56½″	64½″
ENCLOSURE LENGTH—TYPES P AND R			19½″	23½″	27½″	31½″	35½″	39½″	43½″	47½″	51½″	59½″	67½″
	Height of Wall Enclosures	Height of Floor Enclosures	sq. ft.	sq. ft.	sq. ft.	sq. ft.	sq. ft.	sq. ft.	sq. ft.	sq. ft.	sq. ft.	sq. ft.	sq. ft.
ENCLOSURE DEPTH 8⅛″	......	18″	14.8	18.8	22.8	27.2	31.2	35.1	39.6	43.6	47.5	55.9	64.3
	14″	20″	16.3	21.3	25.7	30.7	35.1	40.1	45.0	49.5	54.4	63.9	73.3
	18″	24″	17.8	22.8	28.2	33.2	38.1	43.6	48.5	53.5	58.4	68.8	79.2
	20″	26″	18.3	23.8	28.7	34.2	39.6	44.5	50.0	55.4	60.4	71.3	81.7
	26″	32″	18.8	24.3	29.7	35.1	40.6	46.0	51.5	56.9	62.4	73.3	84.1
	32″	38″	19.3	24.7	30.7	36.1	41.6	47.0	53.0	58.4	63.9	74.7	86.1

RITTLING COPPER CONVECTORS

(Continued from previous page)

RATINGS FOR RITTLING COPPER CONVECTORS

*(Note: Ratings are given in sq. ft. E.D.R., based on 215 deg steam and 65 deg entering air)

ENCLOSURE LENGTH			16½"	20½"	24½"	28½"	32½"	36½"	40½"	44½"	48½"	56½"	64½"
	Height of Wall Enclosures	Height of Floor Enclosures	sq. ft.	sq. ft.	sq. ft.	sq. ft.	sq. ft.	sq. ft.	sq. ft.	sq. ft.	sq. ft.	sq. ft.	sq. ft.
ENCLOSURE DEPTH 4⅛"	......	18"	8.9	11.4	13.9	16.3	18.8	21.3	23.8	26.2	28.7	33.2	38.1
	14"	20"	9.9	12.4	15.3	17.8	20.3	23.3	25.7	28.7	31.2	36.6	42.1
	18"	24"	10.4	13.4	16.3	18.8	21.8	24.7	27.2	30.3	33.2	39.1	45.0
	20"	26"	10.4	13.4	16.3	19.3	22.3	25.2	28.2	31.2	34.2	40.1	46.0
	26"	32"	10.9	13.9	16.8	19.8	22.8	25.7	28.7	31.7	34.6	41.1	47.0
	32"	38"	10.9	13.9	17.3	20.3	23.3	26.2	29.7	32.7	35.6	42.1	48.0

ENCLOSURE LENGTH			16½"	20½"	24½"	28½"	32½"	36½"	40½"	44½"	48½"	56½"	64½"
	Height of Wall Enclosures	Height of Floor Enclosures	sq. ft.	sq. ft.	sq. ft.	sq. ft.	sq. ft.	sq. ft.	sq. ft.	sq. ft.	sq. ft.	sq. ft.	sq. ft.
ENCLOSURE DEPTH 6⅛"	......	18"	16.3	20.8	25.7	30.2	34.6	38.6	43.1	48.0	52.5	61.4	70.8
	14"	20"	16.8	21.8	26.2	30.7	36.5	40.1	45.0	49.5	54.6	63.9	72.8
	18"	24"	17.8	22.3	27.2	32.2	37.1	41.6	46.5	51.5	56.4	66.3	76.3
	20"	26"	18.3	22.8	27.7	33.2	38.1	43.1	48.0	53.1	58.4	68.3	78.7
	26"	32"	18.3	23.3	28.2	33.2	38.6	44.1	49.0	54.0	59.4	69.3	79.7
	32"	38"	20.3	26.2	32.2	37.6	43.6	49.5	54.9	60.9	67.3	78.7	90.1

ENCLOSURE LENGTH			16½"	20½"	24½"	28½"	32½"	36½"	40½"	44½"	48½"	56½"	64½"
	Height of Wall Enclosures	Height of Floor Enclosures	sq. ft.	sq. ft.	sq. ft.	sq. ft.	sq. ft.	sq. ft.	sq. ft.	sq. ft.	sq. ft.	sq. ft.	sq. ft.
ENCLOSURE DEPTH 8⅛"	......	18"	20.8	26.7	32.2	38.1	43.6	49.5	55.4	60.9	66.8	78.2	90.1
	14"	20"	21.3	27.2	33.2	39.6	45.5	51.5	57.9	63.4	69.8	81.7	94.0
	18"	24"	21.8	27.7	34.2	40.1	46.0	52.5	58.4	64.3	70.3	82.7	95.0
	20"	26"	22.3	28.7	34.6	40.6	47.0	53.0	59.4	66.3	72.3	85.1	97.5
	26"	32"	22.8	29.2	35.6	42.1	49.0	55.4	61.9	68.3	75.2	88.1	101.0
	32"	38"	23.8	30.7	38.1	44.5	51.5	58.4	65.8	72.3	79.2	92.6	106.9

ENCLOSURE LENGTH			16½"	20½"	24½"	28½"	32½"	36½"	40½"	44½"	48½"	56½"	64½"
	Height of Wall Enclosures	Height of Floor Enclosures	sq. ft.	sq. ft.	sq. ft.	sq. ft.	sq. ft.	sq. ft.	sq. ft.	sq. ft.	sq. ft.	sq. ft.	sq. ft.
ENCLOSURE DEPTH 10⅛"	......	18"	21.8	28.2	35.1	40.1	44.5	52.0	58.4	64.8	70.3	82.2	95.0
	14"	20"	24.3	31.7	38.1	45.0	51.5	58.9	65.3	72.3	79.2	92.6	106.4
	18"	24"	25.7	33.2	40.6	48.0	55.4	62.4	69.8	77.2	84.6	99.5	113.8
	20"	26"	26.7	34.2	42.1	49.5	57.4	65.3	72.3	80.2	87.6	103.0	118.3
	26"	32"	27.7	36.6	44.5	52.5	60.4	68.3	76.7	84.6	92.6	108.9	124.7
	32"	38"	29.7	38.6	47.0	55.4	63.9	72.8	81.2	90.1	98.0	115.8	132.7

ROME-TURNEY RADIATOR COMPANY

Canal Street, Rome, New York

Robras Convectors

Enclosure Types and Measuring Instructions

(Ratings shown below are continued on the following page)

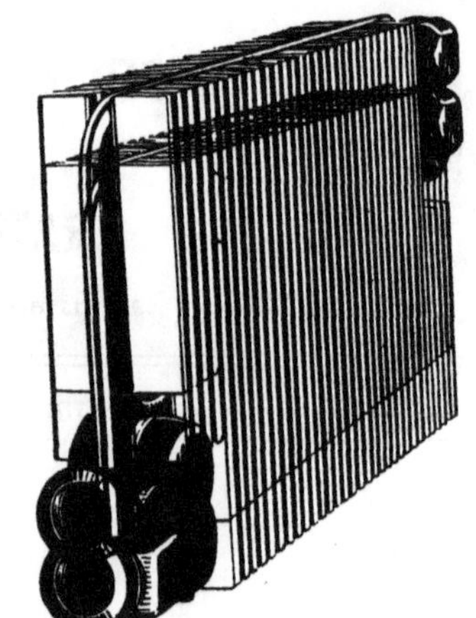

Right: Robras convector element. For identification, note especially the fin and header arrangement.

RATINGS--ROBRAS TYPE "L" CONVECTORS--FACE OUTLET--ELEMENT HEIGHT 5½"*

*(Note: Ratings are given in sq. ft. E.D.R. based on 215 deg steam and 65 deg entering air temperature.)

ELEMENT LENGTH			18″	22″	26″	32″	38″	44″	50″	60″	70″
			sq. ft.	sq. ft.	sq. ft.	sq. ft.	sq. ft.	sq. ft.	sq. ft.	sq. ft.	sq. ft.
ELEMENT DEPTH 3½″	Enclosure Height	16″	10½	12½	15	18¼	21½	25	28¼	34	39¾
		20″	11¼	13½	16	19¾	23½	27	30½	36¾	43
		23″	12	14	16½	20¾	24½	28¼	32¼	38½	45
		26″	12¼	14¾	17¼	21¾	25½	29¼	33½	40¼	47
		29″	12¾	15¼	18	22½	26½	30½	34¾	41½	48¼
		32″	13	16	18½	23	27	31¼	35¾	42¾	49¾
		36″	13½	16½	19	23¾	28	32¼	36¾	44	51¼
		48″	14½	18¾	20¾	25½	30	34½	39¼	47	54¾

ELEMENT LENGTH			18″	22″	26″	32″	38″	44″	50″	60″	70″
			sq. ft.	sq. ft.	sq. ft.	sq. ft.	sq. ft.	sq. ft.	sq. ft.	sq. ft.	sq. ft.
ELEMENT DEPTH 5½″	Enclosure Height	16″	13½	16½	19½	24	28½	32¾	37	44½	52
		20″	14¾	17¾	21¼	26	30½	35½	40½	48½	56½
		23″	15¼	18¾	22¼	27¼	32	37½	42¾	51	59½
		26″	16	19½	23	28½	33½	39	44¾	53	62
		29″	16½	20¼	24	29½	35	40¼	46¼	55	64¼
		32″	17	21	24¾	30½	36	41½	47½	56½	66
		36″	17¾	21¾	25½	31¾	37¼	42¾	49	58¼	68¼
		48″	19	23½	27½	33¾	40	45¾	52¼	62	73

ELEMENT LENGTH			18″	22″	26″	32″	38″	44″	50″	60″	70″
			sq. ft.	sq. ft.	sq. ft.	sq. ft.	sq. ft.	sq. ft.	sq. ft.	sq. ft.	sq. ft.
ELEMENT DEPTH 7½″	Enclosure Height	20″	20	24½	29	35½	42¼	49	56¼	66¼	77½
		23″	21	25¾	30¾	37¾	45	52	59½	70½	83
		26″	22	27	32	39¼	47	54½	62	74	87
		29″	22¾	27¾	33¼	40¾	48¾	56½	64½	77¼	90½
		32″	23½	28¾	34¼	42	50¼	58¼	66¾	80	93¾
		36″	24½	30	35½	43½	52	60¼	69	83	97
		48″	26¾	32½	38¾	47	56	64¾	74½	90	105½

ELEMENT LENGTH			18″	22″	26″	32″	38″	44″	50″	60″	70″
			sq. ft.	sq. ft.	sq. ft.	sq. ft.	sq. ft.	sq. ft.	sq. ft.	sq. ft.	sq. ft.
ELEMENT DEPTH 9½″	Enclosure Height	23″	23	28¼	33½	41½	49	56½	64½	77½	90½
		26″	24	29¾	35¼	43½	51½	59½	67½	81½	95
		29″	25	31	36¾	45	53¾	62	70½	84¾	99
		32″	26	32	38	46½	55¾	64½	73	87½	103
		36″	26¾	33	39½	48¼	57¾	67¼	76	91½	107
		48″	29½	35¾	42¼	51¾	62½	73¾	83½	100	116½
		60″	31	37½	44	54	66	78	88½	105¾	122¾

ROME-TURNEY RADIATOR CO.

(Continued from previous page)

RATINGS FOR ROBRAS TYPE "L" CONVECTORS

ELEMENT LENGTH		18″	22″	26″	32″	38″	44″	50″	60″	70″
		sq. ft.	sq. ft.	sq. ft.	sq. ft.	sq. ft.	sq. ft.	sq. ft.	sq. ft.	sq. ft.
ELEMENT DEPTH 11½″	Enclosure Height 23″	23¼	29	34	42	50½	58	66¼	80	93½
	29″	26½	32¼	38	47	55½	64	73	88	102½
	36″	28½	34½	41¼	51	60¼	69½	79	94½	110½
	48″	31	37½	44½	55¾	65¾	75¾	86½	103¾	120
	72″	33½	40½	48¼	60¾	71½	82½	95¼	113½	130¾
	120″	35	43	51	63	75	87	99½	119½	140

RATINGS--TYPE "L" ROBRAS CONVECTORS--TOP OUTLETS--ELEMENT HEIGHT 5½″*

*(Note: Ratings given in sq. ft. E.D.R. for steam at 215 deg and entering air at 65 deg)

ELEMENT LENGTH		18″	22″	26″	32″	38″	44″	50″	60″	70″
		sq. ft.	sp. ft.	sq. ft.	sq. ft.	sq. ft.	sq. ft.	sq. ft.	sq. ft.	sq. ft.
ELEMENT DEPTH 3½″	Enclosure Height 16″	11¾	14½	17¼	21	25½	29	33½	39¾	47
	20″	12½	15¼	18¼	22½	26¾	30¾	35½	42½	50
	23″	13¼	15¾	19	23½	27¾	32	36¾	44	51¾
	26″	13¾	16½	19¾	24¼	28¾	33	37¾	45½	53½
	29″	14¼	17	20¼	25	29½	34	38¾	47	55
	32″	14½	17½	20¾	25½	30¼	35	39¾	48	56¼
	36″	14¾	18	21½	26¼	31	35¾	40¾	49	57½
	48″	15¾	18¾	22½	27¾	33	38¼	43½	52½	61½

ELEMENT LENGTH		18″	22″	26″	32″	38″	44″	50″	60″	70″
		sq. ft.	sq. ft.	sq. ft.	sq. ft.	sq. ft.	sq. ft.	sq. ft.	sq. ft.	sq. ft.
ELEMENT DEPTH 5½″	Enclosure Height 16″	15½	18¾	22½	27½	32¾	38¼	43½	52¼	61½
	20″	16	19½	23½	28¾	34½	40	45¾	54¾	64½
	23″	16¾	20¼	24¼	29¾	35½	41¼	47	56½	66½
	26″	17¼	20¾	24¾	30½	36½	42½	48¼	58	68½
	29″	17½	21½	25½	31½	37¼	43½	49½	59¼	69¾
	32″	18	22	26¼	32	38	44	50½	60½	71
	36″	18½	22½	26¾	33	38¾	45¼	51½	62	72½
	48″	19½	23¾	28	34½	41	47¾	54¼	65¼	76¼

ELEMENT LENGTH		18″	22″	26″	32″	38″	44″	50″	60″	70″
		sq. ft.	sq. ft.	sq. ft.	sq. ft.	sq. ft.	sq. ft.	sq. ft.	sq. ft.	sq. ft.
ELEMENT DEPTH 7½″	Enclosure Height 20″	24¼	30	35½	43½	52½	61	69½	83½	97½
	23″	25¼	31	37	45½	54½	63	71½	86¼	100½
	26″	26¼	32	38¼	46¾	56¼	65	73¾	88½	103½
	29″	26¾	32¾	39	48	57½	66½	75½	90½	105½
	32″	27½	33½	39¾	49	58¾	67¾	77	92½	107½
	36″	28¼	34½	40¾	50	60	69¼	78½	94½	110¼
	48″	29¾	36½	42¾	52½	62½	72½	82½	98¾	115¾

ELEMENT LENGTH		18″	22″	26″	32″	38″	44″	50″	60″	70″
		sq. ft.	sq. ft.	sq. ft.	sq. ft.	sq. ft.	sq. ft.	sq. ft.	sq. ft.	sq. ft.
ELEMENT DEPTH 9½″	Enclosure Height 23″	29	36	42½	52½	62½	72½	82½	99½	116¼
	26″	29¾	36¾	43¾	54	64	74¼	84¾	102	119
	29″	30½	37½	45	55¼	65½	76	86½	104	121½
	32″	31¼	38¼	45¾	56¼	66¾	77½	87¾	105¾	123½
	36″	31¾	39	46½	57¼	68¼	80	89½	108	126
	48″	33½	41	48½	59¾	71¼	82¾	93¾	112¼	131¼
	60″	34½	42	49½	61¾	73½	85½	96¾	115½	135¼

ROBRAS CONVECTOR RATINGS

ROBRAS TYPE "L" TOP OUTLET RATINGS (Cont'd.)

ELEMENT LENGTH			18″	22″	26″	32″	38″	44″	50″	60″	70″
			sq. ft.	sq. ft.	sq. ft.	sq. ft.	sq. ft.	sq. ft.	sq. ft.	sq. ft.	sq. ft.
ELEMENT DEPTH 11½″	Enclosure Height	23″	32½	40	47½	58½	69¼	80½	91½	110½	129¼
		29″	34	41½	49¾	61¼	72½	83½	95½	115	134½
		36″	35½	43	51¼	63¼	75	86¼	98½	118½	138½
		48″	37	45¼	53½	66	78	89¾	102½	123	143½
		72″	38½	47	56	69½	81¼	93¾	107	128	149½
		120″	39	48¼	58	71	83½	96¼	110	132	154

RATINGS--ROBRAS TYPE "H" CONVECTORS--FACE OUTLETS--ELEMENT HEIGHT 10¾″*

*(Note: Ratings given in sq. ft. E.D.R. based on steam at 215 deg and entering air at 65 deg)

ELEMENT LENGTH			18″	22″	26″	32″	38″	44″	50″	60″	70″
			sq. ft.	sq. ft.	sq. ft.	sq. ft.	sq. ft.	sq. ft.	sq. ft.	sq. ft.	sq. ft.
ELEMENT DEPTH 3½″	Enclosure Height	20″	13¼	16½	19¾	24½	29	33½	38	46	54
		23″	14½	18	21½	26¼	31½	36¼	40¾	49½	58
		26″	15½	19¼	22¾	28	33½	38½	43¼	52¼	61
		29″	16½	20½	24	29½	35	40½	45½	55	64
		32″	17¼	21½	25	30¾	36¾	42½	47¾	57¼	66¾
		36″	18¼	22½	26¼	32¼	38½	44½	50	60¼	70
		48″	20½	25	29½	36	43	49½	56¼	67½	78½

ELEMENT LENGTH			18″	22″	26″	32″	38″	44″	50″	60″	70″
			sq ft.	sq. ft.	sq. ft.	sq. ft.	sq. ft.	sq. ft.	sq. ft.	sq. ft.	sq. ft.
ELEMENT DEPTH 5½″	Enclosure Height	20″	18½	23	27¼	33½	40	46	52½	63½	74
		23″	20	24¾	29½	36¼	43	49½	56½	68¼	80
		26″	21½	26¼	31¼	38½	46	53	60¼	72½	84½
		29″	23	28	33¼	40¾	48½	56¼	63¾	76¾	89½
		32″	24	29½	35	43	51	59	66½	80¼	93½
		36″	25½	31	36¾	45¼	53¾	61½	70¼	84¾	98
		48″	28¼	34¾	41	50¾	60¼	69¼	79	95	109½

ELEMENT LENGTH			18″	22″	26″	32″	38″	44″	50″	60″	70″
			sq. ft.	sq. ft.	sq. ft.	sq. ft.	sq. ft.	sq. ft.	sq. ft.	sq. ft.	sq. ft.
ELEMENT DEPTH 7½″	Enclosure Height	23″	27½	33¼	39½	49	57½	67	76½	92	109
		26″	30¼	36	42¾	53	62	72	82	98½	117
		29″	32½	39	45½	56½	66¼	76½	87½	105	123½
		32″	34½	41¼	48	60	70	81	92	110½	129
		36″	36½	44	51¼	63½	74½	86	98	117½	136
		48″	41	49¾	58¾	72¼	85	98	112	133	152½

ELEMENT LENGTH			18″	22″	26″	32″	38″	44″	50″	60″	70″
			sq. ft.	sq. ft.	sq. ft.	sq. ft.	sq. ft.	sq. ft.	sq. ft.	sq. ft.	sq. ft.
ELEMENT DEPTH 9½″	Enclosure Height	26″	30½	37	44½	55¼	65	76	86	104	121½
		29″	33[illegible]	40	47½	59	69½	81½	92	111	130
		32″	35¼	42½	50½	62¼	73½	85½	97½	117	137
		36″	37½	45½	53¾	66	78½	90½	104	124	145
		48″	42¾	51½	61¼	75	88½	102½	117¾	140	163
		60″	46½	56	66¼	81	95¾	111	127¼	151	175

ELEMENT LENGTH			18″	22″	26″	32″	38″	44″	50″	60″	70″
			sq. ft.	sq. ft.	sq. ft.	sq. ft.	sq. ft.	sq. ft.	sq. ft.	sq. ft.	sq. ft.
ELEMENT DEPTH 11½″	Enclosure Height	29″	34	42	50	60½	71½	83½	94½	113	132½
		36″	38	47	56½	68	80½	94	106½	128	149
		48″	42¾	53	63¼	78	91½	106½	120½	144	168
		72″	49	60½	71¾	89½	105	121¼	137	164	191½
		120″	55½	68	80½	99½	118½	136½	157	188	220

ROME-TURNEY RADIATOR CO.

(Continued from previous page)

Robras Convectors

RATINGS-ROBRAS TYPE "H" CONVECTORS-TOP OUTLETS-ELEMENT HEIGHT 10¾"*

*(Note: Ratings given in sq. ft. E.D.R. based on steam at 215 deg and entering air at 65 deg)

ELEMENT LENGTH		18″	22″	26″	32″	38″	44″	50″	60″	70″
	Enclosure Height	sq. ft.	sq. ft.	sq. ft.	sq. ft.	sq. ft.	sq. ft.	sq. ft.	sq. ft.	sq. ft.
ELEMENT DEPTH 3½″	20″	15½	18¾	22½	27¾	33	38½	44	53¼	62
	23″	16¼	20	23¾	29¼	35	40¾	46¼	56	65½
	26″	17	20¾	24¾	30½	36½	42¾	48½	58½	68¼
	29″	17¾	21½	25¾	31¾	37¾	44¼	50	60½	70¾
	32″	18½	22½	26¾	33	39	45½	51½	62½	73
	36″	19¼	23¼	27¾	34¼	40½	47½	53½	64½	75½
	48″	21	25½	30½	37½	44½	51½	58½	70½	81¾

ELEMENT LENGTH		18″	22″	26″	32″	38″	44″	50″	60″	70″
	Enclosure Height	sq. ft.	sq. ft.	sq. ft.	sq. ft.	sq. ft.	sq. ft.	sq. ft.	sq. ft.	sq. ft.
ELEMENT DEPTH 5½″	20″	24	29½	34¾	43	50½	59	67	81	94¾
	23″	24¾	30¾	36¼	44¾	52¾	61½	70	84½	98¾
	26″	25¾	31¾	37½	46¼	54¾	63½	72½	87½	102½
	29″	26½	33	38¾	47¾	56½	65½	74¾	90	105½
	32″	27½	33¾	39¾	49	58	67½	77	92½	108¼
	36″	28¼	35	41	50½	60	69¾	79½	95½	111½
	48″	30½	37½	44¼	54¼	64½	75	85¼	102½	119¾

ELEMENT LENGTH		18″	22″	26″	32″	38″	44″	50″	60″	70″
	Enclosure Height	sq. ft.	sq. ft.	sq. ft.	sq. ft.	sq. ft.	sq. ft.	sq. ft.	sq. ft.	sq. ft.
ELEMENT DEPTH 7½″	23″	32	39	46¼	57	67½	78¾	89	107½	126½
	26″	34	41½	49¼	60¾	71½	83½	94½	114	134½
	29″	35½	43¾	51¾	64	75	88	99½	119¾	140¾
	32″	37¼	45½	53¾	66½	78½	91½	103½	124¾	146½
	36″	39	47¾	56½	69½	82½	95½	108½	130½	152½
	48″	43	52¼	62¼	76½	91¼	105¼	119½	143½	166½

ELEMENT LENGTH		18″	22″	26″	32″	38″	44″	50″	60″	70″
	Enclosure Height	sq. ft.	sq. ft.	sq. ft.	sq. ft.	sq. ft.	sq. ft.	sq. ft.	sq. ft.	sq. ft.
ELEMENT DEPTH 9½″	26″	39½	48¼	56½	70½	84¼	97½	112	134	158½
	29″	41	50½	59¼	73¾	88	101¾	116½	140	164½
	32″	42½	52½	61½	76½	91	105¼	120	144½	169
	36″	44	54¼	63¾	79¼	94¼	109	124	149½	174¾
	48″	48	58¾	69	85¼	100½	116¾	133	159¾	187
	60″	50¾	62	72¾	89½	105	122	138¾	166¼	195½

ROBRAS TYPE "H" RATINGS CONTINUED

ELEMENT LENGTH		18″	22″	26″	32″	38″	44″	50″	60″	70″
		sq. ft.	sq. ft.	sq. ft.	sq. ft.	sq. ft.	sq. ft.	sq. ft.	sq. ft.	sq. ft.
ELEMENT DEPTH 11½″	Enclosure Height 29″	47	57½	67½	84	99	115½	131½	158	185
	36″	50	61¼	72¼	89	106	123½	140½	169	197¾
	48″	54	65¾	77½	95¾	113¾	132	149¾	180½	210¾
	72″	58¾	71	83¾	103	122	141	159¾	193½	225½
	120″	62	75	88½	109	130	149	169½	203	238

ROME-TURNEY RADIATOR CO.

Rocop Convectors

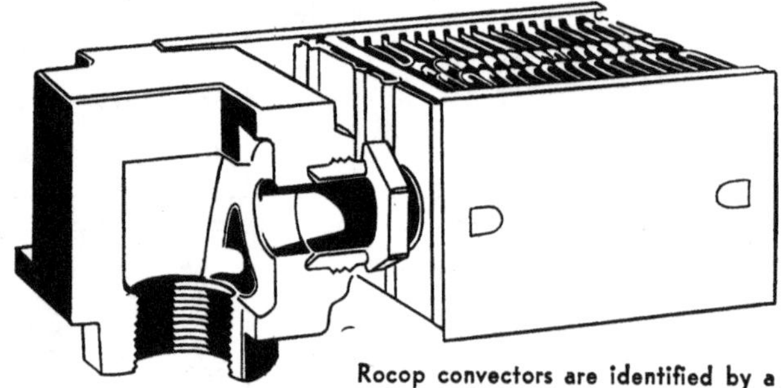

Rocop convectors are identified by a decal on the side of the element.

RATINGS FOR ROCOP CONVECTORS WITH TOP OUTLETS*

*(In sq. ft. E.D.R., steam at 215 deg.; E.A., 65 deg)

ELEMENT LENGTH		18″	22″	26″	30″	36″	42″	48″	54″	60″	66″	72″
		sq. ft.	sq. ft.	sq. ft.	sq. ft.	sq. ft.	sq. ft.	sq. ft.	sq. ft.	sq. ft.	sq. ft.	sq. ft.
ELEMENT DEPTH 3½″	Enclosure Height 16″	10½	13½	16	18¾	22½	26¼	30¼	34	38	42	46
	20″	11½	14¾	17¼	20¼	24¾	29	33½	37¾	42½	46½	51
	23″	12	15½	18¼	21½	26¼	30¾	35¾	40	45	49¼	54¼
	26″	12¾	16	19	22¼	27½	32¼	37½	42¼	47¼	52	57
	29″	13	16¾	20	23¼	28¾	33¼	39¼	44	49½	54½	59½
	32″	13½	17¼	20¾	24	29¾	35	41	46	51¼	56	61¾
	36″	14	18	21½	25¼	31	36¾	42½	47¾	53½	58½	64¼
	48″	15½	19½	23½	27¾	33¾	40¼	46	52	58	64	70¼
	60″	16¼	20¾	25	29	35¼	42	48	54½	60½	67½	74¼

ELEMENT LENGTH		18″	22″	26″	30″	36″	42″	48″	54″	60″	66″	72″
		sq. ft.	sq. ft.	sq. ft.	sq. ft.	sq. ft.	sq. ft.	sq. ft.	sq. ft.	sq. ft.	sq. ft.	sq. ft.
ELEMENT DEPTH 5½″	Enclosure Height 16″	16	20½	25	30	36¼	42¾	49½	56	63	69	76
	20″	17	22	26¾	32	39	46	53½	61	68½	75½	83
	23″	18	23	28	33¼	40¾	48	56¼	64	72	79½	87½
	26″	18¾	24	29¼	34¾	42½	50	58½	66½	74¾	82¾	91
	29″	19¼	24¾	30¼	36	44	52	60½	68¾	77½	85½	94½
	32″	20	25¾	31¼	37	45¼	53¾	62¼	71	80	88	97
	36″	20¾	26¾	32¼	38¼	47	56	64¾	73½	82½	91	100¼
	48″	22¼	29	35	41½	51	60½	70	79½	89	98½	108½
	60″	23¾	30½	37	43¾	53½	63½	73	83¼	93¼	103½	114

ELEMENT LENGTH		18″	22″	26″	30″	36″	42″	48″	54″	60″	66″	72″
		sq. ft.	sq. ft.	sq. ft.	sq. ft.	sq. ft.	sq. ft.	sq. ft.	sq. ft.	sq. ft.	sq. ft.	sq. ft.
ELEMENT DEPTH 7½″	Enclosure Height 16″	21½	28	34½	40¼	50	59	68½	78½	87½	97	106½
	20″	23	29¾	36¾	43	53½	63½	73½	84	94½	104½	114½
	23″	24	31	38¼	45	56	66	77	87¾	98¾	109	119½
	26″	24¾	32	39¾	46¾	57¾	68½	79¾	91	102½	113	123¾
	29″	25½	33¼	41	48¼	59¾	70¾	82¼	93¾	105¾	117	127¾
	32″	26¼	34	42	49¾	61¼	72½	84½	96¼	108½	120	131
	36″	27	35¼	43½	51¼	63½	75	87¼	99½	112	124	135½
	48″	29	38	47	55¼	68¼	80¾	94	107	120¾	133½	147
	60″	31	40	49	58	71	84½	98½	112¼	126½	140	155½

ROME-TURNEY RADIATOR CO.

(Continued from previous page)

RATINGS FOR ROCOP TOP OUTLET CONVECTORS CONTINUED

ELEMENT LENGTH		18″	22″	26″	30″	36″	42″	48″	54″	60″	66″	72″
		sq. ft.	sq. ft.	sq. ft.	sq. ft.	sq. ft.	sq. ft.	sq. ft.	sq. ft.	sq. ft.	sq. ft.	sq. ft.
ELEMENT DEPTH 9½″	Enclosure Height 20″	26¾	34	42	49½	60½	72	83¼	94½	106	117½	129½
	23″	28	36	44	52	63¾	75½	87½	98¾	111	123½	136
	26″	29¼	37½	46	54¼	66½	78½	91	103	115½	128½	141
	29″	30¼	39	47½	56¼	69	81½	94	106½	119½	133	145½
	32″	31¼	40¼	49	57¾	71	83¾	96¾	109¾	123	137	150
	36″	32½	41¾	50¾	59¾	73¼	86¾	100	113½	127	141	154½
	48″	35	45	54¾	64½	79	94	108	122¾	137½	152½	167
	60″	36¾	47	57	67½	83	98½	113½	129¾	145	160½	176
	72″	38	48½	59	69¾	85½	102	117¼	134	150	166	182
	84″	39	49¾	60¼	71	87½	104	120	137	153½	169¾	186
	96″	39½	50¼	61	72	88¾	105½	121½	139	156	172	189
	120″	40	51	62	73	90	106¾	123½	140	158	175	192

ELEMENT LENGTH		18″	22″	26″	30″	36″	42″	48″	54″	60″	66″	72″
		sq. ft.	sq. ft.	sq. ft.	sq. ft.	sq. ft.	sq. ft.	sq. ft.	sq. ft.	sq. ft.	sq. ft.	sq. ft.
ELEMENT DEPTH 11½″	Enclosure Height 23″	32½	41¼	50	58¾	71½	85	98½	111	124	137	150½
	26″	34	43	52¼	61¼	75	89	102½	116	129	142½	157
	29″	35½	45	54¼	64	77½	92	106	120	133¾	148	162½
	32″	36¾	47¼	56	66	80	95	109½	123¾	137½	152	167
	36″	38	48	58	68	83	98	113	128	142½	153¾	173
	48″	40¾	51¾	62¼	73½	89¾	106	122¾	138½	155	171½	188½
	60″	42¾	54	65½	77	94¼	111	129¼	146¼	164	181½	199
	72″	44	55¾	68	79½	97½	114¾	133¾	151¼	170¼	188	206½
	84″	45	57	69½	81¼	100	117½	136¾	155	174½	192½	211¼
	96″	46	58	70½	83	101¼	119¼	139	157¼	177	195½	214¼
	120″	47	59½	72	84½	103	121¾	141	160	179	198	217

RATINGS FOR ROCOP CONVECTORS WITH FACE OUTLETS*

*(Note: Ratings given in sq. ft. E.D.R. based on 215 deg steam and 65 deg entering air)

ELEMENT LENGTH		18″	22″	26″	30″	36″	42″	48″	54″	60″	66″	72″
		sq. ft.	sq. ft.	sq. ft.	sq. ft.	sq. ft.	sq. ft.	sq. ft.	sq. ft.	sq. ft.	sq. ft.	sq. ft.
ELEMENT DEPTH 3½″	Enclosure Height 16″	8	10¼	12¼	14½	17¼	20¼	23	26	29	32	35
	20″	10	12½	15	17¼	21	24¾	28½	32¼	36	39¾	43½
	23″	11	13¾	16½	19	23¼	27¼	31½	35¼	40	44¼	48½
	26″	12	15	17¾	20½	25¼	30	34½	39	43½	48	52½
	29″	12½	16	19	22¼	27	32	37	41½	46¼	51½	56¼
	32″	13	16½	19¾	23¼	28½	33½	38½	43¾	48¾	53¾	59
	36″	14	17½	21	24¾	30	35½	40½	45¾	51½	56¾	62
	48″	15½	19¼	23¼	27¼	33¼	39	45	50¼	56½	62½	68½
	60″	16¼	20¼	24¼	28½	34¾	41	47½	53	59¼	65½	72½

ELEMENT LENGTH		18″	22″	26″	30″	36″	42″	48″	54″	60″	66″	72″
		sq. ft.	sq. ft.	sq. ft.	sq. ft.	sq. ft.	sq. ft.	sq. ft.	sq. ft.	sq. ft.	sq. ft.	sq. ft.
ELEMENT DEPTH 5½″	Enclosure Height 16″	11½	14½	17¼	20	24¾	29½	34	38½	43	47½	52
	20″	14	17½	21½	26	32	38	44	50	55¾	61½	67½
	23″	15¼	19½	24	28¾	35¼	42	48½	55	61½	68	74½
	26″	16½	21¼	26	31	38¼	45¼	52½	59½	66¼	73½	80¾
	29″	17¼	22½	27¾	33	40	47¾	55¼	63	70¼	77½	85¼
	32″	18	23½	29	34	41¾	49¾	57¾	65¾	73	81	89
	36″	19	24¾	30½	35¾	44	52½	60½	69	76¾	84¾	92¾
	48″	21¼	27½	33½	39	48¼	57½	66	74¾	83¾	93	102
	60″	22¾	29	35½	41½	51	60¾	69½	78¾	88¼	97½	107

ROCOP CONVECTOR RATINGS

ELEMENT LENGTH		18″	22″	26″	30″	36″	42″	48″	54″	60″	66″	72″
	Enclosure Height	sq. ft.	sq. ft.	sq. ft.	sq. ft.	sq. ft.	sq. ft.	sq. ft.	sq. ft.	sq. ft.	sq. ft.	sq. ft.
ELEMENT DEPTH 7½″	16″	14¼	18¼	22½	26½	32½	38½	44¾	51¼	57	63¼	69½
	20″	18¼	23¾	29¼	34¾	43	50¼	59¼	66½	74¾	82½	91¼
	23″	20½	26	32	38	47	56	65	74	83	91½	100½
	26″	21¾	28	34½	41	50½	60¼	69½	79½	90	98¼	107¾
	29″	23	29¾	36½	43	53	63	73	83½	93½	103¾	113½
	32″	24	31	38	45	55	65½	76	86½	98	108	118
	36″	25	32¼	39¾	47	57¾	69	79	90½	102½	113	123½
	48″	27	35	43¾	51¼	63	74¾	86½	98½	111½	123	136
	60″	28¾	36¾	46¼	54	66½	78½	91½	103¾	117	130	143½

ELEMENT LENGTH		18″	22″	26″	30″	36″	42″	48″	54″	60″	66″	72″
	Enclosure Height	sq. ft.	sq. ft.	sq. ft.	sq. ft.	sq. ft.	sq. ft.	sq. ft.	sq. ft.	sq. ft.	sq. ft.	sq. ft.
ELEMENT DEPTH 9½″	20″	21¼	27	32¾	38½	46½	55¼	64	71½	80½	88	97½
	23″	23¾	30	36¼	42½	52¼	61¾	71¼	81	90¼	99½	108¾
	26″	25¾	32½	39	46	56½	67	77	88	98	108¼	118½
	29″	27½	34¼	41½	48¾	59½	70½	81¼	92¼	103¼	114	124¾
	32″	28¾	36	43¾	51	62¼	73¾	85	96½	108	119½	130½
	36″	30	37¾	45¾	53¾	65¼	77¼	88½	100¾	112½	124½	136
	48″	32¾	41	50	58½	70½	84	96¾	110	122½	136	149¼
	60″	34¼	43	52½	61¼	74¼	87¾	102¼	115½	129¾	143½	157½
	72″	35½	44¼	54½	63¼	77	90½	106	119½	134½	149	163½
	84″	36¼	45½	55¾	64¾	78¾	92½	108½	122½	138	152½	167½
	96″	37	46	56½	65¾	80	94¼	110	124½	140	154¾	170
	120″	38	47½	57½	67¼	81½	96½	111½	126¾	142	156½	172½

ELEMENT LENGTH		18″	22″	26″	30″	36″	42″	48″	54″	60″	66″	72″
	Enclosure Height	sq. ft.	sq. ft.	sq. ft.	sq. ft.	sq. ft.	sq. ft.	sq. ft.	sq. ft.	sq. ft.	sq. ft.	sq. ft.
ELEMENT DEPTH 11½″	23″	27½	33½	40	47	57	67½	77½	87½	97½	107	117
	26″	29¾	36½	43½	51	62	73¼	84	95	105¼	116	127
	29″	31½	39	46½	54½	66¼	78	89½	101½	112½	123¾	135¼
	32″	33¼	40¾	49¼	57	69½	81½	93¾	106½	118½	130½	141¾
	36″	34¾	43	51¾	60	72½	85½	98½	111½	124½	137¼	149½
	48″	37¾	46½	55¾	64¾	78½	93	106¾	120¾	134½	148¾	162½
	60″	39½	48½	58	67¼	81¾	97	111	125¾	140	154¾	171
	72″	40½	49½	59½	69	83¾	99¾	114¼	129½	144¼	159	176¾
	84″	41	50½	60½	70	85½	102	116½	132¼	147¼	162½	180½
	96″	41½	51	61¼	71	86½	103¼	118	134	149½	164¾	183
	120″	42	51¾	62½	72½	89	105	121	137	153	169	185

SHAW-PERKINS MFG. CO.

Philadelphia 19, Pa.

Perkins Copper Convectors

Measuring Instructions and Convector Ratings

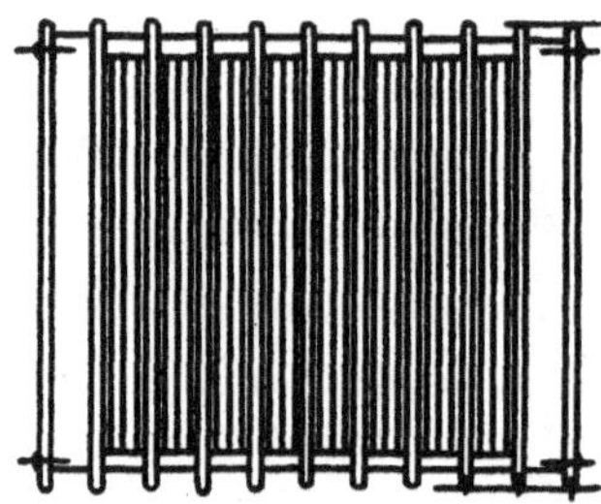

Left: Ceiling mounted Perkins convector unit. These can also be found wall mounted.

Right: This drawing shows the Perkins convector heating element. It is of copper tube, has tie rods running lengthwise through the convector.

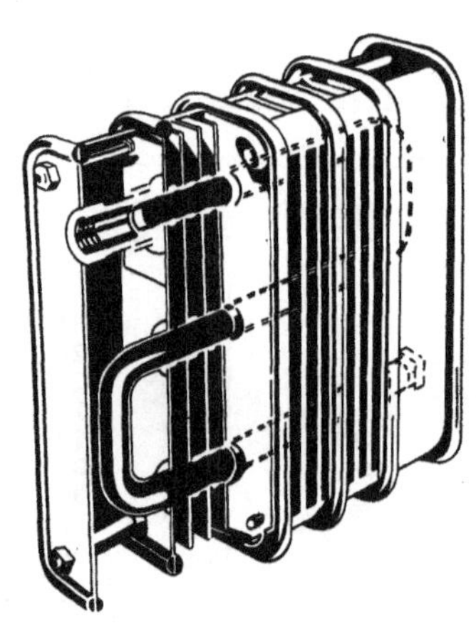

(Continued on following page)

PERKINS CONVECTOR RATINGS CONTINUED

WALL MOUNTED										
No. OF SECTIONS		10	15	20	25	30	35	40	45	50
TOTAL LENGTH		25″	37½″	50″	62½″	75″	87½″	100″	112½″	125″
Enclosure Height		sq. ft.	sq. ft.	sq. ft.	sq. ft.	sq. ft.	sq. ft.	sq. ft.	sq. ft.	sq. ft.
	14½″	14	24	33	43	52	62	71	81	90
	23½″	23	37	52	67	82	96	111	126	141
	32½″	31	51	70	90	109	129	148	168	187

CEILING MOUNTED										
No. OF SECTIONS		10	15	20	25	30	35	40	45	50
TOTAL LENGTH		25″	37½″	50″	62½″	75″	87½″	100″	112½″	125″
Enclosure Height		sq. ft.	sq. ft.	sq. ft.	sq. ft.	sq. ft.	sq. ft.	sq. ft.	sq. ft.	sq. ft.
	14½″	19	30	42	53	65	76	88	99	111
	23½″	27	45	63	82	100	118	137	155	173
	32½″	38	62	86	110	134	158	182	206	230

SHAW-PERKINS MFG. CO.
Philadelphia 19, Pa.

Shaw Copper Convectors

Measuring Instructions and Convector Ratings

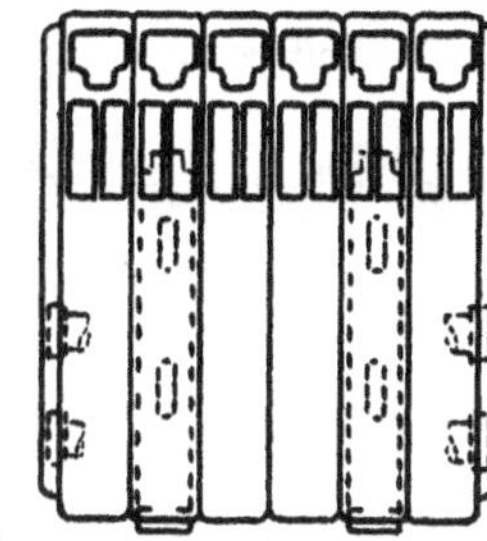

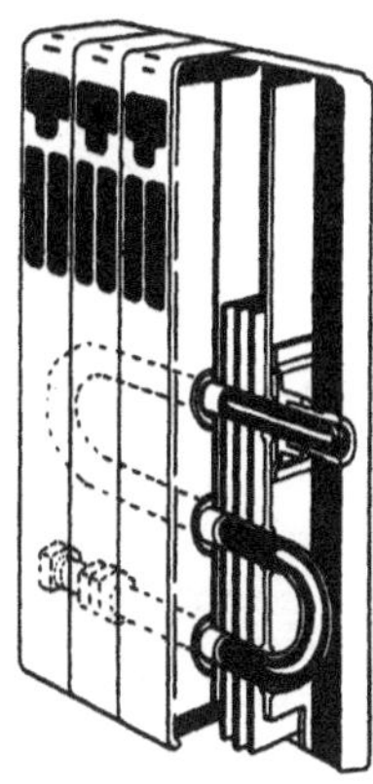

Left: Model "B" front air outlet Shaw Convector.

Right: Model "A" front air outlet Shaw Convector.

RATINGS FOR SHAW CONVECTORS*

*(Note: Ratings given in sq. ft. E.D.R. based on 215 deg steam and 65 deg entering air)

No. OF SECTIONS		5	6	7	8	9	10	11	12	13	14	15	16	17	18	19	20	21
TOTAL LENGTH		11″	13″	15″	17″	19″	21″	23″	25″	27″	29″	31″	33″	35″	37″	39″	41″	43″
Enclosure Height		sq. ft.	sq. ft.	sq. ft.	sq. ft.	sq. ft.	sq. ft.	sq. ft.	sq. ft.	sq. ft.	sq. ft.	sq. ft.	sq. ft.	sq. ft.	sq. ft.	sq. ft.	sq. ft.	sq. ft.
	14″*	3.9	4.8	5.7	6.6	7.5	8.4	9.2	10.1	11.0	11.9	12.3	13.6	14.5	15.5	16.3	17.2	......
	14″	5.3	6.5	7.6	8.8	9.9	11.1	12.3	13.4	14.6	15.8	16.9	18.1	19.2	20.4	21.6	22.7	23.9
	17″	6.4	7.8	9.2	10.6	12.1	13.5	14.9	16.3	17.8	19.2	20.6	22.0	23.4	24.9	26.3	27.7	29.1
	20″	7.5	9.2	10.8	12.5	14.2	15.8	17.5	19.2	20.8	22.5	24.2	25.8	27.5	29.2	30.9	32.5	34.2
	23″	8.5	10.4	12.3	14.2	16.1	18.0	19.9	21.8	23.7	25.5	27.4	29.3	31.2	33.1	35.0	36.9	38.8

No. OF SECTIONS		22	23	24	25	26	27	28	29	30	31	32	33	34	35	36	37	38	39	40
TOTAL LENGTH		45″	47″	49″	51″	53″	55″	57″	59″	61″	63″	65″	67″	69″	71″	73″	75″	77″	79″	81″
Enclosure Height		sq. ft.	sq. ft.	sq. ft.	sq. ft.	sq. ft.	sq. ft.	sq. ft.	sq. ft.	sq. ft.	sq. ft.	sq. ft.	sq. ft.	sq. ft.	sq. ft.	sq. ft.	sq. ft.	sq. ft.	sq. ft.	sq. ft.
	14″	25.1	26.2	27.4	28.5	29.7	30.9	32.0	33.2	34.4	35.5	36.7	37.8	39.0	40.2	41.3	42.5	43.6	44.8	46.0
	17″	30.5	32.0	33.4	34.8	36.2	37.6	39.1	40.5	41.9	43.3	44.7	46.2	47.6	49.0	50.4	51.8	53.3	54.7	56.2
	20″	35.9	37.5	39.2	40.9	42.5	44.2	45.9	47.5	49.2	50.9	52.5	54.2	55.9	57.5	59.2	60.9	62.5	64.2	65.9
	23″	40.7	42.6	44.5	46.4	48.3	50.2	52.1	54.0	55.9	57.7	59.6	61.5	63.4	65.3	67.2	69.1	71.0	72.9	74.8

SHAW COPPER CONVECTOR RATINGS CONTINUED

No. OF SECTIONS		5	6	7	8	9	10	11	12	13	14	15	16	17	18	19	20	21
TOTAL LENGTH		11"	13"	15"	17"	19"	21"	23"	25"	27"	29"	31"	33"	35"	37"	39"	41"	43"
Enclosure Height		sq. ft.	sq. ft.	sq. ft.	sq. ft.	sq. ft.	sq. ft.	sq. ft.	sq. ft.	sq. ft.	sq. ft.	sq. ft.	sq. ft.	sq. ft.	sq. ft.	sq. ft.	sq. ft.	sq. ft.
	14"	6.9	8.4	10.0	11.5	13.0	14.6	16.1	17.7	19.2	20.7	22.3	23.8	25.3	26.9	28.4	30.0	31.5
	17"	7.7	9.4	11.2	12.9	14.6	16.3	18.1	19.8	21.5	23.2	25.0	26.7	28.4	30.1	31.9	33.6	35.3
	20"	8.4	10.3	12.1	14.0	15.9	17.7	19.6	21.5	23.3	25.2	27.1	28.9	30.8	32.6	34.5	36.4	38.2
	23"	9.1	11.1	13.1	15.2	17.2	19.2	21.2	23.2	25.2	27.3	29.3	31.3	33.3	35.3	37.3	39.4	41.4

No. OF SECTIONS		22	23	24	25	26	27	28	29	30	31	32	33	34	35	36	37	38	39	40
TOTAL LENGTH		45"	47"	49"	51"	53"	55"	57"	59"	61"	63"	65"	67"	69"	71"	73"	75"	77"	79"	81"
Enclosure Height		sq. ft.	sq. ft.	sq. ft.	sq. ft.	sq. ft.	sq. ft.	sq. ft.	sq. ft.	sq. ft.	sq. ft.	sq. ft.	sq. ft.	sq. ft.	sq. ft.	sq. ft.	sq. ft.	sq. ft.	sq. ft.	sq. ft.
	14"	33.0	34.6	36.1	37.6	39.2	40.7	42.3	45.3	45.3	46.9	48.4	49.9	51.5	53.0	54.5	56.1	57.9	59.2	60.7
	17"	37.0	38.8	40.5	42.2	43.9	45.7	47.4	49.1	50.8	52.6	54.3	56.0	57.7	59.5	61.2	62.9	64.5	66.4	68.1
	20"	40.1	42.0	43.8	45.7	47.6	49.4	51.3	53.2	55.0	56.9	58.8	60.6	62.5	64.4	66.2	68.1	69.9	71.8	73.7
	23"	43.4	45.4	47.4	49.4	51.5	53.5	55.5	57.5	59.5	61.5	63.6	65.6	67.6	69.6	71.6	73.6	75.7	77.7	79.7

THE TRANE COMPANY

La Crosse, Wisconsin

Trane Copper Convectors

No Identification on Either Element or Enclosure

Left: Types "A" and "FK" Trane convectors. Use actual measurements for height, length and depth.

Right: Type "SK" Trane convector. For measurements use: Actual length less 3", actual height less 1½" and actual depth.

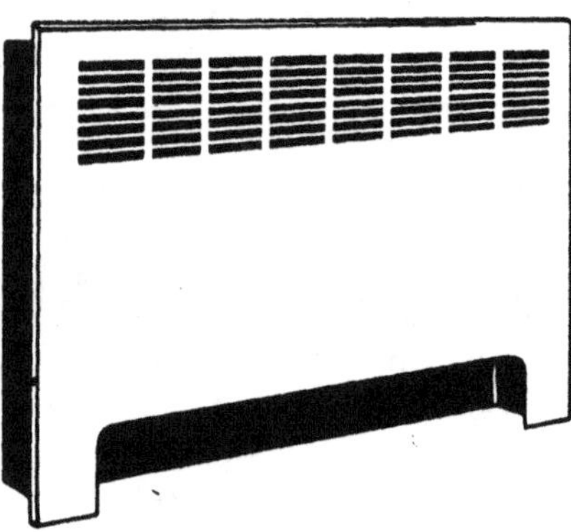

Left: Type "RK" Trane convector. Use actual length less 3", actual height less 1½" and actual depth.

Right: Type "PK" Trane convector. Measurements: Use actual length less 2¼", actual height less 1" and actual depth.

(Continued on following page)

THE TRANE COMPANY

(Continued from previous page)

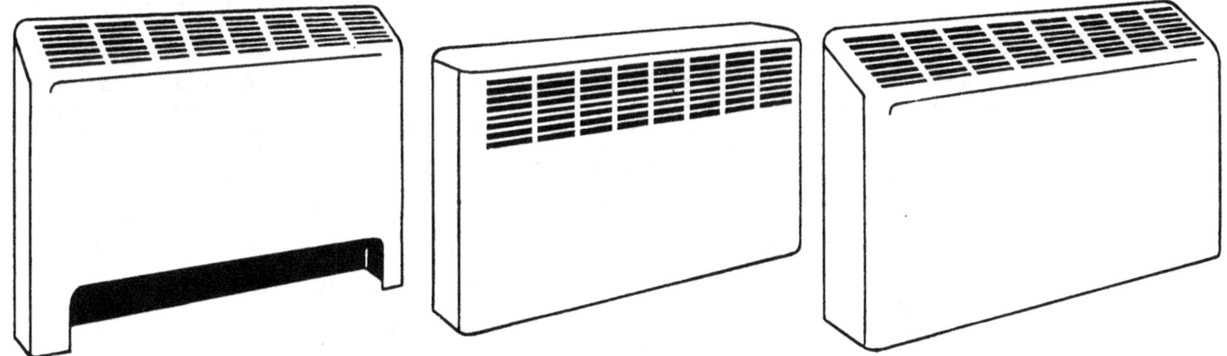

Type "SFK" Trane convector. Measurements: Use actual length less 3/8", actual height and actual depth.

Type "W" Trane convector. Measurements: Use actual length less 3/8", actual height and actual depth.

Type "SW" Trane convector. Measurements: Use actual length less 3/8", actual height and actual depth.

RATINGS FOR TRANE COPPER CONVECTORS, TYPE "A"*

*(Note: Ratings given in sq. ft. E.D.R., based on steam at 215 deg and entering air at 65 deg)

ENCLOSURE LENGTH			20"	24"	28"	32"	36"	40"	44"	48"	56"	64"
			sq. ft.	sq. ft.	sq. ft.	sq. ft.	sq. ft.	sq. ft.	sq. ft.	sq. ft.	sq. ft.	sq. ft.
ENCLOSURE DEPTH 6"	Enclosure Height	20"	16.0	19.5	23.0	26.5	30.0	33.4	37.0	40.5	47.5	54.5
		24"	18.5	22.5	26.5	30.5	34.5	38.5	42.5	46.5	55.0	63.0
		32"	20.0	24.0	28.5	33.0	37.5	42.0	46.0	51.0	59.5	68.5

*(Note: Ratings given in sq. ft. E.D.R., based on steam at 215 deg and entering air at 65 deg)

ENCLOSURE LENGTH			20"	24"	28"	32"	36"	40"	44"	48"	56"	64"
			sq. ft.	sq. ft.	sq. ft.	sq. ft.	sq. ft.	sq. ft.	sq. ft.	sq. ft.	sq. ft.	sq. ft.
ENCLOSURE DEPTH 8"	Enclosure Height	20"	....	....	....	35.5	....	45.5	....	55.0	64.5	74.0
		24"	....	....	....	38.5	....	49.0	....	59.0	69.5	80.0
		32"	....	....	....	41.0	....	52.0	....	63.0	74.0	85.0

*(Note: Ratings given in sq. ft. E.D.R., based on steam at 215 deg and entering air at 65 deg)

ENCLOSURE LENGTH			20"	24"	28"	32"	36"	40"	44"	48"	56"	64"
			sq. ft.	sq. ft.	sq. ft.	sq. ft.	sq. ft.	sq. ft.	sq. ft.	sq. ft.	sq. ft.	sq. ft.
ENCLOSURE DEPTH 10"	Enclosure Height	20"	....	....	....	....	....	50.0	....	60.5	71.0	81.5
		24"	....	....	....	....	....	57.0	....	69.0	81.0	92.5
		32"	....	....	....	....	....	62.0	....	75.0	88.0	101.0

TRANE COPPER CONVECTOR RATINGS, TYPES "FK", "W", "SK", "RK" and "PK"*

*(See measuring instructions on pages 49 and 50)

(These ratings are continued on following page)

ENCLOSURE DEPTH	Height of Wall Hung Enclosures	Height of Floor Mounted Enclosures	16″ sq. ft.	20″ sq. ft.	24″ sq. ft.	28″ sq. ft.	32″ sq. ft.	36″ sq. ft.	40″ sq. ft.	44″ sq. ft.	48″ sq. ft.	56″ sq. ft.	64″ sq. ft.
4″	......	18″	7.5	10.0	12.0	14.0	16.5	18.5	20.6	23.0	25.0	29.0	33.5
	14″	20″	9.0	11.5	14.0	16.5	19.0	21.5	24.0	26.5	29.0	34.0	39.0
	18″	24″	10.0	13.0	16.0	18.5	21.5	24.5	27.0	30.0	33.0	38.5	44.5
	20″	26″	10.5	13.5	16.5	19.5	22.5	25.5	28.5	31.5	34.5	40.5	46.5
	26″	32″	11.0	14.0	17.0	20.0	23.0	26.0	29.0	32.0	35.0	41.5	47.5
	32″	38″	11.0	14.0	17.5	20.5	23.5	26.5	30.0	33.0	36.0	42.5	48.5

ENCLOSURE DEPTH	Height of Wall Hung Enclosures	Height of Floor Mounted Enclosures	16″ sq. ft.	20″ sq. ft.	24″ sq. ft.	28″ sq. ft.	32″ sq. ft.	36″ sq. ft.	40″ sq. ft.	44″ sq. ft.	48″ sq. ft.	56″ sq. ft.	64″ sq. ft.
6″	......	18″	11.0	14.0	17.5	20.5	23.5	26.5	29.5	33.0	36.0	42.0	48.5
	14″	20″	12.5	16.0	19.5	23.0	26.5	30.0	33.5	37.0	40.5	47.5	54.5
	18″	24″	14.5	18.5	22.5	26.5	30.5	34.5	38.5	42.5	46.5	55.0	63.0
	20″	26″	15.0	19.0	23.0	27.5	31.5	36.0	40.0	44.0	48.5	57.0	65.5
	26″	32″	15.5	20.0	24.0	28.5	33.0	37.5	42.0	46.0	51.0	59.5	68.5
	32″	38″	16.0	20.5	25.0	29.5	34.0	38.5	43.0	47.5	52.5	61.5	70.5

ENCLOSURE DEPTH	Height of Wall Hung Enclosures	Height of Floor Mounted Enclosures	16″ sq. ft.	20″ sq. ft.	24″ sq. ft.	28″ sq. ft.	32″ sq. ft.	36″ sq. ft.	40″ sq. ft.	44″ sq. ft.	48″ sq. ft.	56″ sq. ft.	64″ sq. ft.
8″	......	18″	15.0	19.0	23.0	27.5	31.5	35.5	40.0	44.0	48.0	56.5	65.0
	14″	20″	16.5	21.5	26.0	31.0	35.5	40.5	45.5	50.0	55.0	64.5	74.0
	18″	24″	18.0	23.0	28.5	33.5	38.5	44.0	49.0	54.0	59.0	69.5	80.0
	20″	26″	18.5	24.0	29.0	34.5	40.0	45.0	50.5	56.0	61.0	72.0	82.5
	26″	32″	19.0	24.5	30.0	35.5	41.0	46.5	52.0	57.5	63.0	74.0	85.0
	32″	36″	19.5	25.0	31.0	36.5	42.0	47.5	53.5	59.0	64.5	75.5	87.0

ENCLOSURE DEPTH	Height of Wall Hung Enclosures	Height of Floor Mounted Enclosures	16″ sq. ft.	20″ sq. ft.	24″ sq. ft.	28″ sq. ft.	32″ sq. ft.	36″ sq. ft.	40″ sq. ft.	44″ sq. ft.	48″ sq. ft.	56″ sq. ft.	64″ sq. ft.
10″	......	18″	15.5	20.0	24.0	28.5	32.5	37.0	41.5	46.0	50.0	58.5	67.5
	14″	20″	18.5	24.0	29.0	34.5	39.5	45.0	50.0	55.5	60.5	71.0	81.5
	18″	24″	21.0	27.0	33.0	39.0	45.0	51.0	57.0	63.0	69.0	81.0	92.5
	20″	26″	22.0	28.0	34.5	40.5	47.0	53.5	59.5	66.0	72.0	84.5	97.0
	26″	32″	22.5	29.5	36.0	42.5	49.0	55.5	62.0	68.5	75.0	88.0	101.0
	32″	38″	23.5	30.5	37.0	44.0	50.5	57.5	64.0	71.0	77.5	91.5	105.0

THE TRANE COMPANY

(Continued from previous page)

RATINGS FOR TRANE CONVECTORS, TYPES "SFK" and "SW"*

*(See measuring instructions on pages 49 and 50)

ENCLOSURE LENGTH	Height of Wall Hung Enclosures	Height of Floor Mounted Enclosures	16″	20″	24″	28″	32″	36″	40″	44″	48″	56″	64″
			sq. ft.	sq. ft.	sq. ft.	sq. ft.	sq. ft.	sq. ft.	sq. ft.	sq. ft.	sq. ft.	sq. ft.	sq. ft.
ENCLOSURE DEPTH 4″	......	18″	9.0	11.5	14.0	16.5	19.0	21.5	24.0	26.5	29.0	33.5	38.5
	14″	20″	10.0	12.5	15.5	18.0	20.5	23.5	26.0	29.0	31.5	37.0	42.5
	18″	24″	10.5	13.5	16.5	19.0	22.0	25.0	27.5	30.5	33.5	39.5	45.5
	20″	26″	10.5	13.5	16.5	19.5	22.5	25.5	28.5	31.5	34.5	40.5	46.5
	26″	32″	11.0	14.0	17.0	20.0	23.0	26.0	29.0	32.0	35.0	41.5	47.5
	32″	38″	11.0	14.0	17.5	20.5	23.5	26.5	30.0	33.0	36.0	42.5	48.5

ENCLOSURE LENGTH	Height of Wall Hung Enclosures	Height of Floor Mounted Enclosures	16″	20″	24″	28″	32″	36″	40″	44″	48″	56″	64″
			sq. ft.	sq. ft.	sq. ft.	sq. ft.	sq. ft.	sq. ft.	sq. ft.	sq. ft.	sq. ft.	sq. ft.	sq. ft.
ENCLOSURE DEPTH 6″	......	18″	16.5	21.0	26.0	30.5	35.0	39.0	43.5	48.5	53.0	62.0	71.5
	14″	20″	17.0	22.0	26.5	31.0	36.9	40.5	45.5	50.0	55.0	64.5	73.5
	18″	24″	18.0	22.5	27.5	32.5	37.5	42.0	47.0	52.0	57.0	67.0	77.0
	20″	26″	18.5	23.0	28.0	33.5	38.5	43.5	48.5	53.5	59.0	69.0	79.5
	26″	32″	18.5	23.5	28.5	33.5	39.0	44.5	49.5	54.5	60.0	70.0	80.5
	32″	38″	20.5	26.5	32.5	38.0	44.0	50.0	55.5	61.5	68.0	79.5	91.0

ENCLOSURE LENGTH	Height of Wall Hung Enclosures	Height of Floor Mounted Enclosures	16″	20″	24″	28″	32″	36″	40″	44″	48″	56″	64″
			sq. ft.	sq. ft.	sq. ft.	sq. ft.	sq. ft.	sq. ft.	sq. ft.	sq. ft.	sq. ft.	sq. ft.	sq. ft.
ENCLOSURE DEPTH 8″	......	18″	21.0	27.0	32.5	38.5	44.0	50.0	56.0	61.5	67.5	79.0	91.0
	14″	20″	21.5	27.5	33.5	40.0	46.0	52.0	58.5	64.0	70.5	82.5	95.0
	18″	24″	22.0	28.0	34.5	40.5	46.5	53.0	59.0	65.0	71.0	83.5	96.0
	20″	26″	22.5	29.0	35.0	41.0	47.5	53.5	60.0	67.0	73.0	86.0	98.5
	26″	32″	23.0	29.5	36.0	42.5	49.5	56.0	62.5	69.0	76.0	89.0	102.0
	32″	38″	24.0	31.0	38.5	45.0	52.0	59.0	66.5	73.0	80.0	93.5	108.0

ENCLOSURE LENGTH	Height of Wall Hung Enclosures	Height of Floor Mounted Enclosures	16″	20″	24″	28″	32″	36″	40″	44″	48″	56″	64″
			sq. ft.	sq. ft.	sq. ft.	sq. ft.	sq. ft.	sq. ft.	sq. ft.	sq. ft.	sq. ft.	sq. ft.	sq. ft.
ENCLOSURE DEPTH 10″	......	18″	22.0	28.5	35.5	40.5	45.0	52.5	59.0	65.5	71.0	83.0	96.0
	14″	20″	24.5	32.0	38.5	45.5	52.0	59.5	66.0	73.0	80.0	93.5	107.5
	18″	24″	26.0	33.5	41.0	48.5	56.0	63.0	70.5	78.0	85.5	100.5	115.0
	20″	26″	27.0	34.5	42.5	50.0	58.0	66.0	73.0	81.0	88.5	104.0	119.5
	26″	32″	28.0	37.0	45.0	53.0	61.0	69.0	77.5	85.5	93.5	110.0	126.0
	32″	38″	30.0	39.0	47.5	56.0	64.5	73.5	82.0	91.0	99.0	117.0	134.0

H. B. SMITH COMPANY

Westfield, Mass.

The Smith Convector

This illustration shows the convector enclosure type used with Smith convectors, For identification check enclosure.

Enclosure Types and Convector Ratings

RATINGS FOR SMITH CONVECTORS*

*(Ratings are given in sq. ft. E.D.R. for steam)

ENCLOSURE LENGTH, IN.		20	25	30	35	38½	43½	48½	53½	58½	63½	68½	72	77	82	87	92	97	102
"L" CONVECTOR LENGTH, IN.		18	23	28	33	36½	41½	46½	51½	56½	61½	66½	70	75	80	85	90	95	100
	Enclosure Height	sq. ft.	sq. ft.	sq. ft.	sq. ft.	sq. ft.	sq. ft.	sq. ft.	sq. ft.	sq. ft.	sq. ft.	sq. ft.	sq. ft.	sq. ft.	sq. ft.	sq. ft.	sq. ft.	sq. ft.	sq. ft.
ELEMENT DEPTH 3⅝″	20″	9.2	11.8	14.3	16.8	18.4	21.0	23.5	26.1	28.6	31.2	33.8	36.3	38.8	41.3	43.8	46.4	48.9	51.4
	22″	9.6	12.2	14.9	17.6	19.2	21.9	24.6	27.3	29.9	32.6	35.3	37.9	40.5	43.3	45.9	48.6	51.3	53.9
	24″	9.9	12.7	15.4	18.2	19.8	22.6	25.3	28.1	30.9	33.6	36.4	39.1	41.9	44.6	47.3	50.0	52.8	55.5
	26″	10.2	13.0	15.8	18.6	20.3	23.1	26.0	28.8	31.7	34.5	37.3	40.1	42.9	45.7	48.5	51.3	54.1	56.9
	29″	10.4	13.4	16.4	19.3	21.0	23.9	26.8	29.7	32.7	35.6	38.5	41.4	44.3	47.3	50.1	53.1	56.0	58.9
	32″	10.6	13.6	16.6	19.5	21.2	24.2	27.2	30.2	33.2	36.0	39.0	41.9	44.9	47.9	50.8	53.7	56.7	59.9
	35″	10.7	13.7	16.7	19.7	21.5	24.5	27.5	30.5	33.5	36.5	39.4	42.4	45.5	48.4	51.3	55.3	58.1	61.0
	38″	10.9	14.0	16.9	20.0	21.8	24.8	27.9	30.9	33.8	37.0	40.0	42.9	46.0	49.0	51.9	55.9	58.7	61.7

ENCLOSURE LENGTH, IN.		20	25	30	35	38½	43½	48½	53½	58½	63½	68½	72	77	82	87	92	97	102
"L" CONVECTOR LENGTH, IN.		18	23	28	33	36½	41½	46½	51½	56½	61½	66½	70	75	80	85	90	95	100
	Enclosure Height	sq. ft.	sq. ft.	sq. ft.	sq. ft.	sq. ft.	sq. ft.	sq. ft.	sq. ft.	sq. ft.	sq. ft.	sq. ft.	sq. ft.	sq. ft.	sq. ft.	sq. ft.	sq. ft.	sq. ft.	sq. ft.
ELEMENT DEPTH 5⅝″	20″	12.2	15.6	18.9	22.3	25.1	28.5	31.9	35.3	38.6	42.0	45.4	48.8	52.1	55.5	58.9	62.3	65.6	69.0
	22″	12.7	16.2	19.8	23.3	26.3	29.9	33.4	36.9	40.4	43.9	47.4	50.9	54.5	58.0	61.5	65.0	68.5	72.0
	24″	13.1	16.7	20.3	23.9	26.9	30.8	34.1	37.7	41.4	45.0	48.6	52.2	55.8	59.4	63.0	66.6	70.2	73.8
	26″	13.4	17.2	20.9	24.6	27.8	31.5	35.2	39.0	42.7	46.4	50.1	53.9	57.6	61.4	65.1	68.9	72.5	76.3
	29″	13.8	17.6	21.5	25.4	28.6	32.5	36.4	40.1	44.0	47.9	51.7	55.1	58.7	62.6	66.5	70.3	74.2	77.4
	32″	14.0	17.9	21.8	25.7	29.0	32.9	36.8	40.7	44.6	48.4	52.4	56.3	60.1	64.0	68.0	71.8	75.7	78.7
	35″	14.1	18.1	22.1	26.0	29.3	33.3	37.3	41.2	45.2	49.1	53.0	57.0	60.9	64.8	68.9	72.7	76.7	80.1
	38″	14.4	18.4	22.3	26.5	29.8	33.8	37.8	41.8	45.8	49.8	53.7	57.7	61.7	65.7	69.7	73.6	77.7	81.6

ENCLOSURE LENGTH, IN.		25	30	35	38½	43½	48½	53½	58½	63½	68½	72	77	82	87	92	97	102
"L" CONVECTOR LENGTH, IN.		23	28	33	36½	41½	46½	51½	56½	61½	66½	70	75	80	85	90	95	100
	Enclosure Height	sq. ft.	sq. ft.	sq. ft.	sq. ft.	sq. ft.	sq. ft.	sq. ft.	sq. ft.	sq. ft.	sq. ft.	sq. ft.	sq. ft.	sq. ft.	sq. ft.	sq. ft.	sq. ft.	sq. ft.
ELEMENT DEPTH 7⅜″	20″	22.4	27.2	31.9	35.9	39.9	44.6	49.6	54.4	59.3	64.1	68.9	73.7	78.5	83.2	88.1	92.9	97.6
	22″	23.2	28.3	33.5	37.5	41.6	46.7	51.8	56.8	61.9	67.0	72.0	77.1	82.3	87.2	92.3	97.5	102.4
	24″	24.1	29.2	34.6	38.7	42.9	48.2	53.4	58.7	63.8	69.1	74.2	79.5	84.6	89.9	95.0	100.4	105.5
	26″	24.7	30.1	35.4	39.7	43.9	49.4	54.7	60.2	65.5	70.8	76.2	81.5	86.8	92.2	97.5	102.8	108.1
	29″	25.5	31.0	36.6	41.0	45.4	50.9	56.4	62.1	67.6	73.2	78.7	84.1	89.8	95.2	100.9	106.4	111.9
	32″	25.8	31.5	37.1	41.5	46.0	51.7	57.3	62.9	68.4	74.1	79.6	85.3	91.0	96.5	102.1	107.7	113.8
	35″	26.1	31.8	37.4	41.8	46.3	52.3	58.0	63.7	69.3	75.0	80.6	86.4	91.7	97.6	105.1	110.3	116.9
	38″	26.5	32.1	38.0	42.6	47.2	53.0	58.7	64.3	70.3	76.0	81.5	87.4	93.1	98.6	106.2	111.5	117.2

ENCLOSURE LENGTH, IN.		25	30	35	38½	43½	48½	53½	58½	63½	68½	72	77	82	87	92	97	102
"L" CONVECTOR LENGTH, IN.		23	28	33	36½	41½	46½	51½	56½	61½	66½	70	75	80	85	90	95	100
	Enclosure Height	sq. ft.	sq. ft.	sq. ft.	sq. ft.	sq. ft.	sq. ft.	sq. ft.	sq. ft.	sq. ft.	sq. ft.	sq. ft.	sq. ft.	sq. ft.	sq. ft.	sq. ft.	sq. ft.	sq. ft.
ELEMENT DEPTH 9⅜″	20″	24.7	29.9	35.3	39.9	44.5	49.9	55.3	60.6	66.0	71.3	76.6	81.8	87.2	92.4	97.8	103.0	108.4
	22″	25.6	31.3	36.9	41.8	46.6	52.2	57.8	63.3	68.8	74.5	80.0	85.6	91.2	96.7	102.2	107.8	113.4
	24″	26.5	32.1	37.9	42.9	48.1	53.5	59.2	65.1	70.7	76.5	82.2	87.9	93.6	99.4	105.0	110.8	116.5
	26″	27.2	33.1	38.9	44.0	49.2	55.1	61.0	67.0	72.9	78.7	84.7	90.5	95.5	102.2	108.2	114.0	119.9
	29″	28.0	34.1	40.2	45.5	50.9	57.0	63.0	69.1	75.2	81.3	87.1	92.1	99.1	105.3	111.4	117.4	122.9
	32″	28.3	34.6	40.8	46.1	51.5	57.6	63.8	69.9	76.0	82.3	88.4	94.6	100.7	106.9	113.0	119.2	124.7
	35″	28.7	34.9	41.3	46.6	52.0	58.3	64.7	70.9	77.1	83.3	89.6	95.8	102.1	108.4	115.4	121.2	127.2
	38″	29.2	35.4	41.8	47.2	52.7	59.1	65.4	71.7	78.1	84.3	90.6	97.0	103.3	109.4	116.6	122.8	129.0

TUTTLE & BAILEY, INC.

New Britain, Connecticut

T & B Copper Convectors

Enclosure Types and Measuring Instructions

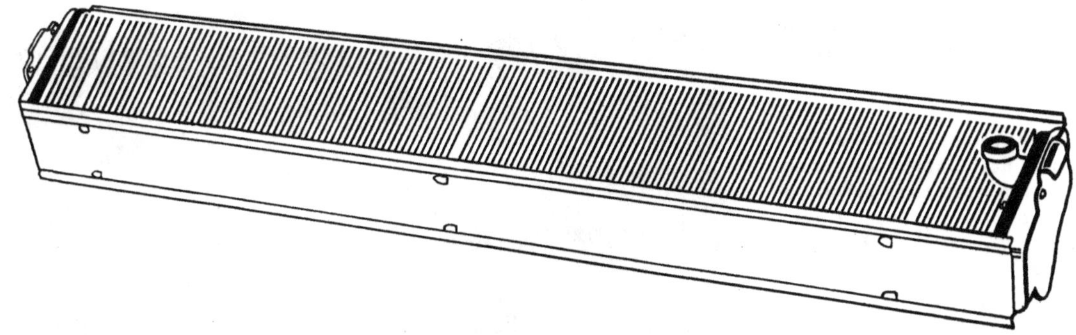

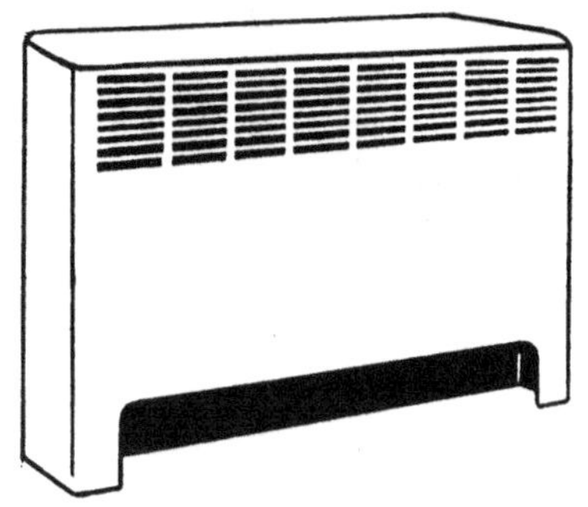

Left: Free standing type T & B convector. Use actual measurements for rating purposes.

Right: Recessed type T & B convector. Measurements: Use actual length less 4", actual height less 1½" and actual depth.

RATINGS FOR TUTTLE & BAILEY COPPER CONVECTORS

*(Note: Ratings are given in sq. ft. E.D.R.)

ENCLOSURE LENGTH			14″	18″	22″	26″	30″	34″	38″	42″	46″	50″	54″	58″	62″
			sq. ft.	sq. ft.	sq. ft.	sq. ft.	sq. ft.	sq. ft.	sq. ft.	sq. ft.	sq. ft.	sq. ft.	sq. ft.	sq. ft.	sq. ft.
ENCLOSURE DEPTH 7½″	Enclosure Height	21½″	......	......	......	......	......	......	45.0	50.0	55.0	60.0	65.0	70.0	75.5
		25½″	......	......	......	......	......	......	48.0	53.5	59.0	64.5	70.0	75.5	80.5
		31½″	......	......	......	......	......	......	......	......	......	......	......	......	......

ENCLOSURE LENGTH			14″	18″	22″	26″	30″	34″	38″	42″	46″	50″	54″	58″	62″
			sq. ft.	sq. ft.	sq. ft.	sq. ft.	sq. ft.	sq. ft.	sq. ft.	sq. ft.	sq. ft.	sq. ft.	sq. ft.	sq. ft.	sq. ft.
ENCLOSURE DEPTH 5¾″	Enclosure Height	21½″	11.0	15.0	19.0	23.0	27.0	31.0	35.0	39.0	43.0	47.0	51.0	54.5	58.5
		25½″	12.0	16.5	21.0	25.0	29.5	34.0	38.0	42.5	46.5	51.0	55.5	59.5	64.0
		31½″	....	18.0	22.5	27.0	31.5	36.5	41.0	....	50.0	....	59.5	....	68.5

UNITED STATES RADIATOR COMPANY

Detroit, Michigan

Capitol Cast Iron Convectors

FRONT OUTLET GRILLE

Ratings for Capitol cast iron convectors are given below, on the facing page and are continued to pages 56 and 57.

Right: This convector enclosure and element identifies Capitol cast iron convectors. The enclosure, pulled to the right, shows the convector element at left.

Use actual convector measurements to obtain convector ratings from the tables. Measure the depth of the element first, then measure the convector length and enclosure height. Turn to appropriate table for the depth of element and convector length, obtain rating.

RATINGS FOR CAPITOL CAST IRON CONVECTORS*

*(Note: Ratings for steam given in sq. ft. E.D.R. at steam temperature of 215 deg. Same ratings for hot water are based on an average water temperature in the convector of 170 deg.)

CONVECTOR LENGTH			15"	20¼"	22½"	24¾"	30⅜"	32⅝"	35⅝"	37⅞"	40⅛"	42⅜"	44⅝"
			sq. ft.	sq. ft.	sq. ft.	sq. ft.	sq. ft.	sq. ft.	sq. ft.	sq. ft.	sq. ft.	sq. ft.	sq. ft.
ELEMENT DEPTH 3½"	Enclosure Height	20"	7.5	10.3	11.5	12.7	15.7	16.9	18.5	19.7	20.9	22.1	23.3
		23"	8.5	11.5	12.9	14.3	17.6	18.9	20.7	22.0	23.4	24.7	26.0
		26"	9.1	12.4	13.9	15.3	18.9	20.3	22.7	23.7	25.1	26.6	28.0
		29"	9.5	13.0	14.5	16.0	19.7	21.2	23.3	24.7	26.2	27.7	29.1
		32"	9.8	13.4	14.9	16.4	20.3	21.8	23.8	25.4	26.9	28.5	30.0
		35"	10.0	13.6	15.3	16.8	20.8	22.3	24.4	25.9	27.6	29.1	30.7
		38"	10.1	13.8	15.6	17.0	21.1	22.7	24.8	26.4	28.0	29.6	31.2
		42"	10.4	14.2	15.8	17.4	21.5	23.1	25.3	26.9	28.5	30.2	31.8
		47"	10.6	14.4	16.1	17.8	21.9	23.6	25.8	27.5	29.1	30.8	32.5
		52"	10.8	14.7	16.4	18.1	22.3	24.0	26.2	27.9	29.6	31.3	33.0
		57"	10.9	14.9	16.6	18.3	22.7	24.6	26.6	28.3	30.0	31.7	33.4

CONVECTOR LENGTH			48"	50¼"	52½"	55½"	57¾"	60"	62¼"	64½"	66⅜"	68⅝"	70⅞"
			sq. ft.	sq. ft.	sq. ft.	sq. ft.	sq. ft.	sq. ft.	sq. ft.	sq. ft.	sq. ft.	sq. ft.	sq. ft.
ELEMENT DEPTH 3½"	Enclosure Height	20"	25.1	26.3	27.5	29.1	30.3	31.5	32.7	33.9	34.9	36.1	37.3
		23"	28.0	29.3	30.7	32.5	33.8	35.1	36.5	37.8	38.9	40.2	41.6
		26"	30.1	31.6	33.0	34.9	36.4	37.8	39.2	40.7	41.9	43.3	44.8
		29"	31.4	32.9	34.4	36.3	37.9	39.3	40.8	42.3	43.5	45.0	46.5
		32"	32.3	33.8	35.4	37.4	38.9	40.5	42.0	43.5	44.8	46.4	47.9
		35"	33.1	34.6	36.2	38.3	39.9	41.4	43.1	44.6	45.9	47.5	49.0
		38"	33.6	35.2	36.8	39.0	40.6	42.2	43.8	45.4	46.7	48.3	49.9
		42"	34.2	35.9	37.5	39.6	41.3	42.9	44.5	46.3	47.5	49.1	50.8
		47"	35.0	36.6	38.3	40.5	42.2	43.9	45.5	47.2	48.6	50.2	51.9
		52"	35.5	37.2	38.9	41.1	42.8	44.5	46.2	47.9	49.3	51.0	52.7
		57"	36.0	37.7	39.4	41.7	43.4	45.1	46.8	48.5	49.9	51.7	53.4

RATINGS FOR CAPITOL CAST IRON CONVECTORS

(Please turn to following page for additional ratings)

CONVECTOR LENGTH			73⅛″	75⅜″	77⅝″	79⅞″	82⅛″	84⅜″	87¾″	92¼″	97⅛″	101⅝″
			sq. ft.	sq. ft.	sq. ft.	sq. ft.	sq. ft.	sq. ft.	sq. ft.	sq. ft.	sq. ft.	sq. ft.
ELEMENT DEPTH 3½″	Enclosure Height	20″	38.5	39.7	40.9	42.1	43.3	44.5	46.2	48.7	51.3	53.7
		23″	42.9	44.2	45.6	46.9	48.2	49.6	51.6	54.2	57.1	59.8
		26″	46.6	47.6	49.1	50.5	51.9	53.4	55.5	58.4	61.5	64.4
		29″	48.0	49.5	51.0	52.5	54.0	55.5	57.7	60.7	63.9	66.9
		32″	49.4	51.0	52.5	54.0	55.6	57.1	59.4	62.4	65.8	68.9
		35″	50.6	52.2	53.7	55.3	56.9	58.4	61.8	63.8	67.3	70.5
		38″	51.5	53.1	54.7	56.4	58.0	59.6	62.0	65.2	68.7	71.9
		42″	52.4	54.0	55.6	57.3	58.9	60.5	63.0	66.2	69.7	73.0
		47″	53.6	55.2	56.9	58.6	60.2	61.9	64.4	67.8	71.3	74.7
		52″	54.4	56.0	57.7	59.4	61.1	62.8	65.3	68.7	72.3	75.7
		57″	55.1	56.8	58.5	60.2	61.9	63.7	66.2	69.6	73.4	76.7

CONVECTOR LENGTH			15″	20¼″	22½″	24¾″	30⅜″	32⅝″	35⅝″	37⅞″	40⅛″	42⅜″	44⅝″
			sq. ft.	sq. ft.	sq. ft.	sq. ft.	sq. ft.	sq. ft.	sq. ft.	sq. ft.	sq. ft.	sq. ft.	sq. ft.
ELEMENT DEPTH 5⅜″	Enclosure Height	20″	11.2	15.3	17.0	18.8	23.2	25.0	27.3	29.1	30.8	32.6	34.3
		23″	12.3	16.9	18.8	20.8	25.7	27.7	30.3	32.2	34.2	36.2	38.1
		26″	13.3	18.3	20.4	22.5	27.8	30.0	32.8	34.9	37.0	39.2	41.2
		29″	14.1	19.3	21.5	23.7	29.3	31.5	34.5	36.7	38.9	41.1	43.3
		32″	14.5	19.8	22.1	24.4	30.1	32.4	35.5	37.8	40.1	42.4	44.7
		35″	14.8	20.2	22.6	24.9	30.8	33.1	36.2	38.5	40.9	43.2	45.6
		38″	15.0	20.5	23.0	25.3	31.4	33.8	36.8	39.2	41.6	44.0	46.4
		42″	15.4	21.0	23.5	25.9	32.0	34.4	37.7	40.1	42.5	45.0	47.4
		47″	15.7	21.4	24.0	26.4	32.6	35.1	38.4	40.9	43.4	45.9	48.3
		52″	15.9	21.7	24.3	26.8	33.1	35.7	39.0	41.5	44.1	46.6	49.1
		57″	16.1	22.1	24.6	27.2	33.6	36.2	39.6	42.1	44.7	47.3	49.8

CONVECTOR LENGTH			73⅛″	75⅜″	77⅝″	79⅞″	82⅛″	84⅜″	87¾″	92¼″	97⅛″	101⅝″
			sq. ft.	sq. ft.	sq. ft.	sq. ft.	sq. ft.	sq. ft.	sq. ft.	sq. ft.	sq. ft.	sq. ft.
ELEMENT DEPTH 5⅜″	Enclosure Height	20″	56.7	58.4	60.2	60.9	63.7	65.5	68.1	71.6	75.5	79.0
		23″	62.9	64.9	66.9	68.8	70.8	72.7	75.7	79.6	83.9	87.8
		26″	68.2	70.3	72.4	74.5	76.6	78.8	82.0	86.2	90.8	95.0
		29″	71.5	73.7	75.9	78.1	80.4	82.6	85.9	90.4	95.2	99.6
		32″	73.8	76.1	78.4	80.7	82.9	85.2	88.7	93.3	98.3	102.9
		35″	75.2	77.5	79.9	82.2	84.6	86.9	90.4	95.1	100.2	104.8
		38″	76.6	79.0	81.3	83.7	86.1	88.5	92.1	96.8	102.0	106.8
		42″	78.2	80.6	83.0	85.5	87.9	90.4	94.0	99.0	104.1	109.0
		47″	79.7	82.2	84.7	87.2	89.7	92.1	95.9	100.8	106.2	111.1
		52″	81.0	83.5	86.0	88.6	91.1	93.6	97.4	102.4	107.9	112.9
		57″	82.4	84.9	87.4	90.0	92.5	95.1	99.0	104.1	109.6	114.8

CONVECTOR LENGTH			48″	50¼″	52½″	55½″	57¾″	60″	62¼″	64½″	66⅜″	68⅝″	70⅞″
			sq. ft.	sq. ft.	sq. ft.	sq. ft.	sq. ft.	sq. ft.	sq. ft.	sq. ft.	sq. ft.	sq. ft.	sq. ft.
ELEMENT DEPTH 5⅜″	Enclosure Height	20″	37.0	38.8	40.5	42.9	44.6	46.4	48.2	49.9	51.4	53.1	54.9
		23″	41.1	43.0	45.0	47.7	49.6	51.5	53.5	55.4	57.1	59.0	60.6
		26″	44.5	46.6	48.7	51.5	53.7	55.8	57.9	60.0	61.8	63.9	66.0
		29″	46.7	48.9	51.1	54.1	56.3	58.5	60.7	63.0	64.5	67.0	69.3
		32″	48.1	50.4	52.7	55.8	58.1	60.4	62.5	65.0	66.9	69.2	71.5
		35″	49.1	51.4	53.8	56.9	59.2	61.6	63.9	66.2	68.8	70.5	72.9
		38″	49.9	52.3	54.7	57.9	60.3	62.7	65.0	67.4	69.4	72.1	74.2
		42″	51.0	53.5	55.9	59.2	61.5	64.0	66.4	68.6	70.9	73.6	75.8
		47″	52.1	54.5	57.0	60.3	62.8	65.3	67.8	70.6	72.3	75.1	77.3
		52″	52.9	55.4	57.9	61.3	63.8	66.3	68.8	71.5	73.5	76.5	78.5
		57″	53.7	56.2	58.8	62.2	64.8	67.3	69.7	72.5	74.6	77.9	79.7

UNITED STATES RADIATOR COMPANY

RATINGS FOR CAPITOL CAST IRON CONVECTORS

(Continued from previous page)

CONVECTOR LENGTH		15″	20¼″	22½″	24¾″	30⅜″	32⅝″	35⅝″	37⅞″	40⅛″	42⅜″	44⅝″
	Enclosure Height	sq. ft.	sq. ft.	sq. ft.	sq. ft.	sq. ft.	sq. ft.	sq. ft.	sq. ft.	sq. ft.	sq. ft.	sq. ft.
ELEMENT DEPTH 7½″	20″	14.1	19.3	21.6	23.8	29.5	31.7	34.7	37.0	39.3	41.5	43.8
	23″	15.4	21.3	23.7	26.2	32.4	34.9	38.3	40.7	43.2	45.7	48.2
	26″	16.8	23.0	25.7	28.4	35.2	37.9	41.4	44.1	46.8	49.5	52.2
	29″	17.9	24.5	27.4	30.2	37.3	40.2	43.9	46.8	49.6	52.5	55.3
	32″	18.5	25.4	28.4	31.4	38.8	41.8	45.7	48.7	51.4	54.6	57.6
	35″	19.1	26.2	29.2	32.3	39.9	43.0	47.0	50.1	53.2	56.2	59.3
	38″	19.5	26.8	29.9	33.0	40.8	43.9	48.1	51.2	54.3	57.4	60.6
	42″	20.0	27.4	30.6	33.8	41.7	45.0	49.2	52.4	55.6	58.8	62.0
	47″	20.4	27.9	31.2	34.5	42.7	46.0	50.3	53.6	56.9	60.2	63.4
	52″	20.8	28.5	31.9	35.1	43.5	46.8	51.3	54.6	57.9	61.2	64.6
	57″	21.2	29.1	32.5	35.7	44.3	47.7	52.2	55.6	59.0	62.3	65.7

CONVECTOR LENGTH		48″	50¼″	52½″	55½″	57¾″	60″	62¼″	64½″	66⅜″	68⅝″	70⅞″
	Enclosure Height	sq. ft.	sq. ft.	sq. ft.	sq. ft.	sq. ft.	sq. ft.	sq. ft.	sq. ft.	sq. ft.	sq. ft.	sq. ft.
ELEMENT DEPTH 7½″	20″	47.2	49.4	51.7	54.7	56.9	59.2	61.4	63.7	65.6	67.8	70.1
	23″	51.8	54.4	56.9	60.2	62.7	65.2	67.7	70.2	72.3	74.8	77.2
	26″	56.3	59.0	61.6	65.2	67.9	70.6	73.3	76.0	78.3	81.0	83.6
	29″	59.6	62.4	65.3	69.1	71.9	74.7	77.6	80.4	82.8	85.6	88.5
	32″	62.0	65.0	68.0	71.9	74.9	77.8	80.8	83.8	86.2	89.2	92.2
	35″	63.8	66.9	69.9	74.0	77.1	80.1	83.2	86.2	88.8	91.8	94.9
	38″	65.2	68.4	71.4	75.6	78.7	81.8	85.0	88.1	90.7	93.8	96.9
	42″	66.8	69.9	73.1	77.5	80.6	83.8	87.0	90.2	92.9	96.1	99.3
	47″	68.3	71.6	74.5	79.3	82.5	85.8	89.1	92.4	95.1	98.4	101.6
	52″	69.5	72.9	75.9	80.6	84.0	87.3	90.6	94.0	96.7	100.0	103.4
	57″	70.8	74.2	77.5	82.1	85.5	88.8	92.2	95.6	98.4	101.8	105.2

CONVECTOR LENGTH		73⅛″	75⅜″	77⅝″	79⅞″	82⅛″	84⅜″	87¾″	92¼″	97⅛″	101⅝″
	Enclosure Height	sq. ft.	sq. ft.	sq. ft.	sq. ft.	sq. ft.	sq. ft.	sq. ft.	sq. ft.	sq. ft.	sq. ft.
ELEMENT DEPTH 7½″	20″	72.3	74.6	76.9	79.1	81.4	83.6	87.0	91.5	96.4	100.9
	23″	79.7	82.2	84.7	87.2	89.7	92.2	95.9	100.9	106.3	111.3
	26″	86.3	89.0	91.7	94.4	97.1	99.0	103.8	111.2	115.1	120.5
	29″	91.3	94.2	97.0	99.8	102.7	105.5	109.8	115.5	121.6	127.3
	32″	95.1	98.1	101.1	104.0	107.0	110.0	114.4	120.3	126.8	132.7
	35″	97.9	101.0	104.0	107.1	110.1	113.2	117.8	123.9	130.5	136.6
	38″	100.0	103.1	106.3	109.4	112.6	115.6	120.3	126.5	133.3	139.5
	42″	102.5	105.7	108.9	112.0	115.2	118.4	123.2	129.6	136.0	142.9
	47″	104.9	108.2	111.5	114.5	118.0	120.8	126.2	132.8	139.9	146.4
	52″	106.7	110.0	113.5	116.7	120.0	123.2	128.3	135.0	142.3	148.8
	57″	108.6	111.9	115.3	118.7	122.1	125.5	130.5	137.3	144.6	151.4

CONVECTOR LENGTH		48⅝″	50⅞″	53⅛″	56⅛″	58⅜″	60⅝″	62⅞″	65⅛″	67″	69¼″	71½″
	Enclosure Height	sq. ft.	sq. ft.	sq. ft.	sq. ft.	sq. ft.	sq. ft.	sq. ft.	sq. ft.	sq. ft.	sq. ft.	sq. ft.
ENCLOSURE DEPTH 9⅛″	20″	57.9	60.6	63.4	67.1	69.8	72.6	75.3	78.0	80.3	83.1	85.8
	23″	63.7	66.7	69.7	73.8	76.8	79.5	82.8	85.8	88.4	91.4	94.4
	26″	69.0	72.2	75.5	79.8	83.1	86.3	89.6	92.8	95.6	98.8	102.1
	29″	73.2	76.7	80.2	84.8	88.3	91.7	95.2	98.6	101.5	104.9	108.5
	32″	76.5	80.2	83.8	88.6	92.3	95.9	99.5	103.2	106.2	109.8	113.4
	35″	78.9	82.9	86.4	91.4	95.1	98.8	102.6	106.2	109.4	113.2	116.9
	38″	80.7	84.7	88.4	93.5	97.3	101.1	104.9	108.6	111.9	115.8	119.6
	42″	82.5	86.6	90.4	95.7	99.4	103.3	107.3	111.2	114.4	118.3	122.2
	47″	84.2	88.2	92.2	97.6	101.5	105.5	109.5	113.5	116.9	120.8	124.9
	52″	85.9	89.9	94.0	99.4	103.5	107.5	111.6	115.7	119.0	123.1	127.2
	57″	87.0	91.1	95.2	100.7	104.8	108.9	113.0	117.2	120.6	124.7	128.9

RATINGS FOR CAPITOL CAST IRON CONVECTORS

CONVECTOR LENGTH			15⅝″	20⅞″	23⅛″	25⅜″	31″	33¼″	36¼″	38½″	40¾″	43″	45¼″
			sq. ft.	sq. ft.	sq. ft.	sq. ft.	sq. ft.	sq. ft.	sq. ft.	sq. ft.	sq. ft.	sq. ft.	sq. ft.
ENCLOSURE DEPTH 9⅛″	Enclosure Height	20″	17.7	24.1	26.8	29.8	36.4	39.2	42.8	45.6	48.3	51.1	53.8
		23″	19.5	26.5	29.5	32.5	40.1	43.1	47.1	50.1	53.2	56.2	59.2
		26″	21.2	28.8	32.1	35.3	43.5	46.7	51.1	54.3	57.6	60.8	64.1
		29″	22.4	30.5	34.0	37.4	46.1	49.6	54.2	57.6	61.1	64.6	68.5
		32″	23.3	31.7	35.4	39.0	48.1	51.7	56.6	60.1	63.8	67.5	71.1
		35″	24.1	32.9	36.6	40.3	49.8	53.2	58.4	62.1	65.9	69.6	73.3
		38″	24.7	33.6	37.5	41.3	50.8	54.6	59.7	63.6	67.4	71.2	75.0
		42″	25.2	34.3	38.2	42.1	51.9	55.8	61.0	64.9	68.8	72.7	76.6
		47″	25.7	35.0	38.9	42.9	52.9	57.0	62.2	66.2	70.2	74.2	78.2
		52″	26.3	35.7	39.7	43.7	53.9	58.1	63.4	67.6	71.6	75.7	79.8
		57″	26.7	36.3	40.4	44.5	54.8	58.9	64.4	68.5	72.6	76.7	80.8

CONVECTOR LENGTH			73¾″	76″	78¼″	80½″	82¾″	85″	88⅜″	92⅞″	97¾″	102¼″
			sq. ft.	sq. ft.	sq. ft.	sq. ft.	sq. ft.	sq. ft.	sq. ft.	sq. ft.	sq. ft.	sq. ft.
ELEMENT DEPTH 9⅛″	Enclosure Height	20″	88.6	91.3	94.1	96.8	99.6	102.3	106.4	111.9	117.4	123.3
		23″	96.6	100.4	103.4	106.5	110.5	112.5	117.0	123.1	129.1	135.6
		26″	105.3	108.6	111.8	115.1	118.3	121.6	126.5	133.0	139.5	146.6
		29″	111.9	115.4	118.9	122.3	125.7	129.4	134.5	141.4	148.3	155.8
		32″	117.1	120.7	124.3	128.0	131.6	135.2	140.7	147.9	155.2	163.0
		35″	120.6	124.4	127.8	131.8	135.6	139.2	144.9	152.4	159.8	167.9
		38″	123.4	127.2	131.0	134.9	138.7	142.5	148.2	155.9	163.5	171.8
		42″	126.1	130.1	134.0	137.9	141.8	145.7	151.6	159.4	167.2	175.7
		47″	128.9	132.9	136.9	140.9	144.9	148.9	154.9	162.9	170.9	179.6
		52″	131.2	135.3	139.3	143.1	147.5	151.5	157.3	165.7	173.9	182.7
		57″	132.9	137.0	141.2	145.3	149.4	153.5	159.7	167.9	176.1	185.0

UNITED STATES RADIATOR COMPANY

U. S. Copper Convectors

Enclosure Types and Convector Ratings

(U. S. copper convector ratings for all types begin on the following page.)

This convector enclosure identifies U. S. copper convectors, Type "F".

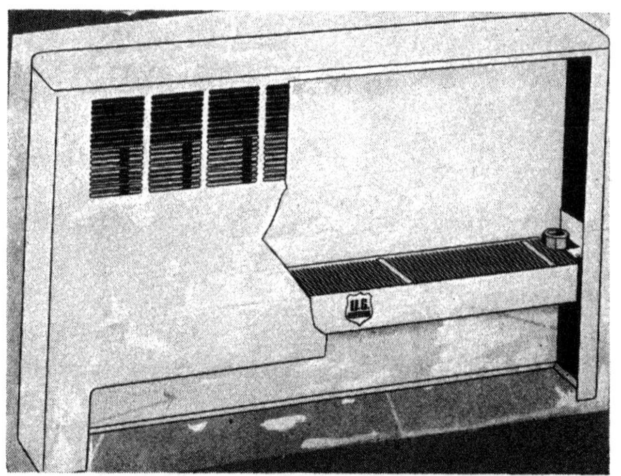

U. S. copper convectors are easily identified by the trade name placed on the front edge of the element, as shown at bottom center of the drawing above.

UNITED STATES RADIATOR COMPANY

(See measuring instructions on previous page)

RATINGS FOR U. S. COPPER CONVECTORS, TYPE "F"*

U. S. Copper Convectors

*(Note: Ratings given in sq. ft. E.D.R. based on steam at 215 deg entering air at 65 deg temperature.)

ENCLOSURE LENGTH			20⅜"	24⅜"	28⅜"	32⅜"	36⅜"	40⅜"	44⅜"	48⅜"	56⅜"	64⅜"
			sq. ft.	sq. ft.	sq. ft.	sq. ft.	sq. ft.	sq. ft.	sq. ft.	sq. ft.	sq. ft.	sq. ft.
ENCLOSURE DEPTH 6"	Enclosure Height	20"	16.2	19.7	23.2	26.8	30.3	33.7	37.4	41.0	48.0	55.0
		24"	18.7	22.7	26.8	30.8	34.8	38.9	43.0	47.0	55.5	63.6
		32"	20.2	24.2	28.8	33.3	37.9	42.4	46.5	51.5	60.0	70.1

ENCLOSURE LENGTH			20⅜"	24⅜"	28⅜"	32⅜"	36⅜"	40⅜"	44⅜"	48⅜"	56⅜"	64⅜"
			sq. ft.	sq. ft.	sq. ft.	sq. ft.	sq. ft.	sq. ft.	sq. ft.	sq. ft.	sq. ft.	sq. ft.
ENCLOSURE DEPTH 8"	Enclosure Height	20"	....	....	....	35.9	41.0	46.0	....	55.5	65.1	74.7
		24"	....	....	....	38.9	44.4	49.5	....	59.6	70.2	80.8
		32"	....	....	....	41.4	47.0	52.5	....	63.6	74.7	85.8

ENCLOSURE LENGTH			20⅜"	24⅜"	28⅜"	32⅜"	36⅜"	40⅜"	44⅜"	48⅜"	56⅜"	64⅜"
			sq. ft.	sq. ft.	sq. ft.	sq. ft.	sq. ft.	sq. ft.	sq. ft.	sq. ft.	sq. ft.	sq. ft.
ENCLOSURE DEPTH 10"	Enclosure Height	20"	....	....	....	....	45.5	50.5	....	61.1	71.7	82.3
		24"	....	....	....	....	51.5	57.6	....	69.7	81.8	93.4
		32"	....	....	....	....	56.0	62.6	....	75.6	88.9	102.0

UNITED STATES RADIATOR COMPANY

U. S. COPPER CONVECTORS, TYPES "FE" and "FB"

Ratings for Types "FE" and "FB" Convectors are Given on the Facing Page.

Left: This enclosure identifies U. S. copper convectors, Type "FE".

Right: Cabinet convector, Type "FB" U. S. copper convector is shown in this drawing of the enclosure.

RATINGS FOR U. S. COPPER CONVECTORS, TYPES "FE" AND "FB"

***(Note: Ratings given in sq. ft. EDR. based on steam at 215 deg and entering air at 65 deg temperature.)**

See Facing Page For Measuring Instructions

ENCLOSURE LENGTH		16⅜"	20⅜"	24⅜"	28⅜"	32⅜"	36⅜"	40⅜"	44⅜"	48⅜"	56⅜"	64⅜"
	Enclosure Height	sq. ft.	sq. ft.	sq. ft.	sq. ft.	sq. ft.	sq. ft.	sq. ft.	sq. ft.	sq. ft.	sq. ft.	sq. ft.
ENCLOSURE DEPTH 4"	18"	7.6	10.1	12.1	14.1	16.7	18.7	20.8	23.2	25.3	29.3	33.8
	20"	9.1	11.6	14.1	16.7	19.2	21.7	24.2	26.8	29.3	34.3	39.4
	24"	10.2	13.1	16.2	18.7	21.7	24.7	27.3	30.3	33.3	38.9	45.0
	26"	10.6	13.6	16.6	19.7	22.7	25.7	28.8	31.8	34.8	40.8	46.9
	32"	11.1	14.1	17.2	20.2	23.2	26.3	29.3	32.3	35.4	42.0	48.0
	38"	11.1	14.1	17.7	20.7	23.7	26.7	30.3	33.3	36.4	42.8	49.0

ENCLOSURE LENGTH		16⅜"	20⅜"	24⅜"	28⅜"	32⅜"	36⅜"	40⅜"	44⅜"	48⅜"	56⅜"	64⅜"
	Enclosure Height	sq. ft.	sq. ft	sq. ft.	sq. ft.	sq. ft.	sq. ft.	sq. ft.	sq. ft.	sq. ft.	sq. ft.	sq. ft.
ENCLOSURE DEPTH 6"	18"	11.1	14.1	17.7	20.7	23.7	26.8	30.0	33.3	36.4	42.4	49.0
	20"	12.6	16.2	19.7	23.2	26.8	30.3	33.7	37.4	41.0	48.0	55.0
	24"	14.6	18.7	22.7	26.8	30.8	34.8	38.9	43.0	47.0	55.5	63.6
	26"	15.1	19.1	23.2	27.8	31.8	36.3	40.4	44.4	49.0	57.5	66.0
	32"	15.6	20.2	24.2	28.8	33.3	37.9	42.4	46.5	51.5	60.0	70.1
	38"	16.1	20.7	25.2	29.8	34.3	38.8	43.4	47.9	53.0	62.0	71.1

ENCLOSURE LENGTH		16⅜"	20⅜"	24⅜"	28⅜"	32⅜"	36⅜"	40⅜"	44⅜"	48⅜"	56⅜"	64⅜"
	Enclosure Height	sq. ft.	sq. ft.	sq. ft.	sq. ft.	sq. ft.	sq. ft.	sq. ft.	sq. ft.	sq. ft.	sq. ft.	sq. ft.
ENCLOSURE DEPTH 8"	18"	15.1	19.2	23.2	27.8	31.8	35.9	40.4	44.4	48.5	57.0	65.7
	20"	16.7	21.7	26.3	31.3	35.9	41.0	46.0	50.5	55.5	65.1	74.7
	24"	18.2	23.2	28.8	33.8	38.9	44.4	49.5	54.5	59.6	70.2	80.8
	26"	18.6	24.2	29.3	34.7	40.3	45.4	50.9	56.5	61.5	72.5	83.0
	32"	19.2	24.7	30.3	35.8	41.4	47.0	52.5	58.3	63.6	74.7	85.8
	38"	19.7	25.3	31.3	36.8	42.4	47.9	54.0	59.5	65.1	76.2	87.6

ENCLOSURE LENGTH		16⅜"	20⅜"	24⅜"	28⅜"	32⅜"	36⅜"	40⅜"	44⅜"	48⅜"	56⅜"	64⅜"
	Enclosure Height	sq. ft.	sq. ft.	sq. ft.	sq. ft.	sq. ft.	sq. ft.	sq. ft.	sq. ft.	sq. ft.	sq. ft.	sq. ft.
ENCLOSURE DEPTH 10"	18"	15.6	20.0	24.2	28.8	32.8	37.3	41.9	46.5	50.5	59.0	68.1
	20"	18.7	24.2	29.3	34.8	39.9	45.5	50.5	56.1	61.1	71.7	82.3
	24"	21.2	27.3	33.3	39.4	45.5	51.5	57.6	63.6	69.7	81.8	93.4
	26"	22.2	28.2	34.7	40.8	47.4	54.0	60.0	66.6	72.6	85.2	97.8
	32"	22.7	29.8	36.4	42.9	49.5	56.0	62.6	69.2	75.6	88.9	102.0
	38"	23.7	30.8	37.4	44.4	51.0	58.0	64.6	71.6	78.1	92.4	106.0

UNITED STATES RADIATOR COMPANY

(Continued from preceding page)

Enclosure Types and Convector Ratings

RATINGS FOR TYPE "S" CONVECTORS

*(Note: Ratings are given in sq. ft. E.D.R. based on 215 deg steam and 65 deg entering air temperature)

This cabinet enclosure above identifies U. S. Copper Convectors, Type "S".

ENCLOSURE LENGTH			16⅜″	20⅜″	24⅜″	28⅜″	32⅜″	36⅜″	40⅜″	44⅜″	48⅜″	56⅜″	64″
			sq. ft.	sq. ft.	sq. ft.	sq. ft.	sq. ft.	sq. ft.	sq. ft.	sq. ft.	sq. ft.	sq. ft.	sq. ft.
ENCLOSURE DEPTH 4″	Enclosure Height	14″	10.1	12.6	15.6	18.2	20.7	23.7	26.3	29.3	31.7	37.3	42.8
		18″	10.6	13.6	16.6	19.2	22.2	25.2	27.7	30.8	33.8	39.8	46.9
		20″	10.6	13.6	16.7	19.7	22.7	25.7	28.7	31.8	34.8	40.8	47.0
		26″	11.1	14.1	17.2	20.2	23.2	26.2	29.2	32.3	35.3	41.8	48.8
		32″	11.1	14.1	17.7	20.7	23.7	26.7	30.3	33.3	36.4	42.8	49.0

ENCLOSURE LENGTH			16⅜″	20⅜″	24⅜″	28⅜″	32⅜″	36⅜″	40⅜″	44⅜″	48⅜″	56⅜″	64⅜″
			sq. ft.	sq. ft.	sq. ft.	sq. ft.	sq. ft.	sq. ft.	sq. ft.	sq. ft.	sq. ft.	sq. ft.	sq. ft.
ENCLOSURE DEPTH 6″	Enclosure Height	14″	17.2	22.3	26.9	31.4	37.3	41.0	46.0	50.5	56.0	65.5	74.7
		18″	18.2	22.8	27.8	33.0	38.0	42.6	47.8	52.8	58.0	68.0	78.0
		20″	18.7	23.2	28.3	33.8	38.8	43.9	48.9	54.0	59.6	69.6	80.2
		26″	18.7	23.8	28.9	34.0	39.5	45.0	50.5	55.2	61.0	71.0	81.8
		32″	20.7	26.7	32.8	38.4	44.4	50.5	56.0	62.1	68.6	80.2	91.8

ENCLOSURE LENGTH			16⅜″	20⅜″	24⅜″	28⅜″	32⅜″	36⅜″	40⅜″	44⅜″	48⅜″	56⅜″	64⅜″
			sq. ft.	sq. ft.	sq. ft.	sq. ft.	sq. ft.	sq. ft.	sq. ft.	sq. ft.	sq. ft.	sq. ft.	sq. ft.
ENCLOSURE DEPTH 8″	Enclosure Height	14″	21.7	27.8	33.8	40.5	46.6	52.8	59.2	64.6	71.5	83.8	96.2
		18″	22.2	28.3	34.8	41.0	47.2	53.8	60.0	65.7	72.0	85.0	97.2
		20″	22.7	29.3	35.3	41.4	47.8	54.0	60.6	67.6	73.7	87.7	99.5
		26″	23.2	29.8	36.4	43.0	50.2	57.0	63.2	69.7	77.0	90.2	103.5
		32″	24.3	31.3	38.9	45.4	52.5	59.5	67.1	73.6	80.2	94.5	109.0

ENCLOSURE LENGTH			16⅜″	20⅜″	24⅜″	28⅜″	32⅜″	36⅜″	40⅜″	44⅜″	48⅜″	56⅜″	64⅜″
			sq. ft.	sq. ft.	sq. ft.	sq. ft.	sq. ft.	sq. ft.	sq. ft.	sq. ft.	sq. ft.	sq. ft.	sq. ft.
ENCLOSURE DEPTH 10″	Enclosure Height	14″	24.7	32.3	38.9	46.0	52.5	60.5	67.0	73.7	81.2	95.0	108.5
		18″	26.3	33.8	41.4	49.0	56.6	64.0	71.6	78.8	87.0	102.0	116.5
		20″	27.3	34.8	42.8	50.5	58.6	66.6	73.6	81.8	89.2	105.0	121.5
		26″	28.3	37.4	45.5	53.5	61.6	70.0	78.8	86.4	95.0	111.5	128.0
		32″	30.3	39.4	48.0	56.5	65.2	74.0	82.1	91.8	100.0	118.0	135.2

RATINGS FOR U. S. COPPER CONVECTORS

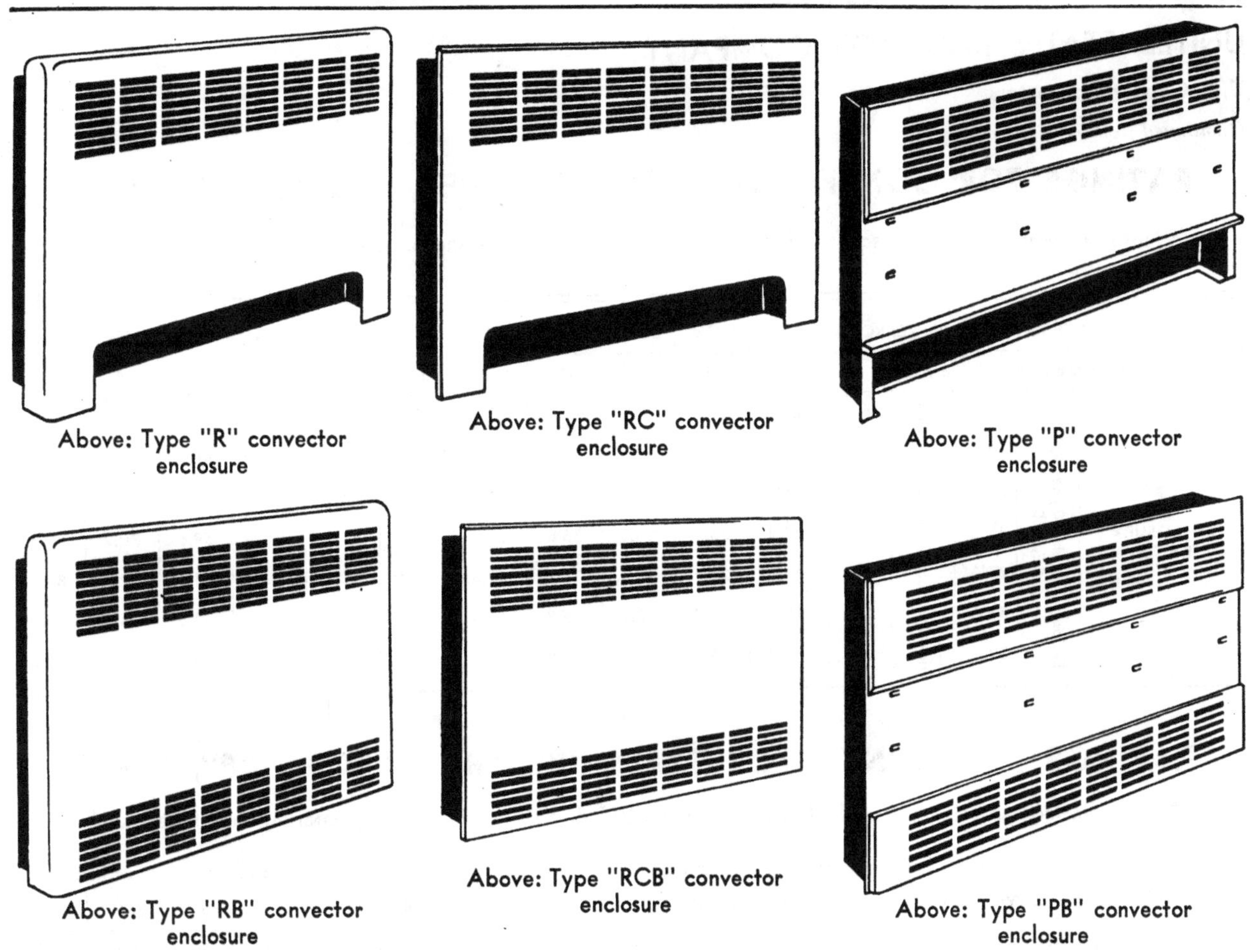

Above: Type "R" convector enclosure

Above: Type "RC" convector enclosure

Above: Type "P" convector enclosure

Above: Type "RB" convector enclosure

Above: Type "RCB" convector enclosure

Above: Type "PB" convector enclosure

RATINGS FOR U.S. COPPER CONVECTORS, TYPES "R", "RB", "RCB", "P", "PB"

ENCLOSURE LENGTHS—TYPES R, RB, RC, RCB			16¼″	20¼″	24¼″	28¼″	32¼″	36¼″	40¼″	44¼″	48¼″	56¼″	64¼″
ENCLOSURE LENGTHS—TYPES P, PB			18″	22″	26″	30″	34″	38″	42″	46″	50″	58″	66″
	Enclosure Height—Types R, RB, RC, RCB	Enclosure Height—Types P and PB	sq. ft.	sq. ft.	sq. ft.	sq. ft.	sq. ft.	sq. ft.	sq. ft.	sq. ft.	sq. ft.	sq. ft.	sq. ft.
ENCLOSURE DEPTH 4″	19½″	19″	7.6	10.1	12.1	14.1	16.7	18.7	20.8	23.2	25.3	29.3	33.8
	21½″	21″	9.1	11.6	14.1	16.7	19.2	21.7	24.2	26.8	29.3	34.3	39.4
	25½″	25″	10.2	13.1	16.2	18.7	21.7	24.7	27.3	30.3	33.3	38.9	45.0
	27½″	27″	10.6	13.6	16.6	19.7	22.7	25.7	28.8	31.8	34.8	40.8	46.9
	33½″	33″	11.1	14.1	17.2	20.2	23.2	26.3	29.3	32.3	35.4	42.0	48.0
	39½″	39″	11.1	14.1	17.7	20.7	23.7	26.7	30.3	33.3	36.4	42.8	49.0

ENCLOSURE LENGTHS—TYPES R, RB, RC, RCB			16¼″	20¼″	24¼″	28¼″	32¼″	36¼″	40¼″	44¼″	48¼″	56¼″	64¼″
ENCLOSURE LENGTHS—TYPES P, PB			18″	22″	26″	30″	34″	38″	42″	46″	50″	58″	66″
	Enclosure Height—Types R, RB, RC, RCB	Enclosure Height—Types P and PB	sq. ft.	sq. ft.	sq. ft.	sq. ft.	sq. ft.	sq. ft.	sq. ft.	sq. ft.	sq. ft.	sq. ft.	sq. ft.
ENCLOSURE DEPTH 6″	19½″	19″	11.1	14.1	17.7	20.7	23.7	26.8	20.0	33.3	36.4	42.4	49.0
	21½″	21″	12.6	16.2	19.7	23.2	26.8	30.3	33.7	37.4	41.0	48.0	55.0
	25½″	25″	14.6	18.7	22.7	26.8	30.8	34.8	38.9	43.0	47.0	55.5	63.6
	27½″	27″	15.1	19.1	23.2	27.8	31.8	36.3	40.4	44.4	49.0	57.5	66.0
	33½″	33″	15.6	20.2	24.2	28.8	33.3	37.9	42.4	46.5	51.5	60.0	70.1
	39½″	39″	16.1	20.7	25.2	29.8	34.3	38.8	43.4	47.9	53.0	62.0	71.1

UNITED STATES RADIATOR COMPANY

U. S. Copper Convectors

(Continued from previous page)

RATINGS FOR CONVECTOR TYPES "R", "RB", "RCB", "P", "PB"*

*(Note: Ratings are given in sq. ft. E.D.R., based on 215 deg steam and 65 deg entering air temperature)

ENCLOSURE LENGTHS—TYPES R, RB, RC, RCB			16¼″	20¼″	24¼″	28¼″	32¼″	36¼″	40¼″	44¼″	48¼″	56¼″	64¼″
ENCLOSURE LENGTHS—TYPES P, PB			18″	22″	26″	30″	34″	38″	42″	46″	50″	58″	66″
	Enclosure Height—Types R, RB, RC, RCB	Enclosure Height—Types P and PB	sq. ft.	sq. ft.	sq. ft.	sq. ft.	sq. ft.	sq. ft.	sq. ft.	sq. ft.	sq. ft.	sq. ft.	sq. ft.
ENCLOSURE DEPTH 8″	19½″	19″	15.1	19.2	23.3	27.8	31.8	35.9	40.4	44.4	48.5	57.0	65.7
	21½″	21″	16.7	21.7	26.3	31.3	35.9	41.0	46.0	50.5	55.5	65.1	74.7
	25½″	25″	18.2	23.2	28.8	33.8	38.9	44.4	49.5	54.5	59.6	70.2	80.8
	27½″	27″	18.6	24.2	29.3	34.7	40.3	45.4	50.9	56.5	61.5	72.5	83.0
	33½″	33″	19.2	24.7	30.3	35.8	41.4	47.0	52.5	58.3	63.6	74.7	85.8
	39½″	39″	19.7	25.3	31.3	36.8	42.4	47.9	54.0	59.5	65.1	76.2	87.6

RATINGS FOR CONVECTOR TYPES "R", "RB", "RCB", "P", "PB"*

*(Note: Ratings are given in sq. ft. E.D.R., based on 215 deg steam and 65 deg entering air temperature)

ENCLOSURE LENGTHS—TYPES R, RB, RC, RCB			16¼″	20¼″	24¼″	28¼″	32¼″	36¼″	40¼″	44¼″	48¼″	56¼″	64¼″
ENCLOSURE LENGTHS—TYPES P, PB			18″	22″	26″	30″	34″	38″	42″	46″	50″	58″	66″
	Enclosure Height—Types R, RB, RC, RCB	Enclosure Height—Types P and PB	sq. ft.	sq. ft.	sq. ft.	sq. ft.	sq. ft.	sq. ft.	sq. ft.	sq. ft.	sq. ft.	sq. ft.	sq. ft.
ENCLOSURE DEPTH 10″	19½″	19″	15.6	20.0	24.2	28.8	32.8	37.3	41.9	46.5	50.5	59.0	68.1
	21½″	21″	18.7	24.2	29.3	34.8	39.9	45.5	50.5	56.1	61.1	71.7	82.3
	25½″	25″	21.2	27.3	33.3	39.4	45.5	51.5	57.6	63.6	69.7	81.8	93.4
	27½″	27′	22.2	28.2	34.7	40.8	47.4	54.0	60.0	66.6	72.6	85.2	97.8
	33½″	33″	22.7	29.8	36.4	42.9	49.5	56.0	62.6	69.2	75.6	88.9	102.0
	39½″	39″	23.7	30.8	37.4	44.4	51.0	58.0	64.6	71.6	78.1	92.4	106.0

RATINGS FOR CONVECTOR TYPES "SF" AND "SFB"

Enclosure Types Shown Below

See Facing Page for Convector Ratings

At left: This drawing shows the enclosure type used for U. S. Copper Convectors. Type "SF".

At right: The enclosure style used with U. S. Type "SFB" convectors is shown here.

RATINGS FOR U. S. COPPER CONVECTORS, TYPES "SF" AND "SFB"

***(Note: Ratings are given in sq. ft. E.D.R., based on 215 deg steam and 65 deg entering air temperature)**

ENCLOSURE LENGTH		16⅜"	20⅜"	24⅜"	28⅜"	32⅜"	36⅜"	40⅜"	44⅜"	48⅜"	56⅜"	64⅜"
	Enclosure Height	sq. ft.	sq. ft.	sq. ft.	sq. ft.	sq. ft.	sq. ft.	sq. ft.	sq. ft.	sq. ft.	sq. ft.	sq. ft.
ENCLOSURE DEPTH 4"	18"	9.1	11.6	14.1	16.7	19.2	21.7	24.2	26.8	29.3	33.9	38.9
	20"	10.1	12.6	15.6	18.2	20.7	23.7	26.3	29.3	31.7	37.3	42.8
	24"	10.6	13.6	16.6	19.2	22.2	25.2	27.7	30.8	33.8	39.8	46.9
	26"	10.6	13.6	16.7	19.7	22.7	25.7	28.7	31.8	34.8	40.8	47.0
	32"	11.1	14.1	17.2	20.2	23.2	26.2	29.2	32.3	35.3	41.8	48.0
	38"	11.1	14.1	17.7	20.7	23.7	26.7	30.3	33.3	36.4	42.8	49.0

ENCLOSURE LENGTH		16⅜"	20⅜"	24⅜"	28⅜"	32⅜"	36⅜"	40⅜"	44⅜"	48⅜"	56⅜"	64⅜"
	Enclosure Height	sq. ft.	sq. ft.	sq. ft.	sq. ft.	sq. ft.	sq. ft.	sq. ft.	sq. ft.	sq. ft.	sq. ft.	sq. ft.
ENCLOSURE DEPTH 6"	18"	16.7	21.2	26.3	30.8	35.9	39.4	43.9	50.0	53.8	62.6	72.2
	20"	17.2	22.3	26.9	31.4	37.3	41.0	46.0	50.5	56.0	65.5	74.7
	24"	18.2	22.8	27.8	33.0	38.0	42.6	47.8	52.8	58.0	68.0	78.0
	26"	18.7	23.2	28.3	33.8	38.8	43.9	48.9	54.0	59.6	69.6	80.2
	32"	18.7	23.8	28.9	34.0	39.5	45.0	50.5	55.2	61.0	71.0	81.8
	38"	20.7	26.7	32.8	38.4	44.4	50.5	56.0	62.1	68.6	80.2	91.8

ENCLOSURE LENGTH		16⅜"	20⅜"	24⅜"	28⅜"	32⅜"	36⅜"	40⅜"	44⅜"	48⅜"	56⅜"	64⅜"
	Enclosure Height	sq. ft.	sq. ft.	sq. ft.	sq. ft.	sq. ft.	sq. ft.	sq. ft.	sq. ft.	sq. ft.	sq. ft.	sq. ft.
ENCLOSURE DEPTH 8"	18"	21.2	27.3	32.8	38.9	44.4	50.5	56.6	62.1	68.2	79.8	91.9
	20"	21.7	27.8	33.8	40.5	46.6	52.8	59.2	64.6	71.5	83.8	96.2
	24"	22.2	28.3	34.8	41.0	47.2	53.8	60.0	65.7	72.0	85.0	97.2
	26"	22.7	29.3	35.3	41.4	47.8	54.0	60.6	67.6	73.7	87.7	99.5
	32"	23.2	29.8	36.4	43.0	50.2	57.0	63.2	69.7	77.0	90.2	103.5
	38"	24.3	31.3	38.9	45.4	52.5	59.5	67.1	73.6	80.2	94.5	109.0

ENCLOSURE LENGTH		16⅜"	20⅜"	24⅜"	28⅜"	32⅜"	36⅜"	40⅜"	44⅜"	48⅜"	56⅜"	64⅜"
	Enclosure Height	sq. ft.	sq. ft.	sq. ft.	sq. ft.	sq. ft.	sq. ft.	sq. ft.	sq. ft.	sq. ft.	sq. ft.	sq. ft.
ENCLOSURE DEPTH 10"	18"	22.2	28.8	35.9	40.4	45.5	53.0	59.6	66.2	71.7	83.8	97.0
	20"	24.7	32.3	38.9	46.0	52.5	60.5	67.0	73.7	81.2	95.0	108.5
	24"	26.3	33.8	41.4	49.0	56.6	64.0	71.6	78.8	87.0	102.0	116.5
	26"	27.3	34.8	42.8	50.5	58.6	66.6	73.6	81.8	89.2	105.0	121.0
	32"	28.3	37.4	45.5	53.5	61.6	70.0	78.8	86.4	95.0	111.5	128.0
	38"	30.3	39.4	48.0	56.5	65.2	74.0	82.8	91.8	100.0	118.0	135.2

UNITED STATES RADIATOR COMPANY

(Continued from previous page)

RATINGS FOR CONVECTOR TYPE "W"*

Right: The enclosure used with U. S. copper convectors, Type "W"

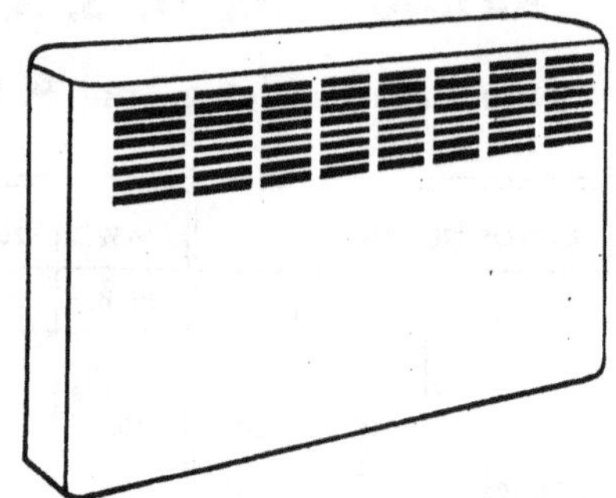

*(Note: Ratings are given in sq. ft. E.D.R., based on 215 deg steam and 65 deg entering air temperature)

ENCLOSURE LENGTH		16⅜"	20⅜"	24⅜"	28⅜"	32⅜"	36⅜"	40⅜"	44⅜"	48⅜"	56⅜"	64⅜"
	Enclosure Height	sq. ft.	sq. ft.	sq. ft.	sq. ft.	sq. ft.	sq. ft.	sq. ft.	sq. ft.	sq. ft.	sq. ft.	sq. ft.
ENCLOSURE DEPTH 4"	14"	9.1	11.6	14.1	16.6	19.2	21.7	24.2	26.8	29.3	34.3	39.4
	18"	10.1	13.1	16.1	18.7	21.7	24.7	27.3	30.3	33.3	38.4	44.9
	20"	10.6	13.6	16.7	19.7	22.7	25.7	28.7	31.8	34.8	40.8	47.0
	26"	11.1	14.1	17.2	20.2	23.2	26.2	29.2	32.3	35.3	41.8	48.0
	32"	11.1	14.1	17.7	20.7	23.7	26.7	30.3	33.3	36.4	42.8	49.0

ENCLOSURE LENGTH		16⅜"	20⅜"	24⅜"	28⅜"	32⅜"	36⅜"	40⅜"	44⅜"	48⅜"	56⅜"	64⅜"
	Enclosure Height	sq. ft.	sq. ft.	sq. ft.	sq. ft.	sq. ft.	sq. ft.	sq. ft.	sq. ft.	sq. ft.	sq. ft.	sq. ft.
ENCLOSURE DEPTH 6"	14"	12.6	16.2	19.8	23.0	26.8	30.4	34.0	37.5	41.0	48.2	55.2
	18"	14.6	18.7	22.8	27.0	31.0	35.0	39.0	43.2	47.2	56.0	64.0
	20"	15.1	19.2	23.2	27.8	31.7	36.4	40.4	44.4	49.0	57.5	66.0
	26"	15.6	20.2	24.2	28.8	33.5	38.0	42.6	46.4	51.8	60.4	69.5
	32"	16.1	20.7	25.2	29.8	34.3	38.8	43.4	47.9	53.0	62.0	71.1

ENCLOSURE LENGTH		16⅜"	20⅜"	24⅜"	28⅜"	32⅜"	36⅜"	40⅜"	44⅜"	48⅜"	56⅜"	64⅜"
	Enclosure Height	sq. ft.	sq. ft.	sq. ft.	sq. ft.	sq. ft.	sq. ft.	sq. ft.	sq. ft.	sq. ft.	sq. ft.	sq. ft.
ENCLOSURE DEPTH 8"	14"	16.7	21.7	26.3	31.3	36.0	41.0	46.0	50.5	56.2	65.5	75.0
	18"	18.2	23.2	28.8	33.8	39.0	44.6	49.6	54.5	60.0	70.5	81.2
	20"	18.7	24.2	29.3	34.8	40.4	45.5	51.0	56.5	61.6	72.6	83.2
	26"	19.2	24.7	30.3	35.8	41.6	47.2	53.2	58.3	64.0	75.0	86.0
	32"	19.7	25.3	31.3	36.8	42.4	47.9	54.0	59.5	65.1	76.2	87.6

ENCLOSURE LENGTH		16⅜"	20⅜"	24⅜"	28⅜"	32⅜"	36⅜"	40⅜"	44⅜"	48⅜"	56⅜"	64⅜"
	Enclosure Height	sq. ft.	sq. ft.	sq. ft.	sq. ft.	sq. ft.	sq. ft.	sq. ft.	sq. ft.	sq. ft.	sq. ft.	sq. ft.
ENCLOSURE DEPTH 10"	14"	18.7	24.2	29.3	34.8	39.9	45.6	50.8	56.1	61.5	72.0	82.8
	18"	21.2	27.3	33.3	39.4	45.5	51.8	58.0	63.6	70.0	82.0	93.8
	20"	22.2	28.3	34.8	40.8	47.5	54.0	60.0	66.6	72.7	85.2	98.0
	26"	22.7	29.8	36.4	42.9	49.5	56.2	63.0	69.2	76.2	89.2	102.0
	32"	23.7	30.8	37.4	44.4	51.0	58.0	64.6	71.6	78.1	92.4	106.0

UTICA RADIATOR CORPORATION

Utica, New York

Utica Cast Iron Convectors *

*(No longer manufactured)

Enclosure Types and Convector Ratings

The illustrations above and at the right show the convector enclosures used with Utica cast iron convectors.

RATINGS FOR UTICA CAST IRON CONVECTORS, TYPE "A"*

*(Note: Ratings are given in sq. ft. E.D.R. for steam)

ENCLOSURE LENGTH, IN.		20	25	30	35	38½	43½	48½	53½	58½	63½	68½	72	77	82	87	92	97	102
"L" CONVECTOR LENGTH, IN.		18	23	28	33	36½	41½	46½	51½	56½	61½	66½	70	75	80	85	90	95	100
		sq. ft.	sq. ft.	sq. ft.	sq. ft.	sq. ft.	sq. ft.	sq. ft.	sq. ft.	sq. ft.	sq. ft.	sq. ft.	sq. ft.	sq. ft.	sq. ft.	sq. ft.	sq. ft.	sq. ft.	sq. ft.
ELEMENT DEPTH 3⅝" — Enclosure Height	20"	9.2	11.8	14.3	16.8	18.4	21.0	23.5	26.1	28.6	31.2	33.8	36.3	38.8	41.3	43.8	46.4	48.9	51.4
	22"	9.6	12.2	14.9	17.6	19.2	21.9	24.6	27.3	29.9	32.6	35.3	37.9	40.5	43.3	45.9	48.6	51.3	53.9
	24"	9.9	12.7	15.4	18.2	19.8	22.6	25.3	28.1	30.9	33.6	36.4	39.1	41.9	44.6	47.3	50.0	52.8	55.5
	26"	10.2	13.0	15.8	18.6	20.3	23.1	26.0	28.8	31.7	34.5	37.3	40.1	42.9	45.7	48.5	51.3	54.1	56.9
	29"	10.4	13.4	16.4	19.3	21.0	23.9	26.8	29.7	32.7	35.6	38.5	41.4	44.3	47.3	50.1	53.1	56.0	58.9
	32"	10.6	13.6	16.6	19.5	21.2	24.2	27.2	30.2	33.2	36.0	39.0	41.9	44.9	47.9	50.8	53.7	56.7	59.9
	35"	10.7	13.7	16.7	19.7	21.5	24.5	27.5	30.5	33.5	36.5	39.4	42.4	45.5	48.4	51.3	55.3	58.1	61.0
	38"	10.9	14.0	16.9	20.0	21.8	24.8	27.9	30.9	33.8	37.0	40.0	42.9	46.0	49.0	51.9	55.9	58.7	61.7

ENCLOSURE LENGTH, IN.		20	25	30	35	38½	43½	48½	53½	58½	63½	68½	72	77	82	87	92	97	102
"L" CONVECTOR LENGTH, IN.		18	23	28	33	36½	41½	46½	51½	56½	61½	66½	70	75	80	85	90	95	100
		sq. ft.	sq. ft.	sq. ft.	sq. ft.	sq. ft.	sq. ft.	sq. ft.	sq. ft.	sq. ft.	sq. ft.	sq. ft.	sq. ft.	sq. ft.	sq. ft.	sq. ft.	sq. ft.	sq. ft.	sq. ft.
ELEMENT DEPTH 5⅝" — Enclosure Height	20"	12.2	15.6	18.9	22.3	25.1	28.5	31.9	35.3	38.6	42.0	45.4	48.8	52.1	55.5	58.9	62.3	65.6	69.0
	22"	12.7	16.2	19.8	23.3	26.3	29.9	33.4	36.9	40.4	43.9	47.4	50.9	54.5	58.0	61.5	65.0	68.5	72.0
	24"	13.1	16.7	20.3	23.9	26.9	30.8	34.1	37.7	41.4	45.0	48.6	52.2	55.8	59.4	63.0	66.6	70.2	73.8
	26"	13.4	17.2	20.9	24.6	27.8	31.5	35.2	39.0	42.7	46.4	50.1	53.9	57.6	61.4	65.1	68.9	72.5	76.3
	29"	13.8	17.6	21.5	25.4	28.6	32.5	36.4	40.1	44.0	47.9	51.7	55.1	58.7	62.6	66.5	70.3	74.2	77.4
	32"	14.0	17.9	21.8	25.7	29.0	32.9	36.8	40.7	44.6	48.4	52.4	56.3	60.1	64.0	68.0	71.8	75.7	78.7
	35"	14.1	18.1	22.1	26.0	29.3	33.3	37.3	41.2	45.2	49.1	53.0	57.0	60.9	64.8	68.9	72.7	76.7	80.1
	38"	14.4	18.4	22.3	26.5	29.8	33.8	37.8	41.8	45.8	49.8	53.7	57.7	61.7	65.7	69.7	73.6	77.7	81.6

(Continued from previous page)

ENCLOSURE LENGTH, IN.		25	30	35	38½	43½	48½	53½	58½	63½	68½	72	77	82	87	92	97	102
"L" CONVECTOR LENGTH, IN.		23	28	33	36½	41½	46½	51½	56½	61½	66½	70	75	80	85	90	95	100
		sq. ft.	sq. ft.	sq. ft.	sq. ft.	sq. ft.	sq. ft.	sq. ft.	sq. ft.	sq. ft.	sq. ft.	sq. ft.	sq. ft.	sq. ft.	sq. ft.	sq. ft.	sq. ft.	sq. ft.
ELEMENT DEPTH 7⅜"	Enclosure Height 20"	22.4	27.2	31.9	35.9	39.9	44.6	49.6	54.4	59.3	64.1	68.9	73.7	78.5	83.2	88.1	92.9	97.6
	22"	23.2	28.3	33.5	37.5	41.6	46.7	51.8	56.8	61.9	67.0	72.0	77.1	82.3	87.2	92.3	97.5	102.4
	24"	24.1	29.2	34.6	38.7	42.9	48.2	53.4	58.7	63.8	69.1	74.2	79.5	84.6	89.9	95.0	100.4	105.5
	26"	24.7	30.1	35.4	39.7	43.9	49.4	54.7	60.2	65.5	70.8	76.2	81.5	86.8	92.2	97.5	102.8	108.1
	29"	25.5	31.0	36.6	41.0	45.4	50.9	56.4	62.1	67.6	73.2	78.7	84.1	89.8	95.2	100.9	106.4	111.9
	32"	25.8	31.5	37.1	41.5	46.0	51.7	57.3	62.9	68.4	74.1	79.6	85.3	91.0	96.5	102.1	107.7	113.8
	35"	26.1	31.8	37.4	41.8	46.3	52.3	58.0	63.7	69.3	75.0	80.6	86.4	91.7	97.6	105.1	110.3	116.9
	38"	26.5	32.1	38.0	42.6	47.2	53.0	58.7	64.3	70.3	76.0	81.5	87.4	93.1	98.6	106.2	111.5	117.2

ENCLOSURE LENGTH, IN.		25	30	35	38½	43½	48½	53½	58½	63½	68½	72	77	82	87	92	97	102
"L" CONVECTOR LENGTH, IN.		23	28	33	36½	41½	46½	51½	56½	61½	66½	70	75	80	85	90	95	100
		sq. ft.	sq. ft.	sq. ft.	sq. ft.	sq. ft.	sq. ft.	sq. ft.	sq. ft.	sq. ft.	sq. ft.	sq. ft.	sq. ft.	sq. ft.	sq. ft.	sq. ft.	sq. ft.	sq. ft.
ELEMENT DEPTH 9⅜"	Enclosure Height 20"	24.7	29.9	35.3	39.9	44.5	49.9	55.3	60.6	66.0	71.3	76.6	81.8	87.2	92.4	97.8	103.0	108.4
	22"	25.6	31.3	36.9	41.8	46.6	52.2	57.8	63.3	68.8	74.5	80.0	85.6	91.2	96.7	102.2	107.8	113.4
	24"	26.5	32.1	37.9	42.9	48.1	53.5	59.2	65.1	70.7	76.5	82.2	87.9	93.6	99.4	105.0	110.8	116.5
	26"	27.2	33.1	38.9	44.0	49.2	55.1	61.0	67.0	72.9	78.7	84.7	90.5	95.5	102.2	108.2	114.0	119.9
	29"	28.0	34.1	40.2	45.5	50.9	57.0	63.0	69.1	75.2	81.3	87.1	92.1	99.1	105.3	111.4	117.4	122.9
	32"	28.3	34.6	40.8	46.1	51.5	57.6	63.8	69.9	76.0	82.3	88.4	94.6	100.7	106.9	113.0	119.2	124.7
	35"	28.7	34.9	41.3	46.6	52.0	58.3	64.7	70.9	77.1	83.3	89.6	95.8	102.1	108.4	115.4	121.2	127.2
	38"	29.2	35.4	41.8	47.2	52.7	59.1	65.4	71.7	78.1	84.3	90.6	97.0	103.3	109.4	116.6	122.8	129.0

RATINGS FOR UTICA CAST IRON CONVECTORS*

***(Note: Ratings are given in sq. ft. E.D.R. for steam)**

ENCLOSURE LENGTH, IN.		20	25	30	35	38½	43½	48½	53½	58½	63½	68½	72	77	82	87	92	97	102
"L" CONVECTOR LENGTH, IN.		18	23	28	33	36½	41½	46½	51½	56½	61½	66½	70	75	80	85	90	95	100
		sq. ft.	sq. ft.	sq. ft.	sq. ft.	sq. ft.	sq. ft.	sq. ft.	sq. ft.	sq. ft.	sq. ft.	sq. ft.	sq. ft.	sq. ft.	sq. ft.	sq. ft.	sq. ft.	sq. ft.	sq. ft.
ELEMENT DEPTH 3⅝"	Enclosure Height 20"	10.2	13.1	15.9	18.7	20.4	23.3	26.1	29.0	31.8	34.7	37.5	40.3	43.1	45.9	48.7	51.5	54.3	57.1
	22"	10.7	13.6	16.6	19.6	21.3	24.3	27.3	30.3	33.2	36.2	39.2	42.1	45.1	48.1	51.0	54.0	57.0	59.9
	24"	11.0	14.1	17.1	20.2	22.0	25.1	28.2	31.2	34.3	37.3	40.4	43.4	46.5	49.5	52.6	55.6	58.7	61.7
	26"	11.3	14.4	17.6	20.7	22.6	25.7	28.9	32.0	35.2	38.3	41.4	44.6	47.7	50.8	53.9	57.0	60.1	63.2
	29"	11.6	14.9	18.2	21.4	23.3	26.6	29.8	33.0	36.3	39.5	42.8	46.0	49.2	52.5	55.7	59.0	62.2	65.4
	32"	11.8	15.1	18.4	21.7	23.6	26.9	30.2	33.5	36.8	40.0	43.3	46.6	49.9	53.2	56.4	59.7	63.0	66.6
	35"	11.9	15.2	18.6	21.9	23.9	27.2	30.6	33.9	37.2	40.5	43.8	47.1	50.5	53.8	57.0	61.4	64.5	67.8
	38"	12.1	15.5	18.8	22.2	24.2	27.6	31.0	34.3	37.6	41.1	44.4	47.7	51.1	54.4	57.7	62.1	65.2	68.5

ENCLOSURE LENGTH, IN.		20	25	30	35	38½	43½	48½	53½	58½	63½	68½	72	77	82	87	92	97	102
"L" CONVECTOR LENGTH, IN.		18	23	28	33	36½	41½	46½	51½	56½	61½	66½	70	75	80	85	90	95	100
		sq. ft.	sq. ft.	sq. ft.	sq. ft.	sq. ft.	sq. ft.	sq. ft.	sq. ft.	sq. ft.	sq. ft.	sq. ft.	sq. ft.	sq. ft.	sq. ft.	sq. ft.	sq. ft.	sq. ft.	sq. ft.
ELEMENT DEPTH 5⅝"	Enclosure Height 20"	13.5	17.3	21.0	24.8	27.9	31.7	35.4	39.2	42.9	46.7	50.4	54.2	57.9	61.7	65.4	69.2	72.9	76.7
	22"	14.1	18.0	22.0	25.9	29.2	33.2	37.1	41.0	44.9	48.8	52.7	56.6	60.5	64.4	68.3	72.2	76.1	80.0
	24"	14.5	18.5	22.5	26.5	29.9	34.2	37.9	41.9	46.0	50.0	54.0	58.0	62.0	66.0	70.0	74.0	78.0	82.0
	26"	14.9	19.1	23.2	27.3	30.9	35.0	39.1	43.3	47.4	51.6	55.7	59.9	64.0	68.2	72.3	76.5	80.6	84.8
	29"	15.3	19.6	23.9	28.2	31.8	36.1	40.4	44.6	48.9	53.2	57.4	61.2	65.2	69.6	73.9	78.1	82.4	86.0
	32"	15.6	19.9	24.2	28.6	32.2	36.6	40.9	45.2	49.5	53.8	58.2	62.5	66.8	71.1	75.5	79.8	84.1	87.4
	35"	15.7	20.1	24.5	28.9	32.6	37.0	41.4	45.8	50.2	54.6	58.9	63.3	67.7	72.0	76.5	80.8	85.2	89.0
	38"	16.0	20.4	24.8	29.4	33.1	37.5	42.0	46.4	50.9	55.3	59.7	64.1	68.6	73.0	77.4	81.8	86.3	90.7

ENCLOSURE LENGTH, IN.		25	30	35	40	43½	48½	53½	58½	63½	68½	72	77	82	87	92	97	102
"L" CONVECTOR LENGTH, IN.		23	28	33	38	41½	46½	51½	56½	61½	66½	70	75	80	85	90	95	100
		sq. ft.	sq. ft.	sq. ft.	sq. ft.	sq. ft.	sq. ft.	sq. ft.	sq. ft.	sq. ft.	sq. ft.	sq. ft.	sq. ft.	sq. ft.	sq. ft.	sq. ft.	sq. ft.	sq. ft.
ELEMENT DEPTH 7⅜"	Enclosure Height 20"	24.9	30.2	35.5	39.9	44.3	49.6	55.1	60.4	65.9	71.2	76.6	81.9	87.2	92.5	97.9	103.2	108.5
	22"	25.8	31.5	37.2	41.7	46.2	51.9	57.6	63.1	68.8	74.5	80.0	85.7	91.4	96.9	102.6	108.3	113.8
	24"	26.8	32.5	38.4	43.0	47.7	53.6	59.3	65.2	70.9	76.8	82.5	88.3	94.0	99.9	105.6	111.5	117.2
	26"	27.4	33.4	39.3	44.1	48.8	54.9	60.8	66.9	72.8	78.7	84.7	90.6	96.5	102.4	108.3	114.2	120.1
	29"	28.3	34.5	40.7	45.6	50.5	56.6	62.7	69.0	75.1	81.3	87.4	93.5	99.8	105.8	112.1	118.2	124.3
	32"	28.7	35.0	41.2	46.1	51.1	57.4	63.7	69.9	76.0	82.3	88.5	94.8	101.1	107.2	113.4	119.7	126.5
	35"	29.0	35.3	41.6	46.5	51.5	58.1	64.4	70.8	77.0	83.3	89.6	96.0	101.8	108.4	116.8	122.6	129.9
	38"	29.5	35.7	42.2	47.3	52.4	58.9	65.2	71.4	78.1	84.4	90.6	97.1	103.4	109.6	118.0	123.9	130.2

ENCLOSURE LENGTH, IN.		25	30	35	40	43½	48½	53½	58½	63½	68½	72	77	82	87	92	97	102
"L" CONVECTOR LENGTH, IN.		23	28	33	38	41½	46½	51½	56½	61½	66½	70	75	80	85	90	95	100
		sq. ft.	sq. ft.	sq. ft.	sq. ft.	sq. ft.	sq. ft.	sq. ft.	sq. ft.	sq. ft.	sq. ft.	sq. ft.	sq. ft.	sq. ft.	sq. ft.	sq. ft.	sq. ft.	sq. ft.
ELEMENT DEPTH 9⅜"	Enclosure Height 20"	27.4	33.2	39.2	44.3	49.5	55.4	61.4	67.3	73.3	79.2	85.1	90.9	96.9	102.7	108.7	114.5	120.5
	22"	28.5	34.8	41.0	46.4	51.8	58.0	64.2	70.3	76.5	82.8	88.9	95.1	101.3	107.4	113.6	119.8	126.0
	24"	29.4	35.7	42.1	47.7	53.4	59.5	65.8	72.3	78.6	85.0	91.3	97.7	104.0	110.4	116.7	123.1	129.4
	26"	30.2	36.8	43.2	48.9	54.7	61.2	67.8	74.4	81.0	87.4	94.1	100.6	106.1	113.6	120.2	126.7	133.2
	29"	31.1	37.9	44.7	50.6	56.6	63.3	70.0	76.8	83.6	90.3	96.8	102.3	110.2	117.0	123.8	130.5	136.6
	32"	31.5	38.4	45.3	51.2	57.2	64.0	70.9	77.7	84.5	91.4	98.2	105.1	111.9	118.8	125.6	132.4	138.6
	35"	31.9	38.8	45.9	51.8	57.8	64.8	71.9	78.8	85.7	92.6	99.6	106.5	113.4	120.4	128.2	134.7	141.3
	38"	32.4	39.3	46.5	52.5	58.6	65.7	72.7	79.7	86.8	93.7	100.7	107.8	114.7	121.6	129.6	136.4	143.3

WARREN WEBSTER AND COMPANY

Camden, New Jersey

Webster System Convector Radiation

Measuring Instructions

(Webster convector ratings are on following pages)

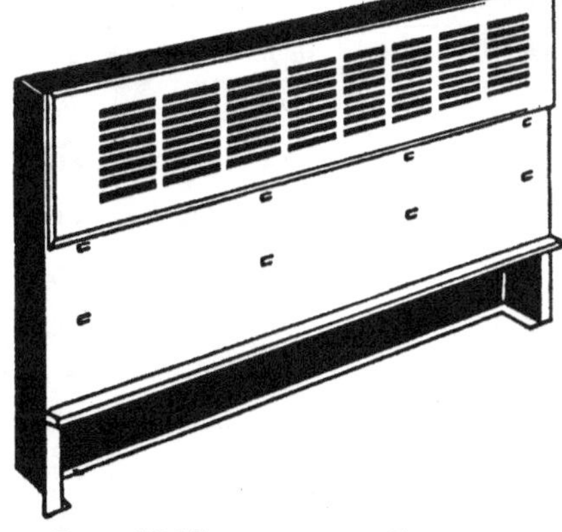

Type "PA" convector. For measurements, use actual length and deduct 2 in.; actual height and deduct $1\frac{1}{2}$ in. and actual depth.

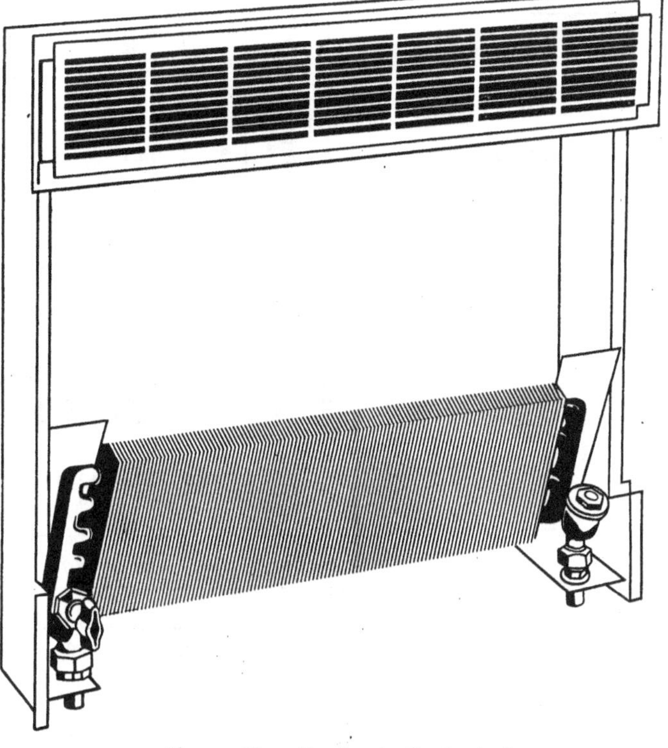

Above: Here the front of a typical Warren Webster convector is removed to show the convector element. Note its position, and identify this make by element construction details.

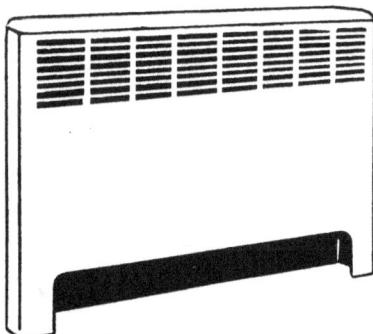

Type "MA", use actual length less 2 in., actual height and actual depth.

Type "FA". Use actual length, height and depth for obtaining measurements to check rating from the tables on the following pages.

Type "SA". Use actual length, height and depth for measurements. Check the rating tables against the obtained measurements for steam rating.

Type "WA", use actual dimensions, including actual length, height and width.

Warren Webster & Company

RATINGS FOR WEBSTER SYSTEM TYPE "PA" CONVECTOR RADIATION*

*(Note: Ratings given in sq. ft. E.D.R.)

ENCLOSURE LENGTH			20"	24"	28"	32"	36"	40"	44"	48"	56"
			sq. ft.	sq. ft.	sq. ft.	sq. ft.	sq. ft.	sq. ft.	sq. ft.	sq. ft.	sq. ft.
ENCLOSURE DEPTH 3½"	Enclosure Height	20"	11.4	14.4	17.4	20.5	23.5	26.6	29.6	32.6	38.7
		24"	12.1	15.3	18.6	21.8	25.0	28.2	31.4	34.7	41.2
		32"	13.1	16.6	20.0	23.6	27.0	30.5	34.0	37.5	44.5
		40"	14.0	17.8	21.5	25.3	29.0	32.8	36.5	40.3	47.7
		50"	15.5	19.6	23.7	27.9	32.0	36.1	40.3	44.4	52.6
		60"	16.8	21.3	25.7	30.2	34.7	39.2	43.6	48.2	57.0

RATINGS FOR WEBSTER SYSTEM TYPE "PA" CONVECTOR RADIATION*

*(Note: Ratings given in sq. ft. E.D.R.)

ENCLOSURE LENGTH			20"	24"	28"	32"	36"	40"	44"	48"	56"
			sq. ft.	sq. ft.	sq. ft.	sq. ft.	sq. ft.	sq. ft.	sq. ft.	sq. ft.	sq. ft.
ENCLOSURE DEPTH 4⅞"	Enclosure Height	20"	16.4	20.8	25.2	29.6	34.0	38.4	42.8	47.2	56.0
		24"	17.7	22.4	27.1	31.8	36.5	41.2	46.0	50.7	60.0
		32"	18.7	23.8	28.8	33.8	38.8	43.8	48.9	53.9	64.0
		40"	19.6	24.8	30.1	35.3	40.5	45.7	51.0	56.2	66.5
		50"	20.9	26.5	32.0	37.6	43.2	48.7	54.3	60.0	71.0
		60"	21.9	27.7	33.6	39.4	45.2	51.0	57.0	62.8	74.5

RATINGS FOR WEBSTER SYSTEM TYPE "PA" CONVECTOR RADIATION*

*(Note: Ratings given in sq. ft. E.D.R.)

ENCLOSURE LENGTH			20"	24"	28"	32"	36"	40"	44"	48"	56"
			sq. ft.	sq. ft.	sq. ft.	sq. ft.	sq. ft.	sq. ft.	sq. ft.	sq. ft.	sq. ft.
ENCLOSURE DEPTH 6"	Enclosure Height	20"	19.0	24.0	29.1	34.2	39.2	44.3	49.4	54.5	64.5
		24"	20.4	25.9	31.3	36.8	42.2	46.5	51.9	57.2	67.8
		32"	21.5	27.3	33.0	38.8	44.5	50.2	56.0	61.7	72.2
		40"	22.5	28.5	34.5	40.5	46.5	52.5	58.5	64.5	76.5
		50"	24.1	30.5	36.9	43.4	49.7	56.1	62.5	69.0	81.7
		60"	25.3	32.0	38.7	45.5	52.2	58.9	65.5	72.5	86.0

WARREN WEBSTER SYSTEM CONVECTOR RADIATION, TYPES "MA", "FA", "WA", "SA"*

*(Note: Ratings given in sq. ft. E.D.R.)

ENCLOSURE LENGTH			20″	24″	28″	32″	36″	40″	44″	48″	56″
			sq. ft.	sq. ft.	sq. ft.	sq. ft.	sq. ft.	sq. ft.	sq. ft.	sq. ft.	sq. ft.
ENCLOSURE DEPTH 4⅞″	Enclosure Height	20″	17.2	21.9	26.5	31.2	35.8	40.5	45.1	49.6	59.0
		24″	18.6	23.6	28.5	33.5	38.4	43.4	48.5	53.5	63.1
		32″	19.7	25.1	30.3	35.4	40.9	46.2	51.5	56.7	67.5

*(Note: Ratings given in sq. ft. E.D.R.)

ENCLOSURE LENGTH			20″	24″	28″	32″	36″	40″	44″	48″	56″
			sq. ft.	sq. ft.	sq. ft.	sq. ft.	sq. ft.	sq. ft.	sq. ft.	sq. ft.	sq. ft.
ENCLOSURE DEPTH 6″	Enclosure Height	20″	20.0	25.3	30.7	36.0	41.3	46.6	52.0	57.4	68.0
		24″	21.5	27.3	33.0	38.8	44.5	49.0	54.6	60.2	71.5
		32″	22.6	28.8	34.8	40.8	46.9	52.9	59.0	65.2	77.1

RATINGS FOR YOUNG CONVECTORS, TYPES "C", "S", "WS"*

*(Note: Ratings given in sq. ft. E.D.R., based on 1 lb steam and 65 deg entering air.)

(See facing page for illustrations)

ENCLOSURE LENGTH			20″	25″	30″	35″	40″	45″	50″	55″	60″
			sq. ft.	sq. ft.	sq. ft.	sq. ft.	sq. ft.	sq. ft.	sq. ft.	sq. ft.	sq. ft.
ENCLOSURE DEPTH 5⅝″	Enclosure Height	20″	18.2	23.0	27.6	31.9	37.4	42.2	46.8	51.8	56.2
		24″	19.6	25.8	31.5	35.8	41.3	46.7	51.7	57.2	62.0
		32″	22.6	28.5	34.3	39.7	45.8	51.7	58.0	63.4	68.8

ENCLOSURE LENGTH			20″	25″	30″	35″	40″	45″	50″	55″	60″
			sq. ft.	sq. ft.	sq. ft.	sq. ft.	sq. ft.	sq. ft.	sq. ft.	sq. ft.	sq. ft.
ENCLOSURE DEPTH 7⅜″	Enclosure Height	20″	....	....	....	38.4	44.7	50.7	56.7	62.7	68.8
		24″	....	....	....	42.4	49.2	55.5	62.1	68.7	75.2
		32″	....	....	....	46.3	53.5	61.0	68.0	75.0	82.3

ENCLOSURE LENGTH			20″	25″	30″	35″	40″	45″	50″	55″	60″
			sq. ft.	sq. ft.	sq. ft.	sq. ft.	sq. ft.	sq. ft.	sq. ft.	sq. ft.	sq. ft.
ENCLOSURE DEPTH 9⅛″	Enclosure Height	20″	....	....	....	....	51.3	58.0	65.7	71.2	77.4
		24″	....	....	....	....	55.7	63.0	70.0	77.2	84.0
		32″	....	....	....	....	61.0	68.8	76.5	84.5	92.2

YOUNG RADIATOR COMPANY

Racine, Wisconsin

Streamline Copper Convectors

Enclosure Types, Measuring Instructions and Convector Ratings

Free standing Type "C" Young convector. For measurements use actual length, height and depth.

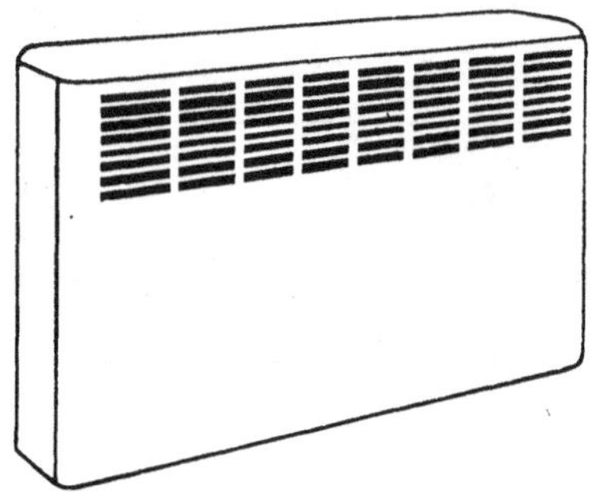

Wall hung Type "W" Young convector. Use actual height, length and depth for measuring.

Partially recessed Type "S" Young convector. For measuring use actual length and deduct 3½ in. Use actual height and depth.

These convectors can be easily identified by the trade name on a rectangular plate fastened to the enclosure.

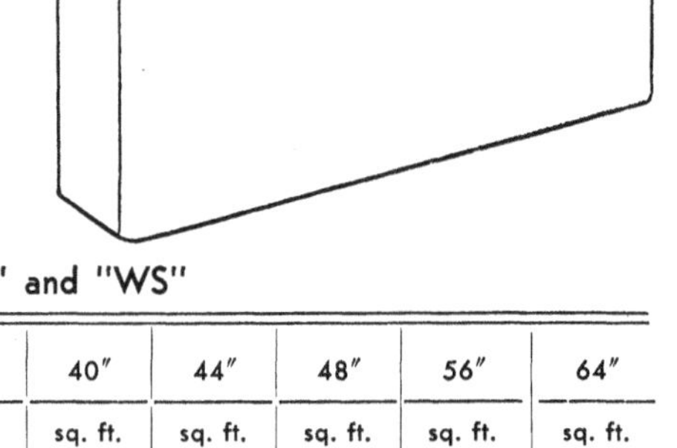

Wall hung Type "WS" convector. Use actual length, height and depth for measurements.

RATINGS FOR YOUNG STREAMAIRE CONVECTORS, TYPES "F" "FR" AND "R"*

*(Note: Ratings given in sq. ft. E.D.R.)

See facing page for ratings on types "C", "S" and "WS"

ENCLOSURE LENGTH			20"	24"	28"	32"	36"	40"	44"	48"	56"	64"
			sq. ft.	sq. ft.	sq. ft.	sq. ft.	sq. ft.	sq. ft.	sq. ft.	sq. ft.	sq. ft.	sq. ft.
CABINET DEPTH 4 3/16"*	Enclosure Height	20"	10.0	12.5	15.0	17.5	20.0	22.5	25.0	27.5	32.5	37.5
		24"	12.0	15.0	18.0	20.5	23.5	26.5	29.5	32.5	38.5	44.5
		32"	13.0	16.5	19.5	23.0	26.5	29.5	33.0	36.0	42.5	49.5

*This depth in Type "FR" only.

ENCLOSURE LENGTH			20"	24"	28"	32"	36"	40"	44"	48"	56"	64"
			sq. ft.	sq. ft.	sq. ft.	sq. ft.	sq. ft.	sq. ft.	sq. ft.	sq. ft.	sq. ft.	sq. ft.
CABINET DEPTH 6 3/16"	Enclosure Height	20"	14.5	18.5	22.0	25.5	29.5	33.0	36.5	40.5	47.5	55.0
		24"	17.5	21.5	26.0	30.5	34.5	39.0	43.0	47.5	56.0	65.0
		32"	20.0	25.0	30.0	35.0	39.5	44.5	49.5	54.5	64.5	74.5

Ratings for Types "F", "FR" and "R" Continued

ENCLOSURE LENGTH			20″	24″	28″	32″	36″	40″	44″	48″	56″	64″
			sq. ft.	sq. ft.	sq. ft.	sq. ft.	sq. ft.	sq. ft.	sq. ft.	sq. ft.	sq. ft.	sq. ft.
CABINET DEPTH 8 3/16″	Enclosure Height	20″	....	....	....	33.5	38.0	43.0	....	52.5	62.0	71.5
		24″	....	....	....	37.5	43.0	48.0	....	59.0	69.5	80.5
		32″	....	....	....	41.5	47.5	53.5	....	65.5	77.5	89.5

ENCLOSURE LENGTH			20″	24″	28″	32″	36″	40″	44″	48″	56″	64″
			sq. ft.	sq. ft.	sq. ft.	sq. ft.	sq. ft.	sq. ft.	sq. ft.	sq. ft.	sq. ft.	sq. ft.
CABINET DEPTH 10 3/16″	Enclosure Height	20″	....	....	....	....	45.0	50.5	....	61.5	72.5	84.0
		24″	....	....	....	....	49.0	55.5	....	68.0	80.0	92.5
		32″	....	....	....	....	54.5	61.5	....	75.5	88.5	102.5

*4 3/16″ depth in Type "FR" only.

RATINGS FOR YOUNG BATHROOM CONVECTORS

Top Outlet Depth 5 3/8″	Height 8″	Length 15 3/16″	Rating 7.0 sq. ft.
Face Outlet Depth 5 5/8″	Height 10″	Length 20 3/16″	Rating 13.3 sq. ft.
Top Outlet Depth 6 3/16″	Height 10″	Length 16″	Rating 10.0 sq. ft.

The illustration at right shows Young bathroom type convectors.

RATINGS FOR YOUNG CONVECTORS, TYPES "C", "S", "W" AND "WS"*

ENCLOSURE LENGTH			20″	24″	28″	32″	36″	40″	44″	48″	56″	64″
			sq. ft.	sq. ft.	sq. ft.	sq. ft.	sq. ft.	sq. ft.	sq. ft.	sq. ft.	sq. ft.	sq. ft.
CABINET DEPTH 4 3/16″	Enclosure Height	16″	10.5	13.0	16.0	18.5	21.0	23.5	26.5	29.0	34.0	39.5
		20″	12.5	15.5	18.5	21.5	24.5	27.5	30.5	33.5	39.5	46.0
		28″	13.5	17.0	20.0	23.5	27.0	30.5	33.5	37.0	44.0	50.5

ENCLOSURE LENGTH			20″	24″	28″	32″	36″	40″	44″	48″	56″	64″
			sq. ft.	sq. ft.	sq. ft.	sq. ft.	sq. ft.	sq. ft.	sq. ft.	sq. ft.	sq. ft.	sq. ft.
CABINET DEPTH 6 3/16″	Enclosure Height	16″	17.5	22.0	26.5	31.0	35.0	39.5	44.0	48.5	57.0	66.0
		20″	20.5	25.5	30.5	35.5	41.0	46.0	51.0	56.0	66.0	76.5
		28″	22.5	28.0	33.5	39.0	45.0	50.5	56.0	62.0	73.0	84.0

YOUNG STREAMAIRE COPPER CONVECTOR RATINGS

YOUNG RADIATOR COMPANY

RATINGS FOR YOUNG CONVECTORS TYPES "C", "S", "W" AND "WS" Continued

ENCLOSURE LENGTH		20″	24″	28″	32″	36″	40″	44″	48″	56″	64″
	Enclosure Height	sq. ft.	sq. ft.	sq. ft.	sq. ft.	sq. ft.	sq ft	sq. ft.	sq. ft.	sq. ft.	sq. ft.
CABINET DEPTH 8 3/16″	16″	....	....	....	40.0	45.5	51.5	....	63.0	74.0	85.5
	20″	....	....	....	46.0	52.5	59.0	....	72.0	85.0	98.5
	28″	....	....	....	51.0	58.5	66.0	....	80.5	95.0	110.0

ENCLOSURE LENGTH		20″	24″	28″	32″	36″	40″	44″	48″	56″	64″
	Enclosure Height	sq. ft.	sq. ft.	sq. ft.	sq. ft.	sq..ft.	sq. ft.	sq. ft.	sq. ft.	sq. ft.	sq. ft.
CABINET DEPTH 10 3/16″	16″	....	....	....	....	54.5	61.0	....	75.0	88.5	102.0
	20″	....	....	....	....	62.0	69.5	....	85.0	100.5	116.0
	28″	....	....	....	....	70.5	79.5	....	97.5	114.5	132.5

Left: Free standing Type "F". Actual length, height and depth for measuring.

Right: Fully recessed Type "FR". When measuring, use actual length and deduct 2½ in. and use actual height and depth.

Left: Semi-recessed Type "R". When measuring, use actual length and deduct 2½in., actual height and deduct 1¼ in. and use actual depth.

Right: Wall hung Type "S". Use actual length, height and width when obtaining dimensions.

INDEX

INDEX

INDEX

INDEX

www.ingramcontent.com/pod-product-compliance
Lightning Source LLC
Chambersburg PA
CBHW080415270326
41929CB00018B/3041
* 9 7 8 0 9 9 6 4 7 7 2 5 3 *